URBAN ECONOMIC ANALYSIS

ECONOMICS HANDBOOK SERIES

Seymour E. Harris, Editor

URBAN ECONOMIC ANALYSIS

WERNER Z. HIRSCH

Professor of Economics
University of California, Los Angeles

McGRAW-HILL BOOK COMPANY

New York St. Louis San Francisco Düsseldorf Johannesburg
Kuala Lumpur London Mexico Montreal New Delhi Panama
Rio de Janeiro Singapore Sydney Toronto

URBAN ECONOMIC ANALYSIS

4 5 6 7 8 9 0   DODO   7 9 8 7 6 5

This book was set in Times Roman by Monotype Composition Company, Inc. The editors were Jack R. Crutchfield and Edwin Hanson; the designer was Rafael Hernandez; and the production supervisor was Joe Campanella. The drawings were done by Eric G. Hieber.
The printer and binder was R. R. Donnelley & Sons Company.

Library of Congress Cataloging in Publication Data

Hirsch, Werner Zvi, 1920–
    Urban economic analysis.

    (Economics handbook series)
    1. Urban economics.   I. Title.
HT321.H57   330.9′173′2   72-5604
ISBN 0-07-029044-X

TO ESTHER

CONTENTS

LIST OF ILLUSTRATIONS

LIST OF TABLES

PREFACE

Cities were first created in the ancient Orient to protect man and advance his well-being. The first urbanites hid behind laboriously constructed moats and fortifications and, with their protection, engaged in production and commerce. Under the exuberant Greeks the city evolved into a cultural showplace designed to promote the good life. More recently the city has become a melting pot and an efficient information producer, while continuing to be the center of culture.

It has been said that the Lord made the countryside but man built the city, and it is in the city that man is inventing and developing new ways and new objects and services designed to satisfy his needs and desires. In a short time span, however, the American city has become in some respects a jungle, and at times even, on balance, an inefficient producer of goods and services. Long ago Ralph Waldo Emerson had already decided that cities give us collision. Some of this has been to the good. However, in recent years collision has taken the form of riots, policemen's and garbage collectors' strikes, and the closing of public schools because of insufficient funds.

Economists have much to contribute to a better understanding of what makes the city tick, of how we can project its future, and of some alternatives that are open for urban public policy and what their main consequences are. They did not seize these opportunities until quite recently, when, in the 1950s, economists began to turn their serious attention to some urban economic issues. This book is built on these efforts.

One can approach urban economics from a number of different directions. Two directions have been taken in the past. One focuses on important urban policy issues; the other proceeds as if urban economics were a subfield or special case of regional economics, which inquires into where a given economic activity takes place and why. Thus this second approach focuses on one spatial aspect of economic activity, i.e., distance and location where economic activity does or should take place. But spatial inquiries can also emphasize nondistance, i.e., proximity and density. Granting that proximity is the inverse of distance, it nevertheless makes a great difference whether, in looking at the urban world, the economist's principal concern is distance or proximity. Specifically, the economist will seek to develop and apply a very different type of economic theory if he is distance-oriented from the type he will be promulgating if he is proximity-oriented, particularly if he sees proximity as going hand in hand with great specialization.

I emphasize in this volume that the urban environment is generally characterized by high levels of proximity, production specialization, affluence, and technology. Great proximity in cities heightens the probability that a decision by one economic actor will affect the utility or production functions of other actors, and thus generate an abundance of externalities. A high degree of production specialization, particularly in the light of low information costs, further contributes to the emergence of interdependencies. At the same time it reduces the options available to those on whom unwanted externality effects are placed, and thereby it increases their vulnerability to conditions imposed by others. Furthermore, the rather widespread affluence of urban areas ensures the making of many externality-producing decisions, which in conjunction with a universally high level of technology tends to greatly extend the scope of externalities. One result of technology is its reduction of effective distance, a phenomenon that further increases the number of economic actors affected by externalities and the degree to which they are affected.

Thus the city is where externalities abound; and it is the prevalence of these externalities that make a city what it is. The city is the place where everything affects everything else. It is clear why this view of urban economics emphasizes so strongly the importance of externalities. In analyzing such a world, this volume could attempt to modify neoclassical economics by introducing spatial considerations, together with externalities, into production and consumption decisions of firms and households. This, however, is an exceedingly difficult undertaking in the present state of our knowledge. Instead, in light of the pervasiveness of interdependencies among firms, individuals, households, and governmental units, this book uses urban markets as the focal point around which urban economics as a discipline is organized. This view does not dismiss the importance of decisions made by individual economic actors; but it seeks to deal with them in a more aggregative manner by paying particular attention to such key urban markets as land and housing, transportation, labor, and public services.

But urban economics, particularly under political federalism, must also take cognizance of some special institutional conditions that affect the nature and quality of governmental decisions. In metropolitan areas decisions are made by a multitude of relevant governments, each of which has limited authority and competence. Furthermore, the prevalence of overlapping jurisdictions and basically noncoterminous economic and political units must be taken into consideration.

We should bear in mind that urban economics is a young field of inquiry. Therefore it does not have a totally coherent framework, and few powerful methods of analysis have emerged. The difficulties inherent in analysis of urban problems are great and will be pointed out in various places throughout this book.

In my attempt to provide an integrated view of urban economic analysis I have drawn almost exclusively on the American experience. I have explicitly mentioned urban conditions in other lands in few—perhaps too few—cases. While this is almost inevitable, much of the analysis provided in this volume can, I believe, be readily generalized, particularly to cities in developed countries. Foreign readers will be alert to their own special conditions and recognize cases where generalization would be hazardous. Mathematical expressions have been kept to a minimum. However, there are a few concepts and methods of analysis—particularly in macroeconomics—where the advantages of using some simple equations appear to outweight the disadvantages.

I am very much aware of the unevenness and difference in levels of sophistication with which by necessity different topics had to be treated. This to no small extent reflects the state of the art in this relatively new field. Much remains to be done. To analyze the great urban policy issues of the next decade, sharper analytical techniques must be developed. It is my hope that some suggestions for the direction of future work have been made in this volume.

In writing this book, I have derived much help, stimulation, and intellectual pleasure from discussions with a large number of colleagues and students. Foremost among these is Dr. Sidney Sonenblum, without whom the writing of this volume would have been impossible. Many ideas were first tried out on him, and he improved and refined them. As a result, many parts of this book, in particular the presentation of urban macroeconomic frameworks and models and the general outlook on urban microeconomic analysis, represent close collaborative effort between Sidney Sonenblum and the author; I am most grateful to him.

I also owe special appreciation to Jerry St. Dennis, who effectively assisted in researching urban macroeconomic models and in helping organize this material; to Robert Butler, who helped in the early stages of research on labor markets; and to Ronald Teeples, who made major contributions to the chapter on urban transportation markets. In probing special aspects of urban economics I greatly benefited from helpful discussions with other colleagues at UCLA—Professors Bryan Ellickson, Michael Intriligator, Harold Somers, Donald C. Shoup, and Jeffrey I. Chapman. Moreover, I was particularly fortunate in being able to complete the manuscript while spending a semester at Harvard University and the Massachusetts Institute of Technology, where many colleagues, in discussions of issues, helped mold my ideas. In this connection my appreciation goes to Professors Kenneth J. Arrow, Martin Feldstein, Robert Dorfman, Richard A. Musgrave, Jerome Rothenberg, and Robert Solow. But I owe no less appreciation to my students, too many to mention, who participated during the last few years in a graduate seminar in urban economics at UCLA. Their challenges to both old and newly proposed ideas and concepts were most stimulating.

Special thanks are due to Mr. Lowden Wingo, Jr., and Dr. Sidney Sonenblum for reading the entire manuscript; to Professor Dick Netzer for reading Chapters 1 and 6 through 13; to Professors Richard F. Muth and Hugh O. Nourse for reading Chapters 2 through 6; and to Professor

Arthur M. Weimer for reading Chapter 3. Their criticism and suggestions were most helpful. Important editorial help was provided by Thomas B. Moule. To Marilyn Schroeter and Elizabeth Bennett I owe thanks for typing and secretarial help. My sincere gratitude goes to all of these.

I also would like to thank McGraw-Hill Book Company for permission to use portions of my book *The Economics of State and Local Government,* and to Praeger Publishers for permission to use portions of the book *Fiscal Pressures on the Central City: The Impact of Commuters, Nonwhites, and Overlapping Governments.*

But perhaps most of all I am indebted to my wife and children for once more putting up with a crammed schedule.

WERNER Z. HIRSCH

CHAPTER 1
INTRODUCTION

I. TODAY'S WORLD—A WORLD OF CITIES

The growth of the cities has been, and still is, one of the strongest, most inexorable developments of the century. In the 1960s, as in the 1950s, this nation's large increase in population was concentrated in about one-fourth of the counties, mostly urban; one-half of the other counties in the United States, mostly rural, actually lost inhabitants. These statistics illustrate the continued massive metropolitanization of America; attracted by the opportunities of urban life and repelled by the lack of rural opportunities, Americans have steadily gravitated from rural areas to the cities and their suburbs. Urban areas thus swallowed up the nation's entire population increase of 24 million; and by 1970, 149.3 million persons—73.5 percent of the total population (compared with 69.9 percent in 1960)—were living in cities of 2,500 or more.[1] Of the fifty largest SMSAs (standard metropolitan statistical areas), all but one showed substantial growth in the 1960s. However, the suburbs grew much more rapidly than did the central-city cores. Whereas the aggregate growth of the central cities of the nation's 243 SMSAs was 5.3 percent, that of the suburban rings was 28.3 percent. By 1970, the suburban population outnumbered that of the cities for the first time—76.3 million versus 63.9 million. These trends are, by and large, duplicated in many of the developed countries of the world.

During the 1960s, there was a slight increase in the number of very large cities—Houston, with more than a million population, became the sixth largest city, and the number of cities with between half a million and a million inhabitants increased from sixteen to nineteen.

This trend has been accompanied by increased slums and crowding; deteriorating public transportation; sprawling suburbs; swelling welfare costs; increasing alienation, violence, and crime; air and water pollution; and severe fiscal pressures, particularly on the central cities.

However, urbanization would not have gone so far but for the positive attributes of urban life. All over the world, people have been moving to the cities for the same reasons: there they can find tremendous opportunities, improved incomes, and diversity of options—many possible employers, many possible careers, and many possible forms of cultural experience and life style.

Thus the great urban dilemma: It is in the cities that people can find and create opportunities; yet, it is in the cities that the quality of living

[1] Philip M. Hauser, "The Census of 1970," *Scientific American,* vol. 255 (July 1971), pp. 17–22.

is perceived as deteriorating. And it is in the cities that the disparity between aspiration and achievement is most apparent.

The cities are places of great interdependence, which is their source of opportunity; yet, their very interdependence makes the millions of heterogeneous residents extremely vulnerable. In the United States, the 1960s have witnessed how vulnerable urban residents can be to determined groups who seek their own objectives. Economics has much to contribute to the analysis of urban interdependences and vulnerability. Often the objectives are economic, in the sense that some groups seek to expand the resources and living standards in urban areas and to change the distribution of these resources among different groups. But beyond that, the analytic tools of economics are concerned with scarcity and allocation issues, and they should be applied specifically to the modern urban scene.

In the late 1960s, two newly powerful groups emerged in American cities—the poor and public employees. These groups can bargain with particular strength because of the increasing interdependence and vulnerability of urbanites. The activities of public employees and the poor have caused some disruptions and contributed to a sense of anxiety and fear; on the other hand, these groups have been instrumental in correcting some of the inequities of the past. However, the persistence of gross and deeply felt inequities continues to be a source of potential and actual trouble, for which remedies must be found and applied soon.

These and similar issues are subjects for analysis by economists. Before we attempt to develop ways to analyze them, we must attempt to define a city and point out those characteristics which constitute the area of interest of urban economics.

II. *WHAT IS A CITY?*

There is a great temptation to define a city, urban policy issues, or urban economics very broadly, perhaps too broadly.[2] For example, one of the most sweeping definitions of the urban scene was indirectly provided by President Richard M. Nixon, who set up an Urban Affairs Council in parallel with the well-established National Security Council, which deals with international affairs. The cabinet-level council was established in order to give "domestic problems equal billing with foreign affairs."[3] By thus being equated with domestic policy issues, urban policy issues are given an extremely broad definition, so comprehensive that it sometimes results in confusion.

What, then, is a city? There are of course many definitions, depending on one's viewpoint and objective. To the economist, a city is a dynamic system of interrelated and interdependent markets characterized by great

[2] Throughout this book the terms "city" and "metropolis" are used interchangeably.
[3] *Business Week* Sept. 27, 1969, p. 72.

density and specialization of economic actors as well as certain institutional conditions that influence decision making by many different governments, each of which has limited authority and competence.[4] These markets serve and are served by large numbers of persons and firms located in relatively close proximity. Cities specialize in efficiently providing households and firms with contacts and flows of information at lower cost than do other spatial forms of social organization.

Significant markets in cities include land and housing, labor, transportation, and public service markets. These markets are closely interrelated in a given metropolitan area, and many are also related with similar markets in other metropolitan areas and the rest of the country. The latter phenomenon stems from the openness of the economy, which does not limit a market to a specified area but offers a relatively free exchange of goods and services within the country.

To be a city, a geographic area must have sufficient size and concentration of economic activities and households to effect scale economies in its private and public sectors. It is clear that the size and character of the city reflect the size and physical requirements of its major markets, and vice versa. Thus a city must provide working space, transportation, and communication for its industries; it must also provide living space, recreation areas, public utilities, logistic support, protection, and other services for its people.

Concentration of people and economic activities, a characteristic of cities, is the direct result of the advantages of close contact—often referred to as "economies of agglomeration." Such economies are in turn responsible for attracting larger and larger agglomerations of people and economic activity. Distance-related costs of transportation and communication shape a market's spatial dimensions (i.e., location of enterprises, residences, and transportation arteries, as well as density of enterprises and households); and the spatial dimensions in turn shape transportation and communication. Another characteristic of cities is production specialization, since producers benefit from the availability of a highly diversified pool of skilled workers, professionals, and entrepreneurs. Because of these resources and the presence of advanced technology and capital intensity, innovation and inventiveness flourish. And large markets ensure scale economies and a great diversity of goods and services, to the benefit of urbanites.

Another characteristic of cities is the circumstances of governmental decision making, which can be discussed in a broader setting. Although the economist is mainly interested in the workings of the urban markets, he cannot overlook how the markets relate to the governmental, social, and physical aspects of the city. Some of the characteristics of a city, and

[4] Jay W. Forrester defines an "urban area (as) . . . a system of interacting industries, housing, and people." *Urban Dynamics* (Cambridge, Mass.: M.I.T. 1969), p. 1.

especially the interplay among them, are responsible for many of the most troubling urban ills. Economists are often tempted to disregard noneconomic concerns, but social likes and dislikes on the urban scene cannot be omitted from consideration, because social behavior influences economic activity.

From a governmental viewpoint, a city is an enormously complicated, and at times an unwieldy and unresponsive, institution. It is virtually never a public policy-making entity, comprising layers of governments e.g., in the United States five layers, on the average, but sometimes twice that many. The vertical relations between federal, state, municipal, county, and school district governments are complex, and the horizontal relations are no less so. For example, many city officials are elected by area and therefore have their own local constituents, loyalties, authorities, and responsibilities, which may be more important to them than the welfare of the larger city. As another example, unlike the central government, city government seldom has a chief executive who controls, and effectively orchestrates, municipal activities. Organizationally, urban government is a jumble of discrete parts, most of the time near chaos, lacking capacity to make comprehensive decisions about the entire city or metropolitan area. Under such circumstances one cannot expect great respect and financial support for urban government.

It might be said that economic functions provide unity to a metropolitan area because they provide employment and income opportunities for the population, whereas social functions create its diversity. But this diversity often generates centrifugal forces that affect behavior of the members of various social groups, including their economic performance. The urbanite may find conflicts between his roles as an economic man and as a social human being, because the city is where ethnic minorities fight most visibly for economic, social, and political advancement.

In cities a variety of people congregate voluntarily or involuntarily into neighborhood groups, often along ethnic, cultural, and socioeconomic lines. Such grouping has profound economic implications. Neighborhoods, although they are not governmental, legal, or economic units, are often the social entities of the city. The evils of involuntary segregation are by now widely understood, but neighborhoods would continue to be distinct even if prejudice were to disappear tomorrow. People tend to sort themselves and form clusters which may be based on ethnic, socioeconomic, or other factors. This tendency stems in part from a psychological need to belong to some group or community with which one can readily identify. The feelings toward members of one's clan or one's territory, strong communal interests and tradition, and common aspirations can produce constructive social action in a neighborhood. But neighborhoods with relatively homogeneous features can also become major antagonists to other neighborhoods that have different backgrounds, interests, or aspirations, particularly those communities along their boundaries. Members of these distinct neighborhoods are customers of and provide personnel for firms, markets, and governments, most of which are located outside the neighborhoods.

In terms of physical characteristics, a city is an artifact created by man. To the architect, a city is an inhabited place of some distinct "imageability."[5] The physical image of a city is defined by its complex of buildings, wires, pipes, roads, and air and water rights and their spatial layout. It is a large, interwoven system that houses and transports people, moves and stores goods and services, and disposes of effluence; many economic features of a city are shaped by this system. In many respects the physical part of a city is a great machine that comes into existence by growth rather than by design. A city grows in response to currently perceived inadequacies at any point in time, unlike smaller machines the lives of which are known and planned for before the decision is made to build them. As a result, the large city machine is in a perpetual state of haphazard and piecemeal construction and congenital imbalance, incapacity, and indisposition.[6] It is replaced and modernized seriatim. Blighted areas and slums are normal characteristics of a city, just as are beautiful, modern homes and villas and up-to-date office buildings. Imbalances and frictions, therefore, are commonplace. Construction of new facilities and repair of old ones go on continually in the modern city, engendering perpetual high social costs in terms of such things as noise, dirt, and congestion.

This review of the important characteristics should prove helpful in taking a look at what urban economics is all about.

III. *URBAN ECONOMICS*

Urban economics is a young field of inquiry even though it has existed in a rather primordial form for some time. It is an outgrowth of the increasing concern of economists with phenomena pertaining to or peculiar to the economic life of cities, and it has gained impetus from the development of regional economics, which emphasizes the spatial dimensions of economic activity.[7]

[5] According to Kevin Lynch, "Imageability is that quality in an object which gives it high probability of evoking a strong image in an observer. It is that shape, color, or arrangement which facilitates the making of vividly identified, powerfully structured, highly useful mental images of the environment." *The Image of the City* (Cambridge, Mass.: Technology Press, M.I.T. and Harvard, 1960), p. 9.
[6] Robert Dorfman, "The Functions of the City" in *Contribution to the Analysis of Urban Problems*, P-3868 (Santa Monica, Calif.: The RAND Corporation, 1968), p. 36.
[7] The development of urban economics in the United States as a discipline was hastened by the establishment of the Committee on Urban Economics (CUE) by Resources for the Future in 1959. This committee was established to guide an experimental program to advance the field of urban economics. The initial member-

Scope

As a subdiscipline of economics, urban economics can draw on the entire body of economic theory. In this connection it is useful to look at two of the perhaps strongest trends underlying civilization—industrialization and urbanization. Economists working to understand industrialization have mainly studied production, while urbanization is essentially the study of human settlement. In the past these two trends have tended to reinforce each other, but it is questionable whether they will continue to do so. Indeed, in some respects industrialization and urbanization are on a collision course, with environmental concern and population growth significant dimensions of a potential clash.

Economics, as a discipline, has been concerned mainly with understanding, analyzing, predicting, and possibly influencing industrialization. Until recently it has not been concerned with urbanization. Urban economics is primarily an effort to bring economics into the study of the city, not to bring the city into the study of economics. Clearly, we know a lot about economics, whereas we know very little about cities and urbanization.[8]

There are different ways the economist can look at the urban world. He can concentrate on the firm and its production; or, as we have chosen to do, he can focus on markets. The reasons for our emphasis on markets are the exceedingly high degree of interdependence among economic actors within a market, and, perhaps more important, the prevalence and intensity of interdependencies among urban markets. We therefore have decided not to look upon urban economics in terms of how mainly neoclassical economic theory would be modified by introducing location and other spatial considerations into production and consumption decisions of firms and households. Instead, because of the pervasiveness of interdependencies among firms, individuals, households, and governmental units, we have selected urban markets as the focal point around which we would like to organize urban economics as a discipline. And it is urban interdependency which leads us to give particular attention to housing, transportation, labor, and public service markets.

As Lowdon Wingo has put it, in the city everything affects everything else:

---

ship of the committee included economists Harvey Perloff (chairman of the committee), Alvin Hansen, Walter Heller, Edgar Hoover, Richard Ruggles, and this author, as well as political scientists Robert Dahl and Robert Wood and sociologist Leo Schnore. The history of the Committee on Urban Economics is well documented by Irving Hoch, *Progress in Urban Economics: The Work of the Committee on Urban Economics, 1959–1968, and the Development of the Field* (Washington, D.C.: Resources for the Future, 1969), pp. ix–x.

[8] I owe the ideas associated with the distinction between the economics of industrialization and urbanization to Sidney Sonenblum.

In the good old days we tackled the slum in a straightforward way by tearing it down. Now we know the slum to be a complex social mechanism of supportive institutions, of housing submarkets, of human resources intertwined with the processes of the metropolitan community as a whole . . . to distinguish favorable policy outcomes from unfavorable ones is no longer a simple matter. Decisions by governments, firms, and individuals in metropolitan areas turn on the state of such interdependent spatial systems as use of recreation facilities, transportation and communication nets, and the markets for land, housing, and even labor, rather than on the highly localized consequences directly elicited by policy actions.[9]

Unlike the economics that focuses on industrialization, urban economics looks at housing not merely as an industry but as a service offered, at different locations, to urbanites who tend to have different ethnic backgrounds, work at varying locations, seek good public services, etc.

Likewise, urban economics looks at transportation as linking urbanites' places of work, residence, recreation, etc. Unlike the economics of industrialization, urban economics looks at urban labor not merely as a factor input but also as a resident who consumes, votes, causes pollution and congestion, and gets into trouble with his neighbors and the law. And finally, urban economics considers the public sector as supplying urbanites with a host of services that not only make them more productive but also enrich their lives through education, recreation, and protection services. Thus throughout, urban economists are concerned with many interdependencies related to spatial juxtaposition, displacement, etc.

Perhaps because urban economics has been born in an age of heightened social consciousness and great visibility of social injustice, and because close proximity can so frequently affect one's neighbor for good or ill, urban economists appear to put somewhat greater weight on distributional considerations than do economists who are concerned solely with industrialization. Also, the time horizon of urban economists tends to be somewhat longer. Concerned with the quality of life, they seek to be farsighted and pursue a process of economic growth in which social cost and social benefit considerations overshadow firms' profits.

Urban economists, aware of the strong linkages between markets and the numerous feedbacks, would greatly prefer to rely on a dynamic general equilibrium analysis. *Ceteris paribus* assumptions and partial equilibrium and static analyses tend to be even more limiting in the study of an urban economy than in a study of the national economy. However, this is not to deny that some partial equilibrium and static analyses can be extremely useful. The interlocking nature of markets within a metropolitan area indicates how important it is for the urban economist to analyze and understand the mix, interplay, and level of local economic activity.

[9] Lowdon Wingo, Jr., "Comment," in Werner Z. Hirsch, ed., *Elements of Regional Accounts* (Baltimore: Johns Hopkins, 1964), p. 144.

The openness of the city's economy requires us to study the urban area's relation to the national economy and pay careful attention to spillovers.

How does urban economics relate to other disciplines? Irving Hoch has stated:

> Urban economics as a field is related to city and regional planning and to geography, political science, and sociology as they concern themselves with the city. But, though related in content and in application to these fields, it appears much more useful for urban economics to retain its autonomy as a subdiscipline of economics, rather than become a component of a subject matter labeled Urban Studies. This follows from the advantages of specialization, for the economist qua economist can bring to bear a highly developed set of theoretical constructs and methodological tools. Within the discipline of economics, the field is closely related to local government finance, transportation economics, real estate economics, land economics, and regional economics.[10]

IV.   MAJOR COMPONENTS OF THE FIELD OF URBAN ECONOMICS

CUE's Five Areas

There are many ways to subdivide the field of urban economics. The Committee on Urban Economics suggested the following five core areas:

1. *Structure and growth of the urban economy.* The city is viewed in its role as a component of the national economy—an element in a national system of cities. Problems of city growth and decline are classified under this head.
2. *Intrametropolitan organization and change.* This subfield focuses on the spatial dimension of the metropolitan economy, in terms of the organization of economic activities within the metropolis and the relation of city form and the allocation of resources. Land use, urban housing, and urban transportation are specific topics of interest.
3. *Urban public services and welfare.* This area involves concern with the urban public economy, addressing problems associated with efficient allocation of public resources and the interaction of the public and private sectors. Topics covered include federal, state, and local finance in a metropolitan context and the demand for and supply of urban public services.
4. *Economics of urban human resources. . . .* Focal topics are households as suppliers of labor services in urban labor markets and urban populations as consumers of final products of the economy. In particular, there is concern with the plight of the urban Negro confronting labor

---

[10] Hoch, op. cit., p. 5.

and housing markets constrained by discrimination. Migration, poverty, and investment in human capital (including education) are examined in an urban context.

5. *Regional accounts.* The systematic organization of flows of information needed for regional economic analysis is the focus of this core area. The urban region is the relevant unit for urban economics application. . . .[11]

It is our objective to show how economic theory can be applied in the context of the key economic characteristics of cities, namely, their spatial, specialization, and decision-making characteristics. In accordance with this objective we have subdivided the field, and this volume, into urban microeconomics, urban macroeconomics, and the urban public sector.

Urban microeconomic analysis focuses on the market behavior of decision-making units such as individuals, households, and firms. Usually the concern is with how these units seek to optimize their position in the market, particularly as they take advantage of such specialization as they possess. Thus urban microeconomic analysis draws heavily on the theory of the firm and the theory of consumer behavior, but takes care to place these theories within a spatial framework. Thus, it heavily relies on location theory. However, not only distance but also proximity considerations must be introduced into urban microeconomic theory. Proximity and production specialization together are responsible for the prevalence of interdependencies among economic actors and markets. Whenever the decision of one economic actor directly affects the utility or production of another, but not through the marketplace, we have an externality.[12]

The specific decision units of urban microanalysis function in many markets, and the markets themselves are highly interrelated. Thus, urban microanalysis should take account of these interrelationships, as it seeks to develop a general theory of urban economics. However, in a situation where many variables are all simultaneously dependent upon one another, it becomes extremely difficult to estimate empirically the microeconomic functional relationships that would test and improve the theory. The state of the art is such that it is more meaningful at the present time to apply microtheory in a partial rather than a general equilibrium framework. That is, it is preferable to analyze individually the specific important markets, including their relationship to other markets, rather than to attempt the description of a general system of simultaneous relationships among urban markets.

Urban macroeconomics is the study of behavior of certain aggregate variables such as consumption and investment expenditures; exports and

[11] Ibid., p. 7.
[12] For more detail, see Chap. 2.

imports; governmental revenues and expenditures; and economywide production, income, and employment, etc., which are seen as "indicators" of the performance of the urban economy. Also, the actors or decision units are usually more aggregative than in microeconomics. Thus, firms become industries, households become income classes, public agencies become governments, individual laborers become occupational classes, etc. Urban macroeconomics is particularly concerned about urban economic change and stability, viewing them as resulting mainly from external forces or from the economic resources and structure of a particular urban economy. Thus urban macroeconomics is concerned not only with issues of specilization in production, but also with how this is affected by government decision making.

High market densities, together with increasing affluence in cities, have generated an environment in which increasing amounts and qualities of services are provided. Inputs into urban services are highly perishable, and many of these services have relatively few substitutes, which conditions tend to make the urban economy sensitive, vulnerable, and unstable. The cyclical instability potential of the urban economy is reinforced by its production specialization and openness. However, great specialization in cities, which at the same time are the centers of technology, innovations, and entrepreneurship, has resulted in economic growth and in high income levels. Thus, urban macroeconomics tends to be much more concerned with the role of services in the city, that is, with what some have called the "postindustrial society."

Urban macroeconomic theory is also helpful in the analysis of the long-run urbanization process. This is the process by which an economy becomes increasingly densely populated, highly specialized, interdependent, and capital-intensive.[13]

While the essential distinction between microeconomics and macroeconomics is the level of aggregation of the variables to which the behavioral relationships are ascribed, there has been little theoretical or empirical success in attempts to aggregate microeconomic relationships to derive a consistent macroeconomic relation between aggregated variables.[14] Even in analyses of specific cities, where one might think it would be easier to do so than for the nation as a whole, it has not been possible to determine exact relations among aggregated urban variables by means of aggregating microeconomic relationships that are known to hold for individuals, households, or firms. It is for this reason that we have kept separate our discussions of urban microeconomics and macroeconomics

---

[13] For more detail, see Chap. 9.
[14] H. A. John Green, *Aggregation in Economic Analysis* (Princeton, N.J.: Princeton, 1964).

even though we recognize they are both concerned with the same set of phenomena.

Inquiries into the economics of the urban government sector, i.e., urban public sector analysis, can be based on modern public goods theory and welfare economics. With their aid, economists can analyze and begin to explain decisions made by urban government officials. Such decisions cover a wide spectrum. Urban public officials are key actors in establishing a favorable environment for efficient operation of the private sector by providing for a generally desirable distribution of government services and tax burdens, by producing goods and services whose production gives them a comparative advantage over private production, and by using their regulatory powers to adjust for externalities. In this manner they are also expected to improve the quality of life.

Analysis of the urban public sector must emphasize particular aspects of taxation and expenditure decisions, since location of taxpayer and service recipient and interdependencies play a major role in their formulation and effects. In relation to tax decisions, particular attention must be paid to the mobility of the tax base as well as the service recipient. In relation to interdependencies, governments must consider their nonmarket effects on the utility and production functions of various economic actors; they also are called upon to improve the efficiency of the urban economy by effectively dealing with externalities generated by the private sector.

However, local urban governments, particularly under fiscal federalism, are faced with a further important phenomenon: interjurisdictional spillovers, which are so abundant in an open urban economy. Such spillovers occur when revenues and expenditures of one governmental unit are directly affected by decisions of economic actors in another jurisdiction.[15] Thus quite frequently expenditures and tax obligations spill over from one jurisdiction to the next without the latter participating in the decisions responsible for these spillovers and the ensuing income redistribution.

We can now summarize and relate the three types of analysis to particularly important urban characteristics presented in an earlier section. This is done in Table 1.1. The rest of this volume is organized in terms of Table 1.1. Chapters 2 through 5 discuss production and exchange in specific markets that operate within distance and proximity constraints in an environment of fragmented decision making. Chapters 6 through 9 discuss the macroaspects of urban production as it takes place in an environment of overlapping governments, political considerations, and extensive vulnerability. Chapters 10 through 13 discuss urban public services as they are provided and financed in the modern urban environment. In more than one instance, important urban characteristics are relevant to more than

---

[15] For more detail, see Chap. 10.

TABLE 1.1   TYPES OF ANALYSIS AND URBAN CHARACTERISTICS

Important Urban Characteristics	Type of Analysis		
	Micro-economic	Macro-economic	Public Sector
Space:			
Distance	✓		
Proximity	✓		✓
Specialization:			
General production	✓	✓	
Decision Making:			
Overlapping governments		✓	✓
Lacking coterminous political and economic entities		✓	✓
Lack of comprehensive city- or SMSA-wide decision making	✓	✓	✓
Frequent government intervention			✓
Vulnerability		✓	✓

one type of analysis. Under such circumstances, the main discussion in this book will be placed where the issue dominates. For example, proximity is mainly taken up in the section on urban microeconomic analysis, while in the public sector section we deal with the issue of one major by-product of proximity, i.e., externalities and spillovers.

CHAPTER 2
INTRODUCTION TO URBAN MICROECONOMIC ANALYSIS

I. *INTRODUCTION*

Urban Microeconomic Concerns

The theoretical tools of microeconomics are designed primarily to facilitate analyses of the behavior of firms—profit maximization—and the behavior of households—utility maximization. Resting on a solid basis of price theory, a belief in the pursuit—if not the achievement—of optimization, and a confidence in the logic of marginalism, microtheorists can spell out the principles of how firms and households can be "expected" to behave. Transactions are the building blocks for microeconomics. A purchase and sale makes a market, and the principles of microtheory are applicable to any market, but they are particularly applicable to the purchases made by households and firms and the sales made by firms.

Microanalysis is most powerful when it focuses on the problems of the firm, particularly when it relates selection of a production function and a scale of operation to prices and earnings. The counterpart microanalysis for households relates consumer budgets to offers of labor and income receipts. In short, microanalyses are strong in consideration of efficiency problems but weak in consideration of distribution problems.

Because of their general utility, the tools of microeconomics should be applicable to the markets and problems associated with the urban scene. But the specific characteristics of an urban place, including space (distance and proximity), interdependencies, production specialization, and consumption diversity, may require that an effective urban microeconomic analysis take on some special characteristics. Thus we should ask whether urban microeconomics, as a special case of microeconomics in general, is called upon to shed light on any problems unique to or particularly important in urban areas, whether it seeks to view markets in some particular way, or whether it requires and has developed any unique tools of analysis.

The first characteristic of cities, which requires some adaptation of standard microeconomic analysis, is that cities are explicitly considered to exist in a spatial dimension. In most of economic theory, space is not a consideration. It is up to us, then, to integrate a means for handling space explicitly. One way of approaching the effect of space is to ask ourselves, What kinds of costs or benefits[1] are associated with space? If there is a distance between two parties to a transaction, then for most kinds of transactions it is necessary that some way be devised to eliminate or reduce that distance, e.g., by moving the parties closer to each other or by linking them through a communications device and then transporting whatever goods are exchanged. In any case, however, a cost is associated with bridging the physical distance, because in doing so some kinds of goods or services must be forgone.

Not only costs, but benefits also, may be associated with distance between actors. These benefits may result from the fact that people simply prefer a little space around them or that they do not work efficiently if they are packed too closely together. It is safe to say, however, that most of the benefits that derive from distance between actors are similar to the costs that arise from physical proximity. Thus there are also costs and benefits associated with proximity of actors.

When people are densely packed into a relatively small area such as a city, their actions affect each other and lead to numerous interrelationships and interdependencies. The importance of this phenomenon is emphasized by a second feature of cities that is relevant to urban microeconomic analysis: production is greatly specialized, whereas consumption is highly diversified. The resulting interdependencies lead to a host of externalities whose effects are imposed upon and unavoided by receivers.

In addition to locational convenience in relation to buyers, producers benefit from specialization by having large numbers of potential workers in a concentrated area. As a result, we find a large number of producers and therefore a greater variety of goods and services to choose from. Furthermore, under affluent conditions many perishable and intangible services are produced. For example, because we do not have the option to grow our own food in cities, we depend on those who bring food into the city and sell it to us. Likewise, we tend to buy relatively large amounts of private services, such as those of restaurants, places of entertainment, and repair shops; and public services, such as those of police and fire departments. Services cannot be stored, and thus if they are not used, they perish and disappear.

The third way in which the theoretical framework of microeconomics must be especially adapted to the characteristics of cities is to acknowledge the existence of certain unique institutional conditions that bear heavily on decision making in cities and metropolitan areas. The main effect of these conditions is on urban government decisions, which are discussed in Chapter 10. However, there also is need for an adaptation of the theoretical framework that allows for analysis of private microeconomic decision making in the presence of numerous, usually uncoordinated, gov-

[1] There is a further discussion on costs and benefits in Chaps. 11 and 12.

ernmental interventions in the urban economy. The purpose of many of these interventions is to alleviate some of the problems that arise as a result of considerations of space (especially density) and of production specialization. Of particular interest to microeconomics is the fact that firms and households must make location, production, and consumption decisions in the absence of concerted, comprehensive planning and control of the city or SMSA. As a result, for instance, a city's land-use pattern results only to a limited extent directly from government decisions. Instead, it evolves as a result of location, production, and consumption decisions made by households, firms, and governments, under governmental influence.

Economists' Interest in Urban Markets and Their Problems

In attempting to identify the great urban problems, we must be careful to distinguish between economic problems found *in* the city and those that are *of* the city. The more interesting issues that fall into the second category relate to urban residential land use and housing markets, transportation markets, labor markets, and certain public service markets. The first three markets not only play a special part in urban America, but also require specific consideration in urban microeconomic analysis. The fourth will be considered separately in the section on the urban public sector. Many of the major problems in urban areas are connected with the operation of these markets.

Most urban problems are also problems in other places, but they can be identified particularly as urban problems because their intensity and perhaps their solutions are influenced by the interaction between the spatial, interdependency, production-specialization, and consumption-diversity characteristics of urban places. The problems of congestion and environmental quality in urban areas are directly influenced by spatial considerations and exacerbated by production specialization and interdependencies. Some aspects of these problems can be analyzed in the context of residential and transportation markets.

Poverty is influenced to some extent by the effects of production specialization and distance on job opportunities. But most of all it is influenced by interdependencies, which means that if one link in the chain of interdependencies, such as adequate education, is missing, the opportunities for passing over poverty thresholds are reduced. In addition, the interdependencies in urban areas often serve to raise expectations, which amplifies the intensity of poverty as a social issue. The evils of discrimination and segregation do not arise from the spatial, interdependency, and production-specialization characteristics of urban places, but they are often intensified by these characteristics, particularly in the labor and residential markets of urban areas.

Urban interdependencies require the provision of a large variety of public services. This, in turn, raises problems of fiscal adequacy that are complicated by differences in attitude concerning what constitutes an equitable distribution of these services and by the spillovers that are associated with governmental fragmentation. Interdependencies also lead to suboptimal arrangements of the physical aspects of cities. As the city grows and changes incrementally, the existing spatial and production-specialization characteristics of the city create a prisoner's dilemma situation for the individual decision maker, and long-run beneficial opportunities are not seized. No landlord can act on his own and improve the quality of housing. Furthermore, because of their densities and interdependencies, urban areas are particularly vulnerable to the demands of any determined group that provides essential services. Not only does this represent a threat to the health and safety of urban residents, but it also contributes to inflationary pressures and reduced growth in real output.

Microeconomic theory is not problem- or social issue-oriented, nor should urban microtheory be so oriented. However, by listing the important social problems associated with urban places we are in a better position to assess the contribution that urban microanalyses, particularly housing, transportation, and labor market analyses, can make to the solution of these problems.

We will turn next to production in an urban environment. Unfortunately, we find it easier to point to important production concerns in cities than to provide rigorously derived new theories or tools of analysis. This will less be the case when we turn in the last sections to the analysis of externalities and spatial aspects of urban markets.

II. PRODUCTION AND DEMAND IN AN URBAN ENVIRONMENT

Production Concerns

One of the major concerns of microeconomic theory is with production economics. We can view entrepreneurship, capital goods, workers, and materials as inputs in the production function, and technology as its operational part. Technology is described and communicated in a set of instructions for combining inputs so they will result in an output of specified characteristics. Like a cake recipe, technology specifies ingredients as well as the sequence of operations. In the neoclassical representation of technological change, improvements in knowledge and techniques result in an alteration of the productivity of inputs; a new production function results.[2]

---

[2] Werner Z. Hirsch, "Technological Progress and Microeconomic Theory," *American Economic Review*, vol. 59, no. 2 (May 1969), p. 36.

At first, production economics was mainly related to agriculture; later it was applied to industrial production. We are concerned with the special environment that urban areas provide the firm for its production of goods and services. There can be little doubt that the most sophisticated entrepreneurship is to be found in urban places. Entrepreneurs are attracted to the city because of the special living and working conditions offered by it. Together with a high level of entrepreneurship in urban areas goes capital intensity of the production process.

Furthermore, the city provides firms with low-unit-cost input factors, for a variety of reasons. There are large and highly diversified pools of skilled labor together with a wide variety of skills and abilities. Firms are not only faced with large numbers of labor sellers in a given occupation or skill category, but they also benefit from the availability of this wide range of types of labor services. This means great opportunity to exploit the comparative advantage of various individuals. As the level of output of a particular good or service grows, opportunities abound for profitably employing these specialized skills. Urban areas also tend to produce low-unit-cost production and marketing information, and the wide variety of alternative suppliers offers flexibility and less costly adjustment in the rate of production. Thus, cities tend to be efficient input factor suppliers. Likewise, they offer a broad array of urban government services.

To complete our consideration of the major contributions the urban environment makes to the firm on the production side, we must briefly consider technology. The progressive entrepreneurship and great capital intensity that we find in cities jointly and separately provide an environment in which high technology as well as inventiveness and innovation flourishes. New production functions are the rule rather than the exception for firms in the urban setting. Even when completely new skills are necessary, the city can generate them quickly because of its good educational and training facilities, which are adaptable to whatever the new demand might call for. Thus, firms need not be worried about changes in production techniques that lead to demands for new kinds of labor.

But cities offer firms more than special production conditions. They also make it possible for firms to operate under special demand conditions that directly affect production. Thus, for example, the large population of cities makes possible a market demand sufficiently large to permit the profitable operation of so-called "threshold" industries, e.g., theaters, specialized medical and professional services, sellers of exotic or imported goods with limited clientele, specialized employment agencies, etc.[3]

In large concentrations of population we usually find close proximity

[3] The "threshold" level of demand is illustrated in Fig. 2.1, where the average total cost (ATC) relation for a representative firm producing and selling a specialized good is represented. The demand for the commodity is considered as a function of income and population in the urban area; and under the usual assumptions about

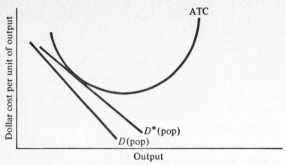

FIGURE 2.1 Representations of the conditions of a threshold activity.

between economic actors. Under this condition, transportation and information costs are reduced and, for example, specialized banking, financial and legal services, etc., can be offered. While population size and density can have these positive effects, they can also impose major costs, many of which are imposed outside of the market.

Finally, the urban environment is one of relatively high personal monetary incomes which are further enhanced by the availability of a broad menu of amenities. Related to high incomes is the fact that urbanites are confronted by a host of options, many of which they might never choose. Still these alternatives, whether they are chosen or not, do have a positive value to the individual. Urbanites appear willing to pay for the value of even unchosen alternatives; this is often also referred to as "option demand."[4] The value of the unchosen alternative can be visualized as the price someone is willing to pay for the "right" to make a purchase at the going market price. Option value is thus closely related to the consumer surplus.

Unchosen alternatives are valuable for a number of reasons. First, they accord urbanites the psychological satisfaction of potential, though unrealized, benefits. Thus, quite a few of those residents who seldom or never go to a symphony, opera, or museum might obtain substantial psychological satisfaction from their knowledge—admittedly often subconscious—that these facilities are available, should they choose to use them.

---

goods, the higher the income, the greater the quantity demanded at any price. Furthermore, the greater the population, the greater the chance that an increasing number of buyers of such a good will exist. Assuming that the market structure is not perfectly competitive, as is realistic for a case in which there are at most a few sellers, it is not possible to derive a supply curve, since the price or quantity offers by the firm in such a market depend upon the demand relation. However, as the diagram shows, there will be no local production of the good until the economy grows to the point where the demand for the product is at least D^*.

[4] Anthony Downs, *The Value of the Unchosen Alternatives*, P-3017 (Santa Monica, Calif.: The RAND Corporation, 1964).

Thus the banding together of people in an urban area, including some who have very little demand for such facilities, makes possible the funding and building of certain urban recreational and cultural facilities.

A second reason is related to benefits associated with the hedge against future declines in the desirability of the chosen alternative. As Downs points out,

> The course of action which is most attractive today may become highly unattractive next week because of some unforeseen change in the environment—including a change in one's own personal inclinations. Even if you plan to do nothing but lie around on the beach on your vacation, it may be worth paying slightly higher rates to go to a resort which also offers a wide variety of indoor entertainment. After all, it might rain, or you might get sunburned, or just bored with such indolence. The existence of unchosen but desirable alternatives thus provides an "escape hatch" for insurance against future misfortunes.[5]

Finally, unchosen alternatives can impart status. For example, many minority members tend to gain psychological satisfaction from knowing that they could join a very prestigious club or move into a wealthy, exclusive suburban neighborhood, even though almost none would actually join or move there. Consequently, many more people would tend to benefit from the provision of such capability in terms of status and psychological gains than the actual number of urbanites who indeed utilized the provision and joined the club or moved into the high-class neighborhood. Altogether, the relatively high personal income in urban areas makes demand functions shift upward and offers increased opportunity for large-scale production and distribution.

The result of the conditions provided firms by cities on both the production and demand sides can be summarized under three major headings: production specialization, scale economies, and a broad menu of goods and services. In an earlier section of this chapter, production specialization was pointed to as one of the main characteristics of an urban economy. The role of such specialization in increasing the dependency and interdependency of urbanites has been stressed. The presence of scale economies underlies many of the production opportunities of cities. For example, production specialization together with scale economies, including large groups of people, supports markets of goods and services that otherwise would not be profitable. And, finally, the large number of producers in urban areas furnish urbanites with a broad assortment of goods and services from which they can choose. This leads to consumption diversity and to improved matching between people's preferences and the large variety of goods and services available.

[5] Ibid.

Production of Information

We would like to consider next the production of a special good that is of particular interest to the urban environment. We are referring to information, to which we alluded earlier. In general it might be useful to separate the production (cost and supply) of information into two sequential dimensions—production and distribution. Information, i.e., bits of ideas and (or) facts, once produced, is distributed by a sender transmitting or communicating it through a channel to a receiver. The transmission can be with or without purpose and therefore either have or not have a message direction. The distribution, transmission, or communication of information has the following dimensions: (1) a sender, (2) a message, (3) a channel, (4) a receiver, (5) attention on the part of the receiver, (6) a common language, (7) time for the process to take place, and (8) one or more purposes to be served.[6]

The information thus produced is demanded by receivers, who, not unlike the senders, have special location characteristics. Since man in his capacity as consumer and (or) producer of information can be in only one place at one moment of time, communication plays a key role in improving an economy's efficiency.

An urbanized economy, because of its size, density, and high technology, can affect in a unique manner the supply of and demand for information. The production costs, in the narrow sense that excludes the distribution of information, can be lower in a highly advanced urban economy than in a less urbanized or in a rural economy. Reasons include such an economy's highly developed state of technology and the fact that much information being produced appears to be multipurpose. Thus, as Meier points out, "On the average there are always more receivers than senders (of information)."[7]

Our main interest centers on the distribution, transmission, or communication of information. The principal channels for communication of information in an urban society are: (1) the written or printed word, (2) the spoken word, transmitted through radio, telephone, television, cinema, recordings, and various other media that separate sender from receiver in time as well as distance, (3) visual images, and (4) touch, odor, taste, etc.

Reference was made before to the purpose to which information is put, i.e., at which receiver the information is directed. Purposeful and directed information can be referred to as information exchange, which can have two major purposes. It can be undertaken for its own sake, e.g., scientists or artists can exchange ideas, or to facilitate financial transactions

[6] Richard L. Meier, *A Communications Theory of Urban Growth* (Cambridge, Mass.: M.I.T., 1962), p. 8.
[7] Ibid., p. 9.

of goods and services. The former exchange mainly raises the level of sophistication and technology, and therefore ultimately the income, of the urban economy. More important, and of particular interest to economists, is the second type of information exchange, that is related to financial transactions between buyers and sellers who hope to benefit from it. The standard transaction requires time for negotiation and is conveniently restricted to one locale. It always involves some exchange of information between individuals or groups in society.

Information exchange tied to financial transactions involves costs and benefits, and we would like to examine how urbanization affects them and is affected by them. In relation to the costs, Armen Alchian points out, "Discovery of the variety of bids and offers and the best path or sequence of actual exchange prices toward an 'equilibrium' requires costly search over the population."[8]

Here then are some major cost components of the sender who distributes and the receiver who searches for information: search for possible buyers or sellers, communication of information about characteristics of the goods of each party, contract information and enforcement, queueing of buyers, provision of price stability, and "buffer inventories" by sellers. Buffer inventories increase the options of buyers, particularly if a diverse inventory is kept. Vacant apartments and large inventories of goods in general have in common a key feature—costs incurred by one party generally reduce the costs of search of another party.

Some of the specific costs that are incurred in information exchange designed to facilitate financial transactions include advertisements, window displays, salesclerks, specialist agents, brokers, inventories, catalogs, correspondence, phone calls, market research agencies, employment agencies, licensing, and certification. These costs are incurred in order to "facilitate the spread and acquisition of knowledge about potential demanders and suppliers and their goods and about prices they can expect to see prevail."[9]

The costs of both types of information exchange are affected by density and technology. Up to a point, information exchange costs tend to decline as the metropolitan area grows in size, for a variety of reasons. Perhaps the two most important reasons are the shortening of distances and the improvement in technology. In addition there is much specialization in the dissemination of and search for information in highly urbanized societies. Furthermore, there is the multipurpose use of information channels. Communication of information is by and large a cooperative attempt on the part of a sender and a receiver to expand the realm of ideas, expressions, and experiences they hold in common. Thus the word *communication* itself derives from the Latin equivalent of *communis*, i.e., common.

[8] Armen A. Alchian, "Information Costs, Pricing, and Resource Unemployment," *Western Economic Journal*, vol. 7, no. 2 (June 1966), pp. 109–110.
[9] Ibid.

Finally, we will turn to the demand for information, which indeed is great in a highly urbanized society. However, while because of high interdependencies and the complexity of decisions, many actions in an urban economy require much information, an increasingly large number of decisions tend to be collective or governmental, i.e., one decision is made for many urbanites. Moreover, since the use of information is made more efficient through the institutionalized contacts provided in cities, e.g., markets, any one decision requires less information.

Thus it appears that highly advanced postindustrialized urban economies are favored by extremely large amounts of pertinent information which, produced and exchanged at low cost, can greatly enhance the economy's efficiency. Under these conditions firms can make even fuller use of their entrepreneurial capacities, inventiveness, availability of capital, and access to new technology. Also, their knowledge of and access to resources, including labor, is improved, together with their understanding of today's and tomorrow's markets. Competition has been sharpened and so has the demand for product, production, distribution, and market innovation.

But households also are likely to benefit. To consumers, more and better information can mean an enlarged menu of goods and services to choose from and a better matching between such offerings and preferences. Prices to consumers might be lowered, both because consumers can make more informed purchase decisions and because of the increased competition among sellers. Furthermore, households in their capacity of labor suppliers can benefit as costs of their own employment search and that of the search for employees by firms are reduced and, with it, frictional unemployment. More and better low-cost information about jobs likely to be open today and tomorrow should improve the chances of workers preparing themselves to take and hold positions. But cities also offer good information on how and where to seek training and retraining for tomorrow's employment opportunities. Yet, for households as well as for firms, more and better information tends to lower costs but also to increase competition. Thus, while it becomes easier to locate employment, there will also tend to be more persons competing for each position.

III.   *EXTERNALITIES IN AN URBAN ENVIRONMENT*

Proximity and specialization of economic actors are important characteristics of urban economies. These two characteristics, particularly in a world of affluence and advanced technology, are responsible for the types and large quantity of externalities occurring in urban areas. In recent years economists have deepened their insight into externalities and have developed methods to analyze them and to advance policy solutions in dealing with them. E. J. Mishan considers concern with externalities as "a new field of specialization within the broader terrain of welfare economics."[10]

Externalities is not a new concept. Alfred Marshall referred to what he called "external effects" as economies external to the firm but internal to the industry.[11] A. C. Pigou elaborated on the concept and pointed to it as a chief cause of divergencies between "private net product" and "social net product" and, therefore, as preventing optimality under conditions of perfect competition.[12]

More recently, contributions to our understanding of externalities have been made by J. Meade and T. Scitovsky; and Kenneth Arrow particularly has helped clarify the concept.[13] However, there is no unaminity among economists at this time as to the nature and definition of externalities. Perhaps the most all-inclusive view is that of James Buchanan and Craig Stubblebine,[14] who talk about a "potentially Pareto-relevant externality," i.e., an interdependency generating "desire on the part of the externally benefited (damaged) party (A) to modify the behavior of the party empowered to take action (B) through trade, persuasion, compromise, agreement, convention, collective action, etc." A similar view can be attributed to E. J. Mishan,[15] who defines an externality as the dependence of someone's utility or output on an unpriced or improperly priced resource.[16] If one of the resources is improperly priced, then gains from trade are possible.

The difficulty with these definitions is not so much that they use Pareto optimality as a benchmark—in theory any other social welfare function could be chosen—as with their implication that any inefficiency is an externality. As Roland McKean points out, ". . . any falling short of either the production-possibility boundary or the 'utility-possibility boundary'

[10] E. J. Mishan, "The Postwar Literature on Externalities," *Journal of Economic Literature*, vol. 9 (March 1971), p. 1.

[11] Alfred Marshall, *Principles of Economics*, 8th ed. (London: Macmillan, 1925).

[12] A. C. Pigou, *The Economics of Welfare*, 4th ed. (London: Macmillan, 1946).

[13] J. Meade, "External Economies and Diseconomies in a Competitive Situation," *Economic Journal*, vol. 62 (March 1952), pp. 54–67; T. Scitovsky, "Two Concepts of External Economies," *Journal of Political Economy*, vol. 62 (April 1954), pp. 70–82; and Kenneth J. Arrow, "The Organization of Economic Activity: Issues Pertinent to the Choice of Market versus Nonmarket Allocation," in *The Analysis and Evaluation of Public Expenditures: The PPB System*, A Compendium of Papers of the Joint Economic Committee (Washington, D.C.: U.S. Government Printing Office, 1969), pp. 47–63.

[14] James M. Buchanan and W. Craig Stubblebine, "Externality," *Economica*, vol. 29 (November 1962), pp. 347–375.

[15] E. J. Mishan, "The Postwar Literature on Externalities," *Journal of Economic Literature*, vol. 9 (March 1971), p. 1.

[16] E. J. Mishan, "Reflections on Recent Developments in the Concept of External Effects," *Canadian Journal of Economics and Political Science*, vol. 31 (February 1965), p. 6.

means that gains from trade are available—or, in Mishan's terms, that some resource is improperly priced."[17]

Ralph Turvey avoids this problem by defining externalities as "the impacts of the activities of households, public agencies, or enterprises upon the activities of other households, public agencies, or enterprises which are exerted otherwise than through the market. They are, in other words, relationships other than those between buyer and seller."[18]

Together with Ralph Turvey, Kenneth Arrow, and E. J. Mishan, we propose that an externality exists whenever the decision of one economic actor, e.g., household or firm, directly affects, through nonmarket transactions, the utility or production functions of other economic actors as well as possibly its own.[19] Externality, thus, results as resources are exchanged in nonmarket situations, commonly involving involuntary exchange.

One individual's (or firm's) consumption can enter into another's utility (or production) function without proper market compensation because of imperfect appropriation of resource rights.[20] Imperfect appropriability of resource rights means that because of technological reasons an individual, household, firm, or governmental unit is unable to fully appropriate (or capture) the marginal value of the benefits each produces or is unable to alleviate costs somebody else imposes.[21] Thus, while from an economic perspective, "resource rights" refer to rights to make decisions about resources and to claim the resulting rewards, there may be reasons why these rights cannot be asserted. Since these rights help shape the household's, firm's, and governmental unit's set of opportunities and tradeoffs, and therefore, their behavior, the effectiveness with which these rights are enforced will also affect behavior.

When there is imperfect appropriability of resource rights, then Musgrave's "exclusion principle" cannot work. This is a principle which postulates that an individual should be "excluded from the enjoyment of any particular commodity or service unless he is willing to pay the stipulated price to the owner."[22] When there is joint consumption, as, for example,

[17] Roland N. McKean, *Appropriability and Externalities in Urban Government*, paper prepared for the Oct. 22, 1971, COUPE meeting in Cambridge, Mass. (processed), p. 10.
[18] Ralph Turvey, "Side Effects of Resource Use," in Henry Jarrett (ed.), *Environmental Quality in a Growing Economy* (Baltimore: Johns Hopkins, 1966), p. 47.
[19] The presence of externalities can be expressed by the following mathematical notations: $F^1 (x_1{}^1, x_2{}^1, \ldots, x_m{}^1; x_n{}^2)$ represents an external effect generated by entity 2 on entity 1; where F^1 stands for the utility (or output) level of individual (or firm) 1, and the x^1's are the amounts of goods $x_1, x_2, \ldots, x_m$ utilized by him (or it) and $x_n{}^2$ is the amount of some good x_n utilized by individual (or firm) 2. Mishan, "The Postwar Literature on Externalities," op. cit., p. 2.
[20] McKean, op. cit., p. 2.
[21] Ethical and institutional reasons may reduce appropriability, though to a lesser extent.
[22] Richard A. Musgrave, *The Theory of Public Finance* (New York: McGraw-Hill, 1959), p. 9.

in the famous lighthouse case, and exclusion is impossible or requires considerable resources, then resource rights will be imperfectly appropriated. In short, appropriability can be made easy or difficult because of technological characteristics of the phenomenon under consideration. It is the high cost of effectively excluding individuals from partaking in joint consumption without proper payment, i.e., high transaction costs, that interferes with the existence of a market and brings about externalities.

This view of transactions requires a major modification of conventional microtheory, since most of that theory implicitly assumes discrete inputs and outputs with perfect appropriability of rewards and burdens. But this is an invalid assumption, particularly in cities where externalities abound and inputs as well as utilities of individuals (and outputs of firms) cannot readily be identified and appropriated.[23]

Since an externality is generated by one or more decision units directly affecting one or more units (often including the first unit) outside the marketplace, several important questions are raised. Which actors initiate the externality and which are affected by it? For example, in the congestion case, many individuals participate in affecting others' utility functions, with virtually complete reciprocity. Thus they all contribute equally and are all equally affected. However, in the pollution case, one or a few individuals (or firms) affect the utility (or production) functions of very many individuals.

Can the externality be traced back to a divergence between what people are individually motivated to do and what they might wish to accomplish together, or is insufficient information at least in part responsible for it? For example, if a driver before entering a highway could learn that it was blocked a mile away because of a traffic accident, he could decide to take a side street and by so doing not impose congestion costs on himself as well as on others.

Is the externality spatial in character, e.g., mainly a function of density, or is it the result of technology or affluence? If space is important, as in the case of neighborhood effects, "an individual's utility depends both on others' behavior (e.g., esthetic, criminal) and on their location."[24]

Now let us consider how externalities and their anatomy are affected by the dominant features of an urban environment. There is much evidence that affluence and advanced technology are responsible for the very large number of externality-producing decisions being made. In an affluent urban society very many activities take place, particularly many involving high technology, which in turn entails numerous externalities. Affluence

---

[23] Matters are further complicated by utilities and outputs being so frequently multidimensional. For example, a house provides not only shelter but also access to jobs, public services, desirable neighbors, etc.

[24] Arrow, op. cit., p. 59. The different externalities will be discussed further in Chaps. 3 and 13.

may be responsible for reducing the concern with externalities in urban areas because it lowers the marginal value of those resource rights which are imperfectly appropriated; on the other hand, if it is precisely those resource rights whose marginal value is increasing (e.g., clean air, tranquillity, and clean water), then the concern with urban externalities will grow.

Similarly, technology might expand the scope of externalities because any one decision affects so very many economic actors. For example, highly advanced communications technology reduces effective distances. Proximity heightens the probability that a decision made by one individual, firm, or government affects directly, though often inadvertently, many others; but the effects might be different. If proximity is great, there is little room for moats and insulation.

Finally, production specialization, particularly in the face of a highly diversified demand for goods and services, tends to reduce the options available to those on whom unwanted utility or output effects are placed. The consequence is that the recipients of these unavoidable and unwanted utility or production effects are highly vulnerable to those imposed losses, against which they have little defense.

We are so greatly concerned about urban externalities because of their allocative significance. In short, when efficient resource allocation is interfered with because of externalities, output corrections are called for, often requiring collective action of some sort. It need not be governmental ownership but can be regulation, taxation, or subsidy. Furthermore, Kenneth Arrow has pointed to the impact of such norms of social behavior as ethical and moral codes. Thus, in the absence of trust in each other's word, costly arrangements are needed for guarantees and sanctions, while at the same time opportunities for mutually beneficial, cooperative, often nonmarket, action are forgone.[25]

IV. TOOLS FOR ANALYSIS OF SPATIAL CHARACTERISTICS OF URBAN MARKETS

Spatial aspects of markets have been the primary focus of regional economics. Considering an urban area simply as a particular type of region, many analysts have directly transferred this spatial emphasis to their study of urban areas. John Kain, for example, argues that spatial considerations are the *only* reasons for considering urban economics as a distinct field of study. Because the extensive literature available on regional economics emphasizes the tools for spatial analysis, this chapter discusses them in only introductory fashion.[26]

[25] Ibid., pp. 61–62. These issues will be taken up in more detail in Chap. 13.
[26] Two recent and excellent texts, the latter being somewhat more technical than the former, are:

The beginning of regional economics can perhaps be dated by the writings of Johann Von Thünen in the early nineteenth century. Alfred Weber then provided the "classical" view of regional economics in the early twentieth century.[27] Three directions of theoretical development relevant to urban economics have emerged from these early works: Consideration of the effects of distance on production, exchange, and location, including consideration of its effects on the spatial extent and shape of markets; consideration of the spatial distribution of cities within a system; and consideration of the spatial sources of growth for a city.

Walter Christaller in the early 1930s was probably the first to provide a firm empirical basis for the observation that cities are distributed not randomly but rather in some ordered relationship to one another.[28] In the 1950s the two "competing" theories explaining the causes of a city's growth were eloquently spelled out and the debate is still raging about whether, as Douglas North argues, demand through export markets is the primary factor in city growth or whether, as François Perraux believes, complex internal factors of supply are more important.[29]

Edgar M. Hoover, *An Introduction to Regional Economics* (New York: Knopf, 1971).

Harry W. Richardson, *Regional Economics* (New York: Praeger, 1969).

More dated, but still relevant overviews are presented in:

John R. Meyer, "Regional Economics: A Survey," *American Economic Review*, vol. 53, no. 1, part 1 (March 1963), pp. 19–54.

Walter Isard, *Methods of Regional Analysis* (New York: Technology Press and Wiley, 1960).

[27] See Carla M. Wartenberg, tr., *Von Thünen's Isolated State* (London: Pergamon, 1966); C. J. Friedrich, tr., *Alfred Weber's Theory of Location of Industries* (Chicago: The University of Chicago Press, 1929).

[28] See:

Prentice-Hall, 1966).

C. W. Baskin, tr., *Central Places in Southern Germany* (Englewood Cliffs, N.J.:

G. Manners, "Urban Expansion in the United States," *Urban Studies*, vol. 2 (1965), pp. 51–66.

Brian Berry, "Cities as Systems Within Systems of Cities," *Papers and Proceedings of the Regional Science Association*, vol. 13 (1964), pp. 147–163.

[29] See the following:

Douglas North, "Location Theory and Regional Economic Growth," *Journal of Political Economy*, vol. 63 (June 1955), pp. 243–258.

François Perraux, "Note on the Concept of Growth Poles," *Economie Appliquée*, 1955 (reprinted in David L. McKee, Robert D. Dean, and William H. Leahy, *Regional Economics*, 1970).

Niles M. Hansen, "Unbalanced Growth and Regional Development," *Western Economic Journal*, vol. 4, no. 1 (September 1965), pp. 3–14.

Edward Ullman, "The Nature of Cities Reconsidered," *Papers and Proceedings of the Regional Science Association*, vol. 9 (1962), pp. 7–23.

Brian Berry and William Garrison, "Recent Developments of Central Place Theory," *Papers and Proceedings of the Regional Science Association*, vol. 14 (1958), pp. 107–120.

Benjamin Chinitz, "Contrasts in Agglomeration: N.Y. and Pittsburgh," *American Economic Review* (May 1961), pp. 279–289.

The costs associated with distance between markets are introduced into urban microeconomics in two important ways.[30] Analyses of urban production and exchange specifically consider the effects of transportation and marketing costs on market size, scale of operation, and substitution possibilities between transportation and other inputs. In addition, distance costs are a basic consideration in the formulation of location theory, which seeks to explain residential location decisions of households and the site location decisions of manufacturing, trade, and service establishments. Some of these locational considerations are also applicable to location of public service facilities.

Concern with the effects of proximity, including the related issues of greater diversity and increased market size, has stimulated further development of benefit-cost analyses. Although such analyses are not a new tool of urban microeconomics, they make extensive use of microeconomic theory and they are likely to result in improved formulations of the basic theory. Finally, urban density, and to some extent deterioration in the urban environment, forces applied microeconomic analyses to explicitly consider land as a factor of production and to take account of its implications for the spatial form of cities.

The Effects of Distance on Production and Exchange

Overcoming distance is a productive activity, and input and opportunity costs are associated with it. Edgar Hoover has used the generic term "transfer" to include not only the transportation costs of moving goods (both inputs and outputs) and people (as consumers and workers) but also the transmission of such intangibles as energy, information, and ideas.[31]

Considerable attention has been devoted in the literature to transportation costs. However, it may be that the costs of the intangible transfers

[30] The effects of distance on production, exchange, location, and extent of market are analyzed in:

Harold Hotelling, "The Laws of Returns under Competitive Conditions," *Economic Journal*, vol. 36 (December 1926), pp. 535–550.

Arthur Smithies, "Optimal Location in Spatial Competition," *Journal of Political Economy*, vol. 49 (June 1941), pp. 423–429.

August Lösch, *The Economics of Location* (New Haven: Yale, 1954).

Walter Isard, *Location and Space Economy* (Cambridge, Mass.: M.I.T., 1956).

Edgar M. Hoover, "Spatial Economics: Partial Equilibrium Approach," in *Encyclopedia of the Social Sciences* (New York: Macmillan, 1968).

Leon Moses, "Spatial Economics: General Equilibrium Approach," in *Encyclopedia of the Social Sciences* (New York: Macmillan, 1968).

Melvin Greenhut, "The Size and Shape of the Market Area of a Firm," *Southern Economic Journal*, vol. 19 (July 1952), pp. 37–50.

[31] Hoover, *An Introduction to Regional Economics*, op. cit., Chap. 3.

are much more significant in production and exchange. For example, marketing costs, the need to supply rapid information to suppliers and customers, and the advantage in being tied into the network of ideas concerning production techniques, potential market changes, new products, etc., will all influence a firm's activities, including its decisions on plant location. Similarly, households require information about job opportunities, the quality and prices of the items they want to purchase, and the location of vendors, all of which will influence their real income and the ways they spend it.

For empirical simplification, unit transportation costs of goods are often assumed to be proportional to the distance traveled; however, the actual distance-cost relationship is not this simple. For example, to ship a good, there are some costs—such as packing and other preparation costs, as well as other costs of loading and unloading—that can be considered fixed with respect to the distance the good must travel. In addition, the technology of transportation is such that for most modes the average costs of transportation, with respect to distance, decrease as distance increases. These two features combine to produce a typical transportation cost function that is nonproportional; however, as long as marginal transportation costs—the costs of transporting a unit an additional increment in distance—are positive, the results of frameworks and models illustrating proportional transportation costs continue to hold.

Another common simplification assumes that for any distance of shipment the marginal transportation costs are a function of the weight of the product being shipped. This simplification neglects the influence on transportation costs of perishability, which is related to length of shipping time. Marginal transportation costs are also affected by fragility and bulk and by any fire or explosion hazards associated with the good. The combined influence of these factors determines the transportation cost of goods that confronts firms and that enters into their production and exchange decisions.

Transportation costs to the individual of personal travel are comprised of two parts: out-of-pocket costs (including any capital purchases) and imputed value of the time spent in travel. The time costs of travel are often more important in the individual's real income and to his decisions concerning work, exchange, and location than are his out-of-pocket costs.

The relation of transportation costs to individual and household decisions is discussed in Chapter 4. Now consider the effect of transportation costs on operations of the firm.

Imagine a buyer of some particular product who demands some quantity and has a normally downward-sloping linear demand curve. The price confronting the buyer can be considered as consisting of two parts, the FOB selling price at the plant or store and the transportation cost to get the product from the plant to the buyer or the buyer to the store. If we assume that the transportation cost is an increasing function of distance, then the amount that would be purchased if there were no transportation cost would be reduced by some quantity because of the added transportation cost associated with distance. Thus the farther a buyer is from the plant or store source of the item obtained, the smaller his demand will be, as determined by the slope of his demand curve, the transportation cost per mile, and the total distance between source and buyer.

Now let us assume that buyers are evenly distributed along a linear corridor from the plant or store, that they have identical and linear demand curves, and that they pay the transportation charges associated with their purchases. The demand for the product of the plant or store at specific places along the corridor can then be shown as a linear function of distance.

Total demand would be zero at the point where the amount which would be purchased if there were no transportation cost equals the amount by which demand would be reduced by transportation costs.

Thus, given the product demand curves, transportation costs, and distribution of buyers, the geographic market area for the seller can be determined: the limits of the market area are smaller, the greater the marginal transportation costs or the higher the FOB selling price; the market area is larger, the greater the demand for the good or the less "responsive" the quantity demanded is to changes in the price.

The simple functional forms used here are not essential to the basic results. If the demand function is nonlinear and nonproportional there would still be a market area limit resulting from the effects of distance on price, although the distance–quantity demanded function would slope downward in a nonlinear fashion.

There are, however, more fundamental modifications that would have to be made to this formulation if it is to be more applicable to the real world. For example, the assumption that buyers are distributed along a single corridor in one direction from the plant would have to be changed to the assumption that buyers are located in all directions from the plant; in this case the quantity demanded–distance relation would take the shape of a demand "cone," assuming that marginal transportation costs are the same regardless of the direction of travel. A modification would have to be made if the density of buyers varies at different distances. Also, if the income of buyers varies with location, then the effects of the different incomes on the individual demand curves would have to be incorporated. Finally, if the seller pays for some or all of the transportation cost, the distance–quantity demanded relationships will be affected.

Once the seller is confronted by different demands at different distances, he has the opportunity of improving his profit position by assuming the transportation cost and including it in the delivered price of the product. He may choose a single delivered price in the market area or a variable price depending on distance. In selecting his pricing policy, however, the seller will need to consider not only the demands for his product, but also the production costs at different scales of operation. Thus, under these conditions, once the prices are set, the quantity of his scales and the range of his market area are simultaneously determined.

To make analyses of the effects of distance on exchange and production more realistic, the assumption of a single seller should also be relaxed. As the later discussion of location decisions indicates, there are some incentives for sellers to locate at different places in order to corner a particular geographic market, i.e., to become "spatial monopolists." When this happens, the production, pricing, and location decisions of firms become intimately interrelated.[32]

Analyses of a situation in which the location of sellers is fixed and the buyers are distributed over space surrounding the sellers are particularly useful in examination of the trading areas of retail or wholesale establishments in the city or of the operations of a plant that is selling materials to many other establishments in the city. However, we should also consider the situation in which a buyer is in a fixed location and the sellers are distributed spatially. Such analyses are useful particularly in labor market analyses and in consideration of a situation in which a single plant is buying materials from a potential variety of vendors in the city. If each supplier of labor or materials is considered to have an upward-sloping supply curve, then a distance–quantity supplied relationship can be derived for each "delivered price" paid by the centrally located buyer. Such a relationship would show that the quantities supplied by various sellers located at various distances from the buyer would decrease with distance and that the location and the quantities supplied at any distance will decrease less rapidly with distance—as the marginal transportation costs become smaller.

For example, consider the provision of labor services by households to firms (which will be discussed more fully in Chapter 5). The buyers of labor services can provisionally be considered as located at a single point such as the Central Business District (CBD) and the sellers of labor services as located around this point in various residential districts. Assuming an upward-sloping aggregate supply curve of labor services with respect to the wage at each point in space, it is then possible to derive for each wage paid at the central location the amount of labor services forthcoming from households located at various distances from the CBD. Although many other factors enter the situation, when these factors are held constant the empirical results generally indicate that the labor supply falls off with distance.

[32] For a discussion of alternative pricing methods of spatial monopolists and their effects on the profits and market area of sellers, see Martin Beckmann, *Location Theory* (New York: Random House, 1968), chap. 2.

The Effects of Distance on Location

It has already been pointed out that the costs associated with overcoming distance from market will influence the choice of location of residence or establishment site. The residential location decision is discussed in Chapter 3; here we consider the location decision of firms.

Clearly it is not only transportation costs that influence location, but also such other factors as land costs, differing tax rates within the metropolitan areas, zoning regulations, labor and other input costs and the assurance of their availability, and the location, density, incomes, and tastes of potential buyers.

The location decision of a profit-maximizing firm should be analyzed within a general approach, accounting simultaneously for the choice of location, level of output, price, scale of plant used, combinations of inputs, and so on.[33] However, to elucidate some of the important relationships it is better to work with relatively simple formulations. Let us begin by considering the case where a firm has a single market, located at some point, and production requires a single input[34] that is located at (originates from) some other point.[35] Thus, there are two distances to consider: the distance that the input is moved, including the sum of the distance from input origin to plant and the distance from the plant to market, and the distance that the output moves from plant to the market. Now let us assume we know the costs of transporting "equivalent" units[36] of inputs and outputs per unit of distance.

With fixed market, plant, and input origin sites, the total transportation cost associated with moving an input first to the plant and then to the market is a constant; i.e., the product of the cost of transporting an equivalent input unit and the distance traversed. Since there is only one input, we might also say that this is the total transportation cost (of both input and output) associated with producing and delivering the product. However, even though only one input is needed to produce the output, we assume that it undergoes some transformation, so that there is a differential cost in moving the input and output over a unit distance. It is necessary

---

[33] For an example of such a model and the difficulties of expressing the locational choice simply, see Harry W. Richardson, *Regional Economics* (New York: Praeger, 1969), pp. 59–90. Also, there is a considerable operations research literature dealing with plant location.

[34] This assumption is not quite as restrictive as it first seems; and this model can be applied as well to the case of multiple inputs where one is "localized," available only at a particular point, and the others are ubiquitous. Ubiquitous inputs are those available at all locations at the same cost; an example is water within a particular urban area.

[35] This discussion is elaborated on with the case of a transshipment point in William Alonso, "Location Theory," in L. Needleman, *Regional Analysis* (Baltimore: Penquin, 1968), pp. 342–347.

[36] An equivalent input unit is defined as that amount of an input used in the production of one unit of output.

to modify the constant term by this differential cost if we are to obtain the true total transportation cost. If, for example, the input gains in weight in the process of being transformed into output, the modification would be to increase the constant term; if it loses weight, the modification would be negative. In order to minimize the transportation costs, therefore, the firm is likely to establish a decision rule that says, "Minimize the distance between plant and market if unit output costs for transportation are greater than unit input costs; but if the reverse is true, then minimize distance between input origin and plant." The minimum value of the distance between plant and market is zero, which puts the firm at the market site, and the maximum value of the distance between plant and market is equal to the distance between input site and market which puts the firm at the input origin site, minimizing the cost of moving the input.

Even if the transportation cost functions are nonlinear or, more important, if they have nonzero constant terms (which can be related to costs of loading and unloading that are independent of distance), the results will be the same. In order to minimize transportation costs of both inputs and outputs, the firm locates at either the market site or input origin unless the cost functions increase at an increasing rate with respect to distance. Assuming that these cost functions tend to exhibit the normal pattern of diminishing marginal cost, this problem will not arise.[37] The important result to keep in mind is that where only two points are involved—an input origin site and a market site—then, whether the cost functions are linear or not, the one of the two points that minimizes cost will be selected as the location site of the firm. The single condition—sufficient, but not necessary—for this conclusion is that transport cost functions do not exhibit increasing marginal costs per unit of distance.

Unfortunately, the simplicity of the two-point model is lost when we consider situations in which there are more than one input site and more than one market location. There are two ways of handling multiple input and output locations. The first method is known as the Weberian Triangle; the second method utilizes isocost maps.

In the Weberian Triangle method,[38] there are three locations to be considered, consisting of two input or materials locations (X and Y) and one market (D). Connecting each of these three points yields a triangle within which lies the cost-minimizing location of the firm that transforms these inputs into an output.

Imagine that a firm has a production function relating its output to two inputs. The transportation costs for each "equivalent" unit of input is equal to the transportation cost per unit of input times the distance moved over the average physical product; the transportation cost of the

---

[37] See Alonso, op. cit., p. 344, for the argument concerning diminishing marginal cost of transport where the margin is distance.
[38] Ibid.

output is its unit transfer cost times the distance it is moved. The total transportation cost is the sum of the two input costs and the output cost. The value for each input and output transportation cost will depend on where the firm locates; changing the location of the firm within the Weberian triangle will cause an input or output transportation cost decrease if any other cost increases. (This is not the case for movements from inside to outside the triangle.) The unit transport costs of the inputs over their average physical product and the unit transport cost of the output can be thought of as weights applied to their respective distances moved. The cost-minimizing location of the firm would be determined by the magnitude of each weight: the larger the weight, the greater will be the "pull" to the input origin or market site, as shown in Figure 2.2. The coefficients determining the input weight or "pull" are the cost of transporting that input through a given distance over the average physical product of input; and the output "pull" is given by the cost of transporting the output.

The solution technique outlined above can be extended theoretically to a large number of cases, although the mathematics becomes difficult after the three-point case.[39]

Where there are many input locations, a second approach to the problem of the firm's location is to develop what is called an *isodapane* map.[40] Again we can assume that there are two input locations and one market location. About each of these three we can draw *isotims*, or lines along which the cost of transporting the good relevant to that point is constant. These will be in the form of concentric circles about the points. The value attached to each successive circle will depend on the characteristics of the transport cost function for that good. In general, these values should increase less rapidly than distance, because of diminishing marginal cost of transportation.

A map such as that shown in Figure 2.3 will show the intersections

[39] See Beckmann, op. cit.
[40] See Alonso, op. cit., pp. 348–353.

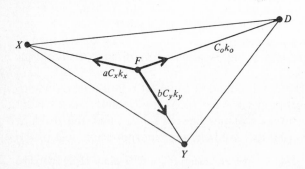

FIGURE 2.2   *The Weberian triangle.*

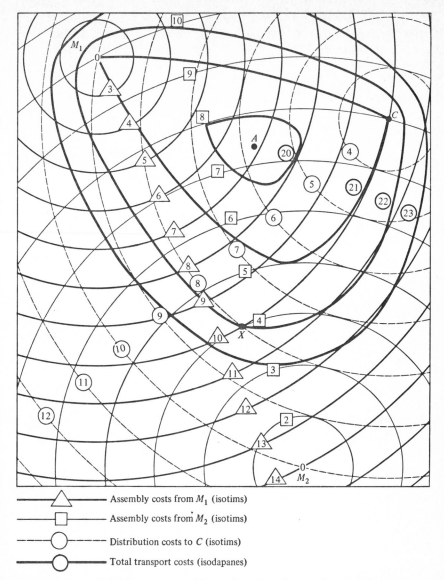

Assembly costs from M_1 (isotims)

Assembly costs from M_2 (isotims)

Distribution costs to C (isotims)

Total transport costs (isodapanes)

FIGURE 2.3 *An isodapane map with two input locations and one market.*
SOURCE: *J. Friedman and W. Alonso (eds.),* Regional Development and Planning (*Cambridge, Mass.: M.I.T., 1964*).

of the three or more systems of circles. By taking note of the total cost at each intersection, or the sum of the values shown on the three curves, we can construct loci of such intersections with equal costs. These loci are the isodapanes, and they represent all the locations at which a firm will have to pay the same total of transportation costs for input and output.

Since the isotims are closed circles, the isodapanes will be closed figures as well, although not necessarily circular. They will also have regularly diminishing values, moving from outside to inside. Thus, the cost-minimizing location for the firm will be the origin or focus of the isodapane map. In the figure this is the point A.

This approach considers the market for a particular good as a point. However, if this assumption is relaxed and the market is considered as a set of potential buyers located at different points in space, as was done earlier, the analysis can account for interdependencies of the location decisions of firms selling the same good. In the presence of more than one supplier of a particular good, the effect of transportation costs is to segment the entire market into geographically separated submarkets or market areas, regions in each of which a single seller is the lowest-cost supplier of the good.

The market area for the firm is the area surrounding it in which buyers prefer to deal with it under perfect competition in every respect other than space. To determine the price that a buyer must pay at any distance from the firm, it is necessary to add the FOB price at the plant or store and the cost of moving the good from the firm to the buyer's location. The way that the price increases with distance is shown in Figure 2.4. The segment at F represents FOB price and the lines going away from the point show the rate of increase in price for distance. The figure shows two such firms for which the slope of the transport cost function is equal and the FOB price is equal. The boundary (b) between the two market areas is a straight line; F has the market to the left of b and F' that to the right of b.

In panel a of Figure 2.5, transport costs are the same, but the FOB price of firm F_2 is higher than that of firm F_1. This results in a hyperbolic boundary between the two firms' market areas, with the locus closer to F_2, the firm with the higher FOB price. In panel b, the FOB prices are equal but the transport cost is greater for F_2. Notice that the transport cost function for F_1 continues beyond the market area for F_2. This means that the market area of the latter is wholly contained within the area of the former.

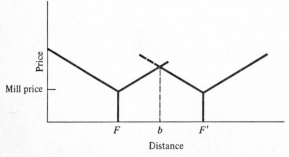

FIGURE 2.4   *Market area boundary with equal prices.*

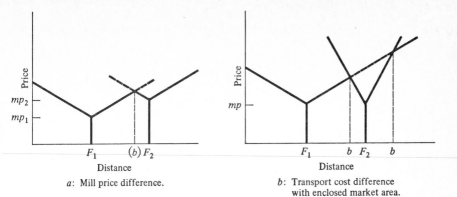

a: Mill price difference.

b: Transport cost difference with enclosed market area.

FIGURE 2.5   *Conditions for hyperbolic boundaries between market areas.*

These diagrams present a picture of the division of buyers among different sellers for given locations of sellers. However, the location *decision* of sellers depends clearly upon the location of other competing sellers. To illustrate the effects of this spatial or locational interdependence, consider the case of a group of buyers distributed spatially over an urban area of fixed size and assume initially that just a single seller of a particular good is located in the area. Then the entire set of buyers makes up the market area for this firm. However, if this firm is earning profits, there is an incentive for other firms to enter the market area so as to earn profits as well. The entry of a second firm (and successive firms) decreases the demand for the firm first established in the area; the entry of other firms may increase the prices that the preexisting firms must pay for inputs as well; but we abstract from such considerations here for simplicity. If buyers are spread evenly throughout the original market area, the entering firms will attempt to locate as far as possible from the existing sellers, so as to gain access to as many buyers (as large a segment of market demand) as possible. If we treat each seller as a spatial monopolist, the entry of additional firms is an example of "monopolistic competition," in Chamberlain's sense.[41] Diagrammatically, this case is presented in Figure 2.6, in which the entry of additional firms is represented by a downward-shifting demand curve faced by each firm. The incentive for entry of new firms is eliminated when the demand faced by the (representative) individual firm has declined to the point that profits are eliminated.[42]

An important type of location activity that takes place in urban areas —one that cannot be analyzed in terms of a profit-maximizing model—is

[41] Edward Chamberlain, *The Theory of Monopolistic Competition* (Cambridge, Mass.: Harvard, 1933).
[42] For a discussion of the shapes that the market areas might take under certain restrictive assumptions, see E. S. Mills and Michael R. Lave, "A Model of Market Areas with Free Entry," in Robert D. Dean et al. (eds.), *Spatial Economic Theory* (New York: Free Press, 1970).

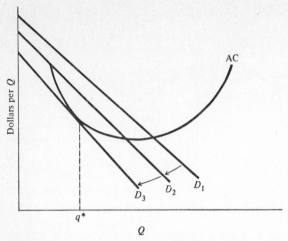

FIGURE 2.6   Equilibrium in spatial monopolistic competition.

the location of public service facilities. These services are often provided from service centers such as city halls, schools, fire stations, courts, police stations, public parks, amusement centers, and so on. Since such facilities cannot be located in terms of profit criteria, other criteria must be substituted, such as minimizing the distance that the public must travel to receive such services, or maximizing the usage of the facilities, or minimizing the costs of providing some given level of quality of public service. Different kinds of public facilities will be influenced by different criteria. For example, the locational aspects of emergency services such as fire and police stations and hospitals may be very different from those for other public facilities such as post offices, parks, waste disposal centers, and public housing.[43] Some of the major influences on public facility location are clear: for example, fire stations and primary schools in some areas must be located so that the travel time to the farthest client does not exceed a given maximum.

While there may be some concepts from private sector location models that are useful in understanding public location decisions,[44] the development of the theory of public facilities location has lagged behind that of private location. A major difference is that public facilities locations in a given jurisdiction are chosen by a relatively centralized decision-making authority, e.g., the fire or police department or the school district, which allows the choice of any particular location to be made in light of other

[43] Charles Revelle, David Marks, and Jon C. Libeman, "An Analysis of Private and Public Sector Location Models," *Management Science*, vol. 16, no. 11 (July 1970), pp. 692–707.

[44] Michael B. Teitz, "Toward a Theory of Urban Public Facility Location," *Papers of the Regional Science Association*, vol. 21 (1968), pp. 35–51.

adjustments in the network or system of similar facilities. By contrast, in the case of selection of location in the private sector, e.g., the location of independently owned grocery stores, the situation is characterized by a set of individual, relatively more independent, decision makers.

There exist many elaborations and refinements of location economics, which we will not take up here. However, we recommend the extensive literature on the subject, mentioned in part in footnote 26, to the attention of readers especially interested in them.

V. THE SPATIAL FORM OF URBAN AREAS

The results of the interactions of the location decisions of households, firms, and the public sector may be observed in the land-use patterns in urban areas.[45] The "atmosphere" in which the separate location decisions are made is very complex, and, as Meyer, Kain, and Wohl have observed,

> . . . the spatial pattern of a city in a free-enterprise society is the collective result of a large number of separate business and household location decisions and transportation choices. These decisions are made in a context of and are influenced by economic, sociological, and technological circumstances, usually beyond the immediate control of the decision-maker. They are also constrained and, to some extent directed by, public policies—zoning ordinances, building codes, transportation policies, and the like.[46]

However, there does exist a general similarity of spatial patterns among cities, as well as some techniques of partial analysis useful for predicting and understanding them. An early technique, developed by Von Thünen,[47] predicts a series of concentric zones centered on a city or market in which those products with higher transportation costs are located nearer the city. The market is the mechanism by which land is allocated to various uses—the firm (or activity) that values the particular site most highly and is willing to pay the highest rent receives use of the land. More recent studies of the spatial structure of urban areas[48] have attempted to understand the

[45] A somewhat different view has been taken by Hans Weigman, who looks at each urban market as having its own characteristics that in turn determine the spatial form of the urban economy. Hans Weigman, "Ideen zu einer Theorie der Raumwirtschaft," *Weltwirtschaftliches Archiv*, vol. 34 (1931), pp. 1–40; and "Standortstheorie und Raumwirtschaft," in W. Seedort and H. Jurgen (eds.), *Johann Heinrich von Thünen zum 150 Geburtstag* (Rostock: Carl Hinstorffs, 1933), pp. 137–157.
[46] John R. Meyer, John F. Kain, and Martin Wohl, *The Urban Transportation Problem* (Cambridge, Mass.: Harvard, 1965), p. 10.
[47] See Chap. 3, p. 53.
[48] Among the more important studies of urban spatial structure are: William Alonso, "A Theory of the Urban Land Market," *Papers of the Regional Science Association*, vol. 6 (1960), pp. 149–157; Eugene F. Brigham, "The Determinants of Residential Land Values," *Land Economics* (November 1965), pp. 327ff.; Richard F. Muth, "Economic Change and Rural-Urban Land Conversions," *Econometrica* (January

myriad of features that influence the value and use of various sites, i.e., including location of similar goods and inputs; transportation facilities; environmental features such as the neighborhood quality; the legal constraints on the allowable uses of the site; the density, often defined in terms of population per square mile but sometimes in terms of a "density gradient" that shows a declining density as the distance from a particularly desirable location increases; the production and cost conditions of building construction;[49] and so on.

Every unit locates itself in space by considering the costs and benefits associated with the transactions it contemplates. In addition, households attempt to satisfy elements in their utility functions that are not directly translatable into costs of distance. These factors are associated with the quality of the environment in which the household situates itself, and include such things as neighbors and scenery.

Figure 2.7 is a flow diagram showing the process by which spatial equilibrium is achieved. There are three tiers or three kinds of decision agents, each of which is seen as having a distinct place in the process, following or preceding other elements. The first kind of decision agent is the firm, which bases its selection of a city in which to locate on a variety of factors, including the location of the bulk of its input materials. Of course, there will be various industries for which the primary considerations are different. Research and development firms, for example, may consider the availability of amenities and a large technical work force to be of overriding importance. Retail firms consider their locations to be almost exclusively determined by the location of potential customers. In the latter case we are really talking about a member of a class of firms that are referred to in Figure 2.7 as "second-order firms," a term that will be explained more fully below.

After determining the city in which it will locate, a firm then must decide where within the city to put its physical plant. The decision factors here include accessibility to materials and markets through the transportation network; the size and concentration of the market itself, where the market is primarily confined to the city; and finally, the access that various locations provide to labor. Having balanced these factors against one another, the firm will finally be able to choose a site within the city for its location. It should be remembered that most of these factors will be reflected in land prices to firms, but to the extent that land enters the

---

1961), pp. 1–23; and Richard F. Muth, *Cities and Housing* (Chicago: The University of Chicago Press, 1969); as well as those cited in Chap. 3 on residential land use.

[49] See Irving Hoch, "The Three-Dimensional City: Contained Urban Space," in Harvey S. Perloff (ed.), *The Quality of the Urban Environment* (Baltimore: Johns Hopkins, 1969), pp. 75–135, for a theoretical discussion of the provision of space in urban areas.

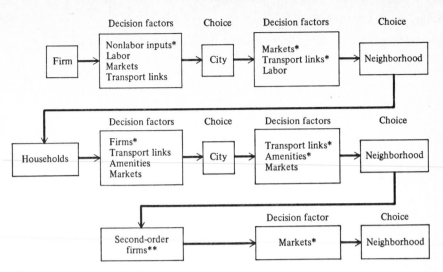

*Factor employed at each decision stage.
**Second-order firms are service firms that are based on low market thresholds.

FIGURE 2.7   A schema for location equilibrium of households and firms.

firm's production function in a distinctive way, the firm will have to consider this as well.

Having located itself in the city, the firm now becomes a part of the given data with which the household begins its own process of choosing a location. The principal determinant of the city in which the household will locate is either wherever the household finds itself to be or, in the case of migration, wherever the appropriate kinds of firms are located. The difference here normally depends on the industry and occupation of the worker. The smaller the industry and the more skilled the occupation, the more likely that the decision of what city to move to will be influenced by the spatial distribution of firms.

The factors that influence the location of the household within a city will be taken up in detail in the next chapter. Here they have been reduced to three: Transportation network characteristics, amenities associated with each location, and the location of markets for both consumption goods and the labor services that the household plans to trade for income. The transportation network plays a pivotal role in this process, since its effect is to alter the isodapane map through which the transportation cost elements of earning and spending income are minimized. The location of markets inside the city is really dependent in an operational sense on how the transportation network is put together.

The amenities associated with each area of a city may be more important than all of the other decision factors. Some of the goods and services that people wish to have, such as schooling and recreation, are parts of the amenity value of any location. Since these facilities may be used extensively, transport costs to and from them may be of great importance. In addition, in larger cities that are broken up into a number of neighborhood areas, it may be that the quality of some of the public services tends to vary widely from place to place. The household may locate so as to take advantage of a given set of such services, and may be concerned about other factors only after it has circumscribed its detailed location choice with the boundaries of a political entity.

Once the household has determined its location, and once households in the aggregate have done so, second-order firms can then profitably choose their locations. A second-order firm is one which requires only a relatively small market to operate efficiently. Examples of such firms are grocery stores, cleaning establishments, appliance repair firms, and medical services vendors. These firms tend to situate themselves in or close to neighborhoods that offer a market of sufficient size for profitable operations. In reality, firms probably could be arranged along a continuum of market thresholds, so that to refer to first- and second-order firms is somewhat misleading. It is convenient to think of a range of goods and services that are provided by community or neighborhood rather than by city, however, and we shall continue to use this terminology.

It has been noted that, in a very general sense, typical spatial patterns in cities have resulted from the millions of separate business and household decisions and transportation choices. While the data are partial, Harland Bartholomew's analysis of a group of 53 American central cities reveals that residential sites make up a fairly uniform 80 percent of the land used by private sector activities.[50] Streets occupy a somewhat less consistent 60 percent of the nonprivate land use. Approximately 70 percent of the land area in any American city is confined to streets and residential sites. John Hamburg found generally consistent land-use organization in Chicago.[51] Again, the strongest regularities show up with respect to residential sites and streets; residential sites as a proportion of all land in use beyond five miles from the Chicago Loop approximated 40 percent, while streets quite uniformly occupied 30 to 35 percent of the land area in the same zone. (Nearly 5 percent of the land area of the Chicago region falls within the five-mile zone.)

The focus of maximum overall accessibility within an urban area is the place at which all the people of the area could assemble with the least total man-miles of travel. This focal point tends to be in the downtown area, and it appears to have shifted only a relatively short distance during

[50] Harland Bartholomew, *Land Use in American Cities* (Cambridge, Mass.: Harvard, 1955).

[51] John R. Hamburg, "Land Use Projections for Predicting Future Traffic," in *Trip Characteristics and Traffic Assignment*, Highway Research Board Bulletin 224 (Washington, D.C.: National Academy of Sciences, National Research Council, 1959), p. 74, Fig. 1.

periods measured in decades and generations. Related to this focal point are a variety of density patterns. One is that of residential densities, whose peaking resembles not so much a sharp, conical mountain peak as a cross-section of a volcano, with a crater of lower gross density in the innermost zone, preempted mainly by nonresidential activities.[52] Density patterns, which can be represented by such descriptive measures as a density gradient, vary considerably among cities; yet they all show a consistent peaking in the central business district and essentially a monotonic decline with distance from it. Irving Hoch points out that "some mappings appear almost spikelike in form."[53] An exponential form of residential density gradient is very common, and it has been found that larger cities have, in addition to higher central densities, lower (flatter) slope coefficients.[54]

The distribution of residential floor area is generally much flatter than that of net population density (population relative to residential land). Total floor space, total trip destinations, nonresidential floor space, and land value data exhibit marked peaking in the CBD and a monotonic decline with distance from the CBD.[55]

There is some evidence of concentric rings of activity, with commercial land concentrated in the CBD and with scattered nodes reflecting shopping centers. Major concentrations of industrial land occur outside the CBD, generally close to rail and water facilities.

Apparently there is also much uniformity among cities as to where the rich and the poor each locate. "The richest families tend to live in close proximity to one another . . . usually . . . on ocean or lake shores or on moderately high elevations, in districts far removed from the smoke and noise of factories and they usually have the fastest transportation to the central business district of the city.[56] The lowest-income areas are often located in the central core of the city, which was the first to be built; they are predominantly on one side of the city, depending upon the topography of rivers, lakes, or oceans. They tend to be where the houses are the oldest.[57] New office buildings tend to be constructed and rented to the best advantage in downtown areas leading in the direction of the high-income areas.[58]

Interestingly, the patterns of land use, population growth, employment locations, and residential choices recorded in recent years have differed

---

[52] Edgar M. Hoover, "The Evolving Form of the Metropolis," in Harvey S. Perloff and Lowdon Wingo, Jr. (eds.), *Issues in Urban Economics* (Baltimore: Johns Hopkins, 1968), p. 249.

[53] Hoch, op. cit., p. 82.

[54] Hoover, "The Evolving Form of the Metropolis," op. cit., p. 250.

[55] Hoch, op. cit., p. 82.

[56] Homer Hoyt, *Where the Rich and the Poor Live* (Washington, D.C.: Urban Land Institute, 1966), p. 7.

[57] Ibid., p. 19.

[58] Ibid., p. 7.

little between those cities that have strong highway orientation and those that have transit orientation. Meyer, Kain, and Wohl conclude that "with or without mass transit, American cities have been decentralizing."[59] Throughout the United States there has been a decline in the relative, and often even the absolute, importance of the central parts of many urban areas. This decentralization, suburbanization, deconcentration, scatteration, or urban sprawl is consistent with the analysis of urban transportation in Chapter 4. First, however, in the next chapter we will consider an analysis of urban residential land use and housing markets. It will be followed by attempts to apply some of the urban microeconomic methods developed in this chapter to urban transportation markets and to urban labor markets.

[59] Meyer, Kain, and Wohl, op. cit., p. 360.

CHAPTER 3

URBAN RESIDENTIAL LAND USE AND HOUSING MARKETS

I. URBAN HOUSING CONDITIONS, DEMAND, AND SUPPLY

Urban Housing Conditions

The urban residential land and housing markets, by any standard, are indeed very large; about three-fourths of privately developed land is being devoted to residential use in urban areas.[1] Furthermore, the average consumer spends about one-fifth of his disposable income on housing. During the first six decades of this century, the percentage of Americans who owned or were purchasing homes has steadily increased, although there are indications that starting in the late 1950s this trend may have been reversed. Much, if not most, of new multifamily dwelling construction appears to be taking place in suburbs and not in central cities.

In the postwar period housing conditions in urban America have improved. The proportion of urban Americans living in truly poor housing has declined. Specifically, census data show that the fraction of urban housing that is below a given absolute quality level declined dramatically during the 1950s.[2] Between 1948 and 1967, nearly 30 million new nonfarm houses and apartments were built, and 20 million of these were in metropolitan areas.[3] During this period the rate of new housing construction outran the rate of population growth. While the population increase in central cities of metropolitan areas was about 8 million during this period, new housing units were built at about the same pace. Since usually more than one person lives in a housing unit, substantial improvements in housing conditions have resulted. During the 1950s, 800,000 substandard

[1] Harland Bartholomew, *Land Uses in American Cities* (Cambridge, Mass.: Harvard, 1955), p. 121.
[2] Richard F. Muth, *Cities and Housing* (Chicago: The University of Chicago Press, 1969), pp. 124–125, 280.
[3] Dick Netzer, *Economics and Urban Problems* (New York: Basic Books, 1970), p. 20.

housing units, which either were dilapidated or lacked full plumbing facilities, were demolished in the central cities of the dozen largest metropolitan areas. Although in 1950 roughly one-fourth of the households in central cities lived in substandard housing units, by 1966 the number had declined to 7 percent. In the same 20-year period, state and local governments invested about $200 billion to improve the social infrastructure of cities by building schools, roads, transit facilities, hospitals, airports, water supply, and sewerage to improve the life of urbanites.

Unfortunately, however, the improvement in housing conditions has not benefited urbanites uniformly. Although, since the early 1930s, when President Franklin D. Roosevelt called one-third of the nation ill-housed, much substandard housing has been demolished and about 800,000 low-rent, publicly owned housing units have been built, many poor people and particularly members of minority groups continue to live in poor housing. In 1966, 16 percent of all central-city nonwhites, compared with 5 percent of all central-city whites, lived in substandard housing.[4] In 1960, 30 percent or more of the housing occupied by nonwhites was slum housing in every American city whose population exceeded one-half million, except in Los Angeles and Washington; and in Negro, Mexican-American, and Puerto Rican neighborhoods, housing conditions were even worse. As Anthony Downs has concluded, ". . . miserable [housing] conditions are not true of all inadequate housing units, but enough Americans are trapped in the hopeless desolation of such surroundings to constitute both a scandal and a serious economic and social drag on our affluent society."[5]

Some Definitions

Writers on housing have devised many special definitions of terms which are most useful for the types of analysis they perform. A review of the various definitions leads to the conclusion that a clear distinction should be drawn between stock and flow concepts and between quantity and quality flows. For our purposes, we define as the housing stock the fixed capital stock that is accumulated for the purpose of sheltering the population. Housing services can be thought of as the services implied by the use of the stock.

The services which are derived from the stock have two dimensions, however. The quantity of housing services yielded by housing stock is normally related to some measure of the physical size of a unit of stock. Quality of services is a vague concept relating to the amount of satisfaction derivable from a given quantity of services. In reality, these two dimensions are not readily separable. Olsen suggests that they be combined

[4] Ibid., p. 22.

[5] Anthony Downs, "Moving toward Realistic Housing Goals," in Kermit Gordon (ed.), *Agenda for the Nation* (Garden City, N.Y.: Doubleday, 1968), p. 142.

into a single measure, simply housing services.[6] We shall use this concept throughout our discussion; however, although this appears to avoid the problem of separating quality and quantity, it does not. In fact, to use such a concept it would be necessary to identify the two elements with the same precision that is required of the disaggregated version. That is, for any given quantity of housing stock, determinations would have to be made of the size of the quality contribution, the size of the quantity contribution, and then some relative "price" between the two in order to build an index number that aggregated them.

Aggregate Demand and Supply

The aggregate demand for urban housing behaves differently in the short run from the way it does in the long run. In the short run, both the stock and the supply of housing services are relatively fixed. It takes a tremendous effort and involves high costs to add significantly to the supply in any short period of time. Thus, in the short run, housing services are mainly controlled by the demand side of the market, with short-run demand largely a reflection of incomes and income expectation and of cost and availability of financing.

In the long run, the aggregate demand for urban housing is related to the size and age distribution of the population as well as the magnitude and distribution of family income, and to relative prices of housing services.[7] The aggregate supply of housing is related to the prices and quantities of land and other inputs to production of housing. Until recently, the demand for housing services was assumed to be inelastic with respect to income. Empirical work by Margaret Reid and Richard Muth, however, indicates that "the income elasticity of housing demand is at least $+1$ and may be as large as $+2$."[8] Muth also found that "the real-income constant price elasticity of housing demand is about -1, though it too may be even larger numerically."[9] Adjusting for the fact that urban land is used

[6] Edgar E. Olsen, "A Competitive Theory of the Housing Market," *American Economic Review*, vol. 59, no. 4, part I (September 1969), p. 613. Olsen attempts to get around the quality-quantity difficulty by asserting that the market for housing services can be thought of as perfectly competitive and that, therefore, the price of housing services (either explicit or imputed rent) serves as the index required. Later in this chapter we shall discuss the rather widespread and important market imperfections associated with housing services. In that section it should become clear why the price is not a feasible index.

[7] Richard F. Muth, "Urban Residential Land and Housing Markets," in Harvey S. Perloff and Lowdon Wingo, Jr. (eds.), *Issues in Urban Economics* (Baltimore: Johns Hopkins, 1968), p. 286.

[8] Ibid., p. 286, and Margaret G. Reid, *Housing and Income* (Chicago: The University of Chicago Press, 1962).

[9] The relative price elasticity of housing demand, measured in various cities in which prices vary mainly because of construction cost differences, also appears to be about unity. Muth, "Urban Residential Land and Housing Markets," op. cit., p. 286.

for other uses as well as housing, Muth reaches the conclusion that the elasticity of demand for residential land is about —0.75.[10]

Concerning the major inputs into housing services, Muth has estimated that for 1946 to 1960 labor and materials each accounted for approximately 43 percent of the cost of housing services, and that land costs amounted to approximately 5 percent. On the assumption of constant returns to scale in the production of housing, the elasticity of substitution of land cost for other housing cost is about 0.75.[11]

The long-run aggregate supply schedule for residential structures appears to be highly price-elastic. Building material prices as well as wage rates paid to construction labor appear to have little relation to the rate of new residential construction. In part this can be explained by the high rate of mobility of firms, into and out of the building industry, little relationship between the incomes of construction firms, and fluctuations in housing prices.

Muth estimates a lower limit of the supply elasticity for urban land to be about +1.2, on the assumption that the supply elasticity of urban land is zero. He argues, "Since the total amount of land in an area is essentially fixed, the supply curve of urban land is this fixed amount less the agricultural demand curve for land. It follows immediately that the elasticity of urban land supply is the negative of the agricultural demand elasticity for land."[12]

The supply curve of urban residential land can be estimated in a similar manner. Muth, using this procedure, concludes that the elasticity of housing supply per unit of residential land is about +14. He further suggests that

> . . . even if the supply of residential land were perfectly inelastic, changes in housing prices are likely to result mostly from shifts in the supply schedule for housing. . . . A less-than-unit elasticity of demand for residential as well as nonresidential urban land would account for the tendency for aggregate urban land rentals to decline with improvements in transportation, which, in effect, increase the supply of urban land.[13]

Briefly, then, the aggregate demand for urban housing is related to population size and age, family size distribution, income level and distribution for families, and relative prices. The aggregate supply of urban

[10] Ibid., pp. 288–291.

[11] The supply of structures is likely to be even more elastic for any given urban area than for the nation as a whole, since differential changes in prices or earnings will, in the long run, result in movement of building materials, as well as construction workers and firms, from one urban area to another. Ibid., p. 287.

[12] The demand curve for the output of local agricultural firms is likely to be highly elastic, since most agricultural products are sold in national markets and the output of the agricultural industry surrounding an urban area is usually a small fraction of the output coming into the national market. Ibid., p. 289.

[13] Ibid., p. 291.

housing is related to the prices and quantities of inputs or factors of production. The most interesting of these factors is land, and we have noted that a large difference exists between the supply elasticity of urban land in the aggregate and that of urban residential land. This difference comes from the substitutability of land on the periphery of a given city as opposed to its substitutability in the aggregate.

Although these are the important factors that determine housing demand and supply in the urban area as a whole, additional factors affect the demand and supply in specific neighborhoods of the city.[14] The additional explanatory factors needed to explain neighborhood housing demand include employment locations, availability of public services including schools, the quality of the environment both in social and in physical terms, and finally, accessibility to other consumption goods not included in this list.

Perhaps the major influence on residential location decisions of households is related to the location of current and prospective places of employment. Commuting to and from work is the most frequent type of trip made from any household. As a result, it can be expected to be of major importance in the process of residential site selection.

The availability and cost of public services also will influence neighborhood housing demand. When a houshold chooses a neighborhood in which to demand residential land or housing, it engages in an all-or-nothing decision with respect to some public services. Each neighborhood is characterized by some range of public services that are available to residents at a zero price (other than taxes) and that are unavailable to nonresidents at any price. For instance, if schooling is of great importance to a family and quality education is available only in one or two neighborhoods, then they will demand housing in those neighborhoods. In addition to the availability of certain important public services, available only to residents of a particular neighborhood, the burden level of financing all public services in the neighborhood also must be taken into consideration. This requires information on the tax burden of property owners and renters in a specific neighborhood.

The strength of demand for housing in a given neighborhood is also responsive to the quality of its environment. There are physical characteristics, such as topographical features, landscape, and weather, and the characteristics of the people who live in the neighborhood. People tend to group themselves by their similarities.

The selection of a neighborhood is also influenced by the access it provides to consumption goods and services such as facilities. For example, the sailing enthusiast who must locate in a very large metropolis that has

[14] Richard Muth has estimated that the relative price elasticity of housing demand, measured in different parts and neighborhoods of a city, is about unity. See Muth, "Urban Residential Land and Housing Markets," op. cit., p. 286.

a single marina on its outskirts would prefer to locate his residence so that the marina is readily accessible. Some neighborhoods might provide access to services which households do not currently require but may demand in the future.

This component of the demand for residential locations is known as "option demand," a notion developed by Anthony Downs.[15] In brief, option demand refers to the demand for availability of goods and services whether they are consumed or not. Thus households, particularly those in cities, appear willing to pay for the value of certain unchosen alternatives. An example might be the somewhat greater demand for space close to a good university by persons who will not necessarily use its facilities but who recognize the possibility that they might.

Harris, Tolley, and Harrell have developed a model, based on consumer demand theory, which considers amenities as well as travel costs as factors determining choice of residence. Total land value per square foot was estimated from the appraisal of land values for tax purposes. This value was separated into travel savings, amenity values, and agricultural value, plus payment for utilities on residential land beyond the travel savings margin. As expected, the highest positive amenity values occur for the most stylish residential areas and the highest negative values are found for the seriously run-down areas.[16]

Another empirical study has been carried out by E. F. Brigham.[17] He stipulates that residential land values in an urban area are related to the particular site's accessibility, amenity level, topography, and certain historical factors including the way the land is being used. Because of serious measurement difficulties, select quantitative proxy variables are used in relation to a sample of land values in Los Angeles County. It is found that accessibility to employment opportunities is positively related to residential land values. However, this relationship is sometimes swamped by the presence of low amenity levels near the primary work centers and is disturbed by the existence of satellite employment and shopping centers located outside the CBD. Amenities are approximated in terms of a surrogate that measures the value of dwelling unit improvements, i.e., the average value of the dwelling unit structure in a given block.

Finally, Ira Lowry and associates have undertaken a study of demand for rental housing in New York City, emphasizing rent control aspects.[18]

[15] Anthony Downs, *The Value of the Unchosen Alternatives*, P-3017 (Santa Monica, Calif.: The RAND Corporation, 1964).
[16] R. N. S. Harris, G. S. Tolley, and C. Harrell, "The Residence Site Choice," *The Review of Economics and Statistics* (May 1968), pp. 241–247.
[17] E. F. Brigham, "The Determinance of Residential Land Values," *Land Economics* (August 1965), pp. 325–334.
[18] Ira S. Lowry et al., *Rental Housing in New York City: The Demand for Shelter*, R-649NYC, vol. 2 (New York: New York City Rand Institute, June 1971), 305 pp.

Expenditures among households are found to vary mainly because of income and location and control status characteristics of rental submarkets. Interestingly enough, age, sex, and ethnic background of the household head as well as the size of his family appeared to have only slight influences on rent expenditures among households of comparable incomes who have housing in the same submarket.[19]

Neighborhood differences do not affect the supply of housing services as importantly as the demand. There are no reasons to expect differences in factor prices or in substitutability between factors from one neighborhood to the next in a given city. The differences that do occur are largely the result of intervention in the market for housing via building codes and zoning ordinances.

Building codes frequently require construction practices that are outmoded, thus denying builders the ability to employ in one neighborhood technological changes they may be able to use in other neighborhoods in the same urban area. The result will be different supply functions for construction output.

Zoning ordinances have two kinds of effect on supply functions. The most obvious is that by disallowing certain land uses in given areas they restrict the supply of land which is available to that use. This raises the price of land, and consequently of services flowing from the land and the structures that can be put on it. In addition, of course, it lowers the price of land in the use toward which the rezoning has been aimed. The effect of zoning can frequently be overcome by the possibility of purchasing variances. Depending on the decision-making apparatus in a given city, variances can be purchased (by expending the resources necessary to persuade the zoning board to grant them) at either high or low prices.

Another effect of zoning on the supply of housing services comes about as a result of the detailed specifications for what is allowable in a given zone. Typically, cities will have several different types of zones for residential land uses. Each zone will allow certain types of structures to be erected within it and will exclude others.

These specifications can be used in several ways. For instance, many suburban cities have used them to create a system of housing segregation by income (and therefore by race). Less explicitly, these specifications often have the effect of preventing neighborhood development along opti-

[19] In addition to the volume on "Demand for Shelter," the New York City Rand Institute has completed the following studies: Ira S. Lowry, *Rental Housing in New York City: Confronting the Crisis*, RM-6190-NYC, vol. 1 (New York: New York City Rand Institute, February 1970), 37 pp.; C. Peter Rydel, *Factors Affecting Maintenance and Operating Costs in Federal Public Housing Projects*, R-634-NYC (New York: New York City Rand Institute, December 1970), 74 pp.; and Michael B. Teitz and Stephen R. Rosenthal, *Housing Code Enforcement in New York City*, R-648-NYC (New York: New York City Rand Institute, April 1971), 58 pp.

mal lines, since the zoning intentions for the neighborhood are incompatible with some elements of the environment which are imposed outside of the zoning system. These effects are similar to those ascribed to building codes in their results on supply functions.

Some recent work has been done that is designed to improve our understanding of the nature and value of housing services. Specifically, four empirical studies of residential property value determinants are available.[20] In most of these studies property values are statistically significantly related to dwelling size, age, and lot size; some of these studies also find accessibility, neighborhood quality, neighborhood prestige, and zoning to be statistically significant. Of particular interest are neighborhood quality variables and zoning, since both can be looked upon as externalities that affect property values. Benton Massell and Janice Stewart find the selling price of a home substantially increased by a generally favorable neighborhood appearance and by the presence in the area of large homes and extensive landscaping. In their view this verifies the advice of real estate brokers, that it does not pay to build or buy a house which is significantly more expensive than the surrounding homes. If brokers were heeded, neighborhoods would tend to be relatively homogeneous.

II.   *FRAMEWORKS AND MODELS OF HOUSEHOLD RESIDENTIAL LOCATION DECISIONS*[21]

The urban economist is interested in how specific markets operate in allocating households to locations and consumption of housing to particular neighborhoods with certain environmental values.

Our first step will be to examine several approaches to the analysis of locational decision making. They were developed to reach several objectives, but all of them have explanatory power for residential location. In addition, most of them have implications for urban form and density. Some of these implications are discussed here, but for the most part treatment of them is left to a later section of this chapter.

---

[20] R. R. G. Ridker and J. A. Henning, "The Determinants of Residential Property Values with Special Reference to Pollution," *Review of Economics and Statistics*, vol. 69, no. 2 (May 1967), pp. 246–257; John F. Kain and John M. Quigley, "Measuring the Value of Housing Quality," *Journal of the American Statistical Association*, vol. 65 (June 1970), pp. 532–548; J. B. Penn, "Using Multiple Listing Service Data to Analyze Determinants of Urban Residential Property Values," *Urban Economics Report No. 39* (Chicago: University of Chicago, September 1970); and Benton F. Massell and Janice M. Stewart, *The Determinants of Residential Property Values*, Discussion Paper No. 6 (Stanford, Calif.: Stanford University Institute for Public Policy Analysis, 1971).

[21] We make a distinction between model and framework, which will be elaborated on in Chap. 6. A framework is a collection of theories or observed empirical relationships useful for explaining certain phenomena. Models are derived from such a framework and have been actually empirically implemented.

Land-Use Framework: Von Thünen

Von Thünen more than a century ago derived notions about the spatial distribution of economic activity from certain postulates about economic behavior and the nature of space. He assumed the existence of a single, large city in the center of a fertile plain, surrounded by wilderness and devoid of navigable waterways. Under such circumstances it was shown that products with high transportation costs, e.g., fruits, fresh vegetables, and milk, tended to be produced nearest the city and that other products would be produced in concentric rings in the order of decreasing transportation cost. The price of a product in the city was shown to be sufficiently high to cover the costs of the most distant producer, including transportation cost. Less distant land was shown to earn a rent attributable to its location and equal to the sum of production and transportation cost to the city at the most distant producing location minus the sum of these costs at the less distant location.[22]

Von Thünen's approach can be readily adapted to help explain and predict the evolution of urban density patterns and urban form. Thus, the Central Business District (CBD) or center of the city replaces the role of the isolated city of Von Thünen, and the land surrounding the CBD is used for residential and other nonagricultural purposes. The CBD is the point of maximum accessibility to all parts of the city, and producers located in it benefit from low transportation costs. Competition for the limited land in and around the city center results in those with large transportation costs or relatively small space requirements locating in or near the CBD. For households the CBD is the most important, although not necessarily the only, place of employment and the purchase of goods and services, and the cost of transporting people to work or shopping tends to be lowest close to the CBD. Not unlike business firms, those households with large transportation costs or small space needs locate near the CBD, and vice versa. Clearly, differences in land rents between any two locations devoted to the same type of use relate to the difference in costs—primarily transportation costs—associated with the two locations.

Income-Related Framework: Park–Burgess

Von Thünen was concerned with agricultural and industrial location, although the implications for residential location are obvious. The first interesting effort specifically related to urban housing location decisions was suggested by Park, Burgess, and McKenzie in the 1920s.[23] They noticed

[22] J. H. Von Thünen, *Der isolierte Staat in Beziehung auf Landwirtschaft und Nationalökonomie* (Hamburg und Rostock, 1826–1863); also see Erich Roll, *A History of Economic Thought* (New York: Prentice-Hall, 1942), pp. 359–362.
[23] Robert E. Park, Ernest W. Burgess, and Roderick D. McKenzie (eds.), *The City* (Chicago: The University of Chicago Press, 1925).

that housing in cities tended to be organized in concentric zones, with wealthier families living in the more distant zones and the poor in the nearer zones. The explanation for this phenomenon was that there was a high income elasticity of demand for *new* housing. The mechanism they suggested to explain the distance of the high-income zone from the center was that high-income people, wishing to purchase large amounts of housing and wanting this housing to be new, economized on the price of land in order to maximize the allocation to other elements of the housing expenditure. They were able to economize on land by moving to the outer, relatively undeveloped land because they were no longer in competition with firms that required land with high access values. This theory fell from grace with the discovery that the predicted pattern of housing was observed in virtually all cities, irrespective of whether they were growing.

Budget Constraint Models: Alonso, Muth, and Siegel

Two more recent models are those of William Alonso and Richard Muth.[24] Although the two models address different parts of the problem of urban housing, they are quite comparable. Each author looks at the process of location selection as a utility maximization procedure which is constrained by income. The theories differ in the forms of the utility and budget functions.[25]

In the Alonso model, the individual is faced with the task of determining the location and quantity of land that will maximize his utility given his budget constraint. Letting the value of all goods other than housing remain fixed, the utility function represents essentially a trade-off between quantity of land (lot size) and distance from the center, since commuting cost increases with distance from the center. As income increases and more of everything is consumed, larger lot sizes will balance greater commuting costs. Since price per unit of land declines as commuting cost in-

---

[24] William Alonso, *Location and Land Use: Toward a General Theory of Land Rent* (Cambridge, Mass.: Harvard, 1964) and Muth, *Cities and Housing*, op. cit.
[25] Alonso maximizes $U(q,k,c)$ subject to $B(p_c c, P[k]q, T[k])$, where q is the amount of land used, k is the distance of that land from the job center, T is the commuting cost and is a function of k, and c is the quantity of the composite good (the quantity of "all other goods"). The budget constraint (B) contains terms for the price level of the composite good (p_c), the price per unit of land at a given distance from the center $(P[k])$, and the cost, $T(k)$, of commuting to the center from distance k. Using the same notation, Muth maximizes $U(h,c)$ subject to $B(p_c c, P[k]h, T[k,y])$, in which h represents a good known as housing services, whose price varies with distance, and commuting costs are made a function of both distance and income (y). Although Muth presents no direct evidence of this relationship (which is negative), Edwin Mills does so in "The Value of Urban Land," in Harvey S. Perloff (ed.), *The Quality of the Urban Environment* (Baltimore: Johns Hopkins, 1969). Notice that in the Alonso model, commuting cost is a function of distance alone.

creases, people who wish to buy relatively large amounts of land will move out farther than those who wish to buy relatively small amounts.[26]

Muth's approach differs from Alonso's in that Muth assumes that housing services combine land and size of structure as well as many other dimensions of the value of housing, and he treats all of these as one entity: housing services. In addition, he includes income as one of the determinants of commuting cost. The constrained maximum found in Muth's model represents an equilibrium location from which no move in any direction can increase utility. Households are induced to locate farther from the center because of the savings available from lower land costs; at the same time they are induced to locate closer to the center because of the decreases in commuting costs available. The equilibrium location is determined in Muth's model by the land price and commuting cost functions at the point where the marginal decrease in expenditures on housing is equal to the marginal increase in commuting costs for small changes in distance. Both the price per unit of land $(-P_k)$ and the commuting cost (T_k) are negatively sloped functions of distance, and the marginal price function has a steeper slope than that of the marginal commuting cost function. Figure 3.1 shows these two functions and the equilibrium solution.[27]

The Muth analysis assumes that the level of housing services has been fixed. However, if both housing services and commuting costs depend on income, then the former cannot be assumed to be fixed. Income increases cause the amount to be saved on land to increase at every distance, since the household wishes to buy more of the income-elastic good, housing services, of which land is a part. In addition, the costs of commuting rise at every distance as a result of increases in income and, therefore, time costs of travel. The change in the distance solution may be positive or negative, depending on the relationship between the income elasticity of demand for housing services and the income elasticity of commuting cost.

[26] The distance response to changes in income is even greater than implied by the Alonso model, which assumes commuting costs are not affected by income. If income were included as one of the determinants of commuting cost (time-wage component), then the distance one would move outward as a result of an increase in income would be less, because of the increase in cost of commuting to a more distant location. This, of course, is restricted to increases in wage income; income from wealth does not have a bearing on hours worked, and therefore increases in income due to increases in wealth do not affect commuting cost.

[27] Note that if the household found itself to the left of k^*, a move farther out from the center of the city would decrease housing cost more than it would increase commuting cost. The converse holds for points to the right of k^*. Of course, if a household found itself not at k^*, it would move only in the event that the returns to doing so (i.e., discounted difference in net savings over the period during which the new and old houses would be used) were in excess of the moving costs. For entire households, moving costs are likely to be relatively high.

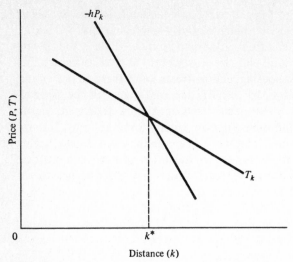

Distance (*k*)

FIGURE 3.1   Distance equilibrium for a household.

If the former is larger, as Muth asserts, then an increase in income will move the equilibrium distance farther from the center, as shown in Figure 3.2.

This assertion is supported in part by research results of M. E. Beesley, who found that expenditures of civil servants in London on transportation to work has an income elasticity of about 1.[28] This conclusion, in conjunction with Muth's finding of income elasticity of demand for housing greater than 1, tends to confirm Muth's assertion. Two further studies have found the income elasticity of housing expenditures to be greater than 1.[29]

Both the Alonso and the Muth models initially make the assumption, originally made by Von Thünen, that all the business activities of a city are located at a dimensionless point in space and that travel costs are equal for equal distances, no matter in which direction one moves. Muth later relaxes this assumption, and so does Siegel, who arrives at the conclusion that density patterns for cities are quite unlike those generated by the simpler Von Thünen-type approach, i.e., jobs can be anywhere in the city, not just in the center.[30]

The demand for a particular residential location, according to Siegel, is related to accessibility, environmental quality (i.e., socioeconomic characteristics of the neighborhood, nature and availability of public services

[28] M. E. Beesley, "The Value of Time Spent in Traveling: Some New Evidence," *Economica*, New Series, 1965, pp. 174–185.
[29] Richard F. Muth, "Demand from Non-Farm Housing," in A. C. Harberger (ed.), *The Demand for Durable Goods* (Chicago: The University of Chicago Press, 1960), and Reid, op. cit.
[30] Jay Siegel, *Intrametropolitan Migration of White and Minority Group Households* (Stanford, Calif.: Stanford, 1970).

and amenities impinging on the site, etc.), and site characteristics associated with the location. A rational household will choose a residential location which maximizes its utility as derived from all three sets of characteristics, subject to its budget constraint. Site costs to be considered in choosing a location include locational rent at the site plus land value and local property taxes, while accessibility costs include costs of transportation, including commuting to the place of employment as well as transportation to other locations in the metropolitan area.[31]

The paucity of environmental quality data forces Siegel to simplify his model and consider only accessibility and site costs, which are measured with respect to a particular reference point, i.e., the CBD.[32] The Siegel

[31] If accessibility, environment, and locational characteristics can be quantified and aggregated, a metric can be constructed completely describing the metropolitan area. The resulting metropolitan map has three dimensions, and every location can be described by a point with indices representing values of each attribute for that site. These values should be explained by a set of exogenous variables, e.g., income, locational rent, family size, education, ethnicity, number of employed persons, and the type of job of the head of household. The corresponding price structure is also included in the exogenous set, while the attributes of a site for a household are endogenously determined. A change in residential location, i.e., intrametropolitan migration, results from changes in the value to a household of the attributes of a given site. The change in value is explained by the change in values of exogenous variables. This induces the household to move to a new location in order to return to a utility-maximizing solution.

[32] These two assumptions reduce the metropolitan area to a one-dimensional ray with the origin at the CBD. This formulation, while not useful for certain questions, is particularly appropriate to study the following questions: Why are people moving from the central city to the suburbs? If industry that employs unskilled labor decentralizes and moves farther out from the CBD, what effect will this have on the residential distribution in the metropolitan area? What is the relative importance

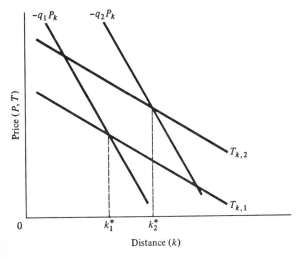

FIGURE 3.2 Change in distance equilibrium from income 1 to income 2.

model combines and extends the Alonso and Muth models by including both accessibility and housing services in the household utility function; thus the household is assumed to derive satisfaction from consuming housing services and accessibility directly. Unlike the other two models, this model does not assume that all jobs are in the CBD, and it enlarges the set of choice variables facing the household.

The choice variables, which are determined simultaneously by the household, cover locational decisions and housing decisions. In connection with the first, the household chooses the location of both home and work. In making a decision about housing services, the household chooses the rent, number of rooms, and type of structure.

Model Implications for Urban Form and Density Pattern

Employing the concepts and information developed in the preceding models, we are now ready to focus more directly on how residential location decisions can be expected to produce a pattern of urban densities. Of the models dealt with, Muth's is the richest in empirical detail; as a consequence, we will focus on the implications of his model for urban form and patterns of density.

In order for a household, with one or more of its members employed in the city center, to maximize its utility with respect to location, two conditions must be met: housing and all other commodities must be consumed in such quantities that the marginal utility per dollar spent is the same for all, and no move, regardless of how small, can increase the household's real income. As a result, the distance from the CBD in equilibrium increases if marginal transportation costs decrease.

The decline in housing prices with distance from the city center is explained by the decline in residential land rentals. Since expenditures on land are only 5 percent—or at most 10 percent—of all expenditures on housing, equal net incomes of firms producing housing in different locations require residential land rentals to decline at a rate ten to twenty times as fast.

The combination of declining prices for land and the fact that construction costs are similar in all parts of cities means that capital will be substituted for land toward the city center and that construction will be relatively land-intensive toward the outskirts. Office buildings, high-rise apartments, and the like, are found in the center, since they have very low space-to-land ratios, while single-family dwellings, outside parking lots,

---

of income and job location in determining residential location? Notice also, however, that this type of measure consistently underestimates distance between job and work, since it assumes lateral movement to be zero.

and so forth, are found at a distance from the center, since these types of structures economize on other inputs relative to land.[33]

Muth has found that as land rentals, and therefore housing prices, decline, the output of housing per square mile declines. Muth discovered that if a price change is given, then the responsiveness of housing output varies directly with the ease of substitution of land for structures in producing housing and inversely with the ratio of expenditures on housing paid out for land.[34]

As the city's population increases, so does housing demand and, therefore, demand for land and for structures which yield housing services. The increased land demand for housing is supplemented by demand increases for land designated for roads and commercial activities, which result in land being bid away mainly from agricultural uses. Residential land rentals increase, resulting in higher housing prices to consumers in all parts of the city. Consequently the rate of distance decline in housing prices is not affected if population growth does not produce other effects, such as reducing transportation cost. Since the value of housing produced responds more rapidly to the increase in housing prices in the outer zones of cities, and expenditures per person remain largely unchanged, population tends to increase most rapidly in the outer zones of cities. These decentralization tendencies stemming from population increases are reinforced by transportation improvements. Declining transportation costs tend to result in a decrease in the rate of decline in housing prices with distance.

Muth has also presented some empirical findings on the pattern of urban population density. He found that population and car registrations per capita as proxies for transportation costs were of overwhelming importance in explaining changes in urban population distribution during the postwar period. The increase in car registrations per capita, of 0.26 in 1950 to 0.35 in 1960, can be interpreted to account for a decline in the percentage of an urbanized area's population residing in the central city from 14 percent to 7 percent. This 50 percent decline closely approximates the actual 65 percent decline for urban areas studied by Muth. He concludes, "Similarly, the increase in land area of the urbanized areas studied averaged about 82 percent from 1950 to 1960. Of this, the increase in car registrations would account for an increase in land area of about 45 percent, while the urbanized area's population growth would account for a land area growth of about 25 percent."[35]

Muth also studied such indicators of the central city's physical condi-

---

[33] See Irving Hoch, "The Three-Dimensional City," in *The Quality of the Urban Environment* (Washington, D.C.: Resources for the Future, 1969).
[34] Richard F. Muth, "The Ghetto in the Local Housing Market," in John P. Crecine (ed.), *Financing the Metropolis* (Beverly Hills: Sage, 1970), p. 441.
[35] Ibid., p. 443.

tion as age of the central city and its dwelling units and the fraction of the latter that is dilapidated and (or) without private bath, average population density in the central city, and the proportion of employment which is in manufacturing. Of these, only the fraction of dwelling units that are dilapidated and (or) without private bath showed a significant correlation (negative) with the relative rate of decline in population density. This fraction of substandard housing, however, showed no clear association with the central city's share in urbanized area population or the latter's land area. Also, the fraction of substandard dwellings declined during the 1950s, from 0.20 to 0.11. Such changes in dwelling conditions would imply recentralization. For this reason, Muth finds that most of the suburbanization of population and growth of urban areas that occurred during the 1950s can be traced to transportation improvements and population growth. Thus, he concludes that these is virtually no evidence to substantiate the claim that these phenomena are a "flight from blight."[36]

III. MARKET IMPERFECTIONS AND HOUSING PROBLEMS

There are a number of sources of imperfections in housing markets. Among the important ones are externalities and the existence of noncompeting groups. The externality imperfections in housing markets are normally referred to as the "neighborhood effect" and partly account for the social problem of "poor" housing. The noncompeting groups market imperfection partly accounts for the social problem of racial segregation in housing markets, a situation in which whites compete with whites and blacks with blacks as buyers of housing services.

Some aspects of the market which are frequently referred to as problems are the result, not of market imperfections, but rather of the operation of the free market. They may still have undesirable results, and therefore be classed as problems, but they are not due to market imperfections. An example is urban sprawl. Advances in the technology of urban transportation, as well as increases in certain types of transport capital stock, have produced urban sprawl. While sprawl represents a response to changes in technology, there are also some changes which have been introduced outside the market mechanism. For example, it is highly unlikely that we would have the urban highway systems developed by governmental agencies if automobile users had been allowed to directly and personally allocate the funds that have gone into them. Similarly, if the financing of home building loans had not been supported by the Federal Housing Administration, it is unlikely that the market mechanism would have produced the

[36] Ibid., p. 443.

same kinds and distribution of housing. These and other policy issues will be discussed in the last section of this chapter.

Neighborhood Degradation

Urban slums mean poor-quality, substandard housing. Edgar Olsen defines a slum dwelling unit as one "which yields less than some arbitrary quantity of housing service per time." For instance, one "might decide to call all dwelling units in a particular locality renting for less than $60 per month slum dwelling units." Olsen goes on to define a slum area as "a contiguous area which contains a high (but arbitrary) percentage of slum dwelling units."[37] Another type of definition of a slum area is that it is a complex of dwelling units occupied by low-income families. Finally, Otto Davis and Andrew Whinston give the slum a welfare economics definition in which a slum dwelling represents suboptimal resource allocation.[38]

On the demand side, a number of reasons have been put forth for the existence of urban blight, and for the tendency of neighborhoods to degrade over time. They include the institutional environment and the income of slum dwellers. We shall consider a third, more general argument which relies directly on the idea of a market imperfection before we discuss the more popular views.

One type of externality is the neighborhood effect, which has been discussed in Chapter 2. The cost of information flowing between neighbors represents a barrier that discourages all of them from making investments in maintenance and improvements because, in the absence of such information, these investments are very risky. For example, in some circumstances no investor would be willing to improve his property unless some relatively large proportion of other homeowners could be expected (or forced) to do the same. The reason is that returns to this investment cannot be entirely captured by the individual but are spread over the entire neighborhood. Thus the only way for an individual to get an expected return from his investment is to induce his neighbor to invest as well, so that some of the investment that he makes, which yields returns to other people, will be balanced by his receipt of returns from other people's investments.

These externalities act to make neighborhood degradation more common than if they did not exist. As long as the information or the contractual agreements are not forthcoming, levels of investment will occur that are suboptimal from a social viewpoint and they will be insufficient to maintain the value of properties in a given neighborhood.

[37] Olsen, op. cit., p. 614.
[38] Otto Davis and Andrew Whinston, "Economics of Urban Renewal," *Law and Contemporary Problems*, vol. 26 (Winter 1969), pp. 106–117.

Richard Muth suggests an alternative demand explanation of the existence of slums. He argues that age, spread of industrial firms, etc., while affecting the supply of housing, do not affect demand for it or the willingness of people to live in such dwellings. For additional substandard housing to be inhabited, its price would have to decline relative to that of good-quality housing. The rentals of land and existing structures in areas of poor-quality housing would decline and the output of poor-quality housing per square mile of land would fall relative to that of good-quality housing. As a result the production of poor-quality housing should be rather unprofitable and land in slum areas less intensively utilized than in comparably located areas of better housing. Muth finds that slums are especially profitable to owners and that population densities and measures of housing output per unit of land are higher, not lower—location being held constant—the higher the fraction of dwellings that are substandard.[39]

Muth's alternative theory of slum formation emphasizes the low incomes of occupants. Muth claims that families with low incomes do not spend much money on housing and thus they buy not only less feet of floor space or rooms per person, but also poorer quality of housing. The latter occurs because it is relatively cheaper for the private housing market to convert already built dwellings than to build new homes when meeting low-income demand for housing. This is especially true for older buildings in multi-unit structures. Muth claims that "such conversions are accomplished partly by cutting larger apartments up into smaller ones, and partly by allowing them to deteriorate in quality through reducing expenditures for maintenance and repair."[40]

There are three major arguments which attempt to explain the existence and extent of slums by reference to supply factors. These include the effects of urban renewal, institutional phenomena which impinge differentially on high- and low-quality housing, and filtering.

Urban renewal was conceived as a method by which downtown areas could be rescued from blight. It is curious that one of its major side effects may actually be to increase the rate of degradation of remaining structures in the city, as well as to raise the price of low-quality housing. One of the major targets for renewal projects is low-quality housing, which often tends to be built on high-value land and which tends to be visually inferior to the nonhousing structures of downtown areas. When renewal projects destroy slum housing in order to replace it either with high-quality housing or with commercial buildings, large numbers of people are displaced from their poor-quality dwellings and must find some new places to live. These people initially lived in low-quality housing because, given their income level, they had no other choice. As a consequence of the tearing down of

---

[39] Muth, *Cities and Housing*, op. cit., p. 240.
[40] Muth, "The Ghetto in the Local Housing Market," op. cit., pp. 445–446.

slums, the housing market is confronted with a large increase in the demand for low-quality housing, i.e., the same type of housing that has been torn down. The ultimate effect is to raise the cost of low-quality housing and possibly to lower the cost of high-quality housing. Thus perhaps the rich are subsidized and the poor are taxed by urban renewal.

The increase in price of low-quality housing cannot be expected to persist over time unless the long-run supply function for low-quality housing is upward-sloping or tends to shift upward under capital stock conversion, which implies the embodiment of technological change in each new wave of replacement structures. Muth discusses how these short-run deficiencies in supply can be overcome through construction.

Muth argues that as the price of poor-quality housing rises, relative to high-quality housing, the quantity of poor-quality housing increases as demand increases. This increase comes about partly by more intensive use of the poor-quality structures and partly by the conversion of high-quality housing. He notes that if structures are not equally easy to convert, then as demand for poor-quality housing increases, buildings that are successively more expensive to convert must be used. Thus, even after there has been an adjustment to a change in demand, the relative price of the poor-quality housing would be higher than before, and therefore the earnings derived from the poor-quality housing would rise. Muth concludes that "previously existing slums, then, become more profitable to their owners as the land area occupied by the slums grows."[41]

Even though slums may exist principally because of low-income housing demand, two issues should be considered. Other forces may contribute to the existence of slums, and the private supply may overreact to demand for poor-quality housing. Muth found that only age of dwellings and a measure of population turnover had significant effect on the presence of slums.

In contrast to Muth, some writers believe that a variety of factors, such as age and obsolescence, spread of industrial and commercial firms into residential neighborhoods, shortage of funds for investment in residential real estate, lack of proper planning and regulation when these areas were initially developed, failure of local governments to supply proper kinds and amounts of local services, etc., have increased the supply of low-quality, substandard housing. Furthermore, property tax features, federal loan subsidy policies in recent years, the intrusion of manufacturing plants and other nuisance industries into good neighborhoods, and the availability of new, relatively inexpensive housing in suburbia have made difficult the redevelopment of older properties and neighborhoods so common in the center of the city.

Of particular importance in this list of institutional factors is the effect

---

[41] Ibid., pp. 446–447.

of current taxes. Property taxes are based on estimated market value of land and structure. Owners of real estate are consequently induced by the laws to minimize the market value of their holdings if they are not consciously attempting to sell them. The result is that a premium is placed on allowing buildings to deteriorate rapidly. Income taxes also aid in the establishment of this bias. Rules for depreciation of capital stock, and the tax benefits implied by them, induce owners to allow buildings to deteriorate at the maximum rate. This is only partly balanced by protection of long-term capital investment.

It is asserted that the decline in housing demand in older parts of cities—usually in the center of the city—has tended to reduce earnings of owners of existing structures in old neighborhoods.[42] At the same time, residents of such neighborhoods have tended to move to the suburbs, and their places have been taken by lower-income households. Many of those newcomers have been members of ethnic minority groups.

Filtering is one process by which housing of low quality is increased in supply. For any kind of housing there are principally three components of supply: existing stock which is inelastic with respect to price, new construction, and conversion or the result of filtering. When structures are converted from one quality to another (usually a lower quality), then they are being filtered.

Since it is apparently unprofitable to newly construct low-quality housing, the supply of such housing depends on the stock at a given time and the relative ease by which structures of higher quality can be converted to low quality. When something occurs either to diminish the current stock (such as urban renewal as discussed above) or to restrict owners' ability to convert their stock (such as building code restrictions aimed at preventing deterioration), then the price of low-quality housing increases. This serves as an inducement to increase the rate of conversion by making conversions which were previously uneconomic.

Housing Segregation

Housing segregation occurs not only along racial lines—segregation by age and income also is common. The concept of the wrong side of the tracks is a part of American tradition; retirement communities and the student sections of college towns are examples of age segregation. There are even examples of occupational and industrial segregation. According to the concentric ring theory, different types of industries can be expected to locate in belts at different distances from the CBD. The labor force for each of these industries would find it most convenient to locate nearby, thus creat-

---

[42] Cf. Muth's findings discussed on the preceding page.

ing industrial segregation. Finally, some industries are characterized by skewed occupational distributions which would result in neighborhoods made up of families headed by people with similar occupations.

Sometimes segregation occurs purely as a result of the economics of location and bears no implications about market imperfections. Some writers see all forms of housing segregation, including racial segregation, as stemming from these cost-minimization motives.[43] However, such motives do no explain the extent of housing segregation that actually occurs. The simplest proof of this is the observation that prices charged to some people for living in a given neighborhood are higher than those charged to people who have the "correct" characteristics—occupation, race, income, or whatever. On a theoretical level, one needs merely to recall that households do not just seek to maximize the difference between cost and return, i.e., profits. They attempt to maximize utility. If the characteristics of neighbors are elements in utility functions, then these characteristics will cause variations in bid and ask prices.

It is generally acknowledged that racial segregation is a social problem. Less often is it recognized that segregation by age, income, or other characteristics could also be a social problem. Yet, since segregation usually leads to narrowness of social contact, and has implications for the physical appearance of neighborhoods, other forms of segregation might also be considered problems.[44] It is probably easier to have social contact only with people who have characteristics similar to one's own. Yet, income segregation, for instance, can lead to the appearance of neighborhoods being dull and repetitive. People with similar incomes tend to have quite similar tastes as well as similar capacities to own homes. An income mix in a neighborhood will lead to a variety of homes and tastes.

A number of different theories have been advanced to explain why residences of ethnic minorities, particularly Negroes, are physically separated from those of other groups. It has been suggested that since Negroes have relatively low incomes and their employment is concentrated in menial, low-paying occupations, they tend to be residentially segregated from others. Carl E. Taeuber and Alma F. Taeuber have studied this hypothesis and rejected it. In their view little of the Negro segregation vis-à-vis the white population can be attributed to income and occupational differences.[45] Using Chicago and Detroit data, Anthony H. Pascal reached a similar conclusion, i.e., that residential segregation does not result from such socioeconomic factors as white-nonwhite differentials in

---

[43] Siegel, op. cit., p. 71.
[44] Jane Jacobs, *The Rise and Decline of Great American Cities* (New York: Doubleday, 1969).
[45] Carl E. Taeuber and Alma F. Taeuber, *Negroes in Cities, Residential Segregation, and Neighborhood Change* (Chicago-Aldine, 1965).

income and wealth, family size and composition, and job location of its working members.[46]

A second explanation for residential segregation of Negroes points to landlords and real estate agents, who are said to cherish a unique aversion—not held by the rest of the community—relative to Negroes, and therefore to discriminate against them. If because of racial bias landlords declined to rent or real estate agents refused to sell to Negroes or other minorities, they would earn less income than their property would otherwise command. Such landlords and real estate agents could profitably sell their business to others who do not have such an aversion.[47] If, however, minorities cannot compete as effectively as other groups in housing markets, discriminatory activities of property owners may lead to a larger economic return.

Closely akin to the aversion theory is the grand conspiracy theory, which assumes that landlords, real estate agents, mortgage lenders, and associated economic actors combine in a grand conspiracy to reap profits from charging Negroes and other ethnic minorities higher housing prices. The foundation of this argument also is indeed flimsy, since thousands of economic units throughout the country would have to join and enter collusive agreements. It should be most difficult to organize and police such an agreement covering numerous, if not all, cities throughout the nation, and particularly in times of adverse market conditions the temptation should be great to sell to Negroes at lower, but still profitable, prices and wreck the agreement.

Somewhat more difficult to dismiss are the theories of Gary Becker and Martin Bailey.[48] Becker's theory of discrimination leads to the conclusion that whites will be willing to pay a premium to live among whites, a premium that is greater than the premium that blacks would be willing to pay to live among whites. The reason is white residents' fear of social and personal implications as well as economic losses likely to result from the influx of minorities into their neighborhoods. Whites fear not only that the entry of nonwhites seriously damages the social status of their neighborhood, but that it induces many white families to move out of the neighborhood and thus disrupt established association patterns.[49] In addition, whites fear that property values in their neighborhood will decline once minority groups are permitted to enter.

[46] Anthony H. Pascal, *The Economics of Housing Segregation*, P-3095 (Santa Monica, Calif.: The RAND Corporation, 1965), p. 1.
[47] Muth, "The Ghetto in the Local Housing Market," op. cit., p. 449.
[48] Gary S. Becker, *The Economics of Discrimination* (Chicago: The University of Chicago Press, 1957), p. 59; and Martin J. Bailey, "Note on the Economics of Residential Zoning and Renewal," *Land Economics*, vol. 35 (August 1959), pp. 288–290.
[49] Luigi Laurenti, *Property Values and Race* (Berkeley, Calif.: University of California Press, 1961), p. 37.

This fear would lead to whites consistently outbidding blacks for housing in white areas and the consequent preservation or extension of segregated living patterns. Unfortunately for the theory, segregation can also be explained by the opposite phenomenon, namely, that blacks are consistently willing to outbid whites for the privilege of living among blacks. It is therefore unclear whether the higher-bid type of hypothesis is evidence of discrimination of whites against blacks or of blacks against whites, unless one assumes the blacks' effective demand for integration is less strong than that of whites for integration. However, it seems reasonable to assume from all the information we have that whites discriminate against blacks.

Bailey looks at the logical result of inclusion of race in utility functions.[50] He develops a model in which residential segregation has already been achieved, with one section in a city allocated to whites and another allocated to blacks. His aim is to answer the question, What will be the difference in price of housing, if any, and what can cause prices to change relative to each other in the two areas? He assumes that whites are willing to pay extra to live away from blacks and the blacks are indifferent. Four housing prices could be generated in such a model—prices to blacks and to whites in the interior of each area and at the boundary between the areas. Since blacks are indifferent, the boundary and interior prices to blacks are equal. But since whites are willing to pay a premium for living among whites, the price to whites at the boundary between the areas will be lower than the interior price to whites. If, as some people have asserted, blacks pay more for housing, then at the boundary the blacks' bid price will exceed the whites' ask price; and if real estate brokers are rational, the boundary will expand into the whites' area. This process will continue until the boundary price to whites rises and the boundary and interior prices to blacks fall so that all three are equal. At that point, however, interior prices to whites will be greater than the other three. This seems inconsistent with the assertion that blacks pay more than whites for housing. Another way of saying this is that even if it were the case that prices to blacks were higher than prices to whites, the situation would be unstable. The only stable equilibrium under Bailey's assumptions occurs when prices to whites are higher than those to blacks—consistent with the prediction of Becker's model.[51]

Social, personal, and economic concerns of whites vis-à-vis the entry of nonwhites into their neighborhoods can bring about "tipping." Tipping is said to occur when a recognizable new minority invades a neighbor-

[50] Bailey, op. cit., pp. 288–290.
[51] The evidence of higher prices to blacks and Bailey's conclusion of higher prices to whites are not necessarily inconsistent. The apparent inconsistency could result from a chronically greater rate of expansion of housing demand of blacks relative to whites. The differential growth in demand could come either from greater rates of immigration of blacks than of whites or from greater increases of income of blacks than of whites in the presence of income-elastic demand for housing.

hood in sufficient numbers to cause the present residents to begin evacuating. The whites' departure may, but need not, be in panic, and the process can take a month or a few years. The process sometimes is accelerated by actions and demonstrations deliberately designed to cause evacuation. Morton Grodzins estimated a 20 percent Negro population to be commonly the upper limit in Eastern cities. He concluded that tipping is a universal phenomenon in America, testifying to the need for control by law if housing integration is to be attained.[52] A study of Chicago found no instance between 1940 and 1952 of a mixed neighborhood (25 percent to 75 percent nonwhite) in which succession from white- to Negro-occupancy was arrested.[53] It was found that succession rarely reversed once the Negro population reached 10 percent.

Schelling has offered a theoretical examination of tipping in which he differentiates between "tipping-in" and "tipping-out" and emphasizes the importance of speculative expectations.[54] Thus, if people expect a neighborhood to tip, their behavior in consequence of that expectation can help it to tip. Within such a framework it is reasonable to assume that the tipping-in point occurs when a very small percentage of the community has suddenly become Negro; however, the expectation is so great that influx will continue.[55]

What is the empirical evidence of the relation between segregation and housing prices? Luigi Laurenti studied seven cities in the 1950s and concluded that "during the time period and for the cases studied the entry of nonwhites into previously all-white neighborhoods was much more often associated with price improvement or stability than with price weakening. . . . no single or uniform pattern of nonwhite influence on property prices could be detected."[56] Factors bearing on the outcome seem to include: intensity of desire of whites to move out and nonwhites to move in, housing choices open to whites and nonwhites, purchasing power of nonwhites, level of house prices, state of the economy, and long-run trends of property values in the neighborhood.

Richard Muth points out that at a given money-income level, expenditures for housing by nonwhites, on the basis of census data, are as much as a third or more greater than expenditures by whites.[57] But census data on contract rent include not only space rent but also expenditures for

---

[52] Morton Grodzins, "Metropolitan Segregation," *Scientific American* (October 1957).

[53] Otis Dudley Duncan and Beverly Duncan, *The Negro Population of Chicago* (Chicago: The University of Chicago Press, 1957), chap. 6.

[54] Thomas C. Schelling, *Models of Segregation*, RM-6014 (Santa Monica, Calif.: The RAND Corporation, 1969), 82 pp.

[55] Ibid., p. 75.

[56] Laurenti, op. cit., p. 47.

[57] Richard F. Muth, "The Variation of Population Density and Its Components in South Chicago," in *Regional Science Association, Papers and Proceedings*, vol. 15, 1965, p. 176.

furnishings and utilities when they are part of the agreed-upon rental payment. Since a larger percentage of nonwhites than of whites live in rental housing, this may bias the results.

In a study of south-side Chicago, Muth found little evidence of any appreciable price differential,[58] and Martin Bailey found sales prices of single-family houses in the Hyde Park area of Chicago lower in Negro than in white areas.[59]

Jay Siegel estimated separate demand functions for housing by whites, blacks, Orientals, and households with Spanish surnames. Independent variables were rent, number of rooms, and type of structure. The estimated underlying behavioral relationships determining the demand for housing services were found to be highly similar for white and black renters but not for white and black homeowners.[60] Furthermore, he found that an equal percentage increase in the quantity of housing consumed, measured in terms of the number of rooms, is associated with lower percentage increase in rent for minority-group households than for white households. Should the number of rooms in a dwelling be a good indication of housing quantity, this result is inconsistent with the hypothesis that minority groups are discriminated against in the housing market. Finally, an increase in the quality of the dwelling unit, i.e., a newer structure, is associated with a larger increase in rent for white than for minority-group households. The coefficient of the age of the structure for whites is almost twice that for minority-group households.

IV. POLICY APPROACHES

We are now ready to apply some of the concepts and theories developed in earlier sections to a consideration of urban housing market policy issues. Attention will be paid to policies related to market imperfections—neighborhood degradation and housing segregation. Then we will turn to policy consideration of urban sprawl, which can be said to have little relation to market imperfection.

Policies to Combat Neighborhood Degradation

Poor housing, urban blight, and slums are the result of a combination of factors. It is useful to distinguish between income phenomena that contribute to the existence of poor-quality housing and slums on the one hand, and high cost and limited-supply phenomena related to market imperfections on the other hand. With this dichotomy in mind, we will discuss

---

[58] Muth, *Cities and Housing*, op. cit., pp. 238–239, 280.
[59] Martin J. Bailey, "Effects of Race and Other Demographic Factors on the Values of Single-Family Houses," *Land Economics*, vol. 42 (May 1966), pp. 215–220.
[60] Siegel, op. cit., p. 71.

policies designed to reduce substandard housing, slums, and blight and, in general, combat neighborhood degradation.

To the extent that low income greatly contributes to people living under substandard housing conditions, policies designed to increase their income would improve housing. The income elasticity of demand for housing services provides an index of the effectiveness of such policies. If the elasticity is low, then the housing gains will be relatively small. Richard Muth and Margaret Reid have concluded that the income elasticity of housing is somewhere between +1 and +2.[61] However, Dick Netzer maintains that housing services have a low income-elasticity.[62] Available evidence is inconclusive.

Even if the income elasticity of housing is larger than unity, policies designed to enhance the incomes of low-income groups face some major obstacles. Should income increases be substantial and sudden, in the absence of excess supply of middle-quality housing, sharp price rises can be expected. Furthermore, a variety of institutional and other impediments are likely to constitute imperfections of the market that prevent certain groups of poor households from getting better housing at reasonable prices; other imperfections make upgrading of neighborhoods costly and therefore unlikely at best.

Urban America in the 1960s underwent profound population changes that promise to continue in the 1970s. Many central cities, including 15 of the 21 largest in the United States, lost population in the decade of the 1960s, while suburbia gained population. As a consequence, while most metropolitan suburbs need more housing units to house their growing population, most central cities do not. One basic problem of central cities is insufficient effective demand to support adequate maintenance of older buildings. Ira Lowry has found that in New York City in 1965–1968, at least 80 percent of landlord losses were in buildings classified as either sound or deteriorating but not dilapidated.[63] He also found that operating and maintenance cost of rental housing increased more rapidly than did the rents tenants were willing or able to pay. As a result, landlords increasingly undermaintained buildings and let them deteriorate.

Under such circumstances a second, more selective, income policy suggests itself, i.e., raising the real income of the poor through rent supplements or certificates. Unlike a general income supplement, rent supplements are earmarked for housing and therefore will be used for that purpose regardless of the income elasticity of demand for housing. In short,

---

[61] Muth, "Urban Residential Land and Housing Markets," op. cit., p. 286, and Reid, op. cit.

[62] Netzer, op. cit., p. 75.

[63] Ira S. Lowry, *Housing Assistance for Low-Income Urban Families: A Fresh Approach*, P-4645 (Santa Monica, Calif.: The RAND Corporation, May 1971), 57 pp.

rent supplements provided to poor families more directly enable them to live in better (or, at any rate, in higher-cost) housing that is otherwise beyond their economic reach. Rent supplements can also counteract housing stock deterioration.

Federal rent supplement programs, first enacted in 1965, require eligible families to pay 25 percent of their incomes for rent, while the federal government pays directly to landlords the difference between the rent and the tenants' payments. The supplement is directly tied to the family (size, etc.) and not to the housing unit. Private, and not public, groups build and operate these low-rent housing units.

Since rent subsidies earmark funds for housing, some inefficiency in resource use can result. The poor are not only poorly housed but are also poorly clothed and fed. On the assumption that the poor know what is best for them, it could be argued that unearmarked or general claims on resources would permit them to purchase those services in greatest demand by them—which do not necessarily include housing.

Also a variety of cost and supply policies can be adopted, designed to reduce urban blight and slums and to upgrade urban housing. They can entail reducing costs of housing services, reducing supply of poor housing stock, or increasing supply of improved housing. Some of these policies can be supplemented by selective income policies, e.g., rent subsidies. Cost-reducing policies include cheaper and more readily available credit, lower land cost, lower construction costs, and tax policies designed to reduce the tax burdens on investors in housing and housing occupants.

In order to provide more readily available and less costly credit, a number of mortgage credit policies can be used. Government, especially the federal government, can guarantee or insure individual mortgages written on far more generous terms than is conventionally possible. By reducing the risk of lenders, interest rates can be lowered and more credit made available. Furthermore, the government can borrow, at substantially lower interest rates, and relend its funds at these lower rates to individual borrowers and builders.[64] Finally, government can lower interest rates beyond those made possible by its borrowing capacity and further subsidize interest rates. For example, the latter policy was followed in sections 235 and 236 of the Housing Act of 1968, which provides for federal subsidies that, at a maximum, reduce the interest cost to the equivalent of a 1 percent mortgage. Tenants pay rents equal to 25 percent of income and homeowners make mortgage payments equal to 20 percent of income; federal subsidies make up the difference between the amounts required for the actual mortgages on the new housing and the rents so established.[65]

[64] The reason why government can borrow at reduced rates stems from its strong credit position and the fact that interest on state and local government bonds is exempt from federal income taxation.

[65] Netzer, op. cit., pp. 89–90.

Making mortgage credit available and at lower cost can, however, have distorting side effects. Producers of housing are induced to make greater capital expenditures and less expenditures for maintenance and for operation than they otherwise would. The result can be well-built public housing that is extremely poorly maintained.

Although land costs amount on the average to merely 5 percent of the cost of housing services, they too can be reduced. Local governments can prescribe rather large minimum lot sizes and in this manner relatively high property tax receipts combined with limited service demands can be expected. Thus, since relatively expensive houses are built, usually on large lots, larger property taxes will be paid by relatively well-to-do households, which tend to have smaller families and therefore make smaller demands on schools and other local services. In order to reduce minimum lot sizes, county or state governments could be assigned the responsibility to determine land uses.

But by far the greatest housing cost item is construction cost. According to the National Commission on Urban Problems this might be reduced up to 15 percent.[66] Building and housing codes, often designed to assure safety and orderly development, however have important cost-raising side effects. Some building codes are outmoded, and yet in many places their revision has been fought by vested interests, i.e., specific building trades and contractors. Perhaps it would be best to adopt uniform statewide building codes, not only in the hope of updating and rationalizing them but also in order to provide for greater uniformity, so that large-scale builders operating in different municipalities can benefit from large-scale purchase of material and standardized construction techniques.[67]

Finally, we can consider taxes, since they impose heavy burdens on housing consumption. It has been estimated that, on the average property, taxes are equivalent to a sales tax of over 25 percent of consumer expenditure for housing exclusive of the tax itself.[68] The percentage appears to be even higher, reaching up to 35 percent, in large urban areas of the Northeast, of the Great Lakes states, and of California and Oregon. No sales tax rates on other consumer items come close to such a high level.

While property taxes raise the occupancy cost of housing, existing federal income tax laws are advantageous to owner-occupants and certain types of investors in rental housing. As a result the overall tax system favors owner-occupied housing in suburban areas, which mainly benefits upper-income groups. The system is most burdensome on low-income

[66] National Commission on Urban Problems, *Building the American City* (Final Report, 1969), p. 16.
[67] It is interesting, though, that an empirical study carried out in Northern Ireland did not discover scale economies in house building (M. C. Fleming, "Conventional Housebuilding and the Scale of Operations," *Bulletin of the Oxford Institute of Economics and Statistics,* vol. 29, no. 2 (1967) pp. 109–137).
[68] Netzer, op. cit., p. 99.

households renting housing in the center of cities.[69] Therefore steps could be taken which would lower property taxes on center-city properties. Then rents could be lowered and housing consumption expanded, particularly if at the same time middle-income households in the center of the city were to demand higher-quality housing. As a consequence, housing formerly occupied by these middle-income families would be vacated and become available to lower-income groups.

Two tax policies are possible. On the one hand, an across-the-board reduction of taxes on center-city housing would provide an attractive policy, with a minimum of distorting side effects. On the other hand, special types of housing could benefit from reduced taxes, as is presently done by exempting from property taxes low-rent federal public housing and, in New York State, state government middle-income housing. The latter policy is selective and tends to generate distorting side effects, likely to interfere with an efficient housing market. Furthermore, property tax laws could take into consideration the desirability of not punishing those who are improving and upgrading their property and thus contributing to the general improvement of neighborhoods.

In addition to these changes in property tax policy, reforms in federal income taxation are desirable. They should go in the direction of reducing the discriminatory effects which favor rich suburbanites in owner-occupied homes and instead particularly reduce the burden on poor renters in the center of the city.

So far we have been concerned with policies designed to reduce the cost of housing mainly in city centers and, in doing so, to improve the supply of better-quality housing there. In so doing we would combat urban slums and blight. However, a further policy would be to reduce supply of poor housing by either increasing the cost to private firms who produce poor-quality housing or by demolishing poor-quality structures and replacing them with upgraded housing. However, a policy to increase the cost to private firms of producing poor-quality housing is unlikely to assure low-income households better housing unless such a program is combined with rent subsidy or other income-enhancing programs. Otherwise, price increases for poor-quality housing relative to good-quality housing are to be expected.

Not only can tax policies be used to raise the cost of private firms in producing poor-quality housing, but also stricter enforcement of building and occupancy codes and public receivership of slum dwellings can have similar results. But in all cases such measures tend to reduce the earnings of poor- relative to good-quality housing. The result will be fewer dwellings being converted to poor-quality housing, reducing in the long run the

[69] The federal income tax advantage of home ownership stems from the tax deduction feature of mortgage interest and property taxes in computing federal income taxes.

housing opportunities for the poor unless supplemented by an income-raising program.

A similar problem exists in relation to demolitions, e.g., under the federal urban renewal program. Such a program reduces the fraction of substandard housing units. It might force low-income households, who otherwise would have lived in inexpensive, poor-quality housing units, to move into better housing; but more importantly, it might force them to occupy such units with more persons per dwelling and thus contribute to the deterioration of such housing. The relative increase from poor- to good-quality housing will induce property owners of the latter to convert it to poor-quality housing. In this manner the supply of substandard dwellings will tend to increase and new slums will result most likely in new areas. Depending on the costs of conversion, demolition might still lead to a net reduction in the fraction of poor-quality housing, and if the price of poor-quality housing would rise, poor households might end up living in poorer housing conditions and (or) greater poverty than before.

If a policy of demolishing slums is to be followed, it would be worthwhile to build new housing for low-income groups before their old slum housing is torn down. We might begin by building new low-income housing on peripheral vacant land, still close to core-oriented public mass transportation. In this manner we would save money, since we would refrain from purchasing land in the densest slums that usually also generate the highest rent and, because of capitalization of net earnings, the highest property values per acre. Having built low-cost housing in peripheral areas and moved into them the poor households from the slums, such properties would tend to fall in price and permit purchase of slum acreage later on at lower cost. Moreover, by producing new housing for low-income families on vacant land, core area slum dwellers could move into better housing earlier and with less discomfort than if dwellings in which they live were demolished first.[70]

Two other policies have been proposed to house the families who are displaced as slums are being demolished. One is a "roll over" strategy that uses mobile housing units near the housing to be replaced. Residents of the latter could move into the mobile units temporarily until they can return to the new housing. These mobile homes could be moved from this clearance site to the next. The shortcoming of such a policy is that the demolition-rebuilding period is too long—on the average, about seven years.[71]

The second strategy that has been suggested calls for the creation of large "temporary way station" housing projects on vacant suburban land. Displaced central-city households would occupy these units until the de-

[70] Wilbur R. Thompson, *A Preface to Urban Economics* (Baltimore: Johns Hopkins, 1965), pp. 296–297.
[71] Downs, "Moving toward Realistic Housing Goals," op. cit., pp. 163–164.

molished dwellings are rebuilt. However, displacing en masse low-income households temporarily from one spot to another has proved to be impossible. There appears to be much resistance against moving from the core city temporarily into the unaccustomed suburban environment.

Finally, policies can be adopted that increase the supply of improved housing, be it through public construction or rehabilitation. Let us analyze the case where government destroys bad housing and constructs in its place improved housing equaling the number of dwelling units demolished. In the short run, if this public construction was unanticipated, the quantity of improved housing services consumed will increase. However, if the market for housing services were perfectly competitive and had been in equilibrium before the public construction of the additional housing, in the long run the consumption of housing services would not increase because of this government action. It would increase only if the public housing activity should be combined with rent subsidies so that both supply and income forces would be at work.[72]

In addition to rent supplements, it might be necessary to provide "displacement grants" large enough to cover most, if not all, of the dislocation costs of poor families to be moved from their slum dwellings to improved housing. The Highway Act of 1968 authorizes such payments for road displacement, and the coverage of the act could be extended to all public programs.

Altogether, it appears proper not to rely on general income-increasing policies to the exclusion of other policies. Richard Muth has proposed such a single-minded attack, while Dick Netzer favors a broader avenue of approach when he states, "A wide range of policies, new and traditional, each of them having a modest impact on the underlying problems, seems necessary if there is to be a massive overall impact."[73]

Policies to Combat Racial Housing Segregation

Various policy approaches are available if we are to attain racial desegregation. If one concludes that segregation results from income differences rather than racial differences, then some of the policy approaches to problems of neighborhood degradation are adaptable in toto. Alternatively, if one concludes that the problem is a manifestation of racial discrimination, as most economists do, then there are two ways in which governments can intervene in the housing market. Subsidies can be offered to whites to overcome their apparent dislike of minority neighbors, or taxes can be imposed on whites who prefer living only among whites.[74]

[72] E. O. Olsen, *Do Public Construction and Rehabilitation Increase the Quantity of Housing Service?* D-17927 (Santa Monica, Calif.: The RAND Corporation, 1968), 10 pp.
[73] Netzer, op. cit., p. 197.
[74] Gary Becker, *The Economics of Discrimination* (Chicago: The University of Chicago Press, 1957).

If one accepts the premise that segregation does not reduce housing consumption by Negroes and other minorities, then one must favor government programs designed to increase the incomes of such groups in order to improve their housing conditions. With this in mind, for example, Muth states, ". . . I would not anticipate that so-called open-occupancy legislation, even if enforced much more vigorously than such legislation has been in the past, would appreciably reduce segregation."[75] Muth believes that such legislation would not prevent whites from moving away from Negroes and that schemes to colonize Negroes in the suburbs would most likely result in Negro enclaves surrounded by whites. Furthermore, Muth believes that while quota systems might prevent the development of new ghettos they would also limit the housing opportunities of Negroes.

Muth's discussion of quotas is particularly of interest in relation to the prevention of tipping. Racial quotas could prevent the widespread expectation and occurrence of tipping. If the nation were to prefer integration to residential separation of minority groups, guaranteed quotas might defuse the expectations that lead to tipping. Enforcement of racial quotas could eliminate speculation that can preclude reaching a desirable racial mix in a neighborhood. However, quotas have a long, antiliberal history of being used to keep down the number of minority-group members in a residential area, a school, a club, or a civil service. Quotas are usually also opposed on economic grounds, because they tend to be inconsistent with efficient resource allocation. At the same time they increase certainty and facilitate the attainment of distributional objectives.

Anthony Downs rejects the notion that poor housing of Negroes can be eliminated by raising their incomes above the poverty level through income maintenance and employment programs, since the supply of housing available to many Negro households is highly restricted.[76] These frictional factors will not yield easily to public remedies, and suddenly raising the incomes of these people would cause their rents to rise sharply. For this reason housing programs per se must remain crucial ingredients if we want to provide Negroes with decent housing. This requires not only integrating nonslum areas in core cities but also opening up the suburbs.

Different policy approaches are available if one accepts the premise that much segregation results from discrimination. One policy would guarantee that whites living in a neighborhood that is to be integrated would not suffer financial losses. If government could guarantee property owners against a decline in property values, not only could a selling panic that aggravates tipping be prevented but the chances of tipping coming about could be greatly reduced. Such assurances, furthermore, induce old-timers

---

[75] Muth, "The Ghetto in the Local Housing Market," op. cit., p. 455.
[76] Downs, "Moving toward Realistic Housing Goals," op. cit., p. 160.

to possibly stay long enough to get accustomed to having a few minority members living among them.

If low-income Negroes are to be integrated into low-income suburban neighborhoods, effective steps must be taken to at least neutralize whites' fiscal self-defense against higher property taxes. Institutional changes have been suggested to remove the economic penalties of accepting low-income residents.[77]

Another policy would provide for a grant-in-aid to suburban governments and particularly school boards, to subsidize them for accepting poor newcomers. A second policy would move taxation and land-use control powers from individual suburban governments to such larger entities as counties or metropolitan areas. Once all households were within a single jurisdiction, movement of low-income households from one portion to another would not create fiscal losses. A third, and possibly most promising, policy would shift funding of education and welfare services to the federal government, a step that would greatly reduce the property tax burden of suburbanites when low-income families move into their areas.

A specific policy proposal is to subsidize middle-class whites for permitting low-income groups, including minority members, to live with them in the same neighborhood. White lower middle-income renters could be subsidized by rent supplements and homeowners by offering them more advantageous credit terms and (or) lower taxes. The Federal Urban Rent Supplement Program of the Housing and Urban Development Act of 1965 provided rent supplements to moderate-income families of between $4,000 and $8,000 annual income.

Let us provide an economic analysis of such a policy. In Figure 3.3 a white, segregated, moderate-income neighborhood is in equilibrium. The demand of moderate-income families for "decent" housing (dd) intersects the market supply curve (ss) at p, i.e., a market-clearing rent. In the short run, the supply is entirely inelastic, as represented in the slope of the supply function.

As a next step we will examine the implications of a government policy designed to provide "decent" housing for low-income families in the midst of this moderate-income neighborhood. The demand function of moderate-income families for "decent" housing will shift downward if they can expect low-income, including minority, families in their neighborhood ($d'd'$). There will be less housing utility to these moderate-income white families than would exist if the entire neighborhood had remained homogeneous. Under those conditions some moderate-income families will seek to leave the neighborhood unless rents are lowered. In the case of Figure 3.3, rents would have to be lowered from p to p', resulting in a

---

[77] Ibid., p. 165.

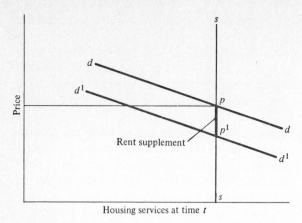

FIGURE 3.3   Derivation of integration-promoting rent supplements.

wealth loss to the apartment house owner. Government can prevent this wealth loss by subsidizing the rents of moderate-income families, who in fact would be paid to stay. Integration without depressing effects on property values could be achieved.

There are indications that President Lyndon Johnson realized the opportunities offered by such a program when he stated in his housing message to Congress on March 2, 1965, "Since the rent supplement is flexible, it will permit us to encourage housing in which families of different incomes, and in different age groups can live together. It will make it unnecessary for the government to assist and even require the segregation by income level which detracts from the variety and quality of urban life."[78]

Another policy approach which acknowledges that discrimination underlies racial segregation, is the taxation of whites (rather than their subsidization). This could be done by government fostering blockbusting. Passage of such laws is facilitated since they do not require appropriations, and their administration is virtually costless. By the government simply stating that it encourages blockbusting, private entreprenuers can be expected to do the rest. Homes in white areas are purchased for nonwhites by third parties. After the nonwhite family moves in, this fact is brought to the attention of the neighbors, along with offers to buy. The new market sales price for homes in that area will be equal to the original market value less whatever whites are willing to give up in order to escape the proximity of nonwhites. In some areas this has been something close to 50 percent of the original market value.[79]

[78] *Congressional Quarterly, Weekly Reports* (January–December 1965), p. 351.
[79] Most writers make the implicit assumption that blockbusting is somehow "unfair" or "bad." This is a difficult position to defend, however. It is virtually the only

Urban Sprawl

Urban sprawl is the leapfrogging development associated with the geographic extension of urban areas far beyond the boundaries which they once had. Cities which used to have identifiable centers and tightly packed residential areas surrounding them have become large metropolitan areas of amorphous collections of many municipalities, shopping centers, multiple centers, and suburbs. Although almost every city has some area in it considered to be "downtown," this label frequently adheres only as a historical phenomenon. In reality, there are many centers of business and high population density in most cities, none of them clearly dominant.

At first glance, the phenomenon of urban sprawl appears to be the result of some kind of market malfunction. In reality, however, the elements of market imperfection which do underlie the explanations for sprawl are exogenous to the city's economic system. Sprawl itself is a rational, and more than likely optimal, market response to these exogenous forces. As a result, we have chosen to discuss the issue in this section of the chapter in preference to the previous section on market imperfections.

There are four major explanations for the existence of urban sprawl as well as a host of minor ones. They are not conflicting explanations, but are reinforcing, some of them even having multiplicative relations rather than simply additive.

One explanation refers to the heavy reliance on property taxes and differential tax rates between the central city and the outlying areas. Another explanation notices that the Federal Housing Administration (FHA) and various housing subsidy plans have produced a built-in bias in the housing market toward the type of family which is most likely to purchase housing farther out from the city center than toward other potential home buyers. A third explanation for urban sprawl concentrates on the expenditures which have been made on transportation capital stock, including the selection of transport modes. Finally, there are several other classes of explanations offered by noneconomists.

---

result of racial discrimination in which whites rather than blacks are made to pay the price for their preferences. In addition, as we have already pointed out, such a policy is extremely low in cost for the government. In effect, laws are written to remove a market imperfection which was originally aided by legislation. The market is allowed to allocate people to housing by race in the fashion desired by those people themselves. The only losses are to whites—and in reality these losses are balanced exactly by their payment aspect. To call the difference between the all-white price and the integrated price a loss is the same as saying that the $6 an individual pays for a book is a loss. It is not, of course. He is exchanging generalized claims on resources for specific goods. The same is the case for whites' sales of their homes at discounts which are determined by the intensity of their desire to live only near whites.

We will examine these four explanations in turn. Mason Gaffney attributes sprawl to cities' heavy reliance on property taxes and particularly their dominating improvement component. He holds this improvement tax mainly responsible for urbanites' flight to the suburbs and the resulting low densities.[80] This argument can be analyzed with the aid of the Muth model, which predicts that, because of price and income elasticities of demand, high-income families tend to live farther from the city center than low-income families. Concentration of low-income families in the central city and its core places, when there is heavy reliance on the property tax, very heavy tax burdens on the other taxpayers in the jurisdiction. Consequently, higher-income families tend to prefer moving into the suburbs. The result has been large numbers of new suburban municipalities which have been chartered for the express purpose of housing and providing a more tailored set of public services to a homogeneous group of medium- or upper-income residents.

In line with Muth's model, FHA and other mortgage subsidy programs have further stimulated urban sprawl. These programs tend to subsidize specially defined social classes of individuals—for the most part, white, middle-class, middle-income families—in their housing expenditures. Given the decline of land, and hence housing prices, with distance from the city center, these families could achieve wealth increases by moving away from the city center. Since the increase in wealth was not directly tied to their earnings, the income increase was not balanced by increases in marginal transportation costs, and the result was a consistently greater distance from the city center representing the equilibrium distance.

Urban sprawl has also been stimulated by greatly improved highways linking central cities with their suburbs. This fact, in combination with some improvements in the private car, has reduced the real cost of automotive transportation borne by users. More will be said in Chapter 4.

There are also several social theories which attempt to explain urban sprawl. The economist is not equipped to judge their significance except as an observer of cities. These theories deal with urbanites' attempts to escape crime and congestion, which seem endemic to the city (until they arrive in the suburbs, where the problems generally persist), and to escape the anomis and isolation which are thought to be generated by the impersonal tensions of urban living. There are other schools, however, which claim these tensions to be the very aspects of urban life which are most appealing to modern city dwellers—they represent the major drawing power which the city exercises on prospective migrants.

While there is much urban sprawl in the United States, it is not clear that such sprawl is or is not desirable. However, if we are to conclude

[80] Mason Gaffney, "Land Rent, Taxation, and Public Policy," *Papers of the Regional Science Association, 1968*, vol. 23, p. 149.

that it *is* undesirable and seek policies to reduce it, the following directions could be pursued: Incentives for urban sprawl would be reduced if local governments would less heavily rely on the property tax, and particularly its improvements component. Shifting more of the financing burden onto higher levels of government also would counteract sprawl tendencies.

A second policy could take the form of reducing the disadvantage that is given residential property in central cities compared to that in the suburbs. One could even go in the opposite direction and favor central-city properties in terms of their financing. Since an urban transportation system has evolved that heavily subsidizes the movement of people and goods between the central city and its suburbs, these practices also could be reversed.

While we do not consider ourselves well equipped to propose policy recommendations based on sociological explanations of urban sprawl, one comment will be made. It has been said that urban sprawl has been fostered by urbanites' desire to escape crime and congestion. These two phenomena well demonstrate the close interdependency between economic actors and human, economic, political, and physical characteristics of cities. It is this interdependency between actors and markets that makes policy solutions so difficult.

Altogether, cities face a large variety of housing and land-use problems, for which economists have been relatively slow to develop powerful analytical tools. The abundance of complicated interdependencies within the urban housing market and between it and other urban markets has posed serious challenges to the economist. However, it is our hope that some of the methods presented here will prove to be of assistance in future efforts.

CHAPTER 4

URBAN TRANSPORTATION MARKETS

I. INTRODUCTION

Throughout our examination of urban economics thus far, the concepts of space in general and of distance and proximity in particular have been central to the analysis. The trade-off between proximity and dispersion is made possible by the transportation system, a crucial element affecting the physical layout and efficiency of operation of all the many markets in an urban area.

Transportation may be defined as the movement of people and goods through space. Urban transportation merely means that the space is densely populated. We are concerned with select urban transportation systems— mainly those involving horizontal, power-driven movement within urban areas.[1]

The economic problem of space—or, better, the scarcity of immediate access to other people's attention or to the resources we want at any moment—would not exist if instant rearrangement and communication were possible at a zero cost. Transportation particularly involves time costs, because distance can be covered only at finite speeds. Furthermore, concern for safety and scheduling implies that individual time costs may dominate direct money-cost constraints when individuals make decisions about the supply of or demand for transportation services. Thus, our discussion of urban transportation must recognize the problems of location or access in terms of relative time costs. Transportation (together with communication in general) is the crucial link between urban markets that makes possible their pronounced interdependency.

An urban transportation system is composed of two major elements. One element is the right-of-way or corridor in space through which individuals and goods can move between locations. In an urban area, the air

---

[1] Transportation thus defined, i.e., the physical movement of people and goods from one location to another, is only one special aspect of the more general issue of communication. Communication is the ability to control and execute various activities at nonproximate locations. In its broadest context of analysis, a communications chapter would consider the relative costs and existing technologies of alternative means of organizing and conducting people's affairs. We will pay no attention to nontransport means of communication, which include telephone services, radio message collection and dispatch systems, on-line, computer-coordinated information systems, verbal and video playback recording systems, high-speed typing and copy reproduction systems, and mail services.

space, land surface, navigable bodies of water, and even underground utility lines and sewers make up an intricate network of legally established corridors for the movement of persons, goods, and wastes.

A second element is the operation of means of conveyance. In addition to obtaining use of a right-of-way or possible route of travel, an individual obtains the services of a means of conveyance. Distinguishing between these two services, rights-of-way and means of conveyance, each of which could be and is in fact marketed by different economic agents, can facilitate our understanding some of our urban transportation problems. The provision of rights-of-way is accomplished by agencies with economic and political motivations or powers that differ from those of the agencies that control the supply of carrier services. By and large, the first are governments and the second are private entities whose responses have differed greatly, quite often for good reasons; one result has been that there are bottlenecks in the transportation system of most larger cities, particularly at peak hours. This conceptual separation between corridors and vehicles also has implications for the descriptions of demand, supply, pricing, and government action relative to transportation.

To place the condition of urban transportation markets into proper perspective, we now briefly review their recent history in America. It has been estimated that during the 1950s and 1960s the United States spent $2.3 trillion moving people and goods around—nearly $200 billion in 1970 alone. Of this amount, about 83 percent went for highway transportation and roughly $109 billion for passenger transportation. Only about 12 percent went for public transport. The rest was used to buy, clean, fuel, insure, repair, and park cars and provide rules for them.[2] The phenomenal upsurge of private-car usage overshadows all other transportation events. Since World War II, the total and per capita number of cars on our cities' highways and streets has continuously increased so that before the 1960s came to an end, more than 100 million cars, buses, and trucks were on our roads, moving more than 1 trillion miles per year. Between the mid-1950s and the late 1960s 3,000 miles of urban freeways were built around and through the central cities.[3]

Well over 70 percent of all transportation related to work trips takes place on urban streets and highways, and probably an even higher proportion of transportation for all purposes takes place on such facilities. Work trips by rail transit account for but a very small fraction of all work travel and are mainly concentrated in a few very large urban areas, with

[2] Gilbert Burck, "Transportation's Troubled Abundance," *Fortune* (1971), pp. 59–60.
[3] John R. Meyer, John F. Kain, and Martin Wohl, *The Urban Transportation Problem* (Cambridge, Mass.: Harvard, 1965), p. 82; and David M. Gordon, *Problems in Political Economy: An Urban Prospective* (Lexington, Mass.: Heath, 1971), p. 408; and "Transportation Problems in Revitalizing Cities," *HUD International Brief* (February 1971), p. 2.

rail transit volume on the five major systems edging up slightly over the last twenty years. During 1950–1969, however, bus transit volume declined by some 39 percent.[4] Thus with the resulting decline in the availability in most cities of alternatives, urbanites' major short-run option is the private car and, in the early 1970s, they spent about $25 billion annually on new automobiles, while public expenditure on arterial highway construction in urban communities amounted to $4 billion a year.

During the last forty years, the technology of urban transportation has changed little. No major functional change with regard to mass transportation has taken place, and private-car users must still put up with the driving burden and must allow their high-cost automobiles to stand idle most of the day when used for work trips.[5] Admittedly, some operating economies have been achieved in bus transportation with diesel engines, and riding quality has been improved by automatic transmissions and moving the motor to the rear.

There is much evidence that throughout the postwar period the quality of publicly provided transit has declined, at least as it is measured by frequency of pickup and delivery services. During the same period, when more and more people took to the private car, there are indications that, by some standards, the quality of private-car travel has improved. For example, during the last decade the average speed on urban expressways during rush periods has increased by as much as ten miles per hour. Also, the period required for evacuating central business districts in the evening rush hours has been greatly reduced, perhaps by as much as 30 to 40 percent, since the late 1940s.[6]

Changes in the demand for publicly provided transportation particularly affected non-rush-hour public transportation, the demand for which declined more rapidly than did that for trips to and from work. Thus, the use of public transportation is mainly concentrated in work trips, whereas superior convenience, mobility, privacy, and relatively low cost—often facilitated by hidden or little recognized subsidies—have given the private car a pronounced advantage for recreational, shopping, and social trips.

The forces and manifestations of these changes are well described by Meyer, Kain, and Wohl:

> Formerly, most urban travel was confined to the dense, central-city core and to heavily built-up radial corridors . . . residential growth and urban

[4] Lyle C. Fitch, "Improving Urban Transportation," in Ernest W. Williams, Jr. (ed.), *The Future of American Transportation* (Englewood Cliffs, N.J.: Prentice-Hall, 1971), pp. 170–171.
[5] Meyer, Kain, and Wohl, op. cit., pp. 309–310.
[6] John R. Meyer, "Urban Transportation: Problems and Perspectives," in James Q. Wilson (ed.), *The Metropolitan Enigma* (Cambridge, Mass.: Harvard, 1968), pp. 42–50; 66–69.

travel were limited by the coverage of transit systems and by what was then reasonable walking distance. Crosstown travel was rare because of the expense, time, discomfort, and inconvenience involved. Over the past fifteen years, by contrast, downtown-oriented travel generally has remained stable or decreased; the growth in urban trip-making has been mainly in crosstown and intrasuburban movement.

The ubiquity of highway systems additionally provides a superior capability to adjust . . . to changes in living patterns, industrial location, and market structure. . . . Bus transit systems and highway and automobile systems have demonstrated at least some ability to adapt to these changes. By contrast, extremely inflexible and long-lived rail transit systems have not been able to bend to these changes without considerable cost and sacrifices in service.[7]

Peaking of transit demand has continued to be serious. And because work trips are concentrated in time, peaking in use rates is more pronounced in rail transit and railroad commuter facilities than it is in private-car travel. In the postwar period, urban bus transit has suffered considerably greater overall ridership declines than has rail transit, yet without equally heavy peaking. Although the length of bus trips has declined, revenue per passenger-mile has somewhat increased.

The pronounced increase in private-car use has gone hand in hand with and has to some extent caused a decline in the relative, and sometimes even the absolute, importance of the central city as a work place and shopping area. Use of the private car has enhanced the relative attractiveness of locations in the outer rings of metropolitan areas. That is, it seems evident that with or without public mass transit systems, American cities have been decentralizing. Residential decentralization has been stimulated by the rapid increases in income levels and the dispersion of work places. Thus an increasing percentage of urbanites each year has reached a position where they can afford suburban locations that have more space, and where they can afford car transportation to reach their places of work.

Externalities and scale economies associated with urban transportation often justify the role of governmental production and control in urban transportation and the various forms such intervention can take. As to the latter, we can, in principle, distinguish between government regulation and standard setting, on the one hand, and government's promotion of urban transportation by direct investment and subsidy, on the other hand. The two forms of intervention can have, however, very similar objectives.

Regulation includes the setting of charges, time schedules, and routes, as well as performance standards and the enforcement of such standards.

---

[7] Meyer, Kain, and Wohl, op. cit., p. 312.

Additionally, there is the licensing of carriers and facilities. Direct governmental promotion has also had far-reaching effects, including possible overinvestment in certain modes or locations of metropolitan areas, and widespread, uncompensated detrimental effects on urban minority groups and property owners. Government's power of eminent domain is often used to establish transportation corridors where organization of routes by private ownership is deemed not practicable.

But in addition to owning rights-of-way, governments have increasingly taken over unprofitable urban transit systems from private companies. By providing such transportation below cost, they subsidize urban commuters directly, and in other cases they provide indirect subsidy in the form of grants and loans to privately owned mass transit systems. Finally, higher-level governments have established areawide transportation authorities to coordinate urban transportation where various local jurisdictions are afforded representation on control boards.

II.   *INTERRELATIONS BETWEEN TRANSPORTATION AND OTHER URBAN MARKETS*

The significance of interdependency among urban markets has been increasingly recognized by transportation planners.[8]

In discussing each major urban market, we have attempted to pay attention to the interdependencies with other markets. Now we deepen our discussion of urban transportation by examining these interrelationships in greater detail, particularly since transportation constitutes such an important "linking process" for all urban activities.

---

[8] Thus, for example, Governor Francis W. Sargent of Massachusetts established the Boston Transportation Planning Review in 1970. Its charge included:

It will be multi-value in orientation. That is, it will give as much consideration to the by-products of transportation investment alternatives as to their intended transportation effects. These by-products will normally include the following:

Effects on the supply of low and moderate income housing;
Effects on the supply of recreational open space;
Air and noise pollution impacts;
Land-use development impacts;
Effects on such social values as racial integration and neighborhood stability;
Local tax base and employment impacts;
Effects on the visual attractiveness and overall congeniality of the urban environment.

(Alan Altshuler in *Hearings on Regional Planning Issues,* Joint Economic Committee, Congress of the United States, part 1, Oct. 13–15, 1970 [Washington, D.C.: U.S. Government Printing Office, 1970], p. 7.)

Transportation Related to Residential Land Use and Housing Markets

The Alonso, Muth, and Siegel models, discussed in the preceding chapter, emphasize the importance to households of the trade-off between housing and commuting costs. Transportation and housing expenditures being substitutes to some extent, workers employed at high-density work places must make a choice regarding the mix of transportation costs and housing costs that they incur. This is particularly true for newly arrived urban residents who are choosing among possible residences. These choices are more complicated and restricted for nonwhites because of racial housing segregation.

With the aid of these models it is also easy to understand how new transportation technology and rising income levels influence housing demand and the overall spatial form of the metropolis: specifically, the increased consumption of single-unit housing with private yards. This consumption pattern has been facilitated by the cost-reducing effects on transportation of tax-financed, zero-priced freeways and the underpricing of suburb-to-city center rail and bus services. Thus, the consumption-work pattern of the suburban dweller who is willing to sacrifice commuting time to central-area job locations has become popular in American cities: a middle- and upper-income-class phenomenon. The lower-income classes typically consume less housing and live in higher-density areas close to central-area job locations, typically engaging in shorter and less convenient and comfortable commuting trips than do the middle-income groups.

The industrial location models that we reviewed in Chapter 2 show how the transportation costs of securing input services from locations, and the transportation costs of marketing outputs from alternative production locations are related. In addition, we considered the relative production costs of vertical and horizontal plant construction and operations. Subsidized construction and operation of both urban freeways and mass transit systems have tended to decrease the relative costs to industry of engaging in more distant, land-intensive, and horizontally expansive techniques of operation. This is especially true of industries that are predominantly staffed by workers who reside in the suburbs.

In earlier chapters we emphasized particularly the stimulating effects on urban sprawl of financing urban transportation systems from resources drawn in part from outside the local communities and, furthermore, of the frequent rationing of transportation system use with near-zero pricing schemes. The latter, underpricing policy not only contributes to more hours being spent in commuting and more distant residential living, but it also promotes peaking in transportation facility use—behavior that we have termed *crowding*. We emphasize here the prevailing urban institutions that tend to yield overinvestment in transportation facilities in order to accommodate peak quantities demanded at zero prices. The great expansion in urban transportation, especially freeways and automobile travel, is largely a consequence of outside subsidies on the condition of underpricing to users. These same inducements have also had the consequence of dramatizing many costs of producing and consuming transport services that are very significant from a social point of view but which do not serve as restraints on the behavior of commuters. For example, the externalities of commuter crowding lead to less efficient functioning of other markets, and increased exhaust emissions lead to greater pollution.

Transportation Related to Labor Markets

Some urban transportation policies have added to rather than alleviated the relative wealth disadvantages of the poor and nonwhite minorities in the urban population, particularly in those cases where transportation policies have fostered racial housing segregation. Older and poorer urbanites not only are being disadvantaged by a declining availability of public rapid transit services, but they also may bear tax burdens that, on balance, serve to subsidize transportation services enjoyed by younger and wealthier suburbanites.

In many metropolitan areas, the centrally located areas that house lower-income families are still served reasonably well by mass transit connections to the central business district. However, the location of blue-collar or less skilled job opportunities has become more decentralized in recent years, with jobs moving to the suburbs and sometimes declining in central areas.[9] As a result, the cost, and particularly the time cost, to the urban poor of commuting to work has increased.[10]

Because of deteriorating mass transportation, the cost to those who do not use the private automobile has increased relative to the costs realized by those who do use it. Thus, the result of urban transportation policies has been to relatively reduce access of the urban poor to geographic areas where their job opportunities are. Using as the pertinent wage one that is the net of transportation and other work-associated costs—i.e., commuting time is considered as part of the work day—the resulting wage differentials indicate that transportation policies have greatly favored those

[9] E. N. Dodson, *Employment Accessibility for Special Urban Groups* (Santa Barbara, Calif.: General Research Corporation, January 1968).
[10] A study by Kassoff and Deutschman has reported that there are 100,000 fewer low-income jobs than low-income workers residing in New York City. (John F. Kain and John R. Meyer, *Interrelationships of Transportation and Poverty* [Cambridge, Mass.: Program on Regional and Urban Economics of Harvard University, 1968], p. 13.) A further study of the Tri-State Regional Planning Commission in 1971 revealed that in New York City subways are not primarily the vehicle of the poor, but that the poor of the region simply do not, or cannot, travel extensively. (*New York Times*, Oct. 18, 1971, p. 1.)

racial and income groups that have a wide selection of residential locations.

As job opportunities decentralize, lower-income white families seek to relocate their residences nearer to their jobs or to transit lines that connect with their jobs. However, many nonwhites face very restricted residential location possibilities, which reduces their opportunities for job search and makes job information more difficult to obtain. Thus transportation policies may have a contributory effect on the relatively higher unemployment rates and longer periods of unemployment among nonwhites. The combined effects of housing market segregation and expansion of public investments to facilitate automobile transit have been closely associated with relatively higher unemployment rates of urban lower-income and nonwhite groups.[11]

New rapid transit developments are not likely to improve this situation for the relatively poor, centrally located residents. For example, analyses of both the San Francisco and Washington, D.C., rapid transit systems indicate that they will yield net benefits for high-income commuters traveling long distances between suburbs and central employment centers, but that they will do very little to improve access for centrally located ghetto residents and suburban employment centers.[12] Furthermore, the urban poor are particularly critical of policies that create new roads or transit facilities in central areas. The result of such "urban renewal" is often a displacement of lower-income and older people who are financially and psychologically hurt by the necessity to adjust to new residential circumstances. For example, it was estimated that the Brookline-Elm alignment of the Cambridge inner belt highway would "displace" an estimated 5,000 people—or about 6 percent of the Cambridge population—the majority of whom are low- and middle-income people.[13]

Transportation Related to the Urban Government Sector

The interactions between urban transportation systems and the supply of other urban government services and revenue yields are complex and often very indirect. To the extent that commuter services are underpriced, urbanites will tend to travel greater distances and longer hours and live farther away from the center or core of the urban area than they would otherwise do. The resulting urban sprawl has been accentuated by government fragmentation as suburban areas have incorporated into municipal and special-service units. In large, balkanized metropolitan areas many families live in one jurisdiction, work in a second, and procure special services from others. Under such circumstances, there may be little corre-

[11] John F. Kain, "Housing Segregation, Negro Employment, and Metropolitan Decentralization," *The Quarterly Journal of Economics*, vol. 82, no. 2 (May 1968).
[12] Martin Wohl, "Income Circumstances of Public Transit Users," *Traffic Quarterly* (January 1970).
[13] Kain and Meyer, op. cit., pp. 14 and 15.

spondence between the family tax costs imposed by a jurisdiction and the services received by the taxed family. The central city has remained the haven of the less mobile members of the urban community, many of them poor and disadvantaged. The resulting concentration of demands for government services and transfer payments in the central municipalities is seldom matched with a taxpaying capacity or liability on the part of the intended recipients. Thus the service demands of central cities are essentially requests for redistributions of resources toward the urban lower-income groups. Furthermore, relatively higher-density living in central cities has tended to greatly increase the unit costs of such services as fire and police protection. Some of the cost-increasing congestion in central areas is directly attributable to those who commute into the center to work but who live in and pay direct taxes to suburban jurisdictions.

Not only have the tax bases of central cities generally declined, but tax burdens have risen, as compared with the tax bases of suburbia, in part as a result of relocation promoted by subsidized transportation. In addition, the building of roads and highways through the central city has taken large amounts of acreage off central-city tax rolls.

In suburbia, the new home developments require large investments in underpriced road, water line, and sewerage services in order to be profitable. The service supplies must pass long distances, often through sparsely populated areas. Thus the excessive peak-period density in the central urban areas and the extremely low-density land use in outlying areas of suburbia both contribute to rapidly rising unit costs of supplying government services.

III. *GOVERNMENTAL INTEREST IN URBAN TRANSPORTATION*

The federal government is heavily involved in the promotion and regulation of transportation. Governmental intervention and some of its abuses were eloquently stated in a message by President John F. Kennedy to Congress:

> A chaotic patchwork of inconsistent and often obsolete legislation and regulation has evolved from a history of specific actions addressed to specific problems of specific industries at specific times. . . . Some carriers are required to provide, at a loss, services for which there is little demand. Some carriers are required to charge rates that are high in relation to cost in order to shelter competing carriers. Some carriers are prevented from making full use of their capacity by restrictions on freedom to solicit business or adjust rates. Restraints on cost-reducing rivalry in ratemaking often cause competition to take the form of cost-reducing rivalry—such as excessive promotion and traffic solicitation, or excessive frequency of service. Some carriers are subject to rate regulation on the transportation of particular commodities while other carriers competing for the same

traffic are exempt. Some carriers benefit from public facilities provided for their use, while others do not; and of those enjoying the use of public facilities, some bear a large part of the cost while others bear little or none. . . .[14]

Interest in what happens to urban mass transit, particularly in the relatively small number of very large cities, is manifested in the Mass Transportation Act of 1964, which provides small amounts of federal subsidy to assist public transit, i.e., about $175 million annually in the late 1960s.[15] The Urban Mass Transportation Act of 1970 provides $10 billion over a twelve-year period.

Reasons for Government Interest

As does transportation in general, urban transportation in particular has certain characteristics that justify government intervention. Following are some key features:

Intraurban travel is accomplished by a network of rights-of-way that traverse many loosely coordinated political jurisdictions. The technology of providing rights-of-way and rail transit services dictates that the number of viable producers be small, if not one. This in turn creates conditions favorable to collusion or single-seller control of each transportation market—conceivably, even intermodal collusion could occur. So-called natural monopolies emerge that tend to undersupply transport services because of the potential for monopoly pricing and because of a desire to prevent entry of resources that would be wastefully expended in search of market shares that are smaller than can possibly persist, given the technologies of production. In short, if left alone by areawide agencies of control, provision of services and coordination of supply tend to be insufficient.

Efficient production techniques for urban transportation services require very large initial capital investments that are thereafter completely sunk and unavoidable, no matter what the uncertain future may bring. Private investors have avoided such investments, in the absence of guarantees of collective risk bearing. This reluctance is of course also an outgrowth of a tradition of enforced underpricing, stemming from regulatory means of preventing monopoly returns on such investments and from the ever-present possibility of direct government provision of competing underpriced urban transportation services. Finally, the assembly of land for new rights-of-way, without the employment by the government of its power of eminent domain, is extremely slow and prohibitively expensive to producers, thus virtually ruling out private action in this area.

The power of eminent domain allows governments to acquire property

[14] Message from the President of the United States, House of Representatives, Document No. 384, 87th Cong., 2d Sess., Apr. 5, 1962.
[15] "Transportation Problems in Revitalizing Cities," op. cit., p. 3.

from private owners without voluntary agreements. That is, although compensation is paid by the government, the amount of payment is determined by formulas of "just" compensation that allow for bargaining, but the understanding is that the private owner must eventually yield. Use of such powers to establish rights-of-way has also led to government ownership and operation of transportation corridors, since property acquired by eminent domain must be used for a "public purpose."[16]

Nodal bottlenecks of national transport systems in urban areas have made governmental coordination on a nationwide basis attractive. National defense considerations and the general increase in mobility of resources have increasingly brought the federal government into the picture. As the physical size and population of an urban area have increased, coordination among the urban residents has become more valuable and at the same time more costly to achieve.

In addition to the government's interest in the functioning of intercity movement, there has been national interest in the relation of urban transportation to other federal policies, e.g., physical appearance, ecological relationships, and livability of our cities. Policies to change spatial arrangements in urban areas—specifically, to reduce urban sprawl, decay, and pollution—must coordinate and, to some extent, control transportation supply.

Furthermore, there has been national interest in urban transportation as it relates to federal government policies of integration of racial and income classes. The relative increase in downtown employment of professional groups and other office workers is accompanied by increased trip demands by low-income employees in the service and retail industries. The future demands for transportation into downtown areas, therefore, may come from opposite poles in the spectrum of social and economic classes. The problem is intensified by racial segregation in housing.[17]

Urban transport services can also be looked upon as social overhead —stimulants for regional economic development. To the extent that such development results in net productivity gains and reduced unemployment, all residents of the area, and particularly the poor, are likely to find some positive benefits from outside-financed transportation investments.

The incentives of urban residents to use private autos for intraurban trips cannot be explained independently of the set of prices that they face,

---

[16] The legal determination of purpose strongly favors continued government ownership of the property and regulation of those who might have a monopoly position in transportation by virture of having exclusive vehicular use of a right-of-way. The public purpose justification often allows regulated public utilities or public carriers to actively plan and manage the use of government powers of eminent domain. In effect, then, particular firms, which obtain franchised use of specific routes and which will use the routes to operate for-hire vehicles, are able to exercise a good deal of control over the use of powers of eminent domain.

[17] Meyer, Kain, and Wohl, op. cit., pp. 362–363.

and prices in turn reflect the underlying system of resource control, including regulatory institutions. Further, given existing institutions and individual investments in suburban property and cars, we should expect that commuters and CBD business owners would resist, by political means, adoption of policies to price curb-lane parking spaces, imposition of user charges on freeways, and restrictions on subsidization of downtown municipal parking.

Powers used to alter regulatory institutions, and thus reallocate resource control, are faced by conflicting desires for lower prices, better service, protection from competitors, greater environmental protection, and, finally, profits to the owners of resources. In urban transportation industries, the licensing of a new entrant or the exit of a failing producer is a rare event. Most political battles are fought over renewals of franchises, bond issues for government or semipublic supply operations, and the fixing of prices and service conditions for authorized producers.

Some Theoretical Considerations

The rejection of open-market price competition in urban transportation is often justified by the assumption that transportation is a natural monopoly.[18] Monopoly, however, is the result of factors including government regulatory policy, which is itself based on the rejection of open-market price competition.[19]

There are other justifications of existing government policies that close transportation markets and suppress price competition, both intra- and inter-modally. These justifications concern the economic efficiency of alternatives to open-market price competition in urban transportation markets.

First, it is argued that nonmarket price competition tends to promote greater than open-market returns to privileged suppliers, these extraordinary profits being necessary to induce the extent of capital outlays that most efficiently provides transportation services. Further, once a proper scale of operation is achieved, wasteful attempts at entry by aspiring competitors must be suppressed. This will spare franchised producers needless defense costs and saves potential entrants from their own folly. However, leaving aside the issue of all avoidable costs borne by monopolists in defense of their barriers to entry and the costs expended by potential entrants, it would seem that an appropriate scale of output and extent of resource employment might be achieved, not endangered, by threats of entry.

Second, it is argued that monopoly returns are necessary in order to achieve cross-subsidization of services provided by franchised producers;

[18]Joseph S. De Salvo, *Proceedings of a Conference on Regional Transportation Planning,* R-706-DOT (Santa Monica, Calif.: The RAND Corporation, March 1971), p. 486.
[19] James R. Nelson, "The Role of Competition in the Regulated Industries," *The Antitrust Bulletin,* vol. 11 (January–April 1966).

greater than open-market returns on some services will compensate producers for other uneconomic services that they are required to supply by the terms and conditions of their franchises. However, monopoly created by protection from price competitors is neither necessary nor sufficient, by itself, to cause desired amounts of unprofitable services to be supplied.

Third, it is argued that once the creation of rights-of-way is treated as a natural government monopoly, governments characteristically will not allocate the use of corridors by price competition in open markets, since public ownership implies open use. Franchise privileges can then be justified on the basis that while transportation services may not be more efficiently supplied by a monopolized industry, given that the right-of-way is treated as a monopoly, then it is relatively more efficient to adopt some form of closed-market, nonprice competition in the provision of services as well.

The creation of a closed market does not guarantee that franchised sellers will realize monopoly returns as an inducement for otherwise unprofitable capital outlays, cross-subsidization of services, or any other action. This is so because franchised suppliers are always made to bear special taxes or to conform to pricing and output constraints. Furthermore, officials who regulate urban transportation are often without a clear mission and criteria on which to base their decisions. Regulators have not been able to reconcile satisfactorily what will constitute a service that is distinct from others, how differences in costs of production should be reflected in rate variations, and which variations in rate schedules are justifiable discriminations among customers.[20]

For example, it has long been held in transportation regulation that user charges for shorter-trip services should not exceed those for longer-trip services. At the same time, regulated rate structures have recognized differences in the value of given services among potential users, e.g., commercial users may be charged higher or lower rates than noncommercial users. Further, the use of flat-rate charges, set independently of the length of trip demanded by the users, introduces price discriminations into transportation pricing that may have no relation to costs of production.

Thus, the stated criteria of rate making are in conflict. As a result, regulators cannot be sure that the resulting prices more or less reflect costs of production, or are more or less discriminatory than alternative regulatory institutions. More importantly, regulators lack the "ideal" open-market results that they are instructed to use as a guide and to imitate. Although many of the regulatory criteria imply that an open market for price competition and long-run equilibrium are an ideal toward which government policies strive, there is no operating model that can serve as a guide. Obviously, it is not believed that such ideal circumstances could be produced in a

[20] Werner Z. Hirsch, *The Economics of State and Local Government* (New York: McGraw-Hill, 1970), chap. 10, "Regulation."

direct, laissez faire method of control, and thus it falls upon regulators to interpret the intent of their authority.

Although there appears to be only limited understanding or agreement among economists on the consequences of alternative regulatory institutions and practices, it is instructive to consider again the view of Meyer, Kain, and Wohl:

> . . . the major consequence of urban transportation regulation today is to keep transit and commuter rail fares lower than they would otherwise be (in an un-price-regulated, closed market). This in turn motivates those providing these services to lower their quality standards in an effort to keep costs within the bounds established by regulation. Lower schedule frequency, antiquated equipment, and abandonment of less-patronized lines are all methods of effecting service and cost reductions. These, of course, in turn improve the competitive attraction of alternative transport (means-of-conveyance services) by private automobile and lead to demands for public subsidies to correct the deterioration of service. Accordingly, less regulation of urban transportation at least deserves consideration in many cases as an alternative to subsidization.[21]

We have stressed that the role of government in urban transportation markets is a major one. The issue is not government intervention versus privately controlled systems. Rather, the question mainly revolves around the consequences of alternative forms of government intervention—specifically, how alterations in government policies are likely to affect the costs and rewards of individual producers and consumers of urban transportation service.

IV. DEMAND FOR URBAN TRANSPORTATION SERVICES

The classical notion of a demand curve as applied to transportation would measure, for passenger transportation, the functional relationship between the money price of trip tickets and the quantity demanded of tickets; or, for goods transportation, would relate the price to move a ton of freight to the quantity of freight movement. However adequate this notion might be for analyses of the behavior of households and firms in the production and consumption of other goods and services, it provides only a limited understanding of the demand for transportation service. This is so for the following reasons, among others.

1. By definition, transportation is a communication service that links markets. The location, activity, and unique requirements of these markets are the sources of interdependencies in transportation demand and demand for other goods.
2. The government plays a greater strategic role in determining the prices

[21] Meyer, Kain, and Wohl, op. cit., p. 357.

and physical characteristics of the transportation supply than it does in other markets.

3. The demand for specific modes of travel is not significantly influenced by price changes in the short run. This is because rights-of-way and residential and work locations are so costly to change that they dominate the short-run decision.

For these reasons we have attempted to distinguish the economics notion of quantity of services demanded from the notion of an urban area's "required needs," given its activity locations, growth projections, assumed tolerances for congestion, and available technology. Most investigations of transportation demand have not been concerned narrowly with the effects of relative transport prices on individual consumption choices. Rather, studies by traffic engineers, highway or transportation agency planners, and so forth, have been concerned with demand as a forecasting problem. These studies have sought to determine the "requirements" of transport services that must be supplied in future periods to meet projected demand.

In most transportation studies, the dependent variable, quantity demanded, is not equivalent to tickets purchased for a particular service or set of services. Rather, the dependent variable is equivalent to a measure of system performance—the amount of "trip making" that will occur. But system performance is the outcome of supply and demand; system performance depends simultaneously on service offers and socioeconomic factors that influence the decisions of demanders. Equilibrium performance or changes in trip making are outcomes of interdependent decisions.[22]

Therefore, whereas a private taxicab firm might be narrowly interested in effects of alternative fare structures on revenue receipts, urban transportation planners have a broader interest—in the complex interrelations between transportation decisions and nearly every other aspect of urban life. This is so because they are interested in answering such questions as:

1. What will happen to the level of accessibility and site value at selected urban locations if proposed transportation policies are adopted and if population changes occur, given existing transportation systems?
2. What capacity of a given transportation mode will be sufficient to handle the quantity of its services demanded in future periods at peak use, where specified schedules and other quality dimensions of the services are maintained?
3. How will residence density and rates of use of various modes of transportation vary in response to proposed changes in the facilities and services offered by one particular transportation mode?
4. What is the relation between government expenditures to create specific

[22] Martin Wohl, *Another View of Transport Systems Analysis*, P-3785 (Santa Monica, Calif.: The RAND Corporation, 1968), pp. 8–13.

changes in transportation facilities and consequent private expenditures on transportation (including private investment in automobile ownership)?
5. What are the interactions between urban income growth or distribution and changes in the urban transportation system, and vice versa?

These and similar questions imply planning problems of such complexity that simple relations between modal-use rates and relative user charges add little to analysis. Depending on one's concerns, the decision to disregard narrowly defined, price-induced substitution effects on quantity demanded is clearly a question of benefits to one's study versus the costs of determining the relation between quantity demanded and price changes. Because of this fact, analyses of transportation demand have for planning purposes generally sought to specify "requirements" or "needed capacity" in a given transportation system, based on projected growth factors of movement that could occur between selected locations if the supply capacity were provided.[23]

A schematic presentation of this view of transportation demand, as adapted from John Meyer, is shown in Figure 4.1.[24] The individual firm or household transportation demand curve (price-quantity relationship) is influenced by a number of factors. Among the important, determining ones are the time price of travel, wealth, some community characteristics, externalities generated by transportation, and the quality of transportation. Transportation demands of households and firms will influence their location decisions, which are also affected by the economic base of the community. Therefore, behind estimates of "what people will produce, distribute, and consume and where they will do so" lie analyses of the present and potential economic base of the area. Data on the urban transportation demands, the economic base, and the locational distribution of people and markets can then be converted into estimates of the transportation or trip requirements that will be generated. Frequently, trip generation will be estimated in terms of origin and destination points as well as by trip purpose, e.g., to school, work, shopping, recreation, etc. However, trip generation is not sufficient, for what is additionally needed is a picture of the routes that will be traveled—that is, the flow of traffic over the transportation network, including particularly the traffic at strategic zonal interchanges. Trip-distribution data are particularly important for estimating the specific transportation mode that will be selected by households and firms.

[23] For example, Z. F. Landsdown, *Analysis of Intercity Transportation Improvements: Forecasting Demand and Evaluating User Benefits,* RM-6255-DOT (Santa Monica, Calif.: The RAND Corporation, May 1970).
[24] John R. Meyer, "The Future and Its Implications for Regional Transportation Planning," in *Proceedings of a Conference on Regional Transportation Planning,* R-706-DOT, J. S. De Salvo, ed. (Santa Monica, Calif.: The RAND Corporation, 1971), p. 382.

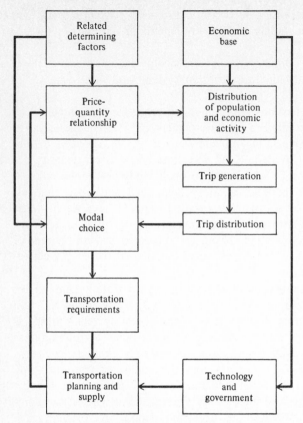

FIGURE 4.1   Determinants of transportation demand.

Modal choice will also be affected by the same factors that influence the transportation demand curve, since this choice will be made in terms of cross-elasticities that affect modal-substitution possibilities.

This analytic process permits estimates to be made of the future requirements for transportation, by mode and purpose of trip. These requirement data, along with considerations of technology and of government regulations and investments (which are influenced by the economic base of the community), will then assist in transportation planning, which, in turn, has a significant effect on the future supply of transportation services. Finally, these supply conditions will feed back an evaluation of the future household and firm demand for urban transportation.

The following sections describe in more detail the components of this analytic process of evaluating transportation demand. However, in these sections we do not take up transportation requirements—which were discussed at the beginning of this chapter—and transportation planning and supply—which will be taken up in section VI.

The Classical Demand Curve

Let us imagine the availability of some transportation service, defined as a right-of-way between locations A and B, and some offer to haul persons over that route at a specified speed and schedule of departure and arrival.[25] The quality of service is given and does not vary; further, no alternative means of transportation exist between A and B (although nontransport means of communication can exist, with given rate schedules). The quantity of tickets demanded will be inversely related to the money price per ticket. That is, we have a classical demand curve, in which the lower the price per ticket, the greater the quantity of ticket sales per period.

However, just as for most demand curves, there is difficulty in making unambiguous references about price-quantity relationships when transportation demand is defined in terms of observed "ticket purchase" or use-rate data. For what is obtained is an observation of what occurred in a given state of the market at a given time; we do not have information concerning what would have been observed if some feature of the market had been different.

As was stated earlier, an individual's demand for transportation services relates quantity demanded to such variables as time price, wealth, community characteristics, externalities, and quality. The aggregate approaches generally involve difficult statistical problems of collinearity, and from a conceptual standpoint yield almost no insight into behavioral changes that could be expected to follow from changes in decision alternatives. Increasingly, studies evaluate quantity demanded relations from the point of view of individual decision makers, by the use of "microvariables."[26]

For example, a study by Charles Lave, using data from a 1956 survey conducted by the Cook County Highway Department, examined the effects of changes in the relative transit characteristics as between automobile and bus travel by individual commuters. His regression analysis produced some elasticities for specific cost reductions in bus travel. The results, typical of those of a number of regression studies, indicated that on the average a ten-minute relative improvement in bus service would divert about 6.7 percent of commuters from cars to buses. A twenty-minute relative time improvement in bus service would on the average divert about 15.5 percent of the commuters to bus usage. When relative money-cost relations were included in the equations, the results indicated that a 10-cent relative price decrease in bus commuting would on the average divert only slightly more than 3 percent of all commuters to bus usage. A 30-cent relative price

[25] Although this section is written in terms of the individual or household demand curve, it can be extended to include firm or industry demands.
[26] For examples of the latter, see S. L. Warner, *Stochastic Choice of Mode in Urban Travel: A Study in Binary Choice* (Evanston, Ill.: Northwestern University Press, 1962); and Charles A. Lave, "The Demand for Urban Mass Transportation," *The Review of Economics and Statistics*, vol. 52 (August 1970), pp. 320–323.

reduction showed nearly 12 percent diversion and a 50-cent relative price reduction showed about a 22 percent diversion to buses. Thus, the estimates were interpreted as saying that a 30-cent price reduction in bus fares (making the service nearly free to commuters) would on the average have about the same effect on diversion as achieving a relative increase in bus speeds to the point where bus usage was on the average no slower than automobile usage. Similar results were obtained for trade-offs between rapid transit and autos, and between train and autos. The results were interpreted by Lave as casting doubt on the chances that large investments in transit systems will be successful in directing commuters away from automobile usage.

In the same view, a 1971 New York City study found that the 21 percent of the people entering Manhattan each day by private transport come from families whose incomes are 50 percent above the city average. Also, they often make additional stops on the way into or out of Manhattan. Therefore they would be insensitive to increased tolls.[27]

Thus, a number of considerations other than price will influence the quantity of tickets demanded, which lies behind the transportation demand curve. The more important of these are discussed below.

Time Price.   Purchasers of tickets must sacrifice not only money but also time in discovering the schedule, purchasing a ticket, boarding, traveling, and finally terminating a trip. Elapsed time in negotiating the procedure of going from A to B can be looked at as a time price implied in conditions of the ticket. If the supplier can reduce the length of travel from A to B, reduce the time required to board a vehicle or to purchase a ticket, or increase the speed of travel, then the time price of his service is reduced. The quantity of tickets demanded is believed to have an inverse relation to the time price implied by conditions of the ticket. The reason is that the time resource of travelers has value in alternative uses that must be forgone in traveling from A to B.

Transportation may provide individuals with a service that is substitutable for nontransport means of communication between locations A and B. Since individuals are likely to economize on money and time outlays for transportation by employing nontransport means of communication, the quantities of tickets demanded will be influenced by changes in relative money and time outlays between transportation and other communication modes.[28]

In addition, the level of demand for a given transport service will be influenced by the existence and pricing policies of alternative means of

[27] *New York Times*, Oct. 18, 1971, p. 36m.
[28] Reuben Gronan, "The Effect of Traveling Time on the Demand for Passenger Transportation," *Journal of Political Economy*, vol. 70, no. 2 (March–April 1970), pp. 377–394.

transport between locations A and B. Since the transportation industry is characterized by government regulation of money prices—primarily for tickets—competition for passengers often takes the form of reducing the time prices of travel. Modal choice has as its base the notion that passengers compare the relative costs—money and time expenditures—of producing a given trip by alternative services.[29] Thus, an increase in the value of time to a passenger will increase the cost of a specified trip, regardless of the mode he may select. But since each mode has its own time-requirement characteristics, the relative costs of the trip change—the amount of price increase—vary among modes. An increase in the value of passenger time is associated with relative increases in the quantity demanded of those transport services that offer relatively low time requirements. Since increases in the value of time resources will increase all trip production costs, as suggested above, and since transportation seems to be a time-intensive form of communication relative to nontransport forms of communication, there may be some decrease in transportation demand as a result of substitution between trips and alternatives to travel as means of accomplishing trip purposes.

Wealth Considerations.   A permanent increase in the value of travelers' time is usually associated with increased wealth. Thus, in addition to substitution effects on quantity of transportation services demanded, there is a wealth effect. Assuming that these services are normal or superior goods, increased wealth to potential travelers between A and B will lead to increases in the quantity of services demanded, for all modes at all prices. However, if a particular mode, e.g., a trolley car service, is an inferior good and some other competing mode, e.g., a cab service, is a luxury good, then a given percentage increase in passenger wealth would be associated with a percentage decrease in quantity of trolley tickets demanded and a greater than proportionate increase in quantity of cab rides demanded. Thus, demanders of transportation services should be segregated by income classes, so that relative levels of demand for the services of various modes can be determined by income class and consequently by location, since residences of demanders are largely grouped into areas of relatively homogeneous income levels.

Community Characteristics.   The above stress upon substitution effects in demand for transportation has implicitly and incorrectly assumed that other influences on levels of demand are invariant. For example, we have discussed indications that relatively low-density, suburban living is a supe-

[29] R. E. Quandt and W. J. Baumol, "The Demand for Abstract Transportation Modes: Theory and Measurement," *Journal of Regional Science*, vol. 6 (1966), pp. 13–26; Reuben Gronan and Roger E. Alcaly, "The Demand for Abstract Transport Modes: Some Misgivings," *Journal of Regional Science*, vol. 9 (1969), pp. 153–156.

rior good. Increases in per capita income will lead to population relocation away from work areas and imply an increase in demand for commuter transportation services. On the other hand, the relocation of urban residences is associated with changing locational patterns of urban-area businesses. Shopping centers, as well as many light and heavier industrial businesses, have been decentralizing, while central cities are becoming more specialized in financial, governmental, and other white-collar types of activities. Further, there is increasing evidence that higher-income urban groups attempt to renew urban centers with open spaces and high-quality, high-density residential structures—even at the not-so-subtle expense of removing the urban poor and unaesthetic buildings to less central locations. A final set of influences that will have great impact for demand includes the secular decrease in the relative cost of nontransport means of communication and the secular increase in the demand for the luxury and convenience attributes of private-auto transportation services.

Externalities. There is little doubt that nearly all modes of transportation involve both desirable and undesirable side effects. For example, the private-automobile mode produces more air pollutants than do alternative modes, whereas underground subways produce less noise for nonusers. Expansion of one mode relative to others may result in a redistribution of wealth within the urban community. The gainers may realize this benefit in the form of increased access to job opportunities.

These "external" effects (external to users) which are associated with the transportation system are not captured by the ticket purchase concept of demand, since nonusers as well as users will benefit or lose by the externalities, and since willingness of nonusers to pay for their demand for externalities is not included in ticket purchases.

Urban transportation industries are conspicuous for the extent to which they produce external effects and for the extent of revenues coming from sources other than user charges. In every major urban area, some form of government or quasi-public transit district is involved in providing alternatives to the private-auto mode of travel. These rapid transit operations generally are carried on at a loss; that is, in the aggregate, massive subsidies are going to urban transit systems, and these losses may represent greater subsidies than those going to automobile users. Total subsidies to alternative systems would of course include the costs borne by governments to establish and extend rights-of-way, to fund the initial setup of rolling and nonrolling facilities, and all lease arrangements enjoyed by the transit operation at rates below capital recovery and existing market values.[30]

Quality. The most frequently advanced schemes for increasing the quantity demanded of declining transit modes have aimed at improving the

[30] Meyer, Kain, and Wohl, op. cit., pp. 100–101.

quality of urban transportation. In this connection, the emphasis has been on increasing the number and comfort of coaches, reducing user waiting time through revised scheduling, and, finally, reducing user charges in money form. Demand-elasticity information, in the desired detail and accuracy, to evaluate these schemes is generally not available. However, the information that is available tends to raise serious doubts about the ability of rapid transit systems to become less dependent upon nonuser charge revenues. For example, ". . . in a recent HHFA [Housing and Home Finance Agency] subsidized experiment, Detroit succeeded in increasing bus patronage somewhat by more frequent scheduling and the institution of more express services, but at a cost of about $2.50 per additional bus rider taken—a figure comparable to taxi fares."[31]

Trip Generation

In order to estimate transportation requirements, a measurable unit of service must be specified. Since urban travel is so heavily dominated by vehicles owned by households and firms, for that travel on streets and freeways on which no user charges (i.e., no tickets) are levied the most popular quantity unit is called a "trip" and is measured by traffic crossing a specified location. A "ticket purchase" demand is therefore a special case of a trip. Since trips may be distinguished by origin, time of departure, traveler purpose, duration, direction, route, mode employed, and (or) destination, any one of a great variety of trip demands can be singled out for estimation.

The most frequently used technique of measuring trips is to station observers at a specific location in the urban area to count vehicles, and thereby to estimate the freight or number of persons passing that point. Such points of observation are frequently established at strategic locations around a central area, e.g., a CBD, in order to get a measure of the change in hourly population within the cordoned area. In general, the larger the cordoned area around a given central location, the smaller the characteristic fluctuations in area population due to commuting. This is so because a great number of relatively short movements become intra-area, and therefore uncounted, trips.

So-called cordon-crossing measures of travel patterns give rise to the familiar peak, off-peak, time distributions of vehicular movement—frequently distinguished by mode—into and out of a given area. The daily peak, off-peak, travel distributions for CBDs of urban areas characteristically indicate that percentage differences between peak and off-peak use are greater for mass transit modes of travel than they are for the private-auto mode. For example, it is common for up to one-fourth of the total passengerload of a commuter rail system running in and out of the CBD

[31] *Ibid.,* p. 102.

to be recorded in one hour out of twenty-four hours of service. Yet, a freeway system leading in and out of the same CBD will record less than 10 or 15 percent of the total daily passenger load during one hour.[32]

In addition to peak, off-peak, trip distributions, cordon measures of trip frequency have yielded a second relation, which can be summed up in what are called "travel-time ratio diversion curves." These curves indicate that the amount of "traffic diversion" to other modes of travel, for a given class of trip, varies with the relative elapsed time required by each mode to accomplish the trip. The general form of such curves is presented in Figure 4.2.[33] The curve in Figure 4.2 shows that as the relative time cost of making a standardized trip by one mode of transportation is increased, the proportion of total trips accomplished by that mode will fall—the percentage decrease being estimated by the measured diversion curves. These travel-time ratio diversion curves are empirical evidence confirming the earlier discussion of the inverse relation between relative quantities of transportation services demanded and changes in relative time costs of obtaining those services.

Now we consider some trip-generation models. Frequently, investigators construct, by using linear regression techniques, statistical trip-generation models that relate the observed frequency of a specified trip to a number of independent variables. The more frequently used determinants of trips are data on family income measures at origin, per capita household or business unit vehicle ownership, land use at origin, distance from the central business district, and land use at destination. Aside from lacking theoretical content, such models usually have important statistical weaknesses. It is common to find intercorrelations between independent

[32] Ibid., p. 97.
[33] B. V. Martin, F. W. Memmott, and A. J. Bone, *Principles and Techniques of Predicting Future Demand for Urban Area Transportation*, Massachusetts Institute of Technology Report no. 3 (Cambridge, Mass.: M.I.T., 1965). For a similar measure of diversion for work trips see: L. N. Moses and H. F. Williamson, Jr., "Value of Time, Choice of Mode, and the Subsidy Issue in Urban Transportation," *Journal of Political Economy*, vol. 71 (June 1963), pp. 247–264.

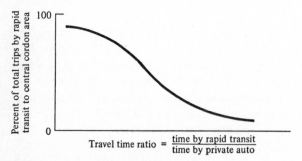

FIGURE 4.2   Traffic diversion curve.

variables used in the regressions, e.g., average family income of a group and average family vehicle ownership in the same group.

The working rationale for producing trip-generation models is that the regression equations will remain stable over time, so that by the incorporation of estimates of future values for the independent variables, the equations will yield estimates of future trip making or "demands" to make similar trips.[34] Thus, projected trip quantities depend upon specific aspects of the urban community. However, forecasts of area populations, levels of economic activity, extent of area vehicle ownership, future land uses, and other aspects of growth become full studies in themselves.

In addition, there is reason to doubt that trip-generation relations will remain strictly proportional to growth measures over time. Existing evidence indicates that certain types of intracity trips may be inferior goods, while other types of transport consumption may be luxury goods. Family income data show that total trips are greater, the higher the income groups or classes (but much less is known about changes in a given family's transportation consumption pattern consequent to family income changes). As aggregate per capita income increases, it appears that trips from residential and recreational origins increase relative to trips originating from industrial land sites. When the origin of trips is distinguished by distance from the CBD, increases in suburban per capita income seem to be associated with modest increases in the relative number of the longer suburb-to-central-city trips. Further, increases in per capita income are believed to be associated with an increase in nonpeak- relative to peak-period trips that originate in the urban area.

The simple trip-generation studies generally assume no significant changes in "modal split" (relative rates of use of various possible modes) over time. However, proportionate expansions of use rates of each distinguishable means of transport have no theoretical justification and surely contradict what little is known about the history of travel patterns in urban areas. Just as railroad use rates have relatively declined for intercity travel, so have there been trend declines in the use rates of some intramunicipal modes of transport. Particularly, street bus and railway systems operated

[34] A trip-generation equation may take the following general form:
$$Y_{ij}{}^{kh} = a_1 x_{i1} + a_2 x_{i2} + \cdots + a_n x_{in} + e$$
where the notion means:

$Y_{ij}{}^{kh}$ = number of person or vehicle trips initiated per time period from the ith urban area of origin to the jth area of destination at the kth hour of day and by the hth route of travel

x_i's = independent variables for the ith area

a's = estimated coefficients derived from current and past data

e = error term

An alternative formulation might then be:

$Y_{ij}{}^{kh}$ = number of person or vehicle trips per time period from the ith area to the jth area for the kth purpose and by the hth mode of travel

by transit companies or transit districts (or departments) of local governments have failed to maintain their share of total intraurban travel.[35]

Trip Distribution

Next we consider how urban trips are distributed. The Transportation studies that attempt to project travel demands within an urban area usually employ a technique that proportions the total number of trips generated by or emanating from any given urban zone among all other potential zones of destination. These interzonal distributions of projected travel are quite often subclassified by trip mode and purpose. The now familiar techniques used to project the distribution of trips among zones have employed theoretical concepts borrowed from the physical sciences.

The oldest generation of trip-distribution models views the flow of traffic as being much like a flow of electrical current or a flow of water. The models of this type assign growth factors to zones in the urban area and then assign traffic, by origin and destination, in such a way as to always maintain a constant interzonal "travel resistance" or equal "attractive forces" over time. The best-known subclass of this type of distribution model is called Fratar techniques.[36] The assumption here is that the volume of trips out of any zone is strictly proportional to the growth factor of that zone, but that the distribution of trips among possible zones of destination is not strictly proportional to absolute growth factors of possible terminal zones. Rather, Fratar techniques assume that trips are "attracted" to zones by a function of relative growth factors among all potential destinations.

A second generation of trip-distribution models has come to be known as "gravity" models. They are premised on the notion that trips emanating from a zone of origin have an "attraction" to possible destinations that is directly proportional to the mass or concentration of attracting forces at each destination, but inversely proportional to the trip distance between the zone of origin and the zone of destination.[37] Although the derivation

---

[35] Meyer, Kain, and Wohl, op. cit., pp. 99–102.

[36] M. Wohl and B. V. Martin, *Traffic System Analysis* (New York: McGraw-Hill, 1967); N. A. Irwin, N. Dodd, and H. G. Von Cube, "Capacity Restraints in Assignment Programs," *Highway Research Board Bulletin*, no. 297, 1961.

[37] Gravity models have the general form:

$$T_{ij}{}^q = K \cdot \frac{M_i{}^\alpha \, M_j{}^\beta}{d_{ij}{}^\delta}$$

where

T_{ij} = trips per period originating in the ith zone and ending in the jth zone for the qth trip purpose

K, α, β, δ = parameters, usually treated as constants

M_i = mass, however defined and measured, of the ith zone

M_j = mass, however defined and measured, of the jth zone

d_{ij} = distance between ith and jth zones

Clear statements of the gravity law using physical science analogies can be found in G. A. P. Carrothers, "An Historical Review of the Gravity and Potential Concepts of Human Inter-

of the so-called gravity law of trip distribution is usually devoid of behavioral assumptions, the gravity models do conform to some data on interstate and intraurban travel patterns. But because of the highly aggregative nature of the gravity models, they are not rich in testable hypotheses about travel patterns.

Recent attempts to explain interzonal travel patterns have made greater efforts to show that gravity type models conform to economic choice analysis. Thus, positive relations between changes in interzonal travel and relative zonal populations in the gravity models are explained by economies from joint production in accomplishing trip purposes.

With equal trip distribution among possible destinations, differing marginal productivity of trips implies a rational reallocation to achieve equal ratios of marginal returns to marginal travel costs. And, the distribution of trips out of a zone among possible destinations should reflect economizing behavior.[38]

A third generation of trip-distribution models are known as opportunity models. The criterion of such models is minimized aggregate travel time, represented by a given number of trips emanating from a given zone, subject to an "acceptability" constraint on destination points. In order to determine trip distributions among zones, all possible destinations must be sequenced by distance from a given origin and a function must be established that will assign acceptance probabilities to possible destinations. These probability functions, of finding a trip destination at a less distant point from the trip's origin, are usually derived from existing trip distribution data. It is customary to assume that the probability assignment function remains unchanged over time.[39]

Modal Choice

Transportation services are specialized in several respects other than routes and locations of pickup and delivery operations. Each mode is also more or less specialized with respect to trip standardization, the uniformity of

---

action," *Journal of American Institute of Planners*, vol. 22 (1956), and W. Isard et al., *Methods of Regional Analysis* (New York: M. I. T. and Wiley, 1960).

[38] J. H. Niedercorn and B. V. Bechdolt, Jr., "An Economic Derivation of the 'Gravity Law' of Spatial Interaction," *Journal of Regional Science*, vol. 9 (Winter 1969); Vijay K. Mathur, "An Economic Derivation of the 'Gravity Law' of Spatial Interaction: A Comment," *Journal of Regional Science*, vol. 10 (1970); J. H. Niedercorn and B. V. Bechdolt, Jr., "An Economic Derivation of the 'Gravity Law' of Spatial Interaction: Reply," *Journal of Regional Science*, vol. 10 (1970).

[39] A probability function assigns to each possible trip destination a probability that the trip originating from the *i*th zone will find the *j*th zone "acceptable" as a terminal location. The probability of acceptance for a *j*th zone is the difference between the probability that a trip originating in the *i*th zone will "find a suitable termination" in any one of closer possible destinations, including the *j*th zone, and the probability that such a trip will "find a suitable termination" in some shorter distance, up to and excluding the *j*th zone.

Although opportunity models suggest that probability assignments would vary depending on the purpose of any given trip, such a distinction is not usually made.

passenger origins and destinations served, and the uniformity of physical shapes or weights of items normally handled by the service. Much of this specialization of transportation services has shown up in measures relating the use rates of various modes of intracity travel to "trip purposes." For example, urban passenger bus and rail services are used primarily for residence-to-job commuting and intra-CBD daytime travel. Private automobiles usually completely dominate as a transportation service for family shopping trips and for what might be called social-recreational trips. Bus limousines offering shuttle services between airports and downtown hotels are an extreme example of a specialized transportation service. Such specialization on the part of demanders seeking transport services greatly reduces the substitutability of modes—even in our simple example of travel between only two locations, A and B. Thus Dick Netzer, in looking at modal-use rate data by types or purposes of trips, observes that private and public transportation are competitive only with respect to the journey to work. He feels that this competition is limited to the rush hours and concludes that it is largely confined to the CBD-oriented trips.[40]

We might rephrase this conclusion to mean that feasible changes in relative comfort, speed, price, wealth, community characteristics, externalities, or any other determinant of relative quantities demanded of specific transportation modes will most likely yield rather small cross-elasticities in short periods of adjustment. For longer periods, however, these factors are likely to have an influence through their effects on transportation planning and supply, by mode. For example, implicit in the Alonso, Muth, and Siegel models of household location of urban residence (see Chapter 3) is a given system of specialized modal services, available at a specified set of relative prices at each potential location. The location of households and business firms and the deployment of government service centers are made in anticipation of trade-offs between transportation costs, proximity, and costs of structures and land area. Having selected a location, such a decision-making unit faces substantial relocation costs. And, private-automobile transportation aside, relocation of or adjustment in transportation supply systems in accordance with altered cost conditions is much slower than it is in less regulated and price-controlled supply systems. Thus, changes in the usual price determinants of quantity demanded will, in short periods of adjustment, yield surprisingly little adjustment by demanders and suppliers. More deferred adjustment, based on reformulated expectations of relative transportation costs and the other determinants of location, will be less costly.[41]

[40] Dick Netzer, *Economics and Urban Problems* (New York: Basic Books, 1970), p. 139.
[41] We should not, however, regard location action and area development to be observed as a lagged consequence of earlier alterations of the exisiting transportation system. Since location decisions and development are based on expectations, such actions will often precede changes in transportation services. And, for this reason,

In summary, the economic content of the term *transportation demand* is the functional relation between quantity of transportation *services* demanded and independent variables that constrain individual consumer choice. However, such demand curves are difficult to estimate or interpret and are rarely used in transportation system planning. But it is also clear that demand estimates, in the sense of projected needs, capacity requirements, or trip movements proportioned among urban zones, lack pure economic meaning. In particular, forecasting of requirements on the basis of trip generation as a function of projected urban growth and land uses, followed by rather arbitrary trip-distribution assignments, holding total generated trips as a given, has little theoretical foundation. What is important to note is that the performance of transportation systems represents the simultaneous solution of complex locational, transport demand, and transport supply decisions that are influenced by social and political as well as economic factors. In the following section we attempt to examine the nature of supply and the most significant interactions between supply decisions and constraints that go into explaining the performance of urban transportation systems.

V. *SHORT-RUN SUPPLY AND PRICING*

We have at our disposal few inquiries into the theory of supply of urban transportation services or investigations of empirical supply functions. This is true of both private and public supply. Urban transportation markets are distinguished by the extent of government ownership, production of services, and regulation of private competition in the supply of services. Yet the supply of urban public services, the behavior of government regulators, and the detailed effects of alternative regulatory constraints on supply decisions are not well understood.[42]

In the textbook sense, supply is the functional relationship between the money price of passenger tickets for a specific transport service and the quantity of passages made available to demanders. All else the same, the general relation is expected to be positive; that is, the higher the price at which a given number of offered tickets can be sold the greater will be the quantity of passages provided by suppliers. We say "general relation" because the urban transportation industry is characterized by institutional and technological conditions that mitigate against our posited textbook supply relation. These conditions include extensive economies of large-

unexpected postponements or cancellations of expansions in the transportation system will have disastrous consequences for developers, households, and firms.
[42] For discussions of the supply of local government services see: Hirsch, op. cit., chaps. 9 and 10; Werner Z. Hirsch, "Cost Functions of an Urban Government Service: Refuse Collection," *Review of Economics and Statistics,* vol. 47 (February 1965), pp. 87–92; Julius Margolis (ed.), *The Public Economy of Urban Communities* (Baltimore: Johns Hopkins, 1965).

scale production, closed-market monopolies, government-regulated fare structures, government control of investment decisions and financing arrangements of capital accumulation, extensive nonprice competition for passengers, and high costs of collecting user revenues and of enforcing exclusion. Further, each mode of transportation—each comprised of a right-of-way service and a means-of-conveyance service—is associated with somewhat unique technological characteristics and therefore often with different institutions that regulate supply.

Price Considerations

The difficulties of conceptualizing a supply function for urban transportation services can be seen from an examination of our most ubiquitous urban transportation mode: an unlimited entry grid of city streets with independent vehicular means of conveyance—private automobiles and trucks, taxis, rented cars, jitneys, buses, and trolleys.

The grid of rights-of-way represented by an urban area's surface streets constitutes a natural monopoly. It is difficult to conceive of a system of open-market production and pricing of streets. Indeed, we usually regard the value of urban locations and the access value of particular sites as depending upon the existence of a well-ordered array of open-entry strips of land. Two beliefs are inextricably interrelated: that city surface streets should all be supplied by a single decision unit, and that direct user pricing of streets is unthinkable. While it may be agreed that more than one producer of city streets directly pricing street use would be a less efficient alternative than a monopoly using a zero-pricing arrangement, it does not follow that the "best" monopoly is a government agency.

Historically, municipal departments that build and service public streets appear to have ignored economic criteria. Decisions regarding the least-cost techniques of constructing and maintaining streets, the quality of streets to produce, the location of lighting, and so forth, have often been made on the basis of political criteria. Although streets are a natural monopoly and user pricing is undesirable because of high collection and enforcement costs, a great many alternatives for organizing production are possible.

For very short periods, we may regard the supply of city streets as given and all of the supply costs as sunk costs—clearly a simplification of reality. (There are such variable costs associated with the supply of street services as daily traffic-law enforcement, accident removal, maintenance, signal operation, and general cleanup to meet health standards of service supply.) The costs of adjusting street services are so great that adjustments are rarely profitable in the short run, and therefore the supply of street services is completely inelastic to price changes.[43]

[43] This does not deny that there is resale value for land and other street resources,

Given the existence of city streets, the services of which cannot be stored and a supply that cannot be converted to an alternative use in the short run, open entry to city streets dictates that when individuals use street services there is no forgone alternative. Unused streets appear to be resources whose alternative uses would have a low value, with playgrounds a possible alternative use. But there is a quality dimension of street services, which depends upon the number of users. Up to some quantity demanded at any given moment, existing street capacity will allow congestion-free travel. However, if individuals continue to crowd onto the streets on a first-come-first-served basis, commute times begin to increase for all street users and quality of street services declines. Congestion has the effect of increasing the expected time cost of all trips, to actual users and potential users alike.

Transportation Vehicles

Although the supply of urban streets is fixed in the short run, the supply of means of conveyance is not. The vehicle supply is influenced by trip prices. Thus we see some evidence of a positive relation between price per unit of service and the quantity of services made available in a short period of adjustment. Both the price and the supply of vehicular services are heavily influenced by means-of-conveyance operating costs. Here we encounter the largest expenditures associated with supplying short-run transportation services within the urban area. The operating costs of means of conveyance are related primarily to distance traveled. Since prices are very often set in terms of costs incurred, ticket prices will usually vary, depending on the length of trip being offered. Thus, individual travelers face a set of relative prices among substitute conveyance services for city streets and a set of relative prices or costs for alternative distances of travel on city streets. The higher the relative price offered for temporary automobile services, the greater the number of cabs that will be pressed into service and the more new and used cars that will be quickly moved onto the fleet lines of rent-a-car services. Likewise, an increase in the price of gasoline, relative to the other costs of operating an automobile, results in some substitution of bus services and, most likely, in a reduction in the mileage put on private automobiles.

Although temporary fluctuations in the prices that vehicular street services can command will result in some short-run adjustments in the services made available, they are probably not extensive; similarly, fluctua-

---

but, again, the short-run conversion costs are such as to leave only the options of devoting these resources to competing transportation uses. Any receipt to the supplier of city street services can be regarded as a quasi-rent—not altering very short-run supply but yielding inducements to consider supply alterations for longer periods of adjustment.

tions in operating costs of vehicular street services will bring about some but not extensive supply response in the short period of adjustment. This is because of the entry and regulation aspects of urban transportation. In most urban areas, the fly-by-night, part-time, and especially the one-man firms offering bus or taxi services in relatively high-priced periods are denied entry. They cannot expand short-run supply when shortages occur in the market. Further, taxi and bus drivers cannot raise and lower regulated fare schedules in order to encourage short-run adjustments in offers.[44] Altogether, much of the short-run adjustment process of market entry, scheduling, routing, and pricing is constrained for government-regulated modes of service supply—more constrained than is the relation of price to quantity supplied that would persist under more open market conditions. Furthermore, short-run cost changes are likely to have a greater effect on modal split than on the aggregate supply of transportation services in the short run.

In addition to the grid of city streets there is in every urban area a set of limited-access rights-of-way that serve more standardized, relatively longer-distance trip demands. These limited-access corridors in the urban space take the physical forms of subway tubes, surface railways, and, more recently, scheduled air routes for use of intraurban helicopter and commuter airline services. Again, and for reasons equivalent to those outlined above for city streets, the rights-of-way for mass transit of people and things constitute natural monopolies. We intuitively perceive the rationale for a monopoly supplier of corridors for each mode of rapid transit in the urban area. However, economists have been particularly critical of the practice of allocating these valuable corridors to users on a zero-price basis.[45]

Pricing Techniques

Grant the simplifications that the supply of urban highway services is completely inelastic to short-run price changes, that all costs of making highway services available in the very short run are sunk costs, and that the vehicular cost function does not change. Under these conditions marginal operating costs are effectively zero and a system of user charges on limited-access highways might be socially beneficial, even if we consider only short-run benefits. User charges can be adjusted so as to prevent congestion—to prevent crowding onto the highway in such quantities that the realized

---

[44] At least, they should not, and could face penalties if caught. We are familiar with tipping and trip-sharing or chartered-trip pricing techniques that allow some circumvention of fixed-fare schedules.

[45] William Vickrey, "Pricing as a Tool in Coordination of Local Transportation," in *Transportation Economics* (New York: National Bureau of Economic Research, 1965), pp. 273–291; Martin Wohl, "Comments—Pricing as a Tool in Coordination of Local Transportation," in *Transportation Economics* (New York: National Bureau of Economic Research, 1965), pp. 293–296.

times of making trips are increased beyond the established quality of highway service or minimum travel speeds. Imposition of a fee that varies with the extent of congestion would cause substitution among alternative periods for making trips. If the period of peak use is assigned the highest user charge, relative to other periods of use,[46] then the substitution possibilities would be among alternative periods of highway use, between alternative modes of mass transit, and between nontransport means of communication for accomplishing given activities.

Also, highway charges would yield high-quality information regarding user demand for the right-of-way services provided.[47] This information is relevant to operating decisions, e.g., the assignment of lanes to traffic on the basis of direction of use demanded, so that demanders of highway use in one direction can bid lanes away from demanders of use in the opposite direction. And user charges information is pertinent to investment decisions, e.g., choices regarding proposed increases or decreases in highway capacity, where it is explicitly recognized that resources such as land, concrete, steel, electric power, and labor have alternative employments for which there are user demands.

We can outline some of the techniques of pricing entry of means-of-conveyance services into the highway system, and some means of pricing the extent of highway use by those admitted. The most common technique locates collection stations at highway entry points and at appropriate distances along the route, requiring vehicles to stop and start again, and contributing to congestion at the stations. Whereas this technique might be well suited for limited-access highways that primarily divert through traffic from city streets, entry to most systems in large urban areas is limited only in comparison with entry to surface streets. The required number of collection stations thus could be very great.

For these reasons, there has been great interest in the development of electronic equipment that could be used to price limited-access highways, in much the same way as individuals are now charged for drawing energy from a common pool of electrical power or for gaining access to central telephone communication networks.[48]

---

[46] Lester B. Lave, *Transportation, City Size and Congestion Tolls,* RM-5874-DOT (Santa Monica, Calif.: The RAND Corporation, April 1969).

[47] Hirsch, *The Economics of State and Local Government,* op. cit., p. 33.

[48] In simple form, each car would have a meter that would be activated by the driver. Both the rate at which the meter is running and its on-off status would be signaled to stations or patrolmen by visual indicators. In a more complicated form, meters would be activated and made to run at different rates by radio signals from roadside equipment. In a still more complex form, vehicular equipment would merely emit identifying signals. Roadside equipment would identify the vehicles and their movements over zone boundaries on highways. This information would be collected by central computers, where periodic billing would take place. (For an early example, see William Vickrey, "Some Implications of Marginal Cost Pricing for Public Utilities," *American Economic Reveiw* [May 1955].)

Such pricing techniques for large-volume use of existing limited-access highways, though conceptually possible, may as yet be too costly to be worthwhile. There are some problems, such as that vehicles without signaling devices will enter the system, or that drivers will disconnect the devices; furthermore, automobiles are frequently sold, and this entails coordination of owner identification with the vehicular devices. More importantly, these pricing techniques involve the use of equipment that has the potential of recording individual movements by date, time, origin, destination, and so forth, and the recording of such information intrudes upon privacy.

Complicated electronic metering systems for pricing limited-access highways can be applied at some future time to city streets in the same way and for the same reasons. William Vickrey has stated:

> Specific charging for street use can also provide conditions more conducive to better adjustment of utilization within [vehicular] modes as well as between modes. For example, much sporadic effort has been spent on promotion of staggered working hours to relieve peak-hour congestion on transportation facilities. However, except in particularly favorable circumstances . . . exhortation seems doomed to only partial success unless backed up by some kind of fare differentiation.[49]

We would only emphasize that short-run adjustments in vehicular traffic, in response to changes in the structure of relative prices for street use, are constrained in urban areas by regulations and customary behavior patterns outside of transportation. For example, working hours are often tightly controlled, so that off-peak periods of activity either are prohibited or require higher operating costs, thus discouraging less intensive peak-period transportation usage.[50]

Nonhighway Transportation

Whereas the corridor itself constituted a natural monopoly, there was no presumption that means of conveyance on highways ought to be monopoly-controlled. On the contrary, we have presumed the existence of an open market for suppliers of vehicular services. However, limited-access corridors such as subway tubes or elevated railways are generally used by only one supplier (or by very few suppliers) of vehicular services—e.g., a

---

[49] Vickrey, "Pricing as a Tool," op. cit., p. 275.

[50] For instance, union restrictions require higher wage payments for off-peak shifts or extranormal working periods. And, in general, organized labor resists employment opportunities that would reduce on-peak labor demand; by preventing the hiring of potential competitors for off-peak periods (by shortening working hours and work week, and increasing work holidays) organized labor can effectively raise the demand facing on-peak work crews. Also, professional organizations and businessmen's associations favor restricting competition in the form of nonnormal hours of operation.

municipal subway authority or private railroad firms that scheduled commuter services for intraurban travel. In such instances there remain two allocation questions: Which competitors will be allowed to supply means-of-conveyance services along a given corridor or right-of-way? and What will be the extent of corridor use by the different suppliers?

In the case of subway services, for example, it would seem that only one supplier would survive in an open market; more than one supplier would lead to more economic waste than is incurred when entry is limited to one supplier. Unfortunately, monopolists, who are protected from wasteful competitive challenges from potential entrants, tend to be wasteful themselves. Either they will tend to undersupply their services in order to reap monopoly prices, or, if they are price-regulated, they will tend to expend resources in ways that would be unprofitable or wasteful as compared with producers in a non-price-regulated open market.

Urban transportation suffers from problems that derive from regulating who will obtain mass transit monopolies. We are often confronted with intractable and inefficient public monopolies or with ineffective regulatory control over private monopolies and the imposition of constraints that produce wasteful side effects,[51] but find it very difficult to force such suppliers out of business.

Even if we can select the best supplier, the question of the volume of services to be supplied remains unanswered. Regardless of whether the markets for producing means-of-conveyance services are relatively open and allow large numbers of suppliers—as was the case in our discussion of highways—or whether such markets are closed and there is only a single supplier—as would be the case for a government-operated commuter train-subway system—the arguments for allocating corridor use by a price system seem less than convincing. Rental fees or use tolls provide revenue for capital recovery schemes, act as prices to bid land use away from alternative, competing activities, and finally, provide information pertinent to planning decisions regarding extensions or contractions of corridor routes in the urban space.

VI. INVESTMENT DECISIONS AND LONG-RUN SUPPLY

Now we consider policy perspectives of economists concerning investment decisions in urban transportation. We are concerned with ways in which economists view the relationship between short-run supply and demand conditions as they influence longer-run conditions. As we have emphasized throughout this chapter, economists view transportation either from the

[51] In this respect we should note that the existence of rivals bidding for a franchise to produce a potential take-over by nonproducing competitors may provide some solutions to the regulatory dilemma. See Harold Demsetz, "Why Regulate Utilities," *Journal of Law and Economics*, vol. II (April 1968), pp. 55–65.

perspective of discovering alternatives for resource use and the consequences associated with adopting such alternatives; or from the perspective of establishing target levels of "necessary" services to meet "required," projected service demands in future periods. Investment decisions and long-run supply analysis can be profitably viewed from either of these perspectives—the former represented by marginal-cost pricing analysis and the latter by benefit-cost analysis.

The highly theoretical marginal-cost pricing literature stresses peak-load charges, treatment of joint costs, and the relation of multiperiod pricing to capital recovery or long-run marginal costs of service variations. Marginal-cost pricing literature is concerned with the relation of price allocation rules to the attainment of economic efficiency.[52]

A second class of economic literature stresses concepts of long-run planning and decision analysis and is largely related to governmental policies and investment officials concerned with investment decisions in urban transportation.[53] The analytic basis for long-run planning and investment discussions is benefit-cost analysis. Both marginal-cost pricing and benefit-cost analyses have relevance to other markets and therefore to other chapters.

Marginal-cost Pricing

Marginal-cost pricing literature has produced some equilibrium conditions of efficiency, using highly abstract models of the real world. Whether conditions of efficiency in economists' models adequately parallel those of the

[52] J. Hewitt, "The Calculation of Congestion Taxes on Roads," *Economica*, vol. 31 (February 1964); Johnson M. Bruce, "On the Economics of Road Congestion," *Econometrica*, vol. 32 (January–April 1964); Alan A. Walters, "The Theory and Measurement of Private and Social Cost of Highway Congestion," *Econometrica*, vol. 29 (October 1961); P. O. Steiner, "Peak Loads and Efficiency Pricing," *Quarterly Journal of Economics*, vol. 71 (November 1957); J. Hirshleifer, "Peak Loads and Efficient Pricing: Comment," *Quarterly Journal of Economics*, vol. 72 (August 1958); O. E. Williamson, "Peak Load Pricing and Optimal Capacity under Indivisibility Constraints," *American Economic Review*, vol. 56 (September 1966); M. Boiteux, "Peak Load Pricing," *The Journal of Business of the University of Chicago*, vol. 33 (April 1960); R. Turvey, "Peak Load Pricing," *Journal of Political Economy*, vol. 76 (January–February 1968); S. C. Littlechild, "Marginal-Cost Pricing with Joint Costs," *The Economic Journal*, vol. 80 (June 1970).
[53] Lyle C. Fitch et al., *Urban Transportation and Public Policy* (San Francisco: Chandler, 1964); H. Mohring and M. Harwitz, *Highway Benefits* (Evanston, Ill.: Northwestern University Press, 1962); D. M. Winch, *The Economics of Highway Planning* (Toronto: University of Toronto Press, 1963); R. M. Zettel and R. R. Carll, *Summary Reviews of Major Metropolitan Transportation Studies in the United States* (Berkeley: University of California, Institute of Transportation and Traffic Engineering, November 1962); M. Beckmann, B. W. Christopher, and C. B. McGuire, *Studies in the Economics of Transportation* (New Haven, Conn.: Cowles Commission, Yale, 1956); H. Mohring, "Land Values and the Measurement of Highway Benefits," *Journal of Political Economy*, vol. 69 (1961); Lowdon Wingo, Jr., *Transportation and Urban Land* (Washington, D.C.: Resources for the Future, 1961); G. M. Smerk (ed.), *Readings in Urban Transportation* (Bloomington: Indiana University Press, 1968).

real world is open to debate. At the very least, however, serious problems of adopting marginal-cost pricing rules in the real world must be faced. First, marginal-cost rules of allocation and investment apply to models that assume away information costs. Second, attempts to change pricing policies or investment practices in the real world must be made in the light of political realities of resource control. Little work has been done on interpreting marginal-cost pricing results for management procedures, and managers of urban transportation services are seldom motivated in the manner assumed by economic models.

Although the marginal-cost pricing literature has produced relatively few rules of efficient operation that can be used in management procedures, it has produced useful insights into the consequences of existing transportation practices. Most important are the conclusions reached concerning the perverse effects of familiar transportation policies on transportation facility congestion, overexpansion, and underutilization because of peak and off-peak-usage patterns. For a number of reasons, highway agencies and transit authorities engage in capital- and land-intensive operations that have very low rates of return, and they overrestrict operating and maintenance outlays. For example, they are often supplied with tax revenues earmarked for land and capital improvement purposes. In addition, subsidies are often granted in the form of free access to capital or land that has been dedicated free of tax liabilities to transportation uses. Furthermore, the pervasive policy of zero-pricing freeway access at both peak and off-peak periods produces congestion. This situation is then used to justify facility expansion and land uses aimed at making peak-period congestion tolerable, with the result that capital and land are underutilized in off-peak periods.

Fare regulations tend to add to the problem. Urban transit fare policies usually grant discounts for volume purchases of tickets known to be used predominantly at peak periods of demand. Round-trip discounts are predominantly used for services in the periods of peak traffic; off-peak, one-way trips in the direction opposite to the dominant direction of traffic flow characteristically pay the highest service charges.[54]

Against this background of practices that contribute greatly to the cause rather than to the alleviation of our urban problems, marginal-cost pricing literature attempts to suggest how alternative pricing policies would result in more efficient resource allocation. For the most part, this literature leaves aside the question raised earlier, as to whether different resource ownership arrangements would lead to pricing practices that produce more efficient supply results.

The crux of marginal-cost pricing arguments has to do with the avoidance of monopoly wastes. If the supplier of a transportation service were

[54] Vickrey, "Pricing as a Tool," op. cit.

an unregulated monopolist, then conceptually he would behave so as to restrict sales to a level that would maximize producer revenues, net of costs; but this would be inefficient, since additional transportation services could be supplied at marginal producer costs per unit that are less than the price customers would pay for the additional services. Inefficient restriction on supply of transportation services can be at least partially avoided by allowing the monopolist to price-discriminate. However, such price-discrimination would increase even further the wealth transfer from consumers to monopolist and restrict the level of demand for transportation services, insofar as the services are normal goods.

Monopoly restrictions on the supply of transportation services might be overcome by subsidy payments that compensate the producer for the loss of wealth he incurs in producing more and selling for less. But, again, there would be a wealth transfer effect, and the important question, How much additional supply should be induced by subsidy? would still not be answered. Strict price regulation might also expand supply, since the monopolist could be confronted with a fare schedule for which maximum profit would occur at greater-than-unregulated monopoly rates of supply. However, how would such a price schedule be determined? Finally, government ownership of the monopoly might replace profit maximization with another criterion of service supply that might approach or even exceed the level of supply associated with price equal to marginal cost. In all cases, however, the norm of efficient operation is not recovery of historical costs or assurances of reasonable returns on past investments—which might be the policy aims of existing transportation regulation. Instead, efficient operation requires that supply be expanded so long as the opportunity cost of additional supply is less than the revealed willingness to sacrifice for additional services.

The emphasis of marginal-cost pricing literature on efficient rates of production relative to rates of quantity demanded does not ignore the "total" conditions of efficiency, i.e., that total receipts or benefits to the operation exceed the total resource costs of supply. If losses are incurred in the transportation operation, such losses may imply that the resources being spent on transportation are so great that alternative production possibilities, for continuing transportation supply at the existing rate, are not being explored. Even if means can be found to assure that service supply will be carried to a desired level of operation, it still remains to be decided whether those transportation services ought to be supplied at the sacrifice of alternative resource uses. Many rail passenger services have been faced with such decisions in recent years. If goods other than transportation are produced by the operation, e.g., smog abatement, noise level reduction, or the like, a value for these other net gains to consumers must be taken into account, particularly when the worth of these additional goods cannot be captured by the producer through sales. In discussing marginal-cost pricing we should not lose sight of the more generally recognized conditions of efficiency regarding the opportunity cost of all resources devoted to a particular operation.

Do marginal-cost pricing results lead to discovery of the right size of investment in transportation facilities—can the information derived from marginal-cost pricing analysis be used to increase the efficiency of long-run planning? The answer to this question does not appear to be a clear yes or no. For example, by marginal-cost pricing taxi services, a taxi company may discover whether a given investment decision in facilities was appropriate (the right size, best location, etc.) for realized, present conditions. But this information might not provide any better knowledge about as-yet-unrealized, future conditions; and yet information about future sacrifice and sales, not past outlays, is relevant to the producer's investment decisions.

Marginal-cost pricing analysis may, however, provide government policy makers with valuable insights into possible techniques of achieving, and even establishing, regulatory aims for transportation production. And even for private producers, efficient investment decisions rely upon correct forecasting of levels of consumer demand and costs of production as well as upon anticipation of the consequences of producing in each future production period so as to yield a clearing price equal to short-run marginal cost. Thus, we should realize that it is anticipation of marginal-cost pricing, rather than realized sales and outlays from following such rules, that most affects the efficiency of investment.

Investment Planning

Marginal-cost pricing analysis stresses the relation between demands for transport services, efficient user charges, and the dependence of long-run investment decisions on employment of alternative short-run pricing policies. Planning analysis stresses the relationship between long-run decisions and benefits and costs, particularly in the context of relative urban land values and use patterns, efficiency of urban markets with consequences for personal wealth, variety of consumer options, and real income resulting from alterations of the aesthetic-quality aspects of the urban environment.[55]

Some of the difficulties to be faced in transportation planning are well stated by Lyle Fitch:

> The community accepted objective of transportation planners . . . is to provide quick and easy movement to any place, at all times. Such unlimited service is beneficial to the community, but it is very costly. . . . Benefits and costs must be more thoroughly investigated: transportation planning should examine the implications for community growth and

[55] The methodology of benefit-cost analysis is discussed further in Chaps. 10–12, where public sector decisions are considered.

economic development of alternative levels of transportation service. . . .
Little attention, . . . has been directed to prices as a determining factor
in the demand for travel and for particular modes of travel. . . . Transportation planning to date has used benefit-cost analysis and other analytical tools only partially and imperfectly.[56]

In the past, urban transportation planning studies have tended to pay
too little attention to indirect benefits and to their distributional consequences.[57] Sources of indirect benefits include *net* increases in urban land
values attributable to increased supply capabilities of the urban transportation system. The land-value increases must be net of decreases in land
values attributable to the supply action, including the impact of altered
tax liabilities or reduced government expenditures elsewhere. Net increases
in human capital values are a similar source of indirect benefits. Such
wealth increases must be net gains, above possible transfers attributable
to the supply decision and net of expected fare payments for the additional services. In considering the indirect benefit for the community as a
whole, it is important to net out some of these benefits so that double
counting does not occur. For example, we would not want to count both
the change in land value and the change in tax liabilities. However, in
considering distributional effects we would want to measure each of the
indirect benefits, since different groups in the community receive them.

On the cost side, it is clear that interest on investment funds and land
costs must be included. And so must costs of taxes, which can be viewed
in several ways. The net loss of tax base due to land being brought into
government (nontaxed) use represents a "loss" of general revenues at the
prevailing tax rate. A more appealing tax allowance scheme is to calculate
the comparable tax liabilities of a similar private, unsubsidized operation
and apply this revenue-loss allowance to the long-run costs of the transportation operation. Such allowances make cost measurements equivalent,
in some rough sense, to the costs of operation imposed on competing
investment decisions in the private community. Although land values are
not always ignored entirely, they are often seriously undervalued because
their value is set at previously assessed worth or at the "official" book value
assigned to plots already in public ownership, rather than at their current
value in alternative uses.

Inclusion of indirect benefits or costs in a study of transportation
supply requires avoiding double counting, i.e., overinclusion. Lyle Fitch
cites some sets of overcounted benefits:[58]

1. Estimates of travel time savings and other gains in convenience,

---

[56] Fitch et al., op. cit., p. 118.
[57] Benefit-cost analysis will be taken up in more detail in Chaps. 10–12.
[58] Fitch et al., op. cit., p. 120.

2. Estimates of increases in real estate values resulting from lower commuting costs and greater convenience, and
3. Estimates of increased real estate tax collections and higher real estate values.

The first steps in planning are: to attempt to expose clearly inferior and wasteful choices; to present objectively the interests of various groups in the community for each considered alternative and each group's prospects for net gains; and to provide a framework for comparing and ranking what has been learned about the considered alternatives. Finally, planning should probably include the function of inventing entirely new alternatives.

Doubtless, the measurement and inclusion of indirect (or secondary) benefits and costs must receive more attention in urban transportation planning efforts. In the absence of pricing of highway use, today's planners must spend most of their efforts devising proxy measures for the value consumers place on marginal expansions in freeway services: decreased travel times, reduced vehicle operating costs, greater comfort, and decreased incidence of accidents—benefits that would be captured in user charges if such facility services were efficiently priced.[59]

R. M. Zettel has argued carefully that in the absence of direct service pricing, the pecuniary externalities of projects show up in greater land-value prices and lower resource and product prices. Thus, inclusion of these net indirect effects tends to result in double counting.[60] On the other hand, such illusive costs of freeway expansion as noise damage to surrounding property may be summarized in resulting decreases to property values.

In line with our distinction between the services of a corridor in space and the services of means of conveyance, noise and air pollution are not properly a cost of highway services per se, but rather externalities of vehicles that gain access to freeways. Thus, highway investment decisions are highly interdependent with policy decisions concerning exhaust-emission controls for licensed vehicles.

Brief reference should be made to arguments that investments in a certain mode of urban transportation should be subsidized in order to "countervail" subsidies that have gone to other, competing modes of travel. For example, it is argued that commuter highways are subsidized by non-

[59] Further, in the absence of direct-benefit pricing there are greater increases in land values than would occur with full user charges. Thus, when highway studies present proxy measures of direct benefits (time and operating cost savings, convenience and comfort gains, etc.) and also include net land-value increases or net lower costs of production in the community as indirect benefits, the study engages in double counting of benefits.
[60] Richard M. Zettel, "The Incidence of Highway Benefits," in *Economic Analysis in Highway Programming, Location, and Design*, Special Report no. 56 (Washington, D.C.: Highway Research Board, October 1960).

commuters, and that therefore potentially competitive, rapid transit modes must also be subsidized to right the implied imbalance. It seems impossible to extract from these claims a nonnormative assertion that could be subjected to study. Yet it seems that one consequence of this general scheme, if it were acted upon, would be to increase the incentives for urban decentralization and increase the land values of distant sites as well as those of core areas in the urban community. To the extent that urban sprawl, induced by subsidized transportation services, results in aggregate net losses of resources to the community's citizens, countervailing subsidy arguments work against the notion that urban transportation systems can be planned to reshape location patterns and yield aggregate net gains. Clearly, such investment decisions will affect different groups differently.

This brings us to the heart of many controversies surrounding transportation planning, i.e., the familiar questions of who pays, who benefits, and by how much. While reliable and specific answers to these questions are extremely difficult to obtain, some impressionistic yet useful information has been generated concerning some consequences to community groups. For example, Danny Beagle, Al Haber, and David Wellman have supplied us with observations concerning the impact of BART (Bay Area Rapid Transit)—the new subway network being built in the San Francisco Bay area.[61] They reason that, all else the same, BART will "greatly encourage" centralization of production and marketing activities and promote greater population growth in the suburbs of the San Francisco Bay area. This will result in greater, not less, congestion and density for residents. They attempt to show the existing conditions that are consistent with that view. New residential building is "BART-oriented," in the sense that development locations have been greatly influenced by the location of subway routes, and second, the magnitude of building has been "stimulated to boom conditions" by the prospect of reduced commuting costs. It is their belief that the extent of high-rise construction in downtown San Francisco is greater than it would be in the absence of BART. In particular, the development of San Francisco's waterfront area—the Embarcadero Center being the first major step—is an immediate and direct consequence of expected increases in centralization of activities, density, and commuters from suburbs to downtown.

Major benefactors of BART will be downtown San Francisco landowners, businesses, and their workers and clients. As the authors note, "... the richest, most discriminating customers are given [more] easy access to the prestige retailers of the downtown complex and the professional services in which it specializes."[62] In this connection, it is their conclusion,

[61] Danny Beagle, Al Haber, and David Wellman, "Turf Power and the Tax Man," cited in David M. Gordon, *Problems in Political Economy: An Urban Perspective* (Lexington, Mass.: Heath, 1971), pp. 438–439.
[62] Ibid., p. 438.

after gaining some familiarization with BART, that the project will redistribute wealth away from lower-income groups in the bay area toward higher-income groups. This is primarily because net increases in wealth due to BART will accrue to land and improvement owners (though substantial relative value adjustments also occur, benefiting locations along BART's routes), and the routing of BART serves primarily to link the more well-to-do suburbs with downtown business and white-collar jobs. Yet taxes will not fall on the beneficiaries in any systematic way; the less-well-to-do will realize net losses due to tax impacts—the tax burdens exceeding any gains, since BART does not link lower-income residential areas with blue-collar job locations and "hinterland" shopping areas.

A rough set of estimates of costs and benefits relative to certain groups were made by Willard Brittain for the Metro Rapid Transit System for suburban Washington, D.C.[63] Metro involves a 98-mile system of rapid transit estimated to cost roughly $2.5 billion. The design of the system is such that it will principally serve the suburbs, yet the District of Columbia, with its 70 percent black population, will bear a disproportionately large share of its costs.[64] Specifically, the suburbs are expected to obtain 80 percent of the benefits and 60 percent of the costs.[65] Brittain thus points to great redistribution of wealth in terms of who benefits at whose cost. Furthermore, he points out, "To the extent that the District's taxes are regressive, the heaviest relative burden of the city's overpayment for Metro will fall on the poor. In fact, the inherently regressive property tax is the largest source of revenue."[66]

Estimated annual benefits of the Metro system to user groups, by 1990, are given in Table 4.1. Present public transit users will receive half the benefits; users newly attracted to the system will receive 30 percent; motorists not using the system but benefiting from reduced congestion will receive 20 percent; and the remainder will be received by the business community.

[63] Willard W. Brittain, "Metro: Rapid Transit for Suburban Washington," in David M. Gordon, *Problems in Political Economy: An Urban Perspective* (Lexington, Mass.: Heath, 1971), pp. 439–443.
[64] Development Research Associates, *Benefits to the Washington Metropolitan Area from the Adopted Regional System* (Washington, D.C.: Development Research Associates, October 1968), p. 5.
[65] Brittain, op. cit., p. 441.
[66] Ibid., p. 442:

	$ Benefits	% of Annual Benefits by 1990	Assigned % of Net Project Costs
Washington, D.C.	37,214,000	20	37.73
Maryland	87,313,840	48	34.35
Virginia	59,542,560	32	27.91

TABLE 4.1   *ANNUAL BENEFITS OF WASHINGTON'S*
METRO SYSTEM BY 1990 (in 1968 constant dollars)

a.	Time savings to those who use public transit now and will continue to do so in the new system	$82,920,600
b.	Auto drivers and passengers diverted to the Metro system	
	1. Time savings to peak-period commuters	11,130,000
	2. Operating costs savings	11,638,700
	3. Parking costs savings to peak-period commuters	15,441,100
	4. Insurance costs savings to commuters	2,177,700
	5. Additional vehicle savings	17,908,400
c.	Nondiverted peak-period motorists	36,750,000
d.	Business community	
	1. Trucking industry (time savings and operating costs savings because of less congestion)	4,620,000
	2. Suburban employers (they will no longer have to provide parking spaces for those who use the Metro system to get to work)	3,484,000

SOURCE: Willard W. Brittain, "Metro: Rapid Transit for Suburban Washington," in David M. Gordon, *Problems in Political Economy: An Urban Perspective* (Lexington, Mass.: Heath, 1971), p. 441.

Finally, transportation planning devotes little effort to discovering the consequences of alternative institutional arrangements. Yet, closed markets in the supply of transportation services are daily being created and perpetuated by government officials—who often also struggle to relieve urban congestion and unemployment and to increase opportunities for private suppliers to serve the urban community. Dick Netzer points out:

> If there were no restriction on the provision of taxi and jitney service (other than such basic things as requirements for adequate insurance coverage and driver licensing), several types of benefits might result. First, there would surely be much more service. . . . The poor, not the rich, are the usual users of jitney service. Second, the expanded service would offer a considerable number of jobs to low-income workers and could significantly reduce the unemployment rate in some cities. Third, if many taxi drivers owned and operated their cabs on a part-time basis (as a second job) and if the off-duty cab could double as a family car . . . incomes are raised, costs of auto ownership are lowered, and the mobility of residents of low-income neighborhoods is increased.[67]

It is a major contribution of economics to show the net gains from greater specialization and gains from further exchange that can follow from removal of imperfections in market organization of competition. Yet planning literature for the urban transportation industry is noticeably weak in its exploration of consequences that can be associated with alternative market structures.

[67] Netzer, op. cit., p. 163.

VII.   *URBAN TRANSPORTATION POLICY*

Finally, we focus the discussion of urban transportation on broad policy issues. Such an effort is complicated by the close interrelation between transportation, housing, and public service and labor markets, as we saw in preceding sections. Moreover, urban transportation is not an end in itself. It is a means for promoting such objectives as facilitating efficient and equitable commutation and goods movement, and linking urban families to work, schools, shopping centers, friends, and recreation.

President John F. Kennedy stated:

> The basic objective of our Nation's transportation system must be to assure the availability of the fast, safe, and economical transportation services needed in a growing and changing economy to move people and goods, without waste or discrimination, in response to private and public demands at the lowest cost consistent with health, convenience, national security and other broad public objectives. . . .[68]

But because of the close interdependencies, urban transportation has as its major policy objectives more than merely fast, safe, and efficient circulation and access to the various parts of the metropolitan area. An additional objective is a minimum of undesirable side effects on land uses, environment, housing segregation, and employability of labor force that are undesirable to a majority of urbanites.

To accomplish these goals, President Kennedy, in the same message to Congress, made some general policy proposals, calling for

> . . . a more coordinated Federal policy and a less segmented approach. It means equality of opportunity for all forms of transportation and their users and undue preference to none. It means greater reliance on the forces of competition and less reliance on the restraints of regulation. And it means that, to the extent possible, the users of transportation services should bear the full costs of the services they use, whether those services are provided privately or publicly.[69]

The importance of transportation policies as a means to change urban life, form, and individual wealth distribution should not be underestimated. For example, Peter J. O. Self holds the view that transportation is perhaps the single most potent means of reshaping life and form in the city.[70] Likewise, Lowdon Wingo and Harvey Perloff claim that "The choice of a transportation system is the core developmental decision that the metropolitan area can make."[71] The costs realized in developing a transporta-

[68] Message from the President of the United States, op. cit.
[69] Ibid.
[70] Peter J. O. Self, "Urban Systems and the Quality of Life," in H. J. Schmandt and W. Bloomberg (eds.), *The Quality of Urban Life* (Beverly Hills, Calif.: Sage, 1969), p. 168.
[71] Lowdon Wingo, Jr., and Harvey S. Perloff, "The Washington Transportation Plan," *Papers and Proceedings of the Regional Science Association*, vol. 7 (1961), pp. 250 and 257.

tion system will affect the productivity of all other resources of the area, both private production and government production of goods, and will affect all citizens' income and quality of life in terms of living, working, and recreation conditions.

In view of the importance of transportation for urban life and form, the attainment of objectives of urban transportation can be influenced by the choice of mode, features of right-of-way and means of conveyance, choice of route, number and timing of trips, and average length of trip. Next we will consider two classes of public policies, consistent with considerations developed in earlier sections of this chapter—cost and supply policies, and demand and income policies. In relation to both classes of policies, cognizance must be taken of the unique advantages and disadvantages of private versus government control of transportation decision making; and of the fact that tastes in the World War II era have greatly favored a system of government-owned, nonpriced roads in conjunction with private cars. This system offers great flexibility to individual drivers but has the disadvantage that the individual marginal out-of-pocket costs tend to be significantly smaller than marginal socially realized costs for given trips. As we pointed out earlier, this system has yielded net burdens on the poor, young, old, and handicapped, left enclaves of minorities with little access to places of work, and has yielded heavy subsidies to private-car users, particularly in peak hours.

Cost and Supply Policies

Achieving net increases in circulation and access to all parts of the city is a most complex undertaking. While some offer only long-run opportunities, some policies are promising in the short run. The short-run cost and supply policies are mainly of two types—levying of proper user charges on private cars, hand in hand with improved routing and scheduling, and improving physical and management arrangements leading to fuller use of available rights-of-way. On pages 112–114 we discussed some aspects of levying user charges. The user charges that we would want to levy would no longer accept the proposition ". . . that the man whose time is worth least, and the man with the least important reason for driving, have the same right to be in the traffic stream, at the same time, as anybody else, regardless of congestion. . . . A more sensible . . . alternative is to ration scarce road space by a system of differential pricing which imposes special charges for the privilege of driving in congestion-prone areas at congestion-prone times."[72] User charges could not only reflect more closely marginal social costs in general, but in particular, higher charges should be charged

[72] Fitch, "Improving Urban Transportation," op. cit., p. 177.

during peak hours in congested areas. Similar results could be obtained by charging parking fees that vary with time and place of congestion. In the past, both these proposals have run into strong political opposition. Even as automatic monitoring systems are becoming technically possible, their use to levy user charges is likely to be strenuously opposed because they intrude on a person's privacy.

Turning next to short-run cost and supply policies designed to improve physical and managerial arrangements of right-of-way and means of conveyance, a large array suggests itself. Here are some of the more interesting ones—giving buses preference at entrances to arterials or at traffic lights; reserving special bus lanes on streets and highways during peak periods; preferential-use permits for certain lanes for buses; off-street loading at major bus terminals; differential pricing of local and express bus operations on different streets; creating special bus lanes or turnouts for loading and unloading; improved entrance, exit, and fare collection on buses; keeping cars out of CBDs; and creating markets for the use of small buses in downtown areas.

While these policies deal mainly with physical arrangements, there are also a number of promising operating procedures. Thus, for example, we can point to improved traffic management, traffic response signaling, and better separation between vehicular and pedestrian traffic. Finally, laws and regulations could be changed to permit jitney service—possibly computerized—extending the licensing of taxis, and, particularly, using at specified times and places private cars as taxis.

While these short-run policies can provide improvements, there are long-run policies which are at least as important. In considering long-run transportation policies, we must keep in mind the size of investments that will be required, long lead time, and politicians' usually short time horizons. (Basically, politicians are reelected every two to six years and cannot wait for ten to twenty years to see urban transportation improved.) Matters are further complicated by the manner in which we separate in various modes of travel between right-of-way services and means of conveyance services—particularly the separation of ownership and control.

Let us next turn to some long-run policy proposals. Their efficacy depends on our judgment as to whether public transit should be favored over the private car, and, if so, whether public transit should have a fixed and exclusive right-of-way. The private car provides for great flexibility and adaptation to new conditions imposed by an uncertain future. But road space used by private cars carrying an average of 1.4 passengers—mainly in peak hours—involves extremely high social costs, including environmental damage, cost of traffic management, and auto theft. However, trains, and particularly subways, are highly specialized in their location and cannot be augmented in a piecemeal fashion by shorter-lived capital in order to respond to changes in population patterns and technology. In contrast, the private car has a much shorter life expectancy and is very much less constrained in routing alterations, regardless of the type of change that occurs.

Buses have far greater flexibility than conventional rail or subway vehicles.[73] Thus one of the important long-run policy alternatives involves the building of new high-speed, high-capacity public transportation systems that basically rely on buses in preference to rail vehicles. Lyle Fitch suggests, "Given the possibility of devising efficient and dependable electronic guidance and control systems, it may be possible to achieve high-speed, high-volume service on reserved freeway lanes, using vehicles that could be manually operated on leaving the automatic system."[74]

Another public transit system began experimentation in Montpelier, France, in 1971. It involves renting small electric cars at random times and places for intracity trips. On city streets rental vehicles would be available, which could be started by placing a token into a slot. Cars would be driven to the passengers' destination and left at a designated station on another street.

Finally, there is also a "dial-a-bus" system—a computerized version of the jitney. A person in need of transportation service would telephone, or, as in Istanbul, hail a vehicle on the street. A computer, tied in with an automatic vehicle monitoring system, would register origins and destinations of requests, and would work them into the routes of taxi-buses already on the streets. They would employ a mathematical routing formula which would select the most efficient routes for the passengers being carried by each vehicle. Clearly, a dial-a-bus could carry more passengers at a time, although it would require more time for an average trip than a taxi. However, it would be cheaper per trip.

In the long run, also, the supply of transportation could be increased and the social cost reduced by improving the balance between road capacity and parking capacity on the one hand, and by inducing urbanites to use smaller cars on the other.

Finally, there are some urban policies, mainly involving urban planning and zoning, that could greatly improve the supply of urban transportation. All too often planning and zoning by municipal governments do not take into consideration the great interdependencies of the different urban markets. Thus, good planning and zoning would require new buildings to be located where there will be adequate transportation and parking facilities. Likewise, building permits could more fully insist on adequate off-street parking being provided by the building.

---

[73] Rail transit involves automatic guidance and exclusive right-of-way. Automation can even cover starting, stopping, speed, acceleration, and braking control. Fitch, "Improving Urban Transportation," op. cit., pp. 183–186.
[74] Ibid., p. 184.

Income Policies

In connection with housing policies we discussed the pros and cons of subsidizing a particular good or service. What makes this discussion particularly urgent in relation to transportation is the fact that at present major subsidies are injected into the system, yet many of them appear to be ill-conceived. All too often they are spent on modes of transit that mainly benefit the well-to-do, while we can identify other modes that, if subsidized, would produce greater external benefits to nonusers or fewer external costs.

External benefits that could be obtained from changing the subsidy system include relatively lower service costs to the young, poor, old, and handicapped; more efficient use of costly urban space; a tendency to make for a more compact metropolitan area in which government services can be rendered more cheaply; improved opportunities for downtown redevelopment so that the existing infrastructure can be used instead of a new one built in suburbia; and a reduction in damage to urban air and visual appearance. Thus, one policy would be to retract subsidies from the road–private-auto mode and subsidize public transit in general and, perhaps, subsidize some special groups such as the poor, handicapped, and unemployed in particular—possibly through vouchers. In theory, these subsidies could be covered by insisting on pricing private cars more in line with their marginal social costs. Furthermore, parking fees could be used to supplement charges on private cars, particularly during rush hours. There could be differential pricing of local and express bus operations on different streets. Finally, steps could be taken to reduce the information costs, particularly to the poor, old, young, and handicapped. However, we must take into consideration that as we improve the real income of the poor, old, and invalid, they will demand increasing amounts of public transportation, possibly leading to further congestion.

There also exist a few long-run policies that could affect the demand for urban transportation in a major way. One of the most promising is staggering work hours, as is done to a minor extent in Washington, D.C. There are obviously many impediments to the staggering of work hours, and some inducements might be needed. One such inducement might be that companies offer on their premises educational or recreational programs free of charge, so attractive that many workers will stay after working hours.

Another long-run policy entails the staggering of work days. Particularly as the work week becomes shorter, it becomes increasingly important to have arrangements that make better use of physical capital. Thus, should the work week decline to three and a half days, it might be possible for one half of the work force to work the first half of the week and then be replaced by the other half. Clearly, these policy proposals vary greatly in political attractiveness.

CHAPTER 5

URBAN LABOR MARKETS

I. INTRODUCTION

The city is made up of people, and the labor market determines whether these people will be employed and at what wage. In that sense, the most important of urban markets is the market for labor. It is perhaps in the consideration of labor markets that the dependence between the various parts of a city's economic system becomes most clear. The locational problems related to the costs incurred by an individual in finding and pursuing a job, living in an environment which he prefers, and getting back and forth between these two important places are directly related to the conditions existing in all of the principal urban markets: land and housing, transportation, public service, and labor.

In earlier chapters we argued that cities were distinguished by such features as concentration of population and transactions, great specialization of economic actors and markets, together with certain unique institutional characteristics that require frequent governmental intervention. We also found that after taking account of such factors, treating urban housing and transportation markets with the tools that the economist has forged in understanding industrialization and studying production raises no real problems. However, this is not the case in relation to urban labor markets, since traditional tools seek to draw out the implications for the demand for and supply of labor by treating labor as a factor of production. In an inquiry into urban labor markets, we must consider labor not only in terms of industrialization but also as it concerns urbanization, and, therefore, see the urban laborer not merely as a factor input but also as a "resident"[1] who not only produces but also consumes, votes, causes pollution and congestion, and gets into trouble with his neighbors and the law.

As we are considering labor as an urban resident (and party to the urbanization process), a number of characteristics stand out. In addition to the conventional production aspects of labor, there are the consumption aspects of the urbanite. Everybody consumes, but only about half of the residents in an affluent urban economy produce. Not only has urbanization proceeded hand in hand with growing affluence, but the city also offers a

---

[1] Mark Perlman, ed., *Human Resources in the Urban Economy* (Washington, D.C.: Resources for the Future, 1963).

large variety of consumption goods—private and public—from which to choose.

Because of the prevalence of externalities in cities, and because of society's increasing concern with social welfare considerations, urbanites are offered many services by government. Under those conditions more options are open if a variety of governments exist within the metropolitan area. This makes it possible for consumers to "vote with their feet" and consume those publicly provided goods they value most.[2]

Urban labor in its role as a consumer relates directly to housing and transportation markets. Thus residential location decisions are influenced by consumption opportunities, including consumption of the convenience to get to and from work.

An examination of urban labor markets also must consider the preparation for a life of work and consumption, including leisure. Since urbanites tend to hold relatively highly skilled positions, have a wide menu of goods to choose from, and can spend much time on leisure, they require quality education of a broad nature and preferably on a continuous basis. Still many members of minority groups are exposed to inferior preparation experiences compared to whites. They seek correction, mainly through improved education and training. Here it is important to realize that urbanites must not merely be prepared for work, but must end up employable. In an age of rapid technological change, particularly in cities, this requires frequent retraining and improved job information. While much of the service to prepare urbanites for a life of work and consumption is publicly rendered, not providing such services can generate demand for other major private as well as public expenditures. Thus those urbanites who are not employable require welfare payments, can require increased police services, and tend to produce fewer taxes.

Another major concern with urban labor markets relates to discrimination and poverty. Because of the close proximity of residents and highly developed means of communication, discrimination and poverty in urban areas are highly visible. Those who suffer the result of discrimination and poverty are very much aware of their status. Yet because urban markets are highly interrelated and urban labor is not only an input factor but also a consumer, the time lapse between consumption and production is shortened. This compactness means that decisions in the production sector, e.g., whether or not to discriminate, have immediate and often far-reaching effects on the consumption side. For example, in the presence of discrimination, the amount of aggregate police protection required by a city can rise and so can welfare expenditures. This, in turn, affects tax revenues, insurance rates, and a host of considerations quite far removed from the initial act. Both efficiency and income distribution considerations are likely

[2] Charles M. Tiebout, "A Pure Theory of Local Expenditures," *Journal of Political Economy*, vol. 64 (October 1956), pp. 416–424.

to stimulate those concerned with economic policies for urban labor markets to seek steps designed to reduce job and housing discrimination, as well as other sources of poverty.

We will begin with a discussion of the national labor market and methods of adjustment to differences in supply and demand at that level. Next we will discuss, separately, urban and intraurban labor markets, considering the theoretical determinants of demand and supply as well as the modifications of traditional concepts required to orient the discussion to the special characteristics of cities. Finally, we will examine various urban labor policy issues, especially those related to labor market inefficiencies, unemployment, poverty, and race.

II. NATIONAL MARKETS: LABOR DEMAND AND SUPPLY

In the short run, the aggregate national demand for labor is derived from the demand for final goods and services, whereas the supply of labor is related to the size and age mix of the population and its labor participation rates. Over the longer run, however, the labor demand is also influenced by technological factors and capital stock changes, while the supply of labor will be additionally influenced by factors affecting the participation rate and the quality of human capital—particularly by education.

There are feedbacks between the demand and supply of labor in both the short run and the longer run. For example, in a closed system, while the aggregate demand for labor is influenced by the demand for final goods and services, the final demand depends, in part, on the level of employment and wages. That is, there is a feedback effect, from employment or wage and salary income to final demand back to employment. Therefore, one of the causes for changing demand for labor is previous changes in demand for labor, causing employment changes and consequently changes in consumption expenditures of workers.[3] But such employment changes, in turn, may cause labor participation rate changes which will affect the labor supply and the balance between labor demands and supplies.

The labor supply tends to increase somewhat even over the short run, because of long-run population growth. If final demand does not change in a way compatible with the growth trend of the labor force, then either tight labor markets or unemployment results. However, even in the short run many market adjustments are likely, including changes in the average weekly hours worked, in labor participation, in criteria for hiring, etc. Over the long run, of course, many more adjustments are possible, includ-

[3] See Axel Leijonhufvud, *Keynesian Economics and the Economics of Keynes* (New York: Oxford, 1969), chap. 2.

ing changes in capital stock, in the relation between labor and capital inputs, and in the quality of labor.

Under certain fairly restrictive assumptions it can be shown that the growth in output is limited by the growth in the labor supply, which, in turn, is limited by population growth. Ordinarily population growth, in a closed system, is viewed as exogenous to labor market characteristics resulting from the balance of births, deaths, and migration. However, each of these is influenced by economic conditions and can, in turn, affect economic conditions, sometimes with equilibrating and sometimes with disequilibrating consequences. For example, it can be shown that with certain assumptions about the population age mix and birth rate, not only will the labor force continue to grow but the ratio of dependents to labor force will continue to rise. Thus per capita incomes will not rise as rapidly as otherwise, which may in turn influence birth rates.

The national, or closed, labor market model is applicable to city labor markets only if some important qualifications are introduced. For example, labor participation rates, birth rates, the quality of labor, and other characteristics of the work force in urban areas differ from those in nonurban areas. Also, the feedbacks between final demand and aggregate labor demand become more complicated in cities, since account must be taken of leakages where local labor produces for final demand markets in other places. Finally, domestic migration plays a large role in affecting labor demand and supply conditions in cities. For example, if supply is sufficiently tight in a given area to cause wages and job opportunities to be greater there than in other regions, then inmigrants can be expected to flow in from labor surplus areas, expand the supply, and bring the wage down to about the level that exists elsewhere. This kind of description is often offered as an explanation of the rural-to-urban migration which has been taking place in the United States during the last century and a half.[4] However, it should be used cautiously in explanation of city labor markets, since many places can be identified as having persistent labor surpluses; and other places consistently have relatively high wage rates, not only because of a favorable industry mix, but also for specific occupations. Migration only partly results in an equilibrating tendency because there are a number of reasons, other than labor market conditions, which influence the migrant flow.

III. *URBAN LABOR MARKETS*

While there are several ways of thinking about urban labor markets, much of what follows makes the implicit assumption that they can be defined by the occupations of workers. Thus there is a market for the services of

[4] An ingenious model of this process, called "Economic Development with Unlimited Supplies of Labour," has been developed by W. Arthur Lewis, *Manchester School* (May 1954), pp. 139–191.

clerical workers, another for the services of private household workers, another for the services of physicians, and so forth. To define the market, we must define the service. In these examples the service is assumed to require some skill and training—in the case of the clerk, not much, and in the case of the physician, a great deal.

Attempting to define labor markets creates another problem: we must deal with space, one of the distinguishing features of urban economics. Markets in space tend to be separated by transport costs; in the case of labor, these are commuting costs. Thus there may be several geographic markets for the same labor skills and occupations, mainly separated by transportation costs.

We agree with Albert Rees and George Shultz that ". . . large metropolitan labor markets are highly complex, and are made up of separate but interrelated occupational and geographical submarkets. Wage determination, job search, and the movement of workers among employers are all influenced by a great variety of forces—economic, institutional, locational, and personal." [5] Thus in cities we find many labor markets, differentiated primarily by skills rather than along geographic lines. Yet some cities, and particularly metropolitan areas, are sufficiently large that markets for the same kind of labor, e.g., occupations, may spring up in different places in the city; but even then, the wage offered does not differ much between the various places.

Individuals will try to adjust to both occupational and geographic market wage differences. All such adjustments are costly, but some— particularly occupational adjustments—are far more costly than others. Therefore they are less likely to occur than are geographic adjustments, which can be made more rapidly, since geographic differences cannot keep markets separated much longer than it takes for information to spill into the next market and for workers to make arrangements and to transport themselves into them. In cities, because of good information, this is a very efficient and speedy process.

This process was already recognized by Adam Smith in his chapter, "Of Wages and Profits in the Different Employments of Labour and Stock," where he states,

> The whole of the advantages and disadvantages of the different employments of labour and stock must, in the same neighborhood, be either perfectly equal or continually tending to equality. If in the same neighborhood, there was any employment evidently either more or less advantageous than the rest, so many people would crowd into it in the one case, and so many would desert it in the other, that its advantages would soon return to the level of other employments. [6]

[5] Albert Rees and George P. Shultz, *Workers and Wages in an Urban Labor Market* (Chicago: The University of Chicago Press, 1970), p. 222.
[6] Adam Smith, *The Wealth of Nations* (New York: Modern Library ed., 1937), p. 99.

Because of greatly improved communication and transportation, we would want to substitute "city" or "metropolitan area" in today's world for Smith's "neighborhood."

While information and mobility facilitate the adjustment and tend to produce separate labor markets, we still find interfirm wage differentials in a given city. Such differentials can be explained in terms of four classes of factors—differentials to offset nonpecuniary disadvantages, differences in labor quality, discrimination, and establishment variables.

Until recently, there was little information on geographical movement of workers within local labor markets, or on spatial wage differentials in such markets.[7] Additional important data are available for the Chicago labor market in 1963, covering eight counties.[8] The Chicago area is tied together by an extensive system of expressways, and 50 percent of the workers in the area in 1960 got to work in private cars. This makes it plausible to think of the eight counties as one labor market area, particularly since in addition several commuter railroads ran from outlying parts of the area into Chicago, bringing a further 5 percent of the workers in the area to work in 1960.

Those differentials which may offset nonpecuniary disadvantages are hard to measure. They include fringe benefits, physical working conditions, and location. A study of the Chicago labor market in 1963 indicates that apparently significant wage premiums are needed to attract female clerical workers to work in nonresidential neighborhoods.[9] Furthermore, the same study also found a strong positive association of wages with distance traveled to work, which may reflect that a compensating differential is needed to draw workers to less accessible establishments.[10]

There is a tendency for occupational wages to show differences among geographic markets within a metropolitan area in the case of low-wage occupations. The lower the wage, the more important a given commuting cost. In such a case—janitors, for example—there are likely to be a number of different geographic markets, each covering part of the metropolitan area, reducing the need of workers to commute very far.

The second class of factors responsible for possibly different wages within a given occupation relates to the quality of labor. This issue can be related to Alfred Marshall's concept of "efficiency earnings"; he argues that

---

[7] Some information on geographical movement between employers in a local labor market is given in Charles A. Myers and W. Rupert McLaurin, *The Measurement of Factory Workers* (New York: Wiley, 1943); and some data on geographical wage differentials within large metropolitan areas are given in Robert Evans, Jr., "Worker Quality and Wage Dispersion," *Proceedings of the Fourteenth Annual Meeting, Industrial Relations Research Association* (Madison, Wis., 1962), pp. 246–259; and Martin Segal, *Wages in the Metropolis* (Cambridge, Mass.: Harvard, 1960), pp. 180–181.

[8] Rees and Shultz, op. cit.

[9] Ibid., pp. 218–219.

[10] Ibid., p. 219.

competition tends to equalize not the hourly money wages of individuals in the same occupation, but rather their earnings per unit of work performed.[11] The Chicago labor market study reveals positive correlations between wages and schooling in seven out of twelve occupations and between wages and previous work experience again in seven out of twelve occupations. To the extent that seniority reflects relevant experience, we might want to point to the high positive correlation between seniority and individual earnings.[12]

A third class of factors involves discrimination, be it by race or sex. Particularly in relation to Negroes, Mexican-Americans, and Puerto Ricans, duplicate markets might be set up in a variety of low-skill occupations, one close to the ghetto area and a second far away from it. The close markets specialize, for example, in Negro labor services, and those far away specialize in nonblack services. A wage differential which may be opened up as a result of race cannot be closed by commuting farther. Albert Rees and George Shultz found in their Chicago study substantial wage differences by color and sex after allowing for the effects of differences among workers in age, seniority, schooling, and experience.[13]

Finally, there are a number of establishment variables, such as the extent of unionization, establishment size, and the nature of the industry. However, we have been unable to identify empirical studies that examine these issues effectively.

Supply

The labor supply in a city depends on the size, age composition, and participation rate of its population. The size of the population depends on births, deaths, and net migration; and the age composition depends on the fertility rate and, in most cases, migration. The participation rate depends on several factors, among them the wage level and unemployment rate, and the age and sex composition of the population.

There are at least two well-defined groups of labor force participants. These are known as *primary* and *secondary workers*. Primary workers are those who are regularly expected to be in the labor force, which is to say either employed or actively seeking work. Secondary workers are in the work force intermittently, or part time.

The primary work force is composed of most males between the ages of twenty and sixty-five. In addition, a smaller proportion of females in the same age bracket are members of the primary work force.

Secondary workers can be thought of as individuals whose nonmarket opportunities and responsibilities normally keep them out of the labor

[11] Alfred Marshall, *Principles of Economics*, 8th ed. (London: Macmillan, 1930), pp. 546–549.
[12] Rees and Shultz, op. cit., p. 219.
[13] Ibid., p. 220.

force. If wages rise sufficiently, some of these people—for instance, house-wives and students—can be drawn into the full-time labor force. Other secondary workers go into the labor force when wages and employment become sufficiently low. For example, among low-income families whose primary workers become unemployed, it is frequently the case that other members, secondary workers, enter the labor force in order to supplement the family income. This situation is due to the inability of these families to finance periods of unemployment out of wealth.

The aggregate supply function of labor, as shown in Figure 5.1, bends backward because at some point the income effect of higher wages over-rides the substitution effect, and workers are induced to prefer more leisure at the expense of income. Variations in the prevailing wage will cause workers to enter or leave the work force by adjusting their participation. Lower wages may induce a worker to work only part time, or only inter-mittently, and still lower wages may cause him to drop out of the labor force altogether.

The supply of labor for any market within the aggregate of urban labor markets depends on relative wages and the distribution of the educational and training attainment of the population. To the extent that distinct mar-kets exist within a city for the same type of labor, then patterns of popula-tion density and the characteristics of the transportation network may also play a role.

Short-run variation in the supply of labor may occur through changes in labor participation rates which have seasonal, cyclical, and even demo-graphic causes. Seasonal variation in supply is caused by the fact that many activities of human beings happen to concentrate at certain times of the year, e.g., schooling and vacations.[14]

---

[14] One example of this is the nine-month season adopted by educational institutions. Originally, this allowed rural children to augment the labor force during a period of excess demand for labor—harvest time. Despite the fact that today much of the seasonal increases in demand for farm labor are normally satisfied by specialists (migrant workers), high school and college students are still released onto urban labor markets every summer. Many businesses, particularly in the trade and service

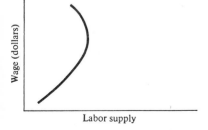

FIGURE 5.1   Aggregate supply func-tions of labor.

Cyclical variability in labor supply is a more serious problem, both because it is less predictable and affects more people and because it lasts longer than most seasonal variations. During downturns in the business cycle, some persons drop out of the labor force while others enter the labor force. The former can be called discouraged workers and the latter added workers. The discouraged and the added workers tend to be women, second workers in the family, young people, and old people, rather than household heads.

There are several reasons why potential workers become discouraged with the labor force. The most important is that during a downturn some persons who would ordinarily enter the work force simply do not enter. Other workers who are laid off hasten their retirement, seek schooling, or return to household work because the wages they can earn in alternative employment are reduced. In addition, however, we can suppose that in a flaccid labor market the cost of finding new employment, once one has left the old employment, is greater than in a normal market, and this provides a disincentive to continue looking for employment. The result is that some workers simply drop out of the labor force. The increased cost of finding employment becomes even more critical when it is associated with the reservation wage phenomenon. A worker is initially unwilling to go back to work for a lower wage than that at which he was previously employed. If the wage level has actually decreased, the amount of time he must spend collecting labor market information is considerably extended if he has a reservation wage, that is, if he is unwilling to work at a lower wage.

The phenomenon of added workers—increases in labor supply during downturns in the business cycle—is believed to be related to low levels of income. For example, a housewife might obtain a job if her husband is laid off, which results in two people rather than one being in the labor force. Jacob Mincer interprets the added-worker effect "as an alternative to dissaving, asset decumulation, or increasing debt in family attempts to maintain consumption in the face of unemployment and other income losses."[15] Mincer points out that this means "the 'additional worker' is more likely to be a low-income person than the 'discouraged worker.' "[16]

---

sectors, arrange their activities to take advantage of this labor supply (for example, using students as replacements for vacationing employees). The usual result is rises in employment, labor participation, and unemployment in urban labor markets. Other illustrations of seasonal changes in labor participation occur as responses to seasonal changes in demand, e.g., Christmas, tourist seasons, etc.

[15] J. Mincer, "Labor Force Participation of Married Women," in Universities-National Bureau Committee for Economic Research, *Aspects of Labor Economics* (Princeton, N.J.: Princeton, for the National Bureau of Economic Research, 1962), p. 75.

[16] J. Mincer, "Labor Force Participation and Unemployment, A Review of Recent Evidence," in Robert A. Gordon and Margaret S. Gordon (eds.), *Prosperity and Unemployment* (New York: Wiley, 1966), p. 95.

However, the additional worker is drawn from both low-income and high-income ranks. Savings are often used by high-income families to tide them over troughs in the business cycle. However, high-income wives also will enter the labor force during downturns, particularly since they often have skills which are in demand. Lower-income families, without savings to draw upon, will find it essential for family members to enter the labor force to supplement income during these troughs when normal sources of income are being curtailed.

Cyclical changes in unemployment may be intensified in urban economies because of the many secondary workers. Thus, for example, second breadwinners who lose their jobs do not often outmigrate, unless the primary breadwinner is also unemployed. As a result unemployment rates tend to differ among urban areas, and unemployment cycles can become somewhat more pronounced.

Cyclical-type variations in labor supply also occur as a result of demographic rather than business cycle phenomena. There tend to be long cycles of birth rate changes, each approximately the length of a generation. If a previously stable population is disturbed by something which induces an increase in the fertility rate, the result a generation hence will be that the increased number of births will be translated into a larger than normal proportion of the population in the labor force and fertile ages. Although this will not affect age-specific participation and fertility rates, it will have the effect of increasing the labor force as well as the birth rate at that time. This temporary rise in the birth rate will produce another wave in another generation. The end result is a very long cycle over which birth rates increase, centering around approximately twenty-five years from the time of the original disturbance, followed by a cycle over which birth rates decrease. Associated with these swings are cyclical changes in the labor supply, resulting from large waves of labor force entrants a generation after the birth rate jump, and large waves of retirements at a still later date.

There are reasons to expect both real wages and labor participation to be higher in urban than in nonurban areas. The aggregate urban labor market consists of a web of highly specialized, specific markets. Thus persons with specialized skills will generally be able to sell their services more easily in the city than in the less specialized, nonurban markets. To the extent that efficiency is improved by specialization, the worker will capture some of this in his wage rate.

In addition, the real wage received by any individual is likely to be higher if we think of the "real wage" as including not only the money component but also some value for the degree of preference the individual has for the type of work he does. For instance, cities have many individuals who are pursuing hobbies as professions; however, there are very few rural towns where it would be possible to support a stamp collector's store, or a pipe shop, or any one of a variety of such enterprises which require a very large population to support them.

Overall labor participation will also be higher in urban areas partly as a consequence of the opportunities people have for working at jobs that have a high psychic income. More important, urban labor participation is relatively high because of demographic differences between the urban and nonurban populations. The rural-to-urban migration process is an age-specific process. This means that younger individuals—people who are specifically oriented toward the labor force—are the ones to migrate. By migrating, they increase the proportion of the population that is in the labor force at the destination, and they decrease the proportion in the place they left. Also, women in rural areas tend to have a lower participation rate partly because of an absence of job opportunities and partly because their responsibilities in the home limit their employability.

However, the differences between urban and nonurban labor markets are diminishing. For example, a considerable portion of farm workers hold part-time jobs in nearby urban areas. Similarly, many nonfarm rural residents have jobs in cities, and to some extent industry location in rural areas is increasing the variety of occupational demands in these areas. Also, population changes in the nonfarm rural areas are causing the mix of demographic characteristics in these areas to become more similar to the mix that is found in cities.

As has been noted, the long-run labor supply is determined by the overall labor participation within the limits of the growth in population of labor force age. The share of the working-age population that is in the labor force has remained relatively constant over the long term. This has resulted because the increasing participation of women has offset earlier retirements for men and later labor force entry for young people. However, there are some aspects of the urban environment which may cause a change in the long-run labor participation rate. For example, the rate of increase in labor participation of women may slow down as it reaches the limits imposed by home responsibilities; the trend toward early retirement may be reversed with improvements in health and job opportunities for the elderly; young people may increasingly seek part-time employment while continuing as students. But more important than these demographic factors are the potential effects of automation on the long-run labor participation. If productivity improves at a very rapid rate, job opportunities may not increase as rapidly as the population of labor force age, and labor participation would likely decline. In effect the long-run labor supply curve is potentially backward-bending and the urban labor supply may be entering the backward portion of the curve in coming decades.

Also of interest to the urban economist are the factors which underlie the long-run supply of skills for specific occupations. Education and training are the principal vehicles for affecting the supply of specific skills.

Through education and training individuals invest in themselves in order to increase the present value of their expected future lifetime earnings. Accordingly they seek that type of education compatible with the emerging occupational demands of society.[17] The result is that educational planning (i.e., the planning of types and amounts of education to be provided by the public and private sectors) becomes an extremely important determinant of the occupational structure of the future labor force and, because of this, also influences such characteristics as labor participation and income distribution.

Although the supply of labor tends to adjust to the demand for labor, it does so in an imperfect manner. The market processes will only partly take care of potential disequilibria and suboptimality. The urban economist is greatly concerned about this problem, realizing that parts of the labor force have strikingly different characteristics—characteristics that appear to be continuously changing. Thus labor supply appears to be determined by factors additional to the demand for labor, particularly by those urban institutions which directly and indirectly participate in preparing urbanites for work. Different groups in urban areas exposed to different work preparation experiences cannot compete equally in the work market. The result will be differential rewards, which in urban economies are highly visible. Thus groups receiving lesser rewards in recent years have demanded of the community either improved work preparation or other types of compensation.

In this connection it is important to differentiate between preparation for work and preparation to be employed. Particularly in an urban economy, changing technology results in changing demands for skills. This requires virtually continuous education and better counseling about future employment opportunities. The call therefore is for urban economies to offer improved information and information dissemination.

Education and training in urban areas also must improve urbanites' ability to effectively fulfill their roles as consumers, including consumption of leisure. Conditioning workers to improve their use of leisure and to retire relatively early in order to benefit from leisure can affect the supply of labor, particularly of older workers.

The long-run supply of skills in specific urban places is also influenced by the migration process. Migration within the United States is sizable. Each year about 15 percent of the population moves from one labor market area to another. In the past a significant part of the increase in urban population was attributable to a rural-to-urban migrant flow. This has largely subsided, so that overall urban population growth is now mostly attributable to natural increase, although population increase in many

---

[17] Comparison of the occupational mix of employment in urban with nonurban areas shows that urban areas require relatively more professional, managerial, clerical, and sales workers.

specific urban places is significantly affected by the migration from other urban places.

The influence of migration on the supply of skills in urban areas is related not only to the number but also to the skill level of migrants. Migrants, on the average, appear to have higher skill levels than nonmigrants, as suggested by the following evidence: migrants are generally younger and better educated than the rest of the population; interurban migrants are generally better educated than the nonmigrant in both the origin and destination cities; there is (in absolute numbers) more white than nonwhite rural-to-urban migration; nonwhite rural-to-urban migrants are better educated than the average nonwhite resident in the rural origin, and are just as likely to be employed as are other nonwhite urban dwellers; a higher proportion of whites than of nonwhites migrate, and migrants tend to have higher incomes than do nonmigrants. It would appear that migrants out of an area tend to be drawn from the best-qualified and most productive people, and these migrants do not generally lower but probably increase the average skill level in the places they go to.

Thus the migration process tends to lower the skill levels of origin places and raise the levels in destination places. In his analysis of gross interurban labor flows, Lowry found that migrants go to places with low unemployment and high income, although the places they leave do not have particularly high unemployment or low incomes.[18] In other words, gross outmigration from an urban place is largely a function of the age distribution in the city, the age-specific propensity to outmigrate being similar for all cities and generally declining as the age brackets grow older. However, the choice of cities to which migrants go is determined by the economic opportunities being offered in the different places—the greater the opportunity, the longer the migration. Since migrants generally find jobs in the destination cities, although for some there is a substantial time lag, so that the expanded labor supply does not cause unemployment, there is a tendency for cities which are growing because of inmigration to continue growing.

From the perspective of the individual migrant, and abstracting from noneconomic considerations, migration can be viewed as an investment in human capital.[19] The individual expects that the lifetime flow of income in the destination city will be greater than the flow of income in the origin city by at least the amount of migration costs—primarily moving costs and forgone earnings. The income flow in the destination city could be

[18] Ira Lowry, *Migration and Metropolitan Growth: Two Analytical Models* (Los Angeles: University of California, Institute of Government and Public Affairs, 1966), 118 pp.
[19] L. Sjaastad, among others, including Gary Becker, has viewed migration in terms of human capital investment models. See Lawrence Sjaastad, "The Costs and Returns of Human Migration," *Journal of Political Economy* (Supplement), vol. 70, no. 5 (October 1962).

larger than in the origin city because his (discounted) real wage rate is higher, his long-term employment is more secure, or his opportunities for training and education are greater and less costly.

Wertheimer has measured the economic returns from migration (the difference between the present value of the lifetime income flow at the destination and at the origin, less costs of migration) and found them to be generally consistent with the assumptions that both migrants and destination places gain by the migration process; the migrants' returns from migration are positive and the destination cities' return from the expanded productive labor supply is greater than the costs associated with any social problems created by the migrants.[20]

There are two somewhat conflicting views as to the effects of migration on urban areas. One view says that migration to the cities is a significant cause of the economic and social problems in the cities. The other view says that migration serves as an equilibrating mechanism to equalize economic opportunity among cities—in effect, to spread the problems around. The preceding evidence throws some light on these issues.

It seems clear, as Wertheimer says, that "Migration to the cities and out of the South is not significant enough nor are migrants' income experiences different enough from their urban and nonurban counterparts to warrant the considerable alarm the migration issue stimulates. The most important policy implication of this is that programs to stem migration to the cities are not likely to have much impact on city problems."[21]

Migration is probably not a significant mechanism for equalizing economic opportunities among different places. Although it probably tends to diminish the difference in unemployment rates among areas, it also tends to strengthen the labor supply and the labor demand in those places where they are already relatively strong.

Although many institutional factors affect urban labor supply, perhaps the most important of these is the process of collective bargaining. The market interdependence and the availability of close substitutes which char-

[20] Specifically, Wertheimer found the following:

Migration out of the South results in a return of about $800 per year, on the average. This return is greater for nonwhites than for whites, quadruples for college-educated migrants, but practically disappears for women.

Migrants from rural to urban areas can generally double their return if they move to larger (over 250,000 population) rather than small cities. Larger cities generally have higher income and wages than small cities.

The return from migration generally comes five years after migration; there is little return in the first five years. As a result the younger the migrant, the longer work life he has in the destination city and the greater his return. A thirty-year-old migrant, e.g., receives less than half the return of a twenty-year-old migrant.

Five years after moving, the migrant has achieved an earnings level equal to that of the destination-city residents of the same education, age, race, and sex.

Richard Wertheimer, *The Monetary Rewards of Migration within the U.S.* (Washington, D.C.: Urban Institute, 1970), pp. 57–61.

[21] Ibid., p. 61.

acterize the economy of cities make collective bargaining arrangements feasible, so that the labor conditions in a city will be considerably influenced by such bargaining instead of by the conditions of classically conceived labor markets.[22]

Interdependence in cities, however, is causing reconsideration of the right to strike, a basic tenet of organized labor. This has arisen particularly in connection with the right of public employees to strike.[23] The implications of this development are not yet completely clear. For one thing, wages and working conditions of public employees deserve to be comparable to those in private industry. For another, withholding essential services makes the city highly vulnerable and can be a distinct threat to the health and safety of its residents.

The issue of collective bargaining in general, and the specific example of new efforts on the part of government employees to bargain, point up one of the most significant aspects of the city's economy: its vulnerability to small groups of labor which hold strategic positions in the system; e.g., the police, garbage collectors, and truckers have all caused urban crises by decisions to withhold their services.

The urban system is vulnerable not only to actors who are discharging purely economic roles. There have been repeated examples (garbage collectors, policemen, and firemen) of the vulnerability of the entire economic system of cities to extremely small groups of dissident individuals who are willing to exploit the interdependence of the economic system in order to force decisions on the larger society, decisions which it would not accept if it were left to its normal decision processes. And even without deliberate exploitation, when breakdowns in some part of the system occur, they may cause the entire system to become temporarily inoperable.

Demand

Microeconomic analysis relates the demand for labor to the demand for the output of the firm. Demand for output is translated through the firm's production function into a derived demand function for labor. The production function of the firm may have several input factors. For our purposes we need look at only four of them. Thus output is a function of land, labor, capital, and technology. Technology, as we shall see, plays a special role in the production function.

The firm chooses that combination of factors of production which

---

[22] Recent evidence points to the possibility that union negotiations may yield labor market solutions which are in no way distinguishable from those which would occur without collective bargaining. This result is based on the notion that the bargaining agents on both sides probably reflect almost precisely the same objectives as the groups for whom they are bargaining.

[23] The Supreme Court, however, has decided that public employees do not have an inherent right to strike.

yields a given output at a minimum cost. The crystallization of the way in which the firm minimizes costs with respect to labor is found in the demand function for labor. This demand function is based on the marginal physical product of labor, which is simply the derivative of the production function with respect to labor. If we assume that all other factors are fixed, then the marginal physical product of labor describes the amount of output which an additional unit of labor input can be expected to produce.

There are three changes which can alter either the shape or the position of the demand function for labor. The first is a relative price change for labor, the second is a change in technology, and the third is a change in demand for final output. Imagine for a moment that the price of labor stays constant but the price of other factors, either land or capital, varies. If the price of one or both of these other factors increases, then the relative price of labor has declined. This would induce a firm to purchase more labor services and fewer of the other inputs. The firm will continue to increase the amount of labor it uses until it has worked down the marginal physical product function of labor to the point that labor's product is equal to the product of other factors at the margin. The converse is also true, of course.

A change in technology can be thought of as an increase or a decrease in the amount of output that can be produced by application of a fixed quantity and mix of inputs. Basically all technological changes which have actually been introduced into production processes have tended to increase the quality or quantity of output produced available from fixed inputs. (New products can be viewed as a quality increase.) Most changes in technologies tend to affect various factors of production differentially. When this occurs, then a change in relative prices of factors occurs also. The factor that is favored by technological change experiences an upward shift of its demand function relative to other factors.[24]

There is another element which can affect the demand function for a factor of production. It derives from the fact that the actual demand function is equal to the marginal physical product of the factor multiplied by the price of the output which the factor produces. If price of the output increases, then the demand function for labor and other factors of production will also shift upward by various amounts, usually depending on the elasticity of supply of output with respect to each factor.

The preceding conceptualization of the effects of relative wage rate, technology, and output changes on the demand for labor is applicable to nonurban as well as urban labor markets. Specific urban considerations require analysis of how these changes operate in the urban environment.

The wage rate relative to other input prices seems to be fairly stable

---

[24] Although technological change is not neutral with respect to utilization of different factors at the micro-level, it appears that, in the aggregate, labor input (measured in value terms) is a relatively constant proportion of national output.

in most urban places. Pressures on land utilization have probably caused a relative increase in the price of the land input, but land costs are usually not a significant part of total production costs. The price of the capital input, however, has probably declined relative to labor to offset the land cost increase.

On balance, technology changes probably tend to favor an increase in urban labor demands. The high-technology industries, which are usually labor-intensive, tend to favor urban locations. Automated plants, with their relatively high labor-saving technologies, tend to locate on the fringe of cities. Also, the low-skilled, labor-intensive industries with little growth potential are increasingly seeking nonurban locations. Finally, technological developments in the service industries appear to encourage increased use of labor at all skill levels, and the service industries generally favor urban locations.

Shifts in demand for an urban area's final output originate in either local or national markets. The consumer budget shift toward services as a result of rising incomes is increasing the importance of the local market as a determinant of urban labor demand. Since demand for services tends to fluctuate less than the demand for manufactured goods, the increasing importance of local markets tends to stabilize urban labor demands. Also, the occupational requirements for a number of different services are similar, so that as demand shifts among services it becomes easier for workers to relocate in new jobs, again adding support to the urban labor demands. Finally, local goods as well as service markets result in fewer income leakages to other areas, which strengthens the base of urban labor demand.

The effects on a city of shifts in national demand will depend on the production base of the export sector of the city. Some cities such as New York and Chicago export a wide variety of goods and services to the rest of the nation. Other cities, such as Pittsburgh and, to a greater extent, Detroit, have relatively specialized export mixes. Thus a very large proportion of Pittsburgh's exports are steel products and a very large proportion of Detroit's output is automobiles. Even small shifts in national demand for these kinds of goods and services can have a very large effect on the economies of such cities.[25]

In general an urban area's demands for labor are highly sensitive to the state of its export markets, and fluctuations in the size of these markets cause still deeper fluctuations in the demand for labor in the area because of income multiplier consequences. The long-run demand for labor is also influenced by the area's export markets. Generally, areas which have a diversified production base and diversified export markets seem to increase

---

[25] The experience of Seattle and Los Angeles in 1969–1971 is a case in point. At that time a relatively small decrease in demand for aircraft and other kinds of military procurements resulted in very large decreases in demand for specialized types of labor in their areas.

their labor demands, over the long run, at a faster pace than do highly specialized areas. For example, Jane Jacobs suggests that if a city must trade off between efficiency in the production of a few important exports and relative inefficiency in the production of a wide variety, then it should choose the latter, even though the short-run gains are small.[26]

There are also seasonal fluctuations in the demand for urban labor, similar to the seasonal fluctuations in the supply of urban labor. Natural seasons—hot and cold—produce alternating favorable and unfavorable conditions for certain kinds of work. These alternations can affect demand directly by changing the demand for the good or service, and the efficiency with which certain work can be performed may be affected by the weather, causing firms to schedule more work at some times than at others.

When it is hot, people increase their demands for air conditioning, baseball games, camping equipment, and beer. When it is cold, all of these things decline in demand and, as a consequence, the people who sell them are confronted with reduced demands for their services. Conversely, when it is cold, demand for football games, hot buttered rum, heating equipment, and ice skates goes up and the people who sell them find that their services are more in demand. The diversity of urban markets allows many of these activities to be engaged in by the same people: air conditioners are frequently sold by the same companies that sell heaters, and the maintenance men who work on the one appliance generally work on the other as well. Some ski equipment companies also sell hiking and tennis equipment, and so forth. These kinds of complementarities make an important contribution to the overall efficiency of urban economic systems.

An example of decreased efficiency being associated with certain seasons is the construction industry. Because builders must work outside, they are unprotected from wind, rain, and cold. This causes their efficiency to decline to the point where firms are unwilling to employ them during inclement weather. The result is that the construction industry is highly regulated by the seasons (although it is becoming less so because of managerial and technological improvements). Construction workers must be paid more per hour in order to be induced to work in an occupation which will yield only a few months of work each year. In the winter, when the demand for their services has disappeared, they must seek other kinds of employment in order to tide them over until spring.

Although cyclical variation in demand is a macroeconomic issue when the labor force is considered as an aggregate, there are some respects in which the microeconomic approach is more directly applicable. One such

---

[26] Jane Jacobs, *The Economy of Cities* (New York: Random House, 1969), p. 88: "Manchester's efficient specialization portended stagnation and a profoundly obsolescent city. For the 'immensity of its future' proved to consist of immense losses of its markets as other people in other places learned how to spin and weave cotton efficiently too."

case is discrimination. If a worker is a member of a group that is not pre-ferred or is discriminated against, he will find that cyclical variations in the demand for his services are different from those which affect the majority of the labor force.

In a downturn, the minority worker will find that demand for his serv-ices often drops off more rapidly than it does for the majority of workers, and that the resulting level of unemployment is much greater for him than it is for the majority of workers. He will also find that, other things equal, he will spend a longer period of time unemployed and that the unemploy-ment rate for his group will stay high longer than it does for the majority group. Once an upturn occurs, however, the recovery of the minority un-employment rate from lower levels will generally be more spectacular than that of the majority group—but this is only because it has a longer dis-tance to go in order to return to its "normal" position.

These observations are based on what is often referred to as the "queueing" theory of minority unemployment, that blacks, or members of any nonpreferred group, tend to be fired first during a downturn and hired last during a subsequent upturn in the business cycle. Although little em-pirical work has been done, a model tested by Lester Thurow appears to support the existence of the queueing phenomenon.[27] It does not, however, attempt to explain the phenomenon through any detailed examination of the behavior of employers.

IV. NEIGHBORHOOD MARKETS

The preceding section considered the adjustment processes that balance labor supply and demand within the urban area as a whole. However, the total labor market area consists of spatially separated markets, with labor being supplied from residential neighborhoods and demanded by work neighborhoods. The adjustment process that takes place between neigh-borhoods is not so much balancing the quantities of labor supplied and demanded as minimizing the costs of movement between the residential and work neighborhoods.

Families will seek to minimize their labor commuting costs. However, they must balance such costs against the costs of housing services (which are usually inversely related to commuting costs), the quality of the neigh-borhood in which they live, and the travel costs for recreational and shop-ping purposes.

Firms will also seek to minimize the commuting costs of their work force by appropriate location decisions. However, firms must balance such

[27] Lester Thurow, *Poverty and Discrimination* (Washington, D.C.: Brookings, 1969), pp. 48–52.

costs against the need to be near an adequate potential work force, the transport costs for obtaining inputs and shipping outputs, the plant site costs, and accessibility to customers. An empirical study of the Chicago labor market in 1963 reveals a wage gradient that is lowest in the northwest corner of the Chicago area and highest in the southeast.[28] This gradient parallels the pattern of location of employment and residences, the north and west regions having a much heavier concentration of residential neighborhoods and the south and east regions having a heavier concentration of nonresidential land uses.

The number of labor markets within a given metropolitan area depends on the size of the city. A larger metropolitan area tends to have more geographical markets, in absolute number even if not on a per capita basis. The occupational characteristics of the work force will also affect the number of markets. A more diversified occupational base probably means more places of labor demand and of labor supply.

However, whether the number of separate marketplaces is large or small will not affect commuting costs. Commuting costs will not even be affected by whether there is less demand than supply for labor places or the reverse. What affects commuting costs is whether the demand (work) places for specific occupations are close to or far from the supply (residence) places for these occupations. Thus the distance between the places where labor is demanded and where it is supplied will vary with the kind of occupational market under consideration.

Five cases can be considered. There can be many or few markets cleared within a single neighborhood, which keeps commuting costs low. Also there can be commuting from many places of supply to many demand places, from a few places of supply to many demand places, and from many places of supply to a few demand places.

When there are many markets whose demand and supply both come from within a neighborhood, they usually relate to low-skill occupations, and these markets are found in a number of neighborhoods in the city. This is because the services being required are oriented toward neighborhood household requirements, such as retail trade and janitorial services. Often the labor is provided by women and part-time workers who cannot afford the time to commute long distances. The wage rates for these occupations may differ between neighborhoods, since they depend on the labor demand and supply conditions within each neighborhood rather than in the city as a whole, because there is an aversion to commuting—and residential relocation is probably not significantly influenced by secondary-worker wage differentials between neighborhoods.

When there are only a few markets whose demand and supply both

[28] Rees and Shultz, op. cit., pp. 176–179.

come from within a neighborhood, they usually relate to high-skilled occupations. The high-skilled worker can often afford to select his residence location in proximity to his job. Also, high-skilled workers with similar occupations may tend to concentrate in specific neighborhoods, seeking similar amenities for their families. As a result some firms requiring such workers may locate in such neighborhoods in order to accommodate this work force.

Those in the intermediate ranges of the occupational distribution will tend to commute between their residences and work neighborhoods. The incomes of workers in these occupations are sufficiently high so that they can choose to live in a wide variety of areas in a city, seeking residential amenities but still constrained by such factors as land prices, tax rates, and commuting costs. As a consequence these workers are likely to be diffused throughout a number of residential neighborhoods in the city. Firms employing such workers tend to consider the citywide occupational supply as their potential labor force, and there are usually a large number of such firms. Since there are many markets of supply and demand, the occupational wage rate tends to be determined on a citywide basis. Some firms will attempt to locate so as to reduce the transportation cost their employees will have to bear. This may mean locating near a variety of residential neighborhoods from which their employees are drawn. For example, the aircraft plants in Southern California have relocated to suburban counties in order to draw their workers from a variety of suburban neighborhoods. In such a case wage rates are not likely to be influenced by commuting costs, since such costs are not likely to be very different among workers.

There are some occupations which may be highly concentrated in a few industries. The firms in these industries may for a variety of reasons seek to be located close to one another. Together these firms employ a sufficiently large work force so that their employees cannot reside in the same neighborhood; as a consequence, the employees live in a variety of neighborhoods. Therefore, in this few-demand, many-supply market situation, some workers are likely to bear higher commuting costs than others. Wage rates, however, are not likely to adjust to this cost differential, since the firms have some degree of monopsony power.

When there are constraints on residential mobility, a situation of few supply markets and many demand markets may arise. The demand for low-skilled occupations is diffused throughout the city. Ghetto residents with low skills must seek their employment in these various markets and bear heavy transportation costs. Since wage rates are low, such costs can be a heavy burden and in some cases may force the real wage below the worker's reservation wage, so that he stops seeking employment. When the labor market is tight, wage differentials among the various markets may arise as a result of transportation costs. To take advantage of such a differential, some firms may choose to locate in or near the ghetto areas.

These descriptions of alternative neighborhood labor market situations point up several possibilities which are not immediately apparent when the labor market is viewed as a whole. There are some occupations whose money wage rate will be uniform throughout the city but whose real wages will vary because of commuting costs; these tend to be low- and intermediate-skill occupations. There are some occupations whose money wage will not be uniform throughout the city because attempts are made to compensate for commuting cost differences. There are some occupations for which there may be a citywide imbalance in labor supply and demand because the neighborhoods where labor is being demanded cannot draw on the supply available in other neighborhoods; these tend to be low-skill occupations. In general, we can say that the greater the variance in a given occupation's wage rates among neighborhoods, the greater the probability of commuting between neighborhoods and the greater will be the expenditures on transportation and information costs; the lower the occupational skill level and the lower the wages, the lower will be commuting between neighborhoods (provided there are no restrictions on residential mobility); the greater the concentration of occupational supply in specific residential neighborhoods, the more likely is it that firms will locate near that neighborhood; the greater the concentration of low- or intermediate-skill occupational demands in specific work neighborhoods, the greater will be the variation in commuting costs among households.

It must be noted, however, that the locational adjustments between firms and residents take place only very slowly because of existing spatial distributions in the city and because of the heavy costs involved in modifying the distribution of the existing infrastructure. For example, if a worker changes his job, he may not seek a more locationally appropriate residence because of the many commitments he has to his present neighborhood; as a firm increases its labor demands, it may be cheaper to expand capacity at its present site than to seek a new location.

V. URBAN LABOR POLICY

The standard of living for most people in the United States is determined by their labor earnings. In recognition of this, national economic policy is directed toward the maintenance of high levels of employment and rising real wages. Thus national monetary policy and national fiscal policy are both directly and indirectly labor policy, and usually have a more pervasive and significant impact on labor markets than do specific labor policies.

In addition there is a corpus of labor law and regulations that have a major impact on labor markets. Child labor, minimum wage, right to work, fair employment, and collective bargaining laws have all been designed to provide protection to groups in society that might otherwise be victims of an impersonal and totally unregulated system of labor markets.

Generally, specific labor policies are not substitutes for overall economic policy and regulation. Rather they are complements to such policy, directed toward labor market conditions that monetary and fiscal policy and regulation, because of their aggregative nature, find difficult to correct. In some cases specific labor policies are required to counteract undesirable conditions actually created as a by-product of desirable aggregate policy.

Thus specific labor policies tend to be localized in both their objective and their effect. Sometimes they are localized in terms of their geographic focus; e.g., rural versus urban areas, depressed versus growing areas, central city versus suburbs, south versus north, etc. More often, however, specific labor policies are localized in the sense that they relate to specific groups in society, i.e., the poor, the unemployed, the unskilled, and minorities. Often, the same people will belong in several of these categories, and they tend to live in urban areas. It is for this reason that specific labor policies are generally urban labor policies.[29]

In the following sections we review several important aspects of urban labor markets that create a need for specific labor policies. Some of these aspects relate to the efficiency with which urban labor markets bring together the supplier and demander of labor. Often many people, employers as well as employees, will suffer because labor markets do not work efficiently.

Policies to improve the efficiency of labor markets are generally viewed with favor since they can be beneficial to many people while being harmful to only a few. Of course improving labor market efficiency does require resources, and the return to such a use of resources is likely to diminish at some point. Thus the question of just how efficient, from a socially optimal perspective, urban labor markets should be becomes an important question.

But even if urban labor markets are optimally efficient, there will be many people whose earnings from labor are inadequate to meet their basic needs. A short-run view, i.e., a dismal view, of such a situation is that since the labor markets are operating efficiently, any attempt to redress these conditions will only lead to still worse conditions. An alternative view, however, is that the market valuation of these suppliers of labor can itself be changed by affecting what they bring to the market. That is, there are specific labor policies designed to bring about such a change.

---

[29] Even policies directed toward rural labor are often urban-oriented. For example, training of migrant workers is designed to improve their chances to obtain urban, not farm, jobs.

We will review such policies by attempting to identify those aspects of poverty, unemployment, and discrimination to which labor policies might be effectively addressed.

Labor Market Inefficiencies

Two aspects of labor market inefficiency are considered: inefficiencies arising from the interaction between labor and other markets, and inefficiencies arising from inadequate labor market information.

Imperfections in the housing, transportation, and public sector markets are likely to be transmitted in an indirect fashion to urban labor markets. What tends to occur is that the extent of the labor market (i.e., distance between job and home) becomes longer than it would otherwise be. For example, when public roads and transportation are underpriced (i.e., do not reflect the social cost of such usage), workers will be willing to travel longer distances to work. When discrimination in housing occurs, workers are compelled to travel longer distances. When public services are imperfectly distributed among neighborhoods, people will tend to move to those parts of a city that provide high-quality services and relatively low taxes, even though this means that they are poorly situated with respect to job location. If the extent of the market is larger than it "should" be, this would tend to lower real wages received, since part of the wage would be invested in commuting costs, and as a consequence the supply of labor might be reduced. It might also raise money wages as workers seek to recoup some of their real wage loss. This might reduce the demand for labor. Even if the supply and demand for labor come into balance, it would be at a lower level than in the absence of other market imperfections.

So far as the operation of urban labor markets is concerned, the imperfections of other markets are taken as given. Although such imperfections are sometimes cited as a "cause" of underemployment and low real wages, labor policies cannot be directed toward reducing the imperfections. Rather, labor policy is made in the context that such imperfections exist.

Labor policies can, however, be directed toward the improvement of labor market information. The costs of job information and search will influence the size of unemployment and wage rates. If these costs could be reduced, labor markets would become more efficient. The complexity of the modern city assures that no individual (employer or employee) can obtain an adequate amount of labor market information unless he is assisted by specialists in the production of such information. Thus policies that improve the U.S. Employment Service and tax deductions for job search which will lead to the use of private employment agencies are effective instruments for improving the efficiency of labor markets.

The theoretical aspects of labor market information have been explored recently by economists who have viewed information as a component of the theory of human capital.[30] In this view information is a good which is subject to the same laws of production to which all goods are subject. If produced in greater volume, it can be expected to be subject to economies of scale; and if produced more rapidly, it can be expected to be more costly. If we consider information about labor markets as a good which is subject to the laws of production, then we can see why an individual may decide to become unemployed in order to increase his efficiency as an information producer.

Alchian explains this by pointing out that unemployed resources (i.e., the unemployed worker) are engaged in the production of information. In the case of labor, this amounts to an entrepreneurial activity, analogous to any other activity in which an individual marshals resources and converts them into something which is profitably exchanged.[31]

We can also see that the city offers the potential for economies of scale in information production, so that its costs can be reduced. As the cost of information is reduced, the amount of unemployment also is reduced. The proximity of markets for the same kind of labor, as well as the prevalence of a combination of markets for labor, leads to a situation in cities where it pays some people to become specialists in the production of information about the labor market. Being specialists, they produce information more cheaply and more quickly than workers who have specialized in some other sort of labor. Similarly, vendors of unspecialized information find it worthwhile to expand their activities to include labor market information. Thus, newspapers, which sell information about a large variety of subjects, include information concerning jobs.

The larger a city, the greater are the opportunities for profit in the production of such information, since the larger is the market for labor and hence the number of workers as well as firms that demand such information. As a result, the city is a place where there are a number of competing entrepreneurs in the business of producing job information.

Workers and employers can try to produce their own information or they can retain specialists to produce it for them. Typically, higher-occupational groups tend to rely for the production of such information on specialists, whose greater efficiency tends to reduce the incidence and term of unemployment of such groups. Conversely, for lower-wage occupations,

---

[30] See, for instance, George Stigler, "Information in the Labor Market," *Journal of Political Economy,* Supplement (October 1962); and Albert Rees, "Information Networks and Labor Markets," *American Economic Reveiw,* Supplement (May 1966). For later work in this area, see John J. McCall, "Economics of Information and Job Search," RM-5745-OEO (Santa Monica, Calif.: The RAND Corporation, 1968).
[31] Armen Alchian, "Information Costs, Pricing, and Resource Unemployment," *Western Economic Journal,* vol. 7, no. 2 (June 1969), p. 109.

where workers produce their own information, or for very specialized occupations in which the number of potential buyers is relatively small, information costs may be high and unemployment also high.

The implication of this analysis is that different information production functions in the city result in different rates of unemployment for different worker groups; also, the more efficient the information-producing industry is, the less unemployment there is likely to be in the city.

Unemployment

The level and rate of unemployment have long been used as summary indicators of economic conditions. Relatively easy to measure and to understand, unemployment statistics have become a barometer by which to gauge the need for designing and implementing labor policies and programs. When these indicators are in an "undesirable" range, pressures for relief build up and programs are triggered. These programs are of two sorts: those which seek to improve general economic conditions, thereby increasing the demand for labor; and those which seek to directly reduce unemployment, usually focusing on improving the characteristics (marketability) of the labor supply. These approaches to labor policy are not alternatives. If only programs to improve general economic conditions are pursued, there is a likelihood that some groups in society will not benefit from these improvements; they will remain unemployed and the use of general economic policy to alleviate such unemployment would eventually become inflationary. On the other hand, no amount of specific programs to improve the labor supply will be successful unless overall economic conditions are such that there will be a market demand for labor.

Unemployment is not a uniquely urban condition. However, its use as a barometer for needed policy is a distinctively urban phenomenon. In rural societies unemployment tends to be disguised. The idea underlying disguised unemployment is that the marginal product of an individual worker is not the basis for payment of the wage. Instead, custom dictates that workers tend to receive wages equal to the average product of the entire group of workers. As a result, it is conceptually possible for someone to have a marginal product of zero yet still receive a reasonable wage, since the fact that he contributes nothing is not noticed and would not be of special importance to the community if it were noticed. Thus, the unemployment of such people is disguised by the compensation convention.

In urban societies, however, the functioning of markets makes productivity a consideration in employment. When people have marginal productivity so low that they fail to meet the market test, they may find themselves unemployed, but not disguised. In urban societies, perhaps because of a loss of a sense of identity with a community, the productive workers are less inclined to share their wage with their less productive neighbors.[32] Until relatively recent years this view was carried to an extreme. That is, if the market judges a person's productivity—and therefore his employability—as being too low, then it was thought that policies could do very little to change this situation. However, it has come to be realized that labor policies can change the terms under which labor is offered and demanded. Particularly in urban areas, with their high interdependencies and market interrelatedness, high levels of unemployment cannot be a stable condition; they must be reduced or unemployment will become still greater.

Although the need for general economic policy can often be guided by the overall unemployment rate, specific labor policies must be guided by the components of unemployment. The aspects of these components include the causes of unemployment and the characteristics of those who are unemployed. Particularly when policies for specific urban places are being formulated, it is important to know these two aspects, since they will not be the same in different cities confronted by a variety of different conditions. The causes of unemployment, reflecting the balance between labor supply and demand, can be identified by using the concepts of frictional, seasonal, structural, and aggregate demand-deficiency unemployment. It is useful to distinguish between these categories of unemployment even though the distinctions are not always precise, since they point to different causes of urban unemployment and imply different polices for containing such unemployment.[33]

Some part of the work force is always "between jobs" as a result of workers' adjusting to changes in their own preferences for type and location of work and to small alterations in conditions of demand, shifting between slowly declining firms or industries and toward expanding ones, and the like. Such factors cause frictional unemployment.

Indicators of frictional unemployment are such things as turnover rates and measurements of job and locational mobility. When an individual migrates from one place to another, he may be unemployed for a short period of time; this period of unemployment is included in the concept of frictional unemployment. Similarly, an individual is frictionally unemployed if he changes jobs and is unemployed for some period between jobs.

It is difficult to measure frictional unemployment because of the difficulties in isolating it from other components of unemployment. It is ordinarily accepted that some amount of frictional unemployment is essential to the efficient operation of labor markets, for if there were none between

---

[32] As the poor become militant, the vulnerability of urban society to their potential pressure may increase the willingness of productive workers to share their wage.

[33] For a very complete and classic treatment of the great variety of types of unemployment, see John R. Hicks, *The Theory of Wages* (London: Macmillan, 1964), chap. 3.

jobs, this would imply very few changes in process for improving production techniques, introducing new products, and upgrading of individuals.

Roughly, it is estimated that efficient labor market operations require about 2 percent of the labor force to be frictionally unemployed. Since such unemployment would be associated with greater levels of aggregate output because of improved efficiency, and no individuals would remain unemployed for a long period of time, such frictional unemployment does not constitute a "social problem." Indeed, there is evidence that frictional unemployment tends to rise slightly when times are good—that is, when the labor market is tight and jobs are easy to find. In such a situation workers perceive an opportunity for upgrading their ultimate real wealth position and are able to finance short periods of unemployment.

However, it is desirable to keep frictional unemployment as low as possible without reducing overall efficiency. One way of doing this is to reduce information and search costs. Thus it is desirable to separate unemployment resulting from lack of information about job opportunities and labor availability from frictional unemployment. Analytic efforts, therefore, should attempt to isolate and to introduce explicitly the information and search aspects of labor market functioning.

This is particularly important for urban areas. The availability of many job opportunities in urban areas probably means that frictional unemployment is lower in urban than nonurban areas (e.g., long-term unemployment is a higher share of total unemployment in nonurban areas than it is in urban areas). However, the many interdependencies among urban markets, the rapidity of technological change, the shifts in occupational requirements, and the birth and death of establishments all indicate that the costs for improving information about urban labor markets would be less than the costs associated with tolerating an unnecessarily high level of frictional unemployment in urban areas. There is, in principle, some optimal position where marginal information costs would equal marginal frictional unemployment costs; it is likely, however, that as urban markets become increasingly interdependent with time, the value of added information will increase, thereby causing this hypothetical optimum to occur at a higher level of information supply.

Programs to decrease the cost of information for both employers and employees are appealing to economists because they make possible a more perfect operation of labor markets. Various actions can be taken by state employment agencies or other agents. Increasing the general level of technology used in job placement firms is most likely to occur. If government provides any subsidies to lower unemployment rates, perhaps some of the most effective would be subsidization of capital investment by job brokers and similar expenditures aimed at reducing the cost of information and the time during which job-matching information can be generated for particular cases.

Seasonal unemployment results from the fact that there are times of the year when the demand for certain types of labor in relation to supply is less than it is at other times. This may be caused by variations in weather, variations in demand for the final output of a certain industry, or variation in labor supply. The most common examples are the seasonality of construction work, which requires clement weather, the seasonality of demand for certain kinds of consumer goods which results from holidays like Christmas and Easter, and the seasonality of demand for recreational facilities related to weather and vacation season.[34]

Seasonal unemployment, in principle, causes the hourly or weekly wage of seasonal workers to be higher than if their labor were in demand throughout the year. This occurs because the seasonal worker is likely to have an annual income expectation (a reservation income), and the seasonal employer includes in the wages he pays some part of the worker's expenses incurred in finding an off-season job as well as some compensation for the probable lower wage that the worker must settle for in his off-season job. Since the incidence of seasonal unemployment can be fairly well predicted, both buyers and sellers of labor can attempt to maximize their profits or utility on the basis of information that is more complete than that which they have in many other labor market situations. However, the probability of finding off-season employment is not equally predictable. Therefore there is a large element of risk for the worker who may find himself unemployed for much of the off-season, particularly if the labor market is flaccid.

In addition, there are institutional factors which will affect the wage bargain which is reached. For example, unemployment insurance will enter into the wage calculation as well as influence the duration of unemployment. Also, much of the demand for seasonal labor is met by overtime work of full-time employees and by part-time employees (e.g., student postal employees during the Christmas season) who enter the labor force only during the peak season (often at a comparatively low wage) in response to the seasonal demands. When seasonal demands are met in this fashion, then seasonal unemployment (more properly called off-season unemployment) does not result.

Seasonal unemployment is high in rural areas because of the nature of farming (although probably diminishing with the use of migrant workers who follow the crops). The farm laborers' response to such unemployment is often to seek off-season urban jobs, and public policies are sometimes designed to make such jobs available. In urban areas the diversity of job opportunities (at reasonably high levels of aggregate demand) makes it

---

[34] In Japan, for instance, bonuses amounting sometimes to half of a worker's annual salary are distributed around Christmas time. This causes truly great seasonality in demand for consumer goods, and therefore for department store workers—much more so than if such payments were spread over the entire year.

possible to contain seasonal unemployment, particularly if programs to make labor market information more readily available are pursued.

Programs responding to seasonal unemployment are also viewed with favor by the economist, to the extent that they contribute to more efficient labor markets.

As we mentioned earlier, the predictability of seasonal unemployment probably leads to greater wage rates during employed periods and to the generation of a greater amount of job information than would otherwise be required. These are social inefficiencies which could be beneficially removed. The ways in which seasonality can be affected are for the most part institutional. For example, it has been suggested that school children need not flood the urban labor market each June and then disappear in September. Earlier in the country's history this was convenient because the demand for labor rose sharply during the summer. But in cities there is little seasonal harvesting, and consequently little seasonal increase in demand. As a result there is an unmatched seasonal increase in supply of labor which leads to unemployment. This could be changed quickly and easily by making schooling an eleven-month process—or, if there is something magical about the nine-month cycle, it could be preserved for individuals while being forgone by the system. The results would be a decrease in seasonal unemployment and an increase in the rate of utilization of school capital stock. As another illustration some urban places seek to take advantage of their seasonal surplus of labor by trying to attract industries which can utilize this labor in off-seasons.

"Structural unemployment" refers to unemployment resulting from shifts in the mix of goods and services being produced or changes in technology that make certain skills obsolete. It implies that as the mix of demand for goods and services, or the way they are produced, changes, then the composition of demand for workers in occupational groups changes—some occupational demands declining and others possibly rising. Even if the declining occupational demands are offset by the rising demands, structural unemployment can occur because of constraints on occupational mobility. This is the kind of structural unemployment associated with the plight of low-skilled workers. But, also, the declining occupational demands may not be totally offset by the rising demands. This is the kind of structural unemployment associated with automation or rapid technological change.

If technological or demand mix changes are large and occur often, then structural unemployment could be high, even if occupational mobility is rapid. Under these circumstances those who are structurally unemployed are likely to be different people each year. When this occurs, structural and frictional unemployment merge into one another, distinguished, perhaps, by their extent rather than their causes. However, in the structural case there is likely to result a significant amount of structural underemployment, where individuals actually find new jobs but at wages considerably below what their skills would normally command. This very often happens in urban areas.

Perhaps of greater social concern is when structural unemployment becomes persistent or chronic. Persistent unemployment occurs when the same individuals remain unemployed for a long period of time because of their inability to adjust to the structural change; chronic unemployment occurs when individuals never become reemployed.

Persistent unemployment may occur because individuals incorrectly anticipate how long it will take for the demand for their skills to be revived. Therefore they do not find alternative opportunities being offered by the market (usually at lower wages) or do not seek training which will develop skills that are in demand. Chronic unemployment occurs when individuals never "learn" the facts of the market or are unable to receive or utilize training to obtain new skills, so that they eventually leave the labor force.

Thus structural unemployment results from structural change but persists because market adjustments are not made. The market failures are important in urban areas, particularly for certain groups. For example, only 60 percent of the urban work force was employed fifty weeks or more in 1968; fewer (on a proportionate basis) urban laborers than other occupational groups, fewer urban Negroes than whites, and fewer urban women than men are employed fifty weeks or more per year; also, urban blacks show a lower rate of full-year employment than do nonurban blacks. About half of the urban unemployed were unemployed for more than five weeks and about one-sixth for more than fifteen weeks (as of March, 1969). The ratio of long-term unemployment to total unemployment among urban blacks was the same as it was among urban whites; however, the higher rate of unemployment for blacks indicates a more serious, persistent unemployment problem.[35]

Structural unemployment probably varies among different urban places, depending on their industrial bases. Industrial places that are dynamic, growing, innovative, and diversified allow for rapid market adjustments. Slow-growing, industrially specialized places are susceptible to periods of great structural unemployment, particularly if people resist outmigration. However, depressed cities are very often able to rapidly reduce their structural unemployment when they develop new industries that can take advantage of growing markets and technological innovations.[36]

---

[35] Data from *Trends in Social and Economic Conditions in Metropolitan and Non-metropolitan Areas,* Special Studies, ser. P-23, no. 33 (1970); *Current Population Reports,* Special Studies, ser. P-23, no. 27, (1969); and *Educational Attainment in Thirty Selected Standard Metropolitan Statistical Areas: 1967* ser. P-20, no. 209 (Washington, D.C.: U.S. Bureau of the Census, Jan. 8, 1971), p. 1.

[36] For an analysis of the existence, extent, and importance of structural unemploy-

Programs for reducing structural unemployment are usually oriented toward increasing the occupational skills of the unemployed. For example, the Manpower Development and Training Act of 1962 had as its chief rationale the reduction of this component of unemployment. The success of the program is now being evaluated by measurements of the effect on the employment status of individuals who participated in the programs. The number who were retrained was so small, compared to the size of the labor force, that it is not likely that any appreciable effect on the unemployment rate will be discerned. In addition, the costs of retraining often seem to be greater than the benefits measured in terms of the future income streams of those who received training. However, these may well be short-sighted measures of the effectiveness of training programs. Their real value may be in breaking the intergenerational cycle of inadequate preparation of specific groups in society, and over the long run, social benefits accruing from such programs may be very large.

Aggregate demand-deficiency unemployment occurs when there is a fall in the demand for labor which is not countered by wage declines, so that involuntary unemployment of individuals results. Such a drop in labor demand may occur, for example, if the federal government embarks on a policy of fiscal restraint so that output falls; with wages unable to drop, the result will be unemployment due to a reduction in demand for output.

Once such a decline in demand has occurred, there are subsequent rounds through which the effect is ultimately felt. Initially a small group of people are offered wage cuts; those refusing to take the cuts become unemployed in order to seek a job in which they feel the wage offer will be sufficiently high. If an aggregate demand decline has taken place, those who refuse the cuts are bound to be disappointed, since no employer is willing to offer more than the reduced wage offered by the previous employers. It will take some time, however, for each worker to "learn" this new fact about the labor market. During this time, he has not been receiving income, except in reduced measure through unemployment benefit programs. As a consequence, his own demand for goods and services has been curtailed, so that added to the original disturbance will be a further decline in demand on the part of the workers who were thrown out of work. This causes more unemployment, which leads to a further decline in demand for final output, and so on.[37] The existence of second- and further-order effects in this process is related, again, to the costliness of information—the fact that adjustments are not made instantaneously.

---

ment, see Barbara Bergman and David Kaun, *Structural Unemployment in the United States* (Washington, D.C.: Brookings, 1967).

[37] Axel Leijonhufvud, *Keynesian Economics and the Economics of Keynes* (New York: Oxford, 1968), chap. 3.

It is conceivable that the initial reduction in output demand results, not in a reduced money wage offer, but in a reduced real wage offer. That is, perhaps because of inflation, wages lag behind other prices. Under such conditions it is far less likely that workers will take the option of becoming unemployed to seek work at the old real wage. That is, the worker may not even be aware of the real wage reduction or may feel that all wages are being deflated at the rate of inflation—that the cut offer is not due simply to the parsimony of his employer. Thus, real wage reductions due to inflation do not carry with them the high-powered reductions in employment which occur when explicit reductions in the money wage are associated with a fall in output demand. The difference is due to the fact that information is far less costly if there is inflation than if there is not.

Aggregate demand-deficiency unemployment has also been interpreted in macroeconomic terms. Estimates of the "potential" GNP under conditions of reasonably full employment are made.[38] The difference between this potential and the actual GNP measures the GNP shortfall. The number of employees who would be needed to produce this shortfall then becomes the measure of aggregate demand-deficiency unemployment. When such calculations are made, they usually indicate that demand deficiency is the most important source of unemployment.

The importance of aggregate demand-deficiency in causing unemployment will vary among different places. For example, a slight decline in the nation's aggregate demand may be concentrated among a few goods, which happen to be produced in only a few cities. As a consequence a demand fall that is hardly perceptible at the national level may induce large-scale unemployment in selected urban places, which becomes even more severe as a consequence of multiplier effects. Indeed, national demand need not fall at all, but only change in its mix, to cause similar kinds of unemployment in specific places—as a number of defense-oriented cities discover whenever a defense procurement change occurs.

The most important policy response to aggregate demand-deficiency unemployment operates at the aggregate level. Theory tells us that this kind of unemployment is due to a temporary decline or slowdown in growth of aggregate demand for final output; this, according to theory, should cause prices of goods to drop and demand functions for labor to shift downward. Such an adjustment process, however, takes time, during which the effect of such declines is borne unequally by different groups in society. As a result there is a desire to avoid adjustments that depend on a declining demand for labor and to utilize policies which will increase aggregate demand and thereby bring about adjustments by increasing the

---

[38] Reasonably full employment is usually identified as a long-term trend or average —ordinarily 3 to 4 percent of the labor force. If the actual unemployment level were used in calculating the potential GNP, the process would become circular and all unemployment would be defined as aggregate deficiency unemployment.

demand for labor. However, such aggregate policies implicitly contain the danger that they might generate an unacceptable level of inflation.

Phillips, for example, found a statistically significant relationship between the number of unemployed and the rate of price change in Great Britain.[39] There is some level of unemployment at which prices remain stable; reducing the number of unemployed below this amount evidently leads to rises in the price level, at higher and higher rates. Thus, the relationship between prices and unemployment can be thought of as measuring the (inflationary) cost of reducing unemployment. The relationship has been tested for several different periods in Britain and found to be quite accurate as a predictor. When it is tested for specific urban places in the United States, however, it becomes a less stable relation.

One possible explanation of why the Phillips curve does not work in urban places relates to the openness of the urban economy. For example, an unemployment change occurring in one city may be associated with price changes which are diffused among many other cities. That is, a city's inflationary cost of reducing unemployment is exported, and the relation between prices and unemployment in a specific urban place becomes obscured. This is one reason why overall demand policy is difficult to implement for specific places, namely, why a city can be an unwilling recipient of costs originating elsewhere and may be unable to keep the benefits from policy within its own boundaries.[40]

[39] A. W. Phillips, "The Relation between Unemployment and the Rate of Change in Money Wage Rates in the United Kingdom, 1862–1957," *Economica* (November 1958), pp. 283–299.
[40] The relation between unemployment and prices in a specific urban place can also be thought of in terms of the job-information-generating capacity of cities. For example, increases in aggregate final demand which lead to increases in demand for labor can be thought of as causing smaller price rises where, because of an efficient job-information-producing industry, matching jobs and workers requires less expenditures of real resources. Thus a city which is an efficient information producer ($P'P'$ in Fig. 5.2) would have a lower rate of change in its price level associated with an unemployment decline than would a less efficient city.

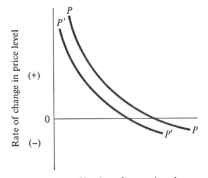

FIGURE 5.2   Phillips curves.

Although it is important in the design of policy to distinguish between frictional, seasonal, structural, and demand-deficiency causes of unemployment, it is still more important to distinguish between the types of people who are unemployed. Until recently, it has been assumed that the mix of people unemployed tends to be about the same regardless of the level of unemployment, and that this mix does not change over time. If such an assumption were accurate, then an aggregate labor policy might be fairly effective in containing unemployment. However, if such an assumption is invalid, then labor policies must become much more specific and be directed toward the specific groups in society who need and can benefit from labor programs.

The outstanding characteristic of recent unemployment in the nation's cities is the relatively small number of white, male heads of households who are unemployed. Even when the overall unemployment rate is high, their number remains relatively small. Even when the overall unemployment rate is low, the number of young, aged, women, and minority persons who are seeking jobs but cannot find them, who have dropped out of the labor force because they cannot find jobs, and who are involuntarily working only part-time, remains relatively high.

While these unemployment-prone groups will benefit most from an overall economic policy which maintains high levels of growth, it is also these same groups which most need specific labor programs to enhance their capability for benefiting from economic progress through their participation in labor markets.

Two broad policy approaches are designed to enable unemployed to benefit from economic progress. An income approach seeks to provide income, through some redistribution process, to those who cannot obtain adequate incomes from their labor earnings. It is assumed that such an approach not only provides support to those who would not, under any circumstances, be able to enter the labor market, but also provides support to those who will at some time be able to successfully enter the labor market but require some temporary assistance.

The second approach seeks to improve the employability of people by enhancing their market value as a human resource. The economic reasoning behind this approach has become embodied in the emerging "theory of human capital."[41] Although there are many ways to enhance the human

---

[41] Theodore W. Schultz relates the economic concept of human capital to the broader concept of human resources as follows:

Thus my interpretation of the term "human resources" is that it encompasses all of the many attributes of a people—physical, biological, psychological, and cultural—that account both for the social values that determine preferences and the economic value of the producer and consumer services that a people render whether they come to them as earnings or as personal satisfactions directly.

Human capital is strictly an economic concept. Although it pertains to particular attributes of man, it is not intended to serve those who are engaged

capital value of unemployed groups, improvements through health and education (training) programs have been the most important.

Both income policies and human capital policies are discussed in the following section, which considers ways to combat urban poverty—perhaps the most serious of urban problems and the most dramatic indicator of economic failure in our cities.

Poverty

An individual or other economic unit is in poverty if his income, including the annuity value of his wealth, is less than some amount that the society deems "adequate." Society tends to periodically adjust its view of what is adequate, which implies that the concept is a relative one, not absolute. In any case, we can still think of those in poverty as a group in the society having less command over resources than most other persons have, and sometimes less than is thought adequate by most people.[42]

Several definitions of poverty have been employed. At the turn of the century, the most widely accepted measure was in terms of cubic feet of housing available per person. Although some consumption measure has always been employed, in the last decade income has been used as a proxy. Galbraith suggested that $1,000 per family was a good cutoff point, representing the minimum acceptable standard of living.[43] Leon Keyserling used the cutoff of $4,000 and the Council of Economic Advisers used $3,000.[44] Victor Fuchs suggested we consider anyone with an income of less than one-half of the median income to be poor.[45]

---

in analyzing psychological, social, or cultural behavior. It is a form of *capital* because it is the source of future earnings, or future satisfactions or both of them. It is *human* because it is an integral part of man.

As quoted by Finish Welch in "The NBER Approach to Human Resource Problems," National Bureau of Economic Research, 51st Annual Report (September 1971).

[42] In addition to having lower money income, poor people may suffer from even lower real income because of higher prices of consumption goods. Evidence has been generated in recent years which suggests that poor people frequently pay more for consumption goods than others do. (See Caplowitz, *The Poor Pay More* [Glencoe, Ill.: Free Press, 1969].) The discussion of the elements of location theory in Chap. 2 indicated that some sellers can take advantage of their location to assert some degree of monopoly power which they derive from the cost of transportation. They can charge prices which reflect the cost to customers of going elsewhere. A spatial monopolist can more easily assert his monopoly power over the poor, who often find it difficult to shop outside their neighborhood because transportation costs are relatively high and also because of various psychological and social factors. Also, business costs are sometimes higher in poor neighborhoods, for such reasons as high incidence of crime, small scale of operation, extra services such as offering credit, etc.

[43] J. K. Galbraith, "The New Position of Poverty," in B. A. Weisbrod (ed.), *The Economics of Poverty* (Englewood Cliffs, N.J.: Prentice-Hall, 1965).

[44] L. Keyserling, *Progress or Poverty* (Washington, D.C.: Conference on Economic Progress, 1964). The CEA material is found in *The Economic Report of the President*, 1964, chap. 2.

[45] Taken from Weisbrod, *The Economics of Poverty*, op. cit., p. 13.

The shortcomings of these single-value cutoff points led to extensive work by Mollie Orshansky of the Social Security Administration, who derived a wide variety of cutoffs for families of various descriptions and for individuals. The detailed calculations of Orshansky did not change the estimate of the number of poor families in the United States. Instead, they considerably changed the composition of the group considered to be poor.[46]

However, even the most detailed calculations cannot offer anything but an arbitrary view of the extent of poverty. Poverty remains measured but undefined. Many people believe that there is no reason to attempt to define poverty because of the conceptual problems which cannot be overcome in choosing levels that are not arbitrary.

Recent developments in the theory of human capital have been used to explain the existence of poverty. The argument goes that there are many individuals for whom the difference between tomorrow's and today's discounted income is too small to justify the outlays. Similarly, there are other individuals for whom the period during which they would benefit from income gains due to training is sufficiently short that the gains from investing in themselves will not be large enough to balance the costs. Finally, some individuals may have such a high rate of time preference that investments which would be considered desirable for others are not considered so by them.

These three cases can be identified in terms of major groups among the poor: For example, in the first case, residents of depressed regions who are contemplating migration but who possess low skills might decide that the difference in incomes available to them in more dynamic areas is not sufficient to warrant the costs of migration. Second, old people whose skills have become outmoded are likely to find that there would be so few years in which to recover the costs of learning a new skill that the investment is unremunerative. Finally, it is sometimes suggested that persons coming from an environment of poverty prefer immediate but modest increases in income to larger but deferred increases.

---

[46] M. Orshansky, "Another Look at the Poverty Profile," *Social Security Bulletin* (Washington, D.C.: Social Security Administration, January 1965). More recent articles have been published in the same bulletin.

In general the new definitions have reduced the number of old people and farm families considered to be poor and increased the number of children included. The basis for the difference was the recognition of three major elements. First, not everyone has the same consumption requirements. Old people and children tend to consume less than do people in the middle age-groups. Second, farm families were acknowledged to have income in kind, which makes money income data for them severely understate the real level of income. The third element was the recognition that ownership of long-term durable consumer goods such as houses represented another form of income which is not included in money income data. Since such ownership is usually positively related to age, the inclusion of the concept diminished the number of old people considered to be poor.

That there are many poor who would not benefit from training and still others for whom training would result in a greater social cost than benefit is undoubtedly true. As a consequence policies to reduce poverty should include several approaches. In addition to human investment there are needed welfare programs, elimination of job discrimination, and, perhaps most important of all, maintenance of high levels of employment.

Economists sometimes also look upon poverty as resulting from insufficient technological advance. Although the city is the seat of much scientific and technological progress, and overall standards of living consequently tend to rise, there remain people not as well endowed genetically or environmentally as others who will remain relatively poor. Thus the urban economist is concerned about whether the market system generates a highly unequal income distribution, leaving some urbanites in poverty and deprivation even as the economy is growing at a high rate. This unequal distribution then has a generational effect. Those who are poor, and their children, remain poor because they cannot invest in themselves as the rich can. Highly developed communication in cities tends to make great income differences unacceptable, forcing the political process to seek redistribution in order to help bring about reduction of the number of families in poverty.

These policies include primarily income support plans. In the United States these policies have historically been directed toward the "deserving" poor—i.e., the aged, the handicapped, children, etc., who are unable to work. Recently, however, as the poor have organized themselves into more powerful bargaining groups, they have argued that the distinction between deserving and undeserving poor is artificial. An adequate income becomes a right to which every citizen is entitled.

It remains to be seen whether this view will become accepted by a broader segment of society. Meanwhile, programs to assist workers who cannot find jobs continue to emphasize human resource development—i.e., improving the skills and health of potential participants in the labor market.[47]

In addition to income support and human resource development programs, there are programs to reduce discrimination in labor markets. Such programs are not only desired for purposes of social justice, but they cut across many of the aspects of labor markets already discussed. They can make labor markets work more efficiently, they have a particular effect

---

[47] Improved skills will be of little value in an economy which provides no market for these skills. The high unemployment rate among the young is particularly serious in this regard. For without job experience it becomes increasingly difficult for unemployed young people to compete on equal terms with their more fortunate, employed peers. For this reason there are a number of government programs designed to provide direct public employment to the young.

for the poor, they have an influence on an important component of the unemployed, and they enhance the value of human capital. It is to an analysis of the economics of racial discrimination that we turn next

Racial Discrimination

While discrimination is the essence of economics—people display their preferences by discriminating between goods—some types of discrimination pose special problems. One of particular concern to urban America is racial discrimination. It is an expression of taste on the part of a large group of people who prefer some characteristics similar to their own. What makes racial discrimination a particularly serious problem is that, being nonpreferred in the terminology of economics, racial minority-group members are frequently made to pay for the luxury of discriminating that is enjoyed by whites, although whites, too, pay for the privilege of associating with each other.

The seriousness of racial discrimination in the United States should not be underestimated. Its economic manifestations are in terms of employment and wages. For example, in the period October 1953 to October 1961 the average unemployment rates for white and nonwhite male wage and salary workers were 5 percent and 10.4 percent, respectively.[48] Not only has there been higher unemployment among nonwhites, but they long have been the first to be let go when a recession sets in.

Nonwhites have been discriminated against also in terms of earnings. Thus mean earnings of blacks in the United States were about 65 percent of those of whites in the late sixties.[49] Various theoretical efforts have been made at explaining the 35 percent lower mean wages for blacks.[50] These explanations have both supply and demand considerations. On the supply side, the noncompeting groups' argument has been advanced, i.e., that on the average the marginal productivity of black labor is lower than that of white. Partly this is because of differences in education, both quantitative and qualitative. Additionally, in terms of age distribution, blacks tend to be younger, and age is positively correlated with earnings.[51] Also, black women participate in the labor force at a higher rate than do white women. Furthermore, although the arguments have been advanced, there is little evidence for such propositions as that there are motivational differences due to cultural variations, and that blacks have a stronger tendency

[48] H. J. Gilman, "Economic Discrimination and Unemployment," *American Economic Review*, vol. 55 (December 1965), p. 1078.
[49] *Economic Report of the President* (Washington, D.C., February 1970), Table C-20, p. 200.
[50] Albert Wohlstetter and Sinclair Coleman, *Race Differences in Income*, R-578 OEO (Santa Monica, Calif.: The RAND Corporation, November 1970).
[51] This differential may be diminishing as the birth rate of blacks approaches that of whites.

to discount the future and, therefore, a lower propensity to invest in themselves. All these supply considerations apparently can at best explain 60 percent of the differences between white and nonwhite mean earnings.

Additional explanations are sought on the demand side, based on the proposition that whites act as though they dislike association with blacks by so much that they do not want to buy from them. Demand analysis of racial employment discrimination best starts with the employers' decisions and their effect on the demand for labor. Even on the assumption that there are no productivity differences between black and white workers, wage differences can be explained in terms of the "taste" of the employer. Thus we might look upon employers as acting to maximize a utility function that depends not only on profits but also on the number of white and black employees. *Ceteris paribus*, the employer has a negative marginal utility for black labor and a positive one for white labor.[52] Since the employer is rewarded through the positive marginal utility for white labor, he will hire white workers up to a point somewhat beyond where their marginal productivity equals their wage. Likewise, the hiring of black labor will stop at a point somewhat before their marginal productivity and wage are equated. Assuming the two types of workers to be perfect substitutes in production, i.e., their marginal productivities are equal and their common value depends only on the total number of workers of both races hired, then an equilibrium can result only when the wages of white workers are above the marginal product of labor and the wages of black workers below. Black workers are less well off, and white workers better off, than they would be under competitive conditions in the absence of discrimination. If entry of workers into jobs is controlled directly by unions with discriminatory attitudes toward blacks, as apparently is the case in the building trades, further discrimination can result, though more likely in unemployment than in wage differentials.[53]

[52] The following discussion is strongly influenced by a discussion with Kenneth J. Arrow of Harvard University and his Marshall Lectures at the University of Cambridge, England, Apr. 14–15, 1970 (Kenneth J. Arrow, *Some Models of Racial Discrimination in the Labor Market*, RM-6253-RC (Santa Monica, Calif.: The RAND Corporation, February 1971).
[53] Gwartney and McCaffree find that the extent of discrimination varies considerably among occupations. They summarize their empirical study as follows:

> In summary, there is persuasive evidence that the intensity of discrimination varies substantially among both major occupational groups as well as among intermediate occupations, both in terms of employment opportunity discrimination and on the basis of relative income ratios between nonwhites and whites. Sales and managerial occupations, some professions where consumer contact is important, and the major intermediate construction and metal crafts generally are areas of high discrimination. Among operatives, most clerical and service workers, especially the postal occupations and occupations somewhat remote from consumer contacts, employment discrimination and low income ratios are less likely to be found. In occupations which may serve a segregated

Kenneth Arrow points to three shortcomings of this type of analysis.[54] The theory neither gives quantitative clues nor provides great specificity. But, perhaps most important, many if not all of the effects of discrimination should disappear in the long run. "In the long run, the less discriminatory will either drive the more discriminatory out of business or, if not, will cause the wage difference to fall. If we suppose that there are some actual or potential employers who do not discriminate at all, then the wage difference should, in the long run, fall to zero."[55] Thus the question is raised of why discriminatory behavior would persist in the long run in spite of competitive pressures. Perhaps we should examine some of the assumptions usually associated with a long-run analysis. One of the major assumptions that Kenneth Arrow examines is that of adequate freedom of entry. There are a number of impediments facing black workers who seek employment, particularly in heretofore virtually all-white urban establishments. As Kenneth Arrow points out, the hiring of workers imposes transaction costs on firms. They are expected to make personnel investments. Furthermore, firing whites to make place for blacks is unlikely to be profitable to the firm that already has personnel capital sunk, the loss of which is not likely to be compensated by slightly lower wages for blacks than for whites. Personnel investments relate to costs incurred by firms in hiring new workers, in training them within the unique environment of the particular firm—a tooling-up cost—and the potential cost associated with firing should the new employee turn out to not meet expectations. Firing costs can be particularly high if unions or other volunteer associations intervene on behalf of the dismissed employee.

In the light of these transaction costs, blackness offers a visible and efficient signal. This signal is not necessarily always perfect and, indeed, often it might be entirely erroneous. However, it might turn out to be an efficient signal under three separate sets of circumstances. First, blackness and work capacity in the eyes of the employer are negatively correlated. Employers discriminate against blacks because they consider them inferior workers, and under such circumstances skin color is a cheap source of information. Second, employers might perceive blacks as having a negative effect on their white coworkers and (or) reduce the demand of whites for the company's output. Third, and this example has been given by Kenneth Arrow, the qualities of the black worker are not known to the employer beforehand.[56] In some respects the worker must make some investment in

clientele, such as teachers, clergymen, and some of the professions, employment discrimination is low but wage discrimination varies substantially.

James D. Gwartney and Kenneth M. McCaffree, "Variance in Discrimination among Occupations," *Southern Economic Journal*, vol. 38, no. 2 (October 1971).

[54] Arrow, op. cit., pp. 9–14.
[55] Ibid., p. 11.
[56] Ibid., p. 21.

himself without the employer knowing that it has been done. These are such subtle types as ". . . the habits of action and thought that favor good performance in skilled jobs, steadiness, punctuality, responsiveness, and initiative. A worker who has made the requisite investment will be said to be *qualified*."[57]

If we now return to the world of the 1930s in American cities, we find many companies without any black employees or with blacks only in menial positions. To this time about 70 percent of the small firms in Chicago have no black workers at all, even though 14 percent of the city's labor force is black. Thus, a virtually all-white firm can remain segregated white, become entirely segregated black, or add black workers to its present white working force. Shifts away from an all-white labor force have been induced in the late 1960s and early 1970s by an increased political power of blacks and the heightened social conscience of whites. But we can also expect nonconvexities in indifference functions in relation to urban minority employment which indicate that rapid and extreme shifts in labor force composition are called for.[58] Perhaps the high transactions costs indicated earlier, which are reduced by using blackness as a signal, can explain why discrimination has existed and extreme shifts from all-white to all-black labor forces have seldom occurred.[59]

There are indications that in the past highly educated blacks seeking higher-level jobs have been particularly heavily discriminated against. Part of the reason might be that the firm's personnel investment increases with job level. Thus a janitor can start within a few hours in a new facility and be as efficient as he was in the one that he cleaned before; while an executive in a corporation or a chemist in a research laboratory will require not only time of his own but also that of others to bring him to a level where he can efficiently discharge his responsibilities. If this is the case, and since cities are the places where upgrading of minorities is emphasized, we might find more discrimination there than we would otherwise expect.

Whatever the mechanism of racial discrimination, its consequences are far-reaching. They place a certain group in society at a disadvantage. That disadvantage is increased in the economic system of a city—but it also may be more amenable to change in cities. The disadvantage is increased as a result of the interdependence of actors and markets in the system. If a man receives less income as a result of being black, then his children

---

[57] Ibid.
[58] M. J. Farrell, "The Convexity Assumption in the Theory of Competitive Markets," *Journal of Political Economy*, vol. 67 (1959), pp. 377–379.
[59] A shift to a dominant black work force would be analogous to the "tipping" which occurs when housing becomes desegregated. Some such incidents have occurred, particularly in trade and service activities, for example, in employment in restaurants and as hospital orderlies.

are likely to receive less education as a result of their parent's smaller wealth; this is in addition to the difference in education that would result purely from the fact that they are black. The smaller educational attainment of the children will lead to expectation of less income, which is further reduced by the same discrimination which applied to their father.[60] A vicious circle or feedback loop is closed around people who are discriminated against in every activity by the majority of the society.

The characteristics proceeding from racial discrimination in a system as opposed to isolated, independent events are interesting. First, one can expect that the income difference resulting from the discriminating system is greater than that in the series of independent events. Second, the difference widens over time, requiring either greater efforts to hold the difference constant or diminishing volatility of the phenomenon. Finally, and most interesting, the system creates a situation which is capable—once direction is reversed, attitudes have changed, and information costs are lowered—of reducing income inequalities among the races more rapidly than in the series of isolated events.

We can conclude that while urban labor markets are perhaps the most important among all urban markets, economists, as we have seen, have been slow to analyze and learn to understand them. This holds both for theoretical and empirical inquiries—most likely a direct result of the complexities of these interrelated markets. However, it is our hope that we have indicated some directions in which further efforts may move.

---

[60] The expectation of discrimination lowers perceived rate of return to marginal investment and probably causes blacks to take less schooling than they otherwise would. Thus the gap will tend to widen, of its own accord.

CHAPTER 6
INTRODUCTION TO URBAN MACROECONOMIC ANALYSIS

I. *INTRODUCTION*

Aspects of Urban Macroeconomics

Macroeconomics is the study of the behavior of certain aggregate variables and groups of decision makers—households, business firms (or "industries"), and government(s). And the aggregate measures of economic activity are variables such as: consumption and investment expenditures, export sales and import purchases, governmental revenues and expenditures, production and employment of certain key commodities, and total economywide production, income, and employment. Macroeconomic analysis attempts to account for mutual interdependence between the aggregate groups of decision makers in order to capture the essential features of an interrelated economy, and in some respects is a more general method in contrast to the "partial" analysis often used in microeconomic analysis. However, in contrast to those of microeconomics, the methods of macroeconomics do not employ explicitly the concepts of utility maximization. Instead, hypotheses about the determinants of the major variables are tested, and these hypotheses take the form of various functional relations, for example, a consumption function, an investment function, an aggregate production function, and so on; and in fact a major portion of the work in macroeconomics has been the investigation of the significant theoretical and empirical determinants to be included in such relationships.

Urban macroeconomic analysis is particularly pertinent to problems of urban economic growth (or decline), economic stability, and urbanization. Economic change and growth as well as economic stability are viewed as resulting mainly from external forces or from the economic resources and structure of a particular economy. Urban macroeconomic analysis can also be applied to urbanization, the process by which a nation's population, production processes, and sociopolitical environment are transformed from a relatively even spatial distribution and an individualistic, labor-intensive organization to one of high density, high production-specialization, and close interdependence, together with a high level of technology, innovation, and entrepreneurship.

In preceding chapters we pointed to special characteristics of urban economies that must be considered in applying conventional microeconomic theory to urban problems. They are spatial characteristics, production specialization of urban economic actors and markets, and institutional characteristics of urban governments and their activities. These characteristics, together with some of their implications, must also be taken into consideration in developing urban macroeconomic models.

Whereas in microeconomics, spatial characteristics were viewed in the context of distance and proximity among markets and actors, in macroeconomics the important spatial concern is with the openness of the urban economy. This openness leads to interdependence between local and non-local markets. It is particularly in the production and marketing of goods—related to the area's comparative advantage—that we find interdependence and interrelatedness between local markets and markets in other metropolitan areas and the rest of the country. Most likely, primarily competing relations exist between industries in separate geographic markets, whereas complementary relationships are likely to prevail among interdependent markets within the same urban area. Specialization in a limited number of producing industries whose demand is exogenously determined is likely to produce instability in the urban economy.

In microeconomics, production specialization was viewed in the context of utility maximization, efficiency, and vulnerability of specific urban markets and key actors. In macroeconomics, concern is with the implications of specialization for urban growth, decline, and stability. One type of specialization refers to the fact that some cities will produce certain kinds of goods rather than others; which kinds is determined by comparative advantages of city resources and made possible by openness of the urban economy, as stated above.

A second type of specialization is concerned with the particular specialty of most urban areas, i.e., production and delivery of services that in many cases in cities have few if any alternative sources of supply and are extremely perishable. The importance of highly perishable services with relatively few substitutes, on whose supply so many households and firms depend, tends to make an urban economy sensitive, vulnerable, and unstable. Specialization and the resulting interdependence show up clearly also in the labor market. The more specialized the skills possessed by any particular worker, the more likely it is that the value of his wage in alternative employment is significantly less than in his specialization. If the demand for a specialized skill decreases in a recession, such specialization causes longer periods of unemployment and job search among the more specialized than among the less specialized urban workers. The reduced consumption expenditures of workers searching for employment will tend to continue for longer periods of time, affect the incomes of other workers in the city, and extend the recession. However, great specialization has also positive macroeconomic effects. Specialization, in conjunction with advanced technology, innovation, and entrepreneurship fostered in an urban environment, produces rapid economic growth and rising income levels.

A third characteristic relates to certain unique institutional issues. In the densely populated city, people can and need to join forces in seeking increasingly many services from their government. In microeconomics this was viewed in terms of the effect of and need for government intervention in specific markets. In macroeconomics it is viewed largely in terms of the increasing importance of government as a market, which can be seen in terms of state and local government employment as a percentage of civilian employment in the United States, which increased from 9.4 percent in 1960 to 11.6 percent in 1968 and is projected to reach 13.5 percent by 1975.[1]

A further institutional issue relates to the absence of overall planning and control over an urban economy as an entity. The governmental and physical environments of an urban economy produce an enormously complicated and yet unresponsive economic entity composed of a jumble of discrete parts, which most of the time are in total disarray. The urban economy has not been planned, and there is no one with power to make effective, comprehensive decisions about its various unorchestrated parts; governmental fragmentation and noncoterminous economic and political units further complicate matters. This absence of effective decision making for the entire urban economy has resulted in haphazard, piecemeal growth of its physical plant and economy, rather than growth by design. Imbalance and grave frictions are commonplace. The result tends to be retarded growth—possibly even a decline, such as we find in large downtown areas —inefficiencies in the growth process, and accentuation of income inequality.

Because of these and other important characteristics of urban economies, urban and national macroeconomic models tend to differ with respect to the variables included and the relative importance of the factors that influence the level of aggregate economic activity. For example, because an urban economy is part of the larger national economy, "the" interest rate, which is usually included as an important variable determined in a national model, is treated as exogenous in urban macroeconomic models. Clearly, the market in which the rate of interest (as a proxy for a set of market interest rates that influence investment and portfolio decisions) is determined is national in scope, mainly because of the high mobility of investable funds.

Another example is the price level, an endogenous variable in many national macroeconomic models. However, the analogous variable—the price level in a given metropolitan area—cannot be readily treated as

[1] National Planning Association, *Metropolitan Area Growth Patterns for the Coming Decade* (Washington, D.C.: National Planning Association, 1970), p. 7.

being determined within the urban area. Except for transportation costs, and to a lesser extent tastes, prices of goods tend to equality within a national area that has a single currency and high mobility of goods.

While some variables are excluded from urban models, other relationships, that are often assumed to be fixed in national models, are treated as endogenous in urban analysis. For example, the size of the labor force is often assumed to be exogenously determined in national models, resulting in a labor supply function, excluding interactions with economic conditions. However, the mobility of workers within a national area means that the size of the labor force in a given urban area should realistically be treated as endogenous; as the level of urban income and employment rises relative to other areas, it can be expected to induce new workers to migrate to the area.[2]

Other features of urban economies require a change in emphasis on the importance of various components of area income and aggregate demand. The urban area economy is much more open than the national economy; any single area, compared to the nation, will be more specialized in the types of some goods that it produces (especially those for which the market area is large), and hence will sell a larger part of its total output of goods to buyers outside the area. These "exports" are proportionately larger and therefore have greater influence on the level of income and employment in an urban economy than on the level in a large national economy.

Another aspect of the relative openness of the urban economy is the greater importance of two kinds of transfers in determining income. The proportion of the income earned by *residents* of an urban area that is earned outside that area will be greater than the proportion earned outside a national economy, because of the relatively greater mobility of funds, the common currency, and the common legal system within a national area. And a greater proportion of the income earned *within* an area will be paid to persons who reside outside the area, for similar reasons.

The relatively high degree of interdependence and interrelatedness of the components of an urban economy has implications for the importance of external influences on the urban economy. Because the various economic units within an area are highly interrelated, markets and individuals

---

[2] Workers' mobility cannot be expected to completely eliminate unemployment rate differences among urban areas in the United States. Not only do these adjustments take time, but also information and transportation costs are involved to overcome imperfections of the market. Furthermore, female workers, who are second breadwinners in the family, are unlikely to move if they lose their jobs unless their husbands are also unemployed. In any case, unemployment rate differences among urban areas tend to be larger in the downswing than in the upswing of the business cycle, particularly if in the recession all urban areas suffer from increased unemployment and, therefore, virtually no urban area offers major employment opportunities.

are especially sensitive to changes in other sectors. Because of the sensitivity of an urban economy, its vulnerability to external effects—such as changing purchase patterns and income levels in the areas to which it exports—is stressed by the use of so-called "impact analysis."

Urban Macroeconomic Indicators

Urban change is described in terms of the economic and demographic characteristics of the area, and to a different extent in terms of its political and social characteristics. These characteristics have three dimensions—depth (quality of the area's environment and ingenuity of its people), diversity of its economy, and scale of activities. It is these dimensions that will often determine the area's comparative advantage, its demands, its production, etc. The characteristics are both the result of previous urban change and the source of further change.

While it is clearly impossible to measure or indicate *all* of the relevant characteristics of a complex urban society, the several important variables that are usually included in a macroanalysis of an urban economy represent an attempt to focus on the major economic characteristics that influence the welfare of its residents. The single variable of primary importance is the level of income produced and distributed within the economy; and the focus on income at the urban level parallels the national interest in the level and rate of growth of income. While this measure has several obvious defects, it is generally used as an informal index of the "standard of living" of residents in the area, perhaps most useful for ordinal rather than cardinal comparisons. The second major variable, which is of course closely related to income, is the level of employment in the area's economy. And at the urban as at the national level, employment or, more usually, the rate of unemployment is considered a highly important measure. Another important variable, but one that is difficult to deal with analytically in a macro model, is the distribution of income, and even more specifically the distribution of income among various ethnic and racial groups.

Some types of expenditures are of interest as well; for example, the level of local government expenditures (in the aggregate as well as by function) and local government revenues provides information about the level of publicly provided services, and for many important goods or services (such as education and maintenance and construction of fixed investment in transportation equipment) the public sector is essentially the major supplier. Also, investment expenditures provide an indication of the growth of the "capital stock" of the area, which importantly influences its ability to grow in future periods. An important, essentially demographic, variable is the level of area population, and the related economic variable is the size of the area's labor force. And finally, the levels of output of certain goods and services in the area are useful indicators of the potential for growth and stability of the economy.

Economists' Concern about Urban Growth (and Decline)

While politicians inherently, and often blindly, tend to favor growth of output and employment, the attitudes of urbanites in general are less clear. Many urbanites, in their capacity as income earners, seem to prefer growth to decline, and yet, in their capacity as residents, they find that growth accentuates such urban ills as congestion, smog, and noise. Economists are interested in issues of urban growth, decline, and stability, since such phenomena affect the efficiency of resource allocation and income distribution. Specific questions are how differential **growth** rates affect comparative costs, location decisions, resource allocation efficiency, demand, differential unemployment of minorities, income distribution in general, and prevalence of poverty in particular.

Urban growth and decline have a variety of highly important side effects. Thus, for example, as long as urban economies grow, it is easier to deal with problems of discrimination and unemployment of minority groups, poverty, congestion, etc. While the need for welfare payments under such conditions grows less rapidly than it does under conditions of decline, rapid urban growth puts pressure on the infrastructure of the urban area, possibly in the short run reducing the availability of public services. Furthermore, a number of external diseconomies may be associated with rapid growth, e.g., congestion, different types of pollution, etc.

Urban economic change analysis involves the study of the processes of economic change within the urban environment and the relation between it and its own surroundings. Almost tautologically, urban economists are interested in growth and decline and stability questions because an urban area's future is determined by its growth or decline patterns. This process can be related to an area's comparative cost advantage, local market demand, and export demand. It might be visualized in the following manner —an urban area has a comparative advantage in the production of a specified good, implying that it earns economic rents. These above-average factor payments imply, in turn, increasing area growth because of higher wages and increased investment, limited by spillouts. Over time, a comparative advantage disappears, partly because of changing technology and the mobility of factors within the country. Detroit is an example of an urban area that once earned rents in the production of cars; but these rents have slowly dwindled away as the result of increased wages, changes in transportation costs that have allowed decentralization of assembly plants, increased foreign competition, etc.

It must be remembered that since urban areas are open economies, they are highly dependent on exports to generate local income and employment. At the same time, fiscal policy at the national level, as well as other national decisions, can directly affect the urban area in a major way.

II. *SOME CONCEPTS: FRAMEWORKS, THEORIES,*
AND MODELS

Before we attempt to propose ways to describe, analyze, project, and possibly plan urban macroeconomic change, it is useful to present a general point of view for systematically dealing with urban change concerns. With this purpose we will attempt to define some key concepts, suggest examples, and relate them to one another.

A framework of urban change is a collection of one or more theories or observed empirical relationships that permits articulation, orchestration, extrapolation, and (or) analysis of urban change. If it is a collection of theories, the framework has a theoretical base and specifies conceptually significant variables; if it is a collection of statistical calculating methods that give expression to observed empirical relationships, it has a statistical base.

A theory is a statement of causality or of relationships between certain variables within a logical framework, e.g., a consumption function, a demand equation, etc. Usually the specific theories are related to one another in either a causal or a simultaneous relationship. The specific theories included in a framework generally depend upon the perspective of those building the framework, an issue that will be discussed below.

A theoretical-base framework provides a logically coherent and general set of hypotheses that specify the conceptual significance of variables and the general form of their functional interrelationships. The virtuosity of the theorists, according to Ira S. Lowry, ". . . lies in rigorous logical derivation of interesting and empirically-relevant propositions from the most parsimonious set of postulates."[3]

The statistical-base frameworks will not ordinarily include well-defined and systematically related theories. Rather, they include some observed empirical relationships that for pragmatic reasons appear useful. They are methods of calculating.

Models, which are empirically implemented frameworks, can be used for planning, projecting, or descriptive purposes. The statistical-base frameworks cannot ordinarily be used for planning models. Thus we have the

[3] Ira S. Lowry, *A Short Course in Model Design*, T-3114 (Santa Monica, Calif.: The RAND Corporation, 1965), 28 pp.

following distinction between the use (model) and content (framework) sides of systematic analysis.

	Models		
Framework	Planning	Projection and Impact	Descriptive
Theoretical	X	X	X
Statistical		X	X

A theoretical-base or statistical-base framework is usually built up from some perspective about the major sources of urban change. At a broad level of aggregation, the causes of urban change can be thought of as originating primarily within the urban area or outside the area. Thus there are three perspectives: external, internal, and mixed external-internal. Perspectives on urban change could also be grouped in a different way, for example, economic forces versus social forces versus demographic forces, etc. We have followed the external-internal dichotomy because it helps to classify specific kinds of frameworks, as follows:

	Frameworks	
Perspective	Theoretical-Base	Statistical-Base
External	Export-Base	Allocation
Internal	Resource-Base	Extrapolation
Mixed	Input-Output	
	Income-Expenditure	Shift and Shares

Here are some brief introductory views of these frameworks:

The export-base framework says that local activity is a function of export demand via a multiplier process. The resource-base framework says that local activity is a function of local factor inputs in the area and their comparative advantage to other areas. The input-output framework says that local activity is dependent on various expenditure, demand, supply, and income equations. However, the emphasis is on the producing (or intermediate-sector) actors.

The income-expenditure framework also says that local activity is a function of various expenditure, demand, supply, and income equations relating to both the local and the external areas. Usually the emphasis is on final demand actors in the economy.

The ratio extrapolation or allocation framework says that a local activity is some share of the comparable national activity. The single-variable extrapolation framework says that a local activity is some function of past changes in the activity, or of past changes in the relationship of that activity to some other activity. The shift and shares framework says that local activity is a function of three components: the change in the national activity, the change in the comparative advantage which the local area has in that activity, and the particular mix of industries in the area.

It should be noted that even those frameworks that have been uniquely related to either external or internal perspectives really have elements of both, i.e., they are mixed. However, we have identified their major perspectives.

A model explicitly details exact functional forms about the more generally stated structural relations within the framework.[4] Thus, the model permits translation of theories in a theoretical-base framework to a concrete case, so that empirically relevant output is generated from empirically based input. Consequently, the model is explicit, where the theory and framework can be vague, compromising between objectives, data availability and quality, costs, and timeliness. While the pure theorist is often satisfied with such general forms as

$$V = f(UVXZ\ldots),$$

the model builder must specify the exact functional forms of the structural relations, e.g.,

$$Y = \log U + a(V - X) - Z^b$$

and ultimately he must fit his variables Y, U, V, X, Z and parameters a, b from empirical sources.[5]

According to Lowry, the model builder, even if he has high appreciation of "theory," usually is forced to build a model ". . . likely to reflect its theoretical origins only in oblique and approximate ways. Mechanisms that work, however mysteriously, come to be substituted for those whose virtue lies in theoretical elegance."[6] In this sense then, also, statistical-base frameworks can be translated into models that detail exact functional forms, although such forms usually do not have a theoretical foundation.

Both frameworks and models can have four major objectives—description, projection, impact analysis, and planning. Therefore, we can distinguish between descriptive, projection, impact, and planning models, being perhaps least interested in descriptive models.

Descriptive urban change models merely attempt to replicate relevant features of the urban change process as it has taken place in the past. Their main use is that they can reveal systematic details of the urban change process by reducing its overt complexity to statements about co-relationships among important aspects of the urban scene. Under the most optimistic circumstances, they might have some applicability to times and

---

[4] Ibid., pp. 7–8.
[5] Ibid., p. 8.
[6] Ibid., p. 7.

places other than those for which the models were originally constructed and supplied.

Projection models are designed to provide information about the future. Unlike descriptive models, which merely need to indicate covariation among variables, projection models must specify these in the form of rigorous and internally consistent mathematical relationships and usually specify change-causing factors by postulating direction and nature of causation, and knowing the future value of the cause makes possible projection of the future value of the effect. Thus projection models translate a logical framework within which some variables stand at the end and others at the beginning of the causal sequence. The latter are introduced into the model on the assumption that they can be plausibly and reliably evaluated as far into the future as may be necessary.[7] In the most general terms, a projection model seeks to identify most probable values or ranges of values for specific outputs, i.e., levels of indicators at some specified future time, with these outputs depending on policy assumptions regarding the causal variables to which the builder has assigned a high probability to be met in the future.

A particular type of projection model is of the conditional variety. This model explicitly stipulates conditions, including some possible but uncertain event outside one's control. One particular conditional projection model involves impact analysis where the focus is on the consequences that can be projected to result from a specified exogenous impact, assuming that other conditions do not change.

Planning models are the most ambitious, difficult, and, so far, least developed. Their purpose is to help choose between either alternative programs or alternative outcomes, i.e., levels of economic and social indicators. A planning model incorporates conditional projection methods but in addition provides for the evaluation of outcomes in terms of specified goals. Lowry has described the following essential steps:

> 1. specification of alternative programs or actions that might be chosen by the planner; 2. prediction of the consequences of choosing each alternative; 3. scoring these consequences according to a metric of goal-achievement; and 4. choosing the alternative which yields the highest score.[8]

III   URBAN CHANGE PERSPECTIVES

The complexities and richness of the real world can never be reproduced in an analytic framework. Rather, the analyst must seek to simplify. He must exclude detail that becomes too cumbersome to manage. But more importantly, he tries to identify underlying principles that can explain a wide variety of observable phenomena.

[7] Ibid., p. 4.
[8] Ibid., p. 5.

Different social scientists try to find these underlying principles in different places. The urban political scientist might look at governmental structure or the interplay among power groups in the city; the urban sociologist might look at community attitudes; the urban geographer might look at the spatial distribution of people and structure; the urban psychologist might look at the stresses created by urban living.

Each of these views is appropriate and can add to understanding of urban living and urban change. It is desirable that the economist be aware of these viewpoints, even though he must necessarily be concerned with urban markets and their consequences for urban living. But even as he looks at urban markets—their trade, their location, their production—the economist must establish a perspective that will allow simplification of analysis and exposition of market activities. Analyses of individual markets, i.e., microanalyses, is one perspective; analyses of the interrelatedness among markets and their consequences for the city as a whole, i.e., macroanalyses, is a second perspective. Both are required for a proper understanding of the economics of cities.

Urban macroanalyses generally seek to explain change in (*a*) the quantity and quality of factor inputs in the area, (*b*) the returns to factor inputs and nonfactor returns that comprise area income and its distribution, (*c*) the area's production (or supply) of goods and services, in the aggregate or by specific sectors, and (*d*) the area's demand (or expenditures) for goods and services, in the aggregate or by specific sectors. Macroanalytic frameworks, however, tend to have differing perspectives on the causes of urban change, including concern with where change is initiated and what is the relative importance of the major classes of change determinants. This is simply another way of saying that there are no completely general analytic frameworks, and that the perspective implicit in each framework indicates how the real world is being simplified for analytic purposes.

One perspective on change occurring within a specific urban place is to identify forces within the city as being the major source of change. This is the internal perspective. The external perspective identifies forces that originate outside the city as being the major source of change.

From the internal perspective, local growth, decline, and short-term instability are conceived of as primarily fueled by conditions prevailing inside urban areas—the environment they offer households and firms, together with the resulting industry mix and its feedbacks. In the resource-base framework, the city is seen as if it were a plant assembling resources to provide goods, services, and opportunities to its residents. Just as a plant has an implicit (and changing) production function, so does a city —an infinitely more complicated production function because of the variety of outputs the city produces and of the resources it requires. To the extent that a given urban area at a moment offers a particular set of conditions, i.e., a particular production function that gives it comparative advantage in the eyes of local and nonlocal consumers and producers, the local population (and labor force) and industry production and plant investment will undergo changes. For example, Wilbur Thompson argues that conditions will change in a given urban area as a result of the creativity of local universities and research organizations; ingenuity and entrepreneurship of financial institutions and leaders of industry, commerce, and government; quality of government in the broadest sense; and quality of physical, aesthetic, and cultural environment efforts. This is the *depth* of the urban area's environment (whereas the area's diversity of its economy is its breadth).[9] These are, perhaps, the critical elements in a city's production function, requiring descriptions of factor inputs that are much richer than the customary ones, of land, labor, and capital.

In any case, urban areas are the seat of innovation and invention that power the nation's progress. This is so not merely because today most of America is urban, but because the proximity of creative people in an exciting setting produces the ferment that modifies the old and produces the new. All this can change the comparative advantage of the given urban area, which in turn alters its attractiveness to potential inmigrants, purchasers inside and outside the area, and new plant investment, bringing about further change in the implicit production function for the city.

The complexity of a city makes the development of an explicit aggregate production function very difficult. As a consequence, the statistical-base extrapolation framework is often used to predict a city's activities by assuming, in effect, that the internal forces will be changing roughly as they have in the past.

From the external perspective, local growth, decline, and short-term instability are conceived of as being primarily fueled by conditions prevailing outside a specific urban area. In the export-base framework, the city is seen as if it were a firm responding to a variety of market forces, in competition with other cities. Thus the export-base framework perceives local growth, decline, and short-term instability as being fueled primarily by what happens to the city's export markets. As these markets change, they influence levels of activity and industry mix in the city, bringing about changes in local markets, labor supply, investment, public services, and so forth; all of which, in turn, affect the city's comparative advantage and therefore its further ability to sell in export markets.

Household, business, and government export markets are not the only external forces that bring about change in the local area. Federal government regulatory, monetary, and fiscal actions have important consequences for local areas, often having differential effects on different areas because

[9] Wilbur R. Thompson, "Internal and External Factors in the Development of Urban Economies," in Harvey S. Perloff and Lowdon Wingo, Jr. (eds.), *Issues in Urban Economics* (Baltimore: Johns Hopkins, 1968), p. 53.

of their unique industry mixes. From the external perspective, changes in technology and tastes are seen as nationwide phenomena that are external to any specific area. These changes are then diffused to specific places through a process of communication, evaluation, and adaptation; however, the rate of diffusion will vary among areas, depending on their capacity and willingness to adapt. Even demographic phenomena such as changes in fertility rate and propensity to migrate can be viewed as nationwide forces, having their basis in nationwide economic and social conditions and therefore external to a specific area. The theoretical basis for estimating diffusion rates of nationwide forces is very weak. As a consequence, the statistical-base allocation framework is often utilized to predict a local area's activities from the perspective of the local consequences of external forces.

Both the external and the internal perspectives are important in explaining urban change. When a theoretical framework emphasizes the external perspective, it does so not because of the irrelevance of internal forces but because the simplification seems warranted that these internal forces will respond in some determinable fashion to export changes—which is often the case for short-term growth and stability analyses. Similarly, when a theoretical framework emphasizes the internal perspective, it is simplifying by assuming that external markets will respond to the comparative advantage resulting from change in internal forces—which is often a valid simplification for longer-term growth and decline analyses.

But because internal and external forces interact with each other, the more powerful theoretical and statistical frameworks are those that incorporate both perspectives. These mixed-perspective frameworks seek not only to include both internal and external forces as causes of change but additionally try to include interactions among local resources, local income, local demand, and local production as change-fostering factors. Input-output frameworks accomplish this by analysis of both internal and external final demand markets and their consequences for the production and purchase activities of specific sectors in the local economy—a framework particularly suited for relatively short- or medium-term growth decline and stability analyses but often misused for long-term analyses. The income-expenditure frameworks also consider both internal and external forces, in the system of simultaneous, or sometimes sequential, equations that spell out the relations among internal and external households, industry, and governments that lead to changes in income, employment, and economic activity in the city.

Some of the urban macroeconomic issues will be taken up in the next three chapters. First, the more significant frameworks will be investigated, to be followed by an analysis of their application in a variety of urban macroeconomic models. Finally, the truly long-run issue of the economics of urbanization will be examined.

CHAPTER 7

FRAMEWORKS OF URBAN MACROECONOMIC ANALYSIS

I. INTRODUCTION

The techniques of urban macroeconomics are similar to the aggregate analyses applied to national economies, and the logic inherent in such frameworks as input-output or income-expenditure is applicable to any economy, regardless of its geographical dimensions or political boundaries. Basic frameworks presented here serve to provide both a description of the important aggregate relationships in the urban economy and the basis for empirical models useful for planners and governmental decision makers.

The export-base frameworks will be examined in the next section. In determining levels of income, employment, and output, emphasis is on the importance of events external to the area itself. It will be followed by a discussion of the urban input-output framework, which in many respects is a more detailed form of economic-base analysis and includes consideration not only of export markets but of the local area's resource base as well. Of a distinctly separate type, the development of which is relatively recent, are multiple-equation, essentially econometric, frameworks that emphasize variables different from either export-base or input-output, but from a mixed external-internal perspective. They are taken up in section IV. Resource-based frameworks, which have primarily an internal perspective, are discussed in section V. Finally, we turn to primarily statistical frameworks—single-variable extrapolation, ratio extrapolation, and shift and share analysis—in section VI.

II. EXPORT-BASE FRAMEWORKS

A major characteristic of most urban areas is that a significant portion of their production is sold in markets outside these areas. Ordinarily, a particular urban area will have little influence on the demand in these export markets. The urban area's exports can therefore be viewed as being exogenously determined. Frameworks that directly relate the income, employment, and production of an urban area to the area's exports are identified as export-base frameworks. The economic process implicit in the underlying export-base framework is that sales to buyers outside the area generate labor and business earnings, some of which are spent on additional purchases of locally produced goods and services and thereby generate still more employment income and production within the area. This process can be summarized in the form of a functional relationship called a "multiplier" that relates the level of the urban area's total activity to its export activity. There are two types of export-base frameworks, one of which is highly aggregative and combines all industries into a single aggregate and then relates total employment to total exports. The other formulation is more detailed and separately identifies the major industries and calculates multipliers for each. These two types of frameworks are very similar, except for the level of aggregation; the discussion in this chapter emphasizes the aggregated framework, and the discussion in Chapter 8 focuses on the more detailed formulation that is often used in impact analysis.

The aggregate export-base frameworks are used to characterize the relationship of total economic activity to exports for the urban area as a whole. Two production sectors are identified: the "nonlocal" sector includes those industries and firms that sell to markets located outside the geographic boundaries of the urban area; the "local" sector sells to markets located within the geographic boundaries of the urban area.[1]

Although a clear, conceptual distinction can be drawn between the local and nonlocal sectors, it may be very difficult to identify these sectors in a given urban area. Whether specific goods and services are exported or are sold locally depends on the characteristics of the items, the marketing practices of the producing firms, and the relationship between the capacity to produce an item and the demand for that item in the area. For example, manufactured or processed goods for which transportation costs are not too high and which are not perishable tend to be exported. However, not all such goods will be exported, because some firms will sell such items in local markets; and, indeed, an area is likely to simultaneously import and export the same kinds of items because of particular marketing patterns that evolve. Services, and some kinds of processed goods, will tend to fall within the local sector because proximity between consumers and producers is preferred; but an area with a large service capacity might also export a significant quantity of services to nonlocal markets. In general, areas will tend to specialize in the production of those items in which they have a "comparative advantage"; these are the items that are exported, and the revenue from such items will pay for the area's imports over the long run. An area's comparative advantage may arise from a

---

[1] In other writings on the export base, these two types of production are called "primary and secondary" or "basic and service," reflecting the emphasis on the "nonlocal" sector as basic to the determination of the level of area income. Since there is considerable debate as to which sector is "more important" for growth and stability of the economy, we denote the two sectors here by more neutral terms.

number of factors, including natural resources, human skills, entrepreneurial talent, locational aspects, efficient plants, etc.[2]

Only a few of the items that are produced in an urban area can be readily identified as being sold either in local markets or in nonlocal markets. Most items are sold in both markets, and the portions tend to change. Market surveys are the most reliable means for identifying the local and nonlocal sectors of an urban area. However, such surveys are time-consuming and costly, so that approximating techniques have been devised. Location quotients, for example, are used to identify an area's exports. A location coefficient is defined as the ratio between the proportion of an area's total employment that is in a specific industry and the proportion of total national employment in that industry.[3] If this ratio is greater than 1, i.e., if the area's proportion is greater than the national proportion, then the implication is that the area is exporting a part of its production of the item. The quantity of the item which is exported is calculated by multiplying the area's production of the item by the share of the area's employment on that item which is assigned to the nonlocal sector.[4]

This method of determining exports assumes that an area will be neither an exporter nor an importer of an item if the proportion of its total employment allocated to that item is the same as the national proportion. This assumption is reasonable only if consumer tastes, the industry mix, and the production function for each industry in the area are all similar to the national average. In order to relax these assumptions and to make the estimates more reasonable and accurate, this approach can be

---

[2] The analysis of elements that influence the location of particular types of production is discussed in Chap. 2.

[3] The location quotient for industry i in a specific area, lq_i, can be expressed as follows:

$$lq_i = \frac{\dfrac{A_i}{A_T}}{\dfrac{N_i}{N_T}} \tag{7.1}$$

where
   A_i = area employment in the production of good i
   A_T = total area employment
   N_i = the national employment in the production of good i
   N_T = total national employment.

[4] The proportion of output of good i that is assigned to the nonlocal sector, i.e., considered as exported, is derived in the following manner: The employment in production of good i that can be considered as nonlocal, NL_i, is given by

$$NL_i = A_T \frac{N_i}{N_T}(lq_i - 1) \quad \text{or} \tag{7.2}$$

$$NL_i = A_i - A_T \left(\frac{N_i}{N_T}\right) \tag{7.3}$$

Then the ratio of nonlocal employment in good i to the area's employment in production of good i is the proportion of output of i that is considered as being exported; that is,

$$\text{Exports of good } i = \frac{NL_i}{A_i} \times \left(\begin{array}{l}\text{area output of}\\\text{good } i\end{array}\right) \tag{7.4}$$

modified. Rather than comparing a particular area to the national economy, we can compare it to a group of economies, e.g., other urban areas of similar size, with more nearly equivalent compositions of consumer tastes, industrial mix, and production techniques. Then, assuming that the one area or economy in this group that has the smallest industry employment share in the production of a given good is neither an exporter nor an importer of the good, the production implied by this employment share reflects only the consumption requirements of residents. This smallest employment share or ratio is called the "minimum requirements" ratio. And an area's exports can then be estimated using equations 7.2 and 7.4 but substituting the minimum requirements ratio for the denominator in the location quotient.

Many items are purchased not only by final consumers but also as inputs in the production process. Therefore, a relatively large location coefficient may reflect not exports from an area, but rather sales to other industries in the area that require the item in their production. Such interindustry, intra-area sales are included in the local sector. Identification of such sales requires specification of the pattern of the interindustry transactions that measure the sales of intermediate goods from one industry to another. With such information, the extent to which production is local or nonlocal can be calculated by a method called "linking." Linking accounts for the fact that, while all production of industry A may be exported, if industry B produces inputs used by A, then part of the production of B should be considered as nonlocal. However, this idea extends to linkages that are more indirect if industry C sells part of its output to B; then logically parts of C's production (and therefore employment and income) should be considered as nonlocal. If B sells 30 percent of its output to A, and if C sells 20 percent of its output to B, then a first step in the linking would show 20 percent $\times$ 30 percent $=$ 6 percent of the output of C classified as nonlocal, and so on to more and more indirect linkages. By specification of the pattern of interindustry sales that, as pointed out above, measure the sales of intermediate goods from one industry to another, the linkage calculation completely classifies all output in the area as local or nonlocal.

The earliest export-base formulations models utilized employment as the measure of an area's economic activity.[5] In part, this reflected a con-

[5] For a detailed discussion of early forms of export base, see Ralph W. Pfouts (ed.), *The Techniques of Urban Economic Analysis* (West Trenton, N.J.: Chandler-Davis, 1960). For an example of a framework using employment as a measure, see G. Hildebrand and A. Mace, "The Employment Multiplier in an Expanding Industrial Market: Los Angeles County, 1940–1947," *Review of Economics and Statistics*, vol. 33 (August 1950), pp. 241–249. A useful overview of the development of export-base frameworks is contained in Theodore Lane, "The Urban Base Multiplier: An Evaluation of the State of the Art," *Land Economics*, vol. 42, no. 3 (August 1966), pp. 339–347.

cern with employment as a policy variable; but primarily it reflected the fact that data on employment were more readily available than data on income in subnational areas. More recent export-base frameworks have used income or value added as a measure of the urban economy; they appear quite similar in this and other respects to macroeconomic analysis of national economics.[6]

In employment terms, the simplest form of export base asserts a stable relationship between the area's total employment and the number of jobs in the nonlocal sector. In this formulation, a certain number of jobs in the local sector are viewed as "supported by" or associated with each job in the nonlocal sector. Then, if the number of nonlocal-sector jobs changes, there will be a corresponding change in the employment in the local sector and therefore in total employment in the area's economy. The dependence of jobs in the local sector on employment in the nonlocal sector is explained by the fact that nonlocal-sector employment generates income for local residents which is spent on goods and services that generate local-sector employment.

The assumed stability of the ratio of local to nonlocal employment is the basis for the definition of the employment "multiplier" that summarizes the export-base framework. In incremental form, the change in total employment is determined as the product of the change in nonlocal empolyment and the employment multiplier; that is,

$$(7.5)$$

$$\text{Change in total employment} = \left(1 + \frac{\text{local employment}}{\text{nonlocal employment}}\right) \times \frac{\text{change in nonlocal}}{\text{employment}}$$

where $\left(1 + \frac{\text{local employment}}{\text{nonlocal employment}}\right)$ is the multiplier.

In this form, the export-base approach is open to strong criticism, because of its failure to specify the internal relationships at work in an area's economy. More recent approaches have presented a more detailed view of the determination of the levels of economic activity.[7] However, the above form does illustrate an emphasis on viewing the economy as being comprised of an endogenous sector (local) that responds to external changes transmitted by an exogenous sector (nonlocal).

Changing the unit of measurement of economic activity from employment to income produces a framework that is very similar to the familiar Keynesian analysis of income determination. The reasoning inherent in

[6] The value-added approach is illustrated in C. L. Leven's study of Sioux City, *Economic Report* (Sioux City, Iowa: City Planning Commission, 1959).
[7] The finding that the local/nonlocal ratio is not at all stable over time has discredited the simple framework as a method for empirical studies. For a discussion of more recent models, see C. M. Tiebout, *The Community Economic Base Study*, Supplementary Paper no. 16 (New York: Committee for Economic Development, 1962).

this form of the export-base framework is as follows. Some of the revenue from the production of goods sold outside the area is paid to residents of the area in the form of wages, salaries, dividends, and so on.[8] Total spending by residents who receive income from the nonlocal sales depends upon the level of their incomes. That part of their spending which is for locally produced goods and services generates income for residents working in the local sector, which causes further rounds of expenditures and income generation.[9]

This process can be summarized by the community- or economic-base multiplier, which shows the dependence of area income upon income earned in the nonlocal sector. The multiplier is defined by the ratio of the area's total income to the income earned in its nonlocal sector.[10] The size of the multiplier indicates the "sensitivity" of income in the area to changes in external economic conditions that influence the level of exports. The multiplier is determined by the propensity to consume and the complement of the propensity to import.[11]

The income formulation of an export-base framework can be expanded to explicitly include the effects of types of expenditures other than consumption and exports. Introducing investment and government expenditures also allows for the specification of a short-run and a long-run form-

---

[8] Income transfers to the area's residents from sources outside the area, such as dividend income earned from investments outside the area, are considered as income earned in the nonlocal sector. Transfers of income earned in the area to residents of other areas are considered as included in the nonlocal portion of consumption spending by households. Alternatively, we can assume that income earned in the area is equal to income received in the area; the distinction is not significant in this simple framework.

[9] This reasoning may be summarized in the following equations:

$$Z = C(Z)d + E, \quad \text{and} \qquad (7.6)$$
$$C(Z) = bZ$$

where

$Z =$ level of area income
$E =$ level of income earned in the nonlocal sector
$C(Z)d =$ income earned in local sector
$C(Z) =$ total income generated by local residents' purchases
$b =$ propensity to consume out of income

But purchases of goods imported from the rest of the world—any place outside the area—do not create income for residents. Therefore d is a coefficient representing that proportion of total purchases of residents which is produced by the local sector. Investment and government expenditures have been suppressed for convenience of exposition, and therefore this is a "households only" framework. A more disaggregated export-base framework that incorporates investment and government expenditures is presented in the final part of this section. Z is used for income in contrast to the usual Y to avoid notational confusion between this section and the following.

[10] More formally, the multiplier is defined as:

$$Z = \frac{1}{1 - bd} E \quad \text{or} \quad Z = kE \qquad (7.7)$$

[11] In a formal sense the economic-base multiplier is exactly analogous to the typical Keynesian multiplier.

ulation. In such a framework, investment expenditures by businesses in a given area, *I*, are in the short run assumed to be independent of the level of area income. However, in the long run it is the level of economic activity in the urban area, measured by income, that influences firms' decisions to invest.

Similar reasoning applies to the level of local[12] government expenditures, *G*. In the short run, such government expenditures are not influenced by the level of or changes in the area's income; but in the long run the capital outlays on sewers, schools, etc., as well as current expenditures on fire, police, and other services, will increase with the growth of the economy and are therefore related to the income level of the urban area.[13]

However, in the longer run, when investment and government expenditures are considered responsive to income levels, the respective propensities to invest, *h*, and of government to spend, *j*, must be taken into consideration. Additionally, allowance must be made for the fact that the proportion of investment and government spending that creates area income may differ from the proportion of consumption expenditures that creates area income. These proportions may also be expected to differ from each other, since business investment may require products produced outside the area (imports), while government expenditures or services include a high proportion of wages and salaries paid to local residents.[14]

Problems With Export-base Analysis

These frameworks illustrate the elements of export-base methods. Although there are more detailed and disaggregated frameworks that use the export-base reasoning,[15] all such frameworks have common problems. The discus-

[12] In this section "local" government indicates those governmental units, e.g., city, district, and county, that are contained within the geographic area of the city; "local" here should not be confused with the "local," "nonlocal" distinction used earlier.
[13] Then, in the short run, the export-base formulation may be expressed as:

$$Z = \frac{1}{1 - bd}(E + I + G) \qquad (7.8)$$

since investment and government expenditures, along with exports, do not respond to income.
[14] In the long run, the export-base framework is formulated as:

$$Z = \frac{1}{1 - (bd + hk + jg)} E \qquad (7.9)$$

where *k* is the proportion of investment expenditures that creates income in the urban area and *g* is the proportion of government expenditures that creates income in the area. For an extended export-base framework of the form of 7.8 and 7.9 that uses seven types of expenditures—private exports, exports to the federal government, local housing investment, local business investment, local government investment, local government current operations, and consumption—see W. Lee Hansen and Charles Tiebout, "An Intersectoral Flows Analysis of the California Economy," *Review of Economics and Statistics*, vol. 45, no. 4 (November 1963), pp. 409–418. This model is an example of the use of a "linking" procedure as discussed above, using employment as the unit of measurement.
[15] For example, Hansen and Tiebout, op. cit.

sion of the simple framework makes clear that the important assumptions are the following: (1) the propensity to consume or the consumption-income ratio is a relatively stable relationship, (2) the proportion of consumption spending that creates local income is also relatively stable, and (3) there are no changes in income associated with anything other than the changes in sales outside the area, i.e., changes in the local sector are determined only by changes in the level of exports.[16] Each of these three assumptions reduces the efficacy of analyses using the export-base framework.[17]

Some of the difficulties with the simple income-consumption relation for an urban area are also experienced with a national consumption function. For example, there are other important variables, such as previous levels of income and wealth, that influence consumption spending, and a simple relationship that excludes and fails to take account of the effects of these variables will be unstable with respect to income. Also, the usefulness of a single relation to represent the spending of a collection of individuals and households, that can be expected to differ widely in their tastes, ignores questions of the distribution of income.

The relatively greater mobility of workers, among urban areas as compared with mobility among national economies, means that an increase in area income tends to be accompanied by a relatively larger increase in area than in national population. An increase in area income accompanied by population growth can be expected to result in a consumption-income ratio different from that in the case of no population change and a rise in per capita income.[18]

The stability of the proportion of consumption spending that creates local income is questionable, because the mix of goods produced within the area can be expected to change as income and population change. For example, as incomes rise, items purchased by consumers tend to shift toward those which tend to be produced locally, such as services. Furthermore, for many goods there exists a "threshold" level of demand, such that if as a result of population and income increases demand rises to this level, the local production of such goods becomes profitable. As a consequence goods that were previously "imported" are supplied by the local

[16] Other implicit assumptions are that all goods are elastic in supply, so that all values can be considered as measured in real terms, and that there are no changes in relative prices.

[17] The corresponding assumptions required in the framework of equation 7.9, about the propensity to invest, the propensity of local government to spend, and the proportions of investment and government expenditures that create income for residents of the area, likewise pose problems for export-base analysis.

[18] However, the impossibility of showing analytically the different effects on the consumption-income ratio under the two cases, even with highly restrictive assumptions about the form of individual consumption functions, is one form of the "aggregation problem" in economics. See John A. Green, *Aggregation in Economic Analysis* (Princeton, N.J.: Princeton, 1964).

sector.[19] This implies that over time the proportion of consumption that creates local income tends to rise, causing the export-base multiplier to rise.

The strong assumption that growth in the local sector is induced only by changes in export earnings denies the possibility of growth-inducing autonomous changes within the urban economy. For example, productivity changes within the local sector could cause growth in this sector, without stimulus from exports. Or local government expenditures might also induce local-sector growth, without export changes. Or improvements in local services or local infrastructure might attract population and industry, which induces a change in exports; that is, the economic base of the area is found in the local rather than in the nonlocal sector.

The assumptions implicit in the export-base framework are quite unrealistic, so that it conveys very little about the behavior of decision units or the economic processes within the urban economy. At best, the framework permits the approximation of levels of economic activity over the short run, during which the distribution of income, the industry mix, and the production techniques used in the urban area are not subject to substantial change. In the hope of reducing some of the conceptual difficulties, we will turn next to the input-output framework.

III.   *INPUT-OUTPUT FRAMEWORK*

An urban economy is an agglomerate of numerous economic actors and markets packed into a densely populated geographic area and with a large number of complex and intimate interrelationships between its own markets and with markets outside its boundaries. Urban macroeconomics is concerned with how these interrelationships influence the levels and mix of area output and employment, the level and distribution of area income, and the rate and stability of area growth. Analysis of such issues requires a framework embodying greater detail of economic actors, i.e., industries, than is ordinarily incorporated in export-base analysis. An urban input-output framework, with its capability for describing detailed transactions among economic units, is especially well suited to the analysis of urban economies.

In contrast to the economic-base approach, input-output or, as it is sometimes called, interindustry economics, takes a more disaggregated perspective in investigating the level and mix of economic activity in an urban economy. Essentially, input-output is a method of tracing and using information about the transactions between buyers and sellers. Sales of so-called intermediate goods from one producer to another, sales from producers to final consumers, as well as sales of primary inputs such as labor

[19] These are sometimes called "import substitutes."

services from households to the producing sectors are recorded and combined by a procedure that provides a variety of types of important economic measures. The input-output framework requires more and different types of information about a particular urban area than does export-base, and the resultant information provided by the procedure is of a much higher level of detail and usefulness.

The Accounting Description

Input-output is, at one level, a theoretical framework with a set of assumptions, well-defined mathematical properties, and close relation to the general equilibrium models of Walras and Cassel. At another level, the technique can be considered as empirical implementation of a special sort of general equilibrium analysis, in which restrictions on the data available and simplifying assumptions convert the technique to a relatively highly disaggregated economic accounting and forecasting tool. It is from this latter perspective that the framework is useful for macroeconomic questions of stability and growth of an urban economy and the effects of urbanization.

The most disaggregated unit in input-output analysis is a "sector," and it is relationships between sectors, and between sector outputs, with which the input-output framework is primarily concerned. In the theoretical formulation of input-output, an interindustry sector is analogous to the microeconomic concept of an "industry," ideally a group of firms producing a single homogeneous output, with highly similar production and cost functions. However, in applying input-output, several compromises are required in this definition, because of the great variety of outputs produced by an industry and differing production techniques used to produce any given product. Even such a relatively finely defined product as writing paper has associated with it a whole array of distinctly different products, and presumably a large group of producers using different technologies in production. But if the number of sectors is to be kept within reasonable bounds, because of considerations of data collection and computation, an application of input-output analysis cannot treat in fine detail every possible good produced in an urban economy. The procedure adopted to keep the number of sectors small enough to be manageable and yet to provide a useful level of detail in the final calculations is to aggregate into a single sector all producers of outputs that can be considered "fairly well" related to each other. As an example, the producers of writing paper might be grouped together with producers of newsprint, cardboard, and all sorts of paper products into a sector called "Paper and Allied Products." Industry classification systems are available that can describe the mix of output of a metropolitan area in terms of industry classification systems.[20]

[20] The most frequently used classification system is the Standard Industrial Classification (SIC) developed by the U.S. Bureau of the Budget.

The empirical basis of input-output analysis is the transactions table or matrix that shows the dollar value of sales and purchases made (1) among interindustry or so-called "endogenous sectors," and (2) between producing sectors and the "final users" of output, including households, government and business investment.

The input-output transactions table or matrix is a double-entry accounting system recording the purchases and sales made by each sector during some specific time interval, ordinarily a year. Each sector in the matrix is shown as a row and as a column; the row entries show the sales by each sector to each other sector, while the column entries show each sector's purchases from each other sector. Thus, each cell entry records simultaneously a purchase by the column sector and a sale by the row sector; a sector's sales include not only its sales to each of the other producing or "intermediate sectors," but also its sales to "final users," ordinarily including households, government, business investment, and net exports. Similarly, a sector's purchases include not only its purchases of goods and services from other producing sectors but also its purchases of primary inputs, ordinarily including labor payments, taxes and other government charges, depreciation, and business profits. By definition, the values of a sector's total sales, total purchases, and total output are all equal. The value of all final users' purchases, in a national table, is equal to the GNP; the value of all primary inputs is equal to the total value added by the economy, which with some accounting adjustments, can also be made equal to the GNP. An example of this matrix, showing just two intermediate sectors, is shown in Table 7.1.

Each interindustry sector appears in the table twice, first as a buyer of inputs from other sectors that supply intermediate goods and primary inputs, and second as a seller of its output to other sectors for intermediate and final use. The columns of the table for the using sectors show

TABLE 7.1 HYPOTHETICAL EXAMPLE OF INTERINDUSTRY AND SECTOR FLOW ACCOUNTS (in millions of dollars)

	Using Sectors				
Producing Sectors	Iron and Steel	Motor Vehicles	Total Inter-mediate Sales	Sales to Final Users	Total Output
Iron and steel	20	45	65	10	75
Motor vehicles	5	30	35	100	135
Total intermediate purchases	25	75	100		
Primary inputs	50	60		110	
Total purchases	75	135			210

the mix of inputs used in the production of each sector's output. For example, Table 7.1 shows that the Iron and Steel producing sector used $5 million worth of inputs purchased from the Motor Vehicles sector as well as $20 million of its own output. In addition, the Iron and Steel sector paid $50 million to households for primary inputs. Thus the value of total purchases is $75 million.

The output of the Iron and Steel sector was distributed in the following way: $20 million of output was used by the sector in its own operations, $45 million worth was used as inputs to the production of Motor Vehicles, and $10 million of sales was made directly to the Final Users. For the Iron and Steel sector, the total value of inputs, $25 million of interindustry purchases and $50 million of primary inputs, is equal to the total value of its output, of which $65 million worth was used up in the operation of the two producing sectors and $10 million worth was delivered to final use or "final demand," as it is usually called; and a similar equality holds for the Motor Vehicles sector. In general, the input-output accounting table makes use of the accounting relationship that the total value of inputs to a sector, including profits or losses, is equal to the total value of its outputs.

The illustration also shows that in total, but not sector by sector, payments to primary inputs are equal to the value of output allocated to final use, and further that the total value of gross income equals gross product, which is $110 million, while the total value of transactions in the area is $210 million.[21]

Table 7.2 shows a general form of the urban accounting system for *n* producing sectors, where additionally the Final Use column has been divided into five subcolumns, four of which show the disposition of final output. In our later analysis the Exports column will be very important, since it is primarily through changes in the demand for an area's exports that the framework is able to trace-through the effects of external forces on the urban economy. In contrast to the export-base framework, this procedure allows us to incorporate a detailed description of the change in exports that we are interested in when we are considering the effect on the urban area's income and output.

This system presents a notation that is useful in discussing the actual input-output framework and allows algebraic expression of the relation-

---

[21] There are a number of specific kinds of accounting conventions that are not described in this simple illustration. For example, dollar flows are usually recorded in producer prices, with so-called "margin" items, e.g., transportation and trade, appearing as separate sectors; secondary product production ordinarily appears twice— once in the sector where actually produced and again imputed to the sector where they are primary products; some transfer payments specifically show up as transactions between the primary input and final demand sectors. Specific accounting conventions will often vary among different input-output tables, although efforts are being made to standardize accounting practices.

TABLE 7.2   URBAN INTERINDUSTRY ACCOUNTING FRAMEWORK

		Purchasing Sectors						
		Interindustry Use		Final Use				
		Sector $1\cdots j\cdots n$	Total Interindustry Use	Invest-ment	Con-sump-tion	Gov-ern-ment	Ex-ports	Total Final Use
Producing sector	1 $X_{11}\cdots X_{1j}\cdots X_{1n}$	W_1	I_1	C_1	G_1	E_1	Y_1
	2 .		.					
	. .		.					
	. .		.					
	i X_{i1} X_{ij} X_{in}	W_i	I_i	C_i	G_i	E_i	Y_i
	. .		.					
	. .		.					
	. .		.					
	n $X_{n1}\cdots X_{nj}\cdots X_{nn}$	W_n	I_n	C_n	G_n	E_n	Y_n
Total pro-duced inputs	U_1 U_j U_n						
Primary in-puts (value added)	P_1 P_j P_n			V_I	V_C	V_G	V_E	
Total pro-duction	X_1 X_j X_n		I	C	G	E	Y

ships used in the accounting.[22] All elements in the table are in dollar terms, although another form of accounting of flows would include entries in terms of physical units of inputs and outputs. In practice, however, it would be very difficult to construct such a table. Many of the sectors, as defined, produce a wide range of differing products that must be consolidated into an aggregate output measure, and the use of dollar values to accomplish this is the easiest statistical procedure.

Table 7.2 and the accompanying algebraic expressions show a general form of the input-output accounting system for interindustry sectors. How-

[22] The X_{ij} entries in the Interindustry section of the table measure the dollar value of the purchases by the jth sector of inputs from the ith sector. The figures in an Interindustry *column* represent the pattern of input purchases of the particular sector. An Interindustry *row* shows the distribution of the value of output of any sector to other, intermediate sectors and to final demand. Total final use includes: the Consumption column (which represents the purchases of households in the urban area), the Investment column (which measures investment in plant and equipment and changes in inventory), the Government column (which includes government procurement), and the Exports column.

ever, it does not make explicit the application of this system to urban areas. Urban input-output tables, like regional input-output tables in general, must explicitly consider the transactions between the set of markets located within the urban area and those in the "rest of the world." This indicates that the geography of the urban area must be defined.

The input-output table must be so structured as to be able to separate the "urban area" from the "rest of the world"; but the criteria for defining an urban area to which input-output analysis can be applied are not determined from the interindustry relationships. Factors important in the choice of the geographic boundaries to be assigned to a specific urban area include the extent to which the area is an economic oasis, population densities at its borders, and political jurisdictions. In general, we would want to define the urban area so that most of the transactions, i.e., purchases and sales, in the three major urban markets (the labor, housing, and transportation markets) are cleared within the urban area. As an example, one of the earliest applications of urban input-output analysis was to the St. Louis metropolitan area.[23] The area included specific political jurisdictions within a relatively densely populated area, surrounded by sparsely populated farming areas, thus clearly demarcating the urban area by the type of products produced—manufacturing and services in the one case and agricultural in the other—and involving relatively little commuting to work from outside the urban area.

Once the urban area has been defined, the area's transactors— industries, households, and governments—can be identified. The structure of the urban input-output table, then, should separately identify those transactions which clear within the urban area and those which are made between the urban area and the rest of the world. An urban area table therefore must elaborate on the exports and imports made by the area's transactors. A static representation of such an elaboration of the transactions shown in Table 7.1 is depicted in Table 7.3, using the same two interindustry sectors as in the previous example but changing the pattern of sales.

There are several differences between Tables 7.1 and 7.3. In Table 7.1 Exports have been explicitly identified as part of sales to Final Users; and here Exports are further classified as being to Intermediate and Final Users in other areas. This allows the clear identification of the purchase pattern of consumers, business (for investment), and governments within the urban area; the pattern can be read from the column, "Final Users within the Urban Area." This column now shows that $80 million worth of output of the Motor Vehicles sector of other areas is imported for final use in the area. Also, the total value of final purchases by governments, households,

[23] Werner Z. Hirsch, "Interindustry Relations of a Metropolitan Area," *Review of Economics and Statistics*, vol. 41, no. 4 (November 1959), pp. 360–370.

TABLE 7.3 HYPOTHETICAL INTERINDUSTRY AND SECTOR FLOW ACCOUNTS, EXPORTS AND IMPORTS EXPLICITLY INCLUDED (in millions of dollars)

| | Using Sectors | | | | | | | |
| | Intraurban Sales | | | | Exports | | | |
Producing Sectors	Iron and Steel	Motor Vehicles	Final Users within the Urban Area	Total Intra-urban Sales	Inter-mediate Users	Final Users	Total Exports	Total Output
Intraurban:								
Iron and steel	15	40	5	60	10	5	15	75
Motor vehicles	4	30	10	44	1	90	91	135
Primary inputs	40	55			0	0	0	
Total intra-urban	59	125	15	104			(106)	
Imports:								
Iron and steel	5	5	0					
Motor vehicles	1	0	80					
Primary inputs	10	5	0					
Total imports	16	10	80	(106)				
Total purchases	75	135	(95)					210

and business (for investment), $95 million, is equal to the total income or value added by these sectors ($40 million + $55 million = $95 million).

However, imports for final use are not the total of imports to the area. The interindustry sectors also purchase output from sectors outside the urban economy. For example, the Iron and Steel sector imported $5 million of Iron and Steel and $1 million of Motor Vericles, and paid $10 million for primary inputs supplied by households and governments outside the area. Overall, the value of the economy's imports, $106 million, just equaled the value of exports. And the total value of purchases and sales transacted in the urban economy is $210 million.

Modifications can be made in the Exports column by taking account of the more important two or three or, in general, *m*, outside areas or regions to which the urban area sells its output. Such an export matrix, containing a column for each particular outside region, is adjoined to the other columns of Final Users. A similar modification may be made to the

Primary Inputs sections by adding a series of rows showing the purchases of the local urban area from several outside supplying regions.[24]

The Theoretical Description

Up to this point, the discussion has been concerned with an economic accounting framework and questions of classifying data on transactions between sectors. However, the major purpose of the input-output table is to aid in the empirical implementation of the input-output framework. Input-output is essentially a set of simultaneous linear relations, one for each sector, showing the distribution of its output to the using sectors. This set of equations, for which the values of the coefficients are derivable from the information in the accounting table, allows a systematic tracing of the effects of production by one sector on the production of other sectors. It also allows estimating the effects on specific sector output and employment of specified levels and mix of final demand, including exports.

There are a number of specific assumptions implicit in input-output, sometimes varying slightly with the particular formulation being used. The most important of these assumptions is that the quantity of each input purchased by a sector depends in a linear way only on the level of output of the using sector. Because this denies any substitution possibilities between inputs, the production function of a sector is obviously of a special form, different from the usual production functions used in microeconomics. And an important concern, when the analysis is implemented, is that the underlying individual production functions should be relatively constant.

Assuming in addition that the prices of inputs remain constant regardless of the amount purchased, the value of a sector's purchases of a particular input can be expressed as a proportional function of the value of the sector's output as:[25]

$$X_{ij} = a_{ij}X_j \qquad (7.13)$$

where X_{ij} is the already defined dollar value of input of sector i used in production of output j, and a_{ij} is the input coefficient or, more properly, the *marginal* input coefficient of i for j that measures the dollar value of purchase by j of input i. The technnology or purchase pattern of any sector is represented by the appropriate set of a_{ij} (e.g., for sector k, the

---

[24] Alternatively, one can disaggregate exports by the industry sectors that are buying the local production, and can disaggregate imports by the sectors that are selling to the local area. Or one can even combine both area and sector disaggregation.

[25] The a_{ij}, or *input coefficients*, as they are called, are estimated from the data in the input-output table as:

$$a_{ij} = \frac{X_{ij}}{X_j} \qquad (7.14)$$

set of coefficients a_{1k}, a_{2k}, a_{3k}, . . . , etc.); for many of the sectors, some of the coefficients will be zero, reflecting no direct input purchases.

However, the expressions of the form of 7.13 may be combined with others showing the purchases of the same input to give the following expression for the distribution of *output* for a particular sector:

$$X_i - [a_{i1}X_1 + a_{i2}X_2 \cdots a_{ii}X_i \cdots a_{in}X_n] = Y_i \qquad (7.15)$$

for any sector i $(i = 1, n)$. This expression states that X_i, the value of total output of sector i, minus the amount of its output used up by that sector and by other intermediate sectors, is equal to the amount of good i delivered to or available for final users. The set of equations of (7.15) when the a_{ij} are calculated from the data in the input-output table is a characterization of the important trading relationships in the economy.[26]

This representation of the economy can be cast into another form, the general solution of the equations of (7.15), that allows both an explicit formulation of the effects of final sales on the levels of output of the producing sectors (the a'_{ij}), and a set of equilibrium values of output for each sector, X_i. The solution to the set of equations, a set of values of output of each sector, may be written as follows for each sector i:

$$X_i = a'_{i1}Y_1 + a'_{i2}Y_2 + a'_{i3}Y_3 + \ldots a'_{ii}Y_i + \ldots a'_{in}Y_n \quad (7.16)$$

where the a'_{ij} must be calculated and depend on all the specified a_{ij}. Equations 7.16 show that all of the output of any sector may be "attributed to" or associated with the deliveries to final demand of all sectors, including its own. The total effect on a sector's output of a change in the final demand for some specific other sector is shown by the relevant coefficients in equation 7.15; for example, a'_{i3} shows the value of output required of sector i per dollar of delivery to final demand of sector 3. This total effect can be separated into "direct" and "indirect" output effects. The direct output effect on sector i may be read from the appropriate structural coefficient of the form of 7.13; for example, the direct output effect on sector i per dollar of increase in output of sector 3 is a_{i3}. The difference between a'_{i3} and a_{i3} is called the "indirect effect."

Cast in this general form, input-output can predict the dollar value of outputs by each of the producing or endogenous sectors in the economy, the X_j, that are required to meet the stipulated level and mix of final demand. In analyzing metropolitan area output, income, and employment

[26] This is a system of n linear equations with n^2 parameters (the a_{ij}), n unknown production levels, the X_i, and a set of autonomous or predetermined variables, Y_i, whose values we shall be interested in varying below. In general, a system of n linear equations in n unknowns, where the constants and the coefficients are specified, is amenable to solution. Although equality of the number of equations and the number of unknowns is neither necessary nor sufficient for the existence of a solution, certain generally satisfied conditions on the a_{ij} ensures that the solution of the system of 7.15 exists.

growth, however, the structural coefficients and final demands should be given a more specific content.

It is through estimates of the structural coefficients in the manner of equation 7.13 that conditions unique to producers in the metropolitan area under consideration are incorporated. The input requirements for a given industry's production may vary from one metropolitan area to another for a variety of reasons. Since metropolitan areas differ in human and physical resource endowments, they are likely to combine their inputs in different ways to produce the same type of product. In some cases they may have to pay different prices for specific inputs, which would influence their input coefficients.[27] Different metropolitan areas are likely to have plants in various stages of obsolescence, implying differing production functions. Perhaps most important is that the interindustry sectors represent aggregations of firms and products. As a result, different areas are not likely to be producing the same product mix in what is ostensibly the same sector. The result could be very different input mixes for producing the same level of output. For all these reasons, it is preferable to develop the structural coefficients for a given area directly from local data. In many cases, however, this becomes prohibitive, so that the coefficients are developed from national tables adjusted for some known local characteristics.

In a national table, the a_{ij} coefficients refer essentially to the technical input requirements for producing a sector's output; there is no need to be concerned with the area that produces these inputs. For a metropolitan area, however, there is need to be concerned with whether these inputs are produced by local firms or are imported. That is, metropolitan input-output analysis must specify not only production relationships but also trading relationships.

One way of handling this problem is to assume a fixed relationship between the proportion of an input that is imported and the proportion that is purchased from local production. If this is done, then the a'_{ij} coefficients can be obtained from an intralocal set of transactions. Equation 7.16 can then be applied in determining sector outputs, given this interpretation of the inverse coefficients. Imports would then be assumed to be elastic in supply and available to meet the input requirements not satisfied by local outputs. Another way of introducing imports is to develop explicit trading equations. For example, it might be assumed that input requirements are initially satisfied by local producers, and it is only when such requirements exceed local capacities that imports are purchased.[28]

---

[27] For an interpretation of input coefficients in terms of isoquants, see Hollis B. Chenery and Paul G. Clark, *Interindustry Economics* (New York: Wiley, 1959), pp. 39–42.

[28] In a more sophisticated form, gravity equations can be developed for each item that make the purchase of an item by some area from some other area a function of (a) the distance between areas, (b) the demands for the item in each area, and

In applying the metropolitan area input-output framework, what final demand elements are stipulated is a matter of option. The choice depends on the analytic purpose of the application. However, it should be emphasized that the framework being described is unilateral—that is, it shows the relationships only between a specific metropolitan area and the rest of the world. In effect, this means that, while the consequences of events in the rest of the world for the metropolitan area activity can be calculated, the effect of the metropolitan area on the rest of the world cannot. To generate feedbacks between the two areas would require a more complex framework, probably, for practical purposes, multiregional in nature and describing the interactions among a number of metropolitan areas or regions.

In the simplified framework being described, we have assumed that the elements of final demand, consumption, investment, government expenditures, exports, and imports can be stipulated and that the primary inputs are perfectly elastic in supply, so that the level of sector outputs can adjust to that required by final demand. With such exogenous stipulations, the sector levels of area production can be determined and the value of primary inputs required to meet this production can be calculated. Depending on the detail in which the primary inputs are stated, estimates of personal income of residents in the area, value added by the area, and government revenues can be derived. Also, along with knowledge of the capacities of production facilities within the area and the level of primary resources or inputs in the area, such an analysis would be useful on identifying bottlenecks or shortages of inputs that would be required to produce the specified level of final output. This sort of information has been of value to economists studying underdeveloped countries with input-output, and it would be of use in urban macroeconomics for anticipating investment and migration trends in the area.

Adjustments can be made to the simple framework specified here that would allow for improved conditional predictions of the level of income in a particular metropolitan area. In this form, it becomes an analysis of income determination, in the same manner as the export-base frameworks discussed above but with much more information content, allowing the calculation of sector income multipliers and sector employment multipliers.

The adjustment would involve deriving, rather than stipulating, the activities of local households, by including them as an interindustry or "endogenous" sector in the structural part of the input-output table. In principle, other local final demand sectors could also be treated as endog-

---

(c) the supply of the item by each area. Use of such equations considerably complicates the input-output analysis but significantly enhances the results. (See Wassily Leontief and Alan Stuart, "Multiregional Input-Output Analysis" in Tibor Barna (ed.), *Structural Interdependence and Economic Development* [London: Macmillan, 1963], pp. 119–150.)

enous sectors; for example, the usefulness of this approach for analyses of fiscal problems of local metropolitan governments can be substantially enhanced by including the local government sector as endogenous.[29]

The local household sector can be included in the interactive or interindustry portion of the framework by representing both its purchases from and its supply of labor services to all sectors. The sales of labor services can be introduced by the inclusion of a new equation of the form of 7.14, as follows:

$$X_h - [a_{h1}X_1 + a_{h2}X_2 + \ldots + a_{hh}X_h + \ldots a_{hn}X_n] = 0 \quad (7.17)$$

Here, X_h represents the total labor earnings of local households and the coefficients, and a_{hi}, represent the labor earnings per unit of output in each sector. The equation shows the distribution of the "output" of the household sector—its sales of labor services to the other using interindustry sectors, including sales to itself. The sales of the household sector to itself represent the direct employment by households of labor inputs, such as domestic service. Except for the change that the deliveries to final demand of this sector are equal to 0, equation 7.17 is strictly analogous to the expressions of this form introduced for the other interindustry sectors.

Just as local labor earnings are made endogenous, it is desirable to make local household purchases endogenous. This can be done by including in each expression for the distribution of the outputs of each producing sector an additional term that represents the sales of the output of that sector to the household sector. These terms, of the form of $a_{ih}X_h$, measure the *consumption* by households of output i. Thus, to the original set of equations (7.15) we have added another row that shows the value of payments to the local household sector from the producing sectors; and we have added another column (an additional term to all equations) that shows the consumption pattern of local households. The variable X_h now represents the level of "output" of the household sector, or, alternatively and interesting for our purposes, the level of income generated within the metropolitan area.

With this transformation, we have essentially moved local consumption from the "final demand" category and reduced that category to include only government purchases, investment, and exports. But now the framework will permit deriving estimates of area income, which will include the multiplier (induced) effects of local consumption on local income. These consumption multiplier effects had not been included in the earlier formulation. In principle, the procedure is the same as before. The framework reduces the transactions within the area to a set of equations in which the coefficients of the linear relationships are estimated from the

[29] See Werner Z. Hirsch, "Input-Output Techniques for Urban Government Decisions," *American Economic Review*, vol. 58, no. 2 (May 1968), pp. 162–170.

information collected and summarized in the accounting relations; and upon the specification of estimates for the reclassified "final uses" sector, the solution gives values of the X_i, here interpreted as the levels of gross output of all the interindustry sectors, and the value of X_h, the estimate of the level of income that would be generated within the area for the specified deliveries to final demand.

If local investment and local government are also made endogenous, then only exports remain in final demand, which is analogous to the autonomous element in export-base. Now input-output analysis can be used to trace the effects or "impacts" on the level of income in the urban area from a change in exports, although the finer detail included in the input-output framework, in contrast to the single homogeneous output implicitly assumed in export-base analysis, allows us to calculate the effects on area income and employment from changes in the level of specific types of exports. As such, input-output allows a more accurate and informative means of tracing the income effects of long-run or cyclical changes in area exports. Discussions of the applications of input-output are presented in Chapter 8; however, here we turn to a discussion of the concepts associated with input-output that allow us to calculate the relative impact on area income from changes in various elements of final demand.

The total income change in the area can be conceptually separated into direct, indirect, and now the "induced" income effects of changes in final demand. In the first formulation of input-output discussed, where consumption expenditures were included in final demand as an exogenous element, it is possible to define a direct and a total income effect,[30] as follows.

The direct income effect is measured by a_{hj}, the coefficient that measures the income payments made to households in the area per dollar of output of the jth sector. For example, the direct effect on income of a \$1 increase in output in the Motor Vehicles sector may be \$0.40, indicating that 40 cents is paid to area residents in wages, salaries, and dividends for every dollar of output produced in that sector. The effect of an increase in sales to final demand of \$100,000 worth of Motor Vehicles would be to directly increase area income by \$40,000. But clearly this is not the entire income effect. The increase in sales to final use of the Motor Vehicles sector requires increased output from the sectors that directly and indirectly supply inputs to this sector. In a manner similar to that used to trace the effects on output of all sectors of an increase in the output of any one sector, we may measure the total income created as the Motor Vehicles sector—call it sector j—buys inputs from other interindustry sectors that also pay out wages and salaries. This is done by first estimating the effect on total output of all sectors from an increase in the

[30] As opposed to the *output* effects discussed then.

sales to final demand of sector j, that is, using the a'_{ij} coefficients that measure the total output effect. Then these terms are multiplied by the respective income payment coefficients of the form of a_{hj} and summed to give the following:

$$I_j = (a_{h1}a'_{1j} + a_{h2}a'_{2j} + \ldots + a_{hn}a'_{nj}) \qquad (7.18)$$

The value I_j measures the direct and indirect increases in income in the area per dollar of increase in the output of the Motor Vehicles sector to final demand.

The direct and indirect income multiplier for any sector—say, sector j—is defined as:

$$K_j = \frac{I_j}{a_{hj}} \qquad (7.19)$$

These sorts of multipliers are especially useful in characterizing and ranking sectors in the urban economy by their influence on the level of income in the area.[31]

For the second specification of the input-output framework in which the level of income is estimated in the input-output technique, one is able to allow for the responsiveness of household consumption expenditures with changes in the level of income. The direct and total effects on income mentioned above lead us to consider another effect, associated with the fact that as households' incomes rise, their consumption expenditures rise, inducing more output of the other sectors, and in turn increase the level of income in the area.

In the general solution of the system of simultaneous equations that represent the input-output framework (of the form of 7.15), after we have included the household sector as endogenous, there is a set of n "new" coefficients, a'_{hj}. These coefficients measure, by the nature of the solution to a set of this sort of equations, another type of *total* effect on income per dollar of increase in output delivered to final demand of sector j. That is, these coefficients measure the direct, the indirect, and the *induced* income effects of changes in the level of deliveries to final output.

We may now calculate the so-called "full-income multiplier" for any sector as follows:

$$K'_j = \frac{a'_{hj}}{a_{hj}} \qquad (7.20)$$

It is important to note here that the multipliers for each of the sectors provide a way in which to rank the influence of the sectors on the level of income in the area: the larger the multiplier, the greater the impact on the income of the metropolitan economy of indirect and induced income

[31] For examples of the numerical values of such multipliers, see Hirsch, "Interindustry Relations of a Metropolitan Area," op. cit., p. 365.

relative to that of direct income, and the more pervasive the effect on the economy.

The foregoing analysis has concentrated on levels of income and output generated by the operation of various sectors of the urban economy. However, the analyses can be conducted in terms of employment, which has direct relevance for analyses of policy-related issues such as unemployment, poverty, transportation systems, and training programs. Some input-output models have been designed entirely in terms of employment flows. Instead of value estimates for the purchases and sales made by sectors, imputed values for employment are placed into the input-output table and the analysis is made with such estimates.[32]

More often, however, employment estimates are derived from the output estimates calculated from the value-based input-output table. This requires estimates of an employment-output ratio for each sector (the inverse of average labor productivity). This ratio could be constant for all levels of sector output, indicating a proportional relation between employment and output, or it could be allowed to vary, allowing for productivity improvements as a function of scale or time.[33]

Using this approach, the "direct" employment effect is defined as the number of workers used by a sector per dollar increase in the value of output, and is measured by the labor input coefficient l_i. But, as in the case above where we dealt with output effects, this direct effect is not the complete picture. Because of the interrelatedness of the producing sectors in the economy, which is captured by the simultaneous equation system, there will be effects on other sectors' employment from an increase in the employment in a particular sector. The effect will be to increase the output and hence the employment of the other sectors.[34]

[32] For an example of this, see Hansen and Tiebout, op. cit. This paper also illustrates the similarities between disaggregated export-base and input-output frameworks.

[33] The employee-output ratio can change even if the labor earnings coefficient remains constant, provided that average labor earnings increase proportionally with the productivity improvement. However, the idea of varying input coefficients is part of a larger discussion of technological change which is not included here.

[34] The total effect on employment in the metropolitan economy from an increase in the value of output delivered to final demand by any particular sector is calculated as follows:

Total employment increase attributable to sector j, $= l_1 a'_{1j} + l_2 a'_{2j} + l_3 a'_{3j} + \cdots + l_n a'_{nj}$ (7.21)

where a'_{ij} identifies for each of the other sectors in the economy ($i = l, n$), the increment in output required per dollar of increased deliveries to final demand of a particular sector, j, and l_i measures the marginal employment-output coefficients. The employment multiplier of any sector can be defined as the ratio of the total (direct plus indirect) employment effects to the direct effects, as follows:

$$L_k = \frac{\sum_{i}^{n} l_i a'_{1k}}{l_k}$$ (7.22)

Problems of Input-Output Analysis

Although input-output analysis takes direct account of certain types of interdependencies among economic units in the urban economy, it has some important weaknesses and limitations. While the usefulness of the method should be judged primarily by the quality of its predictions or forecasts, the properties—especially for longer terms—of the forecasts for urban areas are not well known. However, the framework has proved to be useful in analysis of national economies.

The criticisms of input-output analysis can be related both to its basic assumptions and to difficulties in implementation. Input-output, by its assumption of a stable and proportional trading relation, is limited in that it does not account for or allow representation of the economies and diseconomies of scale present in urban production. The assumption of fixed trading coefficients has further consequences, too. If the coefficients are interpreted as representing an underlying technology, then technological change and innovation will work to change the coefficients. If the coefficients are interpreted as value ratios representing purchase patterns in effect at the time of the data collection, then changes in relative prices would stimulate substitution among input purchases and therefore change the actual trading pattern from that represented by the estimated coefficients. Although both of these limitations, imposed by the assumption of the form of the trading relations, represent potentially important problems with input-output, there is no reason to expect that their effects will be any more damaging to an urban than to a national analysis.

Because of the essentially static nature of the framework presented here, input-output is not well suited to analysis of such obviously important commodities as housing and capital stock. To incorporate the investment behavior without making the framework explicitly dynamic (and much more difficult) requires the use of extensive side calculations made outside the framework itself. This illustrates a weakness of the basic structure of the approach, namely, that behavioral representations, except for the interindustry trading or production relations, must be made outside the framework.

The major problem with the implementation of input-output is the amount of data required to estimate the trading relationships. Because of the high cost of collecting data on a particular urban area by survey or other means, the coefficients are sometimes taken from a national model and adjusted so as to more accurately represent the particular area. However, features that influence the industrial structure of a particular econ-

---

Such a multiplier, calculated for each sector, provides another means of ranking the effects of the various sectors on area economic activity. Alternatively, such a multiplier can be interpreted as showing the total change in employment in the area when employment in a sector changes.

omy tend to make the process of adjusting coefficients difficult and to increase the chances that adjusted coefficients will not accurately represent the actual transactions structure. And finally, the time lag, caused by the extensive data requirements, between data collection and the implementation of the model increases the potential for divergence between the actual transactions pattern and the one that is estimated.

IV. *INCOME-EXPENDITURE FRAMEWORKS*

Next we discuss multiple-equation, essentially income-expenditure, frameworks. We do so by describing a representative framework, one that consists of a collection of definitions and behavioral relations designed to capture the essential elements of an urban economy and to estimate aggregate variables such as output, income, and employment. These frameworks are especially applicable to large, consolidated metropolitan areas, and they represent a relatively new technique in urban macroeconomic analysis. Such frameworks face formidable data problems that make estimation of the structural relations difficult, but they are useful in forecasting and in relatively long-run growth analysis.

The basic procedure is identification of the major influences on aggregate expenditures for the output of the area. The components of aggregate demand are expenditures for consumption (C), investment (I), government (G), and net exports $(E - IM)$. The justification for classifying expenditures in this way is that each of these elements is influenced differently by specific economic and demographic factors. Levels of employment are calculated either by use of a simple employment-output relation or by use of an aggregate regional production function. At least two income measures are relevant for urban areas: factor payments received by residents and businesses in the area, and disposable income of residents of the area. The first income measure can be calculated as the sum of factor payments; the second can be derived, with appropriate specification, from levels of area output.

Concepts of Area Income and Product

Gross output produced in a particular area, X, is defined similarly to Gross National Product and measures the area's contribution to GNP. In terms of expenditures, gross output produced in the metropolitan economy may be expressed as the sum of final expenditures made for the area's output—

$$X = C + I + G + (E - IM) \tag{7.23}$$

Alternatively, gross output produced can be considered as the total of sales of area output to final users located both inside the area and in the rest of the national economy.

Income attributable to production in the area, Y_p, is the total of factor payments arising from production in the area. However, for a subnational area such as a large metropolitan area, the difference between the income originating in an area and income accruing to residents in much larger than for a large national economy like that of the United States. The difference is accounted for in two ways. A certain portion of the income earned in the area is paid to factor owners (individuals and businesses) who reside in other areas, V_0, in the form of wages, profits, dividends, etc. Conversely, businesses and residents of the area will receive payments of income earned in other areas, V_i. This suggests one possible formulation for an income measure that can be included in an urban macro framework, namely, to estimate total factor payments originating in the area by estimating the various types of factor payments, wages and salaries, dividends, interest, etc., which in turn depend upon different elements of the urban economy.[35] Then V_0 can be considered as depending upon the level of gross output produced, X, and V_i can be considered as depending upon levels of economic activity outside the area, perhaps upon GNP. Thus, factor payments received by residents and businesses, V_R, is:[36]

$$Y_R = Y_p - V_0(X) + V_i(GNP) \qquad (7.24)$$

An alternative measure is area disposable income, Y_d, which is defined as follows:

$$Y_d = X - T_d - T_{id} - T_f + TR_g + NF_h - D \qquad (7.25)$$

where

$T_d =$ direct area taxation (state and local)
$T_{id} =$ indirect area taxation
$T_f =$ federal taxation
$TR_g =$ governmental transfers to area
$NF_h =$ net factor payments to area households
$D =$ depreciation[37]

Area disposable income can be incorporated into a macro framework in a number of different ways, the most detailed of which is to estimate separately the respective transfer and tax items. For example, regional transfer payments can be specified as depending upon unemployment and popula-

---

[35] For an example of an approach similar to this, see Laurence C. Chau, *An Econometric Model for Income and Employment in Hawaii* (Economic Research Center, University of Hawaii, June 1970), in which he argues that estimating the components of income rather than of expenditure is appropriate in an open economy.

[36] The notation $V_0(X)$, for example, indicates that V_0 depends upon X.

[37] See Lawrence R. Klein, "The Specification of Regional Econometric Models," *Papers of the Regional Science Association*, vol. 23 (1969), pp. 105–115, for a detailed presentation of a similar approach. The term NF_h is factor payments to households in the area from other areas minus factor payments made to households in other areas.

tion levels, while indirect area taxation depends upon the value of gross production in the area, etc. In contrast, disposable income can be estimated as follows:

$$Y_d = Y_d(X)^{38} \qquad (7.26)$$

The *level* of income received in an area can be used as a means of roughly indexing the standard of living of the residents over time, or as a means of measuring growth in the economy. However, the *distribution* of income may be even more valuable in considering many urban problems and can be expected to influence many of the relationships in a macro framework, e.g., the consumption function, investment in housing, and the levels and types of public services. However, such frameworks usually do not deal with the distribution of income, reflecting the conceptual problem of specifying a macro theory of income distribution.[39]

Determinants of Output and Employment

Area output is estimated by determining separately the major components of expenditure as specified in equation 7.23. The value of consumption expenditures by households in the area on goods produced in the area is stated in its simplest form as a function of disposable income.[40] There are various possible specifications of the consumption function with regard to the variables that can be included.[41] Levels of income in recent previous periods or wealth measures can be included to approximate the effect of permanent income. Or, with a more detailed specification of income, two separate consumption functions can be specified, one for income earned in the area, the other for income payments received from other areas. The justification for this separation is that income earned in the area will consist primarily of wages and salaries, and that income earned in other areas will be primarily nonwage payments and will be associated

---

[38] The two different possible specifications of Y_d, represented respectively by 7.25 (plus the equations required to estimate T_d, T_{id}, T_f, TR_g, D, NF_h) and by 7.26 emphasize the point that nearly all relationships included in a structural framework could be specified in greater detail with an improvement in the correspondence between the framework and the actual workings of the economy under study. However, the form of any framework as finally implemented represents the results of a trade-off between the accuracy of representation, including accuracy of forecasts, and manageability of the framework.

[39] For an attempt to specify certain measures of the distribution of income in an urban economy using many demographic variables, see John M. Mattila and Wilbur R. Thompson, "Toward an Econometric Model of Urban Economic Development," in Harvey S. Perloff and Lowdon Wingo, Jr. (eds), *Issues in Urban Economcis* (Baltimore: Johns Hopkins for Resources for the Future, Inc., 1968), pp. 63–78.

[40] Specifically,

$$C = C(Y_d) \qquad (7.27)$$

[41] There are also variations in the functional forms. However, throughout this section the forms of the empirically fitted relationships are not specified.

with a lower propensity to consume.[42] In addition, there may be other variables that are important for inclusion in a consumption function for an urban area, as distinct from the formulation usually used in frameworks for national economies.

The investment component of aggregate demand includes those expenditures on products produced in the area to maintain or increase the level of the "capital stock" (K). Although precise definition of the theoretical concept of the capital stock is difficult, the concept has been found useful in analyses of national economies and refers to a collection of relatively long-lived physical assets.[43] Expenditures on such assets can be separated into two subtypes, investment in housing, I_h, and investment by business, I_b. Total investment, I, is the sum of these two components.

Investment in housing, or additions to the stock of housing units, can conceptually be derived in two steps. First, the aggregate demand for housing services is considered as depending upon the level and distribution of income received in the area, and on the level of—or, more properly, on the change in—area population. Then the (flow) supply of housing services from the available stock is determined. And from this flow supply and demand analysis, a demand for increments in the housing stock can be derived. This sort of derivation is not in practice included in such frameworks, primarily because of the difficulty of determining the flow measures of housing services. Investment in housing is more usually related to changes in population (ΔN), a representative interest rate (r), and income received in the area.[44]

Investment by businesses is assumed to depend upon the level of gross area output, a representative market interest rate, and previously existing levels of the capital stock (K_{t-1}).[45] The theory of investment behavior implicit in 7.29 is that higher levels of aggregate regional production will induce increases in the desired level of the capital stock, that a higher market interest rate will decrease the present value of many prospective investment projects and thereby decrease the level of investment, and that

---

[42] See Harold T. Moody and Frank W. Puffer, "A Gross Regional Product Approach to Regional Model-Building," *Western Economic Journal*, vol. 7, no. 2 (December 1969), pp. 391–402.

[43] However, the relevance of this concept for urban economies has not been investigated.

[44] Specifically,

$$I_h = I_h \, (\Delta N, r, Y_R) \qquad (7.28)$$

[45] Specifically,

$$I_b = I_b \, (X, r, K_{t-1}) \qquad (7.29)$$

or the functional form can be formulated explicitly to include a form of accelerator mechanism. For a functional specification of the investment relation that directly employs a "desired" and an actual capital stock for the state of Massachusetts, see Fredrick W. Bell, "An Econometric Forecasting Model for a Region," *Journal of Regional Science*, vol. 7, no. 2, pp. 109–127.

the higher the level of the capital stock in preceding periods, the smaller will be the level of investment.

Some frameworks include a greater level of detail by specifying separate investment functions for goods of special interest. For example, for an area in which the production of certain goods, such as automobiles or aircraft, is an important part of the economy, business investment can be disaggregated and separate investment functions can be added. Such functions relate investment for the production of these goods to, among other things, the levels of gross national income, reflecting the larger market area in which automobiles and aircraft are sold. The usefulness of a separation of the investment function depends upon the nature of the economy of the area being studied, and of course different specific goods would be identified for different economies.[46]

The relationship for estimating the value of exports from the area to the "rest of the world," but essentially to other parts of the national economy, can be specified in various levels of detail. In the most aggregative specification, exports depend upon the levels of economic activity in the area to which the exports are made, usually the level of gross national output.[47] In the case of highly specialized production, such as automobiles, the export function can be disaggregated into two or more functions, a separate function for automobiles and one for all other products. In such a case the exports of automobiles can be made dependent upon other national variables besides GNP, such as the growth in the national population and the existing stock of automobiles.[48] An alternative, and more detailed, specification of exports can be made by identifying the trading relationships with the major places to which the area exports. Then separate export functions can be introduced, with the level of income in each area as the independent variable.

Imports to the area can be thought of as being of two kinds of goods: goods purchased by final users, households, and government; and intermediate goods purchased by producers, business firms, and governments. While separate import functions could be introduced for final and intermediate goods, the basic form of the relationship is that imports are a

---

[46] For a framework that relies heavily on the production of automobiles in determining an area's income, see W. L. L'Esperance et al., "Gross State Product and an Econometric Model for a State," *Journal of the American Statistical Association*, vol. 64 (September 1969), pp. 787–808.

[47] Specifically,

$$E = E(GNP) \tag{7.30}$$

where the area's share of GNP is assumed to be small enough so that GNP can be considered an exogenous variable.

[48] On the assumption that there are substantial differences in prices between various regions, Lawrence Klein, op. cit., additionally specifies that the relative price level of an area and the national price level be included in the export function.

function of area product.[49] If the form of the import relationship is specified so as to explicitly include a marginal propensity to import, then the propensity can itself be made a function of the level of output of the area such that as the area output rises, the propensity to import falls, reflecting the effect of the production of import substitutes as the market size of the area grows.[50]

Government expenditures include all nontransfer expenditures by state, local, and federal government in the area. The most aggregated specification of this section of the framework relates government expenditures to the level of output in the area, since requirements for many types of government services, such as fire and police departments, can be expected to follow the level of economic activity in the area, while others, such as education, are related to personal income. Also, the level of output influences the revenues and thereby the expenditures of local governments. Additionally, the size of the urban population influences expenditures for such things as schools and medical services. The simplest form of the relationship is to make government expenditures a function of area product and population.[51]

An alternative specification disaggregates governmental expenditures into such programs as fire-fighting, police, education, and health services, and separately estimates each of these components. This method of introducing governmental expenditures has the advantage that it clearly specifies expenditures on certain especially important goods, such as education, that are useful in dealing with major urban problems. Another alternative is to specify separately governmental investment in major projects such as urban renewal or transit or freeway systems.

Employment in the area, L, can be added to the framework of equations 7.23 and 7.26 through 7.32 most simply by making employment a function of gross area product. However, a more detailed specification that additionally requires knowledge of the area's wage rate, w, includes an aggregate area production function.[52] Then an explicit formulation of the

[49] Specifically,

$$IM = IM(X) \tag{7.31}$$

which allows for both final and intermediate goods imports. Klein, op. cit., also allows for the effect of relative prices in the import relationship.

[50] Note that, in contrast to the export-base model, with this model the propensities of various types of spending to create income in the urban area are not used. The openness of the urban economy is allowed for by separate estimation of the import function.

[51] Specifically,

$$G = G(X, N) \tag{7.32}$$

[52] The production function makes output a function of capital and labor,

$$X = X(K, L) \tag{7.33}$$

See Bell and Klein, op. cit. Bell specifies a Cobb-Douglas form for 7.33.

employment-output[53] relation makes employment a function of area product, capital, wage rates, and interest rates.[54]

A more detailed method of including employment involves specification of demand and supply functions for labor. In this case, the wage rate in the area is made endogenous. A further extension is to allow the area wage rate to influence the population in the area through the effect of the wage rate on migration of workers.[55]

There are several properties of the broad framework presented here. First, such frameworks link the open urban economy to the national economy in different ways from that of either export-base or input-output. National influences are transmitted through the effects of GNP on exports, through the effects of a representative market interest rate which is assumed to be determined in national markets, and through the effect of area wages on the area's labor force and population.

Also the multiple-equation framework allows the calculation of multipliers useful in impact analysis—those that show the effect on each of the endogenous variables of changes in the exogenous variables. In the framework above, for example, the effects of changes in a policy variable, say governmental expenditures, or changes in the population of an area can be calculated once the functional form of the relationships is specified.[56]

However, the most significant feature of the type of frameworks presented here is the relative flexibility they allow for long-run considerations of area income, employment, and expenditures of various types. The specification of the functional forms of the relationships discussed above

---

[53] However, estimates of employment in various types of industries are often much more useful than overall employment. In this case, subframeworks for the level of output and employment of certain sectors are appended to the framework presented here. Input-output, which essentially specifies a collection of production functions and employment-output relationships, is well suited for employment calculations, as discussed in sec. III. However, some econometric models estimate area employment by separately estimating employment in the major producing sectors in the area economy. See Chau, op. cit.

[54] Specifically,

$$L = L(X,K,w,r,) \qquad (7.34)$$

[55] See, for example, Bell, op. cit.

[56] This is known as solving the structural specification into its "reduced form." Anderson has argued that because of data limitations, economists consider the estimation of reduced forms rather than structural forms (Robert J. Anderson, Jr., "A Note on Economic Base Studies and Regional Econometric Forecasting Models," *Journal of Regional Science*, vol. 10, no. 3, pp. 325–334). He also shows that the multipliers used in export-base can be interpreted under certain conditions as equivalent to the coefficients of the reduced form of a simple multiple-equation forecasting formulation. Also, Isard and Czmanski have shown that multipliers derive from export-base, income-expenditure, and input-output models are of the same order of magnitude (W. Isard and S. Czmanski, "Technique for Estimating Multiplier Effects of Major Government Programs," *Papers, Peace Research Society* [International, 1965], pp. 19–45).

can be designed to introduce the effects of, for example: changing productivity (through the aggregate production function), changing consumption patterns as a result of changing demographic conditions (through the consumption function), changing import propensities as a result of changing population size, and changing area income levels (through the import function). Changes such as these in the underlying structural relations that characterize an area economy are much easier to introduce in multiple-equation models than in either export-base or input-output.

Problems of Income Expenditure Frameworks

Although the econometric approach to aggregate urban analysis is flexible and can be modified to account for many and various types of behavior, the approach is severely limited by the availability of data. The numbers both of observations available on any particular variable and of the variables for which series exist for urban areas are so small that structural parameter estimates generated by the standard econometric techniques are subject to relatively large errors. The consequence of this is that forecasts derived from such a framework are also imprecise.

Urban macro frameworks of this type also face the problems common to other econometric approaches, namely, that the empirically observed variables often do not measure the conceptual variables required by the theoretical formulation, and therefore proxy variables are often used. In addition, a theoretically satisfying analysis often requires a dynamic specification that further increases the number of observations required for accurate fitting of the relations; and as the framework is modified to more fully represent real world behavior, the number of equations and variables increases rapidly, making the framework much more complex and difficult.

V. RESOURCE-BASE FRAMEWORKS

Up to this point, we have concentrated on frameworks which include an external perspective of the causes of urban change, which, as discussed in Chapter 6, is primarily a "demand side" orientation. However, there are many important features of a particular urban economy—even a highly open economy—which are internal. And of major importance in a "supply side" analysis are consideration of the quantity and quality (and the closely related concept of the age) of the physical capital, the human capital embodied in the residents of the urban area, the transportation facilities, and in general the social environment, as well as natural resources associated with the area. In contrast to the class of frameworks we called export-base or economic-base, there are relatively few explicit and self-contained frameworks that are useful for analysis based primarily on the "resource base" of an urban economy.[57] This does not mean that the resources, and in general the production and cost conditions, of the urban economy are in any sense less important than the demand conditions; rather, the many and diverse factors that influence the supply side of an economy are not as easily brought together into a single analytic framework as are the demand conditions.

However, there is one type of framework, which has proven to be of interest in the medium- to long-term analysis of national economies, that allows a unified treatment of some of the major influences on the productive capacity of an urban economy. The use of a single, aggregated production function,[58] if it is well specified, allows analysis of the effects of factors such as changing technology and changing labor and capital stock on the output of the economy. In a counterpart to the assumption implicit in the demand side frameworks, that the supply of factors is highly elastic, the use of aggregate production function analysis generally assumes that there is sufficient demand so that output will be determined primarily by the production capabilities of the economy.

Production functions, which relate measures of aggregate inputs to measures of aggregate output, are often considered a convenient framework for exploring the determinants of economic change. At the national level, they have proven to be very powerful tools, since the early formulation of Cobb-Douglas have been refined, by Robert Solow and others,[59] to account for interactions among different types of labor and capital inputs and their effects on output. Specific urban area production function analyses, however, are virtually nonexistent. Part of the reason is that only in recent years have measures of urban output, comparable to measures of the national output, become available. A more fundamental reason relates to the conceptual foundation of an aggregate production function, namely, that the "basis for believing in the existence of a simple and stable relationship between a measure of aggregate input and a measure of aggregate output is uncertain at best."[60] However, the aggregate production function

[57] However, the basic input-output framework can be used for a supply side analysis that allows calculation of the effects of changes in the supply of primary factors such as labor, capital, and imported inputs. See Edgar M. Hoover, *An Introduction to Regional Economics* (New York: Knopf, 1971), pp. 234–238.

[58] In this section, we are concerned with production functions as an analytic framework. Often, however, simplified aggregate production functions are included as part of the system of equations in the income and expenditure framework.

[59] Two complementary discussions of the general types of production functions previously applied to both industries and national economies are: A. A. Walters, "Production and Cost Functions: An Econometric Survey," *Econometrica*, vol. 31 (1963), pp. 1–66; and Murray Brown (ed), *The Theory and Empirical Analysis of Production* (New York: National Bureau of Economic Research, distributed by Columbia University Press, 1967).

[60] Richard R. Nelson, "Aggregate Production Functions and Medium-Range Growth Projections," *American Economic Review*, vol. 54, no. 5 (September 1964), pp. 575–606.

has proven fruitful for analysis of national eonomies and for international comparisons, as well as for providing an essential component in the highly theoretical development of modern growth theory. It is to be hoped that it can prove to be of similar usefulness in urban macroeconomics.

A simple Cobb-Douglas function[61] indicates that the output (O) change is determined by the productivity (A) change, the labor input (L) change, and the capital (K) input change.[62] The parameters, b and $1-b$, equal the elasticities of output with respect to labor and capital, respectively, which under competitive assumptions represent proportionate payments (factor shares) to labor and capital. Ordinarily, they are estimated from regression analyses and are therefore heavily influenced by the period chosen for observation. Whether these coefficients are stable, or whether they sum to 1, as in the Cobb-Douglas formulation, has been seriously challenged with respect to a nation's aggregate production function, and would be even more dubious with respct to an urban function.

The productivity change is also estimated from the regression equation and represents a "residual" after the effects of the quantity of labor and capital on output have been accounted for. To obtain more meaningful productivity estimates, it is necessary to specify in the equation characteristics in addition to the quantity of labor and capital inputs. Particularly, it is important to specify, in some way, the quality of labor and capital, so that the "residual" represents a closer approximation of "true" technological change.[63]

The productivity parameter is estimated as a residual, dependent on

[61] Specifically,

$$\Delta O/O = \Delta A/A + b \, \Delta L/L + (1 - b) \, \Delta K/K \qquad (7.35)$$

[62] A more general form of aggregate production function, which includes Cobb-Douglas as a special case, is the so-called Constant Elasticity of Substitution (CES) functions of the following form:

$$O = g(dK^{-r} + (1 - d)L^{-r})^{-v/r}$$

where
  g = an "efficiency parameter"
  d = a "distribution parameter"
  v = a "returns to scale parameter"
  r = a "substitution parameter"
  g = >0
  d = $(0, 1)$
  v = >0
  r = >-1

[63] Equation 7.36 shows one such expansion used by Richard Nelson (retaining the Cobb-Douglas assumption that factor shares sum to 1).

$$\Delta O/O = [\Delta A^*/A^* + b\lambda_L + (1 - b)\lambda_K - (1 - b)\lambda_K \Delta \bar{a}] + b\Delta L/L + (1 - b)\Delta K/K \qquad (7.36)$$

Thus the bracketed term in (7.36) equals the $\Delta A/A$ of (7.35), where $\Delta A^*/A^*$ represents a closer approximation of technological change than does $\Delta A/A$, since the λ parameters represent changes in the quality of labor and capital and $\Delta \bar{a}$ equals the age of capital. But what confidence can be attached to the stability of these parameters in an urban setting?

local labor and capital. Yet it is probably most significantly influenced by technological improvements made elsewhere and their rate of diffusion. The quality of labor is influenced by migration as well as internal demographic forces. The quality of capital is likely to be highly variable, because the extent of public and private capital obsolescence in an area is heavily influenced by the degree of prosperity in the city. And interpretation of the factor shares becomes difficult because of the extensive flow of labor and property transfers to and from the region.

Furthermore, there is considerable interaction between the supply of labor and capital in a city, because of the relationships between migration and job opportunities. Thus the production function for an urban area would have to introduce leads and lags regarding labor, capital, and productivity, about which very little is currently known and which are ordinarily disregarded at the national level. Thus it would seem that including only the classical labor and capital inputs is too simple an approach for urban production function analysis. It is necessary to go behind these inputs in terms of what has previously been called the "depth" of an urban area.

In the case of the production function that contains only labor and capital inputs, it is possible to rely on some of the explicit functional forms for empirical investigation. However, the incorporation of some of the factors that comprise the depth of the urban area must be more suggestive than rigorous, in the sense that it is not possible to find an appropriate functional form, and that in some cases the "inputs" are, even at the conceptual level, indexes rather than easily measurable quantities. For example, a generalized aggregate urban production function would include as important internal determinants of growth: capital stock, labor, land, technology, transportation resources, and the social system.[64] Not all of these elements are considered in the same way; for example, the technology and the social organization influence how the standard inputs of land, labor, and capital are combined, while the transportation resources are "derived" factors of production. As Horst Siebert points out, both technical knowledge and social organization are not easily defined so as to be operational and would have to be measured by appropriate proxy variables in any particular application. However, the social organization can be considered to include elements such as the creativity and behavioral patterns of the residents, the overall public policy and quality of leadership, and in general the social environment of the area.

[64] Specifically, the production function could be of the form

$$O = f(K, L, Q, T, Tr, So) \tag{7.37}$$

See Horst Siebert, *Regional Economic Growth: Theory and Policy* (Scranton, Pa.: International Textbook Company, 1969), pp. 24–45.

As a natural consequence of the formulation of the production function as (7.37), the framework can be expanded in several ways. For example, the stipulations for labor and capital can be made in a more detailed manner, accounting in the case of the labor input for migration to the area, perhaps as a function of the area wage rate or relative wage rate. The capital stock and investment behavior can be treated best with a dynamic specification of the framework. Similarly, the interest in factor payments is motivation for an examination of the income side of the production relationship. And finally, additional relationships could be added so as to indicate the influence on the social organizaton of factors such as education.

VI. STATISTICAL URBAN MACROECONOMIC FRAMEWORKS

Up to this point we have been concerned primarily with frameworks based in varying degrees on certain theoretically justified hypotheses. However, since there are some empirical relationships about key urban variables that have been observed to hold reasonably well, several frameworks that incorporate and in fact rely primarily on these relations have been constructed, although the basic relationship has not been theoretically established. Such frameworks have been particularly useful for descriptive and predictive models.[65]

Statistical frameworks start from the premise that some economic variables very often display a certain consistency in the way that they change over time. Such consistency is rarely accidental, but results from the way in which institutions and people in the city behave and interact. Often, therefore, such results stimulate theoretical developments. Even when there is no clear indication of why this result occurs, statisticians can take advantage of the fact that it does occur, by projecting the historical consistency to repeat itself into the future. The weakness of such a framework is, of course, that without a theoretical explanation of causal relationships, we have less confidence in the expectation that this particular form of historical consistency will repeat itself in the future. In addition, it is often the identification of turning points, of changes in trend, that is of most interest. Yet this framework, and procedures to implement it, severely limits the possibility of such identification.

Two classes of statistical frameworks, particularly for trend projections, are often used in urban macroanalysis—the single-variable extrapolation or time-trend framework and the ratio extrapolation or allocation framework. There is a third framework that combines the single-variable

---

[65] These statistical frameworks are not to be confused with the various statistical techniques that are used in implementing the theoretical frameworks.

and the ratio extrapolation frameworks, i.e., the differential-proportional or shift and shares framework.

Single-variable Extrapolation Framework

The single-variable extrapolation framework relates the change in a variable to time. It raises such questions as, Has employment in the city increased by about 2,000 jobs per year over the past decade, or at an average rate of 2 percent per year, or perhaps at an annual rate that is one-half of 1 percent greater than the preceding year's increase? Evaluating the historical pattern to determine what pattern of change can be defined as "consistent" is often difficult, and the choice is arbitrary. Standard statistical tests of reliability can be used to help make such decisions. Ordinarily, the curve adopted to describe a consistent trend will be selected from a constant absolute change in the variable over some time interval, a constant rate of change, or a constant movement in the rate of change. More complicated curves are usually not adopted in the application of such a simple statistical framework.

Ratio Extrapolation or Allocation Framework

The ratio extrapolation or allocation framework relates an urban variable to the comparable variable for some larger area—for example, a city's employment as a share of the state or national employment. The empirical reason for using an allocation framework is that many of the important macro indicators in specific urban places—e.g. employment, income, and output—will often show a greater consistency in trend when they are described as a share of some larger area than when they are described in absolute terms. Their consistency is probably a reflection of the slowly changing comparative advantage that a given urban place has over other urban places in the larger urban area.

When the allocation framework is used for projections, a reliable projection of the larger-area variable is required.[66] Because data are more

---

[66] Defining the single-variable extrapolation framework as

$$U_t = aT \tag{1}$$

where
U = the urban variable
T = time

and the ratio extrapolation framework as

$$U_t = bN_t \tag{2}$$

where
N = the larger-area variable, then we can say that (2) is preferred to (1) only if N is exogenously predictable and a is more variable than b. If N is not "predictable," the ratio extrapolation framework will not produce reliable projections. If a is highly variable, then the single-variable extrapolation is not reliable. Even if b is variable within some limits but N is predictable, the ratio framework would probably produce more "accurate" results than the single-variable extrapolation.

abundant and analyses more theoretically secure at the national (or state) than at the urban level, projections of national (or state) variables are likely to be more "accurate" than those of urban variables. Projecting urban indicators by ratio extrapolation takes advantage of out present state of theoretical and empirical understanding; and until we obtain a deeper understanding of urban process, the ratio extrapolation framework will be a pragmatic, relatively cheap, and useful way to project urban indicators.

The major disadvantage of the allocation framework is that at any point in time a number of urban places are likely to be at threshold points marking the beginning of a significant change in the trend of their shares in relation to the larger area, and the allocation framework cannot identify such places. Although the allocation framework implicitly builds in the trend (but not threshold) effects of external events on the specific urban area, it fails to identify why the external events are occurring. Furthermore, it offers little opportunity of identifying how an urban area can plan for changing its response to the external event. Thus, although the allocation framework is relatively easy to apply and probably is more reliable than the single-variable extrapolations, it does not deepen our understanding of the urban economy.

Not only can the allocation framework be applied to a specific urban area, but also all areas within the state or nation can be considered simultaneously. The advantage of working with all areas is that it permits comparison of ratio trends among specific urban areas, so that each one can be extrapolated in relation to others and to the total overall area. This, in effect, represents a shortcut, implicit method for handling trade and other relationships between areas; also, the constraint imposed by allocating no more or no less than the overall area activity reduces the chance that a specific area's extrapolation will be markedly unreasonable. This kind of multiarea allocation requires a considerable amount of information about many areas and is most useful when the intent is to provide extrapolations for a variety of areas, rather than an in-depth analysis of a single area.

Single-variable extrapolation focuses on what is happening within the urban area; ratio extrapolation focuses on the relation between a specific urban area and other areas. These two frameworks can be combined into the statistical framework variously identified as differential-proportional and shift and shares.

Shift and Shares Frameworks

Shift and shares analysis is a framework for both describing and projecting secular changes in selected macroeconomic variables for subnational areas such as regions, states, counties, and urban areas. The framework combines key features of single-variable and ratio extrapolation relative to major industrial sectors; it involves comparisons over some time period between a particular urban area and a reference or benchmark economy, usually the national economy. Although the framework can conceptually be used for value-added or income calculations, in the past it has been most often applied to employment. Once again, this result is due to the difficulty of finding data on the other variables for each industrial sector for relatively small geographical areas such as counties or Standard Metropolitan Statistical Areas (SMSAs). In addition, employment is a highly useful macroeconomic variable in itself and, in conjunction with outside information on wage rates for each industrial sector, provides a description of a major portion of the picture of an urban economy from the income side.

The major feature of the shift and shares framework is that it partitions the change in the employment of a particular sector into three collectively exhaustive components, each of which has an interpretation reflecting different features of the urban and national economies. There is, of course, no single method of partitioning such a change that is best for all uses; ways of resolving the change that are different from that commonly used by shift and shares may provide useful results for other purposes. However, the division employed by shift and shares has the advantage that it isolates a portion (the so-called "competitive share") of the total change that can be attributed primarily to the comparative advantage that a particular area enjoys for the production and marketing of a particular good or goods.

The basic relation used both for description and for projection of shift and shares is formed from the identity stating that regional employment in the ith industry at the end of the period (E_i^*) equals regional employment in the ith industry at the beginning of the period (E_i) plus the change in employment over the period for the industry (ΔE_i^*).[67] The industrial sectors that are identified are those that constitute a substantial portion of the employment in the urban economy. Then the change in employment (E_i^*) is partitioned into three components measuring the influence of national industry change, area industrial mix, and area industry comparative advantage.[68] The industrial mix and the competitive components are considered as "shifts."[69]

[67] Specifically,
$$E_i^* \equiv E_i + \Delta E_i^* \tag{7.38}$$
The notation used here, while it may be confused with that used in the export-base discussion, is standard in shift and shares discussions.
[68] Specifically,
$$\Delta E_i^* \equiv E_i[(US^*/US) - 1] + E_i[(US_i^*/US_i) - (US^*/US)] \\ + E_i[(E_i^*/E_i) - (US_i^*/US_i)] \tag{7.39}$$
where
US_i = national employment in ith industry at beginning of period

Now, using the shift and shares method as a purely *descriptive* framework, all the individual values in (7.39) would be known, and the result of the calculation for a particular sector is a set of values, one for each of the components. The interpretation of the components is as follows: The national share is the increment in employment the sector would have had if it had changed at the aggregate (for all types of industries) national rate. The industry mix component accounts for the change in employment in the sector that is due to the fact that the industry as a whole is growing at a rate different from the average of all industries. And the competitive position component accounts for the fact that the particular industry in the area is growing at a rate different from the national average, i.e., the average of all areas, for that industry.

The sum of the three components will, of course, always add up to the change in employment over the period; however, for purposes of inter-sector comparisons or for identification of the character of a particular sector, it is the magnitude and sign of the elements that are important,[70] and attention is usually focused on the two shift components. For example, a positive competitive position component is interpreted as giving partial evidence of the relative attractiveness of the particular area for the location of a particular industry. This can occur, of course, with an industry that is either growing or declining nationally; all that is required is that employment of the industry in the particular area be growing more rapidly (or decreasing less rapidly) than the national industry. In either case, the method identifies the number of jobs that can be considered as due to the fact that the area's industry is growing more rapidly than the national counterpart. In the case of a negatively signed competitive position component, the interpretation of the value is as a measure of the number of jobs "lost" (actually, not gained) in that industry, presumably because other area are more attractive locations for that industry.

The industrial mix component identifies those industries for which the growth is different from the national average for all industries. The interpretation of the industrial mix component becomes clearer when the analysis is presented in aggregate terms. Consider the case where the competitive position component is zero for each industrial sector and therefore

---

$US_i{}^*$ = national employment in ith industry at end of period
US = total national employment at beginning of period
US^* = total national employment at end of period

The three terms on the right-hand side of (7.39) are called, respectively, the "national share," the "industrial mix," and the "competitive position" components.
[69] The discussion of shift and shares includes several terms for each of the components: national share (national growth, regional share); industrial mix (proportionality shift, compositional mix); competitive position (differential shift, regional component).
[70] The sign of the national share component is nearly always positive, reflecting the steady growth of the United States national economy.

for the total of all sectors. Then, if the increment in total employment is greater than the aggregate national share component, the particular area has an industrial mix different from the national economy and contains, on balance, industries that are growing faster than the average.

The two shift components are interpreted as measuring the effects of two distinctly different economic influences on the individual sectors in the area. The industrial mix component reflects the influence of "the changing total demand and supply relationships for the individual industries, including such elements as income elasticity of demand, changing tastes, technological developments,"[71] and other industry-related influences. The competitive position component "arises out of the fact that some regions gain, over time, a differential advantage (vis-à-vis other regions) in their access to important markets and inputs for each of one or more specific activities. An understanding of this effect involves an understanding of regional input-output relationships for specific activities and sources of their changing form One must become deeply involved in location analysis."[72]

Shift and Shares as a Projection Framework

While the preceding discussion has focused on the properties of the shift and shares framework as a descriptive tool, the method can be used in several ways as a basis for projecting urban change over medium-term periods. As a method of projection, shift and shares has two different formulations; the first preserves the threefold partitioning of the increment in a particular industrial sector's employment and the second combines both of the shift components into a single value and estimates the combined shift component. We turn to these two formulations in turn.

Using the same reasoning as in (7.39) and (7.38), the future or projected increment in sector employment, ΔE_i^{**}, can be written as follows:

$$E_i^{**} \equiv E_i^* + \Delta E_i^{**} \tag{7.40}$$

where E_i^{**} is the projected value of employment of the ith sector in the urban economy. The projected increment in employment can be written as:

$$\Delta E_i^{**} \equiv E_i^*[(US^{**}/US^*) - 1] + E_i^*[(US_i^{**}/US_i^*) - (US^{**}/US^*)] \\ + E_i^*[(E_i^{**}/E_i) - (US_i^{**}/US_i^*)] \tag{7.41}$$

Values of US^{**} and US_i^{**} are necessary to calculate E_i^{**}. If independent projections of the first two values are available, ΔE_i^{**} can be estimated by the shift and shares method. The exogenously given projections of US^{**} and US_i^{**} permit calculations of the national share and the industrial mix components for the urban area's industry. However, to com-

---

[71] Harvey S. Perloff, Edgar S. Dunn, Erich E. Lampard, and Richard F. Muth, *Regions, Resources, and Economic Growth* (Baltimore: Johns Hopkins, 1960), p. 74.
[72] Ibid., p. 74.

pletely estimate (7.41) it is necessary to estimate the competitive position component.[73] There are several ways to do this. However, the method that gives the most precise results (in terms of lowest mean squared error) is to use the previous period's competitive position component as the estimate of the future competitive position component. Now this fact, of itself, indicates that the framework is poorly suited to projection, since merely using the past-period component makes no allowance for a *change* in the competitive position. The formulation of this especially naïve projection model is as follows:

$$E_i^{**} = E_i^* + E_i^*(US^{**}/US^* - 1) + E_i^*[(US^{**}/US^*) - (US^{**}/US^*)] \\ + E_i[(E_i^*/E_i) - (US^*/US_i)] \quad (7.42)$$

Now (7.42), and the other formulations tested by H. James Brown, are clearly examples of what we have called statistical frameworks, in the sense that no explicit attempt is made to introduce the effects of any economic forces on an area's competitive position component.[74] In addition, the formulation of the projection model requires estimates of the overall benchmark economy growth rate as well as of the aggregate industry growth rate.

Criticisms of the Shift and Shares Framework

The basic issue in evaluating shift and shares for a description of urban employment change is the relative usefulness of partitioning the change in the manner suggested. The purpose of the technique is to provide "a rational and orderly method for sorting out the factors which relate to the differences in the rates of employment growth among regions."[75] More specifically, the method identifies which areas and which industries within a particular area have had features that are favorable to growth, as indicated by a positive competitive position component. However, as (7.39) reveals, it is only the competitive position component that reflects any value specifically associated with the urban area, namely (E_i^*/E_i); and this feature accounts for the fact that most empirical efforts concentrate on the competitive position component. Neither of the other two components reflects any local conditions, other than the employment in the sector at the beginning of the period; the coefficients of both the national share and the industrial mix components are the same for all urban areas.

Another weakness of the framework concerns the degree of independence between the two shift components. Ideally, each of the components

[73] This discussion follows that in H. James Brown, "Shift and Share Projections of Regional Growth: An Empirical Test," *Journal of Regional Science*, vol. 9, no. 1 (April 1969), pp. 1–18.
[74] Ibid.
[75] Lowell D. Ashby, *Growth Patterns in Employment by County, 1940–1950 and 1950–1960* (Washington, D.C.: U.S. Government Printing Office, 1965), p. ix.

would reflect the effects of different influences on the particular industrial sector or economy. However, they are not independent, in two senses. First, the particular area's growth rate (E_i*/E_i) influences the national rate of growth for that same sector (US_i*/US_i), since the growth of employment in the area is part of the national growth. However, more important is the fact that certain economic influences will affect both the components directly, thereby eliminating the isolation of effects that the method tries to achieve. For example, consider the case of a technological change that results either directly or indirectly in an increase in employment in a particular industry. This change will influence the industrial mix component, as claimed, but it will also influence the competitive position component to the extent that the industries in the particular area take advantage of the new technology.

A third problem is that the framework takes no account of *changes* in the industrial structure in the area during the period under observation.[76] That is, suppose that the period is long enough so that a set of policies, directed at reducing the area's dependence upon an industry that is declining or growing very slowly nationally, has effect. In such a case, the calculation of the industrial mix component introduces a bias, since the magnitude of the component is calculated on a base, E_i, that reflects the industrial structure at the beginning of the period. However, in the case of a policy to reduce employment in the sector, the more appropriate weight is that of employment at the end of the period, or perhaps some intermediate value[77] that reflects the industrial structure of the area more accurately.

In addition to the problems involved in using shift and shares for description, an examination of the efficacy of projections based on the formulation of (7.42) reveals that this characterization of shift and shares is not very effective in contrast to either of two very simple, but not shift and shares, methods. Better predictions of area industry employment can be made by projecting employment by the urban area's industry at either the industry national growth rate over the preceding period or at the predicted industry national growth rate.[78] In addition to providing better predictions, the alternative methods require less data than the shift and shares framework, since they do not include the all-industry national growth rate estimate.

[76] This is a less serious weakness, the shorter the time period; however, some of the empirical applications have involved periods of five to ten years.
[77] For a discussion of the properties of variously chosen weights, see Lowell D. Ashby, "Changes in Regional Industrial Structure: A Comment," *Urban Studies,* vol. 7, no. 3 (October 1970), pp. 298–304; and F. J. B. Stillwell, "Regional Growth and Structural Adaptation," *Urban Studies,* vol. 6, no. 2 (June 1969), pp. 162–178.
[78] See H. James Brown, op. cit., pp. 4–9, for a careful evaluation of the relative merits of the three methods applied to SMSAs.

Shift and Shares as a Theoretical Framework

While the purely statistical approach toward projection with shift and shares is a relatively weak procedure, the basic concept of estimating the change in employment of an industry that is due to factors influencing the comparative advantage of a particular area is useful. The factors that influence comparative advantage include those bearing on access to inputs to the industry and on the particular markets for final products of the area's industry. A framework which allows for identification and quantification of the factors that influence an area's comparative advantage (and thereby its industries' employment) must employ at least a twofold partitioning of an industry's employment. The twofold distinction is necessary because influences other than comparative advantage, which is a supply side consideration, affect an industry's employment. The other influences, such as changing tastes, technology, and prices of substitute goods, can influence the increase or decrease in the demand for the goods produced by a particular industry and thereby in the industry's employment.

A shift and shares framework that has proved useful for projecting employment for subnational economies, such as states or counties, is based on the following identity:[79]

$$E_i(t) = E_i(t-1) \frac{US_i(t)}{US_i(t-1)} + C_i(t) \tag{7.43}$$

where $E_i(t)$ is industry employment in the area in year t, $E_i(t-1)$ is industry employment in the area in year t minus 1, and $US_i(t)$ and $US_i(t-1)$ have similar interpretations. There are two differences between this formulation of shift and shares and the formulation of (7.39). First, the framework has an explicit yearly period specified while the previous form of shift and shares is based on an unspecified time span. The second and major difference is the division of $E_i(t)$ into just two components. The first term on the right-hand side of (7.43) is what employment would be in industry i if the regional rate of growth were the same as the national rate. The last term, called the "competitive effect," takes on positive or negative values according to whether the regional industry grows faster or slower than the national industry. Expression (7.43) holds as an identity when applied to historical data, $C_i(t)$ being defined simply as the difference between actual industry employment and what industry employment would have been had it grown at the national rate for the industry. And such a twofold partitioning may be useful for describing past patterns of

[79] This framework has been developed by Curtis C. Harris, Jr., in "State and County Projections: A Progress Report of the Regional Forecasting Project," Occasional Paper series, Bureau of Business and Economic Research, University of Maryland, January 1969.

change in the same sense as the descriptive shift and shares method discussed above.

However, for projection purposes the formulation of (7.43) is to be considered as an equation by which national projections of industry employment, $US_i(t)$, can be allocated to regional and urban economies. Such national projections can be allocated to subnational economies by assuming that all areas grow at the national rate; but by projecting the competitive effect it is possible to obtain more realistic regional projections. The competitive effect is interpreted as a measure of the advantages and disadvantages of particular areas for various industries. And the basic procedure for this framework is the specification of the various factors that influence $C_i(t)$ and the estimation, by regression analysis, of the magnitude of their influences on the competitive effect.

The magnitude of the competitive effect for an industry is influenced by: the prior competitive effect, interindustry effects, prior employment levels of the industry, income and population, and specialization of the area's economy. The prior competitive effect acts as a proxy for the many influences that affected the previous location of an industry and that may influence the location of the expansion of employment. For example, an industry may have grown in the past in an area because of its favorable location with respect to markets for inputs, to intermediate goods, or to skilled labor. If such market conditions have not changed, a positive $C_i(t-1)$ may indicate a positive $C_i(t)$. In fact, even if transportation and input costs have changed unfavorably for the industry, the relative costs of relocating or expanding at the present location may be such that it is not profitable for the industry to move. On the other hand, certain industrial sectors, perhaps those with relatively low fixed costs and highly competitive markets for their output, may be especially sensitive to changes in input costs, and the prior competitive effect, reflecting only past conditions, may not be useful for projection.

The interindustry effects are those effects on a particular industry due to the changes in employment (and implicitly, output and input purchases) of other industrial sectors in the area. For example, the change in employment in the fabricated metals sector will influence the employment in primary metals industries; similar relationships exist between the automobile industry and the metals products industry, and between the furniture and the lumber and wood products sectors. A method of accounting for the interindustry effects is to relate the competitive effects of industry i in the present period, $C_i(t)$, to the past-period competitive effect in the related industries, $C_j(t-1), C_k(t-1)$, etc.

The increments in employment in a particular area for an industry have been found on the basis of past performance to be related negatively to the level of employment in the industry. While this result is well established empirically, its theoretical justification is unclear, perhaps related to the concept of the S-shaped time-related growth curve of an industry and so-called "mature industries."[80] Another relationship concerning employment in some industries is that when an industry is of major importance in the economy, it tends to have slow rates of growth, and where the industry is of minor importance in the economy, it tends to have larger rates of growth. Two sorts of measures can be used to capture the relative specialization of an economy—the proportion of an area's employment that is provided directly by a particular industry and the area's "export status" for the industry. The export status is defined as the difference between direct employment of an industry and the employment it would have if it had the national proportion of employment in the industry.[81]

The final variables included in the estimation of $C_i(t)$ are area income and population changes. For some industrial sectors, such as primarily service industries, changes in population and income influence the demand for the industries' output, and the effect on employment is obvious. Industrial sectors that sell primarily to areas outside the urban economy are not influenced by such income and population changes. Rather, the demand for such output is affected by national factors. And the national influences are included in the first term of (7.43) rather than in the competitive effect.

The projection framework presented here is essentially a way of allocating an exogenous forecast of national industry growth. The method requires much more information than does the simple shift and shares formulation. Observations are required on area population, income, industrial specialization, and previous competitive effects for the related industries in the area. In addition, the technique requires several observations on each variable, so as to obtain sufficient confidence in the relationships estimated by regression methods. However, the accuracy of estimates based on the method is much higher than that of the simple projection method of (7.42); for example, variation in the competitive effect explained by the method, when applied to a single state or to counties within a state, is consistently over 70 percent. In addition, the basic framework here is amenable to further modification, in which account can be made, for example, of (1) changing transportation costs, (2) the fact that the effects of externalities on one industry by another can be introduced directly instead of through the prior competitive component of the other industry, and (3) the effects of policy instruments, such as the quality of the area's

---

[80] See Wilbur R. Thompson, *A Preface to Urban Economics* (Baltimore: Johns Hopkins for Resources for the Future, 1965).
[81] The "export status" is similar to the location quotient-based estimate of nonlocal employment of Chap. 7, part II.

transportation system, and other publicly provided features that influence the desirability of the area for location of industries and workers.

The examination of urban macroeconomic frameworks is incomplete until their efficacy has been subjected to the test of implementation. The next chapter will deal with the task of converting the frameworks into models and investigating their applicability to urban macroeconomic analysis.

CHAPTER 8

APPLICATION OF URBAN MACROECONOMIC FRAMEWORKS

I. INTRODUCTION

The frameworks that were discussed in the preceding chapter are the basic macroeconomic techniques employed in urban and regional analysis. Now we will turn to models that are derived from them and have actually been used. They are exceedingly diverse, reflecting the different purposes and resources of individual research efforts.

Two broad groups of features of these models are discussed here. First, we make some general observations about the models constructed for various uses and their characteristics with regard to the periods used, variables included, relative difficulty of implementation, and data requirements. Second, in applying any of the frameworks discussed above to a particular urban area, the resultant model reflects a series of decisions by the researcher about which transactions to associate with the urban economy, which sectors are sufficiently important to capture the essential features of the economy of interest, what is the appropriate level of detail of the structure of the model, and what data to use to calibrate the model in the fitting or estimating procedure. These features, as well as illustrations of the types of information available from models based on different frameworks, are presented in the latter part of the chapter. In addition to illustrating the basic frameworks with models, we will note some of the ways in which they have been modified, partially as a result of experience with models, to improve urban macroeconomic analysis. The final section of this chapter presents a discussion of the problem of choosing and evaluating the policies available to both local and federal governments to influence the growth and stability of urban economies.

II. CONCEPTUAL ISSUES OF PROJECTION, IMPACT, PLANNING, AND DESCRIPTIVE MODELS

All of the frameworks presented in Chapter 7 rely on certain exogenous events, or stipulations of the flow rates of different sorts of variables, to provide the stimulus for change within the urban economy; and the predictions (or, more broadly, the results) of the models are conditional upon the exogenous stipulations. There are three important theoretical features relative to the dependence of the models on the exogenous stipulations. First, the reliability of the results of the models depends heavily on the accuracy of the stipulations; and a general principle is to avoid making the model itself more sophisticated than the specification of the exogenous events. For example, the usefulness of the individual sector predictions from an input-output model is limited by the accuracy of the stipulations of final demand components. This potential difficulty with applied models is partially avoided by the concentration of the analysis on the appropriate coefficients or multipliers (as discussed in Chapter 7), and by using the model not so much for its absolute predictions as for the descriptions of the potential effects of changes in the exogenous stipulations.

A second feature common to many urban models is that the change-inducing stimulus primarily represents reaction to conditions that take place outside the area being analyzed. For example, the expansion of export sales by a particular sector, or the introduction of a new industry (or plant) in the area are influences on the area, but the cause of these changes is an assumed change in conditions outside the area. That is, there is no provision in the models that we are familiar with for changes (such as technological change or the introduction of completely new forms of industries) originating strictly within the urban economy.[1] All of the changes in the urban economy are the result of the linkage of the urban area with the rest of the national economy. Earlier models made strong assumptions about the relation of the urban economy and the rest of the world, which resulted in the urban area being treated as a completely passive respondent to forces that originate outside the area. In more recent models, allowance is made for the influence of relative urban/national conditions on the magnitude of the linkages between the urban economy and the "rest of the world." For example, in the labor supply portion of an income-expenditure model, relative regional and national wage rates influence migration and thereby the labor force and area population.[2] And there have been suggestive formulations of urban frameworks in which relative urban/national prices influence the export sales of the area.[3]

The third major feature is concerned with the way(s) in which the external effects are introduced into the urban models. In a large proportion of models, the urban economy is influenced only through its sales to

[1] If a framework is calibrated for a particular urban area, it is possible to *simulate* the effects of changing technology (or, more broadly, a changing internal structure) and trace the consequences for the economy. So far, however, simulation methods have been applied only to urban microeconomic models for investigation of land use, retail sales patterns, etc.

[2] Fredrick W. Bell, "An Econometric Forecasting Model for a Region," *Journal of Regional Science*, vol. 7, no. 2, pp. 109–127.

[3] Lawrence R. Klein, "The Specification of Regional Econometric Models," *Papers of the Regional Science Association*, vol. 23 (1969), pp. 105–115.

other areas.[4] This implicit assumption is usually justified by asserting that, in the short run, export sales are the single most important variable and that introducing other forms of external influence is both analytically and empirically difficult. However, a direct incorporation of the effects of such important factors as credit and monetary conditions, population, and national income is desirable. In the simple models that use sales as the only form of linkage between the national and the urban economy, the effects of the important national variables are transmitted primarily through the implied effects of these variables on sales of the area. However, more recent and sophisticated models attempt to incorporate these forms of influence more directly.

For the models that use sales to buyers in "the rest of the world" as the major linkage, a twofold distinction as to the purchasers is often employed. Private sector purchases from the area, reflecting the purchase patterns of industries and persons, are generally treated as "more stable" than are the public sector purchases. This reflects the role of government (primarily the federal government) as a major consumer and employer; and many impact analyses, especially, have investigated the consequences of a decrease in purchases of defense-oriented goods.

While there is considerable variety in the actual models constructed, the majority of these models can be classified by the use to which they are put. Many models are used for multiple purposes, since the uses are not mutually exclusive and in fact are complementary; however, the following fourfold distinction is useful: projection, impact analysis, planning, and descriptive models. For projection models, the primary interest is in measuring the total compounded effect on the area's economy of several separate changes in the economic structure and in predicting values of the endogenous variables for the area at some time in the future. That is, a projection model usually attempts to account for as many of the important changes in the area's economy as is feasible, so as to increase the accuracy of forecasts and to provide a detailed representation of the economy. Additionally, the estimates of a projection model are usually made for a specifically identified date in the future.

In contrast, the basic feature of an impact analysis model is its focus on estimating measures of the consequences for an area of a change in a single condition, or at most very few. For example, an impact analysis

[4] There is a growing body of theory and applied work on the interrelations between various subnational areas. Much of this work has been concerned with the relations between "regions," often states or groups of states, and has attempted to specify the major influences on interarea flows of goods. See, for example, Karen Polenske, "Empirical Implementation of a Multiregional Input-Output Gravity Trade Model," in A. P. Carter and A. Brody (eds.), *Contributions to Input-Output Analysis* (Amsterdam: North Holland Publishing Company, 1969), and several research reports of the Harvard Economic Research Project.

might be concerned with the effects on the total level of employment and (or) income in the area of a change in the output or employment of a single major employment sector in the economy. And the period of adjustment to the "impact," as the cause of the change is frequently called, is often not specified. This means, for example, that the increase implied by an export-base framework in total area employment in a major industrial sector is properly interpreted as the value of additional employment toward which the economy will tend after the increase in nonlocal employment has had its complete effect on the economy. This lack of explicit specification of the time of adjustment causes no particular problems for impact models, except for very short-term measures of the impact, since most users of such models are interested primarily in the state of the economy after all changes have had sufficient time to be transmitted. Some of these issues will next be taken up in detail.

Projection Models

Urban macroeconomic models used for projection purposes can be further classified with respect to several important features: periods used, variables included, and relative difficulty of implementation and of satisfying data requirements. Of course, many of these features are not independent of the basic theoretical frameworks, but considerations of these features are the primary conceptual or theoretical issues that arise in the transition from framework to model. The major time-related issue for projection models concerns the time span of the projection.[5] The time span exhibited in combined urban and regional models ranges from very short (three months or a year) to very long (twenty years or more); however, most urban models are used for from one- to five-year estimates.

There is a definite relationship between the type of framework used for the model and the time span of the estimates. The simplest statistical frameworks provide the basis for most of the very short-term projections. These models use extrapolation and simple trend predictions and incor-

---

[5] Another issue is the period used in the structure of the model. By the "periods" of the structure of the model we mean the length of the lag period used in inclusion of lagged values of either endogenous or exogenous variables in the behavioral relations that make up the model. Virtually all models based on the export-base, input-output, and shift and shares frameworks that we present here are "timeless," in the sense that they contain no lagged variables; however, models based on an income-expenditure framework sometimes contain one-period lagged values of area income or output in the behavioral equations. Some statistical projection models, usually for short-term projections, estimate the future-period values of the variable as current-period values plus a trend or growth factor; e.g., Daniel B. Suits, *An Econometric Model of Michigan* (Michigan: Department of Commerce, State Resource Planning Program, Technical Report no. 3 [1966]); here, however, the use of lagged variables is primarily to increase the accuracy of estimation rather than to indicate functional dependence of the next period's values on the current values.

porate a good deal of the researchers' intuition.[6] For projections of periods of from one to about five years, the theoretical frameworks form the basis for many models, and the projection formulation of shift and shares is used also. For longer-term estimates, say of over ten years, primarily input-output frameworks are used.[7] However, there are also sets of projections that are derived from the simultaneous use of several, often informal, models that deal with specific parts of a regional economy. For example, the resultant long-term estimates for an area are often based on a projection of population, estimates of the level of activity of the industries currently included in the economy, estimates of new forms of industrial activity in the area, projections of the national economy, etc. While clearly these estimates are not independent, especially for the highly interrelated urban economy, they are often combined—by the judgment of the researchers rather than by the use of a formal structure of interrelations.[8]

Many individual models, once they are calibrated, are used for multiple-term projections, i.e., for one-, five-, and ten-year forecasts. Sometimes the models have both a short-term and a longer-term version, which share a common core of estimated coefficients. However, such projections must be considered as essentially separate estimates, since virtually all urban projection models are inherently static, in the sense that they generate (a series of) point estimates of the values of the endogenous variables rather than of the time paths of such values. While most large-scale national macroeconomic models share this feature,[9] presumably because of the difficulty of constructing, estimating, and even understanding the properties of dynamic models, the lack of dynamic specification and estimation is particularly disturbing for models of the interrelated urban economy, especially when it is evident not only that the values of many variables are interdependent but that their rates of change are also related.[10] Another result of the lack of dynamic specification of the models is the absence of

---

[6] On such simple short-term projections, see William H. Miernyk, "Forecasting Short-Term Regional Economic Activity," paper presented before the Regional Science Association, December 1958, pp. 1–5.

[7] The form of very long-term input-output-based projections sometimes differs from that presented in Chap. 7, in that attempts are made to incorporate changes in the structural coefficients that result from changing technology and trading patterns. See William H. Miernyk, "Longe-Range Forecasting with a Regional Input-Output Model," *Western Economic Journal*, vol. 6, no. 3 (June 1968), pp. 165–176.

[8] For example, the work done on the New York metropolitan area in Raymond Vernon, *Metropolis 1985* (Cambridge, Mass.: Harvard, 1960). Another example is Irving Hoch, *Forecasting Economic Activity for the Chicago Region: Final Report*, Chicago Area Transportation Study (May 1959).

[9] For a condensed presentation of the properties of the major national models, see Marc Nerlove, "A Tabular Survey of Macro-econometric Models," *International Economic Review*, vol. 7, no. 2 (May 1967), pp. 127–175.

[10] A notable exception is W. E. Oates, E. P. Howery, and William J. Baumol, "Public Policy in Dynamic Urban Models," *Journal of Political Economy*, vol. 79, no. 1 (January/February 1971), pp. 142–153.

any explicitly cyclical model of the urban economy. Although some of the specifications of the income-expenditure framework include an accelerator type of investment relationship, which would allow a simple multiplier-accelerator process, most urban macro models do not include a distinct treatment of cycles in activity.[11]

A final point with respect to the periods used in the various models concerns the comparative suitability of the various models for short- and longer-term projections. While no empirical investigation has fully determined the relative accuracy of the various models, it is clear that the "appropriate" period of forecasts depends partially upon the degree of confidence that one has that the structural aspects of the urban economy incorporatd into a model will approximate the actual structure in the future. From this point of view, the income-expenditure frameworks may be the most useful; they generally include the least restrictive assumptions and the most flexible relationships and have proven to be the dominant form of macro model for national economics.

The variables incorporated in projection models are of two types: those that are estimated or projected (endogenous variables) and those in which the projections are considered to be conditional (exogenous variables).[12] The models can be classified, with respect to their endogenous variables and to the transactors identified, as essentially "industry" models or "economywide" models; and the various frameworks are used for both types of models. For example, the input-output framework can be used to project just the levels of industrial-sector output and employment, in which case it can be considered as a detailed "industry" model, and the shift and shares method is clearly suited fon an industry-by-industry analysis. However, an input-output model in which the household and local government sectors are included as endogenous is an economywide model, in that it incorporates the behavior of the major transactors in the urban area: consumers, government, and business firms. Income-expenditure models are generally economywide models, representing investment, consumption, and fiscal behavior of governments, although in some cases such models treat specific, major industries in the economy separately.

The variable estimated in industry-based models is either employment or industry output, and the most frequently used variable is employment.

---

[11] Considerable work has been done on the concept of regional cycles, essentially for state economies, which has concentrated on collecting empirical evidence for subnational cycles and making interregional comparisons, e.g., George H. Borts, "Regional Cycles of Manufacturing Employment in the United States, 1914–1953," *Journal of the American Statistical Association,* vol. 55 (March 1960), pp. 151–211, and references cited there.

[12] Some short-term forecasting has concentrated on an index of regional industrial activity as the "endogenous" variable; however, such measures are rarely as informative as the other variables mentioned here. (William H. Miernyk, op. cit., "Forecasting Short-Term Regional Economic Activity.")

Although input-output models can be used to estimate only industry output and employment, most industry-based studies are done with shift and shares or industry-specific, export-base models. And although neither of these methods is restricted to estimating employment by any property of the theoretical framework (they are also applicable to measures of value added or output), they have dealt almost exclusively with employment as the unit of measure, because of the availability of the data. In economy-wide models, an income or product measure is most usually the major endogenous variable. And although the "income received" measure is probably the most informative of the income variables, in the sense that it more fully represents the income available to the residents, "income produced" is the most frequently used endogenous variable, because of the difficulty of finding data on and estimating the interarea transfers.[13]

Some economic-demographic variables such as population and labor force are included directly in models based on income-expenditure frameworks; however, these variables are more often either incorporated in side calculations appended to the main economic model or alternatively not included at all. In input-output-based models, for example, there is not a direct way to include the projected level of population into the structural relationships, yet for longer-run projections the level of population clearly influences the area's economy. Therefore the effects of population are included in the estimates of final demand deliveries, or in the consumption relationship if households are introduced as an endogenous sector. For shorter-run projections, the effects of demographic variables such as population, distribution of income, and size of the labor force are often not included explicitly; the assumption is made that these variables change relatively slowly over time and therefore can be considered as remaining constant or growing at past historical rates.

The issue of the relative ease of implementation of projection models based on the various frameworks depends almost entirely upon the relative availability of the data required by the frameworks. In this regard, models based on input-output frameworks are the most difficult to construct,[14] ideally requiring information on the specific trading patterns of firms in the particular urban area; but in the past many subnational input-output models have taken the coefficients from the model of the Office of Business Economics, U.S. Department of Labor, for the United States economy and made certain adjustments (often based on location quotients) to obtain coefficients that, it is hoped, represent the particular regional

---

[13] However, Laurence Chau, *An Econometric Model for Estimating Income and Employment in Hawaii* (Economic Research Center, University of Hawaii, June 1970), has estimated income received.

[14] For example, the cost of the Philadelphia input-output model, probably the largest-scale urban input-output research project, is estimated to be a quarter of a million dollars.

structure.[15] By contrast, models based on the simple form of export-base framework generally use less detailed data and require a much more modest amount of effort to implement them.[16] The econometric income and expenditure models seem to be intermediate between input-output and export-base models with regard to the data requirements. Econometric models, however, require a series of observations over past periods (rather than surveys) to determine current employment and trading patterns, and the longer the series, the more precision is allowed in the estimation of the structural relationships. However, the development of these models is at such an early stage that it is difficult to generalize about their data needs. Projection models based on shift and shares seem to have relatively modest data requirements, since the estimates of national growth rates for the industrial sectors are generally available to a researcher from other sources. However, as the shift and shares projection model has been refined, its data requirements approach those of econometric income-expenditure models.

Impact Models

An impact analysis, which concentrates on measuring and estimating the consequences for an urban economy of a particular stimulus or set of closely related exogenous stimuli, can be either the major reason for the construction of a model or the result of a combined projection and impact analysis interest in the economy. If impact analysis is the primary reason for creating the model, a basically simple export-base framework is usually used, in which a few major industrial sectors are identified and for which the multipliers are calculated.[17] However, when both projection and impact analyses are based in the same model, the majority of such applications have used an input-output framework.[18] And these more detailed

---

[15] This technique is so popular because it is relatively inexpensive; and substantial analytic work has been done to determine the properties of such adjustments, e.g., Stanislaw Czmanski and Emil E. Malizan, "Applicability and Limitations in the Use of National Input-Output Tables for Regional Studies," *Papers of the Regional Science Association,* vol. 23 (1969), pp. 65–77; and William S. Schaffer and Cong Chu, "Nonsurvey Techniques for Constructing Regional Interindustry Models," same issue, pp. 83–101.

[16] Cf. C. Tiebout, *The Community Economic Base Study,* Committee for Economic Development, Supplementary Paper no. 16 (New York, December 1962), in which he estimates the cost of an export-base model at around $5,000; also, the export-base model discussed in sec. III below required only six weeks of data collection and statistical analysis.

[17] This is the type of analysis illustrated in the export-base model example presented in sec. III below.

[18] For example, Walter Isard and Thomas W. Langford, Jr., "Impact of Vietnam War Expenditures on the Philadelphia Economy: Some Initial Experiments with the Inverse of the Philadelphia Input-Output Table," *Papers of the Regional Science Association,* vol. 23 (1969), pp. 217–265. Another example is William H. Miernyk, Ernest R. Bonner, John H. Chapman, Jr., and Kenneth Shellhammer, *The Impact*

impact models make up most of the more recent impact analyses. In such cases the core of the model, which is the matrix of estimated production or trading coefficients, can be used both for projections and for impact analyses with the calculation of the appropriate multipliers, as discussed in Chapter 7. The advantage of using an input-output framework is, of course, that it accounts for the numerous interrelations among producing sectors and allows for a detailed "tracing out" of the effects of a postulated change in a particular sector (or in strongly related sectors, as in the case of the Philadelphia model, where the many sectors associated with the requirements for military activity were considered together).

The income-expenditure framework allows calculation of impacts as well, although the use of such models for this purpose has been limited so far. The impact coefficients in such a simultaneous equation model are the so-called "reduced form" coefficients that show the change in the endogenous variable(s) caused by changes in the values of the exogenous variables. While such models often contain relationships for a few major industrial sectors, and hence are amenable to the same sort of industrial-sector impact analysis as is done with input-output, they also allow different sorts of direct calculations of the impacts of, for example, changing the tax rate or changing money wage rates in the urban area.[19]

Impact analyses can be done by means of variously calculated "impact coefficients"; however, the technique of simulation is another way to measure the magnitude of the impact, with the impact estimated as the difference in the values of the endogenous variables projected upon different stipulations of the exogenous variables. If, for example, when the area wage rate is $4 per hour, employment is estimated to be 100,000, and when the wage rate is $5 per hour, employment is estimated to be 80,000, then the "impact" of a $1 increase in the wage rate is a loss of 20,000 jobs. In the case of exogenous variables included explicitly in the model, the result of this sort of simulation is formally equivalent to the results obtained by the use of impact coefficients. However, this procedure allows another type of impact evaluation that is of significant interest, in which a two-step method is used.[20] Consider the question of evaluating the impact on an urban economy of a change in national monetary and fiscal policy. Then, because the urban economy is linked to the national economy through export sales and other means, the effect on the level of GNP,

of Space and Space-Related Activities on a Local Economy, A Case Study of Boulder, Colorado (Boulder, Colo.: Bureau of Economic Research, Institute of Behavioral Science, July 1965).

[19] R. J. Green, *A Long-Range Econometric Forecasting Model for Illinois* (Bureau of Economic and Business Research, University of Illinois, March 1967), has analyzed the consequences of changing tax rates in such a model for the state of Illinois. See also Norman J. Glickman, "An Econometric Forecasting Model for the Philadelphia Region," *Journal of Regional Science,* vol. 11, no. 1, 1971, pp. 15–32.

[20] Glickman, op. cit., pp. 30ff.

and thereby on export sales, of changing monetary conditions can be evaluated with a national economic model. The direct effects on the area's economy can then be estimated with the urban model that incorporates the effects of changing levels of GNP, interest rates, etc. The results of such estimation clearly depend heavily upon the accuracy of the estimates used in the national model. Although there has been no formal analysis of the efficacy of indirect simulation, such analysis seems to be a promising area for further work and has some application to input-output models as well.

Planning Models

The ability to simulate, with reasonable accuracy, the consequences for a particular economy of various conditions, some of which may be under the control of public decision makers, is a necessary tool for effective urban macroeconomic planning. Up to the present time, "urban planning" has dealt almost exclusively with topics that are microanalytically oriented, such as land-use requirements, densities and the spatial growth of the urban area, the effects of various transportation projects, and urban renewal. As urban centers increase in size and as they form clearly delineated economic entities, interest in planning for such macroeconomic goals as income, employment, price stability, and quality of life will tend to increase.

In this kind of macroeconomic planning, the frameworks presented can provide the basis for development of explicit planning models. In the terminology of Chapter 6, the macroeconomic frameworks we have discussed here require the additional specification of appropriate measures of the degree to which certain "goals" for an economy are attained, so as to allow evaluation to be made of the desirability of various alternative programs or policies. The formal development of appropriate measures or "indicators" of goal achievement and, more importantly, of trade-offs between indicators of conflicting goals has been as slow for urban economic analysis as it has for national economies.

However, some tentative, often informal, planning models have been applied to urban economies. For example, one of the results of an impact and projection analysis, like the example of the St. Louis area discussed in section III below, is the identification of certain sectors that contribute to destabilization of the urban economy or of sectors that contribute relatively little to the growth of the area's income and employment. And although no "objective function" is formally specified in such a case, the information about the features of the various sectors is often used by economists, planners, and governmental officials in directing efforts to induce certain "desirable" industrial firms to locate in the area.

Furthermore, the frameworks discussed here can be used in fiscal or "financial" planning of local governments. Once again, the St. Louis model provides a good illustration of how a basic input-output model, with appropriate side calculations, can provide estimates of the consequences for local government of increases in the level of output of various interindustry sectors that might be occasioned by an urban industrial development policy. Additionally, the work of R. J. Green[21] shows the effects on the fiscal status of a subnational governmental unit of different combinations of taxation and expenditure policies. Although, in general, the local government sector included in income-expenditure models for urban areas is too "coarsely" specified to provide a detailed estimation of the fiscal status of local government, a carefully specified submodel of the urban government[22] can be constructed and contained within or appended to an urban macro model.

Another example of the potential in planning for the frameworks discussed here is the application of an input-output framework to questions of the "quality of urban life," a broad concept that includes such elements as the quality of the physical environment, occupational mobility, and the distribution of income. The essential feature of the method of dealing with such concepts is the association of certain by-products or externalities with the level of output of each of the various interindustry sectors.[23, 24] Then the effects on the elements of the quality of urban life, such as the amount of pollutants emitted or the changes in the distribution of income in the area, can be calculated for various stipulations of final demand.

Although none of these tentative applications of the major frameworks of urban macroeconomic analysis to planning has specifically included a "metric of goal achievement," it is clear that the techniques are useful in evaluating the effects of various policies, by presenting estimates of the array of results most likely to follow from a particular development or growth program.

Descriptive Models

Although the descriptive models, which attempt to describe past patterns of urban change, are the least interesting from the analytic point of view, they provide information useful for at least two purposes. Since in one

[21] R. J. Green, op. cit.; W. L. L'Esperance, G. Nestel, and D. Fromm, "Gross State Product and an Econometric Model of a State," *Journal of the American Statistical Association,* vol. 64, no. 327 (September 1969), pp. 787–807, contains several tax rates and other policy variables which would allow similar calculations.

[22] Sidney Sonenblum, Werner Z. Hirsch, and Morton J. Marcus, *A Conceptual Framework for State and Local Fiscal Analysis,* MR-158 (Institute of Government and Public Affairs, UCLA, February 1971).

[23] Werner Z. Hirsch, Sidney Sonenblum, and Jerry St. Dennis, "Application of Input-Output Techniques to Quality of Urban Life Indicators," *Kyklos,* vol. 24, no. 3 (November 1971), pp. 511–533.

[24] The concept of "by-product" is discussed in E. J. Mishan, "The Post War Literature on Externalities: An Interpretive Essay," *Journal of Economic Literature,* vol. 9, no. 1 (March 1971), pp. 1–28.

sense any statistical characterization of the structure of an area's economy is descriptive, the calibrated models that are based on theoretical frameworks, such as input-output, income-expenditure, and projective shift and shares, are descriptive models that allow interarea comparisons of the stage of development or the structure of the various economies. However, as discussed in Chapter 6, the purely descriptive models represent an important step in the further development of understanding of the properties of urban areas. For example, the descriptive shift and shares model is only one of many ways in which data on past changes in the level of employment of the industrial sectors can be arranged. However, its usefulness lies in the fact that it provides the basis for an analytical approach to the questions of comparative advantage and industrial location.

III. SPECIFIC MODELS

This section presents detailed examples of models based on the major types of frameworks: export-base, input-output, income-expenditure, and shift and shares. These examples indicate the types of results available from the various approaches, the kinds of urban areas to which they have been applied, and the problems encountered in applying the frameworks. Most of the models illustrated here are useful for projections or impact analyses, and to lesser extent for planning.

Export-base Analyses

The export-base framework has provided the basis for many analyses of urban areas. However, the simplest and most aggregate form, as discussed in equation 7.5, which attempts to represent the economy with a single multiplier, has been modified and extended in recent applications. Most export-base models include a greater level of detail by specifying certain industries or producing sectors of key interest and then estimating multipliers specific to each sector. Additionally, the primary use to which such models have been put has been impact analysis; other frameworks have proven to be more useful for projection purposes. While the trend has been toward more detailed models, estimated by more sophisticated methods, the fundamental viewpoint of export-base analysis about the relation between local and nonlocal employment (sales, income, and other variables) has remained the same.

We will present a study of the Portsmouth, New Hampshire, economy[25] as a representative example of an export-base model; it is an application to a relatively small urban center. Export-base is a method that is

[25] Steven J. Weiss and Edwin C. Gooding, *Estimation of Differential Employment Multipliers in a Small Regional Economy*, Research Report to the Federal Reserve Bank of Boston, no. 37 (November 1966).

probably best suited to smaller economies, in which the local and non-local sectors are distinguished relatively easily; furthermore, a small economy is generally more open and hence amenable to export-base analysis and its stress on the importance of nonlocal export activity.[26] Export-base uses employment as the unit of measure, in contrast to income analysis, primarily because employment data are more available. It is an impact analysis by its emphasis on export sales to the federal government, which are of sizable magnitude in the area's economy and are potentially highly volatile.

The actual area studied is the extended Portsmouth, New Hampshire, area, which contains about 60,000 workers and their families. The major employer in the area is the Portsmouth Naval Shipyard, which employs approximately 8,000 workers. Another major federal government influence in the region is the Pease Air Force Base; together these two government installations accounted for approximately 20 percent of employment in the area during the decade for which the study data were available. The large private sectors of the economy are the following: food and kindred products, printing and publishing, glass and clay products, leather and leather products, lumber and wood products, and tourism. Portsmouth is a small, open economy, without a broadly based "local sector," and the nonlocal sector is concentrated in the production of relatively few goods and services; clearly, the economy is not highly diversified.

In making the transition from framework to model, regardless of the type of theoretical or statistical framework, the choice of which people, jobs, and transactions to include within the economy depends more on the judgment of the researcher than on any well-established guidelines. In this case, the exact geographical boundaries of the area were determined by employment and residence patterns; the boundaries were drawn such that about 80 percent of the residences of shipyard workers were included in the area studied.

The primary reason for the study was that in Portsmouth, as in many other areas of the United States in the middle 1960s, there was serious concern on the part of local residents and planners about the repercussions of possible reduction in local defense activities. The levels of output and employment in the naval shipyard are particularly susceptible to fluctua-

[26] However, the export-base framework has been applied to large areas, although less frequently. For an example of the application to the Los Angeles area economy, see George H. Hildebrand and Arthur Mace, Jr., "The Employment Multiplier in an Expanding Economy," *Review of Economics and Statistics*, vol. 32 (August 1950), pp. 241–249. Another example is B. B. Brown, Jr., *Export Employment Multiplier Analysis of a Major Industrial Community* (Houston: Center for Research in Business and Economics, University of Houston, 1964). A model that incorporates the export-base framework along with a separate analysis to predict industrial location is Michael Goldberg and Gerald R. Walter, "Forecasting Employment and Industrial Location in the San Francisco Bay Area," *California Management Review* (Summer 1968), pp. 13–26.

tions in the national priority assigned to the naval defense force, which is a policy-determined variable completely outside the control of the residents or governments in the area.[27]

The procedure used to classify employment in the area as local or nonlocal is quite simple. Approximately 63 percent of employment was allocated on an a priori basis as being in the nonlocal sector. The nonlocal sector includes all employment in the shipyard and air force base and in tourism industries. State and local government, construction, retail and wholesale trade, and professional, financial, and personal services employment were allocated directly to the local sector.

The method of location quotients was used to classify approximately 22 percent of manufacturing employment. The technique used was that illustrated in Chapter 7, with the feature that the benchmark economy was not the national economy; rather, the New England area was used as the basis for comparison, in an attempt to account for regional differences in taste and production functions. The remaining employment, about 16 percent, was allocated to the nonlocal sector by a rule-of-thumb procedure.

The impact multipliers calculated in the study are the following:

Sector	Multiplier—k
Private export employment	1.8
Civilian employment at the naval shipyard	1.6
Employment at the Pease Air Force Base	1.4

The relatively larger multiplier for the private export sector as contrasted to either of the defense-oriented sectors may be due to the fact that the military base provides for itself many "service" or local functions, such as facilities for shopping, recreation, and medical care. A large military base is fairly self-sufficient and economically cut off from the private local sector. Additionally, the response of local-sector employment tends to be limited if the level of activity at a military or defense-related establishment is expected to be unstable or temporary; and both the shipyard

---

[27] Interest in effects on an area from changes in defense-related spending has been the motivation for many studies of this sort (as well as for some using input-output frameworks); e.g., Ian Donald Terner, *The Economic Impact of a Military Installation on the Surrounding Area: A Case Study of Fort Devens and Ayer, Massachusetts,* Research Report to the Federal Reserve Bank of Boston, no. 30, 1965, which uses an export-base approach. A much larger study, incorporating but not relying entirely on export-base, is *Community Readjustment to Reduced Defense Spending: Case Studies of Potential Impact on Seattle-Tacoma, Baltimore, and New London-Groton-Norwich* (United States Arms Control and Disarmament Agency, Washington, D.C., December 1965).

and the air base had experienced in the time prior to the study a series of wide fluctuations in employment. The low multipliers may reflect a certain learning behavior on the part of local employers.[28]

Since the shipyard offers fewer services or local facilities for its personnel, it is reasonable for it to have a multiplier that is larger than that of the air force base. However, because many of the material inputs to the shipyard are not provided by the relatively small Portsmouth economy, the proportion of total shipyard expenditures that create local income is smaller than it is in the case of private exports. In addition, since the wages of shipyard workers are substantially higher than the average for the area, it may be that shipyard workers have a higher propensity to purchase goods produced outside the area than do those who are employed in private export production. This also would account for a lower impact multiplier.

There are several different methods of calculating the multipliers for an export-base model; and for the highly aggregate, single-equation characterization of an economy, the simplest technique is to form the ratio between local and nonlocal employment. However, because the simple ratio has been strongly criticized, more recent export-base models have used other methods of estimation. For this model, the multipliers were estimated with single-equation, least-squares regression methods; they essentially attempted to measure the marginal effects on total employment of the three important sectors by estimating each multiplier as a transformation[29] of the regression coefficient of the linear relation between total employment and the employment in each of the sectors. In contrast to the single-observation base-ratio method, which tries to predict future employment levels on the basis of the local-nonlocal relationship at a particular time, the regression method for this model used a series of ten observations; hence the regression coefficients and the resultant multipliers are a type of weighted average of past local-total employment patterns.[30]

An additional feature of the Portsmouth study is the attempt to uncover statistically the length of time of the impact on total employment of changes in the employment in the nonlocal sectors. A series of simple distributed-lag hypotheses were tested, and the results provide preliminary indication that a lag of approximately six months exists before the total

---

[28] This is the source of a criticism of the export-base framework in which changes in nonlocal employment are asserted to have the "full" multiplier effect, regardless of whether the changes are anticipated to be relatively long- or short-run.

[29] Specifically, the multiplier is estimated as the regression coefficient plus 1.

[30] There have been several investigations of the features of estimation of export-base multipliers with regression analysis, including: Edwin F. Terry, "Linear Estimators of the Export Employment Multiplier," *Journal of Regional Science*, vol. 6, no. 1 (Summer 1965), pp. 17–34; Se-Hark Park, "Least Squares Estimates of the Regional Employment Multiplier: An Appraisal," *Journal of Regional Science*, vol. 10, no. 3 (December 1970), pp. 365–374.

impact of changes in nonlocal employment is completely transmitted through the economy.

Aside from the models that embody the more standard type of export-base analysis, there are several models that are derived from the fundamental assumptions and viewpoint of export-base; and as we relax the definition of what constitutes a strictly export-base model, we are led to consider a series of additional studies, some of which are quite similar to input-output or income-expenditure models. A major feature of such models is a greater amount of detail in the specification of the producing sectors in the economy and a more extensive specification of the external factors that influence the economy. For example, in an "intersectoral flows analysis," which is a hybrid of both export-base and input-output, using employment as the unit of measure, the final sales include consumption and investment in housing, plant, and equipment, as well as exports to private buyers and the federal government, among others.[31] And impact coefficients, similar to multipliers, are calculated that show the direct plus the indirect and induced employment effects, analogous to these effects as discussed in input-output. In fact, the "linking" method of assigning a sector's employment to exports or other final uses can be utilized by means of the inversion of a matrix similar to the procedure used in input-output.

Urban Input-Output Analyses

Input-output models have proven to be useful macroeconomic tools for large metropolitan economies.[32] In addition to being applied primarily to large economies, these studies generally are used for multiple purposes, including projections for various periods in the future as well as for impact analysis. Both of these features of input-output models are probably due to the relatively high cost of implementing and maintaining an input-output model. There is considerable variety among the models with respect both to their size, measured in terms of the number of endogenous sectors, and to the type of data used to calibrate the technical coefficients matrix. The approximate range of the models is from 20 to 500 sectors; some rely on survey data taken from the local economy, while others make certain adjustments on coefficients taken from national models. A final feature

[31] W. Lee Hansen and Charles M. Tiebout, "An Intersectoral Flows Analysis of the California Economy," *Review of Economics and Statistics,* vol. 45 (November 1963), pp. 409–418. This is an example of the "extended" export-base framework discussed in Chap. 7.

[32] A sampling of the major metropolitan areas for which input-output models have been constructed includes: Boulder, Colorado; Chicago; New Orleans; Boston; St. Louis; New York; and Philadelphia. For a bibliography of subnational input-output models, see Phillip J. Bourque and Millicent Cox, *An Inventory of Regional Input-Output Studies in the United States,* Occasional Paper 22 (University of Washington, Graduate School of Business Administration, 1970).

common to most of the models is that the basic input-output model forms a core from which other sector-related variables may be estimated; or the model may be used in conjunction with other information about the area, such as its projected population growth, the projected location of new industries, and its patterns of growth.

As a detailed example of the urban input-output framework we will present its application to the St. Louis area in 1955;[33] it was one of the earliest studies in which the transactions matrix and therefore the coefficient matrix were constructed primarily with data gathered by extensive survey of the urban economy. The input-output model itself forms the basis of calculations not only for a series of projections and the impact coefficients for sector outputs, income, and employment, but also for extended side calculations measuring impacts on local government revenues and expenditures.

The geographic area included in the study is coincident with the St. Louis Standard Metropolitan Statistical Area, which, in 1954–1955, consisted of five counties with a total population of 1.8 million. The area is far removed from other metropolitan areas and is surrounded by a sparsely populated and mainly agricultural hinterland. Very little labor mobility exists between the metropolitan and adjacent areas. Thus, in many respects the St. Louis SMSA is a distinct, closely interrelated economic entity.

Its economy is highly diversified. In 1955, it produced an output totaling $15.6 billion. Of this output, $11.6 billion was sold to the local economy and $4.0 billion was exported. Thus, about 74 percent of local output was produced for direct local use. Both exports and imports varied greatly from industry to industry. The larger magnitude and greater diversity and complexity of the St. Louis economy, in contrast to that of Portsmouth, New Hampshire, require that a more detailed type of framework be implemented to accurately characterize it.

The St. Louis model is an open, nondynamic equilibrium model in which, under equilibrium conditions at a given time, a limited number of goods and service flows are balanced. The St. Louis model relied for its implementation mainly upon company and government records. Secondary data sources were used in connection with households and the state and federal governments. The model was implemented in two basic forms: with household and local government sectors included as elements of final demand, and with households and local government included in the interindustry matrix as endogenous sectors. The inclusion of these sectors as endogenous appears to be appropriate for urban areas, since the activities

[33] Werner Z. Hirsch, "Interindustry Relations of a Metropolitan Area," *Review of Economics and Statistics,* vol. 12, no. 4 (November 1959), pp. 360–370; and Werner Z. Hirsch, "Application of Input-Output Techniques to Urban Areas," in Tibor Barna (ed.), *Structural Interdependence and Economic Development* (London: Macmillan, 1963), pp. 151–168.

of the household and government sectors are closely related to the level of economic activity in the area.

The St. Louis input-output model is designed to give a structural description, as complete as possible, of the transactions occurring in the area during a given period. The model can be considered to be represented by an interindustry flow table composed of three subtables—a local matrix that represents local sales to local sectors; an export matrix that represents local sales to nonlocal sectors; and an import matrix that represents nonlocal sales to local sectors. However, since the main concern is with output, employment, income, and governmental expenditures within the St. Louis metropolitan area, and not with the external supplying industries, the import matrix is compressed into a single import row.

Within the input-output framework, the primary source of change-producing forces is in the levels of sales to final demand by the various producing sectors. With the household and local government sectors included as endogenous sectors, the model allows direct calculation of coefficients that measure the impacts on sector outputs and on income resulting from changes in various sectors' sales to final demand. While the impact of changes in the levels of sales to final demand on the output of various sectors provides important information for planners and businessmen in itself, the primary usefulness of estimates of changes in sector outputs is that they allow further calculations about the impacts of employment and governmental expenditures and revenues.

As in the discussion of Chapter 7, the total income impact is conceptually separable into direct and indirect effects; and when the household sector is included as endogenous, an induced income effect is also considered. The direct income impact of an increase of $1 million in sales to final demand of a particular sector is the amount of income that would be paid out by the particular sector if it were to increase the value of its output by $1 million. The indirect income effect accounts for the total repercussions on outputs and income payment of all sectors associated with the increased sales to final demand of a particular sector. The induced income effect is that impact on income in the area which is attributable to the inclusion of the household (and local government) sector as endogenous.

Considering the formulations of the model in which the household and local government sectors are endogenous, calculations of the total income impacts per dollar of change in final demand revealed one industry having six times the impact of another industry.[34]

---

[34] For example, assuming a $1 million increase in sales to final demand, the lowest total direct, indirect, and induced income impact is associated with the products of the petroleum and coal sector, in which the income increase is $220,000. The manufacturing sector with the largest total income effect was the printing and publishing industry, for which the impact was $870,000. In contrast, the largest total impact for all sectors was for the medical, educational, and nonprofit sector, in which the income increase was $1.34 million.

However, the magnitudes of the total income increases do not tell the whole story, since sectors also differ widely with respect to the relative importance of the direct, indirect, and induced effects. For example, the relative unimportance of the indirect effect for the transportation equipment sector is an indication of this sector's reliance on imported inputs that generate income changes outside but not inside the St. Louis area. In contrast, the low relative importance of the indirect effect for the medical, educational, and nonprofit sector reflects the fact that this sector uses few inputs other than from local households and therefore generates little indirect income.

Employment levels were related to changes in sector outputs by use of employment-output relationships, estimated from survey information that included time series data on employment and output patterns of firms in the area. The result was a series of employment-output coefficients with which production changes can be converted to direct and indirect employment impacts. The employment impacts were measured in man-years, and, assuming a $1 million change in final demand, the sectors with the largest changes were trade (258 man-years) and medical, educational and nonprofit (283 man-years).

The employment multiplier relating the direct plus indirect employment changes to the direct changes indicates the extent to which total area employment is affected by changes in man-year employment in a given sector. These multipliers vary from a low of 1.12 in the transportation equipment sector to a high of 1.49 in the eating and drinking places sector.

For both income and employment considerations, not only the magnitude of the impact but the potential variation of sales to final demand determine a sector's influence on the stability of the urban economy. The detailed final-use matrix identifies final sales of each sector which are made to industrial sectors outside the area. Such data allow preliminary identification of those sectors likely to be destabilizing. For example, the transportation equipment sector sold 97 percent of its output outside the area to the federal government (64 percent) and transportation equipment (33 percent) sectors. This heavy dependence upon two export markets, both of which often encounter substantial demand changes, suggests that transportation equipment is an unstable sector. However, the overall impact of this sector on the instability on the St. Louis economy is reduced by its low income and employment impacts.

The St. Louis input-output model also facilitated an analysis of the effects of industrialization on expenditure and revenue considerations of local governments. The particular governmental function to which the model was applied was education; and the impacts were evaluated through a series of side calculations.

The impact of a change in final demand sales on the three sources of revenues for education (residential property tax, commercial and industrial property tax, and state aid to schools) was traced in the following way (see Figure 8.1). From the input-output model, the impacts on sector employment were calculated as above; then the number of family units associated with each sector was linked to employment by use of a worker-family ratio. With the aid of data on family income by sector and an income-residential property value coefficient, residential property values per worker per sector were estimated and totaled, to give estimates of residential property values per sector. In addition, estimates of commercial and industrial property value were related to the value of sector outputs. Then changes in property values were multiplied by the prevailing school tax rate to give an estimate of the locally raised school tax revenues. State aid to local schools was estimated for each sector by a worker-student enrollment ratio, and the resulting enrollment was multiplied by a figure for state aid per enrollee.

The effect on school expenditures was linked to sector employment by the following method (see Figure 8.2). With estimates of the number of public school children per worker, employment was translated into estimates of students per sector, and then cost-per-student relations were used to calculate school costs attributable to each sector. Comparing the revenue and expenditure impacts results in a "net fiscal resources" impact that shows the effects on the school district of changing the output levels of various sectors. These calculations revealed that low-wage sectors such as textiles and apparel products had a negative impact on the net resources position of the school district; a high-income sector such as products of petroleum and coal had a positive impact.

An urban input-output model can also provide a detailed characterization of the economic structure of an area. It can be incorporated with informal models of population change and residential and industrial location to provide a series of comprehensive projections of many features of a major metropolitan area. Another interesting use of an input-output model has been to evaluate the effects on the local economy of trade with other countries.[35] A supplementary use of an input-output model is to identify sectors forming an industrial cluster with strong internal and relatively weak flows so as to guide investment policy on the part of urban decision makers. For example, if clusters of highly related sectors can be identified, then fostering the establishment of new complementary plants may promote the development of a fully developed industrial complex.[36] Investments that might be rejected, if examined in isolation, might prove

[35] Werner Hochwald, Herbert E. Striner, and Sidney Sonenblum, *Local Impact of Foreign Trade* (Washington, D.C.: National Planning Association).
[36] Stanislaw Czmanski, "Some Empirical Evidence of the Strength of Linkage between Groups of Related Industries in Urban-Regional Complexes," paper presented to the Seventeenth Annual Meetings of the North American Regional Science Association, November 1970.

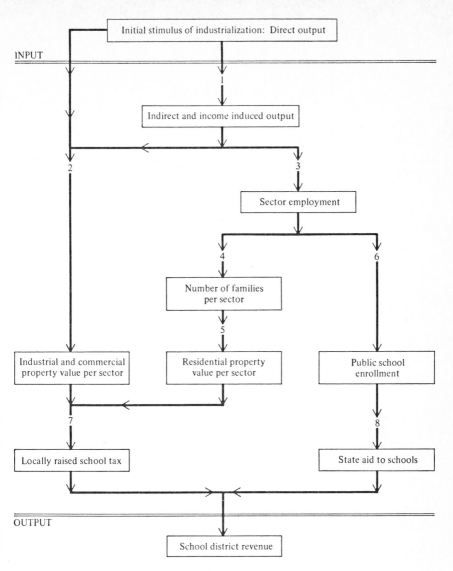

FIGURE 8.1 *Flow chart of revenue side. Source: Werner Z. Hirsch, "Fiscal Impact of Industrialization on Local Schools,"* Review of Economics and Statistics, *vol. 46, no. 2, p. 193.*

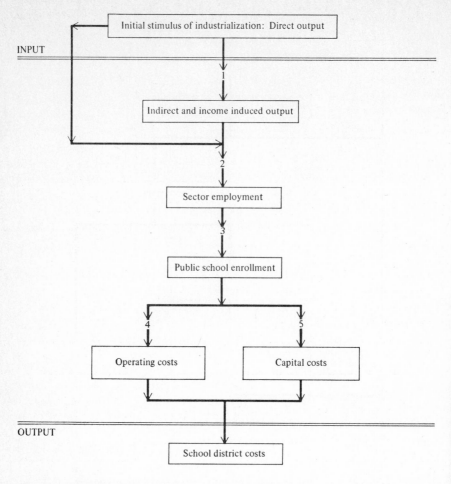

Legend of coefficients:

1 Inverse regional input-output
   matrix
2 Sector output-employment ratios
3 Worker-enrollment ratio
4 Per pupil operating cost
5 Per pupil capital cost

FIGURE 8.2   Flow chart of cost side. Source: Werner Z. Hirsch, "Fiscal Impact of Industrialization on Local Schools," Review of Economics and Statistics, *vol. 46, no. 2, p. 194.*

to be more efficient because of long-run economics of agglomeration associated with industrial complexes.

There are two other urban examples of large-scale input-output models. The first is a study of the Boulder, Colorado, economy and the income and employment effects on it of expenditures related to space explorations

(NASA expenditures).[37] The data for the forty-sector model were collected by a survey of businesses and households to establish both trading and consumption patterns. The household sector was included in some calculations as an endogenous sector so as to allow calculation of induced income and employment effects. Various types of consumption-income functions were used to account for nonlinearities in the relationship and to distinguish between the effects on consumption of increased income of established residents and the change resulting from population growth as new workers are attracted to the area by new job opportunities. In addition to evaluating the impacts of space and space-related expenditures on the Boulder area, additional calculations were made that show the direct effects of such expenditures on the Denver area, the rest of the state of Colorado, and the rest of the world.

The second study,[38] originally conceived to evaluate the effects of NASA expenditures but used also to evaluate the effects of the Vietnam war on the Philadelphia economy, represents a very comprehensive (500-sector) input-output model. In addition, final demand was disaggregated into eighty-six classifications; and a submodel was developed for a major country within the Philadelphia SMSA. One of the most interesting features of the model is its extension into environmental quality analysis, in which the economic system is represented by the input-output model and the influences of the economic system on the ecological system are transmitted through relationships that show the amounts of pollution of the water associated with various levels of production.

Income-expenditure Forecasting Analyses

As an application of econometric techniques to the estimation of what is essentially an income-expenditure framework, we have selected a study by Norman Glickman of the Philadelphia SMSA; it illustrates the major advantages and disadvantages and the potential of this form of urban macroeconomic model.[39] The model represents one of the first applications of the income-expenditure framework, and although it departs in some respects from the eclectic framework presented in Chapter 7, it shares the common properties of such models.

The Philadelphia model consists of twenty-six structural equations and definitions (and an equal number of endogenous variables); while there

---

[37] Miernyk, Bonner, Chapman, and Shellhammer, op. cit.
[38] Walter Isard and Thomas W. Langford, Jr., *Regional Input-Output Study: Recollections, Reflections, and Diverse Notes on the Philadelphia Experience* (Cambridge, Mass: MIT, 1971), and Walter Isard, Thomas W. Langford, Jr., and Eliahu Romanoff, *Philadelphia Region Input-Output Study, Working Papers* (1966–1968), vols. 1–4 (Philadelphia: Regional Science Research Institute).
[39] Norman J. Glickman, Jr., "An Econometric Forecasting Model for the Philadelphia Region," op. cit.

are eight exogenous variables, the urban economy is tied to the national economy almost exclusively through export sales of an aggregated "manufacturing" sector. Total production of marketed goods and services (gross regional product) is divided into three components: manufacturing, wholesale trade and services, and other production. The level of output of the wholesale trade and services and that of the other—production—sectors are related to personal income in the area through two separate "consumption" or, more properly, "expenditure" functions (since the major components of aggregate demand, such as consumption, investment, export, and governmental purchases, are not separately identified). It is in this sense that this model could perhaps be termed an "income and production" model in contrast to the strictly "income and expenditure" aspects discussed in Chapter 7. The output of the manufacturing sector is determined solely by United States gross national product. This formulation is consistent with the reasoning in export-base analysis, where some sectors are identified as "local" and others, which sell primarily to buyers outside the area, are termed "nonlocal."

Investment behavior is included only for the manufacturing sector, and a simple form of a "stock adjustment" model is used, in which investment in a given year depends upon the level of output for that year and upon the level of the capital stock in the preceding year. The statistical investigation reveals that such a simple characterization of the investment decision works only moderately well and that a more fruitful approach might be to use distributed lags, as is done in many national econometric models.[40]

Three employment-output relations are included, one for each of the producing sectors. In Chapter 7, these relations were derived from sector production functions. In contrast, this model estimates the employment-output relation statistically as the simple linear regression between number employed and the value of output. And although such a procedure is not justified analytically, the results are apparently good enough to make the method useful. With the addition of essentially a simple trend formulation for the estimation of the area population, the model allows calculation of the unemployment rate.

An interesting feature of the model is the estimation of the money and real wage rates of the producing sectors as well as of an overall urban price index. The money wage rate for each sector is a function of the corresponding national sector (average) wage rate and the level of unemployment in the urban economy, so as to capture the effects of both national and local labor market conditions. The hypothesis that local firms must pay nationally "competitive" wages to keep laborers from migrating to

[40] For example, Dale Jorgenson and James A. Stephenson, "Investment Behavior in U.S. Manufacturing, 1947–1960," *Econometrica*, vol. 35, no. 2 (April 1967), pp. 169–220.

higher-wage areas is confirmed by the data, but local labor market conditions, indexed by the level of unemployment, are not statistically significant in the regression function.[41] An exceptionally simple form of estimation was used for the area price level, and the results indicate a high degree of explanatory power. The consumer price index is a function of average unit labor costs (the ratio of the total wage bill to the gross regional product) and total employment in the area. The first variable implies that firms set prices as a markup over unit labor costs. The total employment variable is used as a proxy for the phases in the "business cycle" of the urban economy, the reasoning being that there are cyclical patterns in price setting, e.g., the average markup will be higher during boom periods (when employment is high) than it is during recessionary periods.

The final major relationships that complete the model structure are seen in two local government equations, one for expenditures and the other for revenues. Local government revenues depend upon area personal income (taken as exogenous from the production-employment-wages block of the model) and the local property tax rate. Local government expenditures are treated as a simple function of local government revenues. Although the fit of both relationships is quite good (the adjusted coefficient of multiple correlation, R^2, is .94), the characterization of the government "block" of the model is clearly its weakest feature. It takes no account of either intergovernmental transfers such as matching funds or, more importantly, of the influence of local government expenditures on the level of gross regional output or income.

The model was estimated with time series data for the period 1949–1966, and most equations were fitted by two-stage least squares. The overall results of the estimation were quite good, as indicated by the comparisons of the estimates and the actual values of the endogenous variables over the sample period. The mean absolute percentage errors for the individual equations (excluding the manufacturing sector investment function) were generally in the 3 to 4 percent range. Although no single measure is commonly used to evaluate the overall effectiveness of a model of this sort, these results compare favorably with the results of other models based on samples of similar size.

An interesting feature of this model is the attempt to incorporate measures of the impact of two alternative programs of the federal government on the Philadelphia economy. The Wharton Economic Forecasting Unit national econometric model was used as the basis for projecting national variables (gross national product and the average wage rates in the three producing sectors), and two separate national forecasts were used, one representing an anti-inflationary, restrictive monetary and fiscal policy

---

[41] Glickman indicates that he experimented with various formulations of the "Phillips" hypothesis of an inverse relationship between (the rate of change of) wage rates and unemployment, and that none of the tests were statistically significant.

and the other representing a more neutral policy. Then two alternative urban area forecasts were prepared, based on the two national forecasts. The differences in the estimated regional variables represent measures of the effects of such national policies on the Philadelphia area and were shown to be rather large.[42]

The basically very simple form of this model (which is a relatively large-scale urban model) illustrates the most serious problem inherent in the econometric estimation of simultaneous equation frameworks. The major constraint on the model, in terms of both possible relationships to be included and precision of fit, is due to the difficulty of finding appropriate data to measure urban variables corresponding to those that have proven to have substantial explanatory "power" in other (primarily national) models of this type. The effect of the difficulty of obtaining the appropriate data results in (1) a bias toward the simplest (in the sense of having the fewest independent variables) formulations of the individual structural equations in an attempt to conserve degrees of freedom,[43] and (2) a tendency toward use of relatively highly aggregated variables. Both of these features are especially damaging in models of urban economies in which there is a degree of interrelatedness that requires the ability both to specify detailed relationships and to account for several independent effects in each relationship.

Shift and Shares Analyses

Shift and shares analysis has been applied to three large urban areas, Cleveland, Pittsburgh, and Cincinnati,[44] in order to describe past patterns of urban employment change, particularly those resulting from the area's competitive position.[45] The benchmark economy was an aggregate of thir-

[42] While the technique itself is interesting but fraught with difficulties (such as having the effect of compounding the estimation errors of two models in the resultant regional forecasts), the results are somewhat unexpected. For example, under the more restrictive policy mix, personal income and gross regional product would be, respectively, $338 million and $309 million less than under the less restrictive mix. And the different policies mean a difference of 8,000 jobs for the area. While these measures of the impacts of federal policies represent relatively small percentage differences, their magnitude is significant.

[43] In response to the paucity of data, Anderson has recommended that structural equations not be estimated directly at all but that the estimation be restricted to reduced forms and multipliers; however, this transforms a multiple-equation framework into essentially an export-base framework, and clearly is an unsatisfactory solution to the problem. Robert J. Anderson, "A Note on Economic Base Studies and Regional Econometric Forecasting Models," *Journal of Regional Science*, vol. 10, no. 3 (December 1970), pp. 325–333.

[44] "Employment Performances of Cleveland, Pittsburgh, and Cincinnati, 1950–1966," *Economic Review* (Federal Reserve Bank of Cleveland, March 1967; January 1968; March 1968).

[45] Other significant empirical works are: L. D. Ashby, op. cit.; Perloff, Dunn, Lampard, and Muth, op. cit.; and the original application by Daniel Cramer, "Shifts of Manufacturing Industies" in *Industrial Location and National Resources* (Washington, D.C.: National Resources Planning Board, 1943).

teen Standard Metropolitan Statistical Areas, and twenty-eight major industry or service categories were identified. The performances of the three cities were different, reflecting the diversity of their economies. The period 1950–1964 was broken into two segments, 1950–1960 and 1959–1964, to isolate the competitive position component for each industry for each of the periods so as perhaps to reveal changing "comparative advantage" over the entire fourteen-year span.

Two sectors in Cleveland showed a large competitive position component over both periods—the printing and publishing sector and the textile mill products sector. Despite the disparity in size—the printing and publishing sector employed about 20,000 people, five times as many as did the textile mill products sector—these two sectors are markedly similar in terms of their total impact on the growth of the Cleveland economy; the magnitude of the competitive position component is similar in both sectors: about 1,600 employees in the first period and over 600 employees in the second. The motor vehicles sector exhibited an unusual pattern: the competitive position component was very large, $+14,382$ jobs, in the first period; but in the second period the change was insignificant, indicating a major change in the relative attractiveness of the area for the production of such vehicles.

By contrast, the motor vehicles sector in Pittsburgh showed a positive and large competitive position component in both periods and was the only Pittsburgh industrial sector to show such growth in the second period. However, while the absolute number of added employees was large, the industry is not a significant part of the economy and employs less than 1 percent of the total employment of the covered industries. The general characterization of the Pittsburgh economy over the two periods is one of declining competitive components reflecting growth slower than industry average or decline faster than industry average by the respective Pittsburgh sectors. The major employment sector—primary metals—declined at a rate greater than the decline of this sector in the thirteen major metropolitan areas. The machinery sector in Pittsburgh also had a negative competitive position component, but in this case it resulted from the sector growing less rapidly than the thirteen-city machinery sector. In addition to the declines in the major industrial sectors, there were accompanying declines in the competitive position component for the retail trade and the professional services sectors. The declines in these sectors, which generally have market areas approximately equal to the urban area itself, probably reflect the slow income and employment growth of the other sectors rather than a decline in "comparative advantage" in the usual sense.

The Cincinnati economy also showed a comparative decline; only one sector—fabricated metal products—showed a positive component in both periods, and the component was relatively small. The machinery sector showed a decline in this area also, which, in light of similar declines in

Cleveland and Pittsburgh, would indicate a regional decline in the competitive position component. Aircraft and parts was the most volatile sector, with a large positive competitive position component in the first period and a large negative component in the second. The thirteen-city aircraft and parts sector employment showed a wide fluctuation, increasing in the first period and decreasing in the second. However, the behavior of Cincinnati's competitive position component reveals that the fluctuations in the area were much greater than those in the thirteen-city average, which identifies this sector as a highly unstable part of the Cincinnati economy.

The major application of relatively sophisticated shift and shares to forecast analysis is a nationwide projection of employment in various industries in both states and counties in the United States.[46] Although the method has not been applied to large urban economies, its extension to them is straightforward and the properties of the framework are well illustrated by Harris's work. Twenty major industrial sectors are identified, and the estimates for national employment levels for each sector are derived from a national input-output model.[47] Because of the unavailability of data, a ten-year time span was used; a yearly version of the model will soon be available. In distinction to the framework presented in Chapter 7, where the method was applied to industry employment only, formulation analogous to equation 7.43 was used to project regional "competitive effect components" for both regional personal income and regional population. These estimates were then introduced as explanatory or exogenous variables in the estimation of the competitive effect for employment in each industry in each area.

We illustrate the properties of the model with the relationships used for the county estimates within the state of Maryland. The results show that the different industrial sectors are influenced in markedly divergent ways by the following variables, among others: the prior competitive effect of the industry, the competitive population effect, the export status of the industry, the competitive income effect, the area employment share of total industry employment, and the region's share of total projected income. However, there are some consistent patterns in the data that indicate the major features influencing industrial employment growth. The single variable that influenced most of the individual competitive effects was the prior competitive effect of the same industry. And in general, for industries that could be potentially located in urban centers (i.e., excluding agriculture and mining activity), the larger the prior competitive effect, the larger the forecasted competitive effect. On the strict interpretation of the eco-

[46] Curtis C. Harris, Jr., *State and County Projections: A Progress Report of the Regional Forecasting Project*, Occasional Paper series, Bureau of Business and Economic Research, University of Maryland (January 1969).

[47] Clopper Almon, Jr., *The American Economy to 1975* (New York: Harper and Row, 1966).

nomic meaning of the prior competitive effect, the results show that whatever factors (such as favorable transportation facilities, pool of skilled labor, favorable prices of inputs, etc.) influenced the decision of the firms in the industry to locate or expand in an area previously, these same factors continue to influence the decision to expand employment in the area.

For the service-related industries, such as communications, utilities, trade, services, civilian government, finance, insurance, and real estate, the "competitive population effect" entered significantly and positively into the resultant regression relationships. However, the population variable also entered significantly and surprisingly into the estimation of the competitive employment effect in sectors that are generally considered to have large export markets, such as chemicals, fabricated metals, fabricated textiles, and textile mill products. The presence of an effect of area population in the relationships for these industries is difficult to interpret and would be expected to disappear with the use of shorter periods in the estimates.

The expected negative effect of area specialization is evident for sectors such as chemicals, printing and publishing, and fabricated metals, and for heavy equipment sectors such as motor vehicles, aircraft, and shipbuilding. For these sectors, the larger the indicators of specialization, or the larger the portion of total industry employment that was located in a particular area, the smaller the competitive effect component tended to be. A similar effect was present relative to the sectors usually considered to be local: trade, services, finance, insurance, and real estate. For these sectors, the larger the population, the less effect population increases tended to have on the level of employment of these sectors. This may perhaps indicate that there is a level of employment in such sectors that is most efficient, a level which is more readily reached by the sectors in more populous areas.

The accuracy of the forecasts, as indicated by the percentage of variation in the competitive effect explained by the various combinations of explanatory variables (not all variables entered every equation), was very high for cross-sector applications; for fifteen of eighteen sectors, over 90 percent of the variation could be associated with the independent variables. Most of the variables discussed above were statistically significant by the usual tests. These results, and similar ones for a cross-sectional analysis of the location of industrial employment among various states, indicate a great deal of promise for this technique in urban projections. In addition to its application to industrial employment, the method appears to have future use as a means for predicting variables.

In an overall evaluation of the shift and shares framework in its present state of development, it is evident that the framework is more statistical than theoretical in nature. It can, however, provide some guidelines to urban or regional development and growth policy to the extent that it identifies those sectors that are contributing relatively more or less to growth and to the extent that shift and shares models can help uncover the locational and compositional factors that have determined the rate of growth of the area.[48] Factors influencing regional growth, such as pollution, congestion, and agglomeration economies of various kinds, can be introduced into an interdependent shift and shares model by allowing them to influence the magnitude of the growth rates of the industries in the area as well as by incorporating the influence of the growth rates of the industrial sectors on the amount of pollution, congestion, etc.[49] And to the extent that such factors can be incorporated analytically, the potential of shift and shares as a guide to policy is enhanced.

IV. POLICY ASPECTS OF URBAN GROWTH AND STABILITY

Urban growth and stability are important policy goals and involve the setting of appropriate targets for the pace and continuity of growth and the determining of the most feasible means for achieving that growth. The overall economic performance in urban areas is, of course, influenced by activities in specific sectors such as transportation, land use, and education. It has already been pointed out that microeconomic models are available which directly facilitate planning in such specific sectors.

It is conceivable that eventually a planning model for overall economic performance could be developed by combination of specific sector models. However, it is not yet feasible, partly because planning models have not been developed for all important sectors, but more importantly, because the techniques for interrelating specific sector models into a more comprehensive planning statement have not yet been developed.

Thus, if we are to establish policy for overall economic performance, we must seek guidance from the macro models which are developed for projection and impact analyses. These models can provide only limited guidance, primarily because they are not capable of spelling out all the relevant costs and benefits associated with alternative plans. However, the macro models can offer crude and (at broad levels of aggregation) piecemeal, aggregate information which is useful. This may provide insights regarding appropriate economic performance strategies, including distributional consequences of different strategies, i.e., what groups are likely to gain and what groups are likely to lose.

Policy relating to urban economic performance can be regarded in

[48] T. W. Buch, "Shift and Share Analysis: A Guide to Regional Policy?" *Regional Studies*, vol. 4, no. 4 (December 1970), pp. 445–450; and the summary article in the same volume by F. J. B. Stillwell, "Further Thoughts on the Shift and Share Approach," pp. 451–458.
[49] H. C. Davis and M. A. Goldberg, "Combining Shift-Share and Inter-Sectoral Flows Techniques: A Hybird Regional Forecasting Model." Paper presented at the Tenth Annual Meeting of the Western Regional Science Association, February 1971.

terms of a nationwide urban policy or a specific urban place policy. In the former sense, issues of urbanization (see Chapter 9) and geographic distribution of economic activity are particularly important. In the latter sense, programs and plans must be tailored to the unique characteristics of specific places. A national urban policy is the concern of the federal government, while specific place policies are the concern of all levels of government. Because the federal government is concerned with both national and specific place policies, it generally seeks to minimize any possible conflict between the two. However, since there are national economic performance policies, e.g., monetary policy (which by definition are not specific place-oriented), and since there is competition among different places, it is not always possible to pursue optimal performance standards simultaneously at both the nationwide and specific-place levels.

In the following sections we are concerned primarily with showing the relation of the frameworks and models discussed earlier to economic performance policies for specific places. However, it is not a long analytic step to go from a discussion of a specific urban place to a discussion of a national urban policy. The major differences would relate to the administrative and financial aspects of implementing policy.

What Growth and Stability Are Desirable?

Policy makers seeking to formulate a national urban policy, as well as those concerned with a specific urban place policy, ask what growth rates are desirable and what stability performance is desirable. Or, perhaps more correctly, the policy makers are interested in avoiding undesirable growth rates, i.e., those that are very high or very low, and great cyclical instability. With regard to secular growth rates Wilbur Thompson has said, "To grow too slowly is to invite chronic unemployment and poverty, the symptoms of which are slums, blight, and crime. To grow too fast is to invite the capital shortages that lead to the irritating delays and expensive congestion that can be just as damaging to the quality of urban life. . . ." [50]

Similarly, unstable growth is likely to mean that capacities and expectations are generated in the rapid growth phase which cannot be fulfilled in the slow growth phase, resulting not only in hardship in the latter phase, but probably also in a lower overall performance over the long run. In addition, unstable economic performance very often contributes to such ills and inefficiencies as, for example, excessive migration (and reverse migration as well), periodic financial difficulties of local governments, and inability to plan for pleasing and efficient city building.

Urban places vary considerably in the pace and stability of their growth in population, employment, and income. Thus, for example, in the 1960s the Orange County, California, SMSA ballooned from 700,000 to 1,400,000

[50] Thompson, op. cit., p. 2.

residents; Jacksonville more than doubled its population (having annexed within its limits the entire large county of which it was the center); Indianapolis gained 56 precent, also because of annexation; and large advances in population were experienced by several cities in the Southwest, Phoenix increasing by 32 percent, Houston by 31 percent, and Dallas by 23 percent.[51]

Most of the nation's oldest and largest cities, however, stopped growing or showed a decline. Of the twenty-five largest cities, twelve lost population during the decade. Among them are Chicago and Philadelphia, the latter dropping below 2,000,000 for the first time since 1940. Four of the twelve—Detroit, Cleveland, St. Louis, and Pittsburgh—lost more than 10 percent. St. Louis, with a 17 percent loss, fell back to its smallest population since the beginning of the century.

The late 1960s and early 1970s have witnessed a cyclical slowdown in economic activities, resulting in large unemployment increases in many cities and metropolitan areas. Among the outstanding examples is Seattle, Washington, which had an unemployment rate low of less than 3 percent for a short time in the second half of the 1960s and a rate in excess of 10 percent a few years later. Other cities encountering similar instabilities in the late 1960s and early 1970s include Los Angeles, California, and Wichita, Kansas. Furthermore, there is some evidence that central cities incur more pronounced business cycles than does suburbia.[52]

Whether a relatively high or relatively low growth rate in a specific place is desirable or undesirable cannot be inferred from such data alone. It depends on additional hard information, as well as on value judgments. On these, there can be differences between, for example, landowners and those concerned about the ecology, between the poor and the affluent, between the resident and the corporate stockholder living elsewhere, etc.

In order to assess the desirability of a particular growth rate, the following kinds of information and capabilities would be useful:

1. Projections of indices of economic and demographic activity,
2. Description of significant relationships among key economic and demographic variables,
3. Comparison of important potential trade-offs such as those between growth and stability, quantity versus quality, relative burdens and costs on the poor versus the rich, etc.,

[51] U.S. Bureau of the Census, *Trends in Social and Economic Conditions in Metropolitan and Non-metropolitan Areas* (Washington, D.C.: U.S. Bureau of the Census, Sept. 3, 1970), *Special Studies*, series P-23, no. 33, pp. 2–7.
[52] Roger Noll, "Metropolitan Employment and Population Distribution and the Conditions of the Poor," in John P. Crecine (ed.), *Financing the Metropolis* (Beverly Hills, Calif.: Sage, 1970), pp. 501–502.

4. Identification of "leverage points" which are particularly crucial in triggering growth and assuring stability,
5. Capability to simulate the economic activity implications of specified impacts,
6. Identification of important potential imbalances, e.g., insufficient capacity, excessive supply of specific labor skills, strains on public financing, etc., and
7. Identification of expected important markets and their size.

The four models that have been discussed in the previous section vary in their capacity for providing such information. The aggregate models, i.e., export-base and shift and shares, can provide reasonable projections of economic activity and estimates of market size—items 1 and 7. Input-output and income-expenditure models include a large number of important relationships which can assist in analysis of all seven items. Input-output models emphasize industrial relationships, which are particularly useful for items 1, 2, 3, and 5. Income-expenditure models, which are concerned more with aggregate variables and include some consideration of resource inputs, can assist analysis of items 4 and 7.

Generally these models can be used to assess desirability of economic performance only when they are supplemented by various side calculations which, in many cases, are by themselves major undertakings. For example, an urban input-output model might show how final demand markets, in conjunction with various industry mixes, are likely to affect the growth of income and employment; and, by building in appropriate leads and lags, it might indicate the stability of such growth. But specific studies would still have to be carried out on whether such growth creates imbalances in the demand for and supply of public services, possible lags in providing adequate public infrastructure, etc. The models are likely to be of only partial help in answering such questions. They might prove more useful to those asking who is mainly affected by changes in growth rates and by different conditions of economic stability in the urban area, although the answers may be very tentative.

How to Produce Specific Urban Macroeconomic Performance?

Even if we could agree on a desirable urban growth rate and stability condition, we would still face the need to choose from alternative strategies in the hope of their having desired effects on specific firms and industries. Some of the strategies mainly involve federal and state officials, while others involve mainly local officials or both.

To influence urban economic growth and instability it is necessary to affect one or more major local industries; local, as well as export, demand;

and (or) local human and physical resources. Strategies available to affect these demand and resource factors can come under six readings:

Geographic Distribution—including location and relocation growth center and rural-urban mix programs

Human and Physical Investment—including training and health education programs; investments in transportation networks, industrial parks, and public service facilities; and tax incentives to stimulate investment

Monetary Strategies—including interest rate, public borrowing, money supply, credit, and other regulation policies

Fiscal Strategies—including tax rates and public expenditures mix

Market Strategies—including programs for improved information flow, government procurement, and regulations regarding production and consumption

Land-Use Strategies—including planning and zoning

National urban policy makers have available mainly the first four strategies, while policy makers of a particular city or metropolitan area can select among investment, fiscal, market, and land-use strategies. Market strategies are open only to a limited extent to public decision makers, and they would, for the most part, take the form of regulation. It is mainly the private sector that can adopt different market strategies, at least in theory.

The models which have been described would probably not provide much useful information relating to evaluation of monetary and land-use strategies. The export-base and shift and shares models are likely to provide a limited amount of information for market strategies. Input-output models can be useful for geographic distribution and market strategies and, to a more limited extent, for investment strategies. Income-expenditure models are likely to be particularly helpful with fiscal strategies, investment strategies, market strategies, and, to a more limited extent, geographic distribution.

In general, while export-base models can be of some use, input-output models and income-expenditure models are likely to prove more powerful, mainly because they are able to identify relationships among important actors in the economy. Simulations on the basis of specified strategies can give some general indications as to their likely effects on growth rates and stability. Furthermore, they can help obtain some information on the differential effects of specific growth rates and instability conditions, insofar as specific industries, occupations, ethnic groups, and income groups are concerned.

Let us briefly indicate how strategies and specific models can be related, or, more specifically, how suggestions concerning appropriate strategies can be obtained from these macro models. Geographic distribution strategies for the most part depend on comparing the activities potential of different places. Therefore, it is desirable to have separate models for each of several important places. (It would be even more desirable to show the linkages among these places.) As we consider the possible effectiveness of, for example, a growth center strategy, we would want to determine the market potential and the labor force availability in specific places, which can be provided by input-output and income-expenditure models. But we would also want to consider the investment costs associated with the building of this center, as compared to other locations, which would require extensive side calculations. In considering relocation programs we would want geographic information on job opportunities, which might come from any of the four models. But we might also want income and wage rate data, as obtained from income-expenditure models, and housing supply data, which would require side calculations.

Similar information and models would be needed were a new towns strategy to be considered. Title VII of the Housing and Urban Development Act of 1970 declares new towns a key element in national urban growth policy, providing aid to state and local public agencies and private developers.[53] Aid includes direct federal development loans as well as grants to cover the initial costs of providing early public services. To qualify for aid, feasibility in terms of potential for economic growth must be shown. Again, market studies will be needed, together with studies which can benefit from input-output or income-expenditure models. Side calculations will be needed to see whether the proposed plan provides adequate public, commercial, and community facilities and services and is likely to enhance the urban environment and welfare of the surrounding area, as required in the Act.

Usually, when the federal or state government selects a particular growth or stability strategy, it will not do so for a single urban area. Instead, it will pursue a general urban policy. Such a policy can be examined in terms of its overall inflationary effects, as well as for its likely effects on particular urban areas. It makes little difference in terms of the analysis whether the funds or other inducements originate with a higher level of government or with the local government.

The six strategies can also be examined in terms of their probable effect on economic stability. Again, these strategies might be initially adopted by federal or state governments on the one hand or local governments on the other. Policies designed to increase the economic stability of

---

[53] Twentieth Century Fund, *New Towns: Laboratories for Democracy* (New York: Twentieth Century Fund, 1971), pp. 5–6.

urban areas can take various forms. Perhaps they are best divided into two major types: disaster aid and preventive aid. Economic disaster aid, particularly that given by the federal government, can take the form of:

Extension of unemployment compensation
Mortgage or rental payments for a specific period upon written notice of foreclosure or eviction
Food coupon allotments and surplus commodities
Job training and retraining, and relocation assistance

Any one or a mix of aid programs would become available once the area is declared eligible. Criteria for qualification could include the existence of an unemployment rate 50 percent above the national average for six of the preceding twelve months in a major labor area.[54]

Prevention is often less costly and painful than waiting until economic disaster has struck. Preventive aid must be directed at sources that can be expected to result in unemployment. Such aid to individuals can include job training and retraining and relocation assistance. Firms can be given loans and guarantees as well as preferential treatment with regard to federal purchases. Federal programs might be judged in terms of their potential employment stimulus; priority could be given to those programs that have large employment multipliers, and urban areas could be ranked in terms of their employment needs for the application of such programs.

Attention must be paid to the special conditions of central cities versus suburban areas. Among the residents of the core cities, a disproportionate number are poor and belong to minority groups. The poor particularly need training and retraining for tomorrow's job opportunities.

One preventive step by the federal government might be to review its purchasing and investment policies from the viewpoint of their possible overheating effect on specific urban economies. A good example is Seattle, Washington, which, because of a number of private and federal aerospace contracts, saw its unemployment rate dip below the 3 percent level in the middle 1960s and climb to a level four times that high a few years later. The major reason for these large shifts in unemployment was federal procurement policy. In selecting specific stability policies, much attention must be paid to the employment and income multipliers that are likely to be associated with specific policies in the economic disaster-aid category, as well as in the preventive-aid category.

Altogether, research on urban growth and stability is in an early stage; it appears, however, to be advanced with the aid of a variety of urban macroeconomic models.

[54] See Economic Disaster Relief Act, S2393, passed in August 1971 by the U.S. Senate, 1st Sess., 92nd Cong.

CHAPTER 9

ECONOMICS OF URBANIZATION

I. INTRODUCTION

Urbanization may be broadly defined as the societal process that creates the dynamic system that we call a city. In studying the economics of urbanization, we are concerned with the process and the problems of change that take place as a rural economy is transformed into an urban economy. Urbanization involves transformation of the population, production process, and sociopolitical environment of a mainly rural economy that is relatively evenly distributed over space, labor-intensive, and individualistic in character into an urban economy of relatively high spatial concentration, high specialization in the production of goods and services, and close interdependence—private and public—as well as of a high level of technology, innovation, and entrepreneurship.[1] It is particularly relevant that associated with the process of urbanization is an increase in spatial concentration—density—which leads to close proximity of economic actors. Close proximity, together with production specialization, results in pronounced interdependencies of various actors in urban areas. Density makes possible efficient collective purchase of goods and services, resulting in increasingly large social infrastructure and governmental budgets.

Closely associated with the process of urbanization is the development of increasingly large industrial capacity, capital intensity, high levels of technology and innovation, and specialization in the production of goods and services, all key elements of industrialization. The interrelationship between industrialization, i.e., the cumulative implementation of industrial location decisions, and urbanization is complicated. Eric Lampard has stated, "If we conceive of a preindustrial, low-productivity population as one in which factors, firms, and to a large extent, therefore, localities are relatively unspecialized and undifferentiated in space, industrialization and urbanization may be regarded as a societal process in which, among other things, factors, firms, and localities become increasingly specialized and,

---

[1] Urbanization in its very advanced stages, particularly in the United States with its high reliance on automobiles, has seen capital-intensive industries moving out of the central city, which is becoming increasingly labor-intensive as it specializes more and more in the production of services. Because of the automobile, urban areas in the very advanced stages of urbanization spread over large areas, and in so doing they somewhat reduce the unevenness of the spatial distribution that existed when central cities played such an overwhelmingly important role.

within their respective market areas, more differentiated."[2] The processes of industrialization and urbanization are often viewed as occurring simultaneously. Thus Allan Pred concludes that the "spatial, as well as the economic and social, processes of nineteenth and twentieth century urbanization and industrialization are not independent. The phenomena that led to the concurrent emergence of the modern American metropolis and large-scale manufacturing are dynamically involuted and nearly always inseparable."[3] Although the processes of urbanization and industrialization are interdependent, there do seem to be several major stages in the life of a city or society in which one or the other dominates. This separation can facilitate the study of the dynamic development of cities.

A review of the literature does not reveal an interest by economists in urbanization. However, we may benefit from the experience of economists in developing growth theories. Growth theory mainly considered technological change and population increase as providing one-time exogenous shocks, and comparative static analysis has been used to analyze and project how these shocks alter the equilibrium of the system. Realizing that these exogenous shocks were occurring almost continuously, never allowing the system to reach its equilibrium, a new approach was started in the early forties. The long-run equilibrium of the system became a path of steady growth, and tools of comparative statics were developed and applied to alternative growth paths rather than to alternative stationary states. Modern neoclassical growth theory relates potential output to the labor force, the state of technology, and the stock of human and tangible capital. Labor force and technology are usually assumed to grow smoothly at rates determined exogenously by noneconomic factors, while capital accumulation depends on the population's thrift. In equilibrium, the growth of the capital stock matches the growth of labor, together with technology, and the growth of output. This model appears to fit well-observed trends of economic growth.[4]

Our inquiry into the economics of urbanization will begin with an examination of factors and environments that initiate urbanization—in short, the prerequisites of urbanization. Thereafter, we will inquire into what it is that ensures continuity of the just initiated urbanization process, and follow with an identification of the general characteristics of an economy in an intermediary stage of urbanization. Next, we will detail the characteristics of an advanced urban economy, with special emphasis on the partic-

---

[2] Eric E. Lampard, "The Evolving System of Cities in the United States: Urbanization and Economic Development," in Harvey Perloff and Lowdon Wingo, Jr. (eds.), *Issues in Urban Economics* (Baltimore: Johns Hopkins, 1968), p. 100.

[3] Allan R. Pred, *The Spatial Dynamics of U.S. Urban-Industrial Growth, 1800–1914* (Cambridge, Mass.: M.I.T., 1966), p. 12.

[4] William Nordhaus and James Tobin, *Is Growth Obsolete?* paper prepared for the National Bureau of Economic Research Colloquium, San Francisco, Calif., Dec. 10, 1970 (processed, 37pp.).

ularly unique and interesting urban characteristics. Finally, some urbanization policies will be examined.

II. FACTORS INITIATING THE URBANIZATION PROCESS—PREREQUISITES OF URBANIZATION

What are the primordial conditions that can trigger the urbanization process? And what are the factors that play crucial roles? We will present two classes of factors. Most likely the dominant one represents the supply side in the form of comparative cost advantages, resulting in production (industrialization)-initiated urbanization. The second factor relates to internal market demand increases and can be described as local market-, and particularly household sector-, initiated urbanization. These two classes of factors will next be taken up in detail. However, it should be remembered that while for analytic purposes it is useful to distinguish between these two classes of urbanization-initiating forces, they will usually act simultaneously in this process. Furthermore, these two classes of factors continue to be mutually reinforcing throughout later stages of the urbanization process.

Comparative Cost Advantage

Let us take an (idealized) hypothetical case, where a small industrial firm located in rural America makes a significant location decision. Thus a community initiates industrial production because at some point in time a firm decides to capitalize on the locality's comparative cost position. Such an advantage relates to production specialization that benefits from certain low-unit-cost input factors, including transportation, and certain economies of scale.

The "minimum threshold" principle may be responsible for either the building of a new, large manufacturing plant or the substantial enlargement of an existing one. The minimum threshold principle implies that a minimum sales volume is required to support a new or enlarged factory.[5] Thus, until a community is surrounded by an effective market to warrant such production, it will tend to import the particular product. Industries oriented toward regional or national markets will not locate in a community until regional or national thresholds are reached. Once this threshold is reached, and subject to the community's comparative advantage, it can become profitable to build or expand a plant to produce a particular product. The market can become large enough to warrant such a step as a result of sufficiently large export demand, which can result from scale economies, industrial innovations, and (or) transport innovations. Clearly, that the threshold has been reached is no assurance that investments will

---

[5] Ibid., pp. 14 and 33.

be made. Still, under such conditions decisions to invest become easier to make and are more likely to be made.

Once economic actors in a community begin to exploit their comparative cost advantage in a particular industry, production, supported by export demand, will increase, and so will employment opportunities and the size of the labor force, managerial talent and entrepreneurship, and population. With the increase in population greater densities also result, and the urbanization process is on its way, initiated by production factors and especially by the cumulative implementation of industrial location decisions, i.e., industrialization. Capital flows into the area and seeks new investments, which, in turn, leads to a growing pool of specialized and well-trained labor that provides external economies to other industries. They, in turn, cause further growth and widening of the economic base.

Internal Market Demand Increases

A second class of urbanization-triggering forces relates to internal demand. Population and income growth within a community can generate local demand, which in turn will stimulate local production and growth. Once such growth has started, the increased level of business activity creates demand for material and service inputs, so that possibly sufficient local demand will be generated to warrant local production rather than continued importation of certain goods.

One of the key contributors to increased local household demand is autonomous inmigration, which has little relation to the economic opportunities available in a particular community. Rather, such inmigration is affected by "push" and "pull" factors. Push factors include the various characteristics associated with depressed areas from which many people seek to escape. Pull factors include retirement, family and friends, welfare payments, and amenities at the destination.

Thus, the local household sector can initiate urbanization through population growth (mainly resulting from autonomous inmigration) and increased income. As a result, increased production for the local market can be initiated, which in turn can lead to increases in employment opportunities, the labor force, population, and, with them, density.

The National View

Comparative cost advantages under conditions of export demand and internal market demand increases not only can help explain the transformation of a rural community into an urban community; they also shed light on the urbanization of an entire region or nation. With improvement of means of transportation and communication, very large numbers of communities have been exposed to potential increases in export demand. There is growth in national demand for an industry exporting to national markets and there is growth in population, income, and business activity in the region in which such a particular community is located; both will tend to lead to broadly based and highly diversified urban growth.

Urbanization of a nation is further enhanced by migration from rural to urban areas. Such migration is related to productivity advances in agriculture coupled with an inelastic demand for its products. Surplus farm labor is generated which moves to cities, since the cities have comparative advantage in manufacturing and service production and therefore offer job opportunities. Such outmigration of labor from rural areas can initiate a chain reaction, in which cities' comparative cost advantages make for further gains because of scale economies, which in turn can facilitate export demand, and so on.

III. PERPETUATING THE URBANIZATION PROCESS

How can we explain the continuity of the urbanization process once it is started? There are a number of economic forces at work, as well as a few institutional ones. Among the economic forces are those that can be related to the "initial advantage" principle, the "cumulative circular causation" principle, and further application of the "minimum threshold" principle.

The "initial advantage-ratchet effect" principle gives expression to a collection of forces that have some interesting economic features. First, established locations tend to exert considerable influence on subsequent plant location decisions; second, concentration of economic actors has a self-perpetuating momentum; third, established locations are generally characterized by enormous inertia together with a temporal compounding of advantages;[6] fourth, as cities grow, they amass large amounts of fixed capital—private and public—often making it uneconomic to abandon this immobile capital; and, finally, the larger the urban area, the more likely it is to be a hothouse that gives birth to new industries.[7]

In slightly different terms Harvey Perloff presented an analysis that might be said to reflect the "initial advantage-ratchet effect principle." The distribution of people and economic activities that has evolved from the past influences current location decisions, because the overwhelming majority of location decisions must take market, input, and transport facilities as given. Thus, the decision of the present or, in other words, the marginal decision is based to an important extent on the locational (price) situation as it has evolved from the past.[8]

The second factor contributing to continuity of the urbanization pro-

---

[6] Ibid., p. 15.
[7] Wilbur R. Thompson, *A Preface to Urban Economics* (Baltimore: Johns Hopkins, 1965), p. 22.
[8] Harvey Perloff et al., *Regions, Resources, and Economic Growth* (Baltimore: Johns Hopkins, 1960), p. 80.

cess relates to the reinforcing interplay between industrialization and urbanization. It is an application of Gunnar Myrdal's principle of "circular and cumulative causation," and views industrial growth and urban development as an interrelated process with one stage of development dependent on the previous one. Forces of industrialization and urbanization are so interlocked in circular causation "that a change in any one induces the others to change in such a way that these secondary changes support the first changes, with similar tertiary effects upon the variable first affected, and so on."[9] This circular causation not only has cumulative results but often tends to gather speed at an accelerated rate.[10]

While it is analytically difficult to carefully specify the interacting spatial processes of urbanization and industrialization, there is much evidence about the parallel timing of the emergence of concentrated large-scale manufacturing and the enormous growth of metropolitan areas in North America, Japan, and Europe during the last 150 years. Allan Pred has observed, "If the late 1840s and 1850s constituted the first youthful burst of American industrialization outside of the textile industries, then the 1860s may be regarded as the onset of adulthood within the continuum of the United States urban and manufacturing growth."[11] Thus, if we examine the fifty-year period starting in 1860, we find that in the United States industrial output and number of factories have run parallel with the growth of cities.

The "minimum threshold" principle continues to work as new and higher thresholds appear for more and more industries. For example, production and (or) transportation innovations are likely to increase the comparative cost advantage of a particular location for a large number of industries. This in turn tends to result in new linkages, as by-products of innovations and the establishment of more and higher threshold levels.

Finally, there are some institutional factors that appear to underwrite the continuity of the urbanization process. Wilbur Thompson, for example, points to power politics, i.e., "With a larger population comes greater electoral strength. . . ."[12]

IV. CHARACTERISTICS OF AN ECONOMY IN AN INTERMEDIATE STAGE OF URBANIZATION

Once urbanization has started and forces for continuity have been generated, urbanizing factors interact in a variety of ways. Many of the characteristics and interplays of the entire urbanization process are presented in flow chart form (see Figure 9.1). Key features of an urban economy

---

[9] Gunnar Myrdal, *Rich Lands and Poor* (New York: Harper, 1957), p. 18.
[10] Ibid., p. 13.
[11] Pred, op. cit., p. 16.
[12] Thompson, op. cit., p. 22.

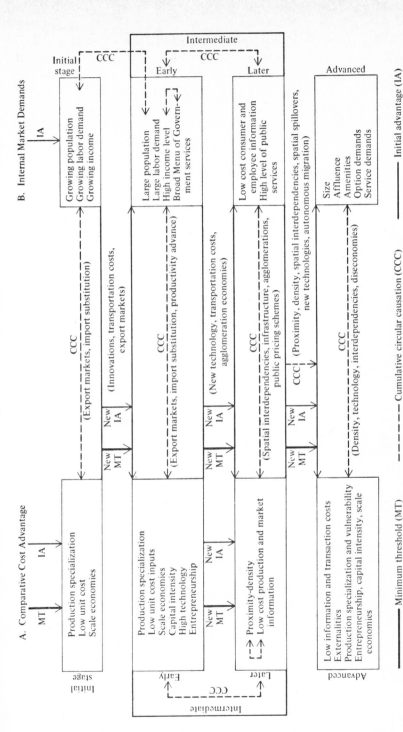

FIGURE 9.1 Urban characteristics, urbanizing factors, and the urbanization process.

in an intermediate stage of urbanization are summarized in Table 9.1. The intermediate stage of urbanization can be separated into two substages— early stage and later stage.

But before we start the examination, we must admit that such stages as the initial, intermediate, and advanced phases of urbanization are quite arbitrary divisions of what is basically a continuous process. Yet, while the boundaries of these phases are not very sharp, their sequence appears to be firmly grounded, and analytic insight into the economics of urbanization can be gained from such a division.

Early Intermediate Stage

At the beginning and in the early stages of urbanization, production specialization, low-unit-cost input factors, and scale economies tend to dominate not only the comparative cost advantage, but also the entire urbanization process. In this early stage the local economy focuses on the building of manufacturing plants, the attraction of labor into the area, and the internalization of production cost advantages in these plants. In many respects this constitutes the secondary stage of economic development described by Colin Clark.[13]

As the demand increases in the community for locally manufactured products, a variety of manufacturing multiplier effects result. Specifically, the increased demand facing a local manufacturing industry generates direct, indirect, and income-induced effects on the community's output; on its employment, labor force, and population; on its government serv-

[13] Colin Clark, *The Conditions of Economic Progress* (London: Macmillan, 1951).

TABLE 9.1 CHARACTERISTICS OF ECONOMY IN EARLY STAGE OF URBANIZATION

A. Comparative cost advantage
  1. Production specialization*
  2. Low-unit-cost input factors*
  3. Scale economies*
  4. Capital intensity
  5. High technology
  6. Entrepreneurship
  7. Proximity-density
  8. Low-cost production (and marketing) information
B. Internal market demand
  1. Large population
  2. High income level (due to industrialization)
  3. Broad menu of goods and services
  4. Low-cost consumer and employee information

* Characteristics also found in the initial phase of urbanization.

ices; and on its income. Not only are the overall levels of these parameters affected, but also their distribution and mix. Thus, for example, not only will the manufacturing multiplier tend to change the community's level of employment, but also its occupational and industrial distribution will change.[14]

As new employment opportunities are generated, the community attracts inmigrants. Many of those migrants to American cities in the past have come from abroad, often bringing highly developed skills.

But there is more to the forces of urban change that have been unleashed.

As the initial multiplier effects make themselves felt, structural changes in the community's economy are likely to take place. They result in part from the fact that as local industry grows, new linkages will be forged—backward linkages through firms that provide primary inputs, and forward linkages through firms that utilize the output of the new factory in the production of other products. As a result, additional increases in output, employment, government services, and income are to be expected, further changing the occupational and industry mix of the local economy.

Another likely consequence is that new local, regional, and national thresholds emerge, which can support new manufacturing activities and additional industrial plant capacity. These new industrial thresholds are likely to come about because new technology in production and transport tends to emerge in cities. Transportation innovations tend to reduce transportation costs, resulting in a pushing outward of market frontiers and the opportunity to realize further scale economies in production. Transport innovations tend to affect numerous industries, but particularly those in which transportation is an important cost item. In general, as transportation costs decline, cities with distant markets and therefore with relatively large transportation costs tend to benefit most and extend their markets farthest. However, this outreaching for new markets is counteracted by other communities' rapid industrialization and urbanization.

At this stage cities tend to benefit from growing entrepreneurship, technology, and inventiveness, which, together with scale economies, improve the efficiency of local industrial firms. This in turn raises the productivity of workers at the margin and therefore tends to lead to higher wages and salaries. Per capita income is further increased in cities because of labor force participation rates that are higher than those in rural areas. High per capita incomes generate demand increases in general and, in par-

[14] Demand increases of different manufacturing industries are likely to have different multiplier effects, which can be readily studied within a regional input-output framework. Not only can one estimate from a regional input-output table the direct, indirect, and income-induced output effects and the income and government service effects, but, also, with the aid of linkage methods, employment, labor force, population, and density estimates can be derived.

ticular, demand for goods and services with high income elasticities. As a result, a disproportionate increase in tertiary activities is stimulated, leading then to the tertiary stage of economic development described by Colin Clark.

With the growth of the local economy and the increasing importance of the tertiary industries, a new set of forces is generated, which further affect output, employment, population, government services, and income. The increased demand for tertiary goods and services manifests itself in additional multiplier effects. They might be referred to as the nonindustrial or secondary multiplier, reflecting increases in the demand for various private and public services. As cities grow, internal markets expand, and local industries increasingly "take in each other's washing" and contribute to the secondary multiplier effects.

Later Intermediate Stage

Population increases coinciding with large-scale agglomeration economies lead to population density increases. Proximity and the easy intracity accessibility to ideas and facts bear on information, technology, capital intensity, and entrepreneurship. Thus the increased proximity of economic actors and markets tends to reduce information and transaction costs and further stimulates inventions and innovation, all of which can contribute additional comparative cost advantages. From the economist's point of view these changes take the form of new production functions of private and public actors in the urban economy.

The increased density has further implications. It permits residents to band together in the purchase of goods and services that benefit all of them but which none could afford to purchase singly. Thus, the ability of city residents to join forces, agree upon a pricing scheme, and then provide public goods by mutually enforcing the pricing scheme results in an enlarged social infrastructure and governmental budget. In turn, urban residents can reap major benefits from this enlarged urban·public sector, benefits not available in a rural environment. This infrastructure, if interpreted broadly, is a major source of local vitality and endurance. Thus, Wilbur Thompson maintains that a pivotal aspect of a highly developed urban area is ". . . the creativity of its universities and research parks, the sophistication of its engineering firms and financial institutions . . . the flexibility of its transportation networks and utility systems and all the other dimensions of infrastructure that facilitate the quick and orderly transfer from old dying bases to new growing ones."[15]

Furthermore, at a time when the importance of government services is on the rise, increased density results in abundant spatial interdependencies. The ensuing massive spillovers call for frequent government inter-

15 Thompson, op. cit., p. 53.

vention in the urban economy. Also, information becomes available in increasing amounts, a subject to be taken up in the next section.

V. CHARACTERISTICS OF AN ADVANCED URBAN ECONOMY

Clearly, the transition from an early to a highly advanced stage of urbanization is gradual and the dimensions of the transition are numerous. Consequently, many of the characteristics of the highly advanced postindustrial urban economy also are found, though with less pronounced manifestations, in earlier stages. Not only have their relative importance and prevalence changed, but also a few new features arise as a society reaches a highly advanced stage of urbanization. At some point even retrogression starts.

Information

It is possible to consider the key features of an advanced urban economy the direct resultant of advanced urbanization. Perhaps the hallmark of advanced urbanization is the high density and specialization, resulting in complex and powerful interdependencies and, with them, a host of externalities. Close proximity lowers information and transaction costs, not only for firms but also for households in their roles of consumers and work-seekers.

Urbanization improves information and communication between economic actors, which in turn fosters further urbanization. Thus, for example, Richard L. Meier asserts, "An intensification of communications, knowledge, and controls seems to be highly correlated with the growth of cities."[16] He goes on to point to one of the many ways in which information and communication can affect location decisions, and with them urbanization. "Opportunities also appear at linkage points in communications systems and entrepreneurs located there obtain access to several independent sources of information first. Thus, change encourages change in the vicinity of a communications focus, and activity is piled upon activity within a small amount of space, subject only to diseconomies associated with intense land use, such as congregation, public disorders, epidemics."

As was shown in Chapter 2, as urbanization progresses, information and other transaction costs appear to decline, potentially benefiting firms and households alike.

Production Specialization, Proximity, and Externalities

In an advanced stage of urbanization, with its high degree of production specialization and proximity among economic actors, externalities become increasingly prevalent. As more and more economic actors and activities

[16] Richard L. Meier, op. cit., p. 43.

are attracted to highly urbanized areas to take advantage of extensive infrastructure, specialized services and markets, and low information costs,
severe externalities will be felt. Excessively large numbers of cars and
people will crowd city streets, particularly in downtown areas that often
were built for the horse-and-buggy age. Crowding and congestion not
merely degrade the urban environment through increasing traffic and parking problems, noise, and the disappearance of even a small measure of
tranquility and privacy in open spaces, but they also greatly reduce the
efficiency with which transactions in highly advanced postindustrial urban
centers are carried out.

Furthermore, Uriel Foa has suggested a further social cost associated
with the late stages of urbanization. In his view urbanization has evolved
primarily for the efficient interaction and exchange of what he calls "uni-
versalistic resources," i.e., money, goods, services, and information. As
concentration and crowding reach a very advanced stage, the magnitude
and frequency of external interactions and stimulation experienced by the
individual multiply. The result can be substitution, which reduces the
amount of time allocated to each input and results in less exchange of
more personal or "particularistic" resources, such as love and status. The
resulting decline of this type of interpersonal resource, in Foa's view, can
generate major social costs through a rise in antisocial behavior—an indirect result of crowding.[17]

Close proximity in an affluent postindustrial and highly mobile urban
society also produces water, air, and noise pollution with far-reaching side
effects. One economic actor under such circumstances is affected by a host
of others. Thus, man ceases to be "king in his own castle." Instead his fate
is in the hands of others, just as their fate is affected by him. More and
more frequently, therefore, government is called upon to intervene. In
doing so, urban government has a number of options. The objectives are
twofold—to reduce the ill effects on the efficiency of resource allocation
and to minimize the inequities brought about by externalities; the latter requires a better matching between the costs incurred by and the benefits
accruing to specific economic actors. Some of the analytic issues surrounding this problem and alternative policy options will be discussed in later
chapters.

Production Specialization and Vulnerability

While in the early stages of urbanization the focus was on firms producing
for export and internalizing cost advantages, this latter issue recedes in
relative importance in the late stages of industrialization. The nature of the
interplay between industrialization and urbanization also changes, with

---

[17] Uriel G. Foa, "Interpersonal and Economic Resources," *Science,* vol. 171 (January 1971), pp. 345–351.

industrialization becoming a lesser stimulus to urbanization than urbanization is to industrialization. Proximity-induced communication economies help take advantage of intra- and interindustry linkages and greatly stimulate entrepreneurship, capital intensity, innovations, and inventiveness found in advanced postindustrial urban economies. As Allan Pred has pointed out,

> The multiplication of interaction among the growing number of individuals engaged in manufacturing and tertiary sectors enhances the possibilities of technological improvements and inventions, enlarges the likelihood of the adoption of more efficient managerial and financial institutions, increases the speed with which locally originating ideas are disseminated, and eases the diffusion of skills and knowledge brought in by migrants from other areas.[18]

Specialization in an advanced postindustrial urban economy, however, has some disturbing side effects. It increases production interdependence and, with it the vulnerability of the urban economy. Vulnerability and sensitivity are particularly damaging in relation to the production and delivery of services with few alternative sources of supply and extremely high perishability, so numerous and crucial in a highly urbanized economy. The result is potential economic instability, not so much of the nation as a whole as of a particular highly urbanized community.

Growth and Size

Next let us consider some size characteristics. Population and labor force size increases have resulted from a variety of origins. However, whereas workers and their families at the start were predominantly attracted to urban areas by employment opportunities and wages—a direct result of industrialization—once a city has reached its maturity and offers its residents a wide selection of jobs, public services, and privately produced goods and services, and good opportunities to match demand preferences with available supplies, autonomous inmigration gains in importance.

Richard F. Muth, in an empirical study examining the relationship between migration and the growth of employment in United States cities in the 1950s, finds evidence that migration and employment growth each affect and are affected by the other. Thus at that advanced stage of American urbanization, it is no longer true that primarily differential rates of migration are induced by differential growth in job opportunities or employment in America's cities. Instead it is perhaps more correct to conclude that to no small extent differential changes in employment are induced by differential rates of inmigration.[19]

As a city grows, the relative importance of export declines and more

---

[18] Pred, op. cit., p. 28.
[19] Richard F. Muth, "Migration: Chicken or Egg?" *Southern Economic Journal,* vol. 37, no. 3 (January 1971), pp. 295–306.

and more of the locally consumed goods are also locally produced. The general increase in the relative importance of internal markets and their demand has been described by Allan Pred: ". . . construction, public utilities, local government, and miscellaneous tertiary activity sectors of the urban economy, just as local market manufacturing, increase aggregate local income through salaries and wages, propagate additional income increases by adding to endogenous income flows, and prevent capital outflows by providing previously imported goods and services."[20]

Urban growth can have some negative effects, mainly resulting from the increasing distances that people and goods must travel. This issue is separate from congestion, although often closely related to it. Furthermore, the delivery of public goods can increase in cost as distances extend.

Although a highly advanced economy is an open economy, it becomes less so as the relative importance of the internal market increases. In some respects the sensitivity to changes in national economic activity and the dependence on it for export markets decline somewhat as cities reach a highly advanced stage of urbanization. This is particularly so as the urban economy becomes increasingly large and its export sector diversified.

Additionally, as the city grows in size and the relative as well as the absolute importance of the internal market increases, a disproportionate gain in its service sector takes place. Specialization in the production and distribution of services that are more income-elastic than many goods, combined with per capita income increases, has greatly stimulated the urban service sector, so much so that today it is quantitatively more significant in urban areas than the manufacturing sector.

But also the size of the government infrastructure and the government sector in general has greatly increased as urbanization advanced. Not only has it become efficient for government to assume additional responsibilities, but also the prevalence of externalities and the huge capital expenditures often required have pushed governments into greater prominence, although often government fails to meet expectations.

Affluence, Amenities, and Option Demand

Finally, we find high income levels in the advanced postindustrial urban economy. An almost meteoric rise in resourceful entrepreneurship and inventiveness, capital intensity, and innovations, and in general sophisticated production specialization, is mainly responsible for this high per capita income. But the high income is only one expression, though admittedly a major one, of the prevalence of affluence in highly advanced urban societies; its people benefit from extensive option consumption that is being met and a variety of amenities that can be satisfied, together with a better matching of supply patterns to a revealed broad menu of preferences.

[20] Pred. op. cit, p. 32.

Affluence can be related to the ability of an individual to maximize utility, subject to the level and manner of generating real income, the range of goods and services available to the individual, and the environment within which he lives. Thus affluence represents the ability to generate high levels of income—income that is not directly tied to production. Affluence means to an individual that he can live in an environment that conforms quite closely to his taste, and to society it means the provision of a wide range of goods and services, including amenities, demanded by its members.

With the increase in diversity of goods and services, as well as in per capita income and leisure time in the urban economy, more and more amenities are demanded. Amenities are those goods and services that enable an individual to live above a level of "subsistence."[21] One can also view amenities as the secondary—by-product—utilities that are provided to the consumer by the acquisiton of some goods with a different primary purpose. For example, an amenity associated with owning an automobile, which is basically a means of transporting oneself from one location to another, is flexibility in choosing the route and timing of travel as well as the prestige associated with owning a particular type of car. Amenities due to urban life are those secondary utilities that are generated by the interactions of the good purchased in the urban environment. Admittedly the line between the "essential" part of the good or service and that producing amenities as a by-product can best be subjectively drawn.

An affluent urban society provides its citizens with a wide range of options or choice. Industrialization has made possible a wide spectrum of options for employment as well as a broad menu of goods and services. Rising income levels and affluence put before urbanites a wide variety of alternatives; even though some of them might never be chosen, societies appear willing to pay the value of the unchosen alternatives. This option demand has been discussed in Chapter 2.

VI. *CITY STAGES*[22]

In addition to looking at the urbanization process and at its organic effects on households, firms, industries, and governments, it might be instructive to examine it in terms of the sequence through which cities might move during this process. The focus could be on the history of the growth of cities, in an attempt to draw generalizations about possible "laws" of city progress.[23] Thus the analytic concern is with defining distinct stages through which cities move and with the conditions necessary for the city

[21] L. H. Klassen, *Social Amenities in Area Economic Growth* (Paris: Organization for Economic Cooperation and Development, 1968).
[22] Most of the ideas in this section I owe to Sidney Sonenblum.
[23] Cities here include both metropolitan and nonmetropolitan urban places.

to move from one such stage to the next, gaining better insight into what affects the probability of cities making the transition and improving our understanding of the length of time a city is likely to spend in a particular stage.

Early work on the hierarchy of cities was undertaken by Walter Christaller, who advanced his central-place theory in the thirties. Through a deductive argument which included considerations of competition between urban places with proximity to one another, Christaller envisioned a system of cities arising, each serving a hexagonally shaped service area. A hierarchy of coincident areas would provide "central places" of the proper size to perfrom the different functions required of the system. Altogether he perceived seven different orders of cities in Southern Germany.[24]

Raymond E. Murphy is convinced that a hierarchical class system of cities exists, and concludes "that larger centers are functionally more complex than smaller centers, with this increasing functional complexity being accompanied by increasing size of the urban complementary region."[25]

The simplest grouping of cities by stages is according to their population size and the kind of economic structure associated with each size class. Table 9.2 shows one such description for the metropolitan areas in the United States as of the mid-sixties.

There is evidence that in recent years the nation's urban population has not shown a tendency to concentrate in cities of any particular size. The largest cities are in fact continuing to grow, and they often exhibit the highest population densities and the highest manufacturing percentages in their labor forces. However, there is some evidence of slippage in the preeminence of New York City, although the evidence is more pronounced for the municipality than for an area that meets a more satisfactory urban definition.

Grouping cities according to their population size or any other such parameter is primarily descriptive. It offers very little theoretical content to the questions of whether cities are likely to grow, at what pace, through what stages, and under what conditions. To provide more theoretical content to the analysis of the growth of cities, it is necessary to describe the forces that cause cities to move from one stage to the next.

One stage classification scheme would distinguish among the following types of cities: national capital, regional capital, nodal center, export specialization city, and small city.[26] These types differ not only in population size, but perhaps more in industry mix, export share of economic activity, demographic characteristics, and geographic location.

[24] Walter Christaller, *Central Places in Southern Germany*, trans. Carlisle W. Baskin (Englewood Cliffs, N.J.: Prentice-Hall, 1966).
[25] Raymond E. Murphy, *The American City* (New York: McGraw-Hill, 1966), p. 95.
[26] This particular classification has been suggested by Lyle Fitch and Sidney Sonenblum.

TABLE 9.2   CHARACTERISTICS OF DIFFERENT-SIZE CITIES

	Largest	Large	Medium Size	Small
1. Population size	Over 1.5 million	800,000–1.5 million	350,000–800,000	Less than 350,000
2. Number of metropolitan areas	14	12	28	148
3. Density as compared with average for all metropolitan areas	Considerably above average	Generally higher than average	Widespread above and below average	Generally below average
4. Industry mix as compared with average of all metropolitan areas	About the same	Concentration on export-type industries, especially manufacturing, and government	Concentration on manufacturing	Concentration on manufacturing and, to a lesser extent government and education
5. Per capita income as compared with average for all metropolitan areas	About the same or above	About the same	Generally lower	Generally lower
6. Recent population growth trends	Generally slower than average—with several exceptions	Generally faster than average	About the average or faster	Generally slower than average
7. Employment participation rates	Generally higher	About average	Generally lower	A wide diversity above and below average

A national capital city is a major source for providing services, particularly transportation, financial, and government services, to the nation as a whole.[27] In the United States there are two national capital cities, Washington, D.C., and New York. While the District of Columbia has been growing in size and diversifying its service base, New York has been remaining relatively stable.

A regional capital city provides services, particularly transportation, financial, and trade, to a broad multistate area. The employment in these

[27] For a careful historical examination of certain location features of capital cities, see Vaughn Cornish, *The Great Capitals: An Historical Geography* (London: Methuen, 1922), 296 pp. Cornish makes the point that great capitals have been either storehouses or important crossways near a storehouse, and that in terms of political geography their location has been forward rather than central. The forward location is determined by the need to deal with other countries.

cities is heavily weighted by white-collar workers. Regional capital cities tend to be stable or expanding, depending on the population growth and economic progress in the regions of which they are parts.

Nodal cities provide transportation, trade, and personal services to their surrounding rural areas and small cities in their hinterlands. There are a large number of nodal cities in each region, some growing rapidly, others remaining stable or declining.

Export-specialized cities serve a national market in some particular good or service. Some of these cities are large; many are small. Some are rapidly growing; others are slowly growing. City growth is dependent on the market for its major product. For example, Detroit is growing slowly because of the slow growth in automobile activity; Miami and its tourist activities are growing rapidly; Seattle's growth is closely tied to defense procurement trends.

Most small cities outside of metropolitan areas are remaining stable or declining in population size because they are losing their economic function. Those that are growing tend to be exurban bedroom communities, university towns, government-oriented cities, and occasionally manufacturing-oriented cities.

This classification is useful in two ways. First, one can identify the number of cities of each type and the nation's population in each type in order to describe the nation's system of cities. Second, one can think of each type as a stage of city development and then speculate about the conditions necessary for a specific city to move between stages and the probability that it will. The stage analysis, appropriately aggregated, would lead to the system of city analysis. For the city stage analysis, we can think in terms of a network presented in Figure 9.2.

Many cities have developed by stages from a village to a small city and then through an export specialization or nodal center stage, some of them then becoming regional capitals. In some cases cities decline and fall back to a "lower" stage, usually as a result of stronger development in competing cities. Some small cities might first become export-specialized and then nodal centers. Regional capital centers emerge only directly from nodal cities. National capital cities emerge in the early period of a nation's development, when some of the strategically located major cities can be considered national capital cities. But as the region grows in size, the number of these national capital cities diminishes.

We can tie the discussion of city stages with the earlier discussion about urbanization forces. Thus, for example, a community may remain a basically rural place or small city, if the linkages and multiplier effects of various activities are weak. For a small city to become an export specialist, it would at first have to be characterized by increasing thresholds and an increasing multiplier effect which would spur further development. Depending on its location and hinterland and the products and services in

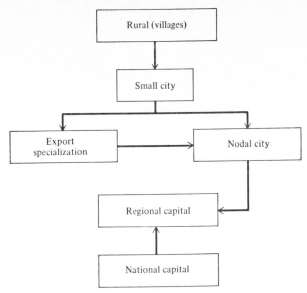

FIGURE 9.2 Classification of cities by growth stages.

which it specializes and achieves comparative advantages, the export-specialization city may then become a nodal city, or a nodal city may become a regional capital.

To assess whether cities are likely to move through the various stages, we should know something about the preconditions necessary for city development. Rostow associates these preconditions with the "takeoff" and identifies the important conditions for national development as: an initial event that makes economic progress possible; a rise in investment, probably supported by capital imports; development of manufacturing activity with rapid growth potential; and the existence of an appropriate political, social, and institutional environment.[28]

These conditions are also relevant to the movement of cities through the various stages. The post-World War II development of Dallas, Texas, for example, can serve as an illustration. In the 1940s Dallas was essentially a small city, serving some nodal-center functions because of a strong retail trade activity. After World War II, technological developments in the electronics field and strong government demands created a market potential. Some imaginative entrepreneurs (mostly recent arrivals in Dallas) saw the opportunities and began to develop the industry. The Dallas financial institutions supported this effort and mobilized the funds needed for expansion, mostly from outside the community, and Dallas moved into its export-specialization stage.

[28] Walter Rostow, *The Stages of Economic Growth* (London: Cambridge, 1960).

As its major manufacturing activities grew, supporting manufacturing activities also came into the city. Added incomes added strength to the retail and wholesale sectors, which increased their markets not only within the immediate area but also within a broader geographic range. Local infrastructure, particularly transportation, also was improved, and Dallas became a strong nodal center during the 1950s.

As rural inmigration continued, the Dallas labor force was strengthened. A greater diversity of manufacturing establishments located in Dallas. Regional headquarters of national companies began to see Dallas as an attractive location. Capital funds to support expansion continued to flow into Dallas. Large centers of wholesale and retail trade gained strength from the expanding incomes in the Southwest region. Transportation access continued to improve, and Dallas emerged as a regional capital during the sixties.[29]

Obviously, not all cities will follow this pattern. Most small cities will not become nodal centers. Indeed, the development of a few nodal centers is likely to cause a decline in small cities as they lose their population and become weaker in their competitive relationship to the nodal cities. Some small cities are likely to develop an export specialty in either some service or some manufacturing activity. Nodal centers are most likely to develop from cities with an export specialty; but only some export-specialized cities will become nodal centers. Indeed, some export-specialized cities can become very large but still not be nodal centers.

The economically strong nodal centers tend to become regional capitals. As population and economic activity in a region grow, the number of regional capitals is likely to increase. In addition, the congestion and diseconomies associated with some existing regional capitals increase the probability that some nodal centers will become regional capitals.

In spite of possible diseconomies, existing regional capitals are not likely to decline. The heavy investments in these areas, their attraction for migrants, and the service amenities they offer all suggest either stability or expansion for existing regional capitals, accompanied by an increased number of regional capitals.

It is unlikely that regional capitals will become national capitals. Apart from the District of Columbia, as the seat of government and perhaps a "showcase" city, there seem to be no strong economic reasons for an additional national capital in the United States. As the large megalopolitan strips develop and the trend toward regional "self-sufficiency" continues, the need for more national capitals such as New York diminishes—and indeed, the need for New York might be diminishing.

As was noted above, the analytic concern of the stages framework is to describe the conditions necessary for a city to make a stage transition,

---

[29] *Goals for Dallas* (Washington, D.C.: National Planning Association, 1970).

the probability of making the transition, and the time likely to be spent in each stage. The first two have been discussed, using a specific stage framework as an illustration. Very little can be said about time spent in each stage, since there are no empirical or theoretical studies of this issue. However, the following aspect of the relationship between time and city growth can be noted. Cities that "took off" in the past tend to grow much more slowly than those which have "taken off" recently. There does seem to be some process causing early-takeoff cities to slow down their growth, so that they remain at whatever stage of development they are at maturity, while the late-takeoff cities are the dynamic places that are still in the transitional process.

As we examine the recent record of American cities within a system of cities, we are left with the following observations: Small cities, not related to metropolitan areas, appear to have changed little in numbers, but their share of national population appears to have been on the decrease. Export-specialization cities appear to be decreasing in both number and share of population. At the same time, nodal cities appear to be increasing in number and share of population while both regional and national capitals appear to account for a declining share of the United States population.

VII. *URBANIZATION POLICY*

We would like to consider briefly some national policies available for influencing the pace and character of urbanization. Particular attention must be paid to the likely effects of such policies, not only on the urbanization phenomenon, but also on the welfare of the American people.

The pace of urbanization of America has been nothing short of phenomenal. While the founding fathers labored in an overwhelmingly rural society and even showed a strong bias against cities, by the end of the nineteenth century America's urban population had reached a size about equal to that of her rural population. The importance of America's urban population has continued to increase in the twentieth century, and by now close to 70 percent of all Americans live in metropolitan areas. The present rural farm population is less than 10 million.

Rapid urbanization has been closely tied to American agriculture's becoming the most highly capitalized and most productive agricultural establishment in the world. One of the by-products has been that during the last thirty years alone about 50 million people—about one-fourth of the current national population—have migrated from rural farm areas to urban areas.[30]

[30] The 30 million people on farms in 1940 would have grown to 60 million on the conservative natural-increase assumptions and zero outmigration rates. Lowdon Wingo, Jr., *Notes on a National Urban Development Strategy for the United States* (Washington, D.C.: Resources for the Future, 1971), p. 4.

During the 1960s about half of our roughly 3,000 counties lost population, and three out of four counties had more persons move out than moved in. Jerome P. Pickard foresees the emergence of twelve large urban regions during the next decades. The largest of these, by far, would be a metropolitan belt comprising the Atlantic Seaboard Urban Region (Boston-Washington) and the Lower Great Lakes Urban Region (Chicago-Pittsburgh). The twelve urban regions would have densities ranging from a low of 250 to a high of 1,040 persons per square mile, with an average of 715. In contrast, the balance of the coterminous United States would enjoy a density of only 33 persons per square mile. According to Pickard's projections, seven-tenths of the United States population would be concentrated in these twelve regions, which, together, occupy only a tenth of the coterminous United States land area.[31]

So much for the record and outlook of urbanization in the United States. Is the national interest best served by such patterns of concentration? What problems do they pose, and what advantages do they offer?

As we observed earlier in this chapter, a very large urban concentration can lead to various diseconomies, including environmental hazards. On the positive side, it permits the preservation of large, sparsely inhabited areas. However, breeding ourselves out of space does not appear to be a major United States problem. Not only did half of the counties in the United States lose population during the last decade, but our average densities are still quite low. Thus, for example, the density of western Europe is approximately seven times that of the United States, and that of England and the low countries is fifteen times as high.[32]

In connection with urban concentration in the United States, a number of policy statements have been made. Thus, for example, President Nixon declared, in 1971, "The concentration of population growth in already crowded areas is not a trend we wish to perpetuate. This Administration would prefer a more balanced growth pattern—and we are taking a number of steps to encourage more development and settlement in the less densely populated areas of our country."[33]

In line with our understanding of the forces that perpetuate the organizational process and the resultants of highly advanced organization, developed earlier in this chapter, we can now turn to an examination of policies that can change population distribution. In the most general way, such a

[31] Jerome P. Pickard, *Trends and Projections of Future Population Growth in the United States, with Special Data on Large Urban Regions and Major Metropolitan Areas, for the Period 1970–2000*, Technical Paper no. 4, Office of the Deputy Under Secretary, U.S. Department of Housing and Urban Development, July 22, 1969.
[32] Peter A. Morrison, *Urban Growth, New Cities, and the "Population Problem,"* P-4515-1 (Santa Monica, Calif.: The RAND Corporation, December 1970), p. 9.
[33] Message from the President of the United States to the Senate on Special Revenue Sharing for Urban Community Development and Planning, *Congressional Record*, 92nd Cong., 1st Sess., vol. 117, no. 29 (Mar. 5, 1971), S2503–S2507.

policy must help manage location of economic activities and people in a manner that produces desirable changes in the distribution of urban populations. Basically, this involves affecting the comparative cost advantages of certain locations as well as internal market demands. Furthermore, steps could be taken to bring about changes in conditions underlying the "initial advantages," "cumulative circular causation," and "minimum threshold" of particular areas. This, most likely, is what the Advisory Commission on Intergovernmental Relations meant, in a general way, when it suggested ". . . a policy . . . for influencing the movement of population and economic growth among different types of communities in various ways so as to achieve generally a greater degree of population decentralization throughout the country and a greater degree of population dispersion within metropolitan areas."[34]

The President's National Goals Research Staff addressed itself to the same issue. It states,

> The trend toward concentration of population in a megalopolis . . . continues, in part because of the strong economic and cultural attractions of the large metropolitan areas, but also in part because of policies—including Government policies and program expenditures—that tend to reinforce existing concentrations of population and economic activity. Hence, the choice of no change in public policy . . . , would run the high risk of bringing about the kind of future in which the communities of both urban and rural America would further deteriorate. It means that hundreds of American towns will continue to lose young people and economic opportunity; and that the large metropolitan areas, already burdened with social and fiscal problems and characterized by fragmentation of governmental responsibility, may reach a size at which they will be socially intolerable, politically unmanageable, and economically inefficient.[35]

While the three criteria are not defined, two of them can be given economic content. Socially intolerable conditions can be related to income distribution, and economically inefficient conditions can be related to resource allocation, particularly within a benefit-cost framework.

Recognizing the need for decisive public policy and action, the report visualizes three basic strategies:

"(1) Spread population by generating growth in sparsely populated rural areas. (2) Foster the growth of existing small cities and towns in non-metropolitan areas. (3) Build new cities outside the large metropolitan regions."[36]

[34] Advisory Commission on Intergovernmental Relations, *Urban and Rural America: Policies for Future Growth* (Washington, D.C.: U.S. Government Printing Office, April 1968), pp. 129–130.
[35] President's National Goals Research Staff, *Toward Balanced Growth: Quantity with Quality* (Washington, D.C.: U.S. Government Printing Office, July 4, 1970), pp. 55–56.
[36] Ibid., p. 56.

Perhaps the most eloquent spokesman of the strategy of generating growth in rural areas has been former Secretary of Agriculture Orville L. Freeman, who stated,

> . . . our metropolitan areas have more people and problems than they can cope with. All around us they are exploding with violence. At the same time, many villages, small towns, and their surrounding countryside are being drained of people and economic vigor. . . . We intend to help people build Communities of Tomorrow. Our objective is to remove the scars of collision between man and his environment and to avert further collisions.[37]

Freeman is proposing a strategy designed to trigger urbanization of small rural economies, which could be accomplished in line with our earlier discussion of factors initiating the urbanization process. Such a policy would mainly tend to change the environment so as to give the rural economy a comparative cost advantage and, to a lesser extent, an internal market demand increase. If successful, then an industrial exporting sector would emerge earning greater than normal profits. This, in turn, could attract inflow of capital and labor, as well as managerial talent and entrepreneurship, with the result that the community would diversify its economic base and grow. Specific steps could include effective encouragement of factories to locate in rural communities, government capital investments, and support for labor-intensive rather than highly automated farming operations.

The efficiency of such a step must be carefully examined. The private benefits of working in such an environment might be relatively small for most people. At the same time, the governmental costs of retaining a small-town population might prove costly, since, under conditions of low density, per capita school, road, hospital, and sewerage costs tend to be very high until the program is indeed successful and a town of a reasonable size has emerged. Moreover, population maintenance at origin is not very responsive to any but the most determined and costly efforts, since young and able people appear strongly attracted to better economic opportunities in the city.[38]

The second strategy involves fostering the growth of existing small cities and towns in nonmetropolitan areas, a step that basically requires an environment where "initial advantage," "cumulative circular causation," and "minimum thresholds" principles tend to perpetuate the urbanization process. Under such circumstances, middle-sized communities of upward of 25,000 inhabitants would be stimulated to incur a self-sustained growth. It would be hoped that such towns, which are located outside congested

---

[37] U.S. Department of Agriculture, *Communities of Tomorrow* (Washington, D.C.: U.S. Government Printing Office, November 1968).
[38] Morrison, op. cit., p. 26.

metropolitan areas, would have beneficial effects on the lagging region by providing new jobs and attracting migrants from surrounding regions. The advantages would include availability of infrastructure and external economies related to city size. Concentration of public investment at such potential growth centers is based on the argument that public services can be provided at reasonable costs and growth becomes self-sustaining without continuous subsidy.[39]

If successful, people in such growing cities would benefit from some of the highly valued urban amenities without the inconveniences of congestion and vulnerabilities so typical of huge metropolitan areas. Disadvantages would include lack of the unique features of our large cities. Furthermore, questions have been raised about the likelihood of success, particularly since ". . . cities with populations in the six-figure range are likely to offer the greatest assurance of self-sustaining growth."[40] Also, there is little evidence that rural Americans in large numbers prefer to move to small rather than to large cities.

It has been suggested that an analysis of a region's system of central places could prove useful in identifying potential growth centers.[41]

To develop alternative growth centers would require some redirection of public expenditures and new forms of partnership between federal, state, and local governments, on the one hand, and private industry on the other.

Finally, there is the policy of building new cities outside large metropolitan areas. It has been advocated by the National Committee on Urban Growth Policy, which recommended a massive new federal program aimed at the construction of 100 new towns with populations of 100,000 each and 10 new cities of 1,000,000 each.[42]

To succeed, new towns would require conditions that trigger and perpetuate urbanization and yet possibly prevent them from becoming overwhelmed by the diseconomies of size and density. It has been argued that new communities would save money through efficient design and construction of facilities, improve the quality of life by developing an adequate sense of community, and maintain a style of life that would provide adequate and reasonable open space and recreational opportunities.

There are, however, also many doubts. Thus it is unlikely that, even if successful, new communities in the next decade would absorb more than a small percentage of the urban population, mainly because of the relatively slow pace at which they can be planned, financed, and built. Moreover, there is the danger that if improperly designed they could aggravate

[39] Input-output analysis can assist in simulating alternative growth policies and in evaluating their likely impact.
[40] Edgar M. Hoover, *An Introduction to Regional Economics* (New York: Knopf, 1971), p. 281.
[41] Ibid., p. 279.
[42] Donald Canty (ed.), *The New City* (New York: Praeger, 1969).

the problems of the cities by siphoning off primarily middle- and upper-income residents, leaving the poor behind in cities stripped of substantial taxpayers.

If we are to build new towns, we need a deep commitment to such a policy. Such a commitment would have to include a plan for the nation to concentrate for the next decade on the building of, let us say, three or at the most five new towns with very large amounts of federal, state, and local funds combined with private funds to be invested. However, in a democracy it is extremely difficult to reach an agreement to focus on the building of such a small number of new towns, mainly because every state has two senators. As a result, it is easy for a much larger number of locations to be designed as new towns, thus diffusing funds and commitment and then, usually, creating conditions that assure failure. This process is not unique to the United States but to different degrees has also occurred in Japan, England, etc.

But there is also the question of whether one could divert huge numbers of migrants into new towns. In this connection, Peter Morrison maintains, "The dynamics of inter-metropolitan migration suggest that new cities would never 'inherit' or 'accommodate' population increase—they would have to compete for it in the same fashion and probably on the same terms that existing metropolitan areas do. It would be difficult to envision any new cities' program that could diminish the overwhelming economic attractiveness radiating from centers . . . like Atlanta, Washington, Dallas, and Los Angeles."[43] Furthermore, existing centers are favored by migrants, since these people so heavily rely on friends and relatives for information on employment in a new locality and for help in adjusting. Thus prior waves of inmigration tend to be self-perpetuating.[44]

Finally, even if inmigrants in sufficient number can be attracted into new towns, the towns would develop a markedly transient population, composed of the most likely candidates for further migration. Migration appeals to groups who for various social and personal reasons are responsive to incentives for movement, and, unfortunately for new cities, such people have a high propensity to move on.

Consequently, Peter Morrison concludes, ". . . the idea of using new cities to deflect growth away from congested metropolitan areas . . . goes against the grain of demographic realities.[45]

In summary, many of the characteristics of urbanization discussed in earlier sections are incorporated into Table 9.3 under four major headings

[43] Morrison, op. cit., p. 19.
[44] A recent study showed that nearly half the inmigrants chose destinations where one of their family already resided, and seven out of ten chose places where there were friends or relatives. (John B. Lansing and Eva Mueller, *The Geographic Mobility of Labor* (Ann Arbor, Mich.: Survey Research Center, Institute for Social Research, 1967).
[45] Morrison, op. cit., p. 24.

TABLE 9.3 *CHARACTERISTICS OF ADVANCED URBAN ECONOMY* (*economic resultants of advanced urbanization process*)

Characteristics	Micro-, Macroeconomic Concerns — Microeconomic Effects			Macroeconomic Effects		
	Household	Firm	Government	Household	Industry	Government
Space						
Proximity-density:						
Interdependence and externalities	x	x				x
Production information		x				
Consumer-employee information	x					
Overlapping jurisdictions:						
Frequent (often ineffective) government intervention						x
Production specialization						
Scale of industrialization:						
Scale economies		x				
Capital intensity		x				
Entrepreneurship		x				
Innovation		x				
Production interdependence:						
Vulnerability, sensitivity, and economic instability					x	
Size						
Population				x		
Internal market and economy's openness		x			x	
Service sector			x		x	
Government budget			x			
Income level						
Affluence	x					
Option demand	x					
Amenities	x					

—Space, Production Specialization, Size, and Income Level. In the same table indications are also provided as to who experiences the primary effects of these characteristics. Thus, we are concerned primarily with microeconomic effects of space on households and firms and its macro effects on governments; the micro and macro effects of specialization on firms and industries; the micro effects of size on firms and government and its macro effects on households and industry; and the micro effects of income on households.

The highly advanced urban economy in a postindustrial society can become the battleground of the gains and losses resulting from side effects of urbanization and industrialization. Excessive size and density generate interdependencies that, on balance, can become negative. Evidence the decline of our central cities. In a postindustrial, highly advanced urban economy emphasis shifts from plant- and firm-building to city-building, from micro to macro concerns, from the production of industrial goods to the provision of services and amenities. Information is the glue that holds together the city's many economic actors and markets and increases the number and efficiency of transactions. Government's role and size have increased, and great attention is given to how the highly scarce land resources of the city are used.

To the economist, perhaps the three most interesting features of the highly advanced urban economy are production specialization-induced resulting from proximity and density, and finally the institutional arrangements that see increasingly many government services and interventions, interdependencies among economic actors and markets, as well as those with impacts on economic growth and stability.

CHAPTER 10
INTRODUCTION TO URBAN PUBLIC SECTOR ANALYSIS

I. *URBAN PUBLIC SECTOR CONCERNS*

Urban public service markets have some major, and perhaps unique, characteristics, many of which are related to the nature of goods and services they produce and the environment in which urban decisions are made. Urban governments provide a host of tangible and intangible services. They regulate, tax, and subsidize in order to facilitate the efficient performance of firms and households as well as to achieve certain socially desirable objectives. Urban governments are not unique in discharging this responsibility; yet the prevalence of externalities in cities greatly increases the need for and frequency of interventions.

Cities are replete with situations in which individual decisions are inconsistent with the collective interest. Urbanites make many decisions that can affect others, not infrequently adversely. Without appropriate organization—mainly by government—inefficiencies can result. Thus urban governments are often called upon to provide institutional arrangements to overcome disparities between perceived individual interest and the larger collective good. This government intervention can be justified on numerous grounds, including the divergence between what urbanites are individually motivated to do and what they might like to accomplish in concert.

Public goods are characterized by jointness or joint consumption—an economic actor produces a good that affects the utility functions of very many consumers, with the consumption by one individual not reducing consumption by anyone else.[1] Battleships, lighthouses, and television are often given as extreme examples. Such jointness exists whenever the marginal social cost of providing a collective good to another person, once it is already provided to someone, is zero.[2] Yet, when the marginal social cost of

[1] Paul A. Samuelson, "The Pure Theory of Public Expenditure," *Review of Economics and Statistics,* vol. 36 (November 1954), pp. 387–389. More recently, Samuelson has used the term *consumption externality,* which exists if a good "enters two or more persons' preference functions simultaneously." Paul A. Samuelson, "Pure Theory of Public Expenditures and Taxation," in J. Margolis and H. Guitton (eds.), *Public Economics* (London: International Economic Association, 1969), p. 102.

[2] J. C. Head, "The Welfare Foundations of Public Finances," *Rivista Di Diritto Finanziario E Scienza Delle Finanze,* 1965, pp. 30–31.

a good is zero, the only price for that good—consistent with Pareto optimality—is also zero. If this is the socially optimum price, then entrepreneurs cannot make a profit at that price. Therefore the good can be provided optimally only by collective action which pays for the good while charging a zero or other nominal price.

In addition to the joint-consumption characteristic, there is a further feature, exclusion, that must be considered in relation to public goods. Musgrave's exclusion principle was discussed in Chapter 2 in connection with inappropriability of resource rights and of externalities. Although apparently most goods with great jointness in consumption also involve high exclusion costs, there are exceptions. A well-known exception is the transmission of television programs: with the aid of a scrambler unauthorized receivers can be excluded at little cost and without damaging the reception for others. Technical exclusion costs are also low for tennis courts and museums. In addition to technical exclusion difficulties that make appropriability of resource rights costly, there can be institutional and ethical reasons. Both may impose costs on an economic actor to fully capture the marginal value of the benefits or to fend off involuntarily imposed costs. All three reasons can impose severe transaction costs. These are resource costs if technological or institutional reasons interfere with appropriability, resource costs and political penalties—defeat at the polls and loss of power —if they are institutional reasons, and loss in social-philosophical values and peace of mind if they are ethical reasons. The latter issue is often discussed under the heading of welfare or distributional considerations, and by Richard Musgrave as involving merit wants.[3]

While a pure public good is one that is produced under conditions of perfect jointness and requires prohibitively high exclusion costs, it is clear that very few, if any, urban public services exist that meet these conditions. Nevertheless urban governments today engage in various activities, many of which exhibit a limited degree of the two above-mentioned characteristics. There is an additional feature that appears to result in government activity: production under conditions of declining average costs, so common to public utilities. It can be readily seen that joint cosumption, i.e., Samuelson's pure public good case, is closely related to the case of an industry where decreasing average costs do not allow marginal cost pricing without running at a loss. Mancur Olson has pointed out that under perfect jointness, in Samuelson's pure public good case, we have a good with a positive average cost and no marginal cost, i.e., the extreme case of the decreasing-cost industry.[4]

[3] Richard Musgrave, *The Theory of Public Finance* (New York: McGraw-Hill, 1959), pp. 13ff., and "Provision for Social Goods" in J. Margolis and H. Guitton (eds.), *Public Economics* (London: International Economic Association, 1969), pp. 143–144.

[4] This view is not entirely correct, since in the joint-consumption case we let average cost vary with the number of consumers and in the declining-cost case we let it vary

There remains the question of what form the government activity should take—service rendering, regulation, or financing. Important considerations include degree of control over outcome and costs. Thus, for example, if the service is rendered by government, it is easier to ensure that agreed-upon social objectives are achieved. At the same time, government-financed but privately supplied services may prove more efficient. By the way, government service rendering can take various forms. For example, city government can have its own department that collects refuse. Notice that still most inputs, e.g., trucks, incinerator plants, etc., are produced by private industry.[5] Or government, without producing the service directly, can be responsible for it by either contracting for it, financing it, or licensing a private firm to do the job.

Finally, there is the question of what level of urban government should be engaged. For the sake of minimizing costs, particularly exclusion costs, we want to select the government unit that best matches the geographic area for which government has responsibility and over which most of the consumption externalities extend.

Let us consider next the environment in which urban governments operate. Some of the institutional circumstances are expressions of the geopolitical aspects of cities under political and fiscal federalism. Governmental fragmentation is typical of metropolitan areas: many governmental jurisdictions overlap geographically, while political and economic entities are seldom coterminous (with urban political entities usually much smaller than economic entities). As a consequence, numerous spatial spillovers result, while few decisions about the area as a totality are made and even fewer are carried out. An interjurisdictional spillover occurs when the revenues and expenditures of one government unit are directly affected by decisions of one or more firms, households, or governments in another jurisdiction. Thus, such spillovers can result from public or private actions, with their effects on expenditures and taxes spilling over from a jurisdiction in which expenditure and tax policies are decided to another that might either benefit or suffer without having participated in the policy determination. These spillovers can cause serious distortions: inappropriate public investments and undesirable distributions of gains and losses among people within or between different urban jurisdictions.

There are two major sources of interjurisdictional spillovers: economic interaction and fiscal interdependence. When residents of one city buy and (or) sell products or work in another city, they are engaged in economic

---

with output. Thus it might be better to consider the two as parallel cases, with joint consumption being an extreme of the first type. Mancur Olson, "Evaluating Performance in the Public Sector," paper presented to the Conference on Research in Income and Wealth, Princeton, N.J., Nov. 4–6, 1971 (processed), pp. 41–42.

[5] By the way, one of the few "goods" that is entirely publicly produced is the Queen of England.

interaction with citizens of the other city; effects are spilled over through the prices of market transactions. Spillovers due to fiscal interdependence occur when taxes collected by an urban government are levied without regard for the residence of or benefits received by the person paying the tax. Such spillovers result even when revenue collection is restricted by place of collection but not by residence of the payer.

The absence of coterminous boundaries for economic and political entities in the metropolis makes regulation of industry in the public interest difficult. A city that wants to prohibit activities considered harmful to its residents cannot extend the prohibition beyond its political boundaries. In fact, prohibiting some economic activities within a city's boundaries may cause the economic market area of the city to expand. If, for example, a good is demanded by residents of a city, but its production is prohibited by the city, then plants might locate nearby but outside the city's political boundary. The effect is extension of its economic boundary, beyond its political boundary. Whatever the city's purpose in prohibiting production of the good, the city has not only failed to achieve it but is unable to control production and distribution of the good. While previously it could have levied taxes, it cannot do so once the firm actually relocates outside the jurisdiction of the city.

Similar problems occur because of the relationships between a city and the region that it dominates economically. Since cities rely mainly on property taxes for revenue, people can escape these by living outside the city, in a suburban community that provides fewer public services and consequently requires smaller property taxes. If enough people do this, it becomes economic for business firms as well to locate outside the city.

Spatial benefit and cost spillovers in American cities are so numerous in part because zoning laws are an extension of the police powers of the state and do not provide for the compensation of those who incur costs as a result of the activities of second parties, even though such parties may reap substantial benefits. Under these circumstances there is little incentive to reduce activities that have major spillovers; the common result is a condition that requires extensive and frequent governmental intervention, if agreed-upon efficiency and distribution criteria are to be met.

The effectiveness of urban government is lessened by the fact that no government has overall planning and control responsibility over an urban economy as an entity. Historically, the urban economy has not been planned, and today no authority has the power to make effective, comprehensive decisions about its various and separate parts. In this respect a city differs in a basic and important manner from a firm, even one that has hundreds or thousands of physical facilities and produces equally many different goods and services. A city resembles somewhat more an industry, although its actors tend to have less in common, since they strive toward more diversified objectives than do members of an industry.

Cities demand not only much regulation, but also many tangible services. So many people living in close proximity and in relative affluence can join forces in demanding more and better services from governments. The great production specialization in the private sector is mirrored in the urban government sector, which, furthermore, produces services for which there are few substitutes. Thus, for example, there are hardly any substitutes (particularly in the short run) for municipal police and fire protection, garbage collection, etc. Equally important is the fact that, unlike automobiles and canned foods that are not perishable, government services cannot be hoarded and kept for periods when public employees may decide not to perform them. The result is that urban economies are very vulnerable because they require the availability of many urban public services. Government intervention, therefore, is called for if the occasions when the city's vital processes are jammed are to be kept to a minimum and major reductions in employment and income are to be avoided.

Finally, in the rapidly growing urban public sector, whose major output takes the form of services, increases in productivity comparable to increases in the private sector have not been forthcoming. As productivity in private manufacturing located in urban areas has increased, the competition between the public and private sectors for the pool of urban workers has resulted in a marked increase in the wages paid to public employees. Such wage increases, together with relatively small improvements in productivity in the public sector and the tendency of the public sector to expand, have resulted in sharply increased costs per unit of public service provided and have contributed to financial crises for metropolitan governments.[6]

II.   *MISSIONS OF URBAN GOVERNMENTS*

Urban governments produce a variety of tangible services or programs, as well as the highly intangible services that are designed to create an environment and rules for the private sector of the economy. While there are numerous ways to arrange a typology of tangible urban public services demanded by urbanites, we suggest five major classes of services (see Table 10.1). First, there are the protection services, which include the criminal justice system and fire protection. The criminal justice system includes police, courts, district attorney's office, public defender's office, penal institutions, probation office, etc. Fire protection is closely related to police protection, with property values and density major determinants of the pattern of spatial distribution of fire houses as well as police stations.

A second group of urban public services relates to human resources

[6] William J. Baumol, "Macroeconomics of Unbalanced Growth: The Anatomy of Urban Crisis," *American Economic Review*, vol. 57, no. 3 (June 1967), pp. 415–426.

TABLE 10.1   MAJOR URBAN PUBLIC SERVICES

Protection services:
  Criminal justice system
  Fire protection
Human resources development services:
  Education
  Recreation
  Cultural activities
  Health
  Welfare
Sanitation services:
  Sewage disposal
  Refuse collection
  Water
Street services:
  Construction
  Maintenance
  Lighting
  Cleaning
  (Transportation system)
General government services:
  Executive branch
  Legislative branch

---

development in urban areas. Such programs include education, recreation, cultural, health, and welfare services, all related through citizens' demand for inputs to their physical, mental, and intellectual health and growth. The main benefits accrue directly to those who are served, although there are also indirect benefits that spill over to others of the population.[7]

Sanitation services are a third class of urban public services. Sewage disposal and water supply can be grouped together into a single service category, since the amount of water taken in by a plant or household largely determines the amount of sewage that leaves it. Thus the demand for these services is mainly related to the number of plants and households in the area. These services, as well as electric and gas utilities, which are sometimes publicly owned, benefit in a major way from economies of scale. Sanitation services are heavily property-oriented. They are truly urban and are seldom publicly rendered to farms, which in former days pumped their own water and disposed of their own sewage and refuse. The size and density of cities have forced people to buy sanitation services from government

---

[7] Major hospitals are found only in cities; urban ghettos tend to have special health problems; education in cities poses certain unique problems, particularly related to ghetto residents; higher education, if placed in the rural community, tends to transform it into a culturally active urban community; and welfare services for the urban poor are likely to be different from those for the rural poor, although municipal governments tend to play a minor role in the delivery of welfare services.

and at the same time have provided sufficiently large markets and, therefore, scale economies.

To some extent street services, which include construction, maintenance, lighting, and cleaning of streets (and transportation systems, to the extent that they are publicly owned), have characteristics similar to those of the sanitation services. Street services depend more on the type of street or highway and its length than on the number of people using them.

Finally, we can point to a group of urban public services often referred to as "general government." They tend to emanate, for example, from the activities that take place in City Hall, in the executive or legislative branch of government. General government can be thought of as producing mainly intermediary goods. For example, a mayor does not provide direct services to urbanites, but instead provides directions and guidelines to departments that actually provide the services.

Services provided by urban government differ greatly with respect to the extent to which they are delivered directly to people rather than to property and parcels of land. Thus, for example, education, welfare, and health services are directly bestowed upon people, whereas street cleaning, refuse collection, and the building of sewage lines are more directly related to physical property, admittedly with the purpose of serving people. Some government services are in part people- and in part property-oriented; police services and some recreational services are examples. Police protection is afforded to people and property alike, and while it is probable that more crimes are committed against property than against people, society usually looks upon crimes against persons as the more serious ones. The issue of urban recreation is somewhat different: urban recreation services are largely people-oriented, although in national parks and monuments the services are more resources-oriented. Distinction between urban public services as primarily people- or property-oriented helps analyze how to finance and provide services and to evaluate their spillover characteristics. For example, the financing of property-related services should rely heavily on an immobile tax base. Such services tend to have relatively few merit-good characteristics. Thus property taxes tend to be more appropriate for property-related urban public services, while personal income and sales taxes tend to be more appropriate for people-related services.

How important are these programs? Because of the large variety of urban governments we seldom find aggregate information on how much money is spent and on what programs. Instead, we have data for different levels of government. One way to get a general indication of the urban government program mix is to look at civilian public expenditures, which in 1967–1968 amounted to about $170 billion. About $30 billion were spent on public schools, $21 billion on health and welfare, $18 billion on highways, $11 billion on higher education, $6 billion on criminal justice and fire protection, $5 billion on transportation (except highways), $4 billion on water supply and treatment, $2 billion on housing programs, etc.[8]

However, if we look at the urban program mix of a particular city, the distribution of expenditures looks quite different. For example, in the proposed 1972 program budget for the District of Columbia 26 percent is to be spent for human resources development, 24 percent for education, 15 percent for public safety, 9 percent for housing and community development, 9 percent for public transportation, 6 percent for protection of urban environments, 4 percent for executive direction, and 3 percent for recreation and culture.[9]

Urban local governments not only play the major role in servicing urbanites, but they also fund most of these activities, aided by grants from federal and state governments. They finance, from their own sources, almost all expenditures on sanitation and police and fire protection services; about 45 percent of local school costs are financed by the higher levels of governments. Netzer has estimated that from local taxes or from charges imposed for services they provide, or by borrowing, urban local governments in 1969 raised roughly $370 per capita of the urban population.[10]

III.   DEMAND

Demand analysis requires a good understanding of the characteristics of urban public services. Thus, meaningful output measures are essential. Service outputs are those amounts, basically expressed in physical units, that result from the production process. Output is measured in terms of the number of basic output units of specified quality characteristics per unit of time. But very few urban services have basic output units with reasonably well-defined physical characteristics. Water delivery and refuse collection are the exception.

Defining and measuring quality of urban government services are extremely difficult. In the abstract, we could view a basic service unit as having numerous quality dimensions that preferably are evaluated from the demand side. Because of great empirical difficulties we often have to rely on proxies for output, output quality, and output quantity value.

Demand functions for many urban public services are often difficult to estimate. For reasons discussed earlier in this chapter, direct money prices are not widely used for many urban government outputs. In the absence of price signals, estimation of the demand for such urban government serv-

---

[8] Adapted from Table 7.1 in Dick Netzer, *Economics and Urban Problems* (New York: Basic Books, 1970), p. 170.
[9] Walter E. Washington, *Program Budget for the City of Washington, D.C., Fiscal Year 1972* (Washington, D.C.: Government of the District of Columbia, 1971), p. vii.
[10] Netzer, op. cit., p. 173.

ices is complex, circuitous, and often unsatisfactory. Under zero pricing of urban public services we fail to obtain valuable information about consumer preferences, and without such price signals estimation of demand for urban government services becomes most difficult. Fortunately, for many urban public services some consumer demand signals can be identified, even though they are quite weak.[11]

A number of approaches are available to make at least partial estimates of the demand for urban public services. If reasonably strong price signals are available, the individual (economic) preference approach can be relied upon. Examples are the variety of public utility services, e.g., water and electricity, for which user charges are imposed. Some urban public services entail associated private costs, as in the case of recreational activities, which may involve travel to and from the recreational facility as well as other expenditures that would not otherwise be made, including entrance fees. Other urban public services have substitutes in the private market, e.g., private education, refuse collection, and police services. The demand for such goods can be estimated with the aid of econometric methods.

A second approach to the estimation of urban public service demand can rely on voting behavior. The behavior of the electorate as well as of legislators and office-seekers can be studied empirically. Furthermore, the effect of "voting with one's feet," or the mere threat of such behavior, on decision makers can be studied. Some theoretical frameworks have been built by political economists in which political institutions are substituted for market processes in efforts to link individual preferences to public expenditures.[12] Such efforts have so far been more in the theoretical than in the empirical realm.

If the demand signals are very weak, the benefit-cost approach can be applied to analyze demand for urban government services. Here the emphasis is on the benefit-cost position of the different important interest groups with regard to specific increments in services. However, rather than revealing effective demand, this approach helps to indicate what the demand ought to be if voters were rational.

Many urban government services have only minor joint-consumption and distributional characteristics, and exclusion costs are relatively small. To the extent that this is true, user charges can be applied to them. A user charge is defined as the dollars per unit of a good or service produced by government that are collected from a recipient; it differs from other government revenues mainly because it involves a direct exchange. User

[11] For greater detail see Werner Z. Hirsch, *The Economics of State and Local Government* (New York: McGraw-Hill, 1970), chaps. 2 and 3.
[12] Anthony Downs, *An Economic Theory of Democracy* (New York: Harper, 1957); and James Buchanan and Gordon Tullock, *The Calculus of Consent* (Ann Arbor, Mich.: The University of Michigan Press, 1962).

charges are levied by officials on the users of particular units of output, and the revenues closely reflect the cost to the government of supplying the output. The effective levy of user charges depends on the ability of urban government to identify all beneficiaries of particular government outputs. User charges can not only provide revenue, but can also aid to ration government output, allocate burdens, and provide demand signals.

In addition to bona fide user charges, urban governments can rely on coupons, e.g., rent subsidy schemes and food stamp plans; special charges, e.g., license fees; and tie-in taxes, e.g., an earmarked excise tax on gasoline which is roughly a user charge on public roads.

Urban governments are already making extensive use of user charges, and technological improvements promise to reduce the cost of administering pricing schemes to a considerable extent. However, greater use of such pricing schemes may involve increased intrusion into the privacy of citizens, and it remains to be seen whether under the circumstances urban governments will extend their reliance on user charges (see the discussion in Chapter 4). The serious fiscal problems facing many cities might persuade them to employ user charges increasingly, in the hope of raising the efficiency with which they allocate scarce resources. On the other hand, increasing affluence might reduce governments' interest in employing such charges. However, there are important opportunities for government departments to charge other departments or clients for services rendered.

In connection with certain property-related services, where conventional demand is so difficult to estimate, a substitute approach is sometimes employed. We refer to it as the "requirements approach to demand," which has been discussed in Chapter 4 in relation to urban transportation and will be discussed in relation to fire and police protection.

IV.   *SUPPLY OF URBAN GOVERNMENT SERVICES*

We will next consider some basic issues relating to the production, cost, and supply of public services provided to urbanites.[13]

Production

An understanding and measurement of production by urban governments require insight into issues associated with defining and measuring output and service quality.

Production is best realized in terms of a production function expressed by an isoquant map that relates different combinations of physical inputs with outputs. Input factors can be divided into labor, capital, resources or material, and management. The management factor can be divided into managerial services—an input—and entrepreneurial capacities—a residual

[13] For greater detail, see Hirsch, op. cit., chaps 7–9.

claimant in the production process. In this view, a city manager, a police chief, or superintendent of schools furnishes managerial services in terms of internal coordination, supervision of external services, etc. The entrepreneurial function is carried out in the public sector by voters, who in part choose to act through elected and appointed officials. The voter's success as an entrepreneur expresses itself in good services and relatively low taxes, which also are reflected in land values.

In addition to input factors, output is affected by service conditions and technology. While input factors by and large can be influenced if not controlled by public officials, service conditions affecting input requirements are by and large given and cannot be changed. Finally, although technological changes take place slowly in the urban government sector, if they do take place they lead to a new production function.

The output of urban government services has both quantity and quality dimensions, which can be traded off against each other. Therefore, service output can be thought of as the product of service quantity (A) and quality (Q). As a matter of fact, since urban governments in many cases are mandated to serve all constituents, officials tend to vary the quality more often than the quantity of the service. In some instances it is not feasible to combine output with quality measures, and then we can think of the quantity of output as being a function of quality, input factors, service conditions, and technology.[14]

By giving explicit recognition to the fact that public service output is a combination of quantity and quality, which can be traded off and is determined by inputs, service conditions, and technology, we have a formulation of the urban government production function which lends itself to empirical investigation.

Urban government production functions can be estimated with the help of technical information provided by engineers or ex post statistical data. So far relatively few empirical production functions have been estimated for urban government services. They pertain mainly to primary and secondary education and measure output in terms of either achievement test scores or annual school continuation rates. Some empirical studies will

[14] More formally, the above discussion can be put into an equation:

$$O = f(I, S, T) \tag{10.1}$$

where the notations are:

I = input factors
S = service conditions affecting input requirements
T = state of technology

$$O = AQ \tag{10.2}$$
$$AQ = f(I, S, T) \tag{10.3}$$
$$A = g(Q, I, S, T) \tag{10.4}$$

where

$$\frac{\partial g}{\partial Q} < 0$$

be presented in Chapters 11 and 12. Throughout, it must be remembered that many externalities are associated with urban government services.

Costs

Costs may be divided into four components based on the distinction between the nature of the resources employed (operating and capital) and the nature of the payments made (direct and indirect) for a public service. A further useful distinction is between agency and social costs. The actual payments made by governments to secure the services of resources (including the value of services rendered by resources owned by governments) will be called "agency costs." Agency payments to labor and the vendors of materials and services usually appear in the budget of the agency. To the extent that such resources are used in the production of current services, they are assignable to the current year's costs; if such resources are capital goods (for use in future years), they must be prorated. In current production, a government agency employs goods secured by payments both in the present period and in preceding periods. Where no payment is made for the use of current services, as in capital utilization of a building constructed in a previous period, we speak of indirect agency costs; conceptually they represent the value of resources (the building's services) in their next best alternative use in the year for which we are attempting to establish current agency costs.

Social costs entail all the resources required for the activity, in terms of the value in their best alternative use, and will usually not equal the costs borne by the government unit that provides the service. Agency costs and social costs may not be equal because other parties, public and private, may incur costs that are neither explicitly charged to the agency in question nor considered in that agency's efficiency and financing deliberations. The same four-part division of costs is applicable. For example, the fire department requires services from the police department in controlling traffic and crowds around a major disaster scene. The police department's costs are direct operating costs but are not part of the fire department's costs. In its inspection and prevention program, the fire department may require that certain types of fire extinguishers be installed in factories and offices. The owners of these facilities incur direct capital costs when they install extinguishers. The sprinkler systems of major buildings are part of the private capital costs incurred to meet fire department standards, and the services of such systems may be imputed annually as part of the total social cost of fire protection in the community. Fire drills detain workers from engaging in other productive exercises and may be considered indirect operating costs generated but not incurred by the fire department.

We should also note that other standard cost concepts are applicable to urban government services. The distinction between fixed and variable costs, while applicable, is likely to be of relatively little consequence in empirical efforts to estimate government costs of those urban government services that are highly labor-intensive.

In developing urban government cost functions, we will concern ourselves with an agency's costs, not with social costs of their activities. Just as urban government production functions can be obtained (see equation 10.4), corresponding average unit cost functions can also be derived. Long-run average unit cost of a given service is affected by the service quality, quantity, prices of factor inputs, service conditions affecting input requirements, and state of technology.[15]

Because most urban government services are labor-intensive, salaries and wages tend to overshadow all other factor prices. Wages usually tend to vary over time, as well as between regions within the United States. However, we would not expect major differences within any one given metropolitan area. Important observed differences, if any, would tend to be reflected to a major extent in manpower quality.

An important issue that can be analyzed with the aid of cost functions, as well as production functions, is the presence of scale economies and diseconomies. Consolidation of local government services often results in control over more already existing units, i.e., further horizontal integration. Under conditions not uncommon among local governments, the average quasi-long-run cost function of horizontally integrated services tends to be reasonably horizontal over a wide range of operations. This condition is favored by the fact that, because labor is the major input of local governments, few inputs are bought to secure major price concessions; moreover, location considerations tend to keep plants relatively small.[16]

Urban governments also provide vertically integrated services, e.g., electricity and water generation and distribution, which appear to benefit from scale economies, at least over a substantial range of operations. Although empirical investigations have not produced entirely uniform results, some have produced results that are consistent with these theoretical propositions. Empirical cost studies will be reviewed in Chapters 11 and 12.

V. DECISION MAKING

Urban governments make investment and operating decisions with regard to tangible services as well as regulatory and financing decisions. For example, among the investment decisions are what facilities to build; how, when, and where to build them; and how to finance them. Operating deci-

---

[15] In more formal terms,

$$AUC = h(Q,A,I,F,S,T) \tag{10.5}$$

where new notations are:
  AUC = average unit cost
  F = input factor prices
[16] Hirsch, op. cit., pp. 273–277.

sions include the quantity and quality of services to render; and how, where, when, and for whom services should be rendered. Regulatory and funding decisions center around the issues of who should benefit and who should pay, and in what manner. Two major approaches to these public decision issues dominate all others: economic and political.

The economic approach, in its extreme, argues that a government first identifies its goals; then it collects information about the various courses of action that seem to be open and about the consequences of choosing alternative paths. The total effects of each alternative are estimated and a preferred solution is selected. As the preferred solution is planned, budgeted, and implemented, the problem is resolved. The political approach has been posited by Charles E. Lindblom, and Aaron Wildavsky, who consider that a rational means-ends calculus is unrealistic in a politically motivated world, where also time and cost do not allow sufficient information for rational choice to be made among alternatives.[17] Instead, Lindblom says, budget makers pursue "disjointed incrementalism," and decision makers do not pursue goals but move away from a problem by following a policy that is only marginally different from the existing one. If one thing does not work, they try something else.

Consistent with the economic approach to public decision making is program budgeting, a planning and management process which applies notions of economic efficiency to public decision making. It involves choice among alternatives in order to achieve the most cost-effective use of resources; involving achievement of the greatest effectiveness for given costs or given effectiveness at minimum cost.

It is useful to look at this planning-management process as having structural, analytic, and administrative-organizational dimensions. These three dimensions, particularly the first two, are interdependent, since an organizationally meaningful budget structure is influenced by the analytic parts of the system, and vice versa.[18]

The format in program budgeting helps to structure and organize funding information. The program budget is output-oriented and composed of convenient, flexible building blocks. This flexibility allows for reformulation of activities to accommodate changes in perspective and objectives of local and state governments. Delineating programs requires careful definition of purposeful missions. The program budget is structured to allow for an extended time horizon so that the future implications of decisions can be better evaluated. Under federalism, a program budget should reflect the sources of funds, who operates the program, and with what discretion.

[17] Charles E. Lindblom, *The Intelligency of Democracy: Decision Making through Adjustment* (New York: Free Press, 1965), 360 pp.; and Aaron Wildavsky, *The Politics of the Budgetary Process* (Boston: Little, Brown, 1964).
[18] Werner Z. Hirsch et al., *Program Budgeting for Primary and Secondary Public Education* (New York: Praeger, 1972).

Analysis and evaluation are an integral part of urban program budgeting and include the study of objectives and of alternative ways of achieving them, of future environments, and of contingencies and how to respond to them. In this connection, benefit-cost analysis is an important analytical tool. By this method, we attempt to compare social benefits and social costs. Social benefits include the total value of added output or satisfaction resulting from choosing some activity. Social costs include all resources required for the activity, in terms of the value in their best alternative use.

Program budgeting analysis can facilitate decision making by government officials mainly on two levels: it can help determine the best mix of subprograms and sub-subprograms and it can help determine the most efficient way of obtaining a given program objective. Empirical benefit-cost studies have been carried out in connection with water, education, recreation, transport, housing and urban renewal, health, welfare, and other programs. Most of these empirical studies are plagued by difficulties in estimating indirect benefits and in handling intangible and incommensurate costs and benefits. Furthermore, no agreement exists on the proper interest rate. More will be said about these matters in the next chapters.

The third dimension of program budgeting is a process for implementing and controlling allocative decisions. Unless administrative problems are solved, program budgeting is unlikely to be introduced effectively into urban government, and if it is introduced, it is unlikely to produce productive results. Identification of informational requirements and the quality of the information obtained are critical for successful operation of program budgeting. Operational methods are needed by which subprograms and sub-subprograms can be assigned to lower-level decision making. It is essential that organizational arrangements and information systems be provided which tend to bring subprograms and sub-subprograms into harmony with the overall performance of the entire program. For the sake of implementing agreed-upon plans, an effective system to monitor and evaluate operations is essential.

Since the federal government began to introduce program budgeting in 1961 to improve decision making, a number of counties, cities, and school districts in the United States have taken steps to incorporate program budgeting into their decision-making processes. In 1967 a State-Local Finances Project was initiated at the George Washington University to develop some operational methods that could be readily applied by city, state, and county governments throughout the country. At the same time the city of New York initiated a sophisticated program budgeting system, aided by the RAND Corporation, which, earlier in the decade, had assisted the U.S. Department of Defense in its program budgeting efforts. Program budgeting was carried out in the city of New York in 1970 by about thirty-five professionals in the Program Planning and Analysis Division of the Bureau of the Budget, in cooperation with about an equal number of professionals in different city agencies. The emphasis has been on analysis, almost to the exclusion of structuring a unified program budget.[19]

About the opposite has been done in the school districts of California, where in 1967 the state legislature established an Advisory Commission on School District Budgeting and Accounting. The predominant efforts have consisted of discussions about goals and objectives, together with structuring of the budget.[20] A quite sophisticated program budget has been implemented by the District of Columbia.[21]

VI. *FUNDING OF URBAN PUBLIC SERVICES*

Earlier in this chapter we indicated that, for many urban government services, pricing—whereby officials obtain revenue, ration output, and receive demand information—is not possible, and is often socially undesirable. Thus, in addition to applying user charges, as discussed above, urban governments rely heavily on taxes and intergovernmental transfers to fund their operations.[22]

A tax is a payment made to cancel a liability imposed by government and for which the government offers the particular taxpayer no specific services directly in return. Urban government taxation raises several major policy questions. The most important normative question is: Who should pay? This issue raises questions about the objectives and criteria of taxes. Two major principles can be applied: The ability-to-pay principle states generally that the amount of tax burden borne by an individual should be related to his economic capability to bear the burden, i.e., the higher his capacity, the higher proportionately the tax take. The benefit principle of taxation rests on the presumption that those who receive benefits from goods and services provided by government should bear the costs for them. The benefit principle automatically links the expenditure and the receipt sides of the government budget.

A second, no less important, question is: Who in fact does pay the tax? In other words, who bears the ultimate burden? To answer this positive question, one must analyze the shifting and incidence of each tax. Tax incidence theory usually assumes that there will be full employment and that some offsetting modification in an expenditure or other tax must accompany a tax change. As a result total government tax collection remains unchanged. We call this technique *differential incidence determination.* Tax

---

[19] Frederick O'R. Hayes, *Creative Budgeting in New York City* (Washington, D.C.: The Urban Institute, June 1971).
[20] California State Department of Education, *Preliminary Planning, Programming, Budgeting System Manual for State of California School Districts* (Sacramento: State of California Department of Education, 1970).
[21] Washington, op. cit.
[22] For greater detail see Hirsch, *Economics of State and Local Government*, op. cit., chaps. 4–6.

shifting results from burden avoidance behavior; as expectations of a tax change become more certain and specific, households alter their behavior in order to avoid the tax burden. Tax burdens are thus shifted from legally liable households to other households who alter their behavior in order to accept part of the tax burden rather than accept the costs implied by complete burden avoidance. Resource specialization, especially geographic specialization, has important effects on the shifting of various taxes.

Urban government taxation can be examined as to its effects on equity of tax burden, economic efficiency, economic growth, and economic stability. These four issues are in a sense criteria by which taxes can be appraised. Basically different tax objectives can be achieved through laws that result in appropriate tax avoidance behaviors.

Another positive question relates to the productivity of taxes: How much in taxes will be paid to an urban government? The tax productivity of a given jurisdiction depends on the income elasticity of tax revenue—which is directly related to the jurisdiction's tax system, structure, and rates—as well as on its tax base—often beyond policy control. The income elasticity of tax revenue must be examined in the light of the progressivity of the tax (and tax system) and the responsiveness of the tax base. Two types of growth frameworks and models can be applied to project tax base changes: regional growth models emphasizing final demand changes, and direct tax base models. Both types are extensions and special applications of the frameworks and models discussed in Chapters 7 and 8.

To the extent that all three levels of government serve urbanites, we could examine tax instruments used by all of them. Instead of doing this, we will concentrate on the tax instruments used by local urban governments.

A review of major revenue sources of urban governments must pay attention to such issues as coverage, collection method, base, and whether it is related to person or transaction. We will keep these issues in mind when taxes are discussed in Chapter 13.

The property tax, although its relative significance has been gradually declining, is still the single most important tax. It is a government levy on certain physical assets, mainly real property and to a lesser extent personal tangible assets. Other taxes include sales and excise taxes and income (or payroll) taxes. Where they are used, general sales taxes are uniformly levied, e.g., on all retail sales. A specific excise tax is one levied on a narrow range of exchanges, i.e., a particular good (automobiles, cigarettes, etc.) or a particular service (telephone calls). Finally, some cities levy a gross income tax. Since such a levy is most readily enforced if it is related to salaries and wages paid by private firms and government, it often amounts to a payroll tax.

Local urban governments also spend moneys raised by state and federal governments and transferred to the former. A variety of intergovernmental fiscal instruments exist. They fall into three main categories: direct transfer of funds to subordinate governments; sharing of the tax base by the federal or state government with local governments, i.e., indirect transfers; and coordination between the three levels of government. Within the first group are such transfer instruments as loans, categorical grants, and unrestricted grants. In the second group are such transfer devices as vacating specific revenue sources, tax supplements, tax deductions, and tax credits. Such instruments are taken up in detail in Chapter 13.

VII.   *REGULATION*

Finally we come to some intangible services that urban governments render. Municipal and county governments seek to provide an environment in which private firms and consumers can thrive in relative harmony. Governments regulate particularly land use and transportation, and with the aid of a variety of techniques seek to abate urban air, water, and noise pollution. Also, they must devise effective rules and arrangements to streamline relations with public employees. In carrying out this responsibility, urban governments must be concerned not only with efficiency but also with income redistribution issues.

For land-use regulation, urban governments heavily rely on planning and zoning. Because land was so abundant in the past, the United States has developed an attitude of being land-wasteful. And now we are visibly confronted by the scarcity of readily accessible land in our cities. Zoning was perceived as a local government "right," and in many states it was started under a state's "home rule" power. Thus zoning limits the use of land, but supposedly only when the restriction is in the interest of public health, safety, and welfare. Because zoning is based on police powers rather than the principle of compensation, it can produce substantial private gains to some and losses to others.

Because of the abundance and seriousness of externalities, urban governments engage in land-use regulation and in pollution abatement, abandoning the venerable precept that "a man's home is his castle." In a highly urbanized and industrialized world in which people closely depend on one another, man can no longer do as he pleases. In cities there are few castles with moats around them. The man who turns on a hi-fi set full blast at 2 A.M. wakes up his neighbor, just as the slaughterhouse pollutes the air for residents many miles away and the plant that pours pollutants into a river harms those who live downstream. To cope with polluters, a number of approaches offer themselves—direct regulation, polluter's charges, and subsidies.

The issues opened up in this chapter will be explored in greater detail in the following three chapters, starting with a consideration of urban public service delivery.

CHAPTER 11

DIMENSIONS OF URBAN PUBLIC SERVICES

I. INTRODUCTION

Among other topics, the preceding chapter has discussed, in conceptual terms, the demand, supply, and decision-making dimensions of urban public services. However, empirical estimation of these characteristics is extremely difficult, because of the paucity of data, uncertainties about data construction, and ambiguities in interpretation of the estimated equations.

For private goods and services the market efficiently produces basic information regarding prices, demand, output, etc. However, in the absence of market signals concerning public services the empirical analyst must turn to administrative data that are not collected for purposes of economic analysis. It is not surprising that under these circumstances directly usable information is scarce or totally lacking. The investigator is therefore often compelled to construct his own data by piecing together information from a variety of sources. Even apart from the considerable time that must be devoted to this preanalytic task there are conceptual difficulties in knowing what to construct. For example, for most public service analyses some proxy must be selected that presumably measures output. Often there are several proxies that could be used but no criteria for deciding which is the most appropriate.

Even after basic data are constructed and incorporated in estimating equations there are ambiguities in interpreting the results of these equations. For example, the identification problem is usually a feature of empirical public service analyses, as are the interpretation difficulties created by the use of cross-sectional regressions for longitudinally defined problems. And, finally, there are considerable variations among studies in the results obtained for different cities and sometimes among studies of the same city for different points in time.

Thus, the empirical investigations of public services undertaken so far suffer from many shortcomings, which should be kept in mind as we review specific empirical studies in this chapter.

II. DEMAND

Two aspects of demand analysis are the source of most conceptual and empirical difficulties. The first is selecting a meaningful output measure for each public service; the second is deciding upon the appropriate variables in the estimating regression.

Output Measures

Urban government service outputs are in concept those amounts, basically expressed in physical units, that result from the production process. Ideally, we would first define the basic service unit and then estimate the number of units produced per some period. But output has quality characteristics as well as quantity characteristics. However, we usually find it extremely difficult to define and measure basic output units and their quality characteristics.

To the extent that urban government provides a collective good, i.e., one typified by jointness in consumption and high exclusion costs, it must expect great difficulty in measuring governmental outputs as they reveal themselves to consumers. In short, the presence of externalities, which prevent resource rights from being fully captured, complicates output measurement.

Attempts at identifying output units and valuing them in terms of quality characteristics have proved most successful in cases where there are few externalities and where basic service units can be defined and quantified, where relatively few important quality dimensions exist, and where to some extent these services are devoid of vertical integration. Refuse collection and water services are such examples. Thus, the basic service unit of refuse collection can be defined as containers of refuse collected per year, while important quality dimensions such as collection frequency, location, and nature (i.e., whether separation of refuse into garbage and trash is required) can be introduced to "adjust" the basic service output units.[1]

Education analyses illustrate the problems associated with trying to select a suitable proxy for output when a variety of candidates are available. Important output measures that have been used in studies of primary and secondary education are percentage rate of annual continuation in school, median change in reading scores between second and sixth grades, average achievement test score, and change in achievement test scores between first and twelfth grades. The first two output measures have been used by Martin T. Katzman; the second measure has been used by Herbert J. Kiesling; and the last measure has been applied to a sample of 1,000 black, male twelfth-grade students by Samuel Bowles.[2] Jesse Burkhead, T.

[1] Werner Z. Hirsch, "Cost Functions of an Urban Government Service: Refuse Collection," *Review of Economics and Statistics,* vol. 47 (February 1965), pp. 87–92.
[2] Martin T. Katzman, *Distribution and Production in a Big City Elementary School System* (Ph.D. dissertation, Yale University, 1967); Herbert J. Kiesling, "Measuring a Local Government Service: A Study of School Districts in New York State," *Review of Economics and Statistics,* vol. 49 (August 1967), pp. 356–367; Samuel

G. Fox, and J. W. Holland, however, prefer four different output measures—eleventh-grade I.Q., eleventh-grade reading score, dropout rate, and extent of post-high school educational intention. The first two measures are found to be superior.[3] Clearly these measures reflect different kinds of outcomes from the education system and imply differential benefits for different groups. Whether one is more appropriate than another often depends on the use to which the output measure is put. However, the various measures may be closely associated, in which case it does not matter which is selected.

Another issue relates to whether output or output changes are the crucial variable in public service analyses. Kiesling, for example, tries to distinguish between level of achievement and gain in achievement output measures in education. Specifically, one output measure is the level of sixth-grade performance, a second measure is gain in performance between grades four and six, and a third measure is sixth-grade level, using fourth-grade score as one of the explanatory variables. Kiesling argues that the last variant is theoretically the most satisfactory if there is much pupil mobility between schools, and that the first variant is best if there is little such mobility. However, his empirical work reveals no significant difference, regardless of which output measure is used, and he concludes that therefore one is able to use level of achievement scores as a surrogate for gain.

A particularly difficult problem arises when the public service is provided to prevent something from happening rather than to provide some more or less tangible service. The difficulty, of course, is how to measure something which might have happened but has not; how can one calculate whether it might have happened? Regulation is a clear illustration of such a service. However, even among the more tangible urban services the problem arises. The major output of police and fire services is in the nature of deterrence; undesirable events are presumably prevented from happening. (These services are discussed more completely in the next chapter.) But other services as well have the deterrence dimension of output. Consider health services: the major output of urban medical and health services takes the form of the reduction in the number of days lost due to ill-health. To some extent this approach was taken by Herbert E. Klarman.[4] An output measure used by Auster, Leveson, and Sarachek was age-adjusted

---

Bowels, "Towards an Educational Production Function," in W. Lee Hansen (ed.), *Education, Income, and Human Capital* (New York: National Bureau of Economic Research, 1970), pp. 11–61.

[3] J. Burkhead, T. G. Fox, and J. W. Holland, *Input and Output in Large City High Schools* (Syracuse, N.Y.: Syracuse University Press, 1967), p. 48.

[4] Herbert E. Klarman, "Syphilis Control Programs," in Robert Dorfman (ed.), *Measuring Benefits of Government Investments* (Washington, D.C.: Brookings, 1965), pp. 367–410.

death rate.[5] Finally, Michael Grossman has used as output measures the number of healthy days enjoyed by an individual in a given year and his total length of life. In connection with the latter, he has developed a survival probability index which is basically 1 minus the death rate.[6]

Demand Estimation

There are relatively few urban service demand studies, defined in the classical sense as the relation between price and output quantity demanded, largely because of the absence of reliable price signals. Therefore private market data and analyses are frequently used. Urban public services differ greatly in the extent to which they involve associated private costs and compete with private substitutes. Higher education and hospitals are good examples of services for which there are private substitutes.

A higher education demand function for the nation has been estimated for the period 1927–1963; to the best of our knowledge, no such function exists for a particular urban university or urban area. Robert Campbell and Barry Siegel used as the demand variable undergraduate degree enrollment in four-year institutions divided by the number of eighteen-to-twenty-four-year-old eligibles (X_1), and as the independent variables real disposable income per household (X_2) and average real tuition (X_3); on that basis they estimated the following demand function:

$$\text{Log } X_1 = 0.7425 + \underline{1.2036} \log X_2 - \underline{0.4404} \log X_3 \qquad (11.1)$$

Both net regression coefficients are statistically significant at a probability level of 0.05 and therefore are underlined. The coefficient of multiple correlation is .9316 and statistically significant.[7]

Gerald Rosenthal has attempted to estimate the short-term demand for general hospital services.[8] He argues that there are two dimensions to the demand for hospital services—admissions rate and length of stay. The former is determined by characteristics of population and is less sensitive than the second to economic variables. Thus, he uses as the demand variable length of stay for twenty medical categories and eight surgical categories. As the independent variable he uses both cash outlay (total bill) and average daily room rate. He finds statistically significant price elasticities of demand for ten of the twenty medical categories and for five of the

[5] R. Auster, I. Leveson, and D. Sarachek, "The Production of Health, an Exploratory Study," *Journal of Human Resources,* vol. 4, no. 4 (Fall 1969), pp. 411–436.
[6] Michael Grossman, *The Demand for Health: A Theoretical and Empirical Investigation* (Ph.D. dissertation, Columbia University, 1970).
[7] Robert Campbell and Barry N. Siegel, "The Demand for Higher Education in the United States, 1919–1964," *The American Economic Review,* vol. 57 (June 1967), pp. 482–494.
[8] Gerald Rosenthal, "Price Elasticity of Demand for Short-Term General Hospital Services," in H. D. Klarman (ed.), *Empirical Studies in Health Economics* (Baltimore: Johns Hopkins, 1970), pp. 101–117.

eight surgical categories. When the average daily room charge is used as the independent or price variable for the medical categories, the price elasticities vary from —0.19 to —0.70, while in the surgical categories the elasticity varies between —0.30 and —0.97.

A second empirical health study illustrates the use of cross-sectional data for estimating income elasticities of medical care demand.[9] The data from a 1964 cross-sectional survey of 2,367 families were used. The dependent demand variable was family expenditure for medical and dental services. Independent variables included income, price, quality, preventive care, and whether patients regularly used specialist, general practitioner, chiropractor, etc. Income elasticities for both medical and dental services were statistically significant, i.e., +0.63 and +1.24, respectively.

A third study sought to construct a demand function for a service provided at zero price. Assuming that in the absence of price there would be other rationing devices, Sidney Sonenblum and Meredith Slobod considered the effects of travel distance (as a price substitute) on clinic usage.[10] Using a 1,000-family sample of Los Angeles members of a prepaid group medical plan, they identified clinic trips (U) as the dependent demand variable. In addition to distance between residence and clinic (D) as an independent variable, they used health status (H), income (Y), education level (E), knowledge about the health plan (K), and family size (F). The demand function they obtained is:

$$U = 4.60 + 0.06H - 0.49Y + 0.22E + 0.42K - 0.28F - 0.11D$$

All signs are in the expected direction and the coefficients are statistically significant. However taken together, the independent variables explain less than 20 percent of frequency of clinic usage.

III. SUPPLY

The supply of urban public services has a number of dimensions; the major ones are production, costs, and supply. Conceptually, no less than empirically, urban government supply functions pose particularly difficult problems. A supply function relates service costs to output. Unlike private firms that have in common a strong profit motive, urban governments appear to pursue a variety of goals, many of which conflict. Marginal cost, an optimality concept useful only when decision makers pursue some rational maximization such as profits, does not readily apply to urban gov-

[9] Ronald Andersen and Lee Bonham, "Factors Affecting the Relationship between Family Income and Medical Care Consumption," in H. E. Klarman (ed.), *Empirical Studies in Health Economics* (Baltimore: Johns Hopkins, 1970), pp. 73–96.

[10] Sidney Sonenblum and Meredith Slobod, *Distance as a Determinant of Demand for Outpatient Medical Services*, MR-157 (Los Angeles: University of California, Institute of Government and Public Affairs, 1971), 52 pp.

ernments. There is no assurance that the least-cost combination of resource inputs and, therefore, the lowest-cost function will be selected by urban governments. A second reason why an urban government service supply function cannot be readily derived from its marginal-cost function arises from the monopolistic characteristics of the markets in which urban government services are offered. Thus, marginal cost is not a supply curve for a monopolist because it does not portray quantities offered at respective alternative prices.

In the light of these difficulties it would be useful to explore alternative formulations of urban government supply. For example, it can be argued that urban government officials usually face a more or less fixed size of budget and number of people to be served; therefore they make adjustments by varying the quality of the service they supply. Thus, instead of moving along a line reflecting the net relation between dollars and quantities supplied, they tend to jump from one line associated with one service quality to a second line associated with another quality.

In this section we will mainly consider production and cost functions and analyze how in particular the latter contributes to analyses of scale economies in the delivery of urban public services.

Production

A production function represents the relationship between inputs of productive factors and outputs per unit of time, subject to certain constraints. Ideally, a production function shows what each set of physical inputs, service conditions, and technologies will produce in terms of specified outputs. Two estimating difficulties are especially important: the multiproduct nature of public service outputs and the selection of appropriate input variables. Since more empirical work on production functions has been done for primary and secondary urban education than perhaps for any other urban public service, we will draw our illustrations from this service area.

We agree with Samuel Bowles that ". . . schools are multiproduct firms; and the composition of output is highly sensitive to the particular combination of inputs used."[11] The schools' multidimensional output has been discussed in such terms as preparation for careers and employment, family and home activity, leisure activity, and civic and social participation.[12] In discussing the multidimensional aspects of school output, Samuel Bowles stresses achievement, cognitive skills, personality, and future economic performance.[13] Kiesling, on the other hand, uses achievement test · scores as output but considers multidimensional output aspects in terms of

---

[11] Bowles, op. cit., p. 24.
[12] Werner Z. Hirsch and Morton J. Marcus with Robert M. Gay, *Program Budgeting for Primary and Secondary Public Education* (New York: Praeger, 1972).
[13] Bowles, op. cit., p. 22.

achievement by different socioeconomic groups.[14] Katzman, however, perceives output as reading scores and the continuation rate in school (i.e., the converse of the dropout rate).[15]

Although the multidimensional aspects of output are clearly recognized, very little has been done to combine these aspects into an overall output measure appropriately weighted by each dimension. Rather, most investigators follow the lead of Bowles, who argues that, depending on the relative valuation of the different outputs, school production functions must be represented by a number of equations, each relating inputs to a different dimension of output. This approach, which is similar to constructing a separate production function for each product in a multiproduct firm, obscures the contribution that each input makes to overall output and productivity of schools.

In Chapter 10, it was argued that production functions for urban services conceptually include three classes of input variables: input factors, service conditions, and the state of technology. However, the empirical studies that have been made do not include any technology variables. Rather, they concentrate on the physical input and service condition variables, and generally find that service conditions are more important than physical inputs in explaining output. This observation about the importance of service conditions seems to hold not only for education but for most public services. This highlights an important difference between public services and private services: the external (to the plant) service conditions seem relatively less important in the private than in the public sector. It also helps explain why productivity may improve more slowly in the public than in the private sector.

Now let us consider some specific production functions that have been developed. Bowles estimates a number of different production functions from a sample of 1,000 black, male, twelfth-grade students, but appears to be most satisfied with the function represented in Table 11.1. Of the ten independent variables, all but two are statistically significant at about an 0.05 level of significance, and together they account for about 30 percent of the variation in output. Two service condition variables—control over environment and self-concept—appear to be powerfully related to achievement, and the proportion of variance explained almost doubles when these two variables are included. Other important service condition variables are number of siblings and parents' educational level; only teacher's verbal ability (and perhaps time spent in guidance) is an important physical input variable.

Not unlike Bowles, also Burkhead, Fox, and Holland, after fitting education production functions for Chicago and Atlanta, also find that service

---

[14] Kiesling, op. cit.
[15] Katzman, op. cit.

*TABLE 11.1   EDUCATIONAL PRODUCTION FUNCTION
WITH STUDENT ATTITUDES MEASURED, BLACK
MALE TWELFTH-GRADE STUDENTS*

Independent Variable (dependent variable is verbal achievement)	Regression Coefficient (*t* in parentheses)	Beta
Service condition variables:		
Reading material in the home	0.4982	0.0212
	(0.7169)	
Number of siblings (positive = few)	1.5287	0.1087
	(3.8885)	
Parents' educational level	1.8746	0.1088
	(3.6768)	
Family stability	0.3818	0.0228
	(0.8489)	
Student's control of environment	4.4059	0.2334
	(8.2159)	
Student's self-concept	4.2721	0.2108
	(7.4439)	
Physical input variables:		
Science lab facilities	0.0355	0.0552
	(1.9383)	
Days in session	0.1814	0.0519
	(1.8571)	
Teacher's verbal-ability score	1.1100	0.1966
	(6.4133)	
Average time spent in guidance	1.7747	0.0964
	(3.0644)	
Constant:	−12.1269	
	(−0.6949)	
R^2 :	0.3036	
$X'X$:	0.3764	
Number of observations:	1,000	

SOURCE: Samuel Bowles, "Towards an Educational Production Function," in W. Lee Hansen (ed.), *Education, Income, and Human Capital* (New York: National Bureau of Economic Research, 1970), p. 22.

condition variables are of dominating importance. The service condition proxy variable included in these studies is median family income, and the physical input variables are age of school building, textbook expenditure per pupil, material and supplies expenditures per pupil, median teacher experience, proportion of teachers with M.A. or higher degree, teacher man-years per pupil, administrative man-years per pupil, and auxiliary man-years per pupil. Both in Chicago and in Atlanta the median family income is of the greatest importance in determining differences in school outputs. Thus current expenditures are concluded to have "very little influ-

ence on school outputs."[16] Only the experience of the teacher, particularly
its impact on reading scores, is an important physical input variable.

Herbert Kiesling undertook two separate studies of the education production function for school districts in New York State. The first deals
with all types of school districts, while the second concentrates on urban
school districts. In both studies, the output proxy was average pupil
achievement test score in the relevant grade. In the first study, inputs are
represented by per-pupil expenditures during the first year of the three-
year study; quantity was represented by school district size, i.e., number
of pupils in average daily attendance (ADA); and service conditions affecting input requirements were represented by an intelligence score, i.e., results of the Lorge-Thorndike Intelligence Examination. This analysis is
carried out for all pupils as well as for six separate socioeconomic groups
in terms of the occupation of the family breadwinner; inclusion of the
breadwinner's occupation is designed to reflect the child's motivation and
desire to learn.[17]

The regression equation for grades 4, 5, and 6, covering all pupils,
was found to be

$$X_1 = -12.78 - \underline{1.269X_2} + \underline{4.362X_3} + \underline{0.174X_4} \qquad (11.2)$$

where

X_1 = average achievement test score
X_2 = size, i.e., number of pupils in ADA (natural logarithm)
X_3 = expenditure per pupil (natural logarithm)
X_4 = intelligence score

All three net regression coefficients are statistically significant at a
probability level of 0.05. The adjusted coefficient of multiple determination is .343, and is also statistically significant at a 0.05 probability level.
Thus about 34 percent of the variation of the achievement test score can
on the average be explained by changes in size, expenditure, and intelligence score, and there is only a 5 percent probability that the difference
between 0 and .343 is due to chance variation.

The statistically significant net regression coefficient of -1.269 can be
interpreted in the following manner. In New York State in the late 1950s
a 1 percent increase in the number of pupils in ADA on the average was
associated with a 1.269 point decrease in the average achievement test
score of pupils (and vice versa), holding constant the effects on achievement of expenditures and intelligence.

In the second study service condition variables include occupational
index of family head of pupil in a given grade and value of school district-
owned property per pupil, while the input variables include the number of

---

[16] Burkhead, Fox, and Holland, op. cit., p. 72.
[17] Kiesling, op. cit., pp. 356–367.

teachers per 1,000 pupils, expenditure per pupil on books and supplies, average salary of teachers in the top salary decile, and expenditure per pupil on principals and supervisors.[18] Production functions are fitted for six different socioeconomic groups, first using composite performance in terms of fourth-grade score gain as the dependent variable, second using arithmetic performance in terms of fourth-grade score gain as the dependent variable, and finally using composite performance level in the sixth grade as the dependent variable. Table 11.2 represents the results of the latter formulation, indicating the importance of the occupational index in explaining output.

Production functions also have been estimated for four metropolitan areas to examine the value of teachers in teaching, by Eric Hanushek and by Henry Levin.[19] Teachers are a physical input factor, and these studies indicate that they are an important influence on output.

Finally, production functions for elementary education in Boston have been estimated by Martin T. Katzman.[20] Katzman estimates two separate production functions; the first uses percentage of annual continuation rate —the converse of the dropout rate—as an output proxy, and the second uses reading score.

The two production functions are as follows:

$$O_6 = 43.8 + \underline{2.047S_{16}} - 0.047E_1 + 0.138E_2 + 0.049E_3 + \underline{0.190E_4} \\ - 0.006E_5 + 0.035E_6 + \underline{0.097E_8} \quad (11.3)$$

$$O_3 = 174.5 + 8.657S_{16} - 0.889E_1 + 2.291E_2 - 0.033E_3 - \underline{1.230E_4} \\ - 1.048E_5 - 0.654E_6 + 0.393E_8 \quad (11.4)$$

where
   output variables are:
   $O_6 =$ percentage annual continuation (in school) rate
   $O_3 =$ median change in reading scores between second and sixth grades
   service condition variable is:
   $S_{16} =$ index of cultural advantage
   physical input variables are:
   $E_2 =$ student-staff ratio
   $E_3 =$ percentage of teachers with master's degree
   $E_4 =$ percentage of teachers with one to ten years of experience

[18] Herbert J. Kiesling, *The Relationship of School Inputs to Public School Performance in New York State*, P-4211 (Santa Monica, Calif.: The RAND Corporation, October 1969), 33 pp.
[19] Eric Hanushek, *The Value of Teachers in Teaching*, RM-6362-C-C-RC (Santa Monica, Calif.: The RAND Corporation, December 1970), and Henry M. Levin, "A Cost Effectiveness Analysis of Teacher Selection," *Journal of Human Resources*, vol. 5, no. 1 (Winter 1970), pp. 24–34.
[20] Katzman, op. cit.

TABLE 11.2 FITTED MULTIPLE REGRESSION EQUATIONS, COMPOSITE PERFORMANCE, GRADE 6, IOWA TESTS OF BASIC SKILLS, URBAN SCHOOL DISTRICTS IN NEW YORK STATE, 1957

Socioeconomic Group (Occupation of Family Breadwinner)	Intercept	Index of Occupation	Teacher-Pupil Ratio	Per-Pupil Expenditure on Books and Supplies	Mean Salary of Teachers in Top Salary Decile	Value of School Property per Pupil	Per-Pupil Expenditure on Principals and Supervisors	N	$\bar{m}$	$\bar{s}$	$R^{2\,a}$
1. Professional persons	7.39 (0.31)	.301 (2.08)*	−.0083 (0.66)	.0052 (0.39)	.0031 (0.47)	−.0063 (0.67)	.010 (3.51)**	44	8.19	0.36	.388
2. Proprietors, managers, officials	6.30 (0.26)	.372 (2.62)*	.0016 (1.33)	.0077 (0.61)	−.0013 (0.23)	.016 (2.22)*	.0045 (1.79)†	44	7.62	0.40	.636
3. Clerks and kindred workers	7.14 (0.30)	.583 (3.38)**	−.036 (2.40)*	−.020 (1.46)	.0077 (1.25)	.014 (1.64)	.0035 (1.19)	44	7.32	0.37	.437
4 and 5. Skilled and semi-skilled workers	7.59 (0.32)	.543 (2.58)*	−.054 (3.31)**	.00029 (0.02)	.0081 (1.22)	.0026 (0.26)	.0047 (1.32)	43	6.98	0.37	.357
6. Unskilled workers and servants	6.72 (0.36)	.951 (4.03)**	−.039 (2.15)*	−.0075 (0.51)	−.0015 (0.17)	−.0022 (0.21)	.013 (2.63)*	43	6.68	0.44	.435
All pupils	6.46 (0.24)	.796 (6.52)**	−.026 (2.38)*	.021 (1.99)†	.0052 (1.04)	−.0022 (0.33)	.0038 (1.59)	46	7.45	0.46	.767

Statistical Significance: † indicates significance at the 10 percent level, * indicates significance at the 5 percent level, and ** indicates significance at the 1 percent level.

ᵃ Corrected for degrees of freedom lost.

SOURCE: Herbert J. Kiesling, *The Relationship of School Inputs to Public School Performance in New York State*, P-4211 (Santa Monica, Calif.: The RAND Corporation, October 1969), 33 pp.

$E_5 =$ percentage of annual teacher turnover

$E_6 =$ percentage of teachers with permanent status

quantity variables are:

$E_8 =$ number of students in district

$E_1 =$ percentage of school crowding

In both cases statistically significant regression coefficients—at a probability level of 0.05—are underlined. The coefficients of multiple determination (adjusted for degrees of freedom lost) are .936 and .711, respectively, and are highly significant at a probability level of 0.05.

Costs

In Chapter 10 it was suggested that the average unit cost of a public service is influenced by the quantity and quality of the public service, the service conditions, physical inputs, state of technology, and the factor input prices.

Although empirical cost curves have been estimated for a number of urban public services, very rarely have they tried to incorporate the variety of relevant independent variables. Perhaps one of the most complete in this respect is a study by Hirsch dealing with refuse collection.

With the use of 1960 cross-sectional data for 24 St. Louis city-county cities and municipalities, an attempt is made to derive a cost function of residential refuse collection.[21] A multiple-regression equation with the following values was estimated:

$$X_1 = 6.16 + 0.000\ 089X_2 - 0.000\ 000\ 000\ 436X_2{}^2 + \underline{3.61X_3}$$
$$+ \underline{3.97X_4} - 0.000\ 611X_5 - 1.87X_6 + \underline{3.43X_7} \quad (11.5)$$

where

$X_1 =$ 1960 average annual residential refuse collection and disposal cost per pickup in dollars

$X_2 =$ number of pickup units, which appears to be a good proxy of the annual amount of refuse collected

$X_3 =$ weekly collection frequency

$X_4 =$ pickup location

$X_5 =$ pickup density

$X_6 =$ nature of contractual arrangements

$X_7 =$ type of financing, where general revenue financing is zero and user charge financing is one.

X_2 can be looked upon as a quantity variable, since it is a proxy of annual amount of refuse collected; weekly collection frequency and pickup

[21] Hirsch, "Cost Functions of an Urban Government Service: Refuse Collection," op. cit., p. 91.

location are service quality indicators; while pickup density, nature of contractual arrangements, and type of financing constitute service conditions affecting input requirements.

The multiple correlation coefficient adjusted for degrees of freedom is .874. It is statistically significant at a probability level of 0.05, as are the underlined net regression coefficients.

The statistically significant net regression coefficient 3.61 can be interpreted in the following manner: In St. Louis County in 1960, increasing the weekly collection frequency by one pickup on the average is associated with a $3.61 increase in refuse collection and disposal cost (and vice versa), holding constant cost effects of number of pickup units, pickup location, pickup density, nature of contractual arrangements, and type of financing.

Most empirical cost studies are less elaborate than the preceding study and have concentrated on the question of whether economies of scale are present in the production and delivery of urban public services. Some of these studies are briefly summarized below. But first we will draw a distinction between horizontally, vertically, and circularly integrated services.

Horizontally integrated services exist when there are a number of "plants" (or a single plant) that produce essentially the same service and a unified policy is pursued with respect to these plants or units. Included would be such public services as police, fire, education (separately for each education level), hospitals, and refuse collection. Horizontally integrated services account for perhaps 80 to 85 percent of urban public services.

Vertical integration exists when there are a number of successive steps in the production and delivery of the service and a unified policy is pursued in the entire sequence of steps. Included would be such services as electricity generation and distribution, water production and distribution, and sewage treatment. Vertically integrated services may account for about 10 to 15 percent of urban public services.

Circular integration occurs when a number of complementary services are provided by different units, but are provided together, and a unified policy is pursued. The administrative activities of city hall or the legislature are illustrations of circular integration, which accounts for perhaps about 3 to 6 percent of urban public services.[22]

A number of cost studies have been developed for horizontally integrated services. As to cost functions of hospital services, we can present

---

[22] Precise classification of a service as vertical, horizontal, or circular is not always possible because of institutional and organizational differences among cities. In addition, the level of aggregation that defines a service may influence the classification. For example, if water service were separated into water production and water distribution, it would change from vertical to horizontal integration.

information produced by Kong Ro for sixty-eight hospitals, mainly in cities of western Pennsylvania for 1952 to 1963, 1956 excluded:[23]

$$X_1 = 29.64 - 0.0145X_2 - \underline{0.0721X_3} + \underline{0.1291X_4} - \underline{0.0356X_5} \qquad (11.6)$$

where

X_1 = inpatient costs per patient-day
X_2 = number of admissions
X_3 = occupancy rate
X_4 = patient care expenses per inpatient operating expenditures
X_5 = patient-days per personnel

In the equation X_2 is a proxy variable for quantity; X_4, for quality; and X_5, for the state of technology. The coefficient of multiple determination adjusted for degrees of freedom was .89 and is statistically significant at a probability level of 0.05, as are the underlined net regression coefficients. Although in this equation no statistically significant scale economies were found—i.e., 0.0145 had a negative sign but was found to be not statistically significant—Kong Ro noted that if he related these four independent variables to inpatient expenditures per admission—instead of per patient-day—statistically significant scale economies were found.

Harold Cohen improves upon the work of Kong Ro in many respects.[24] He uses data from forty-six short-term hospitals in New York City in 1965 and seeks to estimate long-run cost curves. He develops a measure of weighted output:

$$S^K = \sum_i W_i Q_i^K$$

where

S^K = service output of Kth hospital
W_i = weight for ith service
Q_i^K = number of service units for ith service in Kth hospital

To estimate total long-run costs (TC), he fits the following total cost curve,

$$TC = 4,100,000 + \underline{0.000052} \, (S^K)^2; \; R^2 = .92 \qquad (11.7)$$

Although the preceding study simply estimates total cost as a function of appropriately weighted output, Cohen also attempts to measure the effect of quality on differences in total cost. The hospitals were classified as affiliated or not affiliated with a medical school, the former representing a higher quality of service. A dummy variable representing this quality characteristic (d) was used, and, as shown in the following equation, it

---

[23] Kong K. Ro, "Determinants of Hospital Costs," *Yale Economic Essays*, vol. 8 (Fall 1968).
[24] Harold A. Cohen, "Hospital Cost Curves with Emphasis on Measuring Patient Care Output," in H. E. Klarman (ed.), *Empirical Studies in Health Economics* (Baltimore: Johns Hopkins, 1970), pp. 279–293.

added little in terms of explanatory power, even though it was statistically significant.

$$TC = 3,700,000 + \underline{0.000049} \ (S^K)^2 + \underline{0.013d}; \ R^2 = 0.93$$
$$(11.8)$$

In equation 11.7 the low cost point is at 280,000 units of service, requiring a hospital of between 560 and 575 beds operating at slightly more than 90 percent of capacity. In equation 11.8 the low point is at 270,000 units of service, requiring a 540- to 555-bed hospital.

Cost functions are also estimated with patient-days replacing service units of output as independent variables; statistically highly significant correlation and regression coefficients are derived. They are, however, somewhat smaller than those obtained using service units. In all cases, scale economies are identified.

While it is difficult to empirically develop bona fide quasi-long-run average unit cost functions, those developed in a case study for police protection[25] and the study of refuse collection discussed earlier in this chapter might be considered reasonable approximations. Each of these cost studies used some proxies in an attempt to introduce quality as independent variables. No significant scale economies were found for either of these horizontally integrated services for communities from 200,000 to 865,000 residents (and 200,000 to 225,000 pickup units). Similar results were found for education, while fire protection showed some small economies of scale up to a nighttime population of about 110,000.[26]

A study by Schmandt and Stephens also can be used to test hypotheses about the quasi-long-run average unit cost function of city police departments, whether they have one or more police stations. Schmandt and Stephens analyzed nineteen cities and villages of Milwaukee County, Wisconsin, and correlated 1959 per capita police protection expenditures with service level and population; no significant scale economies were revealed.[27]

Herbert J. Kiesling checked for economies of scale in primary and secondary New York State schools. He found no economies of scale in school district performance, and indeed had to fall back upon geographical differences between school districts to avoid finding diseconomies.[28]

[25] Werner Z. Hirsch, "Expenditure Implications of Metropolitan Growth and Consolidation," *Review of Economics and Statistics,* vol. 41 (August 1959), p. 237.
[26] Ibid., pp. 238 and 239.
[27] The partial correlation coefficient relating per capita expenditure and population size was .22, which is statistically insignificant for a sample size of 19. Henry J. Schmandt and G. Ross Stephens, "Measuring Municipal Output," *National Tax Journal,* vol. 8, no. 4 (December 1960), p. 374.
[28] Herbert J. Kiesling, "Measuring a Local Government Service," op. cit., pp. 356–367.

John Riew analyzed 109 Wisconsin senior high schools (ninety-two four-year and seventeen three-year high schools) using 1960–1961 data.[29] Per pupil in average daily attendance (ADA) operating costs were correlated with the number of pupils in ADA as a scale measure. Three quality proxies were used—average teacher salary, number of credit units offered, and number of courses taught by average teacher; and two growth variables—growth in the number of pupils and percentage growth in classrooms. A significant parabolic relationship between the pupil cost and enrollment was found. The trough of the cost function was found to be at an enrollment level of 1,675 students. Riew attributed the economies of scale mainly to the fact that senior high schools require a high degree of specialization with regard to teaching staff and facilities, much more so than primary schools.

Robert Will found significant economies of scale in the delivery of fire protection services up to a city size of 300,000 population.[30] Over that size, economies of scale barely existed.

Some cost studies of vertically integrated electric, water, and sewage treatment services are available. Long-run water delivery cost functions have been estimated for selected Wisconsin communities.[31] A few dozen individual plants were analyzed, using data from 1945 to 1957. During that period, and longer, virtually no technological changes took place. There are two different water delivery techniques, i.e., underground and surface sources of supply. Costs vary because of service conditions, such as the size and density of the community to be supplied, as well as the terrain.[32] In order to neutralize terrain as a factor in the final cost of water delivery, power and pumping expenditures can be left out of operating costs. Separate average fixed, variable, and total cost functions are fitted for surface water and underground water sources of supply, as well as for plant investment including and excluding power and pumping expenditures.

Since plants can operate at different capacity levels, capacity is introduced as one independent variable and size, with adjusted plant investment as its proxy, as a second. The following is an average total cost function for a surface water source of supply with operating costs, excluding power and pumping expenditures:

[29] John Riew, "Economics of Scale in High School Operation," *Review of Economics and Statistics,* vol. 48, no. 3 (August 1966), pp. 280–287.
[30] Robert E. Will, "Scalar Economies and Urban Service Requirements," *Yale Economic Essays,* vol. 5 (Spring 1965), pp. 1–62.
[31] Lawrence G. Hines, "The Long-Run Cost Function of Water Production for Selected Wisconsin Communities," *Land Economics,* vol. 45 (February 1969), pp. 133–140.
[32] Production and distribution of water entail collection at source of supply, i.e., stream, lake, reservoir, or underground; a treatment system; and a system to distribute water for various uses, e.g., domestic consumption, industrial purposes, and fire protection.

$$X_1 = 342.3376 - \underline{2.7880X_2} - \underline{0.00001530X_3} \qquad (11.9)$$

where
    X_1 = average total cost, excluding power and pumping expenditures, for a surface water source of supply
    X_2 = percent capacity utilization
    X_3 = adjusted plant investment per capacity utilization, excluding investment in power and pumping facilities and equipment

Thus in surface water production in the selected Wisconsin cases, where power and pumping expenses are eliminated in measuring plant size, scale economies are realized.

Walter Isard and Robert Coughlin have produced 1953 operating cost data for secondary-treatment sewage plants in Massachusetts.[33] A correlation analysis of these data reveals a statistically significant, negatively sloping unit cost function.

Marc Nerlove has examined returns to scale in electricity supply, using public utility, not governmental, data. He correlated production costs with physical output and labor, capital, and fuel prices on a firm basis. The coefficient of multiple determination for 145 privately owned utilities in 1955 was .93, and statistically significant increasing returns to scale were indicated.[34]

A number of gas and electricity cost studies were also made in the United Kingdom. K. S. Lomax found long-run average cost functions declining in relation to gas supply.[35] Likewise, J. Johnston found long-run average cost of electricity supply declining.[36]

A Model of Scale Economies in Public Services

Whether or not scale economies are present in public services has important implications for efficiency, government organization, and city size. Let us consider the circumstances under which scale economies may arise.

It has already been noted that in the private manufacturing sector, external (to the plant) effects on costs may be relatively less important than the effects that service conditions have on urban public services costs. With this in mind and considering the empirical results of the preceding chapter, as summarized in Table 11.3, we try to describe a quasi-dynamic model in which service costs are related to service conditions and type of integration.

It will be recalled that under horizontal integration a government con-

[33] Walter Isard and Robert E. Coughlin, *Municipal Costs and Revenues* (Wellesley, Mass.: Chandler-Davis, 1957), p. 76.
[34] Marc Nerlove, *Returns to Scale in Electricity Supply* (Stanford, Calif.: Institute for Mathematical Studies in the Social Sciences, Stanford University, 1961), p. 11.
[35] K. S. Lomax, "Cost Curves for Gas Supply," *Bulletin of the Oxford Institute of Statistics*, vol. 13 (1951), pp. 243–246.
[36] J. Johnston, *Statistical Cost Analysis* (New York: McGraw-Hill, 1960), 197 pp.

TABLE 11.3 PRESENCE OR ABSENCE OF
ECONOMIES OF SCALE IN URBAN PUBLIC
SERVICES

Horizontally integrated services:	
Police	No
Primary and secondary education	No
Refuse collection	No
High school education	Uncertain
Hospitals	Uncertain
Fire	Yes, but very minor
Vertically integrated:	
Water	Yes
Sewage	Yes
Electricity	Yes

trols a number of units, all furnishing a single service under a unified policy. If a government unit (or plant) renders a number of services that complement one another, circularity (or complementarity) exists. A circular horizontally integrated government controls a number of units that furnish complementary services under a unified policy. A vertically integrated government controls a number of different operations, under a unified policy, in the production of ingredients that enter into rendering a service. Clearly, there can be different combinations of these three basic types.

Government consolidation can permit control over a larger number of existing units, i.e., further horizontal integration.[37] However, except for centralization of administrative offices, relatively few changes can be made in the short run with regard to school buildings, police stations, fire houses, libraries, sewage and water treatment plants, etc. The consolidated government will tend to use the facility about as it is. Only when replacements are built can facility size reflect the needs of the consolidated government; it will seldom operate under genuine long-run conditions. Instead, quasi-long-run conditions are usually encountered.

With these considerations in mind, let us speculate about the shape of quasi-long-run cost functions of some horizontally integrated services. For example, police protection in a small community will tend to face a short-run cost function until it reaches a size where an additional station is needed. Deductive reasoning suggests that this short-run cost function should have a flat-bottomed U shape. Its left-hand portion declines, on the assumption that a community needs, on the average, one police officer per 1,000 residents to provide good police protection; around-the-clock service can thus be rendered by a department of no less than four full-

[37] The following consolidation plans have received most attention: annexation by the core city, city-county consolidation, federation or borough plans, urban or metropolitan county plans, and single- or multipurpose metropolitan district plans.

time officers. Once these four men are effectively deployed, and serve up to 4,000 residents, the addition of officers will tend to change per capita costs relatively little, until territory and distances increase substantially. The end of the flat bottom will occur when there are some tens of thousands of inhabitants. Yet the police department may seldom operate in the rising expenditure phase, since location considerations produce diseconomies of scale and can lead to the opening of branch stations. Libraries, schools, and parks also have indivisible but highly adaptable fixed plants. The law of diminishing returns applies, and leads to a U-shaped short-run cost function. Since all four service units are basically flexible, their average cost functions tend to have substantial flatness.[38]

If services of equal quality are rendered regardless of the scale of operation; if plants are of about equal size, have about equal service functions, tend to be operated at about optimum capacity, and can be readily added or closed; and if factor prices are fixed, then the long-run average unit cost function tends to be horizontal.[39] The evidence suggests that by and large these assumptions tend to be met.

Scale economies exist in private industry because of lower factor costs, larger and more efficient plants, and induced circular and vertical integration. But when local urban governments grow or consolidate, these conditions are often missing. Cities and counties purchase a highly diversified array of factors, except for labor; few factors purchased are in quantities large enough to obtain major price concessions. Unionization of public servants, however, can produce diseconomies. Also, the nature of local government services, particularly location considerations, tends to keep plants relatively small. Legal restrictions on salary levels of top officials and on permissible debt interfere with good administration and retard technological economies. At the same time, serious diseconomies can accompany a large local government that loses efficiency because of political patronage and administrative top-heaviness.

Thus on a priori grounds, growing or consolidating local governments can approximate conditions under which long-run cost functions for horizontally integrated services will not show economies of scale. Since, however, the size of some plants (and the caliber of its officials) is fixed, the quasi-long-run cost functions will resemble a U with a flat bottom over a very wide range. Furthermore, since most horizontally integrated services incur relatively little overhead, the short-run and long-run functions will tend to approximate one another. They coincide in their flat-bottom por-

---

[38] The characteristics of a fire house are slightly different in that some portion of the fixed plant, i.e., the fire-fighting equipment, is divisible and adaptability is limited. A fire house extends its scale of operation by adding a fire engine and increasing the number of firemen who operate it.

[39] Don Patinkin, "Multiple-Plant Firms, Cartels and Imperfect Competition," *Quarterly Journal of Economics,* vol. 61 (February 1947), pp. 173–205.

tion. Net economies are responsible for a negative slope to the left of this area and net diseconomies for a positive slope to the right of it. The more units that are horizontally integrated, the flatter the short-run function. All this seems consistent with the empirical evidence.

In a similar way we could speculate about the shape of the cost functions of circularly integrated services. This has been done elsewhere,[40] and it was concluded that on a priori grounds, short-run average unit cost functions for such multipurpose single-plant services could be expected to be U-shaped, with the trough in medium-size communities.

A similar analysis of vertically integrated services concluded on a priori grounds that the quasi-long-run average unit cost function for such services tends to decline until a very large scale of operation is reached. This also is consistent with the evidence that has been cited.

IV. DECISION MAKING

Never before the 1960s had there been such intense concentration on developing methods for rational decision making. As we will see, the results have been mixed, leading Alice Rivlin to conclude, "Considerable progress has been made in identifying and measuring social problems in our society. . . . Systematic analysis has improved our knowledge of the distribution of the initial costs and benefits of social action programs. . . . Little progress has been made in comparing the benefits of different social action programs. . . . Little is known about how to produce more effective health, education, and other social services."[41]

Studies designed to improve rational decision making have many motives. An important motivation is the absence of market forces and price signals in the urban public sector, which requires for rational decision making some quantitative estimates of the benefits and costs of alternative programs. Decision makers are faced with various problems. For some purposes a decision maker may want to approve a program on the basis of whether the resulting benefits exceed the costs of the program; he may choose to make this decision on the basis of the total social costs and benefits involved or on the basis of a more limited set of costs and benefits that are incurred by persons most directly involved with the program. These are program evaluation studies.

But a decision maker is also confronted with evaluating programs that have positive net benefits. He cannot approve all of them, so in making his selection he may prefer those that have the largest net benefit or benefit-cost ratios. Thus he may require studies that explicitly compare the

[40] Werner Z. Hirsch, "Expenditure Implications of Metropolitan Growth and Consolidation," op. cit., pp. 234 and 235.
[41] Alice M. Rivlin, *Systematic Thinking for Social Action* (Washington, D.C.: Brookings, 1971), p. 7.

benefits and costs of specific programs. Cost-effectiveness studies, which compare the cost alternatives of achieving some given objective, are a special case. They are interprogram comparison studies.

In addition to such program comparisons the decision maker is also interested in who bears the burden and who receives the benefits of the program, because he may choose to base his decision on distributional criteria rather than on the overall benefit-cost relationship. These are intergroup comparison studies.

In this section we will review some of the benefit-cost studies in the public services areas of human resources, sanitation, transportation, and urban renewal and development (police and fire protection as well as recreation services are discussed in the following chapter). Many of these studies will incorporate estimation of production, cost, and (or) demand functions.

Rather than organize these studies by public service we have grouped them according to whether they are primarily program evaluation, interprogram comparison, or intergroup comparison studies. Since the specific studies are often complex, there is a degree of arbitrariness about assignment to a group.[42]

Program Evaluation

A number of studies in the human resource development area and one program evaluation study of street services are discussed below.

Burton Weisbrod made a benefit-cost study of dropout prevention. His sample consisted of about 800 St. Louis high school students, sixteen years of age and over and with an IQ of at least 80.[43] A control group

[42] In addition to the studies that are described below, a number of empirical studies of higher education have been carried out, emphasizing monetary returns to educational investment and factors affecting it. (Herman P. Miller, "Income and Education: Does Education Pay Off?" in Selma J. Mushkin (ed.), *Economics of Higher Education* [Washington, D.C.: U.S. Government Printing Office, 1962], pp. 129–146; Shane J. Hunt, "Income Determinants for College Graduates and the Return to Educational Investment," *Yale Economic Essays,* vol. 3 [1963], pp. 305–357; Orley Ashenfelter and Joseph D. Mooney, "Graduate Education, Ability and Earnings," *Review of Economics and Statistics,* vol. 49 [February 1968], pp. 78–86; and Burton Weisbrod and Peter Karpoff, "Monetary Returns to College Education, Student Ability, and College Quality," *Review of Economics and Statistics,* vol. 50 [November 1968], pp. 491–497.) Furthermore, a number of studies have considered some of the conceptual issues and crucial empirical elements of benefit-cost analyses of urban transportation. (Martin Wohl, *A Conceptual Framework for Evaluating Traffic Safety System Measures,* RM-5632-DOT [Santa Monica, Calif.: The RAND Corporation, April 1968]; Herbert Mohring, "Urban Highway Investments," in Robert Dorfman (ed.), *Measuring Benefits of Government Investments* [Washington, D.C.: Brookings, 1965], pp. 231–291; and James R. Nelson, "The Value of Travel Time," in Samuel B. Chase (ed.), *Problems in Public Expenditure Analysis* [Washington, D.C.: Brookings, 1968], pp. 78–118.)

[43] Burton A. Weisbrod, "Preventing High School Dropouts," in Robert Dorfman (ed.), *Measuring Benefits of Government Investments* (Washington, D.C.: Brookings, 1964), pp. 117–161.

received normal school services, while an experimental group received additional special counseling services, assistance in getting placed on jobs and remaining on jobs, and special assistance on the job from employer and school personnel. By the end of two years, 44.1 percent of the experimental group and 52 percent of the control group had dropped out.

Weisbrod estimated two resource costs per dropout prevented—direct prevention costs of $5,815 and additional instruction costs of $725. He divided benefits between internal and external benefits per dropout prevented, and was able to estimate only one internal benefit, i.e., increased present value of lifetime income of $2,750 per dropout prevented. For such external benefits as increased productivity of cooperating resources, increased social and political consciousness and participation, decreased social costs of crime and delinquency, and decreased social costs of administering transfer payments, Weisbrod could make no empirical estimate, although he considered all of them to have positive values.

The quantifiable items add up to a total net cost of $3,800 per dropout prevented. After discussing some of the shortcomings of the analysis, Weisbrod concluded, "Subject to the many qualifications . . . the particular prevention program . . . was found to be 'unprofitable'—in terms of measured benefits and costs—even before benefits were deflated for the effect of such noneducation factors as ability and ambition. . . ."[44]

Now we will consider a health service, specifically rehabilitation, under the Vocational Rehabilitation Act of 1965, which assists disabled persons in obtaining or retaining productive employment or in locating more productive employment. Ronald Conley estimates that the more than 170,000 disabled persons who were rehabilitated through the state-federal vocational rehabilitation program in 1967 increased their lifetime earnings by about $5 for each $1 of the social cost of rehabilitation services, using a 4 percent discount rate.[45] The study finds that rehabilitants with the highest earnings at the end of the rehabilitation program also tend to be those with the highest earnings at acceptance, and they are the most expensive to rehabilitate. This leads to the conclusion "that from the standpoint of economic efficiency, it may be as desirable to rehabilitate the less productive disabled as the more productive."[46]

An earlier study of the same rehabilitation program by a team of program analysts of the Department of Health, Education, and Welfare estimated higher benefit-cost ratios than did the previously reported study.[47] Specifically, it finds that for 1965 each $1 spent on rehabilitation sets in

[44] Ibid., p. 147.
[45] Ronald W. Conley, "A Benefit-Cost Analysis of the Vocational Rehabilitation Program,"*Journal of Human Resources,* vol. 4 (Spring 1969), pp. 226–252.
[46] Ibid., p. 226.
[47] Office of the Assistant Secretary for Program Coordination, *Program Analysis of Selected Human Investment Programs,* 1966–10 (Washington, D.C.: U.S. Department of Health, Education, and Welfare, October 1966), pp. 4–7.

motion a stream of outputs with a present value of about $12 to $13, using 4 percent and 8 percent discount rates.

The urban Job Corps also has been evaluated. Members of the Job Corps are confined to a Job Corps center, except for occasional weekend leaves or vacations. The urban center provides housing, meals, and medical care, as well as social and psychological counseling, physical conditioning, recreation, remedial basic education, work experience, job training, job counseling, and job placement. Thus it is an expensive program. V. Rawlins estimates the monthly cost of training in an urban Job Corps center as roughly $515 per trainee.[48] The study finds that education on entry to the program, length of training, and completion of training program are among the variables that appear to have a significant impact on post-training earnings. Though the study indicates that when trainees are able and willing to complete the training course such a program has a positive impact on earnings, no rigorous indication is offered as to whether the social benefits are likely to exceed social costs.

Worth Bateman has attempted to estimate benefits and costs of the Work-Experience Program, funded under Title V of the Economic Opportunity Act of 1964.[49] Ideally, one would estimate the economic benefits of such a program by considering both the short-run benefits of the output produced by people working who would otherwise be unemployed and the long-run benefits of reduced dependency and improved potential for economic independence and self-support. Unfortunately, the past earnings of individuals enrolled in the program are unknown and the existing follow-up data on post-enrollment earnings are completely unreliable. Therefore a break-even analysis is used. It shows that to break even, expected future earnings from either higher wages or employment rates would have to rise from 1 percent to 3 percent in those education categories where work-experience participants are most likely to be concentrated.

A benefit-cost analysis has also been made of an augmented family planning program in Los Angeles County. If the national perspective is taken, i.e., federal, state, and local benefits and costs are included, the benefit ratio varies from 1 to 20. Assuming that the county government compares mainly savings and welfare payments with program costs, the benefit-cost ratio of the program varies from 3 to 35. If the county officials look upon the money they receive from the federal government to run the program as "free," i.e., they think that if they do not introduce the family planning program they will obtain an equivalent amount of funds for other purposes, the county officials would want to compare the total program

[48] V. Lane Rawlins, "Job Corps: The Urban Center as a Training Facility," *Journal of Human Resources,* vol. 6 (Spring 1971), p. 223.
[49] Worth Bateman, "An Application of Cost-Benefit Analysis to the Work-Experience Program," *American Economic Review,* vol. 57 (May 1967), pp. 80–91.

costs (rather than the county government's costs) with the county government's savings on welfare payments. In this comparison there are basically no net benefits.[50]

Now to look at street services. We will present a transportation benefit-cost study of the Victoria Line (VL) in a London Transport Underground railway from Victoria at its southern end to Walthamstow in northeast London.[51] It is assumed that five and one-half years will be required to build VL, and that it will be in operation for fifty years. For the calculations a 6 percent discount rate was assumed. Costs were divided into initial capital investments and operating expenses. They were estimated to amount to £1.413 billion. Annual costs at a 6 percent discount rate were £55 million.

Benefits are grouped in terms of beneficiaries: diverted traffic benefits of all those who will use VL in place of other means of transportation; undiverted traffic benefits of those who will not divert to VL, but will benefit indirectly through faster, better, and more comfortable transit; and generated traffic benefits that relate to new traffic which will result from the fall in cost of transport, not only on the VL, but because of the VL. Discounting at 6 percent, benefits to undiverted traffic are about 52 percent of the whole, and benefits to diverted traffic about 34 percent of the whole.

Under these three benefit categories, we find benefits due to time savings, fare and cost savings, and comfort and convenience. The most important single benefit, amounting to about 25 percent of the total, is found to be time savings from reducing congestion in London streets. If the other effect of decongestion—savings in vehicle operating costs—is added, the two make 35 percent of total benefits. Further major benefits are savings in bus costs (9 percent), time savings of VL traffic diverting from buses (8 percent), savings in vehicle operating costs to motorists diverting to VL (9 percent), and the value to undiverted passengers on the Underground of the increased probability of getting a seat, i.e., a comfort and convenience item (6 percent).

A feature that distinguishes this study from previous efforts (for example, by T. Coburn et al.)[52] is an attempt to measure comfort and convenience and savings accruing to people not directly connected with, using, or operating the Underground system, i.e., road users benefiting from de-

[50] Bryan C. Conley and Moshe Shelhav, *Local Government Program Budgeting for Welfare*, MR-144 (Los Angeles: University of California, Institute of Government and Public Affairs, 1970), pp. 56–65.
[51] C. D. Foster and M. E. Beesley, "Estimating the Social Benefit of Constructing an Underground Railway in London," *Journal of the Royal Statistical Society*, vol. 126 (1963), pp. 46–58.
[52] T. M. Coburn et al., "The London-Birmingham Motorway," *Technical Paper*, 46 (London: Road Research Laboratory, 1960).

congestion. Interestingly, these two categories account for 46 percent of all benefits.

The empirical findings can be summarized as follows: Discounted at 6 percent, the present value of benefits is £86 million, the present value of costs is £55 million, and the present value of net benefits is £31 million. The benefit-cost ratio is 1.57. The rate of return that allows for the effect of time is obtained by calculating the surplus of benefits over current cost of the VL for each year of its life separately. Discounting these back to the present, and expressing the total as a level annual rate of return over the period of construction and operation on the present value of the capital invested turns out to be 11.6 percent at a 4 percent discount rate, 11.3 percent at a 6 percent discount rate, and 10.9 percent at an 8 percent discount rate. The internal rate of return, which equates the rate of interest with the present values of benefits and costs, is approximately 10.5 percent.

Interprogram Comparison

First we describe two straightforward cost-effectiveness studies in education, which compare the costs of alternative ways of achieving a given objective. Then we describe some benefit-cost studies which specifically compare the benefit-cost relationships between programs—there are such studies in the human resource area, one for sanitation services and another for urban renewal.

Henry Levin has undertaken a cost-effectiveness analysis of teacher selection,[53] first estimating education production functions for black and for white sixth-grade students in four major Northern city schools in 1965–1966. Student verbal scores are consistently related to two key teacher characteristics: teacher verbal score and teacher experience. He estimates that for each additional point of teacher verbal score, Negro students gain 0.175 points and white students 0.179 points in student verbal score. For each additional year of teacher experience, test scores of Negro students are 0.108 points higher and test scores of white students 0.060 higher. When the cost of an additional point of teacher's verbal score ($24) and the cost of an additional year of teaching experience ($79) are estimated, the cost-effectiveness of these two particular strategies is revealed. The analysis indicates that recruiting and retaining teachers with higher verbal scores is five to ten times as effective per dollar of teacher expenditure in raising achievement scores of students as is the strategy of obtaining teachers with more experience.

A cost-effectiveness analysis of vocational-technical education programs carried out by Richard Kraft finds, in relation to 1965–1968 grad-

[53] Levin, op. cit., pp. 24–33.

uates of various vocational-technical programs in Florida, a positive rate of return exceeding returns to capital in the rest of the economy.[54]

Hirsch, Marcus, and Gay have undertaken a benefit-cost analysis of three options faced by the Los Angeles School District in April 1967, when it was forced to reduce its projected expenditures by $12 million a year.[55] The alternatives were a reduction in the amount of student transportation provided by the school district, a reduction in the number of hours of instruction provided in the ninth and tenth grades, and a reduction in the maintenance activities of the district.

The results of the analysis of these three alternatives, assuming a 5 percent discount rate, are presented in Table 11.4. In terms of net benefit considerations the alternative that reduces the length of the school day is the least attractive and reducing transportation is the most attractive.

A partial benefit-cost analysis was undertaken in relation to the efficiency of providing either an additional year of junior college or its equivalent in summer school sessions during the last five years of secondary education to students who would ordinarily end their education at high school graduation. The costs and benefits of these programs have been calculated in terms of (1) capital costs, operating costs, forgone earnings of the student, and other selected costs and (2) benefits in terms of added income that can be expected as a result of the additional education.

The resulting benefit-cost ratios, tentative estimates only, were: (1) one additional year of junior college—male students, 1.66, and female students, 0.64; five additional years of summer school—male students, 3.23, and female students, 1.47.[56] These benefit estimates are only partial and do not consider such benefits as a decline in demands for public services that might result from fewer social and personal disorders, traceable to more adequate schooling, etc.

T. Hu, M. Lee, and E. Stromsdorfer have investigated the relative desirability of vocational and comprehensive high school education in terms of earnings and employment. A sample of 2,767 high school graduates in three major cities was studied and earnings and employment of those who graduated from vocational high school programs were compared with those of graduates from comprehensive, college preparatory high schools who did not go on to college. Standardizing for a number of socio-demographic characteristics of students, vocational high school program graduates earned $512 per year more on the average than did those who

[54] Richard H. P. Kraft, *Cost Effectiveness Analysis of Vocational-Technical Education Programs* (Tallahassee, Fla.: Florida State Department of Education, 1969), p. 118.

[55] Hirsch, Marcus, and Gay, op. cit.

[56] For details see Werner Z. Hirsch and Morton J. Marcus, "Some Benefit-Cost Considerations of Universal Junior College Education," *National Tax Journal* (June 1966), pp. 48–57. The 1.66 and 0.64 ratios for one year of junior college education are somewhat smaller than those for two years given in the reference.

TABLE 11.4 SUMMARY OF THREE BUDGET REDUCTION OPTIONS, LOS ANGELES UNIFIED SCHOOL DISTRICT, 1967–1968 (in thousands of dollars)

	Transportation		Length of School Day		Maintenance	
	Series A	Series B	Series A	Series B	Series A	Series B
Increased school district costs	833	3,258	1,320	1,586	3,402	4,374
Increased private costs			338	799	35	70
Reduced private benefits	30	72	4,041	7,523	945	2,268
Total cost increases and benefit reductions	863	3,330	5,699	9,908	4,382	6,712
School district budget reduction (net)	1,975	1,975	3,100	3,100	2,613	2,613
Net gain (loss)	1,112	(1,355)	(2,599)	(6,809)	(1,769)	(4,099)

SOURCE: Werner Z. Hirsch and Morton J. Marcus with Robert M. Gay, *Program Budgeting for Primary and Secondary Public Education* (New York: Praeger, 1972).

graduated from comprehensive high schools. On the average, vocational high school graduates were employed about five weeks per year more than were comprehensive high school graduates. The marginal cost for vocational high school education was $525, and that for comprehensive high school education $321. The present value of net benefits of vocational high school education over comprehensive high school education for a six-year period is $2,031, using a 6 percent discount rate (and $1,534 using a 10 percent discount rate), per graduate.[57]

A somewhat watered-down, and therefore less costly, version of the Job Corps is the Youth Training and Employment Project of East Los Angeles, which serves youths sixteen to twenty-one years of age, mainly of Mexican-American descent. The program includes testing, counseling, training, and job placement. Bryan Conley and Moshe Shelhav undertook benefit-cost analyses regarding decisions about alternative prevocational training activities and on-the-job training versus prevocational training. The alternative training activities include maintaining a household service course, job placement of additional graduates, and filling other training courses. The benefit-cost ratio of the first alternative was 20:50, of the second was 2:150, and of the third was 34:90.

The study made a trade-off analysis between an on-the-job training effort, where recruits are trained in an employer's plant or office, and prevocational training, where youths train in the social agency's own quarters. A 6 percent discount rate was assumed and the benefit-cost ratio for on-the-job training was 21:45 and that for prevocational training 11:27. The authors conclude, "While it is clear that each of the programs is desirable from the viewpoint of trainees and society, it is more difficult to make a choice between them, allowing for the approximations involved in the estimating procedures. . . ."[58]

We make brief reference to an empirical study of costs in the sanitation services area, i.e., extending sewer service at the urban-rural fringe.[59] Specifically, the study examines the economics, under various assumptions, of extending the community sewage disposal system into areas previously served by septic tanks. It was assumed in one case that the subdivision was adjacent to an area already being served by the community system, and in the second case that the subdivision was not immediately adjacent to such an area. Spillovers were neglected, although they are particularly important in this case. The marginal cost of community sewage disposal is compared with private septic tank costs. Economies of scale in sewage

[57] T. Hu, M. Lee, and E. Stromsdorfer, "Economic Returns to Vocational and Comprehensive High School Graduates," *Journal of Human Resources*, vol. 6 (Winter 1971), pp. 25–50.
[58] Conley and Shelhav, op. cit., p. 94.
[59] Paul B. Downing, "Extension of Sewer Service at the Urban-Rural Fringe," *Land Economics*, vol. 45 (February 1969), pp. 103–111.

collection and treatment are indicated as density increases. Some marginal-cost estimates of septic tank service are provided, as well as marginal costs of extending community sewer services.

Finally we consider a benefit-cost analysis of urban renewal. A careful study of urban renewal has been carried out by Jerome Rothenberg, which includes a case study that in many respects is illustrative.[60] Rothenberg undertakes a benefit-cost analysis of five renewal projects in Chicago: Michael Reese, Hyde Park A, Hyde Park B, Blue Island, and Lake Meadows. Michael Reese, Hyde Park A, and Lake Meadows are large projects, while the other two are small. Most of these projects were started in the mid-fifties, and the post-project situation was assumed to be that in 1962–1963.

On the cost side, gross project costs were estimated, and from them the initial value of land was deducted. Three types of benefits were estimated: internalization of externalities in neighborhood land use and their resulting neighborhood effects; income redistribution effect through changes in the structure of the housing stock; and changes in the social costs generated by slums. For example, it was estimated that in the Michael Reese-Lake Meadows complex in 1955–1963, externalities accounted for a 28 percent benefit increase; such a finding points to the importance of including externality estimates.

Income-redistribution effects concern transfers of real income through the price changes attendant on changes in the structure of the housing stock. Here the question is: To what extent do dislocatees lose, on balance, and the people who subsequently move into the redeveloped area gain, on balance? For example, it was found that in the Hyde Park B area, 98.3 percent of the housing was substandard, yet 82 percent of the relocatees from this section subsequently obtained residence in standard dwellings.

With regard to social costs of slums, four types of benefits have been identified, each connected with the amelioration of a slum-generated social cost: decreased fire hazards, decreased illness, decreased crime, and decreased damage to personality development. The benefit-cost estimates of the five projects are summarized in Table 11.5. The Lake Meadows project turned out to promise a net benefit of $4.7 million, while at the other end of the spectrum the Michael Reese project promised a $2.9 million net loss.

Intergroup Comparison

There is much interest in who benefits from and who pays for urban public services. In Chapter 4 we presented some rough estimates of benefits and costs certain groups can be expected to incur once the Metro Rapid

[60] Jerome Rothenberg, *Economic Evaluation of Urban Renewal* (Washington, D.C.: Brookings, 1967), pp. 176–197.

TABLE 11.5 BENEFIT-COST SUMMARY OF URBAN RENEWAL NUMERICAL ILLUSTRATION (*in thousands of dollars*)

Benefit and Cost Categories	Blue Island	Hyde Park B	Hyde Park A	Michael Reese	Lake Meadows
1. Resource cost of project					
a. Gross project costs (*GPC*)	396	638	10,534	6,235	16,761
b. Less initial value of land (L_0), equals	46	49	6,449	1,596	8,777
c. Total resource costs (*TC*)	350	589	4,085	4,639	7,984
2. Benefits produced by project					
a. Increased productivity of site land ($L_1 - L_0$)	29	30	5,016	1,719	12,711
b. Increased productivity of neighboring real estate	+	+	+	+	+
c. Decreased social costs associated with slums (ΔSC)	+	+	+	+	+
3. Total costs not offset by site land benefit (1c−2a)	321	559	−931 (gain)	2,920	−4,727 (gain)

SOURCE: Jerome Rothenberg, *Economic Evaluation of Urban Renewal* (Washington, D.C.: Brookings, 1967), p. 196.

Transit System for Washington, D.C., is operational. Now we would like to present four intergroup comparison studies. The first is a study of the distribution of benefits and costs of Boston's public schools. Norton Grubb analyzes the Boston public schools in 1960, seeking to determine how benefits and costs are distributed by income and race.[61] Like so many other central cities in New England, Boston contains merely a small percentage of the metropolitan area's population. Many of the white, wealthier residents have fled to the suburbs, leaving the city with a sizable black ghetto, low per capita income and tax rates, and schools that are generally inferior to those in the suburbs.

Public costs of public education are measured in terms of the taxes that support it, and particularly the distribution in terms of the incidence of these taxes. While recognizing a large variety of education benefit elements, Grubb estimates merely the increment in expected lifetime earnings attributable to education.

Making a number of assumptions, he estimates two indexes. The first index describes the income-redistribution effects of public education. Benefits to children are related to parents' income. As a descriptive measure it implicitly assumes that educational benefits should be compared with parental income. An egalitarian system of education would want to educate all children equally, not equally in relation to their parents' incomes.

The second index, benefits per person, seeks to ascertain whether all children benefit equally from the educational system. Thus the indices focus on (1) redistribution, measured by the ratio of net benefits to income, and (2) equality, measured by the benefits per person.

Here are the major findings: the index of income distribution, giving net benefits as a percentage of income, indicates net benefits of elementary and secondary education to be regressive, i.e., "pro-poor." Thus public education tends to equalize the distribution of income within racial groups, for both whites and nonwhites. But at all income levels, the net benefits of education as a percentage of income are lower for nonwhites than for whites, indicating that education redistributes income from nonwhites to whites. The index of equality reveals that benefits per student for first through twelfth grades are slightly progressive overall, with some regressivity over the middle-income range. Benefits per student are uniformly lower for nonwhites than for whites. At every income level the benefits per person for nonwhites are approximately one-half of those per person for whites; and within a race, the children of upper-income parents are offered greater educational benefits than are their poorer classmates. This leads Grubb to conclude, "The results indicate that public education redistributes income from rich to poor and from nonwhites to whites. In abso-

---

[61] W. Norton Grubb, "The Distribution of Costs and Benefits in an Urban Public School System," *National Tax Journal*, vol. 24 (March 1971), pp. 1–12.

lute terms, education benefits children from upper-income families more than poor children, and whites considerably more than nonwhites."[62]

Next we turn to a program administered by the Office of Economic Opportunity and designed to improve the welfare of the poor. Walter Garms analyzed the private and social benefits and costs of the Upward Bound Program for four groups: white males, white females, nonwhite males, and nonwhite females.[63] Older siblings of the same sex were used as a control group. The sample consists of 7,236 students entering Upward Bound between June 1966 and August 1968. Social benefits are limited to lifetime income differentials of those who enroll in the Upward Bound Program, taken before taxes, as a measure of the increased production of those who take part in the program. External as well as intangible benefits are neglected. The social costs include direct costs of the Upward Bound Program to the government, less the amount paid in stipends; costs of the Upward Bound Program to the participating colleges; costs of educating the Upward Bound students both in high school and in college; extra living costs of students while in school; and forgone income.

While private net benefits are estimated to be positive for all sex-race classifications at discount rates of 5 percent and 10 percent, social net benefits are positive at 5 percent discount rate but negative at 10 percent. Specifically, at a 5 percent discount rate, net social benefits are as follows: white males, $3,632; white females, $1,625; nonwhite males, $1,491; and nonwhite females, $4,453.[64]

The Neighborhood Youth Corps Program, under the Economic Opportunity Act of 1964, has also been examined. A study by Michael Borus et al. included 604 participants in Neighborhood Youth Corps Programs in five urban areas in Indiana and 166 eligible nonparticipants, in 1967.[65] The earnings gain as a result of the Neighborhood Youth Corps Program is substantial for males, and high social benefit-cost ratios are obtained. Female participants, however, increased their post-program earnings very little, and their benefit-cost ratios for society are almost always below 1. Thus, benefit-cost ratios for males vary from a low of 1.8 to a high of 7.4, and those for females from a low of 0.0 to a high of 2.1. High school dropouts benefit more from the program than do graduates from high school, and the longer the participant remains in the program, the greater the increases in his post-program earnings.

Finally, intriguing and very detailed benefit-cost analyses have been undertaken by Nathaniel Lichfield in relation to city planning. He has

[62] Ibid., p. 1.
[63] Walter I. Garms, "A Benefit-Cost Analysis of the Upward Bound Program," *Journal of Human Resources,* vol. 6 (Spring 1971), pp. 207–220.
[64] Ibid., p. 219.
[65] Michael E. Borus et al., "A Benefit-Cost Analysis of the Neighborhood Youth Corps: The Out-of-School Program in Indiana," *Journal of Human Resources,* vol. 5 (Spring 1970), pp. 139–159.

engaged in such analyses in England regarding alternative development patterns for Cambridge as well as for Ipswich. Lichfield compares a select group of alternative plans for the development of the city, involving either new works of construction on open or already developed land, or no such work. These changes are visualized as a series of projects, to be implemented by public and private development agencies. Sectors of the various "producers" and "operators" (individuals or groups who play a part in creating and running the services to be realized from the project) are identified. As far as possible, each producer or operator is compared with the appropriate "consumers," i.e., individuals or groups who consume the services produced. Each linked or associated pair of producers-operators and consumers is considered to be engaged in a transaction whereby the former produces services for sale to the latter. These transactions are not confined to goods and services directly exchanged in the market but include, for example, traffic noise "sold" to the occupier of an established house by the builder of a new traffic road nearby. An account with all these transactions is established and the benefits and costs that result from each transaction are estimated. By providing detailed estimates of this sort, Lichfield identifies preferred city development plans.[66]

The preceding pages testify to the large variety of dimensions that must be considered when analyzing urban public services. Despite great complexities, substantial progress has been made in recent years. Still, there is great unevenness in our knowledge about specific urban public services, and this should become even clearer in the next chapter, which probes select services in detail.

[66] Nathaniel Lichfield, *Cost-Benefit Analysis in Town Planning: A Case Study of Cambridge* (Cambridge: Cambridgeshire, an Isle of Ely County Council, 1966); Nathaniel Lichfield, "Cost-Benefit Analysis in Town Planning—A Case Study: Swanley," *Urban Studies,* vol. 3 (November 1966), pp. 215–249; and Nathaniel Lichfield and Honor Chapman, "Cost-Benefit Analysis in Urban Expansion: A Case Study, Ipswich," *Urban Studies,* vol. 7 (June 1970), pp. 153–183.

CHAPTER 12

FOUR MAJOR URBAN PUBLIC SERVICES

I. INTRODUCTION

The preceding chapter has reviewed some of the concepts and empirical techniques for analyzing the demand and supply sides of urban public services, as well as decision making about them. Illustrations were drawn from studies of various urban public services. In this chapter we take up the more detailed consideration of four important urban public services—police, fire, recreation, and cultural services.

II. POLICE PROTECTION SERVICES

Environment and Goals

Criminal justice is administered by a complex, multifaceted system. It includes the police; the courts; the District Attorney's office; the Public Defender's office; penal institutions, including those for juveniles; probation office; etc. These public agencies, and more, play key roles in providing urbanites with criminal justice, although they often act independently and not necessarily efficiently and effectively. In this discussion we confine ourselves to police services and emphasize those that are particularly important, if not unique, to city conditions.

By the middle 1960s the United States was spending annually over $5 billion on the criminal justice system. More than 40,000 police agencies accounted for over $2.5 billion—greater than 50 percent—of the total system expenditures. Well over $1 billion was allocated to police patrol—the single most significant police law enforcement expenditure.[1] While we do not have precise information about how much is spent by urban police departments, it certainly is well over two-thirds of these figures.

Four important aspects of police services can be noted. First, crime in the 1960s was on the increase in the United States, at the same time that

[1] President's Commission on Law Enforcement and Administration of Justice, *The Challenge of Crime in a Free Society* (Washington, D.C.: U.S. Government Printing Office, 1967).

social and economic well-being in our cities was greatly improved and that public expenditures on police protection were increased.[2] Second, crime rates are higher in cities than outside of cities, and higher for large cities than for small cities.[3] Third, there is great diversity among cities in the resources devoted to police services and in the relationship between these services and crime rates.[4] Finally, the crime-fighting work of urban police departments is made difficult by the fragmentation of governments in metropolitan areas and by intergovernmental division of responsibilities.[5]

[2] For example, between 1960 and 1968 the reported national rate of forcible rape per 100,000 population increased 65 percent, that of aggravated assault 67 percent, and that of robbery 119 percent. (National Commission on the Causes and Prevention of Violence, *Violent Crime* [New York: George Braziller, 1969], p. 35.) Between 1960 and 1965 expenditures by all levels of government for police protection rose 39 percent. Recently, no doubt the expenditure increase was even more pronounced, particularly between 1967 and 1971. (President's Commission on Law Enforcement and Criminal Justice, *Task Force Report: Crime and Its Impact—An Assessment* [Washington, D.C.: U.S. Government Printing Office, 1967], p. 55.)

[3] For example, the "index crimes" (homicide, forcible rape, aggravated assault, robbery, burglary, grand larceny, and auto theft) amounted to 1.8 crimes for every 100 Americans in 1966. In cities over 250,000 the rate was 3.2, and in cities over 1 million it was 3.6, or more than double the national average. In suburban areas alone, including suburban cities, the rate was only 1.3, or just over one-third the rate in the largest cities. (National Advisory Commission on Civil Disorders, *Report of the National Advisory Commission on Civil Disorders* [New York: Bantam Books, 1968], p. 266.) Urban areas stand out in their demand for services to cope with traffic and congestion and, in recent years, with urban uprisings and riots. Thus, for example, the summer of 1967 alone saw nearly 150 cities reporting disorders in Negro—and in some instances, Puerto Rican—neighborhoods. (National Advisory Commission on Civil Disorders, op. cit., p. 32.)

[4] A study of six major police jurisdictions, including the Los Angeles City Police, Los Angeles County Sheriff's Department, Phoenix Police, St. Louis Metropolitan Police, and two departments who requested that they not be identified, gives some indication of the diversity. For example, annual Part I crimes per capita varied from 0.03 to 0.14; police budgets per capita varied between $13 and $85; uniform patrol strength per 1,000 residents varied between 1.0 and 2.5; patrol cars on the street per shift per square mile varied between 0.045 and 2.7; calls for service per patrol car per shift varied between 2.5 and 11.5; annual Part I crimes per uniformed patrolman varied between 26 and 70; and annual Part I plus Part II arrests per uniformed patrolman varied between 22 and 79. Police strength or police per capita during the 1960s increased less rapidly than reported crime per capita, although police per capita outpaced population change. For example, reported Part I crime per capita has grown at least 50 percent in two of the six jurisdictions and as much as 180 percent in two others, whereas uniformed patrolmen per capita have increased by only 12 to 43 percent. Work load per patrolman has grown, too, but not as rapidly as reported crime per capita. Calls for service per patrolman increased by 30 to 45 percent and reported crime per patrolman increased by 35 to 160 percent. (James S. Kakalik and Sorrel Wildhorn, *Aids to Decision Making in Police Patrol*, R-593-HUD-RC [Santa Monica, Calif.: The RAND Corporation, February 1971], pp. 28–52.)

[5] The responsibility for providing police protection is largely at the local level; local governments account for 79 percent, state governments for 13 percent, and the federal government for only 8 percent of all expenditures for police protection. (President's Commission on Law Enforcement and Criminal Justice, op. cit., p. 55.) There are more than 40,000 police forces in the country, 90 percent of them with fewer than ten full-time personnel. Yet, it is generally conceded that a ten-man force

Police services are closely interrelated and interdependent with various other urban markets. Traffic control activities of urban police departments are directly related to transportation, and land use and its planning directly affect the demands made on urban police departments for services. Urban police forces are related to urban labor markets in at least two ways: they draw on urban labor pools for recruits, and during industrial strikes they are called upon to protect property and lives. In drawing on the available labor pool, they compete particularly with urban fire departments for recruits.[6] In other respects, fire and police departments have complementary relationships and support one another. Thus, in case of riots, fire as well as police departments are often called upon, and a fire alarm usually also brings a police car to the scene.

There is no need to emphasize the close cooperation between police and other parts of the criminal justice system. For example, policemen spend a not insignificant part of their time in court. The failings of our education system as well as of the home very often place large burdens on the police in terms of drug addiction and other violations.

Finally, B. M. Fleisher has shown that male unemployment rates are significantly related to juvenile arrest (and presumably crime) rates.[7] Under those circumstances, not only is the urban police force imposed upon because of inappropriate or ineffective national full-employment policies, but the question of a countercyclical police budget also arises.

Donald Shoup and Stephen Mehay have stated:

> While the overall mission of the legal system is social order, the more

usually is unable to provide adequate protection. Information for 1967 on size of police forces and their number in major metropolitan areas is summarized in the following tabulation:

Size Class of Metropolitan Area (population)	Number of SMSAs	Number of Local Govts.	Number of Organized Police Forces	Size of Police Force				
				1–10	11–20	21–50	51–150	Over 150
1,000,000 and over	30	3,415	1,403	352	351	391	216	93
			(100.0%)	(25.1)	(25.0)	(27.9)	(15.4)	(6.6)
500–999,999	18	849	229	66	56	50	26	31
			(100.0%)	(28.8)	(24.5)	(21.8)	(11.4)	(13.5)
250–499,999	19	511	134	46	24	25	18	21
			(100.0%)	(34.3)	(17.9)	(18.7)	(13.4)	(15.7)
50–249,999	24	428	02	21	20	23	22	6
			(100.0%)	(22.8)	(21.8)	(25.0)	(23.9)	(6.5)
Total	91	5,203	1,858	485	451	489	282	151
			(100.0%)	(26.1)	(24.3)	(26.3)	(15.2)	(8.1)

SOURCE: Advisory Commission on Intergovernmental Relations Compilation from the following sources: U.S. Bureau of the Census, *Employment of Major Local Governments*, 1967 Census of Governments, vol. 3, no. 1; F.B.I., *Uniform Crime Reports—1967*, Tables 55–56; International City Management Association, *Municipal Year Book—1968*, Table IV.

[6] Eugene J. Devine, *Analysis of Manpower Shortages in Local Government: Case Studies of Nurses, Policemen, and Teachers* (New York: Praeger, 1970), 171 pp.

[7] B. M. Fleisher, "The Effect of Unemployment on Delinquency," *Journal of Political Economy*, vol. 71 (December 1963).

specific mission of the police is to ensure the public peace and security. As to security, the police seek to minimize the cost of illegal actions to society—both the harm done by criminals and the cost of both police and private efforts to prevent it. The objective of the police is not to reduce the level of crime to zero, but to reduce the amount of crime to some "optimal" level below which the cost (in terms of additional police resources) of reducing crime further is greater than the resulting benefit (in terms of a reduction in the harm caused by crime).[8]

They also suggest that more specifically police have the six goals of reducing to some optimum levels (1) violations of property rights, (2) violations of individuals' rights, (3) violations of moral conduct regulations, (4) collective civil violations, (5) traffic violations, and (6) providing noncrime public services of various sorts. To do this, most large urban police departments organize themselves in a manner that facilitates their carrying out five major activities: (1) preventing future criminal activities by altering the conditions that lead to crime, (2) deterring potential criminals by maintaining a conspicuous and continuous presence in the community and responding quickly to a reported crime, (3) apprehending individuals who have committed crimes, (4) engaging in activities relative to traffic and congestion, and (5) providing noncrime public services of various sorts.

In seeking to minimize the cost of crime to society, police should consider possible trade-offs among these activities. It is for this reason that demand, supply, and benefit-cost studies are important. Thus, urban police departments commonly face the question of whether in the light of their present mix of prevention, deterrence, apprehension (or investigation), and other activities, investing additional resources in prevention efforts, e.g., undercover efforts in the Negro community or on university campuses, would reduce the cost of crime more than would the same resources devoted to investigation and apprehension, e.g., new crime laboratory equipment.

Furthermore, decisions must be made about what areas and what groups are to be protected and given what services. In many cases geographical location is a good proxy for the socioeconomic characteristics of

[8] Donald C. Shoup and Stephen L. Mehay, *Program Budgeting for Urban Police Services,* MR-154 (Los Angeles, Calif.: University of California, Institute of Government and Public Affairs, 1971), p. A-1. Note that this approach accepts the traditional law enforcement (or protection) mission of the police and the conventional alignment of police organizational structures with this mission. Recently, it has been pointed out that the police actually spend more time in noncrime-related activities than in dealing with serious criminal events. (Gordon E. Misner, "The Urban Police Mission," *Issues in Criminology,* vol. 3 [Summer 1967], p. 38, and James Q. Wilson, *Varieties of Police Behavior* [Cambridge, Mass.: Harvard, 1968], pp. 17–19.) As a result, it is suggested that "order maintenance" is a more important function than law enforcement and that the present orientation of police activities around the latter tends to misallocate resources. (Misner, pp. 38 and 46; Wilson, pp. 67–69 and 291–293.)

its residents, and therefore by allocating different amounts of police services to specific geographic areas, different recipient groups receive different amounts of services and impose differential costs. Thus decisions must be made as to the extent to which each of the goals is to be attained and through what mix of activities; how the services are to be distributed geographically and by groups; and who is to finance these services and how.

Decisions can be made within a benefit-cost framework and with the aid of demand, production, and cost functions about the extent to which illegal activities are to be minimized, how this can be done efficiently, how far this effort should go in relation to specific illegal activities, and who is to foot the bills.

Property rights violations include robbery, burglary, grand theft, auto theft, larceny, and fraud. Violations of property rights lead to destruction or transfer of property, and wealth losses to society occur when property is destroyed by such crimes as arson or vandalism. When property is illegally taken from the owner, as in burglary or embezzlement, involuntary wealth transfers in society occur. The loss to the victim of the crime is, of course, the same from either type of crime, but in the transfer case stolen property at least continues to be of use to someone within society. However, the criminal also invests some resources in the pursuit of his illegal activities, and therefore some real costs are incurred.[9]

In addition to the loss in welfare from a crime-induced shift in consumption patterns, inefficiencies may result from crime-induced shifts in production patterns. Thus, firms exposed to crime tend to incur higher operating costs due to actual loss of goods and destruction of property, increased insurance rates, increased private protection expenses, and possibly higher wages to employees to compensate for personal risk of injury. Finally, perhaps the most visible cost relates to public and private expenditures to protect property from crime. They include expenditures by police agencies on property crime prevention, deterrence, and investigation; and for the criminal justice system at large, prosecution, incarceration, and rehabilitation. Private costs include guard services, burglar alarms, safes, locks, and the overhead cost of providing property insurance.[10]

Violations of individuals' rights include homicide, manslaughter, aggravated assault, and rape. Some of these crimes are frequently committed jointly with property violations. When an individual is injured by crime,

---

[9] The President's Commission on Law Enforcement estimated that in 1965 crimes against property (both transfers and losses) amounted to almost $4 billion, of which about 8 percent represented net losses to society through arson and vandalism. (The President's Commission on Law Enforcement and Administration of Justice, op. cit., p. 44.)

[10] The President's Commission estimated that in 1965, $1.35 billion was spent for private crime-preventive service wages, and that at least $200 million more was spent for purchase of protective equipment. (Ibid., pp. 57 and 58.)

society loses in terms of the present discounted value of his forgone earnings, plus any medical expenditures required; in the case of death, this would amount to the full discounted value of all future earnings at the time of death. In addition to the direct cost of crime against persons just described, large public and private expenditures are incurred to prevent such crimes, and there is also the private cost related to the "fear of crime." The latter affects the individual's decisions about where to live, where to work, and what form of transportation to use. Shifts due to such fear can result in added resource costs.

Thus,

> The potential of crime against individuals raises the expected cost to individuals of any activity that involves exposure to such crime. This change in relative costs would shift the consumption pattern away from the no-crime pattern to a less preferred pattern that takes into account the possibility of being a crime victim. The shift in consumption pattern is, of course, no benefit to the criminal sector of society . . . , and the cost involved is *wholly a cost to society.*[11]

Violations of moral conduct regulations, often also referred to as "crimes without victims," are based on a consensus of society that certain actions are to be prohibited. Economically, these crimes represent neither pure redistributions nor complete losses, but resemble transactions where voluntary exchanges between buyers and sellers satisfy both parties. Thus gambling, prostitution, narcotics, etc., are services produced and distributed by profit-making entrepreneurs.[12]

Collective civil violations, e.g., uprisings and riots, are not a new phenomenon in the United States, but in recent years they have received increasing attention. In the late 1960s many urban police departments instituted new riot control programs. Costs include collective violations of individuals' rights and property as well as costs incurred by urban police forces to train, be ready, and in fact deal with civil violations.

The fourth area relates to traffic violations involving a person who, by carrying out the prohibited activity, say of speeding, will impose damages upon himself and others. Economic costs of traffic accidents include output reduction due to injuries and death, medical expenditures, damages to property, and private and public agency costs associated with traffic accidents, including the police, safety equipment on autos, and administrative costs of auto insurance companies.[13]

[11] Shoup and Mehay, op. cit., p. 27.
[12] The President's Commission on Law Enforcement estimated the annual cost of crime involving illegal goods and services to be about $8 billion. (The President's Commission on Law Enforcement and Administration of Justice, op. cit., p. 52.)
[13] Perhaps the most significant cost is the human suffering occasioned by traffic accidents. The national cost of traffic accidents in 1967, in terms of wages lost as the result of death and injuries, medical expense, insurance administrative costs, and property damage, was estimated to amount to $10 to $11 billion. National Safety Council, *Accident Facts on the Line* (Chicago, 1968), p. 5.

Finally, there is the provision of miscellaneous public services by urban police departments. Gordon Misner[14] has found that frequently more than 80 percent of patrol officers' on-call time is spent dealing with noncriminal matters. These general community services are rendered by the police principally because much of their time is spent performing preventive patrol rather than actually responding to crime calls, mainly because apparent cost is quite low. While opportunity costs are incurred, e.g., reduced probability that the patrol officer will be able to respond speedily to a crime call, the cost of an additional governmental agency responding at all hours to the wide variety of emergency matters that the police now deal with would probably be very large. In addition, the police benefit indirectly from providing these services, since they improve police-community relations.

Demand

Although urban police protection is not a pure public good, it is publicly rendered. It includes some joint consumption, exclusion is not always easy, and society wants everybody to have some police protection. It has private market substitutes and some associated private costs. Insurance premiums are a market indicator of a private service that is to some extent the substitute for police protection. To the extent that police protection fails to prevent losses, insurance can be relied upon for compensation.[15]

To reduce the possibility of losses, citizens can also purchase various services and devices that can prevent unauthorized entrance to premises or facilitate immediate detection of intruders, such as sophisticated locks, private police services, burglar alarms, etc. Altogether, only weak price signals for police protection can be detected.

There has been only one effort made to estimate a classical police demand function, to our knowledge. Jeffrey Chapman has developed a four-simultaneous-equation model which relates arrest rates to property and violent crimes, police labor to arrest rates, and police wages and the crime

---

14 Misner, op. cit., p. 38.

15 Insurance is a form of risk shifting whereby the costs of losses are transferred from individuals to second parties who pool risks of a large number of persons. We can assume that the amount an individual pays (his premium) for insurance against each type of potential loss (e.g., theft, burglary, vandalism, or personal assault) approximates his individual evaluation of a potential loss from such an occurrence. His premium, or the approximate expected value of potential loss, could be interpreted as equivalent to the individual's valuation of the quantity of police services that would be sufficient to prevent such a loss or, in other words, as his demand for police services. His additional purchases of theft insurance from private insurers imply either increases in theft-susceptible wealth and (or) an increase in the possibility of a loss. His additional premiums for theft insurance would approximate the amount he would be willing to pay for a quantity of police protection sufficient to reduce the size of the potential additional loss.

rate to police labor.[16] Under the assumption of a perfectly elastic supply of police labor, this last equation is the demand for police as a function of the price of police—an example of a demand for a factor input.

Chapman found, for seventy-seven California cities in 1960, using two-stage least squares as an estimation technique, the following:

$$PL = .0014 - .00000010W + .049PRAPE + .061V + .027P$$
$$\quad (3.36) \quad (1.11) \quad\quad\quad (.09) \quad\quad\quad (.45) \quad (1.92)$$
$$\quad\quad\quad + .00022VAL - .0000089OC - .000016PUB$$
$$\quad\quad\quad\quad (4.99) \quad\quad\quad (2.72) \quad\quad\quad (1.65)$$

$R^2 = .49$ (*t* statistics in parenthesis)

with:

$$\begin{aligned}
PL &= \text{per capita police labor} \\
W &= \text{police wage} \\
PRAPE &= \text{per capita rapes} \\
V &= \text{per capita murders and assaults} \\
P &= \text{per capita burglary, robbery, grand theft} \\
VAL &= \text{per capita property value} \\
OC &= \text{percent employed in manufacturing} \\
PUB &= \text{percent of labor force who take public transportation to work}
\end{aligned}$$

The two major findings from this result are that the wage rate, while negatively related to police labor, is not significantly different from zero at the 90 percent level, and that the marginal product of property crimes with respect to police is significantly different from zero while none of the marginal products of the other crimes differ from zero at the 90 percent level.

In addition, the St. Louis, Missouri, Police Department has undertaken a bivariate, linear regression analysis to project selected variables which were thought to represent the community's demand for police services. In that study, community demand for police services is assumed to be measurable in terms of five indicators: St. Louis Police Department Index crimes, FBI Part I crimes, radio calls for service, total reported traffic accidents, and personal injury and fatal traffic accidents. Historical data for 1948–1966 are employed to compute linear regression lines for each of the five indicators, which are then used to project the demand for police services in 1975 and 1980. (See Table 12.1.)[17] What is of interest in this rather simple regression analysis is that the police department views crime as a demand variable whereas deterrence of crime is a more appropriate community demand.

[16] Jeffrey Chapman, *A Model of Crime and Police Output,* unpublished doctoral dissertation, University of California, Berkeley, 1971, p. 188.
[17] St. Louis Police Department, *Allocation of Patrol Manpower in the St. Louis Police Department,* OLEA Grant no. 39 (July 1966) (processed), pp. 2 and 3.

TABLE 12.1   REGRESSION SUMMARIES OF DEMANDS FOR POLICE
SERVICES IN ST. LOUIS FOR THE YEARS 1948-1966, INCLUSIVE

Series	Equation*	Standard Error of Coefficient	R†	Current Growth Rate†
Index crimes	$Y = 984T - 36,986$	75	.91	3.3%
Part I crimes	$Y = 2,278T - 96,130$	145	.94	3.9%
Radio calls	$Y = 24,828T - 1,012,291$	2,104	.89	3.7%
Reported traffic accidents	$Y = 630T - 23,103$	70	.83	3.2%
Personal injury and fatal traffic accidents	$Y = 162T - 3,655$	18	.83	2.2%

* T represents the last two digits of the year: $T = 48, 49, \ldots, 66$.
† Calculated as the ratio of the predicted growth during the year to the predicted value o
the corresponding series for 1968.
SOURCE: St. Louis Police Department, *Allocation of Patrol Manpower in the St. Louis Police
Department*, OLEA Grant No. 39 (July 1966) (processed), pp. 2 and 3.

Supply

Analysis of the delivery and cost of police services by urban police departments is in an early stage of development. Generally, the studies consider the aggregate of police activities rather than the important components. One could proceed by estimating separate production and cost
functions for the six major police goals or programs mentioned above,
i.e., reducing violations of property rights, violations of individuals' rights,
violations of moral conduct regulations, collective civil violations, and
traffic violations and providing noncrime public services of various sorts.
Another approach would seek to estimate functions for the five police
activities, i.e., prevention, deterrence, apprehension, traffic, and noncrime
services, or any of their major components. The ideal approach would be
to analyze the activities within programs.

One such study has estimated production functions for deterring property crimes through police patrols, which in most police departments account for 40 to 50 percent of total operating expenditures.[18] Since a major
goal of patrols is deterrence of criminal events, a relevant output measure
is reduction of the victimization rate, i.e., number of actual crimes for a
given population. Although not all offenders are equally susceptible to
deterrence by probability of arrest, property thefts tend to be the result
of cold calculation.

With this in mind, Donald Shoup and Stephen Mehay, using reported
property crime rates as measures of patrol output, have estimated a police
service production function to determine the extent to which the police in-

[18] Shoup and Mehay, op. cit., p. A-25.

fluence criminal activity of property offenders.[19] Also, the rate of all reported Part I crimes was used to compare the differences, if any, between the effects of patrol inputs on all major crimes and their effects on property crimes alone. Additionally, arrest rates for both property crimes and all Part I crimes were used as a dependent variable to compare the effect of patrol inputs on arrests—primarily a performance indicator—with their effect on crimes.

Least-squares multiple-regression equations are estimated for fifty-two independent cities in four Southern California counties (excluding the cities of Los Angeles and Long Beach), using data collected by letter survey. The property or visible crime index,[20] an index of total crime,[21] and indices of visible and total arrest (where all indices were expressed as rates per 1,000 population) are regressed on independent variables representing patrol inputs and service conditions. Some of the more interesting linear equations (with *t*-values in parentheses and with net regression and multiple-determination coefficients at a 0.05 probability level underlined) are shown in the following equations.

FBI visible

$$\frac{\text{crimes}}{1,000 \text{ population}} = 74.35 - \underset{(1.086)}{19.368PT} + \underset{(1.114)}{27.6VEH} - \underset{(.790)}{2.743SCH} - \underset{(.153)}{.470SM}$$

$$+ \underset{(\underline{4.402})}{1.468NW} + \underset{(1.196)}{4.039W} \qquad \underline{R^2 = .33} \quad (12.1)$$

Calif. visible

$$\frac{\text{crimes}}{1,000 \text{ population}} = 6.588 + \underset{(.640)}{.789PT} - \underset{(.403)}{.669VEH} - \underset{(1.590)}{.426SCH} - \underset{(\underline{2.470})}{.555SM}$$

$$+ \underset{(\underline{6.141})}{.135NW} + \underset{(\underline{4.150})}{.948W} \qquad \underline{R^2 = .76} \quad (12.2)$$

---

[19] Ibid., p. A-26.

[20] The property crime index used in the regression analysis includes crimes thought to be more susceptible to deterrence through the activity of visible field patrol. It is termed a "visible" crime index because the majority of the crimes occur in public places. The index is made up of robbery, burglary, larceny-theft (both grand and petty), and auto theft, with FBI data and crime statistics from the California Bureau of Criminal Statistics as data sources.

It is assumed that the ability of the police to deter visible property crime depends on their effect on the relative costs and gains to wealth-maximizing potential offenders. The ability of the police to affect a potential violator's decision to commit crimes thus depends upon the level, quality, and deployment of available resources (including managerial ability); on methods of combining inputs; and on environmental (or service) conditions—such as social or economic characteristics of an area's population or physical characteristics of the area—which are beyond the control of the police.

[21] The crimes added to the visible crime index are homicide, forcible rape, and aggravated assault.

Total FBI

$$\frac{\text{crimes}}{1,000 \text{ population}} = 72.226 - \underset{(1.055)}{11.760PT} - \underset{(2.125)}{11.015U} + \underset{(2.063)}{12.844NPT} - \underset{(.990)}{2.523SCH}$$

$$- \underset{(1.030)}{2.393SM} + \underset{(4.567)}{1.021NW} + \underset{(.649)}{1.467W} \qquad R^2 = .60 \quad (12.3)$$

Total Calif.

$$\frac{\text{crimes}}{1,000 \text{ population}} = 61.030 - \underset{(1.033)}{8.706PT} - \underset{(2.967)}{11.635U} + \underset{(2.037)}{9.593NPT} - \underset{(1.253)}{2.416SCH}$$

$$- \underset{(.879)}{1.545SM} + \underset{(5.228)}{.884NW} + \underset{(.557)}{.953W} \qquad R^2 = .68 \quad (12.4)$$

Total adult

$$\frac{\text{felony arrests}}{1,000 \text{ population}} = 18.524 - \underset{(1.615)}{1.660U} + \underset{(3.148)}{3.350PPT} - \underset{(2.804)}{1.217SCH} - \underset{(1.658)}{.683SM}$$

$$+ \underset{(3.540)}{.161NW} + \underset{(4.980)}{1.386W} \qquad R^2 = .67 \quad (12.5)$$

where

PT = number of sworn officers who perform visible patrol duties

VEH = number of patrol vehicles, a proxy for capital input

SCH = median school years completed, persons twenty-five years of age and older

SM = number of street miles

NW = percentage of total population nonwhite

W = assessed valuation of property, or "wealth"

U = the percentage of all regularly assigned patrol units which are one-man

NPT = officers who are not visible patrolmen

PPT = percentage of total police force that is visible patrolmen

The results indicate that, just as for so many other urban services, outputs (whether measured as crimes or arrests) are more influenced by service conditions than by police inputs. Indeed, for the visible-crime equations none of the patrol inputs are statistically significant at the 5 percent probability level. The number of visible patrolmen has no significant effect on either visible or total crimes. Interestingly, nonvisible patrolmen appear to have an effect on the nonproperty crimes, while the proportion of patrolmen who are visible also has a significant effect on arrests. Finally, on the basis of the California data (equations 12.4 and 12.2) it would appear that the independent variables explain total crimes about as well as visible crimes (although the former are better explained when the FBI data are used).

A study by the RAND Corporation also attempted to estimate a police production function. It used data from the 1968 *Kansas City Police Department Survey,* selected crime measures from 1968 *FBI Uniform Crime Reports,* and population, area, and population density for thirty cities in the United States. A total of nineteen different equations were estimated, many of them with the number of index crimes as the dependent variable.[22] The authors conclude that the following equation has the greatest predictive value for index crimes:

$$X_1 = -2076 + \underline{13.13X_2} + \underline{19.96X_3} \qquad (12.6)$$

where
  $X_1 =$ number of index crimes
  $X_2 =$ number of police
  $X_3 =$ population$/1,000$

The coefficient of multiple determination is .80; this and the two net regression coefficients are statistically significant at a probability level of 0.05.

Density also was introduced as an independent variable but proved to be statistically insignificant. The fact that reported crimes are positively related with police strength is somewhat puzzling and deserves to be investigated further, preferably by using disaggregated time series data for one city. The cross-sectional data used here may reflect the number of crimes committed in the presence of police less than the number of police assigned in the light of crimes being committed. That is, we may have here an identification problem where a demand rather than a production function is being measured.

A similar effort was made by Douglas Morris and Luther Tweeten to estimate police production functions.[23] This study also finds a statistically significant positive relationship between crime rates and police.

Next we will take up police cost functions. While in Chapter 10 we presented a general discussion of urban government cost functions (see equation 10.5), estimation of police cost functions poses many special conceptual and empirical problems. For example, here too certain independent variables present a difficulty in separation: Should they be part of a police cost function or a demand function? Thus the value of the property to be protected has a direct bearing on the cost of the service, but it also reflects ability to pay for it. Furthermore, a variety of factors, including inertia, can encourage government officials to operate at above minimum cost. Finally, data problems are most severe, since so many urban

[22] Kakalik and Wildhorn, op. cit., pp. 78–93.
[23] Douglas Morris and Luther Tweeten, "The Cost of Controlling Crime," *The Annals of Regional Science of the Western Regional Science Association,* vol. 5 (June 1971), pp. 33–49.

police departments do not collect the kind of data needed for cost estimation.

We present here a police cost function that was estimated with the aid of 1955–1956 cross-sectional data for sixty-four St. Louis city-county police departments.[24]

$$X_1 = 3.14 - 0.000\,0103X_2 + 0.000\,000\,000\,00351X_2{}^2 + 0.000\,550X_3$$
$$+ 0.000\,00946X_4 + \underline{0.00315X_5} + \underline{0.00949X_6} - 0.000\,00212X_7$$
$$+ 0.000\,946X_8 + \underline{0.107X_9} + \underline{0.000\,219X_{10}} \quad (12.7)$$

where

$X_1 = $ per capita total costs of police protection
$X_2 = $ nighttime population
$X_3 = $ total miles of streets
$X_4 = $ nighttime population density per square mile
$X_5 = $ percentage of nonwhite population
$X_6 = $ percentage of nighttime population under twenty-five years of age
$X_7 = $ combined receipts of wholesale, retail, and service establishments
$X_8 = $ number of wholesale, retail, and service establishments
$X_9 = $ index of scope and quality of police protection
$X_{10} = $ average per capita assessed valuation of real property

In this equation, X_2 and X_3 are service quantity proxies; X_9 is a quality proxy, and the other variables reflect the service conditions affecting input requirements. The coefficient of multiple determination adjusted for degrees of freedom is .90, which is statistically significant at a probability level of 0.05, as are the underlined net regression coefficients.

Thus, on the average, statistically significant positive associations with changes in police cost existed with percentage of nonwhite population, percentage of nighttime population under twenty-five years of age, index of scope and quality of police protection, and average per capita assessed valuation of real property.

There is also the issue of how to allocate the supply of police services to different geographic areas and groups. Clearly, different criteria exist, and deciding on any particular criterion will have a major effect on who benefits from police protection and, depending on circumstances, who therefore should pay for it. Urban police services can be supplied in line with one of three major distribution rules. First, service distribution based on an input equality rule requires that resource *inputs* per service recipient be equalized among all service areas. Second, distribution based on an output equality rule requires that service *output* per recipient be equalized

[24] Werner Z. Hirsch, *The Economics of State and Local Government* (New York: McGraw-Hill, 1970), pp. 170–171.

among all service areas. Third, there is what might be called the efficiency rule, which requires that the marginal product of resource inputs be equal in all uses or, stated equivalently, that the marginal cost per unit of output be equal in all uses. The efficiency rule corresponds to the goal of maximum *total* output, using given resources. Thus, in considering service distribution we have the same conflict between equity and efficiency criteria that arises in discussions of income distribution. In addition, with government service distribution we lack good measures of units of output.

Local police protection, unlike national defense, is not automatically provided in about equal amounts to all citizens of a police jurisdiction. In national defense, essentially the same protection from foreign aggression is provided to all citizens of the nation, and although different persons may value differently the protection thus afforded, they all receive the same amount of protection. However, even within the jurisdiction of a single local police department the quantity and quality of police service given different groups often vary significantly. We are constrained to organize distribution of police protection according to geographic area or division instead of specific recipients, such as income class or race. But in many cases geographic location is a good proxy for the socioeconomic characteristics of its residents, and information on a geographic breakdown can be very illuminating.

The potential conflict between our first two distribution criteria, input equality and output equality, is illustrated in Figure 12.1. Consider two police divisions, 1 and 2, within a city. Assume that because of social forces, e.g., lack of employment opportunities, in division 1, for any given number of police per capita, the crime rate is higher in 1 than in 2. Given the total number of police resources (including policemen and equipment), an allocation of police officers that would result in an equal crime rate per

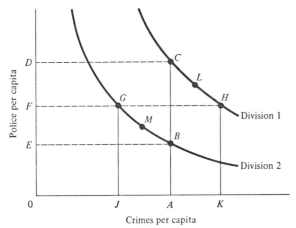

FIGURE 12.1   *Police-crime relationship.*

capita in divisions 1 and 2 would necessarily involve a much higher ratio of police per capita in 1 than in 2. Such a situation is illustrated in the diagram, where each division has the same crime rate A, while division 1 has D and division 2 has E police per capita. If instead each division were allocated the same number of police per capita (equality in an input rather than an output sense), division 1 would have a much higher crime rate than division 2.

Carl Shoup has demonstrated the conflict between the goal of output equality in terms of equal crime rates among divisions and the goal of minimizing the total number of crimes in the city.[25] Minimization of the total number of crimes occurs when, with an allocation of police that produces equality among all divisions in terms of the crime rate, the marginal product of a police officer is higher in one area than in another. This corresponds to our third distribution rule, that of efficiency. In terms of Figure 12.1, suppose police resources are allocated to produce equal output per capita, so that the crime rate in each division is A; i.e., there are D police per capita in division 1, and E police per capita in division 2. Also suppose that an additional police officer in division 1 reduces the number of crimes per year by 5, and that an additional policeman in division 2 reduces the number of crimes per year by 10. In this situation, the total number of crimes in the city would be reduced by 5 if one officer were removed from division 1 (increasing the number of crimes there by 5) and assigned to division 2 (decreasing the number of crimes there by 10). In general, the total number of crimes in the city will be minimized only when the marginal effect of an additional policeman on the number of crimes is the same in each division. Otherwise, it would always be possible to reallocate police resources from a division in which the marginal product of police resources was lower to one in which the marginal product was higher, and thereby reduce the total number of crimes in the city. However, this would then lead to a departure from the criterion of equal output distribution and to a conflict between the output equality and efficiency rules of distribution, in addition to the previously mentioned conflict between the input equality and output equality rules.

Decision Making

Benefit-cost and cost-effectiveness analyses provide an appropriate analytic framework for decisions regarding which activities to pursue in achieving the goals of police services. At the beginning of section II, the social and individual costs resulting from criminal behavior were described. Therefore a reduction of these costs through police activities represents the benefits of police services. The costs are generally represented by the

[25] Carl S. Shoup, "Standards for Distributing a Free Governmental Service: Crime Prevention," *Public Finance*, vol. 19 (1964), pp. 386–390.

resource costs (direct and indirect) required to provide the police service.[26]
We now illustrate some benefit-cost analyses for police patrol, apprehension, and traffic enforcement activities.

Police Patrol Services. In order to efficiently and equitably provide crime-deterrent patrol, urban police departments must make decisions with respect to three major issues: patrol force strength, distribution of patrol services by police district and tour of duty, and operational policies and tactics for police patrol.[27] Patrol force strength decisions require analyses of the trade-offs between deterrence and other police activities, mainly prevention and apprehension. Force distribution decisions relate to who shall get what patrol services, and how these services are most effectively delivered—an issue that spills over into operations and tactics of patrol.[28] Thus, urban police departments need to predict the incidence of crime and calls for service by type, geographic area, and time period; specify criteria and desired target levels of performance; estimate number of men required to achieve specified target levels of performance; and, finally, allocate patrol manpower in response to these demands.

Presently, many urban police departments use a variety of criteria and methods in deciding about police patrol-type activities. The criteria used include "command discretion," simple resource input measures, conglomerate hazard ratings, and the percentage of calls for service that cannot be immediately dispatched to a free patrol car.[29]

With a view to analyzing alternative operational policies, Donald

[26] It should be noted that for most public services the costs in a benefit-cost calculation include not only the resource costs but also the indirect social costs associated with the program. But for a deterrence activity such as police, it is precisely reduction in the social costs that represents the benefits resulting from the service.

[27] Kakalik and Wildhorn, op. cit., p. 1.

[28] The patrol organizations of most large urban police departments have similar geographical command hierarchies; and decisions on basic beat assignments and reassignments during shifts of patrol resources are generally the responsibility of district commanders. While dispatching operations are centralized, most departments operate under an informal, rather than formal, priority policy in responding to calls for service from the public. (Ibid., p. 6.)

[29] "Hazard formulas" are widely used for allocating manpower by time and geography. This method takes into consideration various factors thought to be relevant to determining the need for patrol services, weights each factor by some subjectively determined rates, and adds them to derive a single hazard number. Patrol units are then distributed in proportion to the relative hazard in an area. Such formulas are deficient in that they reflect past rather than future conditions, assume that relations between factors are additive, and do not relate meaningful measures of effectiveness to operational policy. In the St. Louis Police Department this method is highly perfected. Demand for police services is predicted by hour and geographic area, and then applied by a mathematical technique to estimate the number of patrol cars needed to immediately answer, without dispatching delay, 85 percent of the predicted incoming calls for service in each geographic area by day and by four-hour time period. The remainder of the patrol force is assigned to preventive patrol. (Ibid., pp. 3, 7, and 8.)

Shoup and Stephen Mehay made a benefit-cost analysis of one-man patrol units. In order to evaluate the deterrent effect of additional one-man patrol units they varied the percentages of patrol units in one- and two-man patrol cars and estimated the value of the marginal product for different percentages. Input changes are interpreted as not involving additions to direct police costs, since a fixed number of inputs are merely reorganized as the proportion of one-man patrol units is changed.

The benefits (or social savings) are defined as the costs that are prevented from being imposed on individuals whose legal rights are violated and on society. Private costs incurred from criminal offenses include damage to person or property, monetary losses, and psychic damages. Although the monetary losses are mainly transfers and not themselves real costs (see p. 353), the involuntary redistribution of property is assumed to constitute a social cost. Estimates of the reduction of pain and suffering and reduction of resource costs in terms of protective devices are omitted because of a lack of data. The number of reported crimes deterred is weighted by a correction factor for nonreporting to arrive at an estimate of the number of actual crimes deterred. To improve the estimates of the average personal loss of each crime, a "seriousness weight" is assigned to the average robbery transfers to adjust for the additional expected cost due to the risk of personal injury associated with this particular offense.

The benefit-cost analysis relies on production functions presented in equations 12.1–5, together with various side calculations. It was found that on the average a 1 percent increase in the percentage of one-man patrol units significantly deterred 1.172 actual robberies, 5.325 burglaries, and 3.093 auto thefts. Estimates of the social savings are obtained by multiplying the change in crimes deterred times the social cost of each crime. A lower-bound estimate of the social saving is obtained by deducting the average monetary value of property recovered by the police (and, presumably, returned to lawful owners) for each crime from the average full dollar loss figure per crime. The low estimate of benefits based on this adjustment is $18,305, whereas neglecting recovery of property yields an upper-bound social saving estimate of $21,045.[30]

A partial benefit-cost analysis of assigning marked police cars to each member of the Indianapolis Patrol Force, to drive when off duty as well as when on duty, was undertaken by Donald Fisk.[31] Patrolmen driving patrol cars to and from work and using them for personal activities while off duty are expected to maintain radio contact and to respond to emergencies in their immediate area. On the basis of an eight-month trial period, implementation of this plan had an annual cost of $650,000 in the

[30] Shoup and Mehay, op. cit., pp. A-36–39, 182–263.
[31] Donald M. Fisk, *The Indianapolis Police Fleet Plan* (Washington, D.C.: The Urban Institute, October 1970), 52 pp.

first year and $450,000 annually thereafter. On-duty patrol time increased by about 7 percent. Reported crime decreased following introduction of the plan: automobile theft decreased absolutely about 15 percent from the previous year and about 22 percent from that expected from past trends. Purse snatching decreased 8 percent and 21 percent, respectively. Traffic accidents decreased 8 percent and 14 percent, respectively; total killed in traffic accidents decreased 29 percent and 33 percent, respectively; and total injured in traffic accidents decreased 1 percent and 5 percent, respectively.

Apprehension Activities. As was mentioned earlier, one of the major police activities is the investigation of crimes and the apprehension of criminals. Peter W. Greenwood has studied this activity of the New York City Police Department, using a partial benefit-cost analysis. He is concerned with determining the preferred allocation of manpower among such apprehension activities as uniformed patrol, investigation, detective patrols by burglary squads, and detective patrols by neighborhood task forces. Estimates are made of the marginal productivity of additional manpower in terms of arrests per man-day.[32]

The study finds that for Part I crimes, the probability of arrest differs vastly between the crimes of passion (homicide, rape, and assault) and the crimes for profit (robbery, burglary, and larceny). This probability is high for crimes of passion; and for example, in the case of assault, arrest probability increases with effort (or input) by police. For crimes for profit, the probability of arrest is very low—robbery, 0.06; burglary, 0.01; and grand larceny, 0.02—and it appears not to increase with effort by police. Average arrest productivities for the four different types of activities are presented in Table 12.2. Shifting men from either uniformed patrol or case investigations to detective patrol activities increases the number of primary arrests likely to be made.[33]

Traffic Law Enforcement. One of the truly urban police services is traffic law enforcement, since it relates to the density of people and buildings and the large number of private cars, taxis, trucks, and buses. In pro-

[32] Peter W. Greenwood, *An Analysis of the Apprehension Activities of the New York City Police Department,* R-529-NYC (New York: New York City Rand Institute, September 1970), 60 pp.

[33] One of the hallmarks of a city is its density and, with it, the incidence of crime. Thus the effectiveness of detective patrol appears to be a function of crime density and observability. As crime density or observability increases, so does the probability that a detective on patrol will be able to spot a suspect and keep him under surveillance. For this reason detective patrols can be expected to be much more productive in high-hazard areas with heavy pedestrian traffic than in areas of low hazard, where there are fewer people on the streets. The arrest productivity of the burglary squads in New York boroughs of different population density clearly substantiates this conclusion. (Ibid., p. 43.)

TABLE 12.2   ARREST PRODUCTIVITY

Activity	Average Arrest Productivity: Primary Arrests per Man-Month
Uniformed patrol	0.22
Investigation	0.86
Detective patrol:	
Burglary squad	0.92
Neighborhood task force	2.15

SOURCE: Peter W. Greenwood, *An Analysis of the Apprehension Activities of the New York City Police Department,* R-529-NYC (New York: New York City Rand Institute, September 1970), 60 pp.

viding traffic law enforcement, a variety of trade-offs is possible, and benefit-cost analysis can help shed light on their implications and desirability. Donald Shoup and Stephen Mehay analyzed alternative methods of traffic law enforcement, seeking to ascertain the optimum level of enforcement on a traffic beat in Los Angeles.[34]

Traffic laws are enforced throughout Los Angeles by units of the patrol bureau. On those surface streets with the greatest number of automobile accidents, the traffic bureau assigns special motorcycle traffic law enforcement officers on the assumption that concentration of enforcement effort at times and places where the most accidents occur will produce the greatest output in terms of accident reduction. Each motorcycle patrolman is assigned a patrol beat that is from three to six miles long. An experiment was designed to establish the relationship between the level of enforcement and the frequency of traffic accidents, and other possible side effects. The objective was to estimate the benefits and costs associated with alternative techniques of motorcycle patrol.

Important cost elements of traffic law enforcement are cost of patrol and reduced speed of traffic flow. Since the cost of patrol represents mostly wages and vehicle costs for the motorcycle officers (90 percent of the total), average costs tend to approximate actual marginal costs. These costs per motorcycle unit for the nine-month day watch are estimated to be $12,000. No cost estimate of reduced traffic flow speed cóuld be made in the study. Traffic law enforcement benefits include those due to accident and crime reductions, which result in savings of lives, injuries, property damage, and travel time.

In the experiment, several alternative patrol techniques were evaluated: manpower allocation remains unchanged, is completely stripped, and is

[34] Shoup and Mehay, op. cit., pp. A-8–A-25, 90–181.

increased by one to four patrol officers on five beats. In addition, on one beat the motorcycle patrol officer refrains from citing traffic law violators (except the most flagrant ones) and merely relies on his *visibility;* and on another beat the officer stops and merely relies on *warning* violators, without issuing citations.[35]

Costs and benefits of these experimental patrol changes are presented in Table 12.3. The authors summarize these results in the following manner:

> The most striking implication . . . is that, with the exception of the warning-only beat, no experimental change resulted in a clearly demonstrated net benefit. Where manpower was increased, the marginal (measured) cost exceeded the marginal (measured) benefit, and where manpower was decreased the reverse was true. Such a uniformly negative net benefit indicates that the existing allocation of resources among these was superior to any reallocation that was tried, and that the saturation technique of concentrated traffic law enforcement resources in a small area is not justified. In no case was the value of the marginal product of an additional traffic officer clearly greater than the marginal cost when there was already one officer on a typical beat. . . . The warning-only beat shows a large benefit at no cost, and this result (is interpreted as) possibly due to the inappropriate reward structure imposed on officers whose output is, at least partially, measured by the number of citations written per day.[36]

[35] Ibid., pp. A-24, 25.
[36] Ibid., p. 169.

TABLE 12.3 SUMMARY OF COSTS AND BENEFITS OF EXPERIMENTAL PATROL CHANGES

Beat	Change in Number of Officers	Change in Cost of Patrol	Benefit of Accident Reduction		Benefit of Crime Reduction	Measured Net Benefit	
(1)	(2)	(3) ($000)	(4) High ($000)	(5) Low ($000)	(6) ($000)	(7) High	(8) Low
1	0 (Visibility)	0	−3	−2.1	0	−3	−2.1
2	0 (Warning)	0	+34	+23.5	0	+34	+23.5
3	3	36	0	0	+1.1	−34.9	−34.9
4	4	48	+38	+26.2	+2.8	−7.2	−19
5	No change	—	—	—	—	—	—
6	1	12	+9	+6.2	+0.4	−2.6	−5.4
7	2	24	+28	+19.3	+0.5	+4.5	−4.2
8	−1	−12	−32	−22	−0.6	−20.6	+10.7

SOURCE: Donald C. Shoup and Stephen L. Mehay, *Program Budgeting for Urban Police Services*, MR-154 (Los Angeles, Calif.: University of California, Institute of Government and Public Affairs, 1971), p. 168.

Motor Vehicle Accident Control.   A team of physicians and economists undertook, in the mid-1960s, a benefit-cost analysis of different motor vehicle accident control programs.[37] The programs ranged from improving driver training and licensing to improving emergency medical services and increasing seat-belt use. Benefits were divided into direct and indirect morbidity savings as well as mortality savings.[38]

Benefit elements associated with the various vehicle accident control programs include: (1) direct morbidity savings—reductions in amounts that would have been spent for hospital care, physicians' services, nursing home care, other professional services, drugs, and medical supplies, if these programs were not undertaken; (2) indirect morbidity savings—earnings gains for those whose injuries and resulting disability would be prevented by the specific accident control program; and (3) mortality savings—the present value of lifetime earnings for persons who would be saved from death due to motor vehicle accidents as a direct result of specific accident control programs.[39] Costs refer to program costs. Surprisingly large differences in benefit-cost ratios were found in relation to nine programs summarized in Table 12.4. Increased seat-belt use has a benefit-cost ratio in excess of 1,300, while at the other extreme improved driver training has a ratio of less than 2.

III.   FIRE PROTECTION SERVICES

Environment and Goals

Fire departments provide protective services, just as agencies in the criminal justice system do. The total annual cost of fire in the United States is estimated at about $10 billion and some 12,000 lives.[40] One reason per capita fire losses are so high in the United States is the high level of urbanization and, with it, the density of inflammable property. While fire protection is also needed in rural areas, a number of somewhat unique circumstances face fire-fighting forces in cities.

In New York City, fire alarm rates more than tripled between 1956 and 1969—from 69,000 alarms per year to more than 240,000. The rate of every type of incident, from false alarms to structural fires, has been increasing exponentially. However, false alarms, rubbish fires, nonfire

---

[37] U.S. Department of Health, Education, and Welfare, *Application of Benefit-Cost Analysis to Motor Vehicle Accidents* (Washington, D.C.: U.S. Department of Health, Education, and Welfare, August 1966), 181 pp.
[38] Michael Jones-Lee, "Evaluation of Reduction in Probability of Death by Road Accident," *Journal of Transport Economics and Policy,* vol. 3, no. 1 (January 1969), pp. 1–11.
[39] U.S. Department of Health, Education, and Welfare, op. cit., p. 65.
[40] National Academy of Sciences, *A Proposed National Fire Research Program* (Washington, D.C.: National Academy of Sciences, 1969), p. 1.

TABLE 12.4 BENEFITS AND COSTS OF ACCIDENT CONTROL PROGRAM, 1968–1972 (in thousands of dollars)

Unit Number	Program	Program Costs	Estimated Benefits					Benefit-Cost Ratio[a]	
			Total	Morbidity Savings			Mortality Savings[d]	Amount	Rank
				Total	Direct[b]	Indirect[c]			
1	Improve driver licensing	$6,113	$22,938	$7,733	$4,278	$3,455	$15,205	3.8	7
2	Improve driver training	750,550	1,287,022	213,471	117,593	95,878	1,073,551	1.7	9
3	Reduce driver drinking	28,545	612,970	144,323	79,673	64,650	468,647	21.5	6
4	Reduce pedestrian injury	1,061	153,110	46,327	25,574	20,753	106,783	144.3	3
5	Increase seat belt use	2,019	2,728,374	617,610	341,207	276,403	2,110,764	1,351.4	1
6	Improve driving environment[e]	28,545	1,409,891	331,730	183,077	148,653	1,078,161	49.4	5
7	Use of improved restraint systems	610	681,452	152,993	84,223	68,770	528,459	1,117.1	2
8	Increase use of protective devices by motorcyclists	7,419	412,754	—	—	—	412,754	55.6	4
9	Improve emergency medical services[f]	721,478	1,726,384	320,080	131,851	188,229	1,406,304	2.4	8

[a] Represents the ratio of benefits to program costs.

[b] Direct costs include amounts spent for hospital care, physicians' services, nursing home care, other professional services, drugs, and medical supplies.

[c] Indirect costs represent losses in earnings for those whose injury and resulting disability prevent them from working. Included is an imputed value for services of housewives prevented from housekeeping as a result of a motor vehicle accident.

[d] Represents present value of expected lifetime earnings for projected motor vehicle fatalities in each year, calculated for each 5-year age and sex group on the basis of 1964 life tables, 1964 labor force participation rates adjusted for full employment (an average 4 percent unemployment rate), 1964 mean earnings, imputed value of housewives' services, 1964 housekeeping rates, and an annual net effective discount rate of 3 percent.

[e] This program unit would also involve the efforts of other Government agencies. The benefits assume such cooperation; however, the costs of the program represent only the DHEW effort.

[f] This cost figure should, for the purpose of this cost benefit analysis, be interpreted in light of the fact that one-third of all emergency medical service is for injury resulting from vehicular accident.

SOURCE: U.S. Department of Health, Education, and Welfare, *Application of Benefit-Cost Analysis to Motor Vehicle Accidents* (Washington, D.C.: U.S. Department of Health, Education, and Welfare, August 1966), p. 11.

emergencies, fires in vacant or abandoned buildings, and deliberate fires now outnumber the accidental structural fires that used to be a fire department's main concern. Indeed, false alarms have been increasing more rapidly than any other type. In 1969, about 30 percent of the alarms were false and 20 percent were for structural fires. A disproportionate share of the increase has occurred in slum areas, most likely because of deteriorating housing and other facilities, continued overcrowding, and under-maintenance, as well as other social ills. Edward Blum finds that between 1962 and 1968, for example, one rapidly deteriorating New York neighborhood experienced a 44 percent average annual rate of increase in alarms, while a stable neighborhood, barely two miles away, saw an average increase of less than 5 percent.[41] He also finds that in 1968 the Brownsville section of Brooklyn—considered by many to be the most deteriorated part of the city—had an annual rate of over 10,000 alarms per square mile, more than thirteen times the citywide average. Costing $35 to $40 per capita, fire protection is the fifth largest public service expenditure in New York City (or in any other city where the urban government is responsible for all urban public services), after welfare, education, health services, and police.[42]

Urban fire departments today are facing some new problems, including riots. There also are indications that while public adulation for the fire fighter is waning in the larger cities, demands on him are increasingly becoming conspicuous symptoms of deeper social ills. These changing public attitudes, deteriorating relations with minority communities, further bureaucratizing in large fire departments of cities, and militancy (including resort to strikes of municipal service unions) all pose serious problems.

Urban fire departments serve large populations who live in close proximity and often work under similar conditions. Their mission is to prevent fires from occurring and to respond promptly and effectively to protect the community when parts of the physical or social order break down. In short, their goal is to achieve an optimal level of prevention and extinguishment of fires.

In order to accomplish this mission, urban fire departments engage in a number of activities: fire prevention (including reducing ignition of material), fire detection (including reduction of its early growth), extinguishment, and reduction of life hazards. Activities concerned with fire prevention and detection tend to be quite different in character from actual extinguishment and reduction of life hazards. The second class of activities

---

[41] Edward H. Blum, *Urban Fire Protection: Studies of the Operations of the New York City Fire Department,* R-681 (New York: The New York City Rand Institute, January 1971), p. 6.
[42] The Fire Department of the City of New York had about 15,000 uniformed men, 1,000 civilian employees, and 400 fire units in 1970. (Ibid., p. 2.)

is of a crisis nature and must be undertaken on short notice and with utmost effectiveness when an alarm is reported. These are, no doubt, the dominating activities of fire departments. Fire engines are dispatched, and pumps, hoses, and ladders are activated. Having arrived at the building, the firemen rescue and evacuate people who may be in danger and put out the fire. Once the fire seems to be out, the tedious work of overhauling begins—finding and quenching embers and hot spots from which the fire could re-ignite and putting the property in order.

Prevention and detection activities can be carried out at a more deliberate pace and in many respects involve participation by other public agencies and private firms.[43] Urban fire service depends heavily on those who formulate and administer building codes, on architects and building contractors, on fire insurance companies (whose rating practices influence private fire protection, e.g., detectors, sprinklers, or brush clearance that property owners provide), on telephone companies, on private or auxiliary services, and on building material and fire detection manufacturers.

Demand

The discussion on demand for urban fire protection services can be brief. Conceptually, there is relatively little difference between the demand for fire and police services, both having many similar characteristics. While no study has come to our attention that attempts to estimate a classical demand curve for fire services, Jan Chaiken and John Rolph have predicted the incidence rate of fire alarms and, on this basis, service requirements. This is similar to the urban transportation demand studies which specify "requirements" in a given transportation system on the basis of projected growth factors of movement.[44]

Chaiken and Rolph, using New York City fire figures for 1958–1968, sought to determine the factors affecting the incidence of fire alarms. They found that different types of alarms have different hourly patterns. Also, alarm boxes of extremely high demand were found to be bunched together in small regions, and neighborhoods can be distinguished by their false alarm ratios.[45] Main streets have demand patterns that differ from those of side streets. In high-incidence areas, the main streets have fewer alarms than side streets, reflecting a smaller rate of false alarms. In low-incidence areas, the main streets have more alarms than the side streets (but, of

---

[43] Urban fire departments in their noncrisis activities inspect or advise on building plans, helping to ensure that materials, wiring, heating units, etc., meet the fire codes and will present firemen as few problems as possible should a fire occur. They also inspect industrial, commercial, and public buildings for possible ignition sources (kindling and fuel), for lack of safe egress, and for other potential hazards.

[44] See Chap. 4, pp. 95–109.

[45] Jan M. Chaiken and John E. Rolph, *Predicting the Demand for Fire Service*, P-4625 (Santa Monica, Calif.: The RAND Corporation, May 1971), 31 pp.

course, lower than main streets in high-incidence areas), perhaps because there are more people around to cause and to spread fires. Other major factors are weather, temperature, and relative humidity.

Having identified the relevant factors, Chaiken and Rolph developed a method for short-term prediction of the incidence rates for various types of fire alarms as a function of location, time (year, season, day of week, and hour), method of reporting (box, phone, etc.), and weather conditions (temperature, relative humidity, and precipitation). They assume a Poisson-type probability model of fire alarms, which assumes independence over time and geography and "no multiple hits."[46] Using a logarithmic functional relationship between fire incidence rates on the one hand and location, time, method of reporting, and weather on the other, apparently a good fit is obtained, suggesting a multiplicative relation with exponential growth.

Supply

Very few cost or production functions for fire protection services have come to our attention. However, one average unit cost function, similar to the police cost function in equation 10.5, was estimated for fire protection of the St. Louis city-county area in 1955–1956:[47]

$$X_1 = 0.63 - 0.000\ 0235X_2 + \underline{0.000\ 000\ 000\ 109X_2{}^2} - \underline{0.0866X_3}$$
$$+ 0.000\ 00170X_4 - 0.00206X_5 - \underline{0.000\ 0108X_6} + \underline{1.889X_7}$$
$$+ \underline{0.00231X_8} \quad (12.7)$$

where the following are notations not found in equation 12.6:

$X_1 =$ per capita total current costs for fire protection
$X_2 =$ nighttime population
$X_3 =$ area in square miles
$X_4 =$ density of dwelling units per square mile
$X_5 =$ 1950–1955 nighttime population increases
$X_6 =$ combined receipts of wholesale, retail, and service establishments
$X_7 =$ index of scope and quality of fire protection
$X_8 =$ average per capita assessed valuation of real property

In this equation X_2 is a proxy variable for quantity and X_7 that for quality. X_3, X_4, and X_5 are indicative of service conditions affecting input requirements; in a sense this holds true for X_7 and X_8, which, however,

---

[46] In this manner, given the type of alarm and method of reporting, the occurrence of that type of alarm is viewed as an independent Poisson point process whose parameters vary with time, geography, and weather. The advantage of this approach is that, given the region, a set of types, and a time period, the number of alarms has a Poisson distribution whose parameter is the integral of the intensity function over the region and time period, and summed over the types. (Ibid., pp. 12–13.)
[47] Hirsch, op. cit., p. 171.

also reflect quantity. The coefficient of multiple determination adjusted for degrees of freedom was .82 and is statistically significant at a probability level of 0.05, as are the underlined net regression coefficients.

Thus fire service cost in St. Louis had, on the average, a statistically significant association with area in square miles; combined receipts of wholesale, retail, and service establishments; index of scope and quality of fire protection; and average per capita assessed valuation of real property. The first two relationships are negative and the latter two positive. Surprisingly, dwelling density turns out to be statistically insignificant, and it is difficult to explain the negative relationship between fire protection costs and sales receipts in the community.[48]

Decision Making

Urban fire departments, not unlike police departments, must make crucial decisions about the size of the fire-fighting force, its distribution over space and time, and operational policy. Thus, for example, there are trade-offs between resources invested in prevention and automatic detection, on the one hand, and fire extinguishment on the other hand. A fire detection device might be designed to implement direct fire-extinguishing action such as the opening of a sprinkler head by the melting of a low-melting alloy; or it might be designed to warn occupants and to signal a distant point for aid; or it might change the vulnerability of a building, such as by closing a fire door or by resetting the ventilation control. With these potential developments in mind, the Committee on Fire Research of the National Academy of Sciences in 1969 reached the conclusion, "A case can be made for the claim that the reduction in annual fire losses would be greater per dollar spent in research on cheaper and better fire protection devices than in any other fire-research area."[49]

Cost-effectiveness analyses that have been carried out so far relative to urban fire protection have been more in the nature of operations research than of systems analytic efforts. Two examples for dispatching and deploying fire-fighting equipment are illustrated below.

Dispatching Fire-fighting Equipment. Dispatching consists of two basic sets of operations: receiving, interpreting, and identifying alarms;

---

[48] Technology was not included as an independent variable, since all departments in the area used quite similar equipment and technology. In general, until very recently, basic fire department practices have changed very little, even with the advent of motorized equipment and mobile radio communications. However, in the late 1960s, particularly under the leadership of the New York City Fire Department, new operational practices, communications, equipment, and procedures, as well as new technology, were being introduced and experimented with.

[49] National Academy of Sciences, op. cit., p. 5.

and allocating and dispatching fire-fighting units to respond. The first set involves counting telegraphic signals, answering telephones, etc., and can constitute a major bottleneck. Empirical data obtained from the New York City Fire Department indicate that the time delay associated with receiving, interpreting, and identifying alarms increases significantly with the number of active incidents. Not only do more incoming alarms need to be processed but also the service of each additional alarm slows down as the more active incidents that need to be considered increase.[50]

In the Brooklyn communications office, the busiest in New York City, alarms are routinely dispatched in less than one minute. A simulation model built by Blum indicates that under the present system, at thirty alarms per hour—a peak-hour load that rising alarm rates are expected to bring shortly—dispatching time would average nearly four minutes, and at thirty-five alarms per hour the average time would soar to nearly eleven minutes. Delays that long are clearly intolerable. Operational procedures were changed by dividing operations at the decision point. With the aid of what amounts to a change in their production function, dispatchers handled without strain or delay twenty-seven alarms in thirty minutes and forty-three alarms in sixty minutes—more than the system had ever been able·to handle before. The new operational procedure increases costs by less than $1,000 while effectively doubling the system's ability to handle peak loads.[51]

Deploying Fire-fighting Units.   The territories served by large urban fire departments differ greatly as to their density, quality of housing stock, socioeconomic characteristics, etc. As a result, different areas have different alarm densities. An important management issue is the allocation of fire-fighting units, i.e., decisions must be made about how many units to have, and how to man and deploy them. The nature of the decision affects both the effectiveness and the cost of providing fire protection.

Historically, a fire department has had the same number of men and units on duty around the clock, even though hourly demand in the afternoon-evening peak period is several times greater than demand during early-morning hours. Similarly, most departments have a uniform "standard response" of men and equipment to alarms at all times, although fire hazards and the likelihood that initially indeterminate alarms might turn out to be serious fires vary greatly with area and time of day. This "standard response" varies greatly from city to city. Thus, in the late 1960s in the city of Los Angeles, the standard response was three engines (pumpers) and two ladder trucks; in Philadelphia and Chicago (for a time at

[50] Blum, op. cit., pp. 8–11.
[51] Ibid., p. 11.

least), it was one engine and one ladder truck; in Washington, D.C., six engines and four ladder trucks.[52]

In most fire departments, including New York City's, when an alarm at a given location is made, dispatchers consult an "alarm assignment" that contains a list of units closest to the site, to see which units to send. The list also gives preplanned move-ups to cover the area around the site, should there be a large fire. In active periods, following this procedure in areas of high alarm densities can quickly deplete coverage. As alarm rates rise, fewer units are available and response time extends. In the late 1960s in New York City, busy periods were often depleting coverage rapidly; some units were responding more than 8,000 times per year. The cost of adding a unit was estimated to be $500,000 per year.

Analysis and projections of high incidence indicated that alarm rates from roughly 3 P.M. until 1 A.M. were and probably would remain at least twice as high as rates for other times of the day. They also showed that in high-incidence areas false alarms, rubbish fires, and other minor incidents are most frequent during these hours. These minor events do not require the same men and equipment as do structural fires. With the New York City Fire Department sending three engines and two ladder trucks to all street box alarms, the standard response tended to strip high-incidence areas quickly during the peak-demand hours.

An alternative deployment—an adaptive response—was developed by varying the number of men and equipment dispatched, depending on the likelihood of given types of alarms and hazards at various locations and times of the day. In 1969 New York City instituted such an adaptive-response policy and new fire-fighting units called "tactical control units." They operate only during the hours of peak demand.

This adaptive-response policy gets the full response to fires faster, on the average, than the standard response does. Furthermore, traditional dispatching rules dictate sending the units closest to an incident. Analysis shows that when nearby units have widely different work loads, other dispatching assignments are superior to this traditional rule—both leveling work load and reducing average response time. Moreover, the gains appear to come essentially free. An evaluation of these new deployment policies, after they were in operation for six months, indicated that the benefits for men and equipment are substantial. Tactical control units provide the impact of full-time units but at 40 percent of the cost, permitting equipment to arrive sooner yet having available additional units for immediate dispatch when needed. It was estimated that to obtain the increased effectiveness through conventional methods would have cost New York City $5 to $15 million annually.[53]

---

[52] Edward H. Blum, *The Rand-New York City Fire Project* (Santa Monica, Calif.: The RAND Corporation, Nov. 8, 1968), p. 3.
[53] Ibid., p. 16.

IV. RECREATION SERVICES

Environment and Goals

According to Morton Marcus, John Kavanagh, and Robert Gay, recreation involves a "use of time, independent of an individual's usual productive activities, in a socially recognized context for the purpose of refreshing the body and mind."[54] Recreation is thus an activity on the part of individuals, alone or in groups; it is not an activity of government. Instead, government provides inputs that complement the time and other inputs of individuals engaged in recreation.

Urban governments have a particular, and in some instances unique, interest in recreation. In rural America, open fields are close to every home. Not so in our large cities, where there are huge distances between average resident and open fields at the edge of town. As a result, cities must have parks and, particularly in the poorer sections of town, playgrounds for the young and rest areas for the old. The tension that is typical of city residents tends to increase the demand for recreation, and this demand is further enhanced by affluence. Many urbanites play tennis and golf and swim.

Local governments in 1967 spent about $1.3 billion on recreational services, of which well over $1 billion was spent by urban governments.[55] Nearly one-third of expenditures for parks and recreation goes for capital outlays, a percentage much larger than that for education, health, protection, or welfare services, though less than for transportation. Since 1957 about 2.2 percent of general local government expenditures have gone for parks and recreation, down from 3.3 percent at the turn of the century. Large metropolitan areas appear to spend more per capita on recreation services than do smaller metropolitan areas,[56] and municipalities within SMSAs seem to spend more than do those outside SMSAs.[57]

Recreation services should provide a variety of year-round leisure opportunities that are accessible, safe, and physically attractive and provide enjoyable experiences. They should, to the maximum extent, contribute to the mental and physical health of the community and to its economic and social well-being and permit outlets that will help decrease incidence of

---

[54] Morton J. Marcus, John M. Kavanagh, and Robert M. Gay, *Program Budgeting and Analyses for Urban Recreation,* MR-164 (Los Angeles, Calif.: University of California, Institute of Government and Public Affairs, 1971), p. 3.

[55] U.S. Bureau of the Census, *Census of Governments, 1967,* vol. 4, no. 5: *Companion of Government Finances* (Washington, D.C., 1969), Tables 8 and 10.

[56] Thus, in 1966–1967, per capita expenditures for parks and recreation amounted to $10.34 for SMSAs with a million population or larger, $7.63 for SMSAs of one-half to one million population, and $5.34 for SMSAs with 50,000–100,000 population. (Ibid.)

[57] Also, municipalities within SMSAs spent nearly 5 percent of their expenditures for parks and recreation, whereas all governments outside SMSAs spent only 1 percent for this program. (Ibid., Table 9.)

antisocial behavior.[58] Recreation services have joint products, which are often produced on multiple-purpose facilities. Thus the open space of a city park can be a ball park for twelve-year-olds on weekday evenings and picnic grounds for entire families on Sundays. In winter, when it is flooded and frozen, the area can serve as a skating rink; and on summer nights rock bands can alternate with the local symphony in providing musical entertainment.

Outputs of a city recreation department are in most cases not final outputs, but inputs to recreation processes. These outputs have production or provision dimensions and demand or utilization dimensions. The production dimension relates to the availability of inputs for individuals' recreation activities, e.g., acres per thousand persons and distance to facilities. The demand dimension relates to the extent of use of a given service or facility and the value to the users of a public recreation service.

In some important respects, it is even more difficult to define and measure the output of recreation services than that of other urban government services. Thus, outputs of education can be described and partly measured in terms of the educational value added—e.g., changes in test scores—that results from the schools' efforts; or change in health status of an individual user of health services can be considered a health output measure. Yet, although we may define recreation output in terms of refreshment of body and mind, describing and measuring such changes in an individual's condition appear to be beyond our ability. The most we are able to do is to state that a given individual was in a certain place for a stated period, allocating his time in a particular manner in conjunction with opportunities provided by a recreation agency.

Some indirect output measurements have been proposed. They include: attendance per participant-hour, participation-nonparticipation, time and distance from facilities, crowdedness, variety, safety, physical attractiveness, perceived recreation satisfaction, delinquency and crime reduction, health, and economic impact.[59]

Demand

Urban recreation services also are far from a pure public good. Governments provide recreation services in part because of distributional considerations, i.e., they wish to make recreational opportunities available to the poor. In some cases, high costs of exclusion are a reason for public provision of recreation. Exclusion costs, in terms of building fences, walls, or toll gates, can be extremely high, particularly for large parks like Central Park in New York, Golden Gate Park in San Francisco, or Griffith

---

[58] Harry P. Hatry and Diana R. Dunn, *Measuring the Effectiveness of Local Government Services* (Washington, D.C.: Urban Institute, 1971), p. 13.
[59] Ibid., pp. 20–37.

Park in Los Angeles. Exclusion costs are much less for tennis courts and swimming pools. Also, some joint consumption is involved.

Joint consumption is not the rule in urban recreation, mainly because of high density and crowding. A park bench occupied by one couple is not available to another. And the same holds for a tennis court. Where the conditions of joint consumption exist, no individual has incentive to reveal his preferences for the service if he believes that others will pay for its production in any case. Nor are there effective market means for giving expression to the option element for a good. Under such conditions, price signals are weak. However, that is true only to a limited extent in relation to urban recreation services.

Because of these characteristics many urban recreation services are priced not at all and others are priced at a relatively low user fee. Thus in 1967 admission and user fees for parks and recreation programs of local governments accounted for only about 15 percent of their expenditures, the remaining 85 percent being financed out of general revenue.

The demand for urban public recreation services can sometimes be analyzed in terms of their private substitutes. Thus the demand for a public golf course can be estimated with the aid of information about a private golf course with similar characteristics. Associated private costs can also be used to estimate recreation demand, particularly demand for extended-use recreation programs, since the costs are larger for extended-use programs than for casual-use programs. Thus, tennis, golf, and boating require larger private investments in equipment than do casual visits to playgrounds during the lunch hour.

There are different demand functions for different types of recreational programs. Such athletic programs as tennis, golf, and swimming have distinctly different demands from those of such environmental programs as nature trails, scenic drives, and visiting waterfronts and monuments. While there have been some empirical demand studies of general recreation, few if any have been made of urban recreation.[60]

Supply

Studies of recreational supply tend to be concerned with how, in social and geographic terms, recreation services are distributed. Target groups include children, aged, minorities, and low-income groups and such geographic areas as the central city and specific suburban neighborhoods. Not infrequently a close relationship exists between geographic and demographic distribution patterns. An additional group are out-of-town tourists and visitors.[61]

[60] See Wayne B. Boyet and George S. Tolley, "Recreation Projections Based on Demand Analysis," *Journal of Farm Economics,* vol. 48 (November 1966), pp. 984–1001.

[61] Another urban case where visitors are important relates to the fact that many

An interesting study of the distribution of recreation services in Berkeley, California, has been made by Charles Benson and Peter Lund.[62] They selected three neighborhoods on the basis of socioeconomic homogeneity and then allocated recreation expenditures to each of them as well as to "other Berkeley" and to "non-Berkeley" groups on the basis of participation in various recreation programs. Since participation in unscheduled events or programs is difficult to ascertain, only selected recreation programs are included. The results are presented in Table 12.5, where supply is allocated in terms of expenditures. Thus, over one-quarter of the allocated expenditures are associated with non-Berkeley residents. Recreation centers accounted for nearly one-third of total expenditures, and these facilities, which substitute for home-provided resources, are heavily used by a low-income area. Instruction for swimming is heavily patronized by higher-income areas, which may be a reflection of middle-class investments in human capital or the user fee charged for the service.

Decision Making

Many years ago Alfred Marshall surmised, "There is no better use for public and private money than in providing public parks and playgrounds in large cities. . . ."[63] However, only recently have empirical benefit-cost

---

central cities have zoos and museums that serve the entire metropolitan area. However, they are mainly supported, and usually entirely controlled, by the central city.
[62] Charles S. Benson and Peter B. Lund with Arthur Dambacher, *Neighborhood Distribution of Local Public Services* (Berkeley, Calif.: Institute of Governmental Studies, 1969), 181 pp.
[63] Alfred Marshall, *Principles of Economics,* 9th ed. (New York: Macmillan, 1961), p. 200.

*TABLE 12.5   PARTIAL DISTRIBUTION OF RECREATION
EXPENDITURES, BERKELEY, CALIFORNIA*

Area	1959 Family Income*	1960 Population†	1964–1965 Expenditures	Percentage of Expenditures
A	$ 5,260	15,072	$ 82,690	14.9
B	6,484	14,826	44,568	8.0
C	10,732	14,684	84,307	15.2
Other Berkeley	6,576	66,686	199,992	36.1
Non-Berkeley	—	—	142,771	25.8
Total			$554,328	100.0

* Other Berkeley: Total Berkeley median family income less A, B, and C areas: population-weighted median family income.
† Other Berkeley: Total Berkeley less areas A, B, and C.
SOURCE: Charles S. Benson and Peter B. Lund with Arthur Dambacher, *Neighborhood Distribution of Local Public Services* (Berkeley, Calif.: Institute of Governmental Studies, 1969), 181 pp.

analyses been made of urban recreation. Before we consider specific empirical benefit-cost studies, it appears useful to identify major social benefit and cost elements of urban recreation services. They are presented in Table 12.6. Although urban recreation also provides some investment benefits, we are usually forced to concentrate on the direct consumption benefits. There is little hope of measuring the "sense of pleasure experienced immediately before, during, and after participation in . . . recreation."[64]

The benefits of general outdoor recreation have been measured by Ruth Mack and Sumner Myers with merit-weighted user-days, a judgmental approach that attempts to simulate a political decision-making context.[65] Perhaps the earliest to suggest methods of benefit estimation for outdoor recreation was Marion Clawson, who emphasized private associated costs.[66] There are also recreation benefits that accrue to nonusers. These are externalities, in many respects typical of an urban environment. For example, people being in parks may result in less noise, vandalism, etc., in the neighborhood. Also, a homeowner adjacent to a playground may gain from having such a facility close by for the use of his children, and his property may rise in value because of this convenience. Furthermore, benefits accrue to people who do not actually use parks but place a positive value on having them available in case they wish to use them. Owners of buildings near a public garden can offer attractive vistas to

[64] Ruth P. Mack and Sumner Myers, "Outdoor Recreation," in Robert Dorfman (ed.), *Measuring Benefits of Government Investments* (Washington, D.C.: Brookings, 1965), p. 73.
[65] Ibid., p. 89ff.
[66] Marion Clawson, *Methods of Measuring the Demand for and Value of Outdoor Recreation*, Reprint no. 10 (Washington, D.C.: Resources for the Future, February 1959).

TABLE 12.6   COMPONENTS OF SOCIAL COSTS AND BENEFITS FOR URBAN RECREATION PROJECTS

Costs	Benefits
1. Planning and analysis	1. Consumption benefits to users
2. Physical capital (site, tax value, development, equipment)	2. Human capital development (skills and attitudes of users)
3. Operating and maintenance of facility and program	3. Nonuser benefits (visual, aesthetic)
4. Resources used by other governments or agencies	4. Private resources released for alternative uses
5. User resource costs (time, travel expenses, equipment, forgone production)	5. Public resources released for alternative uses
6. Other social costs (noise, congestion, property damage)	

their tenants. Not only may rents go up, but also some of the appreciation is capitalized into land values; consequently, tax assessments might rise and with them returns to taxpayers.

Recreation costs should be valued by the next best alternative use of resources devoted to the project at hand. Major cost elements have been identified in Table 12.6. They include costs for planning and analysis, physical capital, operating and maintenance, resources used by other agencies, resources employed by users, and some urban pollution.[67]

Now we look at three benefit-cost analyses of urban recreation: rooftop parks, rooftop plazas, and vest-pocket parks.

Rooftops as Park Sites. As the density of population in our cities increases and land values rise, some of the options that can be explored for recreational facilities are rooftops. The typical roof size for high-rise buildings is one-quarter to one-half an acre; some of the area is taken up by elevator housings and ventilators. A wide variety of facilities can be housed on rooftops. They include rest areas (plazas, dining facilities, and sunbathing areas), children's play areas (playgrounds and swimming and wading pools), teenage and adult physical activity areas (swimming pools, handball and volleyball courts, driving ranges and putting greens, and basketball and tennis courts), and cultural and social areas (gardens, concert areas and stages, dance areas, and arts and crafts centers). Usually a mix of facilities would be provided.

Major benefit components of rooftop parks include direct recreation benefits, value from use by others, visual externalities, and option demand value. The value of recreation benefits from a given park depends on the amount of use it receives. This in turn is affected by the price charged or, more generally, by the total cost to the individual of using the facility, as well as the cost of substitutes and complements. Total usage of and benefits from a given park also depend on characteristics of the community it serves. Direct recreation benefits are among the most important ones. But several types of nonuser benefits must be considered as well as certain costs. Rooftops involve important physical capital, i.e., equipment purchase, installation, and maintenance; such incremental building costs as structural modifications, added elevator capacity, and incremental build-

---

[67] Fees paid by users to a recreation agency are not a cost element to be included in a benefit-cost analysis. They are an alternative means of financing the real resources employed in the recreation experience. In benefit-cost analysis we look at the real resource costs first, and may supplement that information with detail on the distribution of those costs among users and taxpayers. Another item not included in social costs, but of some importance to decision makers, is the reallocation of activity from the private to the public sector. If, for example, a city government builds an ice-skating rink, local privately operated rinks may lose business, as may other privately and publicly controlled recreation substitutes. The decreased revenues of the private operators are not a social cost.

ing maintenance; and opportunity costs of the site. Among the user resource costs are travel costs, and among the social "bads" are incremental congestion of the building and adjacent area.

Marcus, Kavanagh, and Gay undertook a benefit-cost analysis of a hypothetical rooftop neighborhood park of about 20,000 sq. ft.[68] The park was planned for West Los Angeles, an area with income higher than average, a representative age distribution of residents, and a relatively smog-free atmosphere. Facilities were suited to the age distribution of the potential users and included a fully enclosed combination basketball-volleyball-tennis court; two handball courts; two shuffleboard courts; a children's play area; and a covered dining-resting area. The park was located on a high-rise commercial building, had lighting, and was assumed to be open to the public twelve hours a day.

The present value of recreation benefits and costs associated with this rooftop park are estimated, using 4, 6, and 10 percent discount rates (see Table 12.7). The net present value is positive at 4 percent and negative at 6 percent and 10 percent, implying that the project probably is not efficient. The more favorable result at lower interest rates is to be expected,

[68] Marcus, Kavanagh, and Gay, op. cit., p. 127ff.

TABLE 12.7   PRESENT VALUE OF THE RECREATION BENEFITS AND COSTS OF ROOFTOP PARK

Description of Costs	Discount Rate		
	4%	6%	10%
1. Equipment			
a. Purchase and installation	$ 40,975	$ 40,975	$ 40,975
b. Maintenance	59,400	45,000	29,340
2. Building costs			
a. Elevator			
(i) Purchase and installation	50,000	50,000	50,000
(ii) Maintenance	79,200	60,000	39,120
b. Structural	200,000	200,000	200,000
3. Supervision			
a. Security officer	185,130	140,250	91,443
b. Parents	50,787	38,475	25,086
4. Injuries and property damage			
a. Injuries to users	19,800	15,000	9,780
b. Injuries and property damage to nonusers	29,700	22,500	14,670
Total present value of costs	$714,992	$612,200	$500,414
Total recreation benefits	$764,280	$579,000	$377,508
Net present value	$ 49,288	(−$ 33,200)	(−$122,906)

SOURCE: Morton J. Marcus, John M. Kavanagh, and Robert M. Gay, *Program Budgeting and Analyses for Urban Recreation*, MR-164 (Los Angeles, Calif.: University of California Institute of Government and Public Affairs, 1971).

since on the average benefits occur further in the future than costs. Most likely the most appropriate interest rate for a project of this type is 10 percent, mainly because such investments have relatively low certainty equivalent values.

Rooftop Plazas. A further use of rooftop space for recreation in downtown areas is the development of rooftop plazas. Marcus, Kavanagh, and Gay assume such a plaza occupies an area of 10,000 sq. ft. in downtown Los Angeles and consists of resting and dining areas that are open nine hours a day, six days a week.[69] They further assume an average of ten users per hour over the year, two-thirds of the users being between eighteen and sixty years of age. The primary users are people who work in the buildings, and shoppers. The present value of benefits and costs is given in Table 12.8; the net value of benefits varies from $188,000 at a 4 percent discount rate to $24,000 at a 10 percent discount rate. Thus net benefits are positive for all three interest rates.

While these benefit and cost estimates are tentative and partial, they have the advantage of being internally consistent with the estimates made relative to the use of rooftops as park sites. On a tentative basis the plazas appeared to be preferable to park sites.

Vest-pocket Parks. In the late 1960s, the city of Los Angeles developed two vest-pocket parks on city-owned land in the Venice district, one

[69] Ibid., p. 143ff.

TABLE 12.8 PRESENT VALUE OF USER BENEFITS AND COSTS OF ROOFTOP PLAZA

	Discount Rate		
Description of costs	4%	6%	10%
Total present value of benefits plus present value of costs	$413,087	$312,945	$204,040
1. Facilities			
a. Purchase and installation	20,488	20,488	20,488
b. Maintenance	29,700	22,500	14,670
2. Incremental building costs			
a. Elevator	15,000	15,000	15,000
b. Structural	100,000	100,000	100,000
3. Injuries and property damage			
a. Injuries to users and property damage to nonusers	59,400	45,000	29,340
Total present value of costs	$224,588	$202,988	$179,498
Net present value of benefits	$188,499	$109,957	$ 24,542

SOURCE: Morton J. Marcus, John M. Kavanagh, and Robert M. Gay, *Program Budgeting and Analyses for Urban Recreation*, MR-164 (Los Angeles, Calif.: University of California Institute of Government and Public Affairs, 1971).

of about 10,000 sq. ft. and the other of about 3,600 sq. ft. These parks were designed to provide residence-oriented, casual-use programs mainly for preschool-age children of lower-income groups. Analysis reveals that these parks were placed in almost entirely white areas with relatively few children, and that if Los Angeles City wanted to help the poor and the minorities, neither location was satisfactory.[70]

A benefit-cost analysis has been made that considers both agency and private cost streams, where agency costs include development and equipment costs, the rental value of the park site, plus the tax stream implicit in the present value of the sites over the life of the park. The private costs include travel and time costs, baby-sitting costs, street congestion costs, property damage, and noise costs. Of the costs, the agency costs and the private travel and time costs appear to make up the greatest part of the project costs. The primary benefits are the valuation of "tot-lot" consumption and the value of time that would be allocated to non-tot-lot uses. Additional benefits include the reduction of property damage and noise, the removal of litter strewn in vacant lots, and the benefits of closer community interaction. Only relatively few cost and benefit elements could in fact be estimated, and their magnitudes are summarized for the Howard Street and McKinley Street parks, assuming 4 percent, 6 percent, and 10 percent discount rates (see Table 12.9). The net present value calculated for a fifteen-year stream turned out to be negative in all cases.

By merely economic criteria, the McKinley site is the more desirable of the two, because in all cases its net present value costs are smaller. Nevertheless, both are operating at net costs, and therefore neither of these two vest-pocket parks is justified on economic grounds.

[70] Ibid.

TABLE 12.9   BENEFITS AND COSTS OF TWO VEST-POCKET PARKS, LOS ANGELES, CALIFORNIA

	Howard Street Park Interest Rates of			McKinley Street Park Interest Rates of		
	4%	6%	10%	4%	6%	10%
Benefits	$89,500	$77,300	$58,300	$58,800	$50,400	$38,100
Costs	97,400	85,900	68,800	60,700	53,100	41,900
Net present value*	−7,900	−8,600	−10,500	−1,900	−2,700	−3,800

* Fifteen-year stream.
SOURCE: J. Michael Kavanagh, "Programmatic Benefit-Cost Analysis of Local Youth Recreation Programs," OR-142 (Los Angeles: University of California Institute of Government and Public Affairs, 1968).

V.   *CULTURAL ASSETS AND ACTIVITIES*

Environment and Goals

The city has historically been the seat of culture. Close proximity and easy access, cultural heterogeneity and clashes, intellectual ferment and flourishing arts, and, more recently, availability of relatively inexpensive studio space have attracted artists to work in the city. Furthermore, because of economies of scale and adequately large markets, the large cities are the places where symphony halls and museums are built and philharmonic orchestras, ballets, and opera companies perform, as well as where great art is being exhibitied. Thus the arts and cultural activities are predominantly, if not exclusively, city-based.

Cultural activities can be defined as those leisure-time activities that are wholly or mainly concerned with the performing and visual arts—leisure-time activities that appeal to the aesthetic development of man rather than *homo economicus*. At any moment, a community has a given stock of cultural resources—assets devoted to cultural activities. There is a long list of cultural resources, and, as we will discuss below, some deserve to be major responsibilities of government while others can be entirely developed by the private sector. These assets can be divided into performing arts and visual (or fine) arts. Important performing arts relate to orchestras, legitimate theater, opera, ballet, modern dance, educational television, etc. Visual arts relate to museums, art galleries, libraries, etc.

Performing Arts.   Altogether, in 1964 an estimated $476 million was spent on admissions to performing arts events, a 142 percent increase from the $197 million in 1953. During this period the rate of increase on such admissions was about 50 percent higher than that on consumer outlays on a long list of leisure-time goods and services and greatly surpassed that for spectator sport and motion picture admissions. In 1963, performing arts admissions amounted to $3.23[l] per capita of American thirteen years old and over, compared to $9.31 for movies; $4.25 for spectator sports; $9.51 for television receivers, records, and musical instruments; and $13.00 for books and maps.[71] It was also estimated that in 1963–1964, attendance at live professional performances amounted to 20 million, i.e., one performance a year for every ten persons in the United States.

In the late 1960s, there were about 1,400 symphony orchestras, located in virtually every city of more than 50,000 people. A total audience of at least 20 million men, women, and children attended more than

[71] William J. Baumol and William G. Bowen, *Performing Arts—The Economic Dilemma* (New York: Twentieth Century Fund, 1966).

11,000 concerts a year. Aggregate expenditures of these symphony orchestras totaled nearly $100 million a year.[72] Of the 1,400 orchestras, William Baumol and William Bowen consider twenty-five to be major orchestras—including the four largest, in Boston, Cleveland, New York, and Philadelphia.[73]

Although it has been estimated that 70 percent of orchestras' activities in the United States are public service in nature (e.g., in 1969 they gave 3,500 concerts for children and students and another 4,000 concerts for the general public in parks and on tours), direct subsidies are rare. However, there are indirect subsidies, about which more will be said below, and in some major cities governments have helped finance the construction of symphony halls.[74]

It is useful to separate legitimate theater into commercial theater, commercial summer theater, off-Broadway-type theater, and regional theater. By far the most important theater center is New York City, which in 1964 had thirty-six on-Broadway theater buildings (down from eighty buildings in the late 1920s). New productions in the mid-1960s were fifty to sixty a year, down from 264 in the peak year of 1927–1928.[75] Off-Broadway-type theaters have gained in importance not only in New York and Chicago but in other major cities in the United States. Such theaters began in the late 1940s, and in 1963–1964 had ninety productions. Regional theaters are on the increase, with more than thirty of them in existence in 1964. Among the important ones are those in Washington, D.C., Boston, San Francisco, Cincinnati, Minneapolis, Milwaukee, Houston, Oklahoma City, and Los Angeles.

There are merely four major opera companies in the whole United States —the Metropolitan, the New York City Opera, the Chicago Lyric Opera, and the San Francisco Opera. In the middle 1960s, the Metropolitan's annual budget amounted to about $9 million and the annual deficit to $1½ million.[76] Throughout the United States in 1963–1964 there were 4,000 professional and amateur operatic performances.[77]

---

[72] The expenses of ninety principal American symphony orchestras amounted in 1963 to $29 million and in 1969 to $67 million, with expenses exceeding receipts in 1969 by more than $5 million. Unlike symphony orchestras in the United States, those in Amsterdam, Berlin, The Hague, and Munich benefit from government subsidies that total more than 75 percent of their budgets. The four London orchestras and the Manchester orchestra are supported by government grants of about 20 to 30 percent of their total budgets. Amyas Ames, "The Silent Spring of Our Symphonies," *Saturday Review* (Feb. 28, 1970), pp. 81 and 82.

[73] Baumol and Bowen, op. cit., pp. 15–18.

[74] For example, the state of New Jersey has financed the building of its Garden State Arts Center to the tune of $6.7 million, and the city of Cincinnati financed the building of a hall in its Eden Park, just as many other cities have done in their major public parks.

[75] Baumol and Bowen, op. cit., pp. 18–24.

[76] Ibid., p. 30.

[77] Ibid., p. 51.

The United States has three renowned dance companies—the New York City Ballet, the San Francisco Ballet, and the American Ballet Theater. In addition, there are more than a dozen leading modern dance groups. In 1964–1965 about 350 professional dance performances were given in New York City.[78]

Visual (or Fine) Arts. In 1966–1967 there were about 6,000 museums in the United States.[79] A study of 2,889 of the more important museums, undertaken in 1966–1967, revealed that about 49 percent were exclusively history museums, 15 percent were art museums, 15 percent were science museums, and the remaining 21 percent included more than one subject area.[80] Of these, 420 were exclusively devoted to arts, and about one-half were run by nonprofit organizations. Educational institutions operated 31 percent of the art-only museums.

Interest in museums appears to have been increasing rapidly, so that recently attendance has tended to double every ten years. Attendance in 1966–1967 amounted to 560 million, of which 212 million was accounted for by art museums. The bulk of attendance is accounted for by relatively few museums. The 1966 budget of museums amounted to about $0.5 billion dollars, $260 million of which went for science museums. The museum staff amounted to 53,000.[81]

In 1966, total circulation of public libraries nationally topped 1 billion books for the first time. About 55 million Americans used public library facilities that year, i.e., on the average about one person in three. Public school libraries, college and university libraries, and the host of specialized library facilities maintained by the private sector probably accounted for yet another 1 billion books in circulation.

In 1968 there were almost 7,200 public libraries and another 2,400 college and university libraries in the United States.[82] In addition there were perhaps as many school libraries. The 1968 budgets of the about 1,100 public libraries in cities with populations of 25,000 or more amounted to about $0.5 billion, of which $432 million was for operating purposes. Public libraries were funded about $360 million by local governments, $25 million by state governments, and $11 million by the federal government. More than $260 million was paid in wages and salaries to

[78] Ibid., pp. 30–32, 51.
[79] The American Association of Museums, *America's Museums: The Belmont Report* (Washington, D.C.: The American Association of Museums, 1969), pp. 3 and 4.
[80] Lola E. Rogers, *Museums and Related Institutions* (Washington, D.C.: U.S. Department of Health, Education, and Welfare, 1969), p. 10.
[81] Ibid., pp. 40, 55, and 69. A study of the fiscal situation of twenty-nine major science museums indicates that public sources account for roughly 40 percent of their budgets. (Ibid., pp. 26 and 27.)
[82] R. R. Bowker, *The Bowker Annual of Library and Book Trade Information* (New York: R. R. Bowker, 1971), pp. 9–17, and 49.

about 50,000 library personnel. Public libraries held about 190 million volumes. Colleges and universities allocate about 3 to 4 percent of their annual budgets to libraries.[83] The 2,400 college and university libraries had an operating budget of $0.5 billion in 1968, of which $275 million went for wages and salaries to pay about 44,000 library staff. These libraries had more than 300 million volumes.

The importance of public libraries in urban areas is exemplified by Los Angeles County, where in 1965–1966 public libraries had about 9 million volumes, while libraries at Southern California colleges and universities had about the same number and those in the public schools had about 7 million volumes. Southern California's public libraries spent $3.18 per capita in 1965–1966, for a total outlay of $38.2 million.

It is difficult to define the mission of cultural services. Culture relates to truly intangible concerns of man, although we can observe that cultural services have consumption as well as investment aspects. Cultural services give much immediate enjoyment, and at the same time enhance man's long-term ability to enjoy life, to grow intellectually, and to live a fuller and healthier life, thus contributing to the mental health of the community. Even if we succeed in carefully describing such consumption benefits of culture as contributing to mental health, refreshing the mind, and providing a sense of pleasure, we do not get very close to measuring the changes in an individual's condition. And even if we could indentify the investment benefits of cultural activities in terms of their contribution to human capital, they are likely to be overshadowed by other investments in human capital provided by society.

Thus in seeking output measures for cultural activities, about the best we can do is state that a given individual participated in a specified cultural experience in conjunction with opportunities provided by a cultural institution. For the time being we are forced to pay major attention to the contributions cultural institutions make in providing opportunities for cultural enjoyment to urbanites, and to assume that these opportunities are in some way related to actual consumption or investment benefits.[84] Such indirect output measures usually take the form of attendance figures combined with information about the price of attending (i.e., entrance fee plus such various associated costs as transportation, baby-sitting, etc.) and weighted by the quality of the "attendance." For example, in the case of libraries, the number of visits to the library per year, perhaps weighted by the number of books taken out, is a partial output measure. Selection and physical conditions are important quality characteristics of the books themselves. And so are the availability of the books requested, good read-

---

[83] Ibid., p. 9.
[84] Anyone who has sat through a poorly performed opera might take serious issue with the assumption that merely being there provides a consumption benefit.

ing room facilities, help to children in selecting books, reference service, and location of library.

In Chapter 10 we identified four characteristics that qualify services to be rendered publicly or provided at zero price.[85] Cultural activities exhibit these characteristics in varying degrees, although they are far from a pure public good.[86] Perhaps the single most important characteristic relates to welfare and distributional issues. On egalitarian grounds and for the sake of educating minors and future generations of mankind, it is argued that government has a responsibility to provide cultural experiences for all, regardless of their ability to pay for them.[87]

Second, there is joint consumption. Writing of the arts, Lionel Robbins argues,

> . . . the benefit is not merely discriminate . . . the positive effects of the fostering of art and learning and the preservation of culture are not restricted to those immediately prepared to pay cash but diffuse themselves to the benefit of much wider sections of the community in much the same way as the benefits of the apparatus of public hygiene or of a well-planned urban landscape.[88]

Up to a point, attendance of another person at a museum or library or

[85] Interesting arguments have been made for cultural activities, although they seem to be less important and convincing to the economist. It is argued, for instance, that certain artistic activities have an "intrinsic" value. Lord Bridges states, "The heart of this matter is surely that the arts can give to all of us, including those who lack expert knowledge of any of them, much of what is best in human life and enjoyment; and that a nation that does not put this at the disposal of those who have the liking and the capacity for it, is failing in a most important duty." (Lord Bridges, *The State and the Arts,* Romanes Lecture, Oxford, June 3, 1958 [Oxford: Clarendon Press, 1958], pp. 12 and 13.) It is also claimed that the arts should not be judged by the market test, just as one does not expect the defense establishment or the courts to cover their costs out of their revenues. Finally, there is the issue of local (and national) prestige. No city wants to be accused of being "a cultural wasteland." In Chap. 9 we discussed option demand and pointed to the benefits associated with the hedge against future declines and the desirability of the chosen alternative as well as the gains and psychological satisfaction of knowing that one lives in a "cultural" city. (Chap. 9, pp. 283–284.) Clearly, these advantages are tied to the indirect business activities sometimes referred to as "loss leaders."

[86] In the United States there is a wide disparity in the extent to which different cultural activities are publicly supported: libraries are public institutions or belong to schools, colleges, or universities, while theater, dance, and ballet receive relatively little public support. Local government support has been small and so has been that of states (with the possible exception of New York). The federal government has come to play an increasingly important role in financing certain cultural activities. In addition, the federal government provides indirect financial support because of its tax exemption provision. Federal tax deductions allowed for gifts to the performing arts in 1962 were estimated to amount to between $30 and $35 million. (Baumol and Bowen, op. cit., p. 354.)

[87] Baumol and Bowen, op. cit., pp. 378–380 and 384 and 385; and Alan T. Peacock, "Welfare Economics and Public Subsidies to the Arts," *The Manchester School of Economic and Social Studies,* vol. 37, no. 4 (Dec. 1969), pp. 329 and 330.

[88] Quoted in Peacock, op. cit., p. 329.

performance does not inflict costs on other visitors. Yet crowding, particularly at "special" events, does occur, to the discomfort of many.

Finally, the costs of exclusion, i.e., setting up some kind of rationing system, are probably not large for most cultural activities. However, if exclusionary devices are adopted, they are likely to penalize precisely those groups whose attendance under the distributional criteria we seek to encourage.

Demand

To the extent that they place user charges on select cultural activities, urban governments receive demand signals directly. In those instances it should not be too difficult to estimate the demand for the activities, particularly if either the same institution changes its user fees from time to time or institutions that are by and large similar make different user charges. The same also holds if private substitutes are used to approximate the demand facing, let us say, a municipal museum that does not charge an entrance fee.

The quantity of tickets demanded, for any particular cultural activity, is a function of ticket prices, income, prices of competing goods, and tastes. There is much evidence that the taste for specific cultural activities varies greatly with ethnicity, occupation, age, and education.[89] Also, there is evidence that the price elasticity of demand for cultural activities is not very great. However, this may reflect offsetting effects from a positive income elasticity, or it may mean that associated costs—transportation outlays, restaurants, baby-sitters, etc.—are more important than the ticket price for attendance.[90] William Baumol and William Bowen's tentative analysis suggests that the demand for attending artistic performances is probably inelastic.[91] A comparison of attendance (in relation to capacity) with ticket prices for the basic eleven major orchestras provides some evidence of a negative relationship between the two. During 1961–1964 prices rose sharply, and the percentage of capacity fell. Attendance at the New York Philharmonic fell in four of the seven cases when prices were increased. Prices for the Metropolitan Opera increased in 1958, 1961, 1963, and 1965, and in three out of these four cases attendance as a percentage of capacity fell temporarily, and it did not fall in any other year. However, the inhibiting effect of price increases appears to be small. In all but one of the cases, the percentage decline in attendance was smaller than the percentage rise in prices.

[89] Germans, Italians, and Jews appear to like musical performances; attendance by people over sixty is much larger than that by people under twenty years of age; professionals are disproportionately interested in art; the more education, the more interest in the arts. (Baumol and Bowen, op. cit., pp. 75–77.)
[90] Baumol and Bowen, op. cit., pp. 273–275.
[91] Ibid., pp. 274–278.

Baumol and Bowen offer additional information, though partial, on the elasticity of demand. In an audience survey, they found surprisingly few persons who tried to purchase less expensive seats. Of all respondents, only 11 percent sought cheaper theater tickets, and 5 percent had tried to purchase more expensive seats. At the ballet, where prices are generally low, the number of persons seeking higher-priced seats actually exceeded the number who wanted less expensive ones. Baumol and Bowen found, in a survey, that in 1963–1964 over 90 percent of attendees of live performances made some sort of nonticket expenditure: 88 percent of the audience spent something on transportation, 31 percent ate at a restaurant, and 15 percent had to pay a baby-sitter. The nonticket expenses, on the average, were almost equal in size to the ticket expenses. The total cost of attending a performance in New York was higher than the national average—it averaged, in 1963–1964, $8.68 per person as compared with the national average of $6.82.[92]

To our knowledge, there are no empirical demand analyses of cultural activities, and this holds for museums. We have observed a large-scale increase in museum attendance, which may also be typical of some other cultural activities. The demand function for museum activities is likely to have shifted upward because leisure time as well as per capita income has increased; the quality of art exhibits may have increased; the mobility of Americans, and therefore access to museums, has increased, which in turn should have reduced the cost of attending; the taste of Americans may have changed, and more people may have become actively interested in the fine arts.

An effort has been made to indicate some indirect quality dimensions of museums. Although they are quite crude, they are informative. Thus, it has been suggested that the following are possible quality characteristics of a museum: cataloged collections, professionally designed exhibits, library, professional staff, educational-cultural activities, substantive publications, published annual report, formal research program, and formal professional worker-training program. It is clearly very difficult to give a relative weight to these characteristics. There were twenty-one museums that reported all nine of the indicators, and eighty-four that reported none. Of those reporting six or more quality indicators, the museums operated by educational institutions indicated the highest frequency.[93]

Supply

The cost structure of the performing arts differs greatly from that of the visual arts. The former, especially operas and symphony orchestras, are very labor-intensive. At the same time, musicians, actors, and dancers are

[92] Ibid., pp. 261–264.
[93] Rogers, op. cit., pp. 102–109.

in professional-technical occupations that are among the lowest-paid.[94] The visual arts are capital-intensive, spending large amounts on acquiring paintings, sculptures, books, etc. Thus, in 1968 public libraries serving areas with populations in excess of 25,000 spent 42 percent of their total operating expenditures on books, serials, films, and other nonsalary items.[95] Likewise, museums spend large amounts of funds on paintings and sculptures. However, these kinds of "investment" are not for purposes of improving productivity. Thus, over the years, relatively little technological change has taken place relative to the performing and visual arts.[96] The performing arts and, to a lesser extent, the visual arts suffer from the fact that they are what Baumol calls a "technologically nonprogressive sector." The substitution of capital for labor is strictly limited, particularly in the performing arts. In the past, the productivity growth of the performing arts was much less than that of many other sectors of the economy. Such unbalanced productivity growth, to quote William Baumol, "threatens to destroy many of the activities that do so much to enrich our existence, and to give others over into the hands of amateurs. These are dangers which many of us may feel should not be ignored or taken lightly."[97]

The cost per performance differs greatly among the different performing arts. Thus, in 1963–1964, the average performance of the Metropolitan Opera cost $36,000, while that of major orchestras cost $7,000, that of musicals $6,500, a Broadway show $3,100, and an off-Broadway-type show $750.[98]

Empirical cost functions have been estimated for major orchestras in the United States. The function that was fitted is a simplified equation where the independent variable is the number of performances of these

---

[94] According to the United States Census, in 1959 male physicians and surgeons had a median income (from all sources) of more than $15,000, while actors' income was $5,600, musicians' and music teachers' income was $4,800, dancers' and dancing teachers' income was $3,500, and median income of female musicians and music teachers was a mere $1,600. However, it should also be noted that in many cases these low incomes reflect only part-time earnings. (Ibid., pp. 102–104.)

[95] Bowker, op. cit., p. 14.

[96] Some modern composers write more and more for small ensembles and attempt to employ devices with some capital intensity. Alan Peacock reports that Peter Maxwell Davies, for example, uses an ancient gramophone and prerecorded tapes in his composition *L'Homme Armé*. (Peacock, op. cit., p. 326.) Furthermore, many modern playwrights, notably Pinter, Becket, and Wesker, call for small casts. Museums attempt to use more television cameras to reduce the number of guards required on their premises.

[97] William J. Baumol, "Macroeconomics of Unbalanced Growth," op. cit., p. 422.

[98] Baumol and Bowen, op. cit., pp. 141 and 142. The per-person cost of a performance was about $10 for the Metropolitan Opera, $5 for musicals and Broadway plays, $5 for the five top symphony orchestras playing in their home auditoriums (although $2 if all major orchestras are put together), and $3.80 for off-Broadway plays. The relatively high per-person cost of off-Broadway-type plays in the light of their relatively low costs per performance stems from the relatively small seating capacity of such plays.

orchestras per year, and the dependent variable is average unit cost per performance adjusted for changes in the purchasing power of the dollar. Since the bulk of the orchestras' expenditures is for salaries of musicians, this figure is used to measure purchasing power.[99] Time series data for 1936–1964 are used for eleven major orchestras. Both linear and curvilinear equations are fitted, the latter providing a somewhat better fit than the former (i.e., coefficient of multiple correlation of .89 versus .79). The two fitted equations relating real expenditure per concert to number of concerts for a specific major orchestra are presented in Figure 12.2.

The cost curves for the eleven orchestras are not the same. However, six of the eleven orchestras fall into similar patterns, even though the curves are by no means identical—they are not equally steep, nor do they begin to level off at the same number of concerts per year. Some orchestras reach their minimum cost level after as few as ninety concerts per year, while others go on enjoying economies of scale until they have played nearly 150 concerts per year. That the unit-cost-minimizing number of concerts varies can be explained in part by whether an orchestra plays the same program only once or to more than one audience. This is because

[99] Ibid., pp. 201–207, and 479–481.

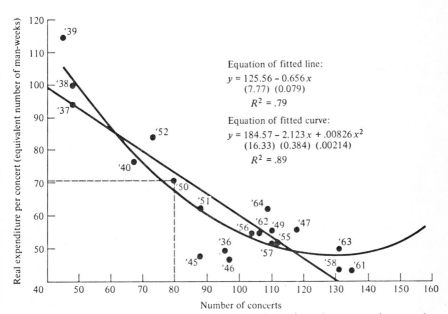

Equation of fitted line:
$$y = 125.56 - 0.656\,x$$
$$(7.77)\ (0.079)$$
$$R^2 = .79$$

Equation of fitted curve:
$$y = 184.57 - 2.123\,x + .00826\,x^2$$
$$(16.33)\ (0.384)\ (.00214)$$
$$R^2 = .89$$

FIGURE 12.2 Real expenditure per concert and number of concerts, for a major orchestra, 1936–1964. Source: *William J. Baumol and William G. Bowen,* Performing Arts—The Economic Dilemma *(New York: Twentieth Century Fund, 1966), p. 202.*

total rehearsal time is about the same whether the orchestra plays a program once or several times during a given week.

With such considerations we would expect the average cost to decline with an increase in number of performances, but to decline at a decreasing rate, up to the minimum AUC.[100] This actually happened in eight of the eleven cases studied. For these eight cases the median value of R^2 is .8. These coefficients are significant at a probability level of 0.01 in six cases and not significant in the others.

When expenditurers on artistic personnel alone, instead of total unit cost, are used, results improve further. For five orchestras the R^2 ranges between .90 and .99.[101] The general shapes of the average cost curves remain much the same even though the minima now generally call for a somewhat larger number of concerts per season. This implies that unit administrative costs typically begin to increase at a number of concerts smaller than the turning point in expenditures on performers' salaries. This runs counter to expectations about administrative costs for most productive activities, where economies of scale for administrative expenses are generally supposed to be a major source of overall declining unit costs. This may reflect the generally primitive state of management techniques in the culture industry.

Baumol and Bowen also indicate that such scale economies are likely to hold for the theater as well as for concerts. The longer the run of a play, the lower the unit cost. Thus they cite figures for the Bucks County Playhouse that enable them to compare the costs of the second week of a two-week run with those of the first week. The figures show that, on the average, the second week's operation costs are 11 percent less than those of the first week.[102]

Decision Making

No benefit-cost studies of cultural activities have been found. This fact may relate to the obvious difficulties of defining benefits and the difficulties in obtaining cost data. However, it is possibly related also to the fact that only in recent years has the culture "industry" begun to attract the attention of economists, and even more recently have advances in organization theory spread to consideration of improving management and efficiency in the industry.

---

[100] In the quadratic equation $AUC = a + bQ + cQ^2$, this would mean that the expected value of b is negative and that of c is positive. See the fitted-curve equation in Fig. 12.2.
[101] The improved statistical fit may result from the elimination from the data of erratic expenses for tours, repairs, etc. (Ibid., pp. 479–481.)
[102] Ibid., p. 205.

The culture industry is preeminently an urban industry. The increased attention it commands by economists is symptomatic of the growing concern with urban economics.

In summary, this chapter should leave little doubt about the substantial progress that has been made in methods of analyzing certain urban public services. In the middle 1950s economists quite suddenly took a strong interest in probing public education; much progress resulted. The same holds for police protection, which began to concern economists in the late 1960s. In contrast, economists have so far neglected research on cultural services, and the state of our knowledge about this service is comparatively limited.

CHAPTER 13

FINANCE, REGULATION, AND CONTROL

I. INTRODUCTION

Urban governments face a number of tasks in addition to delivering a variety of tangible services. First, they must raise funds to finance the services, and second, they are intent on providing an environment and rules of the game in which the private sector can effectively operate. This second function they can fulfill through imposition and enforcement of laws and regulations in relation to land use and transportation. However, a particularly interesting case of control relates to the recently emerging concern about the quality of the environment. Urban governments are faced with important decisions about how best to abate such urban public bads as air pollution, water pollution, noise pollution, and congestion. As we will see, pollution abatement can use a variety of mechanisms, including outright control and fees to compensate those who are hurt by pollution, and subsidies to encourage industry to curtail its pollution.

In the following pages we first examine major revenue sources for urban governments and some fiscal imbalances and pressures. The third section is a consideration of an especially important fiscal issue, i.e., the fiscal plight of the central cities. In the next section we review government intervention, particularly as it applies to land use (since regulation relative to transportation has been taken up in Chapter 4), pollution abatement, and regulation of public employment relations. The final section considers some urban public policies.

II. FINANCING

Local governments, the principal suppliers of services to urbanites, are forced to fund most of these activities. In 1966–1967, total direct local government expenditures amounted to $65.8 billion, of which all but $20.4 billion was raised by local governments. Local funding varied from about 100 percent in the case of refuse collection to about 14 percent in the case of welfare. (See Table 13.1.) Dick Netzer has estimated that from local taxes or from charges imposed for services they provide, or by borrowing, urban local governments in 1969 raised roughly $370 per capita of the urban population.[1] Of the $45 billion raised locally in 1966–1967,

---

[1] Dick Netzer, *Economics and Urban Problems* (New York: Basic Books, 1970), pp. 173 and 185.

TABLE 13.1 FINANCING OF SELECTED URBAN SERVICES, 1966–1967

Selected Urban Services	Amount Spent by Governments Actually Providing the Service (in billions of dollars)			How State-Local Spending Is Financed (percent)*		
	State	Local	Com-bined	Fed-eral Funds	State Funds	Local Funds
Welfare	4.3	4.0	8.2	51	35	14
Health and hospitals	3.4	3.3	6.6	6	48	46
Housing programs	—†	1.5	1.5	47	6	47
Public schools	0.3	27.8	28.1	7	38	55
Police, correction, and fire	1.2	4.5	5.7	—	21	79
Transportation (except highways)	1.3	2.1	2.4	4	12	84
Water supply and water treatment	—‡	4.3	4.3	2	2	96
Local parks and recreation	—‡	1.3	1.3	3	4	93
Sanitation (except sewerage)	—	0.9	0.9	—	—	100
Libraries	—†	0.5	0.5	10	10	80
Total, selected services	9.4	50.1	59.5	13	31	56

* These columns describe the source of funds for the state-local direct expenditure shown in the preceding columns. The federal funds shown in this table include only federal aid to state and local government.
† Less than $50 million.
‡ There is some direct state government expenditure for urban water supply and for urban parks, but it is small and difficult to separate out from published data.
SOURCE: Dick Netzer, *Economics and Urban Problems* (New York: Basic Books, 1970), pp. 172 and 185.

the major portion was raised by taxes, but perhaps up to one-third was raised by user charges and fees.

Revenue Sources[2]

In considering the tax sources of urban governments, particular emphasis must be placed on mobility of the tax base—a most significant distinguishing feature of taxation by local urban governments. Fragmentation of governments in densely populated urban areas does not permit us to assume, as is so often done on the national level, that the costs of avoiding a tax through relocation are sufficiently great to preclude such behavior as a major factor in tax incidence. Moreover, for the same reason we cannot assume that the beneficiaries of government activities are the citizens of the government that supply the services. As a result the question of who

[2] This section draws heavily on chaps. 4–6 of Werner Z. Hirsch, *Economics of State and Local Government* (New York: McGraw-Hill, 1970).

pays what taxes and who benefits from the services financed by these levies assumes great importance.

Fees and User Charges.   To fund their operations, urban governments depend on locally raised fees as well as on taxes and intergovernmental transfers. Depending on how broadly or narrowly one defines fees and user charges, these account for somewhere between 29 percent and 35 percent of total local government revenue from its own sources. Because of their characteristics, the application of user charges is clearly limited. Particularly, services with important welfare aspects, such as education, libraries, and health services, not to speak of welfare services, cannot be funded by user charges. Likewise, services with very high exclusion cost, e.g., air pollution abatement and mosquito control, do not readily lend themselves to financing through user charges. However, since for example it is difficult in the short run to expand CBD-oriented urban expressways, and the poor do not rely heavily on private cars, imposition of street user charges during rush hours could speed up traffic at a minimum cost to the poor. Thus, transportation services illustrate the presently inept application of user charges, since transit fares, on-street parking, gasoline taxes, and license charges for cars tend to be flat fees.

Altogether, fees and user charges have distinct advantages in that they can improve public decision making about the supply of urban government services and the allocation of them among users. They provide price signals on the basis of which the rationing of services can be improved and costs and benefits can be better matched. In particular, user charges can reduce problems associated with geographic spillovers, the cost of which can seldom be recaptured by means of taxation. An urban government cannot always tax outsiders who may be benefiting from the public services it provides. But many cities have user-charge structures that are perversely designed. They provide quantity discounts on commuters' tickets even though commuters typically travel at rush hours.

Relying on user fees is attractive when potential users have different urgencies of use or intensities of demand for the service, since such fees enable those with the more urgent need to use the facility. Only those to whom it is worth the price will use it. User charges will also be appealing when the alternative is to distribute coupons whose nontransferability is not readily enforced. Finally, user charges appeal when the urgency of need is visible and higher prices can be charged to those who have the greater need. Clearly, user charges can be inequitable because they do not take into consideration ability to pay. But poverty should be dealt with through federal income redistribution.

Property Taxes.   A property tax is a government levy on certain physical assets that are claims to future services in kind. Property taxes are mainly levied on real property, although they can also be levied on specific personal tangible assets. Since the administration of the personal property tax base is difficult and costly, governments have been discouraged from using it.

Real property taxes have been a significant source of urban government revenue. They are levied by 71,000 local government units, nearly 18,000 of which are in metropolitan areas. Property tax revenues rose from $4.5 billion in 1942 to $26.3 billion in 1967, providing about two-thirds of the revenue from all local sources and seven-eighths of local tax revenues.[3]

The median effective property tax rate among 122 large cities in the United States in 1967 ranged from 0.36 percent to 4.3 percent of assessed value. Half of these cities showed a median rate of at least 1.85 percent.[4] Most effective rates among United States cities in the Northeast are higher than those in other regions, particularly in the South and West. Effective tax rates tend to be higher in core cities than in suburbs. For example, of sixty-three large cities (where the city and the large suburban areas adjacent to it employed the same assessing agency in 1967), thirty-nine cities showed a higher, fifteen a lower, and nine about an equal median effective rate for houses in the core city compared with houses in the city's suburbs. It has been estimated that property taxes in the large urban states are equivalent, in revenue yield, to a flat-rate tax on personal income (after personal exemptions) of 10 percent or more, and that property tax rates in urban areas are equivalent to sales tax rates of 25 percent or more.[5]

The fact that the property tax is distinguished by immobility of its base has some interesting implications. For example, highway improvements that benefit residents by allowing better and more rapid movement about the city can lead to a decline in the value of certain lands and improvements close to the highway. Yet many urban government services are site-oriented, e.g., fire protection, refuse collection, street cleaning, etc., and much of the benefit received by citizens can be taxed by levying liabilities on real property. Under these circumstances, there is a close link between real property tax burdens and benefits received from these urban government services. Yet, in general, real property holdings are a poor proxy for ability to pay.

There have been different views about the effects of the property tax. Alfred Marshall has stated that a tax levied on capital on a specific site will be borne by the owners of the land, although he also says that a universal property tax may be shifted to consumers.[6] Earl Rolph and George

[3] Ibid., p. 95.
[4] U.S. Bureau of the Census, *Census of Government: Property Tax Rates in Selected Major Cities and Counties* CG-P-5 (May 1968), pp. 1–30.
[5] Netzer, op. cit., pp. 191–192.
[6] Alfred Marshall, *Principles of Economics*, 8th ed., app. G.

Break assert that the property tax will be paid by all site factors whose elasticities of supply are less than infinite.[7] Dick Netzer holds that a tax on improvements of existing structures will be fully forward-shifted to consumers.[8] Nonresidential property owners have greater ability to shift the tax than homeowners, even though L. Orr finds in either case little forward shifting in the Boston area.[9] Wallace Oats has examined the effects of local property taxes and local expenditure programs on property values. He concludes that if property taxes are raised but services are not increased, the bulk of the tax increase will be capitalized and find its expression in lower property values. This is not the case if increased taxes go hand in hand with improved services.[10]

Many complaints have been registered against the property tax. It has long been argued that the property tax places a disproportionately heavy burden on the poor. Empirical studies of the income elasticity of the property tax appear to indicate that it is slightly higher than 1, i.e., between 1 and 1.3.[11] If, however, ability to pay were to be measured with greater regard for wealth changes, and if consistent assumptions regarding shifting were to be maintained for all types of property taxes, it is likely that these taxes would be found to be less regressive than earlier studies have concluded.[12]

A further problem with the property tax relates to its administration. It is both costly and poorly carried out. Making tax assessment more professional by providing for effective statewide review of assessments, and possibly shifting the assessment burden from government to the asset holder, could streamline property tax assessment. Since property tax rates are at present locally set and placed on a specified local tax base, location decisions, particularly those about industrial sites, can be affected, as well as those about rental property. Because the central city relies so heavily on the property tax, industrial activity and the needed rebuilding of the

[7] Earl R. Rolph and George Break, *Public Finance* (New York: Ronald, 1961), p. 343.
[8] Dick Netzer, *Economics of the Property Tax* (Washington, D.C.: Brookings, 1966), pp. 32–66.
[9] L. L. Orr, "The Incidence of Differential Property Taxes on Urban Housing," *National Tax Journal*, vol. 21 (September 1968), pp. 253–262.
[10] Wallace E. Oats, "The Effects of Property Taxes and Local Public Spending on Property Values," *Journal of Political Economy*, vol. 77 (November-December 1969), pp. 957–971.
[11] Hirsch, op. cit., pp. 97–99. These studies are time series analyses of the tax base for geographic aggregates; they are not cross-sectional among income groups and say little about regressivity.
[12] Property tax relief programs are being tried out in some instances. Tax credit to low-income elderly in Wisconsin appears to have made the property tax for the elderly poor more progressive. K. E. Quindry and B. D. Cook, "Humanization of the Property Tax for Low Income Households," *National Tax Journal*, vol. 22 (September 1969), pp. 357–367.

central city's housing stock are often impeded. At the same time, industrial enclaves that keep out residential land uses, and therefore are tax havens, are possibly encouraged.

Why, then, has the property tax remained so attractive to urban governments in spite of these disadvantages? The fact is that in recent years the percentage increase in property tax collections has exceeded that in gross national product. One reason is its large revenue-raising capability. Another relates to the fact that it is an appropriate tax for property-oriented services with relatively minor merit-want characteristics. And finally, it is a tax that has proved to have great revenue stability.

These advantages would be further enhanced if the tax were levied on land alone and not also on the improvements on the site. While this idea was espoused by Henry George a century ago, Dick Netzer is one of its modern proponents.[13] In his view, a land tax could provide appropriate incentives for urbanites to make judicious use of the city's most limited natural resource.

Nonproperty Taxes.   Urban governments also levy sales taxes, excise taxes, and income (or payroll) taxes. On the average, these account for a relatively small part of the tax revenue raised by local governments, i.e., less than one-seventh of all tax revenue, although there is much variation among different places. For example, school districts basically raise no taxes other than property taxes. Also, local nonproperty taxes are not used in some parts of the country. General sales taxes are widely used by urban governments in sixteen states. Local income taxes are widely used in five states and by a small number of large cities in three other states. Very large cities use either sales or income taxes, and New York City uses both. The forty-three of the largest cities, combined, get nearly 40 percent of their tax revenues from local nonproperty taxes, and in some of them the local nonproperty taxes exceed the property tax in importance.[14]

General sales taxes are levies on a great variety of exchanges; in the United States they are levied on retail sales of most final consumption goods. A specific excise tax is a levy on a narrow range of exchanges, i.e., a particular good or service. Since New York City started collecting general retail sales taxes in 1934, about 3,000 other local governments, mainly in Illinois and California, have imposed this tax. If an increase in general sales taxation is offset by a reduction in neutral tax liabilities, altered retail shopping behavior is likely to result. For example, shoppers may seek to purchase goods either by traveling to, or importing from, markets outside the taxing jurisdiction. An empirical investigation of New York City

[13] Netzer, *Economics and Urban Problems,* op. cit., pp. 196–199.
[14] Ibid., pp. 199–200.

by William Hamovitch bears out this hypothesis and indicates that locally marketed retail goods are highly price-elastic.[15]

John Mikesell in a study of 173 central cities of metropolitan areas produces similar results.[16] Specifically he concludes that in the early 1960s there was 95 percent probability ". . . that the loss of per capita sales from a 1 percent change in the sales tax variable will be between 1.69 and 10.97 percent."

This consumer behavior tends to reduce the ability of suppliers in the urban economy to shift burdens forward to the consumer. Furthermore, there would be some outmigration of factors of production as a result of the backward shifting to these factors in which local suppliers might engage. The effects of backward shifting of sales taxes in terms of reduced factor wages and factor relocations are much more difficult to evaluate. We can expect relatively more unemployment to occur as shifting to avoid the new tax liabilities progresses.[17]

Selma Mushkin and Gabrielle Lupo have estimated the income elasticity of the general sales tax to be 1, somewhat higher than that of specific excise taxes, for which the elasticity was estimated to be 0.7.[18] Excise taxes are levied mainly on cigarettes, liquor, gasoline, and entertainment. By 1968, all but one state (North Carolina) had imposed a tax on cigarettes, varying from 2½ cents to 13 cents per pack. The income elasticity of tobacco product taxes was estimated to be 0.4, that of alcoholic beverage taxes 0.6, and that of motor fuel taxes 0.6.

A single city in a metropolitan area cannot impose a sales tax without incurring a major sales decline. Thus, prior to 1965, New York City had a sales tax while adjacent New Jersey and the surrounding suburban counties in New York State did not. Henry Levin estimates that the city's 4 percent sales tax, by itself, was responsible for the diversion of nearly 25 percent of the city's retail sales of house furnishings and apparel to suburban areas.[19] On the other hand, such taxes have the advantage of enabling the central city to tap the taxpaying capacity of the larger metropolitan economy, by taxing sales to nonresident shoppers and visitors.[20]

The same advantage accrues also when a city levies an income (or payroll) tax. Gross income taxes are levied by about 3,000, mainly small,

[15] William Hamovitch, "Sales Taxation: An Analysis of the Effect of Rate Increases in Two Contrasting Cases," *National Tax Journal,* vol. 19 (December 1966), pp. 411–420.
[16] John L. Mikesell, "Central Cities and Sales Tax Rate Differentials: The Border City Problem," *National Tax Journal,* vol. 23 (June 1970), pp. 206–213.
[17] For detail, see Hirsch, op. cit., pp. 92–93.
[18] Selma J. Mushkin and Gabrielle C. Lupo, "Project 70: Projecting the State-Local Sector," *Review of Economics and Statistics,* vol. 49 (May 1967), p. 243.
[19] Henry M. Levin, "An Analysis of the Economic Effects of the New York City Sales Tax," in *Financing Government in New York City* (New York: New York University Graduate School of Public Administration, 1966), pp. 635–692.
[20] Mikesell, op. cit., pp. 206–213.

cities located predominantly in Kentucky, Michigan, Ohio, and Pennsylvania, as well as by such large cities as St. Louis and Kansas City. New York City levies a net income tax with graduated rates, as do counties in Maryland. If only gross incomes or payrolls are taxed, the income elasticity of the payroll tax would not be high, and would possibly even be regressive.

Grants-in-aid. Other important sources of funds of urban governments are grants-in-aid and other intergovernmental transfers.

Under the impetus of increasing urbanization, mobility, and local government "fiscal crises," federal-state-local government relations have undergone major changes. The year 1932 has been cited by Roscoe Martin as representing a kind of geologic fault line in the development of federal-local government relations in general and federal-city relations in particular.[21] The years 1950 and 1965 represent more recent fault lines in federal assistance, particularly for urban governments. By the end of 1965, the federal government was administering more than seventy-five grant programs for urban governments, and more than three-quarters of these were authorized after 1950. Congressional enactments in 1965 included grants for basic water and sewer facilities, advance acquisition of land, open space for urban beautification, neighborhood facilities, code enforcement assistance, demolition of unsafe structures, rent supplements, and support for councils of locally elected officials—all as parts of the Housing and Urban Development Act of 1965.

Federal grants to state and local governments have been increasing rapidly: federal aid as a percentage of state and local sources of general revenue increased from 8 percent in 1942 to 11 percent in 1948, to 15 percent in 1965, and to 20 percent in 1967. The amount of federal aid in 1967 was about $16 billion.[22]

The amount of federal aid varies greatly among the fifty states. In 1967, state and local governments in Delaware received $40 million from the federal government, while those in California received $2.3 billion. Admittedly, the difference was much smaller on a per capita basis.

States have responded, often quite creatively, to the increased federal interest in state and local governments as well as to the serious fiscal problems of local governments. In addition, federal legislation in some cases stipulates states as indispensable administrative partners in carrying out programs.

States have in recent years set up state offices or departments of local

[21] Roscoe C. Martin, *The Cities and the Federal System* (New York: Atherton, 1965), p. 111.
[22] Advisory Commission on Intergovernmental Relations, *State and Local Finances, 1966 to 1969*, M-43 (Washington, D.C.: U.S. Government Printing Office, 1968), p. 20.

government, community affairs, or urban affairs, as well as coordinating offices to provide effective liaison for intergovernmental programs.

More important, perhaps, during the twenty-year period from 1948 to 1967 the amount of annual state payments to local government multiplied almost sixfold, from $3.2 billion to $19.1 billion. Throughout this period, however, such payments made up a fairly consistent fraction of the annual nationwide total of the states' general expenditures. Between 1952 and 1967, for example, this percentage relationship ranged merely between 33 percent and 37 percent.[23]

State governments differ widely in the amounts they pay to local governments. For example, state intergovernmental expenditures in 1967 ranged from $178 per capita in New York to $21 in New Hampshire. Payments to all local governments totaled almost 36 percent of all state government general expenditure in 1967; however, the percentage ranged widely among the states, from less than 10 percent in Hawaii and New Hampshire to more than 54 percent in New York. During the past twenty-five years, state-local fiscal relations have become more uniform. In the forty-six states subject to direct comparison, there was an increase in the number whose payments to local governments ranged from 20 percent to 40 percent of state general expenditure: The numbers of such states increased from twenty-two in 1942 to twenty-six in 1952, and to thirty-two in both 1962 and 1967.[24]

Most of state aid is for four local government programs. Thus, in 1967, of all state aid, 62 percent was given to education, 15 percent to public welfare, 10 percent to highways, and 8 percent to general local government support. In terms of types of governments, 50 percent went to school districts, 25 percent to counties, 21 percent to municipalities, and the rest to townships and special districts.[25]

Reasons why urban governments deserve to be financially helped by state and federal governments are numerous and include interjurisdictional spillovers of costs and benefits and regional income disparities. These and other reasons will be discussed in the section analyzing the reasons for the fiscal plight of central cities. Clearly an important consideration is fragmentation of governments that serve densely populated urban areas in a highly mobile and industrialized society, and the ensuing numerous, extensive spillovers. These cost and benefit spillovers are particularly significant in relation to services connected with human resource development—education, health, and welfare services—since people tend to migrate. Additionally, some urban services—transportation, environmental control, etc.

[23] U.S. Bureau of the Census, *Census of Government, 1967: State Payments to Local Governments* (1968), vol. 6, no. 4, pp. 1–4.
[24] Ibid., p. 2.
[25] Ibid., pp. 3 and 4.

—have many spillovers, since their technology rules out easy confinement of benefits and costs to relatively small geographic areas.

Also, there are great fiscal disparities between different parts of the country and between central cities and suburbs. One way to bring about a greater equality is for federal and state governments to share their revenues with those cities that possess inferior tax bases. Reducing the inequality among different parts of the country is clearly a federal responsibility, which can be discharged either by providing grants-in-aid to the poorer cities or by directly subsidizing the poor.

Of the different intergovernmental fiscal instruments mentioned in Chapter 10, categorical grants-in-aid have benefits that are by far the most significant to urban governments. In the early 1970s, there has been much agitation for the federal government to provide unrestricted grants to cities, often associated with discussions about revenue sharing. Five criteria, not necessarily consistent with one another or of equal importance, can be applied to evaluate the desirability of different intergovernmental fiscal instruments: equity in income and service distribution, economic efficiency, economic growth, stability of revenue and economic activity, and autonomy and pass-through of funds. The complexity of such evaluation is dramatized by the fact that there are at least three different types of economic efficiency considerations, two relating to the effects of these instruments on the efficiency of the public sector, and one on the efficiency of the private sector.

These intergovernmental transfers can, and ordinarily do, affect the expenditures of the urban governments which receive them. Depending on circumstances, such aid can increase expenditures financed by recipient governments, distort the allocation of resources between the recipient government and the private sector, and distort the allocation of resources between different government services offered by the recipient urban government.

The United States is an exceedingly heterogeneous country, heavily industrialized and urbanized, and its society is very mobile. As a result, geographic income disparities exist, together with major benefit and cost spillovers, particularly in relation to such merit goods as welfare, education, and health services. A good case can therefore be made for the federal, and to some extent the state, government to assume increasing responsibility for the financing of welfare, education, and health services or to provide for revenue sharing whereby a fixed percentage of federal receipts would be earmarked for the support of urban governments. There is a tendency to reason that revenue sharing should provide unearmarked funds to urban governments, to be used by them as they see fit. The argument for block grants states that urban governments know best for what to use these funds. The opposing argument goes that such governments are not well equipped to assure the responsible use of these funds and that it is the responsibility of the federal government to assure that these funds are used not only efficiently but also consistently with the national interest.

In order to safeguard the efficient use of grants-in-aid to urban governments, the basis of awards might shift from a need or opportunity basis to a performance or accountability basis. Such a change is particularly promising for education, where recent research promises to make it possible to know with some accuracy how to achieve specific educational outcomes. For example, knowledge has been increasing about the frequency, duration, and intensity of particular educational activities needed to produce definite types of behavior in students of different ages, aptitudes, and interests. As a result, we may reach a stage where we can begin to determine cost-effective means to accomplish specific educational objectives. While state and federal funds could be used to assure minimum performance, educational improvements could be stimulated with the aid of state and (or) federal matching grants. The cost of educational improvement should take into consideration the service conditions of particular schools, i.e., whether the same improvements might be more expensive in one district than in another. Other services where grants-in-aid might be based on performance are higher education and health services.

Fiscal Imbalances and Pressures

Urban governments have been encountering serious fiscal pressures and imbalances. In the next section, we will consider the somewhat unique issues of the fiscal plight of central cities, a subset of problems facing urban governments in general.

All governments, to the extent that they rely on taxation to fund activities, must face the fact that the political process separately determines who benefits from specific public services and who pays for them. Reliance on taxation prevents governments from receiving price signals that could help make rational decisions about inputs and outputs. Fragmentation of governments in urban areas, together with massive commutation and great mobility, can produce major imbalances, under- or over-investments, and possibly an undesirable match between tax payment and service receipt.

Great concern is also caused by substantial differences between the income elasticity of tax revenues and that of expenditures in urban areas, or revenue elasticity and expenditure elasticity, for short. The magnitude of revenue elasticity is directly related to the jurisdiction's tax system, structure, and rates, which together determine the level of future revenue. There is a close relationship between revenue elasticity, tax progressivity, and tax yield. As a matter of fact, highly progressive tax sources tend to be revenue-elastic and produce large tax yields as income increases over time. Yet, as we have discussed above, local urban governments rely heavily on a relatively inelastic real property tax. Therefore, their tax yield increases tend to be substantially smaller than those of the federal government if personal income increases and the tax base and rate are not changed.

Expenditure elasticity presents a quite different picture. There are indications that expenditure elasticities of such urban government services as education, health services, and street services are substantially above +1. As a matter of fact, in recent years a change in mores has resulted in greatly increased expenditure elasticity for welfare services. Thus, while Americans were previously often ashamed of misfortune and concealed it, in recent years welfare payments are claimed as a matter of right.

In many urban public services the substitution of capital for labor is strictly limited, and therefore productivity increases are difficult to come by. William Baumol has observed that ". . . inherent in the technological structure of . . . [municipal government, education, the performing arts, and leisure activity] are forces working almost unavoidably for progressive and cumulative increases in the real costs incurred in supplying them." He designates many urban public services as technologically nonprogressive activities which, in Baumol's eyes, are the opposite of ". . . technologically progressive activities in which innovations, capital accumulation, and economies of large scale all make for a cumulative rise in output per man hour and . . . per unit only sporadic increases in productivity."[26]

Not only are many urban public sectors technologically nonprogressive, but in addition city charters frequently provide that municipal employees be paid wages similar to those paid workers in comparable positions in the private sector. Since money wage improvements in the private sector tend to move with or even outdistance productivity improvements, urban public sector cost per unit of output tends to rise more than that of the rest of the economy.

Since the mid-1960s, two new important power groups have emerged in American cities—the poor and municipal employees. The poor have often, even militantly, demanded more and better services; municipal employees have organized and bargained successfully for substantial wage and salary increases. Yet there are indications that productivity increases in urban government are distinctly smaller than either government wage and salary increases or productivity increases in industry.

These matters were not helped by a period of rapid inflation resulting from the Vietnam war. Not since 1948 have price increases been as rapid, thus putting particular strain on local urban governments; property tax receipts have not increased at an equal rate, partly because of delayed reassessment.

---

[26] William J. Baumol, "Macroeconomics of Unbalanced Growth: The Anatomy of Urban Crisis," *American Economic Review*, vol. 57 (June 1967), pp. 415–416.

A further source of concern has been the apparent fact that responsibilities for too many urban public services have been assigned to local governments, which cannot adequately finance many of these activities under present circumstances.

Finally, there are many imbalances resulting from governmental fragmentation of densely populated urban areas. In an age of industrialization and mobility, fragmentation is responsible for widespread cost and benefit spillovers. These and other issues are perhaps most effectively examined in relation to the central city and its surrounding suburbs. This we will do next.

III. THE FISCAL PLIGHT OF THE CENTRAL CITY

Particularly in the large central cities of America there is today a grave imbalance between people's aspirations for public services and their willingness and ability to pay for them—an imbalance that to some extent applies to private goods as well. Most likely, this imbalance is unusually painful today because in earlier decades central cities were well-to-do and thus could afford to meet reasonably high aspirations for services, whereas in recent years many have been unable to maintain existing or slowly rising service levels with their existing revenue structures or with feasible improvements in those structures.

Other than in terms of political boundaries, which are precisely defined, characterizing the central city and distinguishing between the central city and its suburbs within the metropolitan area is not easy. Typically, the central city is older, is larger in area, and continues to provide a variety of cultural and financial services for which a central location is advantageous, and it is no longer growing in terms of either population or area.

Unlike the central city, the area around it within the metropolitan area contains a large number of considerable diversity of governmental entities as well as a mix of land uses. Further, unlike the central city, the suburbs are growing, both in number of communities and in population. The result has been that, in terms of area, in the first sixty years of this century the relative size of the central city has fallen from two-thirds to one-third of the metropolitan area.

Reasons for the Central City's Fiscal Plight

Basically, there are three reasons, quite closely interrelated, that might explain why central cities are finding it increasingly difficult to finance urban public services:

1. Central cities are the havens of the poor and of disadvantaged minority groups, with the result that a slow-growing revenue base is combined with relatively high expenditure levels.

2. Large central cities have certain unique physical and organizational characteristics—aging structure; congestion, despite much land devoted to roads and streets; outmigration of high-income groups and of industry and commerce; diseconomies of scale; etc.—as a result of which the relative deterioration in the revenue base has not been accompanied by a decline in costs.
3. Governmental fragmentation under federalism has been producing major interjurisdictional spillovers due to commutation, migration, and fiscal interdependence, as well as spatial externalities associated with the movement of nonhuman resources. On balance, these spillovers have gone against the central cities.

Central Cities—Havens of the Poor.   To the extent that the central cities of America have become the homes of the poor, a significant impact on cities' revenues and expenditures is to be expected. On the revenue side, the effect of continued inmigration of poor people and outmigration of relatively more affluent people is to reduce the tax base. The prevalence of poor people in central cities has distinct cost and expenditure implications.

The 1970 census indicates that while the population of the United States as a whole increased by 12 percent since 1960, the population of metropolitan areas increased by 15 percent. However, within the metropolitan areas virtually all, if not all, population growth during the 1960s occurred in the suburbs.

These overall population changes have been accompanied by changes in the characteristics of the population.[27] For example:

About half of the nation's poor now live in metropolitan areas; in absolute numbers, twice as many poor people live in central cities than live in suburbs (our definition of poverty is that developed by the Social Security Administration in 1964).

Between 1959 and 1967, the proportion of people who are poor declined by almost half in the nation as a whole, but this decline has been slower in central cities. In relative terms there are twice as many poor living in central cities as in suburbs.

Median family income in central cities of metropolitan areas with more than 1 million residents in 1967 was 20 percent below the family income in the suburban rings of those cities.

In the thirty largest metropolitan areas in 1967 one-half of the central-city residents over the age of twenty-five had not completed high school, as compared with about one-third in their suburban rings.

[27] U.S. Bureau of the Census, *Trends in Social and Economic Conditions in Metropolitan and Nonmetropolitan Areas,* Special Studies, Series P-23, no. 33, 1970.

Negroes are sharply increasing their share of the population in the central cities of large metropolitan areas; but they are only slightly increasing their share in smaller metropolitan areas. Negroes now comprise one-fifth of all central-city residents and one-fourth of the central-city residents in metropolitan areas of over 1 million population.

The central city is often characterized as caught in a permanent downward trend in employment opportunities, business investments, and middle- and upper-income population, which is coupled with a permanent upward trend in low-income, disadvantaged residents.[28] In an examination of some fiscal implications of the fact that the central city houses many of the poor, particularly Negro and other immigrant poor, Lyle C. Fitch has pointed out, "Because of the high incidence of poverty and its corollaries of low education and skills . . . , immigration has added heavily to the burden of providing social services, education, public protection, and other poverty-necessitated benefits and services."[29]

Furthermore, as we have noted, the 1960s saw a major rise in the bargaining power of the poor, expressed in demands for increased public services. A logical deduction would be that the income elasticity of demand for urban government expenditure for the average central-city resident has increased over time and perhaps is larger than that for the suburban resident. The relatively high expenditure elasticity of central-city residents stands in distinct contrast to the city's relatively low income elasticity of revenue, particularly for the dominant tax base of central cities—the property tax. This imbalance is made possible because payment for services is separated from receipt of services. Expenditures by the nation's five largest cities with populations of over 1 million increased by 72 percent between 1962 and 1968. The largest increases were in education (104 percent), public welfare (211 percent), health and hospitals (102 percent), and police (53 percent). These four items combined rose by 114 percent, while expenditures in other categories rose by 36 percent.[30]

Further, partial evidence is presented by Henry Terrell, who finds that expenditures of central-city governments were relatively high, particularly if compared with revenue receipts.[31] In the early 1960s nonwhites—be-

[28] J. R. Meyer, J. F. Kain, and M. Wohl, *The Urban Transportation Problem* (Cambridge: Harvard, 1965); J. F. Kain, "The Distribution and Movement of Jobs and Industry," in J. Q. Wilson (ed.), *The Metropolitan Enigma* (Washington, D.C.: Chamber of Commerce of the United States, 1967); and E. Ginzberg et al., *Manpower Strategy for the Metropolis* (New York: Columbia University Press, 1968).
[29] Lyle C. Fitch, "Governing Megacentropolis: The People," *Public Administration Review*, vol. 30, no. 5 (September–October 1970), p. 483.
[30] Ibid., p. 484.
[31] Henry S. Terrell, "The Fiscal Impact of Nonwhites," in Werner Z. Hirsch et al., *Fiscal Pressures on the Central City: The Impact of Commuters, Nonwhites, and Overlapping Governments* (New York: Praeger, 1971).

cause they were poorer than whites—tended to raise educational expenditures, partly because of their much greater tendency to utilize public education. He also finds that as the central city's nonwhite population increases, police expenditures increase.

Physical and Organizational Matters. It is easy to argue that their tax base tends to be eroded as central cities age, as more and more of their land is devoted to streets, and as middle- and upper-income groups outmigrate together with some industry and commerce. However, it is much more difficult to decide what portion of the tax base erosion of central cities is due to their physical and organizational characteristics and what portion is due to inmigration and the presence of the poor. The same uncertainty holds for the impact of these characteristics on central-city costs and expenditures.

We would expect the high density of central cities to produce undesirable by-products. Thus, almost universal congestion, particularly at certain hours of the day, makes circulation more difficult and costly in central cities than in suburbia. Likewise, we would assume that the cost of providing police and fire protection is significantly increased because of high density in general and high-rise buildings in particular, as well as because of underemployed youths. Thus, for example, crime rates in the central cities of the thirty-seven largest metropolitan areas were on the average 100 percent greater than those in the suburbs.[32] Yet how can we disentangle the effects of the physical characteristics of cities on crime from the effects of poverty?

Callahan and Gabler found, using 1960–1967 data, that population density had a significantly positive relationship to per capita police expenditures.[33] Similar results in relation to density and such expenditures had been found by other research.[34]

Concerning organizational characteristics of cities, there appears to be some evidence that very large city governments suffer from diseconomies of scale.[35] Their size also makes them distant from their constituents, who are increasingly alienated and are seeking local participation in and control of government. Although there is no unequivocal evidence, it appears that in the absence of closer local participation and local control,

[32] Advisory Commission on Intergovernmental Relations, *Metropolitan Disparities—A Second Reading* (Washington, D.C.: Advisory Commission on Intergovernmental Relations, January 1970), Bulletin no. 70-1, p. 2.

[33] John J. Callahan and L. R. Gabler, "The Economics of Urban Police Protection: A Research Note" (unpublished manuscript, 1971), p. 7.

[34] Harvey Brazer, *City Expenditures in the United States* (New York: Bureau of Economic Research, 1959); Roy Bahl, *Metropolitan City Expenditures* (Lexington: University of Kentucky Press, 1968); Oliver Williams et al., *Suburban Differences and Metropolitan Policies* (Philadelphia: University of Pennsylvania Press, 1965).

[35] Hirsch, *The Economics of State and Local Government,* op. cit., pp. 176–181.

the population has become increasingly reluctant to be taxed by large urban governments. Furthermore, our large central cities are increasingly subject to strong wage demands from bargaining representatives of municipal employees. They provide, under conditions of great dependence and interdependence, services for which there are few substitutes. Thus, for example, over the past decade city employees in New York City have won a 49 percent average salary increase, while the cost of living has increased by only about 20 percent.[36]

Governmental Fragmentation under Federalism and Spillovers.   Metropolitan areas are fragmented into a large number of independent jurisdictions. Thus, for example, the Chicago metropolitan area is composed of 6 counties, 114 townships, 250 municipalities, 327 school districts, and 501 special-purpose districts. There are 1,198 separate units of government, or one local government for every three square miles, or one for every 5,550 inhabitants. Some of these governments merely abate mosquitoes or light the streets; others do nothing at all.

Such fragmentation causes large-scale interjurisdictional spillovers which are said to occur whenever the revenues and expenditures of one government unit are directly affected by decisions of one or more firms, households, or governments in another jurisdiction. Spillovers can be into the central city, out of it, or in both directions. These spillovers are mainly due to commutation, migration, and fiscal interdependence. Although they are interrelated, each type of spillover deserves separate attention, to see how it affects the fiscal health of central cities. In addition there are spatial externalities associated with the movement of nonhuman resources.

Commutation spillovers.   The "central-city exploitation thesis"—that residents of the suburbs benefit from central-city services but do not compensate the central city either for the basic costs incurred by the city or for the values to the suburbanites of the benefits received—is directly related to commutation spillovers. Commutation spillovers can be related to working, shopping, and recreation trips between the central city and its suburbs as well as to pass-throughs. As a result of these trips, benefits and costs can accrue to the central city and to its suburbs.

A number of studies, starting in the early 1950s, have attempted to test this thesis.[37] More recently, William Neenan has tested the exploitation

---

[36] Two reasons why such increases may not be "excessive" are that at the beginning of the decade city employees may have been at a relatively low wage rate; and that a productivity improvement of 30 percent per decade is not unusual, at least in the private sector.

[37] For a review of studies by Amos H. Hawley, Julius Margolis, Harvey S. Brazer, and James M. Banovetz, see Werner Z. Hirsch, "The Fiscal Plight: Causes and Remedies," in Werner Z. Hirsch et al., *Fiscal Pressures on the Central City: The Impact of Commuters, Nonwhites, and Overlapping Governments* (New York: Praeger, 1971), pp. 18–19.

thesis in regard to Detroit, employing a willingness-to-pay model to evaluate public services. A willingness-to-pay index of government benefits is used as an alternative to the measurement of benefits by their costs. Assuming that voters are maximizers, he examines voting data, since they should offer insight into the pattern of perceived benefits and costs of various expenditures and tax decisions and thus suggest normative guidelines for metropolitan public finance. Neenan stipulates a utility function for citizens in the public sector that relates utility to disposable income and public sector goods and services.[38] He concludes, "In all instances the revenue flows to Detroit fail to compensate fully for the public sector benefits flowing from Detroit to the municipalities. Consequently, all the municipalities enjoy a welfare gain from Detroit through the public sector ranging from $1.73 per capita for Highland Park to $12.58 per capita for Birmingham."[39]

Phillip Vincent looks upon commutation in metropolitan areas as having mainly four purposes—working, shopping, recreation, and pass-through.[40] In these activities commuters may benefit the central city through increased tax collections, state and nonstate intergovernmental aid, and central-city user charges, as well as by increased personal income of central-city residents. Work commutation into the city, in conjunction with either technology changes and (or) demand increases for goods or services in which the central city has a comparative locational advantage, can lead to the construction of additional commercial and industrial buildings. This in itself increases the demand for workers.

Commuting for shopping purposes produces direct additional returns to central-city businesses through increased sales (and, in turn, increased sales tax revenue to the city government) and to central-city property owners. If a central city is attractive for shopping, demand of retailers and their suppliers for central-city property is generated (which, in turn, can increase the city's property tax receipts).

Phillip Vincent finds that in 1960, central cities that attracted relatively substantial numbers of workers and shoppers from their suburbs incurred significantly higher per capita city government expenditures. However, at the same time, workers commuting into the city had a statistically significant positive, though weak, impact on the per capita income of central-city residents. This personal income increase for central-city residents, associated with increased commutation, appears to more than compensate for the additional municipal costs of serving commuters. More generally, the central city gains through workers commuting in from the suburbs, by in-

---

[38] William B. Neenan, "Suburban-Central City Exploitation Thesis: One City's Tale," *National Tax Journal*, vol. 23, no. 2 (June 1970), pp. 119–129.
[39] Ibid., p. 139.
[40] Phillip E. Vincent, "The Fiscal Impact of Commuters," in Werner Z. Hirsch et al., *Fiscal Pressures on the Central City: The Impact of Commuters, Nonwhites, and Overlapping Governments* (New York: Praeger, 1971).

creases in central-city personal income and nonresidential real property tax revenue, while statistically significant positive effects of sales by central-city retailers to suburban residents are associated with increases in central-city nonproperty tax revenue. If all these factors are combined, excepting some results from nonstate intergovernmental revenues, statistically significant gains accure to the central city which by far exceed the costs associated with commutation. A medium estimate of both total taxes and expenditures suggests that the central-city government receives a per capita net gain of $6 from both types of commuters combined, although it apparently loses in relation to shoppers and gains greatly from commuting workers.

Migration spillovers.   Migration can affect the fiscal health of the central city in a number of ways; it transfers the human tax base and with it educational and health capital from one jurisdiction to another. As a result, some costs and benefits resulting from a public service provided in one jurisdiction are ultimately realized by residents of another. For example, if a student educated in the central city outmigrates, the central city incurs a loss of future tax base, and therefore a benefit spillout has occurred. But clearly the outmigrant not only stops paying taxes to the central city but also stops requiring services. Thus the spillovers due to migration must be considered from the revenue as well as the expenditure side.

There is considerable evidence that central cities have experienced inmigration that is, on balance, composed of many relatively poor people, and outmigration that, on balance, is composed of many members of middle- and upper-income groups. The importance of poverty and the impact of poor people on the fiscal health of central cities as shown by Henry Terrell have been discussed in the section on poverty. Furthermore, a study by Ronald Crowley concludes that internal migration to the cities in the 1959–1960 period has imposed heavy financial burdens on them. In the short run it poses serious difficulties because the city's outmigrants are on balance more well-to-do than its inmigrants. The 1955–1960 migration into cities in the United States, according to Crowley, has been selective of the "inferior elements," i.e., inmigrants as a group tended to have such characteristics that economically desirable features were underrepresented and economically undesirable features were overrepresented.[11] In only two

[11] Ronald W. Crowley, *Internal Migration: A Study of Costs Imposed on Cities in the United States* (unpublished doctoral dissertation, Duke University, 1968). Migrants from rural areas were a significant proportion of total inmigration. Only 30 percent of the total population was classified as nonurban in 1960, yet in only one of the twenty-five cities examined was a smaller percentage of its inmigrants so classified. While these percentage differences do not imply that inmigration from nonurban areas has been increasing, a decrease in inmigration might be expected in view of the declining nonurban proportion of the total population.

out of ninety-four cities do inmigrants impose a smaller net cost than do the residents of the receiving area.[42]

Finally, an empirical study of public education cost and benefit spillovers of Clayton, within the St. Louis metropolitan area, in 1959–1960 bears out the fact that large net cost spillins into the central city, i.e., the City of St. Louis, occur as a result of migration as well as of fiscal interdependence.[43]

But if instead of taking a short-run, basically one-period, view of the effects of migration, we are concerned with its long-run impact, then we see migration serving as an equilibrating mechanism that tends to equalize economic opportunity among different parts of the country. An analysis based on such a long-run view has been undertaken by Richard Wertheimer and is summarized in Chapter 5, p. 143.

Thus for a central city that incurs large-scale in- and outmigration, serious short-run fiscal difficulties are likely to result if the net "inferior" inmigration increases rapidly. Given time, this problem may become less severe or even fade away if the relative importance of "inferior" inmigration does not change over time. The inmigrant after a while, i.e., after about five years, tends to resemble in earnings the average resident of the central city with similar characteristics.

Fiscal interdependence spillovers.   Since the central city and its suburbs are closely interrelated in terms of both tax and expenditure decisions, cost spillovers can result. Cost spillovers are related to the revenues that finance the jurisdiction's public sector activities. Different revenue sources can have different spatial tax incidence patterns, and their analysis helps to place the ultimate cost burden. The net amount of the central city's resources apportioned to its public sector is determined by the type and level of taxes levied on its taxpayers, their spatial burden pattern, and the proportion of local tax revenues that is spent on public services provided within the city's boundaries. Together these factors determine the net balance between the ultimate resource costs or tax burden of the central city and the amount of resources ultimately utilized for the provision of public services. The latter is the expenditure incidence.

A special type of fiscal interdependence exists when a higher level of government, such as a county, performs certain services for only some parts of its jurisdiction, such as unincorporated urban areas, or sells services below cost to some of its municipalities, while levying taxes on all of the taxpayers in its jurisdiction. When an urban county like Los Angeles

[42] Ibid., pp. 153–155 and 181–185.
[43] Werner Z. Hirsch et al., *Spillover of Public Education Costs and Benefits* (Los Angeles: University of California Institute of Government and Public Affairs, 1969), pp. 301–303.

County pursues such a policy, there can be a tendency for central-city residents to subsidize those unincorporated areas and suburban municipalities that contract with the county government for services.

Let us examine both types of fiscal interdependence spillovers. To the extent that some of the central city's public services are subsidized (as in the case of education) by state and federal governments that have progressive tax systems, poorer central cities will gain more or lose less from net spillins than will the richer suburbs. This position is substantiated in an empirical study of the suburban Clayton School District, which finds that the public education net spillover is generally consistent with the nation's progressive fiscal policy.[44]

Specifically, the study examined six areas: Clayton, the rest of St. Louis County, the City of St. Louis, the rest of St. Louis SMSA, the rest of Missouri, and the rest of the United States. Clayton has had a per capita income higher than that of the other five areas. Clayton incurred net benefit spillouts in relation to four of the five areas. These net spillouts amounted to $1,013,000 in relation to the rest of the United States, $874,000 in relation to the rest of Missouri, $389,000 in relation to the City of St. Louis, and $177,000 in relation to the rest of the SMSA. In relation to the fifth area, St. Louis County, a very small net benefit spillin of $8,000 occurred. By and large, the poorer the area, the greater the net benefit spillin.

As an example of the second type of fiscal interdependence spillover, we point to a study of the Los Angeles County Sheriff's Department as to the allocation of expenditures and benefits in a system of overlapping governments.[45] The findings indicate that there is significant subsidization of law enforcement services to the unincorporated portion of Los Angeles County out of tax revenue collected countywide. Los Angeles County can improve service coordination and help take advantage of economies of scale in the production of local government services for a metropolitan area containing many small local governments. In 1968, thirty cities chose, for example, to contract with the Los Angeles County Sheriff's Department for law enforcement services rather than to provide these services themselves. There is evidence that in Los Angeles County law enforcement services are sold to contracting cities (or provided to unincorporated areas) below the marginal cost of providing them; the result is a subsidy to the contracting cities (or unincorporated areas) at the expense of cities that maintain independent police departments at their own expense.[46]

[44] Hirsch et al., op. cit., p. 191.
[45] Donald C. Shoup and Arthur Rosett, "Fiscal Exploitation by Overlapping Governments," in Werner Z. Hirsch et al., *Fiscal Pressures on the Central City: The Impact of Commuters, Nonwhites, and Overlapping Governments* (New York: Praeger, 1971).
[46] Shoup and Rosett estimate that in 1967–1968 the subsidy for law enforcement was about $6.1 million to the unincorporated areas of Los Angeles County and $5.1 million to the cities that contract for police services from the Sheriff's Department.

In summary, if we include public education and welfare services (which benefit from major state and federal subsidies) in the central-city public sector, net spillovers due to fiscal interdependence are likely to favor the central city.

Nonhuman movement externalities. Nonhuman resources, also, move into and out of the central city, and by so doing impose differential costs and benefits on its residents. Perhaps the most significant externalities are the various forms of water and air pollution. While there is little empirical evidence about the geographical balance of the different types of pollution, we can deduce some tentative conclusions.

Because of the high density and heavy automobile traffic, particularly in the downtown area, of central cities it is likely that, on balance, they are imposing heavy externalities on residents of suburbs. This is the result not only of high concentrations of cars using the central city, but also of traffic congestion, which forces cars to stop and go and to move slowly; as a result their exhausts emit tremendous quantities of pollutants. Yet many of the car users are residents of suburbia. The picture in relation to water pollution is less clear, although there can be little doubt that serious costs are spilled out to downstream towns. To the extent that many polluting industries are located in the central city, they are likely to pollute rivers, lakes, and oceans and impose burdens on suburban areas. However, the situation in some metropolitan areas is just the reverse, in that water pollution may originate outside the city. The residents of central city and of the suburbs are also likely to affect one another by noise pollution. This particularly holds for airport noises, which commonly originate outside the central city, where most large airports are located.[47]

Potential Remedies

The preceding section indicates that there are disproportionately many more poor people in central cities than in suburbia. These poor are a major factor, perhaps *the* major factor, in the central city's fiscal plight. The physical and organizational characteristics of central cities have tended to retard revenue and stimulate expenditures disproportionately. Concerning the impact of governmental fragmentation, migration spillovers and fiscal interdependency spillovers due to overlapping governments appear to go against the central city; other fiscal interdependency spillovers appear to favor the city; evidence about commutation spillovers is contradictory; and

---

Since most of the people in Los Angeles County live in the central city, central-city residents paid most of the subsidy.

[47] However, attention must be paid to the fact that while the airport may be located outside the central city, it may be heavily used directly or indirectly by central-city residents.

the direction of nonhuman resource spillovers depends on the location of the major polluters in each area.

Thus while we have at best partial answers as to what is primarily responsible for the fiscal plight of the central city, it appears that the presence of disproportionately many poor people dominates all other considerations. While an attack on the poverty in central cities can succeed only if we maintain full employment, balanced growth, and reasonable price stability in the national economy, a variety of more specific programs can be tried. The same holds for improving organizational arrangements, including better matching between revenues and expenditures in the presence of large-scale governmental fragmentation.

For example, fiscal interdependency spillovers due to overlapping governments can be regulated by requiring county governments to compensate cities that provide their own services, through tax rebates. Likewise, the tendency of counties to perform contract services at cut-rate charges, in order to build empires, can be counteracted by the establishment of county commissions that not only set contract fees but also supervise the level and quality of contract services delivered to municipalities.

Furthermore, in those situations where the suburbs do heavily exploit the central city, municipal income taxes, which are usually in the form of payroll taxes, might be imposed. Such commuter taxes, which today are levied by more than 3,000 jurisdictions, place a tax on earnings in the jurisdictions in which they occur.

The above are merely a few examples. The package of remedial steps that is chosen should focus on the fact that the central city has been burdened by a disproportionately large number of poor Americans. Therefore, perhaps policy remedies should be more people-, i.e., poor-oriented, than location-, i.e., city-oriented, particularly in the long run. High priority might be given to policies that will bring about a greater similarity of poor-rich and black-brown-white mixes in the suburbs and in the central cities.

IV. GOVERNMENTAL INTERVENTION

Urban governments impose various regulations to provide an environment and "rules of the game" within which households, industry, commerce, and governments can well perform their activities. Regulation—although it does not produce as tangible a product as does transportation, water delivery, or refuse collection—can have a major effect on production, costs, and supply and demand for the private as well as the public sector. As a result, it can change benefit-cost relations as perceived by private and public decision makers and thus affect welfare. We will concentrate on regulation of land uses, since certain aspects of regulating transportation have been taken up in Chapter 4. While urban governments also regulate some other activities, such regulation neither constitutes a unique urban problem nor is of major magnitude. The exception, to some extent, relates to air and water pollution. This issue will be taken up separately, since their control can take forms other than regulation.

The importance of regulation can be demonstrated in relation to its impact on decentralization and urban sprawl. For example, Irving Hoch identified four government activities that can lead to decentralization; three of the activities are regulatory in nature. They are zoning of building height limits, zoning prohibition of mixed land uses, and pricing of the infrastructure.[48]

Government can use a variety of legal instruments to regulate land uses and abate pollution; they differ mainly in their comprehensiveness and definiteness. The most comprehensive instrument of regulation is outright government ownership, though it is more frequently used in relation to the transportation-communications network than to land use and pollution. The second instrument is the legislative directive, which can take the form of a law that applies specifically to the operation or performance of private firms (e.g., utility lines must be underground) or that is general (e.g., a pollution control law prohibiting the burning of certain types of fuel). The third approach to regulation is through a commission, a quasi-legislative-judicial-administrative body, the members of which are given some discretion in establishing and changing rules. The commission approach is intended to bring the public interest to bear on the issue without involving the government in the ownership or management of the operation. This approach usually is supplementary to the initial legislative authority. Finally, a government can use a variety of indirect or informal controls, e.g., taxation, subsidies, depreciation allowances, and master planning.

In addition to examining governmental intervention in relation to urban land use and pollution abatement, we will pay attention to an internal problem of urban governments—labor relations. Municipal employees perform certain essential services of which urbanites must be assured. Their delivery affects the utility functions of most urbanites and the production functions of most firms in cities. Yet municipal employees must be assured of sufficient bargaining power to be treated about as well as workers in the private sector. This subject will be discussed last.

Land-use Regulation[49]

Considering instruments used to regulate land uses, we can begin with a master plan that is implemented with the aid of a city zoning ordinance. By "zoning" we mean:

> The division of land into districts having different regulations . . . such

[48] Irving Hoch, *The Economics of Vertical Transportation, Air Rights, and Land Use* (Washington, D.C.: Resources for the Future, 1968), p. 2.
[49] This section draws heavily on chap. 10 of Werner Z. Hirsch, *Economics of State and Local Government,* op. cit.

regulations shall be made in accordance with a comprehensive plan and designed to lessen congestion in the streets; to secure safety from fire, panic, and other dangers; to promote health and the general welfare; to provide adequate light and air; to prevent the overcrowding of land; to avoid undue concentration of population; to facilitate the adequate provision of transportation, water, sewage, schools, parks and other public requirements. Such regulations shall be made with reasonable consideration, among other things, of the character of the district and its peculiar suitability for particular uses, and with a view to conserving the value of buildings and encouraging the most appropriate use of land throughout such municipalities.[50]

Zoning can be used for such diverse purposes as enforcement of building codes, regulation of factory operations, restriction of floor space relative to site area, and control of population density. The unique feature of zoning, compared with other municipal regulations, is its discriminatory nature. Different zoning regulations apply in different parts or districts of a community.[51] The zone or district approach of the United States is based on two notions: (1) like users belong together, and such groupings are "natural" and reasonable, and (2) certain areas of the community, because of terrain or location within the community, are most appropriate to a particular land use.[52] Municipal zoning relies on three zoning instruments —zone change, zone variance, and conditional-use permit.

Regulation by urban governments is designed to promote what is often loosely referred to as the "general welfare." Authorization for this function is provided by the 1928 Standard City Planning Enabling Act of the U.S. Department of Commerce. The act states: "The plan shall be made with the general purpose of guiding and accomplishing a coordinated, adjusted, and harmonious development of the municipality and its environs which will . . . best promote health, safety, morals, order, convenience, prosperity, and general welfare, as well as efficiency and economy in the process of development. . . ."[53]

What is meant by promoting an area's general welfare? Seeking to attain a resource allocation efficiency criterion is not the same as promoting the general welfare, for it promotes only one aspect of the general welfare. To illustrate this point: It might be highly efficient to allow the old or disabled members of our society to starve to death, or to endow 1 percent of the population with 99 percent of the wealth of the economy, but neither

[50] Edward M. Bassett, *Zoning* (New York: Russell Sage, 1940), pp. 52–53.
[51] Zoning originated in the early days of the Industrial Revolution in Germany and Sweden. The first American zoning ordinance was enacted in New York City in 1916 to keep glue factories and other dirty, noisy, or bustling plants away from residential areas and retailing centers.
[52] Jacob B. Ukeles, *The Consequences of Municipal Zoning* (Washington, D. C.: Urban Land Institute, 1964), pp. 28–29.
[53] U.S. Department of Commerce, *A Standard City Planning Enabling Act*, secs. 6, 7 (1928).

would promote the general welfare. Equitable distribution of income, economic stability, and economic growth are objectives to be considered as well as efficiency.

The four objectives mentioned will conflict when an economy attempts their simultaneous achievement. The widespread conflict between efficiency and equity goals is dominant in any economic consideration of regulation in general and land-use planning in particular.

The main concern of regulation by urban governments should be economic efficiency. As was mentioned earlier, the federal government holds major, if not exclusive, responsibility for the attainment of distributional, growth, and stability objectives. Given ideal assumptions and definitions, the attainment of economic efficiency would be tantamount to the maximization of aggregate income with a given set of resources and distribution of income. Aggregate income would include items that are intangible in their financial value, since by their nature they do not pass through the market.

There are several defects in our economy that prevent the attainment of efficiency—most noticeably, externalities, which were defined earlier. Coping with externalities is of particular concern to land-use regulation. It is important to find institutional devices by which the impact of the externalities will be compensated for or prevented. Thus, land-use planning and zoning are founded on the necessity of correcting for externality effects that are not handled adequately in any marketplace. Were a marketplace able to accomplish the appropriate corrections for externality effects, there would be no need for land-use regulations. It is the externality problem, perhaps more than any other, that brings the land-use regulator into the allocative process. Land-use planning and zoning must be designed to ensure that private and public decision makers act in such a manner that the external effects produce the largest net social benefits for the community. Or, in negative terms, the land-use regulator primarily seeks to prevent potentially harmful steps that would reduce the income (broadly construed) of the community. In short, zoning can be looked upon as a government intervention to correct a market defect.

The land-use regulator can adjust external effects in various ways. One method is to intervene in the ongoing interplay of market forces in order to try to create an environment in which efficiency can be attained. Zoning ordinances, compulsory dedication requirements, and urban renewal are examples of this method.

Zoning in the United States derives its legal basis from the police powers of state government. Unlike laws based on the right of eminent domain, zoning regulations do not require compensation for losses in property value or income to private individuals. Since zoning can make one person better off at the expense of another person, without the latter being compensated, zoning tends to defy Pareto optimality conditions.

Now to consider some of the effects of rezoning a district from business-residential to exclusively residential use. In this connection it should be remembered that zoning ordinances can control the location in which specified activities or establishments are permitted (and from which others are excluded), the location in which specified population densities and floor space are permitted, and the location in which a certain level of bulk and spacing of structures is permitted.[54]

However, zoning regulations cannot be retroactive: a land use existing prior to the enactment of the regulation cannot be changed. Businesses located in the area prior to the rezoning remain there, on a "nonconforming use" basis. Therefore, if the nonconforming uses (e.g., businesses) are functionally related to the dominant activity (e.g., residences), zoning does not eliminate the scattered use. Instead, zoning gives monopoly status to the existing scattered businesses because additional similar activities are not allowed to locate in the same zone. Thus, the nonconforming uses (e.g., businesses) tend to be perpetuated, and the monopoly tends to reduce the welfare of the area.

Increasing the minimum lot size per dwelling unit or reducing the maximum number of families per dwelling unit for a residential zone has similar effects on an area. A short-run shortage in residential land as well as urban decentralization could result from either measure.

Limiting the number of stories and amount of floor space for an office building, relative to site area, in a business zone might turn out to be inconsistent with economic efficiency and could adversely affect the area's welfare. The same result could come from limiting the level of smoke, noise, and vibration of factories in an industrial zone. Increasing the regulation of "nuisances" could increase the cost of factory production and make the area less attractive to industry. This in turn could reduce per capita income and decrease employment and economic growth. On the other hand, the amenities of life might be enhanced, and this might outweigh the other effects.

Finally, let us consider zoning vacant land for future industrial use. This is frequently done by designating an area as an industrial park. City planners argue for industrial parks on the grounds that the city will run out of land suitable for industrial use in the future. However, this type of ordinance can constrain the land market's choices for use of the land, and the planners' argument assumes a major imperfection in the price mechanism of the land market. Without zoning constraints and market imperfections, land with a higher value in an industrial use than in its present use will be bid away from the existing use.

Thus, zoning as a resource allocator has advantages and disadvantages. The great advantage of zoning is its ability to correct market defects that

[54] Ukeles, op. cit., p. 32.

result from externalities. It is on the basis of this feature that zoning has been advocated.

However, zoning can also interfere with efficiency. For example, since zoning regulations cannot be retroactive, zoning gives rise to geographic monopoly of existing businesses. By limitation of the number of stories and total floor space relative to site area, constraints are imposed upon the production function of builders, possibly preventing them from building the most efficient buildings. By segregating into one geographic area industries that create external diseconomies, zoning can increase the overall cost of external diseconomies. Zoning ordinances, by allowing zone variances, tend to have associated with them bribery and graft, which in turn reduce respect for local government officials and laws.[55] Finally, there are administrative costs of creating and enforcing zoning ordinances and there are time costs of property owners who have to wait for zone variance permits.

We must keep in mind the fact that zoning and rezoning take place as parts of a political process. Take the case of a single-family residential district in which some property owners seek to buy out residences and construct commercial improvements. This requires a zone change that is likely to result in external diseconomies for those property owners who retain residential housing in the area. Facing the conflict of interests, the public officials can vote for or against granting variances or completely rezoning the district. The greater the number of property owners who resist a zone change and the more political power they can bring to bear, the more costly it is for the public officials to vote for the zone change.

If, for example, the area had multifamily apartment buildings instead of single-family residences, and all property owners favored replacing apartment houses with business buildings, the officials might face a more difficult decision. The owners are few in number and might not even be living in the district. However, the renters might take a very negative view, if for no other reason than that moving is costly. The more renters with a negative view, the less rewarding a zone change will be for the public official.

Finally, consider the case in which a land developer has constructed and sold single-family residences on half of his land, while an identical second half has not yet been developed. Suddenly, the undeveloped part is facing a zone change as part of the adoption of a new master plan. The land developer may tend to favor keeping the second half zoned for the same use as the developed half. However, residents of the developed half will tend to favor upgrading, by stricter restrictions than those imposed on their property, so that they will benefit from higher-quality residences adjacent to their own. The votes of residents who would benefit from external

---

[55] Not infrequently in American politics, a mayor apparently appoints persons to the board of zoning adjustment after they have made contributions to the mayor's campaign fund.

economies will outnumber the vote of the developer by far, and unless the public official can visualize other rewards such as campaign contributions, he will tend to "overzone" the undeveloped half of the parcel, i.e., give it a higher zoning classification than is warranted. The issue would be more complicated if the developed half had multifamily apartments instead of single-family residences. Tenants would not be so directly concerned about property value effects, but instead would be concerned about the possibility that overzoning might result in higher rents but not necessarily in nicer future neighbors, since tenants will tend to be shorter-term residents of the neighborhood.

Abating Urban Pollution

Contrary to previous American experience, some resources now appear to be in limited supply, particularly in cities. Thus, clean air, clean water, and tranquility, and rapid movement on sidewalks, streets, and highways are becoming increasingly scarce. Instead we increasingly encounter air and water pollution and massive congestion in cities—all the consequence of modern, large-scale consumption and production activities under conditions of great density and interdependence. Since congestion was discussed in Chapter 4, only infrequent reference will be made to it here.

There are basically two types of pollution, both quite common in a densely populated, industrialized, and mechanized urban society. One class of pollution relates to the fact that the capacity of the environment to assimilate residuals is limited. Thus certain production and consumption processes are at variance with the fundamental physical law of conservation of mass.[56] The limited capacity of the environment to assimilate residuals is exacerbated by the prevalence of externalities. One person's use of such natural resources as water and air can inflict damage on other people who are in no position to secure compensation.

The second type of pollution does not involve a materials disposal problem and therefore does not involve a nonreplenishable resource. Noise pollution and congestion are of this sort and result mainly from improper resource allocation and rationing associated with externalities.

Although the assimilative capacity of air and water has become a scarce resource, they continue to be provided free of charge as common property to anyone with waste to dispose of. Under such circumstances air and water resources are likely to be overused because of biased incentives. For example, while each of the millions of cars contributes its small bit of the Los Angeles and New York smog, and each driver may suffer from watering eyes, coughs, and perhaps even lung disease due to exhaust emissions, any one driver's responsibility is negligible. Likewise, because high-

[56] Allan V. Kneese et al., *Economics and the Environment: A Materials Balance Approach* (Baltimore: Johns Hopkins, 1970), pp. 4 and 5.

sulfur fuel is cheaper than low-sulfur fuel to produce, the former is burned in many cities and sulfur dioxide wastes are dumped into the air. Although residents pay in terms of damage to plants, human health, and painted and metal surfaces, only part of the full social costs become private costs, and therefore the influence of costs on private decisions is distorted. The same is true for upstream factories that deposit waste in a river or raise its temperature. This is virtually costless to the upstream factory but involves major costs of water purification downstream when a city wants to use the same water for drinking or recreation.

The close relation between pollution and urban settings is recognized by Allan Kneese, who states, "These external diseconomies are quantitatively negligible in a low-population, economically undeveloped setting, but they become progressively (nonlinearly) more important as the population rises and the level of output increases (i.e., as the natural reservoirs of dilution and assimilative capacity become exhausted)."[57] Speaking merely of air and water pollution, he offers some admittedly crude estimates of the external costs associated with residuals discharge, surmising that these costs are "already in the tens of billions annually."[58]

This estimate is confirmed by the 1971 report of the White House Council on Environmental Quality. According to the report, in 1968 air pollution damage totaled $16 billion: $6 billion in health costs, $5 billion in damage to crops and other vegetation, and $5 billion as a result of lowered property values in areas with heavy air pollution. The cost to control environmental pollution over a five-year period ending in 1975 is estimated to amount to $105 billion.[59]

Externalities and pollution associated with them can also be appraised in a different manner, as is done by James Buchanan and Gordon Tullock. They conclude that as economic development proceeds, "congestion" tends to replace "cooperation" as the underlying motive behind collective action. In short, controlling external diseconomies tends to overshadow cooperation designed to help realize external economies.[60]

Some significant questions face officials concerned with pollution abatement: What level of pollution is socially acceptable? What approach is likely to achieve this standard and do so efficiently and equitably? How can costs be allocated fairly to those who contribute to air pollution?[61] We consider these questions after briefly reviewing major pollution phenomena.

[57] Ibid., p. 14.
[58] Ibid., p. 6.
[59] Council on Environmental Quality, *Environmental Quality, Second Annual Report* (Washington, D.C.: U.S. Government Printing Office, 1971).
[60] James W. Buchanan and Gordon Tullock, "Public and Private Interaction under Reciprocal Externality," in Julius Margolis (ed.), *The Public Economy of Urban Communities* (Baltimore: Johns Hopkins, 1965), pp. 52–73.
[61] Ronald G. Ridker, *Economic Costs of Air Pollution* (New York: Praeger, 1967), p. 1.

Pollution Characteristics.   We referred above to two classes of pollution, those with and those without materials disposal problems. They have in common externalities, in densely populated, industrialized, and urbanized societies.

Water pollution results from a variety of causes, including complex changes in receiving waters. Pollutants that enter watercourses result from man's domestic and industrial activities and are mainly of the conservative and nonconservative types. Conservative pollutants are not altered by the biological processes that occur in natural waters; they are mainly inorganic chemicals. Nonconservative pollutants are affected by biological, chemical, and physical phenomena; by far the most widespread source of nonconservative pollutants is domestic sewage.[62]

Air pollution results mainly from manufacturing, combustion of fuels, incineration, and transportation, with perhaps 60 percent emitted into the air by transport vehicles. Air-polluting substances are mainly of two classes —stable primary pollutants that are not changed in the air, i.e., dust, smoke, gas fumes, and droplets, and pollutants produced by photochemical or physiochemical interactions between primary pollutants in the air.

In terms of physical and chemical classification of air pollutants, six stand out—carbon monoxide, sulfur oxides, nitrogen oxides, hydrocarbons, particulates, and photochemical smog.[63] Air pollution varies from city to city, depending on sources of pollutants, weather conditions, and local topography. According to George Hagevik: "At one extreme is Los Angeles, where a large percentage of the air pollution is photochemical smog caused by automobile emissions. Somewhere near the opposite end of the continuum is New York City, where sulfur dioxide and particulate matter are major air pollutants and the contribution of automobile emissions to ambient air pollution is judged to be, in a relative sense, less significant."[64]

Noise pollution too has numerous causes, e.g., heavy car and truck traffic on highways, earthmoving equipment, power-driven factory equipment, and airplanes. It has distinctly damaging consequences. Noise over 70 decibels begins to stimulate the sympathetic nervous system, causing a temporary decrease in the size of blood vessels, which in turn sends adrenalin to the blood, leading to the contraction of muscles, an increase in the pulse rate and breathing rate, and irritation of the pupils of the eyes. Prolonged exposure to noise at 80 decibels causes hearing damage.

Air pollution, particularly in large cities, differs in major respects from water pollution. Although meteorologists build mathematical models of the atmosphere, they find movements of air much less predictable than

---

[62] Allan V. Kneese, *Water Pollution: Economic Aspects and Research Needs* (Baltimore: Resources for the Future, 1962), pp. 5–7.
[63] George H. Hagevik, *Decision-Making in Air Pollution Control* (New York: Praeger, 1970), pp. 3–5.
[64] Ibid., p. 4.

those of watersheds. Also, the number of polluters of the air is usually much larger than the number of waste sources along a watercourse. Robert Solow points out:

> Air pollution is rather like automobile congestion. Just as each driver in a traffic jam is inflicting delay costs on every other driver (as well as himself), so is every polluter of the air in a city polluting everyone else (including himself), and inflicting costs on the property and the health of everyone else. . . . For this reason, it is much more difficult to imagine optimum planning of pollution abatement in a city than to imagine it in a river basin. A system of effluent charges would involve metering altogether too many emissions: from industrial stacks, from domestic heating, from automobiles, from office buildings, and from public utilities. Moreover, the seriousness of air pollution often depends on photochemical reactions in the atmosphere which cannot be directly connected with any particular polluter . . . urban air pollution presents difficulties because it could be inefficient to treat it in isolation from other modes of waste disposal. A city could easily clean its air by disposing of most of its wastes in water; or it could just as easily protect its water by concentrating its wastes and incinerating the residues. Nor can the burden be thrown entirely on solid-waste disposal, because that has become an equally costly and difficult process in most areas of dense population. Rational management of waste materials in a city will require something more complicated than a model of a single river basin.[65]

Estimating the Social Costs of Pollution. In the hope of considering efficient and equitable choices for pollution abatement, we need information on the costs of pollution or the benefits that can be expected from pollution control measures. Specifically, we are interested in cost (or benefit) information in order—

1. To determine the socially desirable level of pollution control, i.e., select controls that maximize net social benefits; and
2. To determine the marginal social cost a pollution source imposes on others so that appropriate effluent fees can be established.

In these efforts it is essential to have information on the causal links between controls and the ensuing benefits, and (or) the costs associated with different pollution levels. Specific economic consequences—benefits—of air pollution control relate to health, property, and aesthetic considerations. There is very little empirical information about these causal links, making cost or benefit estimations very difficult at best. Matters are further complicated by the fact that combating, for example, air pollution can reduce resource use for treating the sick, cleaning windows, painting

[65] Robert M. Solow, "The Economist's Approach to Pollution and Its Control," *Science,* vol. 173 (Aug. 6, 1971), pp. 501 and 502.

houses, etc., and yet, at the same time, it can also increase resources used to build devices and engage in activities for pollution reduction.

Ronald Ridker has made an effort to provide some estimates of the economic costs of air pollution.[66] Major emphasis is placed on the effects on health, soiling and materials damage, and property values. A number of studies have been made to estimate the effect of air pollution on house values, and while most of them have indicated a statistically significant negative relationship, a recent empirical study for St. Louis, Missouri, by Kenneth Wieand shows that the author was unable to find a statistically significant relationship.[67]

Approaches to Controlling (and Abating) Pollution. John Stuart Mill wrote in his essay *On Liberty,* "The only purpose for which power can be rightfully exercised over any member of a civilized community, against his will, is to prevent harm to others." Since the market mechanism not only fails to cope with pollution, but possibly even is in part responsible for it, Mill's dictum can be readily applied to pollution control.

Controlling and abating air, water, and noise pollution is basically a matter of reducing pollutants coming from a source, uprooting the source, shifting location of the source or the recipient, or changing the timing of emission release. So far, abatement has focused on the first step, i.e., reducing levels of pollutant emissions.

To abate air pollution, stationary sources can be controlled by changing manufacturing or combustion processes, utilizing more efficient equipment, substituting raw materials used, changing fuels, and better operating and maintaining equipment.[68]

---

[66] Ridker, op. cit.

[67] Kenneth F. Wieand, "Property Values and the Demand for Clean Air: Cross Section Study for St. Louis," paper presented at the Committee on Urban Economics Research Conference, Sept. 11–12, 1970 (processed), 11 pp. Earlier studies include: Hugh O. Nourse, "The Effect of Air Pollution on House Values," *Land Economics,* vol. 42 (May 1966), pp. 181–189; and Robert J. Anderson and Thomas D. Crocker, "The Site Value Approach to the Measurement of Economic Losses Due to Air Pollution," presented to the Annual Meeting of the Air Pollution Control Association, June 22–26, 1969, New York, N.Y., 11 pp.

[68] For example, emissions from space heaters can be reduced by turning from high-sulphur coal and oil to low-sulphur oil and natural gas, as well as by the use of more efficient combustion processes. Refuse incinerator emissions can be abated by controlled high-temperature, multichamber furnaces with auxiliary fuel injection, installation of dust control apparatus, etc. Industrial emissions from the petroleum industry, by electric power plants, and from metallurgical and chemical processes can be reduced by improving combustion efficiency as well as by air and gas cleaning devices and by curtailing product leakage and evaporation. However, perhaps most important is the installation of recovery equipment, e.g., electrostatic precipitators and mechanical cleaners at point of emission. (Hagevik, op. cit., pp. 59–73.) Technology of air pollution control is reviewed in U.S. Department of Health, Education, and Welfare, *Air Pollution Engineering Manual* (Washington, D.C.: U.S. Government Printing Office, 1968), Public Health Service Publication 999-AP-40.

Three approaches to abating pollution have been widely recognized.[69] The three techniques are direct regulation through licenses, permits, registration, zoning, standards, and their enforcement through regulatory bodies and the courts; polluter's fee that is based on the costs associated with damage resulting from the polluter; and payments and subsidies to polluters so as to induce them to reduce pollution at the source.

Each of these three approaches will be considered in some detail. Direct regulation is used more widely today than are the other two approaches. In relation to air pollution, direct regulation can use the zoning powers of government to physically separate emitter and receptors. Thus power plants and major polluting industries can be zoned out of certain residential areas. The procedure involves setting minimum quality standards and providing for enforcement. Among its advantages are its relative effectiveness and ease of administration as well as its flexibility, which permits government to take interim steps even in the absence of hard information on relevant measurements.[70]

However, direct control can be inefficient. Thus, under normal circumstances it ignores that some sources of pollution are more readily eliminated than others. For example, if two factories producing different products both contaminate the same stream to the same extent, control directives are likely to require each to reduce its contamination by the same percentage. Most likely, the incremental cost of such a reduction in pollution would be distinctly different for the two factories, if for no other reason than that they are likely to use different production techniques. From an efficiency viewpoint, the factory with the smaller incremental cost should be required to pollute a little less while the other would be permitted to pollute a little more. As a result, the total amount of pollution would be the same, but total cost of accomplishing the given percentage reduction would be smaller. Thus, since it is the total amount of pollution that should be reduced, the cheaper possibilities of pollution abatement should be pursued first.[71]

The second approach entails charging a polluter's fee, with the objective of minimizing the total pollution damage costs and the costs incurred to alleviate that damage. Such a fee can help screen out the less essential or less worthwhile activities that harm the rest of us. Thus pollution abatement should result from the least costly combination of means available,

[69] As examples, see Allan V. Kneese, *The Economics of Regional Water Quality Management* (Baltimore: Johns Hopkins, 1964), pp. 193–195; Edwin S. Mills, "Economic Incentives in Air-Pollution Control," in Harold Wolozin (ed.), *The Economics of Air Pollution* (New York: Norton, 1966), pp. 43–44; Hagevik, op. cit., pp. 60–73; and Solow, op. cit., pp. 499–501.
[70] P. Gerhardt, "Some Economic Aspects of Air Pollution," paper presented at the Mid-Atlantic States Section, Air Pollution Control Association Conference, Oct. 4, 1967; and Hagevik, op. cit., pp. 60–63.
[71] Solow, op. cit., p. 499.

and the costs of any decrement of pollution should not exceed the benefits obtained by the reduction.[72] The damage to each receptor from pollution would be computed, indicating benefits to be expected from proposed abatement. The costs to each pollutant source of abating its emissions in varying degrees would be computed, and "The optimal allocation of the air resource would then require that pollutants be prevented from entering the atmosphere at levels that would inflict more marginal damage on receptors than the marginal cost to the source of preventing the pollution."[73]

Operationally, damage done by emission of incremental amounts of pollutants at any given location and time would be estimated, and the corresponding charge assessed against the emitter. The polluter's fee would reflect the marginal cost that the sources impose on others, with the view of providing an economic incentive for allocating the resource—the waste-assimilative capacity of the environment. This pricing technique is similar to peak-load pricing, discussed in Chapter 4.

Internalizing the cost of pollution by means of a polluter's fee provides incentives for the economic unit to seek the best adjustment in light of the costs and benefits expected to be received. Firms that can reduce emissions at a cost below the government charge will tend to do so and avoid the charge. Those unable to reduce emissions at a cost below the charge will tend to pay it, though continuously seeking methods to reduce emissions. As a consequence, at least in theory, the optimal level of pollution abatement will be approached in a manner least costly to society as a whole.

Once the fee is set, private firms rather than government make the major decisions. The advantages in relation to water pollution can be stated as follows: polluter's charges concentrate automatically on the cheap abatement of pollution and not on any artificial allocation of the abatement burden on polluters. These charges induce polluters to search for new and cheaper methods of waste treatment and waste reduction, including changes in their own production methods. Furthermore, there is room for decentralized decision making which also provides information helpful to decision making by the central authority that controls the river basin. In a sense, this arrangement offers the best of both worlds: information for the central authority about characteristics of stream flow and social costs of poor water quality; and freedom of individual polluters, who tend to know much about the costs of reducing pollution at their own locations, to act in their self-interest. Finally there are strong incentives for innovation and improvement.

There remains the question of what to do with the revenues collected

[72] Hagevik, op. cit., p. 63.
[73] Ibid., p. 63; and Thomas D. Crocker, "The Structuring of Atmospheric Pollution Control Systems," in Harold Wolozin (ed.), *The Economics of Air Pollution* (New York: Norton, 1966), pp. 61–86.

as a by-product of the environmental policy. Two major uses come to mind: revenues from polluter charges can be applied toward the costs of research and investment in major public activities designed to facilitate pollution abatement. Revenue can also be applied to assist workers in marginal enterprises made unprofitable by the taxes, and to help them find new jobs elsewhere. In a similar manner, since polluter's fees are levied regardless of ability to pay, and they therefore constitute an especially heavy burden on the poor, some of the revenue could be redistributed to the poor. Here, however, attention should be paid to the fact that the major responsibility of officials concerned with pollution abatement is efficiency and not income redistribution.

A final approach is payments and subsidies. The payments approach is the obverse of the polluter's fee approach. Selective cash grants can be made to polluters to motivate them to restrict emissions to an optimal degree. These cash grants could in principle be equivalent to the off-site costs imposed by increments of waste discharge and vary with conditions as well as quantity and quality of effluent. This sort of payment resembles the polluter's fee scheme in theory, but its approach is the opposite, and therefore criticisms discussed in relation to the latter would also apply here. The strongest criticism has been made by Edwin Mills, who declares,

> They are simply payments for the wrong thing. The investment credit proposal will illustrate the deficiency that is common to others. An investment credit on air pollution abatement equipment reduces the cost of such equipment. But most such equipment is inherently unprofitable in that it adds nothing to revenues and does not reduce costs. To reduce the cost of such an item cannot possibly induce a firm to install it. The most it can do is to reduce the resistance to public pressure for installation. Common sense and scattered bits of evidence suggest that these payments policies are costly and inefficient ways to achieve abatement.[74]

This approach is likely to be inefficient in that it will frequently stimulate the purchase of special equipment when other methods might be superior. Further, it would be difficult to determine who should be subsidized and by how much. Also, taxpayers' feelings of equity might be violated, since the industrial firm, in not having to consider pollution abatement a cost of production in the same sense that labor and capital are, would rely on payments raised at least partially by higher taxes on other taxpayers. Apparently, the only advantage that payments and subsidies have to recommend them is political. It is easier to subsidize than to tax, although ultimately subsidies have to be raised in terms of taxes or fees.

A strong case has been made in favor of comprehensive approaches to pollution abatement in preference to piecemeal efforts. Many items affect

[74] Edwin S. Mills, "Federal Incentives in Air Pollution Control," *Proceedings,* National Conference on Air Pollution, Dec. 12–14, 1966, p. 576.

the capacity of the environment to assimilate residuals, and they should all be looked upon in a totality. There is close interrelation between air pollution, water pollution, solid waste disposal, sewage, old automobiles, plastic containers, and many other accessories of affluent city life. Separately and jointly they pose a serious challenge to the management of material residuals of production and consumption. In the light of this phenomenon, Edwin Mills has proposed that government collect a materials-use fee on specified materials removed from the environment.[75] The fee would be paid by the original producer or importer of raw materials. It would be set for each material to equal the social cost to the environment if the material were eventually returned to the environment in the most harmful way possible. Fees would be refunded to anyone who could certify that he had disposed of the material, the size of the refund depending on the method of disposal. Recycled materials would be exempt from the materials-use fee, which is equivalent to a full refund; disposal in a preferred way, relatively harmless to users of the environment, would earn a large refund; disposal in some moderately harmful way would earn a moderate refund; and disposal in the most harmful way would earn no refund at all.

Under those conditions, as to materials serving the same purpose, the fees would reflect social costs, including disposal, rather than merely private costs. Original choices of materials would tend to be more socially optimum. If the refund schedule closely reflects social costs of various disposal methods, the fees can provide a correct guide to individuals and private and public agencies in choosing a method of disposal in view of the direct costs and the accompanying refund. While it would avoid many difficult measurement problems and place the burden of proof on the individual and not on the pollution-control agency, the scheme poses serious problems. It would have to apply over a wide geographic area to avoid refunds being made in one place, to those who disposed of the materials, whereas the original fee had been paid elsewhere. Also perhaps price correction for materials incorporated in very durable objects would be needed. Equity would be a problem, since owners of deposits of certain materials would suffer an immediate capital loss with the institution of such a fee. Finally, for some materials detection of their first removal from the environment, or verification of the disposal method, would be virtually impossible.

Municipal Employment Labor Relations

In cities we buy many public services for which there are no substitutes, or at best there are very few, and often poor, substitutes; these services cannot be stored, and thus, if not used, they perish and disappear. It is therefore essential that cities be assured of a continuous supply of police

---

[75] Edwin S. Mills, *User Fees and the Quality of the Environment,* cited in Solow, op. cit., p. 502.

and fire protection services, for which there are, in the short run, no good substitutes. The delivery or nondelivery of these urban services affects the utility functions of virtually all individuals and the production functions of virtually all firms in the city. At the same time provision must be made to assure public employees of bargaining power to improve their working conditions, no less than that of workers in the private sector.

We realize the importance of the issue if we look at the spectacular growth of employment in the public sector: in the last thirty years public payrolls have more than tripled.[76] The largest and fastest-growing industry in the United States today is government employment, especially at the local and state levels. Public employment has been rising not only in absolute terms, but also as a percentage of the total civilian labor force. In 1940 there were approximately 3.5 million government employees, representing about 6.5 percent of the civilan labor force. By 1950, government employment had climbed to 5.5 million, or 9 percent. In 1960 it had reached 7.8 million, or 11 percent. By mid-1970, the total number of employees on government payrolls had reached 12.6 million, or about 15 percent of the civilian labor force (10 million were on state and local government payrolls).[77] All indications point to a further increase in public employment in the United States, mainly in urban areas. The U.S. Department of Labor predicts that during the 1970s municipal employment will increase by 52 percent while the nation's total work force will rise 23 percent.[78]

The rise in payrolls of local and state governments has been accompanied by increased employee organization activity. Teachers, nurses, social workers, policemen, fire fighters, garbage collectors, technicians, maintenance workers, clerks, lifeguards, and even zoo attendants have demanded the right to organize and bargain collectively on wages, hours, and working conditions. Membership has risen steadily in unions representing public employees:[79] by 1970 the number of organized municipal employees had passed the 2 million mark, and was continuing to grow. In cities of more

---

[76] Paul Prasow, *The Crisis in Public Employment Labor Relations* (Los Angeles: University of California Institute of Industrial Relations, 1970), processed, pp. 1–2, 5, 11–17.

[77] This percentage figure is only slightly smaller than that in England (20 percent) and in Sweden (about 22 percent).

[78] *Fortune*, October 1971, p. 94.

[79] The increase in public union membership has significantly expanded the scope of bargaining between employee organizations and the employing governmental agency. Public professional employee organizations and white-collar groups have considered negotiations not only as a means of improving wages, hours, and working conditions. Teachers, for example, demand a voice in determining basic educational policy; they bargain about school curriculum, class size, and the quality of education. Nurses bargain about professional standards; social workers insist upon negotiating the level of benefits for welfare recipients; and policemen want to regulate the number of men on a given patrol and the relationship between law enforcement officials and suspected law violators.

than 10,000 population, three out of five government employees belonged to unions or associations.[80] The largest single union, the American Federation of State, County, and Municipal Employees, had some 450,000 members and in less than one decade moved from nineteenth to seventh place among affiliates of the AFL-CIO.

Union militancy also has been on the rise. In the first quarter of 1971, more than twice as many strikes were called against local government in the eastern half of the United States as in the preceding year. Strikes by sanitation workers led the list of seventeen; ten walkouts by either policemen or firemen were also recorded.

On January 12, 1962, on the basis of recommendations of a Task Force appointed by him in the preceding year, President Kennedy issued Executive Order 10988, which guaranteed to most federal employees the right to join or not to join a labor organization, granted the right of exclusive recognition to an employee organization that represented a majority of employees in an appropriate unit, and provided for advisory arbitration in any dispute over the scope of an appropriate unit. The Order had a profound effect on labor relations in government service. It directly stimulated employee organization and negotiations not only in the federal service, but also indirectly at the state and local level as well.

Other forces, also, came to the fore in the 1960s. Felix Nigro has argued, "Not just teachers, but all government workers are influenced by the effectiveness of civil rights marches, open-housing demonstrations, student sit-ins, and other forms of noncooperation or civil disobedience."[81] Also, personnel management in urban governments has been archaic, particularly in comparison with that in the private sector. Furthermore, with the Supreme Court's reapportionment decisions of the early 1960s, state legislatures became more sympathetic to organized labor in general and to municipal employees in particular.

In the light of these developments we should examine some special characteristics of municipal employment. Derek Bok and John Dunlop remind us that,

> In the private sector, union demands are usually checked by the forces of competition and other market pressures. Similar limitations are either nonexistent or very much weaker in the public sector. While budgets and corresponding tax levies operate in a general way to check increases in compensation, the connection is remote and scarcely applicable to particular units or groups of strategically located public employees.[82]

---

[80] Ibid., pp. 94–95.
[81] Felix A. Nigro, "Collective Negotiatons in the Public Service," *Public Administration Review* (March–April 1968), p. 115.
[82] Derek C. Bok and John T. Dunlop, *Labor and the American Community* (New York: Simon and Schuster, 1970), pp. 334–335.

In addition, municipal negotiations are usually trilateral rather than bilateral, as they are in private industry. There is a built-in, often hidden, tension between elected officials and professional managers. An excellent description of this internal conflict on the municipal level is the following:

> The mayor of a city is rarely on the municipal bargaining team, but he may have a significant effect on negotiations. Besides being chief executive of the city, the mayor is also a politician. The dual nature of the job often leads mayors to undercut the position of their own bargaining team; their political interests may be completely divorced from the interests of their constituents. For example, in one city the mayor unilaterally reopened contract negotiations prior to a mayoralty election and gave city workers one of the best public employee pension plans in the nation. The mayor was reelected by a small plurality, thanks to union assistance in his election campaign.[83]

In New York City, municipal employees not only make large financial contributions to the mayor's election campaign, but also turn out en masse to ring doorbells for him. Some reciprocity is hard to rule out.

Furthermore, in municipal bargaining the department heads have limited authority to negotiate; many terms and conditions of employment are prescribed by civil service regulations and legislation. Frequently, a department has authority to negotiate on some issues but not on others that are citywide. Even the chief administrative officer is limited, in that he has no authority to determine the ultimate distribution of funds.

Finally, there appears to exist little capacity to negotiate effectively. Particularly, employers in the municipal field have failed to develop machinery and competent staff, as the private sector has done.

The great unresolved issues are the right to strike, the right to organize and negotiate, and the scope of negotiations.

The strike as the ultimate economic weapon of organized employees in the public sector is not only prohibited by federal law, but also proscribed in the vast majority of state statutes and judicial decisions. There are three different views: One is that strikes should be allowed except when the public health or safety is clearly jeopardized. Another is that they should be prohibited by law, and any impasse should be settled by compulsory arbitration. A third view is that strikes should be outlawed and that instead a fact-finding board should hold hearings and submit a report of findings and recommendations; if the report should prove unacceptable to either party, the legislative body would then review the entire dispute and enact legislation prescribing terms and conditions of employment. The current trend is to avoid making strikes illegal and to permit them on a restricted

[83] Michael H. Moskow, J. Joseph Loewenberg, and Edward Clifford Koziara, *Collective Bargaining in Public Employment* (New York: Random House, 1970), p. 109.

basis. In 1970, two states enacted laws that legalized strikes by public employees.[84]

Much less controversial than the strike issue is the right of public employees to form or join unions. Many urban public jurisdictions deny their employees this right if the purpose of the organization is to engage in collective negotiations. However, most state and local government jurisdictions lack statutes on public employee relations.[85]

Finally, there is much debate about what issues are to be excluded from negotiations. In recent years the area of bargaining has been gradually extended to include many subjects formerly considered inappropriate.

In summary, collective bargaining by public employees in the United States in general and its cities in particular is distinguished by laws that have proved ineffective, e.g., the nonstrike laws, and the lack of capability of employers and employees to bargain effectively. The nonstrike clauses have failed to prevent municipal strikes. Despite the potential of severe penalties, strikes are on the increase. Because of the sheer numbers of participants in a strike neither wholesale replacement of strikers nor imposition of penalties is feasible.[86] Thus the basic problems remain of balancing the public's right to receive essential services without interruption and the public employee's right to protect and improve his economic interests through

[84] Pennsylvania granted to its state employees the right to strike where bargaining, mediation, and fact finding have been exhausted; and where a strike would not create a clear and present danger to the public health, safety, or welfare. Whether a potential strike would create such a threat is left to the courts to decide. The strike weapon is still denied to policemen, firemen, and mental hospital workers, and court employees.

Hawaii passed a comprehensive public employee labor statute. The law provides for mandatory mediation and fact finding in the event of an impasse. A bargaining schedule allows thirty days for mediation and fact finding, and then further permits enjoining the strike for at least another seventy days. The Hawaii Employment Relations Board determines whether a threatened stoppage would endanger the public health or safety. If it does occur, the Board is empowered (after hearings) to declare the strike unlawful and to petition the court for a restraining order.

Under a Canadian law passed in 1968, employee organizations in the public service have the option of deciding in advance whether they wish to exercise the right to strike or to submit the dispute to compulsory arbitration. Restrictions on the right to strike pertain to certain industries which may seriously affect public safety and security. If the government agency decides that a strike would jeopardize public safety, the employees may be requested to refrain from using the strike weapon. In the first two years no disputes were submitted to arbitration.

[85] Note that in 1968 Martin Luther King, Jr., was assassinated in Memphis during his active support of that city's sanitation workers' attempts to achieve recognition and the right to negotiate terms and conditions of employment. No legal machinery existed in Memphis or in Tennessee to deal with this matter. The issue of union recognition continues to be the most frequent cause of work stoppages in local and state public employment.

[86] Consider the walkout of hundreds of thousands of postal workers in the spring of 1970, each committing a criminal act under the Taft-Hartley Act, which states that a person who strikes against the United States Government commits a felony and may be fined $1,000 and imprisoned up to a year or both (Section 305, Labor-Management Relations Act of 1947).

an effective system of negotiations. Both rights are legitimate and must be recognized. We will find means of compromise only when we recognize that while the right to strike must be subordinated to the right of the community to be protected against a threat to public health and safety, we also recognize that government as an employer has an inescapable obligation to provide a viable alternative to the strike weapon, involving some variant or combination of mediation, fact finding, and compulsory arbitration.

Theodore Kheel advocates permitting strikes by public employees, asserting that genuine collective bargaining cannot take place without the right to strike. He argues that strikes by government workers should not be banned outright, but should be permitted and then evaluated on a case-by-case basis. If such a strike should produce an emergency, it could be dealt with ex post facto by injunction and be restrained only after it could be demonstrated that the public health and safety were jeopardized.[87]

As the main proponent of the opposing view, Arvid Anderson argues that strikes by government workers are invariably inappropriate and that the strike weapon should not and cannot be a part of the negotiating process in public employment. Anderson rejects the contention that the strike plays the same role in the public as in the private sector, pointing out that in government the political process is the substitute for the strike weapon as an orderly method of dispute resolution. He stresses that decisions affecting wages, hours, and working conditions of public employees are primarily political rather than economic in nature.[88]

It might be noted that England and Sweden basically have no legal restrictions on the unionization of public employees and they permit strikes.

In the light of these considerations, the following directions are indicated: provide for compulsory arbitration of impasses involving such essential groups as policemen, fire fighters, and prison guards; and permit strikes by other categories of public workers, subject to subsequent court restraints should a strike prove to be a threat to public health and safety. Nine states, including Michigan and Pennsylvania, already require binding arbitration in labor disputes involving policemen and firemen. The same holds for the cities of Eugene, Oregon, and Vallejo, California, with New York City carefully considering such a law.

However, in addition steps can be taken to improve negotiation capacity and machinery. On the basis of the experience of England and Sweden, it might be desirable to establish a joint council that bargains for employees of all municipalities or all policemen in a state. In turn, cities could organize a joint council that would bargain on their behalf. While as a result collective bargaining agreements could be reached for all municipal em-

---

[87] Theodore W. Kheel, "Resolving Deadlocks without Banning Strikes," *Monthly Labor Review*, vol. 92, no. 7 (July 1969), p. 63.
[88] Arvid Anderson, "Strikes and Impasse Resolution in Public Employment," *Michigan Law Review*, vol. 67, no. 5 (March 1969), p. 957.

ployees or all policemen in a state, explicit adjustment could be made for cost-of-living differences among communities as well as differential ability to pay. This would provide for the benefits of centralization without excessive standardization. The result would be that both employer and employee associations would end up with competent staffs to engage in collective bargaining.[89]

V.   URBAN PUBLIC POLICIES

The development and implementation of urban public policies in the United States involve a large number of actors who are faced by a host of interdependencies and externalities. Governmental fragmentation under federalism further complicates matters. Better understanding of the policy options available and their implications requires powerful tools of analysis, which are not yet fully developed. Thus, with the techniques that are available, we will consider some public policy issues that relate to the delivery and financing of urban public services, the possible restructuring of urban government, and various forms of governmental intervention.

Efficiency in Service Delivery

One of the key efficiency questions is, Who should produce what services? Specifically, we must decide what level of government should engage in the production, and whether or not certain services could be produced by private firms, perhaps under supervision, licensing, or contracting by government. There is much merit in the view that most urban public services should be locally produced, so that government can be responsive to the needs of the people. This does not deny the necessity for higher levels of government to provide incentives and, in some cases, instructions that promise relatively efficient and equitable service delivery. However, there is no need for government to produce all urban public services; it can seek bids from other public bodies and private firms and contract for services. In this manner, competition is fostered and possibly efficiency is increased.

Efficiency in production can also be increased through the creation of "joint efficiency teams"—composed of city government officials and employees, possibly assisted by a neutral party that can also provide technical competence—to explore ways to increase the efficiency of city government operation. Prior agreement should ensure the right of public employees to participate through their various organizations in developing and implementing proposals that might affect hours and working conditions. No dismissal of municipal employees should result from such an effort; employees

---

[89] For example, in England local authorities have formed an employers association with an excellent staff located in London—the Local Authorities' Conditions of Service Advisory Board (LACSAP).

should be assured of sharing with taxpayers in the cost savings resulting from greater efficiency and increased productivity. Furthermore, efficiency can be improved through greater reliance on user charges, since they can induce more rational consumption.

Finally, we could experiment with performance accountability systems. Not only could such a system be used to evaluate the performance of those who participate in the production of urban public services, but state and federal grants-in-aid could be slowly shifted from a per capita to an output performance basis, at least in part. For example, instead of subsidizing local school districts through conventional per capita grants that provide a given amount of money for each pupil, states could experiment with making grants only if stipulated performance criteria are reached or surpassed.

In the mid-sixties, and to some extent since, interest has been expressed in the application of program budgeting to improve the planning-management process in urban government. In many respects, it is a story of unfulfilled promises. However, while a comprehensive program budgeting system is most likely neither possible nor necessary, such efforts as have been made in various cities and other urban governments have shown the potency of analytic studies. Systems analysis and operations research can become important tools for increasing the efficiency of service delivery.

Financing Urban Governments

As in the past, two large funding questions remain: What level of government should have what funding responsibilities? and, What tax sources should be how heavily relied upon? Answers to these questions must be framed in the light of the great governmental fragmentation in our metropolitan areas. There can be little doubt about the need for a better match between expenditure beneficiaries and revenue sources. The funding of such people-oriented public services as welfare, health, and education can increasingly come from federal income taxes and, in the case of education, also from state income taxes. Not only do people deserve to receive such services, regardless of their incomes, but also these services benefit the entire nation. Furthermore, property taxes, presently used to fund such people-oriented services, are an improper source of such funding. Once central cities and other local governments are relieved of the funding of all welfare and most education services, the conventional tax revenues will become more nearly adequate to support those municipal services for which central cities should indeed be responsible, e.g., police and fire protection, street cleaning, etc.[90]

An alternative to shifting the financial responsibility for welfare, and

[90] This suggestion is consistent with the notion that income redistribution should be principally the mission of the federal government, the states playing junior parts. Likewise, local urban government should not seek to assume responsibility for stabilizing the economy nor have as a major objective the nation's economic growth.

perhaps education, to the federal and, to a lesser extent, state government, is for state and local governments to share in the federally raised income tax. Federal revenue-sharing is likely to be of relatively little help to central cities unless the aid comes to them directly from the federal government. Unlike the giving of earmarked grants, which in the past have had egalitarian effects, the giving of block grants to states will not be likely to serve the interests of central cities and their poor. The one-man, one-vote rule, although it was once expected to be of particular advantage to the central city, has shifted political power to the suburbs. Not only can the suburbs very often outvote the central city, but also they often join rural areas in opposing such state programs as special services to poor minorities, low-income housing, and urban mass transportation. Furthermore, in the light of the extremely strong bargaining power of municipal unions, large portions of unearmarked federal funds are likely to end up in higher wages without necessarily improving municipal services.

As we ponder the question of what local tax sources to tap, we must be cognizant of the mobility of the tax base in metropolitan areas. Under federalism this mobility is of dominating importance. Nevertheless, as we indicated earlier, there is merit in placing greater emphasis on user charges and on deemphasizing the use of property taxes to finance people-oriented services. Furthermore, major steps could be taken to improve the administration of the property tax, making it not only more efficient but also more equitable. Recent court decisions relative to the equal protection clause of the Constitution can open the way to nationwide standards of assessment practices and ratios to be applied to the property tax.

The Restructuring of Government in Metropolitan Areas

The structure of government in the United States evolved over the years under the impetus of political and fiscal federalism. Government structures that might have been appropriate for a rural America are much less so for the very large metropolitan areas. Ever since the end of World War II, much discussion has taken place about the possibility of restructuring metropolitan area government, a step which could also improve the matching of revenues with expenditures. However, the past record of metropolitan consolidation in the United States is poor. In addition to bringing about equity in financing services, metropolitan consolidation has also been advocated as a means to benefit from scale economies and from coordinated and orderly planning for growth. In Chapter 11 we have shown that scale economies are likely to be less important than was earlier claimed. In terms of economies of scale, urban governments serving relatively small cities, i.e., perhaps as few as from 50,000 to 100,000 urbanites, might be most efficient in the supplying of important services.

The second claim for consolidation concerns coordinated and orderly planning for growth. It is argued that spillovers, if they are internalized through consolidation, facilitate the orderly growth of the area. However, this advantage is somewhat counteracted by a sacrifice of freedom to act individually and independently. Furthermore, large organizations have often proved unable to anticipate, recognize, or adjust to change. This brings us then to the third virtue claimed for consolidation—improved matching between revenues and expenditures, together with greater equity. This claim is in many respects valid, although there are alternative means of obtaining better matching—mainly shifting financing responsibility to higher levels of government.

In the late 1960s, strong forces against consolidation emerged. Particularly in the ghettos of large cities, minority leaders have been arguing for local participation in, and local control of, various urban public services. Perhaps the strongest effort has been made in relation to public schools.

Recognizing the importance of economies of scale as well as local control in metropolitan areas, the Committee for Economic Development proposed a two-level governmental system: "To gain the advantages of both centralization and decentralization, we recommend as an ultimate solution a governmental system of two levels. Some functions should be assigned in their entirety to areawide government, others to the local level, but most will be assigned in part to each level. . . ." In addition to an areawide level, modern metropolitan government should contain a community-level government system comprised of "community districts." These units might consist of existing local governments with functions readjusted to the two-level system, together with new districts in areas where no local unit exists.[91]

More Systematic Intervention

Because urban America is replete with interdependencies and externalities, frequent government intervention is mandatory. Land-use planning and zoning by local governments have proved to be not only piecemeal and ineffective, but at times outright corrupt. We might experiment with arrangements by which local planning commission rulings can be appealed to county commissions, and by them, in turn, to state commissions. Furthermore, land use might improve if compensation were more frequently provided to those who incur losses because of rezoning.

Recent years have seen increasing interest in abating congestion and pollution. Of the various intervention methods that are being explored, i.e., regulation, taxation, user charges, and subsidies, it appears that user charges are particularly promising.

[91] Committee for Economic Development, *Reshaping Government in Metropolitan Areas* (New York: Committee for Economic Development, 1970), pp. 19–20.

There is an area where, in the past, by law, government has intervened on a large scale, but by and large ineffectively. Thus, state and federal laws have tended to outlaw strikes by public employees. These laws have proved mostly ineffective, and labor unrest in urban governments has been on the increase in both numbers involved and seriousness. Urban governments could make major contributions by bringing about the development of employers' and employees' bargaining counsels designed to increase the competency and therefore the efficiency with which collective bargaining can be carried out.

Some Further Thoughts

We have emphasized efficiency of urban governments, since it is the responsibility of the federal government to attain a desirable income redistribution for the country as a whole. We note with great interest recent court decisions designed to reduce service disparity between the rich and the poor. In order to reduce such disparities, suits have been filed in Michigan, California, Illinois, Texas, Virginia, and Mississippi alleging violation of the Fourteenth Amendment of the United States Constitution and, in some instances, identical provisions in state constitutions. Early in 1971 when the first case was adjudicated, the Fifth Circuit Court ruled that the town of Shaw, Mississippi, must move to provide equal services for all its citizens. In a somewhat similar move, the Supreme Court of California ruled in August 1971, by a 6 to 1 vote, that raising school funds through local property taxes invidiously discriminates against the poor, because it makes the quality of a child's education a function of the wealth of his parents and neighbors. These are important decisions whose full impact is yet to be felt.

There is also the question as to whether the federal government could, and possibly should, institute programs to reduce the incentives of rural Americans to leave for the city. There are some indications to that effect in President Nixon's 1971 State of the Union message in which he speaks about encouraging a balanced national growth, growth that will revitalize our rural heartland and enhance the quality of life throughout America. Such statements, together with the emphasis on "balanced growth," could be interpreted as designed to slow, or perhaps eventually even reverse, the population flow from rural areas to cities by moving more federal resources into the former. However, in the light of higher welfare payments, superior education, employment, and living conditions in metropolitan areas, outmigration from rural areas is hard to counteract. Yet the population of rural America has shrunk so much that migration to the city must taper off in years to come.

NAME INDEX

SUBJECT INDEX